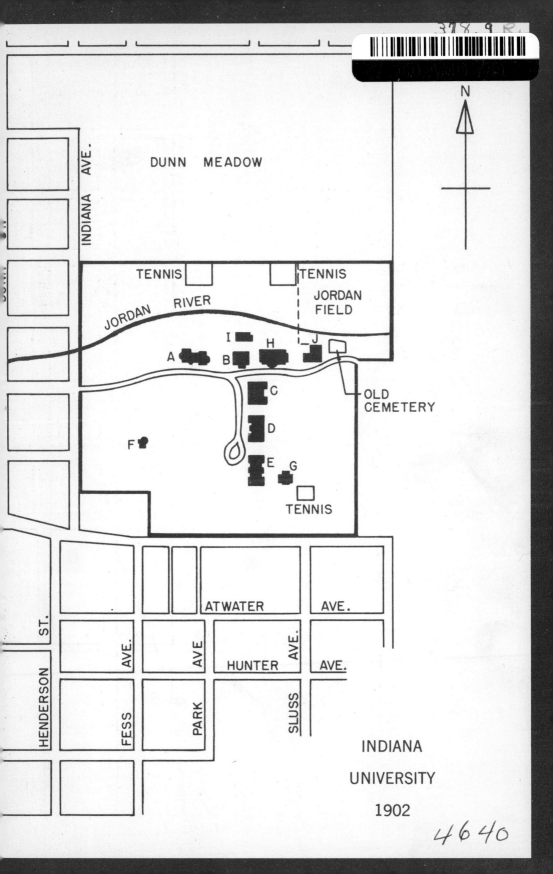

HISTORY OF
INDIANA UNIVERSITY

VOLUME II

1902–1937

BURTON DORR MYERS

HISTORY OF
INDIANA UNIVERSITY

VOLUME II

1902-1937

THE BRYAN ADMINISTRATION

By BURTON DORR MYERS, M.D.

Dean and Professor Emeritus
Indiana University School of Medicine
(at Bloomington)

EDITED BY

IVY L. CHAMNESS

and

BURTON D. MYERS

PUBLISHED BY

INDIANA UNIVERSITY

1952

Printed in the United States of America by R. R. Donnelley & Sons Company
Chicago and Crawfordsville, Indiana

For sale by Indiana University Bookstore
Bloomington, Indiana

WILLIAM LOWE BRYAN IN 1921

FOREWORD

FOUR HISTORIES of Indiana University, one following another, tell its story. The authors were alike as men with the training and the conscience of the scholar. They knew how to find what must be found so that the story should be truly told. They met the implacable demand of the historian that every page must have authority from authentic records. Each of them had also intimate personal acquaintance with the events and the persons whose story he wrote.

The present work, Dean Emeritus Burton Dorr Myers, author, is the largest of the four. This has been necessary because in the expanding life of the University events and records have multiplied almost beyond computation. The minutes of the Board of Trustees at a single session may now require more pages than were necessary for the records of twenty years before 1900. Those pages must be read by the historian. Dr. Myers has read them. He has been merciless with himself as the scholar must be. He has read also the minutes of the faculty and whatever other records are relevant in the archives of the University and of the state of Indiana. He has not failed to garner reminiscence from every quarter, but likewise has not failed to check memories by official records.

The author has, of course, and rightly, taken full advantage of the work of his predecessors. He has then, also, unearthed from obscure records a wealth of important new materials. But again, like his predecessors, he does not end his work with pages of statistics.

For example, statistically, the financial history of the institution begins with a zero and arrives at so-and-so many millions. This story is here told with a completeness never before attained. But behind this arithmetic is the story of the *idea* of a free public school system including a state university. An idea at first without a penny, that grew against inertias and great oppositions to become more and more the will of the people to provide at whatever necessary cost for the complete enlightenment of our society.

Dr. Myers is a starred scientist. Exactly what does that mean? At seven periods (1903, 1909, 1920, 1926, 1932, 1937, 1943) there have been published (*American Men of Science*) lists of men in twelve sciences who were judged worthy a place in that company. Each man was chosen, judged, and rated by a competent committee of his colleagues. The men in each science judged to belong to the highest group were designated by stars. Of the many thousands of American scientists since 1903, 2,607 were starred. Of these, 1,440 were alive in 1946. Dr. Myers is one of them. He was not by profession a historian. He brings to his present task as a historian the mind and method of the scholar.

All will join the author in warm appreciation of those who have contributed chapters or parts of chapters to this history: William A. Alexander, Joseph W. Piercy and Lloyd Wilkins, Fernandus Payne, Velorus Martz, William A. Rawles, Barzille Winfred Merrill, Cedric C. Cummins, Ivy L. Chamness.

Among those who have given generous aid to Dr. Myers in his work one has been pre-eminent. This history of Indiana University, like that of Dr. Woodburn, is under great obligation to the expert Editor of University Publications, Miss Ivy Leone Chamness.

WILLIAM LOWE BRYAN

Dr. Myers died February 28, 1951. On November 25 I had written him a letter which I am permitted to add to the Foreword.

Dear Dr. Myers:

I am sorry to hear that you are not so well. I shall hope soon to hear better news of you.

Often I run over in mind the long story of our life as comrades—since first Dr. Mall introduced us—when you were in the flush of your success at Leipzig and your appointment at Hopkins.

It took a team to win the fight we made. We had good men on the team. But often I say: But without *that* man we could not have won. You were *that* man. Then you have capped your life as starred man of science with your master work as historian.

Along with everything else you were my friend and brother.

These things and many more I say often to myself.

Sincerely
W. L. BRYAN

TABLE OF CONTENTS

ILLUSTRATIONS

INTRODUCTION

IN contrast with early periods of the history of Indiana University, the records of which, with only a few exceptions, were destroyed on the night of July 12, 1883, in the fire which consumed the main University building with its contents, the records of the Bryan administration are intact. Since 1937 records have been kept in the fireproof Archives of the Administration Building, behind steel doors with combination locks, in custody of a competent archivist, where the files should never again be broken, by fire or forgotten withdrawal.

While various sources of information are available for the history of the Bryan administration, the reports of the President to the Board of Trustees are definitely among the most important. These are intimate periodic surveys of the status of the University, its growth, its vital needs, its objectives, its difficulties, etc. With the growth of the University, reports naturally have become more extensive, more detailed, and better organized. As schools were added, school reports became a part of the President's reports. As departments multiplied, departmental reports were included, and the time arrived when reports from every functional unit of the University were incorporated in reports of the President to the trustees.

The minutes of the board are not exciting reading, although of major importance as a source of information for the history of this administration. For the greater part they are the records of actions taken by the board on the reports and recommendations of the President. They show what recommendations of the President were approved, what projects were given the "go sign," what and when expansions were authorized, and so on. But they reveal almost nothing of the discussion, sometimes prolonged, which preceded action on important matters. At times, in reading these minutes it is a bit difficult to realize that the trustees were men who could laugh, exchange witticisms, and experience the emotions of the mine run of men, and not some highly organized composite thinking machine into which the problems of the University were poured, a lever pulled, and a logical answer delivered.

The minutes of the Executive Committee are another source of information. This committee, which consisted of the President and the two Monroe County trustees, with John W. Cravens serving as secretary during the Bryan administration, was authorized to act on a wide range of minor routine matters and on special matters referred to it by the board. Through this committee quick action could be secured on various minor matters of buildings and grounds and on minor adjustments in teaching staff and other personnel. Small appropriations could be and were made. With the growth of the University the activity of this committee increased greatly. At convenient intervals actions of the committee were presented to the board for approval.

Reports of the trustees to the Governor gave an annual accounting of receipts and disbursements of the University as required by legislative act since the establishment of the institution. They were originally reports of the treasurer, but later the annual report was submitted by the president of the board to the Governor, who transmitted it to the auditor of state for verification of financial statements. These reports are not merely authoritative statements of financial matters, but from time to time they have included important statements submitted by the President of the University, or by the Finance Committee, bearing on the status of the institution.

For the first ten years of the Bryan administration the President prepared reports to the Legislative Visiting Committee. These were, of course, first considered by the trustees and on occasion were signed by the president of the board. The Visiting Committee carried these reports away for deliberate examination. Later the President and trustees were invited to a conference in which they were asked to agree to certain budgetary requests which the Visiting Committee was prepared to support. This procedure, carried out with other state institutions, led to a recommended budget.

The minutes of the faculty for the entire period of the Bryan administration are on file. Certain recommendations of the faculty are submitted to the trustees for their approval. These recommendations of the faculty are made after extended discussion and deliberation and with approval of a substantial majority of the faculty and always receive most thoughtful consideration by the board. I find no instance of their rejection, though reconsideration of certain sections may be suggested. Some recommendations involving a change of policy, the faculty has understood, could be put into effect only over a period of years.

The minutes of the State Board of Education from 1855 to date have been of great value in determining the exact time of election of trustees and the files of the alumni secretary have been helpful.

In connection with such matters as the influenza epidemic of 1918 or the water famines of the first two decades of the Bryan administration, contemporary publications have been of great value. Among these are the various University publications, the files of professional journals, and those of Bloomington and Indianapolis newspapers. Correspondence on University matters of importance is found on file in the Archives.

ACKNOWLEDGMENTS

It has been a pleasure to be able to submit successive chapters, as written, to President Bryan for reading and comment. His reminiscences invariably have been accompanied by the admonition: "But you have to verify it." Other persons have been helpful in connection with single chapters, among them being Ward Biddle, who read the chapter on the Bookstore, and Messrs. Clevenger, Moenkhaus, and Sembower, who read the chapter on athletics.

As a member of an early committee on publication, Professor Albert L. Kohlmeier offered the wise suggestion: "Take time. Do not hurry the work." Happily, being retired, I could do this. Two years were devoted to the first writing of this history. It was then laid aside, for eighteen months, while I was writing the biographical sketches for the *Trustees and Officers of Indiana University*. That work completed, the following eighteen months were devoted to a radical revision of the manuscript of the *History of the Bryan Administration*. After an interval of twelve months during which the biographical sketches were rewritten, the manuscript was again taken up and a year was devoted to editing under the experienced leadership of Miss Ivy L. Chamness. Many chapters were again reorganized and some were largely rewritten.

B. D. M.

EARLIER HISTORIES OF INDIANA UNIVERSITY

THREE earlier publications on the history of the University have been published, appearing in 1890, 1904, and 1940.

Since most early official records of Indiana University were lost by fire, it is fortunate that Theophilus A. Wylie, who was elected to the Indiana University faculty in 1837, wrote of the early years of the institution. Except for two and one-half years at Miami University, 1852–55, he spent nearly half a century as a teacher in Indiana University. He became professor emeritus in 1886. The valuable subject matter compiled by Professor Wylie was "revised, condensed, and arranged" for publication by David D. Banta, at the request of the Board of Trustees. Dean Banta contributed a chapter on "Indiana Seminary" to this volume. Trustee Robert S. Robertson wrote the chapter on "The Indiana University as Fostered and Developed by Legislation." This volume, *Indiana University, Its History from 1820, When Founded, to 1890,* was published in 1890.

The *History of Indiana University, 1820–1904,* was prepared for the Louisiana Purchase Exposition at St. Louis under the able editorial supervision of Samuel B. Harding. William A. Rawles wrote the brief (thirty-page) historical sketch. The rather extensive "Development of the Course of Study" was prepared by Lewis C. Carson. Many people contributed to the compilation of the 150-page bibliography. This long list of titles of publications of present and former faculty members, of alumni and students is evidence of the productivity of faculty and students in this period prior to formal organization of the Graduate School.

The James A. Woodburn *History of Indiana University, 1820–1902,* edited by Ivy L. Chamness, was planned as a series of volumes to be completed down through the years. The first six chapters by David D. Banta cover the history of the early period of the University. All six were delivered as Foundation Day addresses, 1889–94 inclusive. Certain special chapters, those on athletics, the curriculum, the School of Law, and others were not completed in time for inclusion in Volume I, and are therefore included in this present volume.

HISTORY OF
INDIANA UNIVERSITY

VOLUME II

1902–1937

CHAPTER I

WHAT WAS INDIANA UNIVERSITY
LIKE IN 1902?

A President Is Chosen

A FATEFUL decision confronted the Board of Trustees of Indiana University at their Commencement meeting in June, 1902.

The report for the past year had been very encouraging. There had been 1,285 students in attendance, an instructional staff of 61, and an income of $129,761.01. Recent growth of the University had been remarkable. Only seventeen years earlier, on January 1, 1885, when David Starr Jordan became president, there had been only 157 students, a faculty of 18, and the income for 1884–85 had been $30,800. The number of students was now eight times, the number of professors and instructors three and one-half times, and the income four times that of 1884–85.

This remarkable growth of the past seventeen years had taken place under the leadership of three great presidents: David Starr Jordan, John M. Coulter, and Joseph Swain. Now it was known that Joseph Swain was about to resign. Would a man be chosen to succeed him under whom the recent development which held so much promise for the future would continue?

Indiana University, in June, 1902, was a large College of Liberal Arts, one of the largest in the country, with a small Law School. Was that to be the future of Indiana University? Some of the strongest men of the faculty hoped so. They feared that the establishment of new schools would sap the resources of the University which they believed should be devoted to the expansion of the arts college.

There were those of broader vision, however, who believed that the best interests of the State University and of the people of the state of Indiana would be promoted by the establishment of additional schools furnishing to Hoosier boys and girls a wider opportunity for an education.

Responsibility for the future of Indiana University on that June day of 1902 rested with the trustees who must choose a new leader under whom Indiana University would become "a sleepy little college in a sleepy little town" as Nicholas Murray Butler once described Princeton in introducing Woodrow Wilson to a Columbia University audience, or it would develop into a real university with additional schools and broadened educational opportunities for the most precious resource of Indiana, namely, Hoosier boys and girls.

The trustees who were to choose a president were: Edwin Corr and Nat U. Hill, of Bloomington; Robert I. Hamilton, Huntington; Charles L. Henry, Anderson; Isaac Jenkinson, Richmond; Robert A. Ogg, Kokomo; Joseph H. Shea, of Scottsburg; and Benjamin F. Shively, South Bend. On that June day the alumni elected James W. Fesler to succeed Mr. Ogg, who had served from 1896.

President Swain, in his report to this board, read on June 16, 1902, stated that the presidency of Swarthmore College had been definitely offered to him, that he had imposed certain conditions of acceptance, which conditions had been met, and he therefore felt an obligation to accept. He had given much thought, he said, to the question of his successor at Indiana University. He concluded:

I have carefully looked over all the available men of my acquaintance and these include the great body of the Presidents of the Colleges and Universities throughout the country, and I have thought very carefully over the available men of our Faculty. When one comes to consider all the possibilities in the case, I am clearly of the opinion that the thing to do is to ask Dr. William L. Bryan, now Vice President, to accept the Presidency of the University. I believe Dr. Bryan is the one man who, in the present situation, can command the unqualified support of all the factions that go to make up the influence of the University and carry the work forward as it is going today.

The minutes of the board for the following day contain a copy of a letter of Joseph Swain in which he expresses appreciation of the uniform courtesy and friendship of all the members of the board and tenders his resignation as president, to take effect August 1, 1902. The resignation was accepted effective on the date mentioned.

The minutes of that morning session of the board then continue:

On motion of Mr. Henry a ballot was taken for selection of a successor to President Joseph Swain. No nominations were made, each one of the eight trustees cast a ballot, and each ballot bore the name of Professor William L. Bryan. On request of the Board, President Jenkinson informed Professor Bryan of his unanimous selection as President of Indiana University, and in response Professor Bryan made a speech of acceptance.

It had been a momentous session of an able board. Meeting at 10:30, in a few hours the resignation of one president had been received and accepted, and, in a single ballot, a successor, a new president, had been elected—a good morning's work.

This record of the election of President Bryan may seem to indicate a somewhat casual attitude of the Board of Trustees. That was not the fact, however. There is a story back of the record.

When President Coulter in March, 1893, decided to resign he crossed the hall in Owen to the classroom of Dr. Bryan, informed him of his intention, and said, "I am going to recommend you as my successor." Jordan, however, had been a member of the faculty of Indiana University for twelve years (1879–91), six years as president. He recommended Professor Swain, then at Stanford, and though Jordan had been away from Indiana for two years his prestige was still great and his recommendation prevailed. There is no record to indicate that any other person was considered. But at the first board meeting under the Swain presidency in November, 1893, the office of vice-president was re-established and W. L. Bryan was elected to that office.

While the vice-presidency was probably intended as a sort of consolation prize, it seems fortunate for Dr. Bryan that he was not elected to the presidency in 1893. For during the years 1893–1902 he did investigative work of great value, the importance of which won for him election as the twelfth president of the American Psychological Association and placed him thirteenth of the fifty psychologists included among the first one thousand American men of science. Those years also provided opportunity for maturity of educational convictions which shaped his policies and contributed greatly to his success as an administrator.

At the March, 1902, meeting of the board, President Swain announced that he had refused the invitation to become a candidate for the chancellorship of the University of Kansas. It is more than possible, however, that the board had discussed available successors.

Though it was not until June, 1902, that President Swain presented his formal resignation, he stated that he had already informed the board of the Swarthmore offer. His resignation, therefore, was not wholly unexpected, nor were the trustees wholly lacking in opportunity to consider the problem presented.

The president of the board, Isaac Jenkinson, and Trustee Corr had been members of the board in 1893 when Joseph Swain had been elected president. Bryan's growth in eligibility had not escaped the observation of the board. Jordan (as he tells us) had been consulted, and when the judgment of the board was fortified by the strong recommendation of Swain and of Jordan, in favor of Bryan, the result of the trial ballot surprised no member of the board.

Now what was the status of Indiana University of which, on that June day of 1902, William Lowe Bryan was chosen president, and what do we know of this man, William Lowe Bryan, who was called to this important position by the unanimous vote of the board of control?

CAMPUS IN 1902

The campus of Indiana University and east central Bloomington as of 1902 are shown inside the front cover. The campus of 20 acres purchased in Dunn's Woods on February 4, 1884, had been increased to nearly 51 acres (50.82 acres, to be exact) by additional purchases in 1897. The 20-acre campus site is included in the map inside the back cover as Area 1, with boundaries indicated by dotted lines. The west boundary of this 20-acre site was 375 feet east of Indiana Avenue.

The Jordan River is shown running east to west through the campus and then sweeping southward to cut the lower border of the map of east central Bloomington about 200 feet east of the original 10-acre campus, a rectangular area (1), lying south of Second Street and between Walnut Street and the railroad.

North of the campus of 1902 was Dunn Meadow. The Dunn farm originally lay between Third Street (as now called) and Tenth Street. Dunn Street marked the west boundary of the farm. It will be noted that Dunn Meadow still extended west to Dunn Street in the block between Ninth and Tenth streets.

The buildings on the campus are identified as: A, Maxwell Hall; B, Owen Hall; C, Wylie Hall; D, Kirkwood Hall; E, Science Hall (under construction); F, Kirkwood Observatory; G, Mitchell Hall; H, Men's Gym; I, Old Gym, later a carpenter shop; J, Power Plant.

PROPERTY AND INCOME

President Bryan, reporting to the Legislative Visiting Committee,[1] November, 1902, gave very detailed information as to the status of the University:

Grounds:
The University Campus of 51 acres was valued at.............. $ 26,000.00
Buildings, and valuation:
Maxwell ....$ 65,000.00
Owen 30,000.00
Wylie 55,000.00
Kirkwood 50,000.00
Men's Gymnasium (later Assembly Hall)........................ 12,000.00
Women's Gymnasium (Mitchell Hall)............................   2,500.00
Observatory 6,000.00
Old Gymnasium (a carpenter shop in 1902)....................   200.00
Power House 2,500.00
Science Hall (under construction)

Total.......... $223,200.00

Library:
The Library, located in Maxwell Hall, contained
43,000 volumes valued at ....$ 43,000.00
Equipment:
Furniture ....$ 8,200.00
Apparatus 24,200.00

Total....... $ 32,400.00
Supplies: ....$ 9,500.00
Summary:
Grounds ....$ 26,000.00
Buildings[2] 223,200.00

---

[1] This is not to be confused with the "Board of Visitors," consisting of high state officials and other prominent citizens, authorized in 1827 to examine the financial and academic status of the institution.

[2] Science Hall, then under construction, is not included. Science Hall was dedicated in January, 1903, when President Bryan was inaugurated and brought the total value to about $450,000.

Equipment (furniture and apparatus)	$ 32,400.00
Library	43,000.00
Supplies	9,500.00

Total.........$334,100.00

The total receipts for the fiscal year ending October 31, 1902, were $129,761.01, derived as follows:

From the state—

Educational levy 1/15 mill tax	$ 90,200.00
Interest on permanent endowment (6%)	21,500.00
Interest on University Bonds @ 5%	7,200.00
Income from other sources, fees, etc.,	10,861.01

Total.......$129,761.01

Disbursements for departmental maintenance for the year ending October 31, 1902, did not amount to $1,000 for any one department.

The report of the President to the Legislative Visiting Committee contains this significant paragraph:

In a word, the University's need of greater income is plain beyond the necessity of argument. We are in the position of a city whose school enrollment has nearly doubled while its funds for school purposes have not increased. Each year, in spite of more rigid requirements, an increasing number of young people from every corner of the state are crowding in upon us. This is the decisive annual vote of the people of the State that they want the opportunities offered here. The University comes as in law and in fact an integral part of the common school system of the State to ask that the State shall provide for its own children.

Faculty in 1902

On November 6, 1902, there were 61 members of the faculty with salaries ranging from $700 to $2,500. Of these 61 faculty members, only three received the maximum, $2,500.

Far more important than the physical plant was this faculty of 61 members which the new administration inherited. Much of the success of Indiana University under this new president depended upon the strength of this faculty. If the faculty were strong, an immediate advance of the educational program might be anticipated. If it were weak, then no matter how capable an administrator the new president proved to be, the institution would be seriously handicapped.

When Jordan became president, maximum faculty salaries ranged from $1,670 to $2,000[3] with only two men receiving $2,000. Even after the shock of the resignation of seven of the strongest of the twenty-nine faculty members (25 per cent) who followed Jordan to Stanford, the maximum professorial salary in April, 1893, when Swain became president, was still only $2,000 with only one man receiving that maximum. By the close of the Swain administration, nine years later, he had succeeded in increasing the maximum to $2,500, with one man receiving that maximum. With this one exception the maximum salary at Indiana University in 1901-2 was $2,200.

Of the faculty for 1902-3, all had served under President Swain except Berry, Carson, Glenn, Hogate, Leckrone, Long, Milburn, Ogg, Springer, and Triplett. Many of these served throughout the Bryan administration and others until their death or retirement and were elements of great strength in that administration.

[3] While these maximum salaries seem pitifully small, they are to be judged correctly only by reference to the socio-economic life of that day. From personal knowledge I am able to give the following measure of the purchasing power of those salaries of 1885. The house I live in, 424 North Walnut, was built by Mr. J. D. Showers in the year Jordan became president of Indiana University (1885) at a cost of $2,800. Ninth Street was then a mere wagon trail, and across Ninth Street began the northward extending woods in which the boys played Indians. This corner lot cost $300. So here was a house costing (house and lot) $3,100.

It is a rather widely accepted economic principle that the average man cannot afford to invest in a house more than twice his annual income. Here then was a house, perhaps above average, which the full professor of 1885 on maximum salary might have built. It was quite as good for its day as a house costing $10,000 to $12,000, twice the maximum professorial salary in 1937.

But this house which today has plumbing, electric wiring, hot water heating, running water, etc., had none of those conveniences when first built. It was lighted by lamps, heated by stoves and fireplaces. The water supply for drinking and washing was a big cistern in the back yard. The one, so-called, modern improvement was a bathroom. The bath was a zinc tub in an oak frame, hinged so as to fold up against the wall when not in use. There was a tank in the bathroom and a force pump connecting with the cistern. Water was pumped into the tank, heated, and let into the bath. The opening of the bath fitted into a drain pipe through which the water, when the plug in the bath was pulled, ran out into a cesspool.

The first city water supply was established in Bloomington in 1894 and modern improvements followed very rapidly so that by the beginning of the twentieth century this house and many others had plumbing and running water, was wired for electricity, and piped for gas. Stoves, fireplaces, and even chimneys were removed and central heating installed. Carpets gave way to hardwood floors and rugs, and a new social era was at hand. But the house as originally built in 1885 met the social standards and possibilities of the time as completely as the good house built today at four times the cost.

FACULTY OF INDIANA UNIVERSITY, 1902-3

William Lowe Bryan, President.

George Louis Reinhard, Vice-President, Dean of the School of Law, and Professor of Law.

Horace Addison Hoffman, Dean of the Departments of Liberal Arts, and Professor of Greek.

Mary Bidwell Breed, Dean of Women, and Assistant Professor of Chemistry.

Gustaf E. Karsten, Professor of Germanic Philology.

James Albert Woodburn, Professor of American History and Politics.

Robert Judson Aley, Professor of Mathematics, and Secretary of the Faculty.

Carl H. Eigenmann, Professor of Zoology, and Director of the Biological Station.

Vernon Freeman Marsters, Professor of Geology and Geography.

Martin Wright Sampson, Professor of English.

Harold Whetstone Johnston, Professor of Latin.

John Anthony Miller, Professor of Mechanics and Astronomy.

Robert Edward Lyons, Professor of Chemistry.

Arthur Lee Foley, Professor of Physics.

David Myers Mottier, Professor of Botany.

Albert Frederick Kuersteiner, Professor of Romance Languages.

Ulysses Grant Weatherly, Professor of Economics and Social Science.

Ernest Hiram Lindley, Professor of Philosophy and Psychology.

John Andrew Bergstrom, Professor of Pedagogy.

Enoch George Hogate, Professor of Law.

Carl Wilhelm Ferdinand Osthaus, Associate Professor of German.

Schuyler Colfax Davisson, Associate Professor of Mathematics.

Louis Sherman Davis, Associate Professor of Chemistry.

Samuel Bannister Harding, Associate Professor of History.

Elmer Burritt Bryan,[4] Associate Professor of Pedagogy.

David Andrew Rothrock, Associate Professor of Mathematics.

Amos Shartle Hershey, Associate Professor of European History and Politics.

William Ellsworth Clapham,[5] Associate Professor of Law.

Herdis Frederick Clements, Associate Professor of Law.

Richard McClellan Milburn, Acting Associate Professor of Law.

Francis M. Springer, Acting Associate Professor of Law.

George Davis Morris, Assistant Professor of French.

Charles Jacob Sembower, Assistant Professor of English.

Frank William Tilden, Assistant Professor of Greek.

Guido Hermann Stempel, Assistant Professor of English.

John Mantel Clapp, Assistant Professor of English.

William A. Rawles, Assistant Professor of Political Economy.

---

[4] Absent on leave, in the Philippines, until August 1, 1903.
[5] Absent on leave, Harvard University, until August 1, 1903.

Alfred Mansfield Brooks, Assistant Professor of the Fine Arts.
Charles Tobias Knipp, Assistant Professor of Physics.
Henry Thew Stephenson, Assistant Professor of English.
Edward Payson Morton, Assistant Professor of English.
Eugene Leser, Assistant Professor of German.
Ulysses Sherman Hanna, Assistant Professor of Mathematics.
William J. Moenkhaus, Assistant Professor of Zoology.
Charles Alfred Mosemiller, Assistant Professor of Romance Languages.
Hamilton Byron Moore, Assistant Professor of English.
Benjamin Franklin Long, Assistant Professor of Law.
Lewis Clinton Carson, Assistant Professor of Philosophy.
Roy Henderson Perring, Instructor in German.
Frank Marion Andrews, Instructor in Botany.
Edgar Roscoe Cumings,[6] Instructor in Paleontology.
Oliver W. Brown, Instructor in Chemistry.
Wilbur Adelman Cogshall, Instructor in Mechanics and Astronomy.
James P. Porter, Instructor in Psychology.
Anton Theophilus Boisen, Instructor in Romance Languages.
John Andrew Stoneking, Instructor in Physics.
Joshua William Beede, Instructor in Geology.
Lillian Gay Berry, Instructor in Latin.
Frederic Austin Ogg,[7] Instructor in History.
Grace Triplett, Instructor in Latin.
Oliver Edmunds Glenn, Instructor in Mathematics.
Charles Leckrone, Instructor in Latin.

Mention should be made of the fact that among the officers in 1902 we find:

William Albert Alexander, an Assistant, for many years Librarian.
John W. Cravens, Registrar, and Secretary of the Board of Trustees.
Ulysses Howe Smith, Assistant to Registrar, later Bursar.
John Porter Foley, Mechanician, who for many years played the University chimes.

Of these sixty-one faculty members, Hoffman, Woodburn, Karsten, Bryan, Eigenmann, Foley, Lyons, and Osthaus were appointed by Jordan. Marsters, Davisson, Mottier, Rothrock, Sembower, and Davis were appointed by Coulter.

Mr. Cravens became emeritus in June, 1936, but Alexander, Smith, and Foley were still active in 1936–37.

[6] Absent on leave, Yale University, until August 1, 1903. As assistant professor he began his service as Head of the Department of Geology in 1903, when Professor Vernon F. Marsters was on leave of absence prior to his resignation.
[7] Absent on leave after August 1, 1903.

Many of the men who remained at Indiana University throughout the Bryan administration refused opportunities for careers elsewhere at a financial advantage. They found themselves bound to Indiana University by ties of various sorts, not the least important of which was the feeling that here they were a part of a worth-while educational program. Also in the early years the promise of the Carnegie retirement program gave them a feeling of future security.

There were still 16 of the original 61 faculty members on the active teaching staff during the last year of President Bryan's administration, 1936–37. They are listed below with dates of expected retirements.

NAME	1937	1938	1939	1940	1941	1942	1943	1944
Frank Marion Andrews					†			
Lillian Gay Berry							*	
Oliver W. Brown							*	
Wilbur Adelman Cogshall								*
Edgar Roscoe Cumings								*
Schuyler Colfax Davisson	*							
Arthur Lee Foley	*							
Robert Edward Lyons		‡						
William J. Moenkhaus					*			
George Davis Morris	*							
David Myers Mottier	*							
Carl Wilhelm Ferdinand Osthaus	*							
David Andrew Rothrock	*							
Charles Jacob Sembower					*			
Guido Hermann Stempel		*						
Henry Thew Stephenson				*				

* Retired June 30 of year indicated.
† Was scheduled to retire June 30, 1941; died November 26, 1940.
‡ Was scheduled to retire June 30, 1940; resigned November 1, 1938.

Of this faculty group one may properly repeat Jordan's reference to his faculty as "the strongest corps of teachers ever gathered together in an institution so scantily endowed."

This then is the picture of Indiana University at the close of the school year, 1901–2. The institution had great potentialities, the greatest of which was its faculty.

Chapter II

WHAT OF THE MAN, WILLIAM
LOWE BRYAN?

"Here, as I think, is the program for our educational system—to make plain highways from every corner of the state to every occupation which history has proved good." William L. Bryan, "Education Through Occupations" (1900), *The Spirit of Indiana,* page 145.

A s to the man, William Lowe Bryan, whom some of us have known throughout the years of his presidency,[1] what was he like in 1902; what was his training for the task he then assumed; did he have a vision of a greater Indiana University; did he have any deep-seated convictions as to the educational policy which the administration should follow; what was his temperament; would he follow lines of least resistance, using Indiana University as a steppingstone to some more promising educational field if the going got hard, or was he a fighter ready to put on armor and do battle, making his broader educational field here at Indiana University?

William Lowe Bryan was first of all a Hoosier. Still more, he was born on a Monroe County farm near Bloomington. His father was the Reverend John Bryan, and, as is well known, college statistics show that sons of ministers develop into able leaders in numbers above their ratio to the student body. He was graduated from Indiana University in 1884, at the age of twenty-three, and received the A.M. degree in 1886.

Dr. Bryan's course of study was twice interrupted. He registered as William Julian Bryan as a Freshman in Indiana University in 1877–78, and as a Sophomore in 1880–81. Then he was out again for a year. When he re-entered as a Junior in 1882, he completed his

---

[1] I met Dr. Bryan in the early spring of 1903, so I have known him almost from the time of his taking office as president. Though forty-two years of age, he gave the impression of being younger. He was dynamic, and seemed a man of great vitality. That this impression was not erroneous, I realized many times in later years. His slightly "baseball" nose hinted unostentatiously that it had not been kept exclusively within books. Much later I learned he was an "I" man, having earned his letter in baseball.

course of study without further interruption. In 1884-85 he was an instructor in English in the University Preparatory Department.

In 1885–86 he is listed in the Catalog as associate professor in philosophy and acting instructor in English. In the departmental announcement his name appears as acting professor, the only man in the Department. There were nine courses listed. The next year he is listed as associate professor of philosophy, absent for the year at the University of Berlin. On his return from Berlin the following year, 1887–88, he was appointed professor of philosophy.

In his report to the board in June, 1887, written in longhand, President Jordan makes the following recommendation with reference to philosophy:

> I recommend the election to the Chair of Philosophy of Professor William J. Bryan. I also recommend that he be made Instructor in Elocution at least for the coming year. In view of the demand for instruction in this branch, Professor Bryan has been making, in the University of Berlin, a special study of the method of training students to speak and read properly. He will, no doubt, give the fullest satisfaction to the students wishing to take up this work.

It is rather amusing that instead of offering justification for advancement of Associate Professor Bryan to a full professorship, President Jordan emphasizes his qualification for appointment as an instructor in elocution.

In his book, *The Days of a Man*,[2] Jordan writes of Bryan and this appointment as follows:

> Bryan, a picturesque writer and most effective speaker, of winning personality, showed marked promise in the new science of Physiological Psychology. On his return from the University of Berlin I appointed him Professor of Philosophy, which then included all forms of mental science. . . . In lecturing over the state I often took Bryan with me to strengthen my influence with young men.

Dr. Bryan is listed as professor of philosophy for fifteen years, 1887 to 1902. During 1891–92 he was absent at Clark University, where he received the Ph.D. degree. As a student and during his early years as a member of the faculty his name appears as William Julian Bryan. On July 11, 1889, he married Charlotte A. Lowe, and took as his middle name, Lowe, instead of Julian, thus compliment-

[2] Vol. I, p. 296.

ing the young woman he was marrying and at the same time obviating possible confusion of identity with another William J. Bryan.

It will be recalled that in the November following the election of Joseph Swain as president the office of vice-president of the faculty was created (really revived). The salary was fixed by the board from time to time and paid in addition to any other salary the person elected to this office might be receiving. From 1893 to 1902 Dr. Bryan's title appears as vice-president and professor of philosophy. He was to "discharge the duties of the president of the faculty in the case of death, absence, or inability of that officer from sickness."

Professor Bryan's salary as professor of philosophy was $2,000, the maximum professorial salary at that time, 1893. His salary as vice-president was fixed at $250 per year. As vice-president he was occasionally consulted by the President with reference to administrative matters, but no more so than would probably have been the case had he been merely Professor Bryan. As vice-president he was not called upon to join the President in attending board meetings. So these nine years as vice-president cannot be regarded as having provided valuable administrative experiences, preparing him for the duties of president. The appointment seems to have been more in the nature of a gesture, possibly an excuse for increasing the salary of a faculty member, already regarded as a man of great promise, without constituting a new high in professorial salaries.

Did William Lowe Bryan have a vision of a greater Indiana and deep-seated convictions regarding the educational program to be pursued?[3]

Let us suppose we are back in 1902 hoping to find in what Bryan had written, or said, or done, a key to how he might be expected to think and act in his new position.

In *The Spirit of Indiana* we find what Bryan calls a "youthfully colored address" of 1889, "The Mortal Immortal," which, he says,

[3] Dr. Bryan has said that in the early days of his presidency he was frequently asked about his educational policies. To these inquiries he gave noncommittal replies. It is possible he was encouraged in this by a story he laughingly recalled as told him by Dean William P. Rogers, of the School of Law. According to him, a man recently appointed to the Supreme Court was being congratulated in grandiloquent terms by an acquaintance on the great opportunity which was now his, profoundly to influence thought, on the honor of becoming one with that immortal group that framed the Constitution by having the opportunity to write Supreme Court decisions having all the force of articles of the Constitution, etc., etc., etc. The new Justice replied: "That's not what's worrying me. What's worrying me is whether I'll be able to carry on in this job without making a ———— fool of myself."

"is included because it is the first expression of my faith that the security of truth and of society is not in their being fixed like a rock, but in their growing like living things."

In 1892 he published the results of an extensive research on "The Development of Voluntary Motor Ability." The study deals with the development of voluntary motor ability in children, with respect to: (1) the maximum rate of rhythmically repeated movement; (2) the precision of voluntary movement, particularly as regards direction and force, with a note on the bilateral development of strength and force. It is an extensive article of eighty small-print pages, with many tables and kymographic charts. In the preface he says: "Work in experimental psychology must meet two requirements. It must be carried out according to the best attained methods of scientific research; and it must contribute something to the knowledge of conscious life." His work here reported well illustrates these rules, and demonstrates his clear conception of the requirements of research work.

Five years later in the *Psychological Review,* Volume IV, Number 1, January, 1897, we find the report of "Studies in the Physiology and Psychology of the Telegraphic Language" by W. L. Bryan and Noble Harter. These studies follow logically, naturally, on his work of 1892. They deal with the development of a *special* motor ability in *adults,* the learning of telegraphy.

In recognition of the high quality of these two studies, fellow psychologists of America elected Dr. Bryan president of the American Psychological Association, the twelfth man to receive that honor. He served in 1903, presiding at the St. Louis meeting. It was in nearly this same numerical position (thirteenth) that he was elected by his colleagues as one of the fifty foremost psychologists of America, and his name, starred,[4] was included in the first edition of *American Men of Science.*

Telegraphy is learned as an occupation. It was natural, therefore, that as a result of these studies on "The Physiology and Psychology of the Telegraphic Language" the attention of Dr. Bryan should be directed to the psychology of occupations. He delivered in 1900 one of the best of his many masterly addresses, entitled "Education

---

[4] The star indicates his recognition as one of the one thousand foremost men of science of America.

through Occupations." It is perhaps the most revealing of President Bryan's writings, and, but for the fact that it is twenty-two pages in length and easily accessible, should be quoted here in full. It is found in *The Spirit of Indiana,* copyrighted in 1917 by the Indiana University Bookstore, and reprinted in *Modern American Prose Selections* by Byron J. Rees, Professor of English at Williams College, whose purpose "was to bring together some twenty examples of typical contemporary prose in which writers who know whereof they write, discuss certain present-day themes in readable fashion."

In this address our search for a key to how Bryan might think and act in his new position is rewarded. It is his conception, here expressed, that every occupation arose in response to a deep social need for a certain service, performed by generations of men forming a sort of brotherhood or guild, whose history extends back to the farthest antiquity. To state his idea still more simply and concisely:

1. There developed a social need for a certain service.
2. Men attracted to that service were able to engage in it if it afforded a means of livelihood.
3. Thus arose (*a*) an occupation and (*b*) a guild.

This Bryan regarded as so fundamental that he said:

. . . no art and no sort of learning was ever vitally present among a people, unless it was there as a living occupation. . . . The fact that an occupation can teach its far-brought wisdom to the men of each generation makes civilization and progress possible. But this on one condition, that many of the people and some of the best of them shall be able to make that occupation their life business.

By "living occupation" it is obvious that he meant an occupation at which one may earn a living, a living which enables one to "make that occupation his life business."

He continued: "Learning has come to us in this sense only within the last quarter-century."

He paid tribute to the learning and service of some few men of classical and scientific training, present on the faculty during the days of the founding of the University.

But one thing they could not do. They could not furnish to society more men who should devote themselves to learning than society would furnish a living for. And the bare fact is that there was a living for a very few such men in America in the days before the War [Civil].

He concluded:

Here, as I think, is the program for our educational system,—to make plain highways[5] from every corner of the state to every occupation which history has proved good.

This thought he elaborated in his inaugural address entitled "Faith in Education" included in *The Spirit of Indiana*.

To summarize, we find that as a result of his researches and his contemplation of the ideas to which they gave rise, Bryan had arrived at the conclusion that the choice of an occupation is a momentous decision. He repeats that the occupation chosen must be one in which a man could earn a living. To train for an occupation in which one could not make a living resulted later in finding one's self trapped.

It was clear that occupations could be followed on an infinite number of planes or levels, high or low, and a man's value to society depended largely upon the plane on which he pursued an occupation.

He felt that there should be no "Road Closed" signs on the pathways to occupations and that it was the function of the University to maintain open pathways from all parts of the state for all able children regardless of their economic status.

He knew that when men came into a new country, such as the woods of Indiana, they lost much, though retaining the potentiality of regaining all they had lost and of moving onward to undreamed-of accomplishments. There might be growing illiteracy and free schools might be retained only by the narrowest margin by vote of the people. But the potentiality of better conditions was always present.

[5] John Oxenham arrived at much the same idea of pathways. He wrote:
"To every man there openeth a way,
And ways,—and A WAY.
And high souls climb the high way,
And low souls grope the low,
And in between on the misty flats
The rest drift to and fro;
But to every man there openeth
A high way—and a low,
And every man decideth
The way that his soul shall go."

He believed that there were always great potentialities in society. He conceived it as "not fixed like a rock but as growing like a living thing." Maintenance of open pathways to any and every living occupation was the salvation of the common man, and the salvation of the common man was the salvation of society.

In the above quotations and summary I think we find what we might well call the platform of the new president of 1902, William Lowe Bryan.

As to his temperament, we find at this time, 1902, no facts that justify important conclusions.

Unhappily, the University did not have many years to wait to see him vigorously repelling one of the most serious attacks ever directed against the institution. They saw him outwardly indifferent to personal thrusts, but unhesitating in meeting thrusts at the good faith or good name of the University.

But all that is another story.

Note:

In undertaking the arduous task of continuing the history of Indiana University, of Dean David D. Banta and Professor James A. Woodburn, through the thirty-five years of the Bryan administration, we are sensible of the fact that it is not to be a biography of William Lowe Bryan.

It has seemed essential to an understanding of this period, however, that in this early chapter we should endeavor to present briefly something of what this man had thought and was thinking as a key to what he might do.

To this end we have made available, in a few pages, quotations from his writings which, we believe, reveal his deepest convictions on educational matters, convictions that would inevitably determine the development of Indiana University under his leadership.

CHAPTER III

THE FIRST YEAR OF THE BRYAN ADMINISTRATION, 1902 - 3

How the Bryan Administration Began

LET US recall that the election of President Bryan was effective as of August 1, 1902. The Executive Committee on July 22 authorized him as president-elect to recommend a teacher of psychology at not to exceed $1,200, and on July 30 to make arrangements for janitor service.

As president, his first Executive Committee meeting on August 6, 1902, ordered an opening in the stone fence opposite Sluss Avenue, the rebuilding with new material of the fence around Jordan Field on the south and west sides, and the advertising for bids on heating and plumbing in Kirkwood Hall.

Thus began the work of the Bryan administration, in simple routine matters of maintenance of buildings and grounds.

The first meeting of the trustees during this administration, a special session, was called for September 3, 1902. At that session all members of the board were present except James W. Fesler, who was seated at the meeting on November 6, 1902. This special session was confronted with a minor crisis arising through the resignation of Dean W. P. Rogers, of the School of Law, to accept a like position in Cincinnati at an increase of $1,000 in salary. The board accepted the recommendation of President Bryan for the advancement of Judge George L. Reinhard to the deanship and concurred in his further recommendations for reorganization of the Law School faculty.

Thus there was presented, at this first board meeting of the Bryan administration, a difficulty which persisted for many years at Indiana University, namely, the loss of some of her strongest men to institutions able to offer more remunerative opportunities. Another matter of great moment at that September meeting was the uncompleted

18

campaign for a fund for a woman's building, the completion of which is described in Chapter VI.

In November, 1902, we find the first of a series of excellent reports made biennially, each even year, to the Governor and Legislative Visiting Committee, during the Bryan administration.

In early legislative acts, the determination of the curriculum and other matters of intimate management of the University had been delegated to the trustees. It was, therefore, quite a shock to the board when they discovered one year at Commencement time that Jordan had abandoned the old form of Commencement program in which all graduates made an address, in favor of a single speaker. They complained of innovations sprung on them without consultation. More and more, following January 1, 1885, when Jordan became president, the president had become an educational leader, advisory to the trustees.

In the Bryan reports you see an educational leader in action, making comparative studies in education in state universities, presenting for consideration of his board well analyzed problems for their consideration, making recommendations to be weighed, modified, rejected, or approved as in the combined judgment of able and devoted trustees might be deemed wisest.

This report of November, 1902, to Governor Winfield T. Durbin is very informative. It begins with a brief history of Indiana University which includes an inventory of grounds, buildings, and equipment.[1] It shows the number of students in attendance and the number of graduates each year from 1828 to the close of the year 1901–2. There is a brief description of the water supply and the sewage disposal system. The major needs of the University are forcefully presented with particular emphasis on the condition of the heating and lighting plant, which had been built in 1897 at a cost of $9,000, $4,000 of which had been taken from fees then charged but now discontinued. The plant was too small and was not equipped for the most economical consumption of coal. The University, however, had done the best it could with money available. To heat Science Hall, then nearing completion, two boilers and a second stack had been added. This patchwork, from the standpoint of the state, was

[1] See Chap. I.

not good business, but from the standpoint of the University it was a necessity. Soon the Student Building, the gift of students, alumni, and friends, would be completed and the University would again confront the problem of heat and light with the plant already heavily overloaded. No additional provision had been made for lighting Science Hall and no funds were available for that purpose.

The problem of heating and lighting arose again and again during the Bryan administration. For many years each new building became an overload for the power plant already operating at peak capacity.

In a statement of needs of the institution, President Bryan said: "The most urgent need of the University is the need for greater income." In support of this statement he gave enrollments and receipts for each year for the previous ten years. In 1891–92, there had been an enrollment of 492 students and an income of $64,728; in 1901–2, an enrollment of 1,285 with total receipts amounting to $129,761.01. During those ten years, whereas the student enrollment had almost trebled, the income had only doubled.

The report complained of the degree to which appropriations for laboratories and library purposes had had to be cut. The need of additional instructors was emphasized, likewise the fact that during the past year six heads of departments had received offers of higher salaries elsewhere. Twelve thousand books were on wooden shelves in the basement of Maxwell Hall where they were subject to deterioration from dampness and hazard from fire. The report concluded:

We ask that the fraction of a mill tax for maintenance of the State University be increased from one-fifteenth of a mill to one-tenth of a mill. We feel that no smaller increase than this one-thirtieth of a mill should be considered. It makes a minimum provision for the maintenance of the University on a strictly economical basis.

The summary of needs was as follows:

Increased income—
Tax to be increased to one-tenth (1/10) of a mill on the dollar
Completion and equipment of Science Hall. $11,892.65
Enlargement and improvement of Heating Plant. 17,750.00
Enlargement and improvement of Lighting Plant. 16,100.00
Fireproof stacks for books now in basement. 5,000.00
Addition to Library Building. 35,280.00

Upon such reports and budgetary requests the Visiting Committee bases its recommendation to the legislature and, after consideration, appropriations are made which determine whether this service unit of the state, the University, will be able to move forward during the biennium, with provisions for the more adequate or the new opportunities for training demanded of Hoosier as of all boys and girls for a place in the sun anywhere in America, or whether, as in Kipling's poem "Boots," the institution must mark time presenting arguments at the next legislative session, and the next, until a majority is convinced and the opportunity for service to Hoosier boys and girls is underwritten by the necessary appropriation.

A review of the acts of this first legislative session of the Bryan administration revealed that this legislature had done what legislatures very often have done—provided for only part of the University's needs. The 50 per cent increase in mill tax and the special appropriation for completion of Science Hall had been granted. But only $20,000 had been allowed for enlargement and improvement of the heating and lighting plant—$13,850 less than requested, and, unhappily, nothing had been done to relieve the critical library situation. If, however, comparison was made with earlier years, it became obvious that the response of the recent General Assembly had been the most generous ever made up to that time.

Though many thought the University had fared very well, the President knew that, even with this increase in mill tax, the income of Indiana University was small in comparison with the income of other midwest universities which drew many students from the same territory. He showed income of seven midwest universities:

University of Chicago	$3,650,539.00
University of Illinois	778,789.00
University of Michigan	741,000.00
University of Wisconsin	575,000.00
University of Ohio	420,006.00
Northwestern University	418,269.00
Purdue University	215,000.00
Indiana University after tax raise	200,000.00

Obviously Indiana University could not do all the things which were done in a university with much greater income. The President concluded:

In this situation we are forced, I think, to only one conclusion. Out of all the things that a University may properly do, we must select the things which we shall undertake, and must deliberately leave many good things alone. If we are to grow corn stalks we must keep down the number of suckers.

INAUGURATION OF THE NEW PRESIDENT

President Bryan was inaugurated on Wednesday, January 21, 1903. The installation was the culmination of two days of impressive ceremonies. Distinguished educators, alumni, and visitors from all parts of the country were present.

The eighty-third anniversary of the founding of the University was celebrated on January 20, with Judge James H. Jordan, of the Indiana Supreme Court, presiding.

There was a long and colorful academic procession before the inaugural ceremonies. Chief Justice John V. Hadley,[2] of the Indiana Supreme Court, delivered the installation address. Judge Hadley defined a university "as being in a technical sense a corporate institution where instruction is offered in the higher branches." "In a more popular sense," he said, "it is a finishing school where young men and women are fitted in a higher character to perform successfully the active duties of life."

The dedication addresses for the new Science Building were given by Dr. Edward L. Nichols, Professor of Physics at Cornell University, Dr. John Coulter, of the University of Chicago, former president of Indiana University, and Professor Arthur L. Foley, Head of the Department of Physics.

In President Bryan's inaugural address he made the oft-quoted statement:

What the people need and demand is that their children shall have a chance—as good a chance as any other children in the world—to make the most of themselves, to rise in any and every occupation, including those occupations which require the most thorough training. What the people want is *open* paths from every corner of the State through the schools to the highest and best things which men can achieve. To make such paths, to make them open to the poorest and make them lead to the highest, is the mission of democracy.

---

[2] It was Judge Hadley who had rendered the Supreme Court decision quoted in Chap. LIII, "The Establishment and Maintenance of Indiana University."

As George Brehm saw the installation reception.

Here was a voice crying in the wilderness, "make straight in the desert a highway." Would it be possible to open these pathways, and to what would they lead?

The President was making a study of the things Indiana University might do to provide opportunity for professional training in other than the teaching field. He was weighing the advantages of expansion in the fields of medicine, engineering, journalism, commerce, library training, etc., to the end that a decision might be reached as to what should be done first.

President Bryan, speaking recently of this period, said:

I thought of sundry possibilities. I called upon Professors Foley, Aley, Lyons, and Miller to make a formal report showing what courses already given in the College of Arts and Sciences were also essential parts of the school of engineering. Their informal reports showed that we were already providing two years of work in fields of engineering, especially in mechanical, civil, and chemical engineering. I knew from the experiences in other states that it would be possible to expand these courses at comparatively little expense. We had before us the definite policy of duplicating engineering in this state as it had been done in many other states. We reached the conclusion that we should not undertake this expansion on the work already provided at Purdue, which would be unfair to the taxpayers of Indiana.

We then turned to consider what might be done in the field of medicine beyond what we were doing.

Organization of the School of Medicine

Imbedded in the records of the Board of Trustees for March, 1903, is an inconspicuous, impersonal, six-line minute which I believe the most important of the thirty-five years of the Bryan administration. It reads as follows:

> On motion of Mr. Shively, seconded by Mr. Corr, President Bryan was authorized to make arrangements for the establishment of a medical department with a two-year course of instruction, and the Executive Committee was authorized to secure a suitable person for the department, all in pursuance of President Bryan's report.

A new era in medical education was dawning. Had the University not availed herself of her right[3] to establish medical education at that particular time she would have lost her opportunity of holding a strategic position in the medical educational developments of the near future. She would have been in no position to defend her long-neglected right in this field two years later. She probably would not have made the fight in the General Assembly of 1907 to maintain her rights in the field of medical education, and had she attempted to do so her position strategically would have been so weak she almost certainly would have lost, in which case Indiana University as we know her today probably never would have come into existence. She would have remained what she was, and what some members of the faculty wished her to continue to be, a fine, an outstanding College of Liberal Arts, but with a decided drift toward becoming a university normal school. She would have been to Indiana what Miami is to Ohio, something fine to be sure—but not a great state university.

[3] The Act of February 15, 1838, had authorized Indiana University to give instruction in law and medicine.

The future of Indiana University hung upon that motion of Senator Shively in March, 1903, in which the University was committed to the policy of establishing professional schools.

The *Indiana University Bulletin* for May, 1903, announced:

NEW MEDICAL DEPARTMENT

The University is about to establish a Department of Medicine. In general the first two years of a four years' medical course are given up to laboratory subjects, such as chemistry, physiology, anatomy, neurology and the like, the last two years being devoted to the clinical subjects. Experience has shown that the first two years' work can be better done in connection with universities than in connection with the ordinary medical schools. For several years a number of medical courses have been given in Indiana University. Graduates of the institution have received something more than a year's credit at the best medical schools. The present plan is to increase the number of medical courses so as to furnish two full years of work.

Thus was launched the Indiana University School of Medicine.

It should be noted that this action establishing the School of Medicine followed logically on Dr. Bryan's study of occupations referred to at length in Chapter II and elaborated in his inaugural address. It also was a first step in providing at Indiana University opportunity for training for professions other than that of teaching, which in another study by Dr. Bryan was found to be the chief activity of the University at that time.

ELECTION OF TRUSTEE ROSE

On May 15, 1903, Theodore Rose, of Muncie, was elected by the State Board of Education as a trustee of Indiana University. He succeeded Charles L. Henry, formerly of Anderson, who had become ineligible by moving to Indianapolis, Marion County. At that time only one trustee might be elected from any one county, except Monroe, where election of two trustees was permissible. Marion County had been represented on the board since June, 1902, when James W. Fesler was elected alumni trustee.

CHAPTER IV

THE SECOND YEAR OF THE BRYAN ADMINISTRATION, 1903 - 4

NEW FIELDS OF STUDY

WHEN, IN the spring of 1903, the trustees decided that, of the various lines of expansion on which the University might properly embark, the establishment of a School of Medicine seemed for various reasons most advisable, the President appointed committees to study and report on various other lines of expansion. In November, 1903, he called attention of the board to the reports of these committees showing the possibility of enlarging the course in commerce and of establishing courses in mechanical, electrical, and civil engineering, in journalism, and in architecture.

Professor William A. Rawles, supported by Professor Ulysses G. Weatherly, submitted a number of courses intended for those who meant to follow a business career. This was an expansion of the work in commerce announced in the Catalog of May, 1902. These additional courses were announced in the *University Bulletin* of May, 1904, and a four-year course of study was outlined leading to an A.B. degree with economics as major, which included nearly two full years of work in courses important for one contemplating a business career. (See Chapter XXXVIII.)

In 1903–4 every university gave courses in mathematics, physics, and mechanics which were identical with those offered in engineering schools. The amount of such work offered at Indiana University at that time was equal to nearly three of the four years required for graduation in the leading schools of engineering. At the President's request Professors Robert J. Aley, Arthur L. Foley, and John A. Miller had outlined a course in engineering, for which, they stated, there would be necessary: equipment for shop work, an additional assistant professor of physics, and an additional instructor in the Department of Astronomy. Believing that duplication of work well done at Purdue was a questionable policy, the President submitted these proposals to the board for discussion, without his approval and recommendation.

Though courses in engineering could have been established for $4,000 as indicated by the Aley-Foley-Miller report, the fact that these courses were well given by Purdue, that the establishment of engineering would have constituted what seemed an unjustifiable duplication and invasion of a field of activity in which a sister institution held a certain priority led the board to omit engineering.

At the suggestion of the President, Professor Martin W. Sampson, Head of the Department of English, submitted an outline for a course in journalism, made almost entirely of work already offered by the University. It was estimated that at the outset the extra cost would not exceed $500.

The fact that students majoring in fine arts under Professor Alfred M. Brooks had been admitted to the Massachusetts Institute of Technology with two and a fraction years of advanced standing indicated a further possible expansion.

Formal action was taken on November 10, 1903, ordering establishment of courses in commerce, manual training, journalism, and architecture.

Eighteen years earlier Dr. Jordan had established here the principle that a graduate should have a major subject—some subject of his own choice in which he had secured a substantial mastery. The thing now proposed was to allow a student to have as his major subject not only particular sciences—chemistry, history, or the like, but also particular groups of sciences, each group leading to some occupation, such as law, medicine, journalism, architecture, or business. President Bryan believed that this policy was educationally sound and that it would justify itself as a practical measure.

The School of Medicine

Many medical matters occupied the attention of the Board of Trustees throughout the year. The year 1903–4 ended with the full expectation that one or both of the old medical schools of Indianapolis would become an integral part of Indiana University, thus providing all four years of the medical course.

THE GRADUATE SCHOOL

A definite "Outline of Scheme for Postgraduate Degrees" was first announced in the Catalog for 1881–82. Graduate students were enrolled in every session beginning with that year.

Up to the time of formal organization as a Graduate School in March, 1904, the degree Master of Science had been conferred on 12 (and one honorary), the Master of Arts on 249, and the Doctor of Philosophy on 14 persons.

At a faculty meeting in February, 1904, the report of the committee on advanced degrees recommending the establishment of a Graduate School encountered spirited opposition. Professor Harold W. Johnston, Head of the Department of Latin, a very able man of keen mentality, was humorously satirical. Others were merely satirical. It was contended, among other things, that Indiana University did not have the library facilities necessary for graduate work. This was a point well taken. But the establishment of the Graduate School soon led to great improvement of the Library. Dr. Eigenmann was the leading advocate of the proposal, which of course was readily defensible in the light of graduate work carried on in past years. The opposition and doubts were part of the "growing pains" experienced in the transition of the institution from a College of Arts and Sciences to a University.

The *University Bulletin* of May, 1904, announced that in order to emphasize the facilities offered by the University for work of an advanced nature the Graduate School had been organized in March, under the immediate control of a committee on graduate work. Regulations relating to admission, graduation, etc. were given.

COOPERATIVE ASSOCIATION

The story of the organization of the Bookstore is told in Chapter XXXVI. In 1903–4 the Cooperative Bookstore was encountering difficulties. Considerable effort was being made to inject politics into its management. In 1910 its charter expired, and the Cooperative was sold. It was purchased by the University and became the University Bookstore.

Effect of Increase in Mill Tax

The increase in the mill tax granted by the General Assembly early in 1903 was too optimistically estimated as producing an increase in income sufficient to total $194,000 for the year 1903–4. Though the total for that year was only $171,871.98, it made possible an appropriation of $250 for the Biological Station, $1,000, "or as much thereof as might be necessary," for the use of the Athletic Association, appointment of a superintendent of buildings, a keeper of grounds, and a University carpenter. The Executive Committee used a part of the appropriation for the Athletic Association to employ Z. G. Clevenger as assistant physical director. One of the University carpenter's first assignments was to change all doors of University buildings so they would open outward.

Instead of using the special appropriation of $20,000 for patching up the old power plant it was decided to make a start at construction of a new power plant to be located north and west of the old plant.

CHAPTER V

INDIANA UNIVERSITY, 1904 - 6

THE FIRST two years of the Bryan administration have been considered separately. Policies were being discussed and inaugurated. Steps were being taken which in time would lead to the transformation of the institution from a university in name to a university in fact.

Though students and faculty generally look upon the semester or school year as the important time unit in university life, from an administrative point of view the biennium, consisting of two fiscal years, was, perhaps, the most important time period of Indiana University. The beginning of the fiscal year has been changed from time to time, but in 1904 it began on October first.

In the fall of each even year a biennial report made to the Governor and Legislative Visiting Committee began with a fundamental review of the status of the institution, based upon departmental, administrative, and committee reports, supplemented by special studies. There was included the report of the treasurer showing essential details of expenditures during the past biennium and also the pressing needs of the University, with request for appropriations for the biennium to come.

REPORT TO VISITING COMMITTEE FOR 1904–6

In the fall of 1904 the President was preparing this biennial report to the Governor and Legislative Visiting Committee in which, among other things, he asked for $250,000 for a new library building and $75,000 for land.

The Visiting Committee appointed by Governor Durbin in 1904 was a very superior group of men consisting of Senator Fremont Goodwin and Representatives Guy Cantwell and Thomas Honan. In his report the President again emphasized the inadequacy of the income of the State University, as compared with neighboring state universities, and cited the resulting exodus of nearly one thousand

30

students from the state of Indiana to educational institutions in other states where more ample university support was being made.

This part of the report is so important and so forcefully presented that it is here quoted in its entirety. The President said:

The financial reports from the Universities of the States which were formed from the Northwest Territory (Ohio, Indiana, Illinois, Michigan, Wisconsin) show that Indiana is far behind all of the others in the appropriation which it makes for higher education. The reports from New York, Minnesota, Iowa, Nebraska, Missouri, Kansas, California, and Texas show that Indiana is in all cases behind the others and in most cases far behind them.

The reports of the United States Commissioner of Education show that the total amount spent for higher education by state and non-state colleges and universities combined is much less for Indiana than for any of the other surrounding states except Kentucky.

The catalogues of twenty-five leading institutions outside of Indiana, for 1903–4, show that they had enrolled 973 students from this State. Of these, 632 were enrolled in the Universities of Ohio, Michigan, and Illinois. The cost of tuition and living expenses at the twenty-five institutions concerned ranges from $500 to $1,000 per student. This means that between one half million and a million dollars of Indiana money went out of the State last year for higher education demanded by our people. On the same scale the amount of Indiana money going into Illinois, Ohio, and Michigan last year ranges between $316,000 and $632,000. The total amount of money sent out of the State for higher education is much greater than the total amount spent by the State for higher education within the State. It is an interesting fact that only 172 of the 973 students attend the great Universities of the Atlantic States. The West is providing magnificently for higher education, but Indiana although it has done much is behind her sister states and is not providing for her own people.

Our common school system, though it requires improvements and the expenditure of more money, is regarded by everyone as one of the best in the country. Our high school system is everywhere looked upon as a model. No youth can better himself by leaving Indiana for an elementary or high school education. But when it comes to higher education, we must confess that we have not in Indiana the bare room to receive all the young people of the State who wish to go to college, and still less have in adequate measure the facilities required by the demands of modern civilization.

The whole scale of our expenditures is necessarily far below what it is in the states mentioned. It is a fact which can be shown item by item that we spend less for buildings, for equipment, for books and for men than the states which are about us, excepting those to the south and not excepting all of those. I wish here to record the warning that if these conditions do not change decidedly in the right direction, they will infallibly change more and more in the wrong direction, and that Indiana will presently send the bulk of the money which it has to spend for higher education out of the state and at the same time have the reproach of being a state that will not adequately support higher education.

The President then stressed the need for special appropriations for completion of the heat, light, and power plant; construction of a new library; and purchase of additional land.

Two years earlier $33,850 had been requested for the heat, light, and power plant. The legislature had appropriated $20,000, a wholly inadequate sum. What should be done? After much consideration, and after consultation with the Governor, it was decided to erect the building necessary for housing the required equipment and go as far toward its equipment as funds would permit. The University, the President stated, now had the required building, with one boiler, one engine, and generator, and space for the further necessary equipment, for which funds were now requested. Meanwhile it was necessary to run the old plant and the one boiler in the new plant, with extra cost for servicing two separate units.

Supporting the request for a new library building, the President said:

The present building was erected fifteen years ago. It was suited in size to the needs of the institution at that time. Since that time the enrollment has increased approximately five hundred per cent. The result is that our library has long been far from adequate. Six years ago the Legislative Committee recognized the inadequacy of the library and so stated in its official report. Since that time the enrollment has increased by a half. Two years ago the Legislative Committee again officially recognized in its report the need of a larger and better library.

To meet immediate needs without taking any account of the future, the building should be twice as large as the present one. It is a plain business proposition that we should erect a building which would be large enough at least to last one generation. It should contain space for the offices of administration. It should be absolutely fireproof.

Emphasizing the importance of securing land, still available east and north of the campus, the President stated:

In 1884 the University purchased part of the present site, paying $6,000 for 20 acres. In March, 1897, an additional tract of 9 acres was bought for $12,000. In June, 1897, a tract of 20 acres was bought for $6,953. The forty-nine[1] acres in the present campus cost $24,953, or an average of $509.26 per acre.

[1] There were fractions in the purchases, which made a total of 50.82 acres.

Meanwhile the city has grown rapidly extending about and beyond the campus and the price of land has greatly increased. The Trustees have long realized the danger of having the campus hemmed in with no possibility of enlargement except at prohibitive prices, but they have had no funds available for the purchase of the adjacent land.

The President summarized University needs as they presented themselves in November, 1904, as follows:

1. If we can organize a complete medical school which shall absorb the two principal Indianapolis schools, the establishment of that school should be our first object. In that event the need of income would be greater than the need of buildings.

2. Next in order of immediate importance is a new library. The present library built in 1890 for $75,000 has long been inadequate. It would be foolish to build another of this size. We ought to build a library including administration offices to cost $250,000, so that the work would be done for a quarter of a century.

3. Though the need for more land is not so immediate as that for a library, it may be thought of greater importance considering the long run.

These three needs take precedence in my judgment of all others however great.

A complete medical school, a new library, additional land, purchased now, before the price went still higher, these three objectives expressed the hopes and ambitions of Indiana University in the fall of 1904.

The months between the report to the Visiting Committee and the adjournment of the General Assembly in March were usually months of anxious waiting and of hopes often vain.

When the board met in April, 1905, they already knew that the legislature had made no appropriation for completion of the heat, light, and power plant, nor for purchase of additional land. Whereas $250,000 had been asked for a library building, only $100,000 had been granted. Under the circumstances, what was to be done? Obviously it was going to be necessary to limp along with the inefficient heating and lighting plant for another biennium.

This failure of the legislature of 1905 to meet the carefully prepared statement of budgetary needs of the University was very disheartening. The legislature may have overestimated the yield of the mill tax voted in 1903. While there were, no doubt, various reasons for this failure of the legislature to come to the support of the state institutions of higher education, perhaps the two most frequently encountered were the tendency to compare the University with the denominational schools of the state and the fear that growth of the University was to the disinterest of these schools.

Library

As to the library building, what could be done with $100,000 toward meeting the pressing need of the University? This is what was done. Librarian William E. Jenkins visited many of the best libraries and with the President examined the plans of many others. Finally it was decided to have plans drawn for a building that could be erected for $100,000 and to which additions could be made.

To this end Architects Patton and Miller, of Chicago, were employed and directed to follow, so far as possible, the plans prepared by Mr. Jenkins. Tentative plans were first submitted on June 16, 1905, but it was not until October 5 that final revised plans and specifications with estimates of costs were accepted and ordered advertised for bids. Further delays were encountered, however, so it was not until January, 1906, that bids were opened and contracts let. Meanwhile so much time had been lost that the state auditor called attention to the fact that $50,000 was now available and the unexpended balance would revert to the state on October 31.

Even with this Statehouse prodding, actual work on construction of the library got under way with incredible slowness. On April 2, 1906, a year after the appropriation was made, the contractor was just getting materials and equipment on the ground between the Student Building and Indiana Avenue, where it had been decided the building should be located.

President Bryan gives an explanation of the slow start in construction of a building so greatly needed:

Construction of the University Library was delayed when the contractor and then also the architects stated that they did not know how to make the ceiling of the large reading room of one concrete slab in such manner that the structure would be safe. A Chicago engineer called in consultation was likewise unable to give satisfactory advice. We then asked three of our professors— Lyons (Chemistry), Foley (Physics), Miller (Analytical Mechanics)—to consider the problem. They made the necessary chemical and mathematical studies and submitted plans and specifications for a safe construction. These were adopted and building proceeded accordingly.

LAND

The administration was convinced that the purchase of additional land was of such great importance that, in spite of the failure of the legislature to make a special appropriation for this purpose—$75,000 had been asked—the interests of the University and of the state made immediate action imperative. Accordingly, Moses Dunn, who owned the land adjoining the campus, was invited to a conference in April, 1905. The conference resulted in options given by Mr. Dunn on: (1) the land between Seventh and Ninth streets and between Indiana Avenue and the old Dunn home, for $37,000; on (2) the Dunn property east of the campus and between Seventh Street and Third Street, for $10,000. The University was given first opportunity to purchase the old Dunn homestead and lands eastward if the first option were taken. There was no mention of land between Ninth and Tenth streets. The University purchased the nineteen and one-half acres east of the campus known as the Forest Place addition to the city of Bloomington.

There can be no doubt of the wisdom of this land purchase, though its necessity was regrettable, for the money used was badly needed for laboratory equipment in various science departments, for Library, and for instructional staff throughout the institution. Ultimately a *part* of the Dunn land north of Seventh Street was purchased at a cost much greater than was being asked for the whole plot in 1905.

THE MEDICAL SITUATION

While Library, land, and heat and light may seem to have been occupying the entire attention of the administration, a union of the two old medical schools with Indiana University was never out of mind.

A crisis was approaching in medical education in Indiana. Things began happening with wholly unexpected suddenness. Matters of great importance and developments of vital interest succeeded one another with bewildering rapidity. The following is a mere catalog of some of the major events of the last year of this biennium.

In April, 1905, conferences were held with representatives of the Medical College of Indiana with reference to their formal proposal for a union. During the spring the establishment of the courses necessary for the work of the first two years in medicine was completed. The Indiana University School of Medicine was inspected by and admitted to membership in the Association of American Medical Colleges.

Then in the fall of 1905 there was announced the union of the Medical College of Indiana with Purdue University. In the spring of 1906 the building in Indianapolis of the Central College of Physicians and Surgeons was purchased by friends of Indiana University and the State College of Physicians and Surgeons was organized in affiliation with the Indiana University School of Medicine, making possible a four-year course in medicine beginning with the fall of 1906.

These matters merely mentioned here are parts of the story told in Chapter VIII.

MISCELLANEOUS

The summer session had become a regular part of the school year. Attendance in the summer of 1904 exceeded that of the University in the fall of 1894.

A chapter of Sigma Xi was established in the fall of 1904, on petition of thirteen members of science departments who were members of the Society by election while students in other universities. Charter members of the Indiana University chapter were Arthur L. Foley, Edgar R. Cumings, Joshua W. Beede, Rolla R. Ramsey, Burton D. Myers, William L. Bryan, Carl H. Eigenmann, John A. Miller, Ernest H. Lindley, David M. Mottier, Robert E. Lyons, John A. Bergstrom, William J. Moenkhaus.

We get a glimpse of the "horse and buggy" days at Indiana University in the following S.O.S.: "It is now impossible for one stenographer to do the work in the administrative offices." The entire time of an additional stenographer was needed, and a like need existed in the Library. A warning was sounded, however, that "the employment of two additional stenographers would mean the purchase of two additional machines." Two typewriters were purchased and two stenographers were employed, one in the Library and one in the administrative office.

John W. Foster, '55, distinguished diplomat and one-time Secretary of State, gave the Commencement address and received the LL.D. degree in 1905.

A fund was made available to the librarian for purchase of bargains in books.

Professor Samuel B. Harding was appointed editor of University publications in addition to his teaching duties.

Miss Louise Goodbody was chosen acting dean of women, to succeed Dr. Mary B. Breed, resigned.

The President was authorized in June, 1906, to formulate a plan for retirement and pensioning of "superannuated professors."

Trustee Isaac Jenkinson, who had served the University longer than any other trustee, announced his retirement in the spring of 1906. He was succeeded by James E. Watson.

Establishment of a school of engineering was again being seriously considered.

Assistant Professor Wilbur A. Cogshall became head of the Department of Mechanics and Astronomy in 1906 when Professor John A. Miller went to Swarthmore.

The Senior Class sponsored two performances by the Ben Greet players in April, 1906: *The Merchant of Venice* and *Macbeth*.

A May Festival, in which students, faculty members, and townspeople sang, was held on two days in May, 1906.

The courses in comparative philology were set off from the Department of English in 1906 as a separate department, headed by Associate Professor Guido H. Stempel, who had been teaching them.

CHAPTER VI

THE STUDENT BUILDING, 1901 - 6

One of the major problems inherited by President Bryan from his predecessor was a lagging campaign for a fund for erecting a woman's building. This project was destined to undergo various changes as it developed.

The idea of a building for women had originated with Mrs. Joseph Swain. In March, 1901, on invitation of the trustees, she had explained to them her plan to raise a fund by private subscription for erecting a building for women on the campus. They passed a resolution heartily endorsing the movement and urging all friends of the University and of education generally to aid Mrs. Swain and her associates in this good work. Her associates were members of the women's clubs of Bloomington whom she had interested in this project. The Local Council of Women of Bloomington had made the first payment.

It should be recalled that after the fire of April 9, 1854, Bloomington citizens had contributed $10,000 toward rebuilding. Again, after the fire on the night of July 12, 1883, Monroe County had contributed $50,000 toward rebuilding. But this was the first time friends of the University throughout the state had been approached in an organized campaign for a fund for construction of anything on the campus of the State University, and the sympathetic and ready response of Bloomington people was giving Mrs. Swain much needed encouragement.

When responsibility for establishment of a State University was written into the Indiana Constitution in 1816, it was the general belief that interest on the fund to be derived from sale of a grant of federal lands would finance the institution. It was fifty-one years later, 1867, that the error of this view and the responsibility of the state were so generally recognized that a small annual appropriation of $8,000 was voted by the legislature for University maintenance.

During the following thirty-four years, 1867 to 1901, though the little appropriation of $8,000 had gradually grown to $87,880, it had little more than kept pace with attendance, which during those same years had increased from 128 to 1,137. On the basis of income per student the institution was therefore not much better off. Meanwhile, though state support of higher education was very inadequate, people had become accustomed to thinking of support of the University solely as the responsibility of the state.

In his report to the trustees in June, 1901, President Swain discussed the progress of the campaign and the difficulties encountered. He and Mrs. Swain had attended meetings of alumni in Chicago, Indianapolis, Louisville, Evansville, and Vincennes. In many places in the state the movement was not meeting with enthusiastic response. In other places it was met with indifference.

It had become evident that to interest alumni and friends in the project a great deal of correspondence and much travel would be necessary. There was needed a secretary, someone who had the interests of the University at heart. An appropriation of $1,000 was recommended for expenses. The President saw in the movement opportunity for greatly strengthening the alumni organization. Requests had come for a brief statement as to why alumni and friends should contribute to erection of a woman's building, as it was still called on the University campus, and he had prepared the following statement:

We are so accustomed to think of the obligation of the state to maintain its institutions that we do not perhaps sufficiently realize the obligation of those who are receiving its benefits to do all in their power to maintain such institutions. While it is true that it pays the state many times over to support its state's educational institutions of higher learning, this does not absolve those who receive special opportunities from their obligations.

For the first time in the history of Indiana University a general appeal is made to its alumni and friends to raise by private subscription the sum of $30,000. This sum is to be used in the erection of a woman's building. The building is to contain a gymnasium, a small auditorium, parlors, rest-rooms, kitchen, etc. It will naturally be the center of the social life of the University. The larger the University becomes the more such a building is a necessity. The question may be asked, Why should anyone give anything to a state university? First, anything which makes the University more efficient makes the degree from it of more value and the institution is of greater service to its graduates and to the state. By strengthening the University every friend of it strengthens himself. Second, every graduate of the University has cost the institution money, time, and devotion. If each graduate made a financial gift to his alma mater every year as well as gave his love and personal service, he could never, let him do all that he would, pay back to his alma mater what her fostering care had done for him. If one stops for a moment to compare what his life would have been without his college training, he would realize something of his indebtedness to her.

Why should a graduate of a state institution, if he is able to do so, not assist his alma mater financially as does a graduate of a private or denominational college? One who thinks of it for a moment must recognize his indebtedness to his alma mater. Why give to the erection of this Woman's Building? First, it is needed. Second, the trustees, faculty, and friends of the University to whom this matter has been presented believe thoroughly in the movement. Third, it is the first general appeal for money from the alumni and friends. Such appeals have been made with success in other state universities. Fourth, the trustees have not the money at present for this purpose and the legislature is not likely to provide it. Fifth, there should be at least one building on the campus which represents the voluntary contribution of its friends. Sixth, if every friend gives according to his ability it will mean a new era for the University. Seventh, whatever may be the feeling of anyone concerning this particular building, all must recognize that the union of all the friends in a common cause of interest to our alma mater must be a great good to the University. This Woman's Building has the field at present. Let each friend do something. The spirit of cooperation will do much for our University. Yea, much more than any building, however necessary.

To desire this building for its own sake, for the comforts and appliances it will afford, is commendable. But far more important than the building itself is that we should have here on the campus a memorial gift which will be a constant expression of the faith, love, and unfailing good will of the children and guardians of the University. Our devotion is so much increased by our gifts.

This statement of President Swain is of general historical interest. Throughout the United States alumni and friends of state universities were startled and even angered at being asked to contribute to anything on a state university campus. They asked why they should contribute. Why not let the state do it? President Swain was doing pioneer work. He was helping Hoosiers take a forward step in a wider conception of civic responsibility. This campaign for $30,000 for a woman's building had significance far beyond the money or building. It was an educational campaign in better citizenship which carried people beyond their own picket fence, beyond the city limits, and called for thinking as citizens of the state. It laid the foundation for the far greater memorial campaign twenty years later.

Subscriptions, however, were coming in slowly. In the spring of 1902 President Swain had accepted the call to Swarthmore. But he and Mrs. Swain had put their shoulders to this woman's building project, so dear to Mrs. Swain. With the clock ticking off his last hours at Indiana the President wrote to John D. Rockefeller asking help. Questions were asked and answered. Then on June 9, 1902, John D. Rockefeller, Jr., wrote President Swain:

> Understanding that $60,000 is required to build and furnish a building for the social and religious needs of the men and women students of Indiana University, and understanding that toward this amount $14,000 has already been subscribed: providing that, including that amount, a total of $30,000 is subscribed in good responsible pledges, on or before January 1, 1903, Mr. John D. Rockefeller will give $30,000.

On June 28 President Swain expressed the appreciation of the board for this gift and informed Mr. Rockefeller that he was leaving for Swarthmore, but that William L. Bryan, Vice-President and President-Elect, who sympathized in every respect with this building project, would carry on.

So it was put squarely up to President Bryan in the first year of his administration to save this woman's building project by raising $16,000 in good pledges. Happily, in March, 1903, he was able to inform Mr. Rockefeller that a total of $36,717.93 had been subscribed for the building.

As the campaign progressed the vision of what this building would and should be had so expanded that the President inquired whether Mr. Rockefeller would match this or an even larger sum.

To this inquiry Mr. Rockefeller, Jr., replied:

> On behalf of my father I hereby make the following pledge. For every dollar which you have raised for a social and religious building, in addition to the $30,000 above referred to [already pledged by Mr. Rockefeller] or which you shall raise on or before July 1, 1903, and which same shall be paid in on or before July 1, 1904, my father will give one dollar up to a total of $20,000.
>
> This makes my father's total pledge to Indiana University $50,000 from him.

This was splendid except that it left the University, which in this case meant the President, again short of the new goal by $13,282.07, a figure which the President remembers today (1945). The canvass of the state was essentially complete. A building costing the full $100,000 was greatly needed. What procedure should be adopted?

As planned, the building for women included a gymnasium for women. The President called attention to this as a legitimate University expense and raised the question whether, under the circumstances, it might be wise for the University to provide the balance needed, $13,300, to secure the whole of the $50,000 from Mr. Rockefeller. This suggestion was followed.

On July 15, 1904, the President sent to Mr. Rockefeller the certificate of Walter Woodburn, Treasurer of Indiana University, showing pledges totaling $50,000 in his hands and available. Ten days later a check for $50,000 was sent by Mr. Rockefeller.

As the campaign for this building progressed the original conception was modified by President Swain to include men. The pledge of $30,000 by Mr. Rockefeller was for the social and religious needs of men and women students. For a time the erection of two buildings, one for women and one for men, was considered. The question was referred to Mr. Rockefeller, who regarded it as a local problem.

With the decision to include men in the project the term "woman's building" became a misnomer. But whether there should be two buildings, one for women and another for men, or a single building for both men and women was still undecided as late as June, 1903.

Ultimately it became clear that there were great advantages in a single building, to be called the Student Building, with a large centrally located auditorium accessible from a wing on each side, the east one for men, the other for women. The site west rather than north of Maxwell Hall was finally selected (January 6, 1904); "the south line of the building was to be on a line with the center of the middle window of the bay window in Maxwell Hall."

In the fall of 1904 various matters in connection with contracts and construction of the Student Building were occupying the attention of the board. A building of such size and cost as to increase the total value of University property by approximately 25 per cent was, very naturally, a major project. Though a master plan for the campus had been prepared, it was now obsolete. The needs of a school of arts and sciences such as Indiana University were comparatively simple. If Indiana began to fulfil her destiny of becoming a University in something more than name, needs would multiply. But the institution was still small, and her real growth just beginning. Even the campus was small, bounded by Third and Seventh streets, Indiana Avenue, and Forest Place. So the problems created by the construction of the Student Building seemed and were very great.

A number of different stone companies had made donations of stone, some of which was regarded as unacceptable or as fit only for foundation purposes or for use in the rear of the building. It was a day when a uniform gray was considered the only desirable stone for building purposes. In a controversy with some of the donors of stone, Henry Woolery and Fred Mathews, local stone men, helped work out an agreement which solved most of the major difficulties.

The desirability of chimes and a clock for the Student Building was officially considered in November, 1904, when it was made known that four classes, 1899 to 1902 inclusive, had subscribed $659.94 for the purchase of chimes. Professor Arthur L. Foley had investigated the cost of chimes and found it ranged from $1,200 to $3,600, the difference in price depending mainly on the weight of the bells. The tone in general improved with increase in weight. The President urged purchase of the chimes even if it made incomplete furnishing necessary. Authorization was given for the purchase. Professor Foley reported that a first-rate tower clock could be purchased for $800.

The architects (Vonnegut and Bohn) were ordered to make preliminary sketches of a tower for the clock and chimes and to secure estimates to be submitted to the Executive Committee, which was authorized to take such action as appeared best. The sketches of the architect were adopted, satisfactory arrangements were made with the contractor, and the bid of the McShane Bell Company to furnish chimes for the sum of $3,650 was accepted.

The first functions were held in this new building at Commencement time, June, 1906. The building contained rooms for social and religious purposes for women, women's gymnasium, lecture room (50 feet by 80 feet, capacity 600 seats) for small assemblies, lectures, etc., rooms for social and religious purposes for men, offices for various student organizations, etc.

It was believed at that time that there should be an east wing for a men's gymnasium, a plan fortunately not carried out.

When first constructed the acoustics of the auditorium were very unsatisfactory. Since this was a particular interest of Professor Foley, he made suggestions which, carried out later, largely remedied this defect.

The story of the erection of the Student Building has been told in detail and given considerable importance but the story is one of 1901–6, and the construction of a splendid auditorium (Music Hall) thirty-five years later, costing ten times as much, was not regarded with greater admiration and wonder in 1941 than this Student Building in 1906.

Today it would be a small project. But it was a great project in the opinion of Mrs. James K. Beck, who baked and sold cakes to pay her subscription. It was not a small project in the eyes of Mrs. William N. Showers, who knit borders to wash cloths and sold them for money to pay her pledge. It was a great project to the 2,000 students, alumni, and friends of the University who subscribed to its construction.

This building was a great boon to the University. It not only served, as it still serves, for promotion of the social and religious activities of the student body, but it served for faculty receptions, alumni luncheons, etc., not to mention the use of the auditorium for the large classes in hygiene. The chimes were a happy addition to the building as originally planned.

A bronze tablet was dedicated in 1906 to Frances Morgan Swain, in recognition of her pre-eminent part in the movement for the erection of this building.

CHAPTER VII

INDIANA UNIVERSITY, 1906 - 8

ANOTHER LEGISLATIVE YEAR

INDIANA LEGISLATURES had not yet learned to support the state institutions of higher education generously. They had not learned that generous support of the state universities did not affect the non-state schools adversely, but, on the contrary, made it easier for the non-state schools to get the better support they needed, as was pointed out by President Francis J. McConnell, of DePauw, at a little later date, at the beginning of the administration of Governor Thomas R. Marshall.

The President in his report to Governor J. Frank Hanly and the Visiting Committee in November, 1906, had stated that the most urgent material need of the University was an appropriation for completion of the power plant. The sum of $337,873.53 had been requested for seven projects, including the power plant.

The President again reviewed the heat and light situation. It had been extremely difficult to know how to use wisely the inadequate appropriation of $20,000 for heat and light, made by the legislature of 1903. It was hoped to make an end to wasteful patching up of an inadequate power plant. Finally, after consultation with the Governor, it was decided to have plans and specifications prepared for a new and complete power plant and then to build as much of that plant as possible with funds available.

It followed, therefore, that in the fall of 1906, the University had a new power plant building, one boiler, one engine and generator, with space and plans for a complete plant. Meanwhile it had been necessary to run both the old plant and the one boiler of the new plant. There was no mechanical stoker, so extra service for the two plants was necessary.

Fortunately, the legislature of 1907 granted the appropriation for completion of this plant. No time was lost. Plans and specifications were ready. It was the purpose to have construction completed and equipment installed and ready for the opening of the school year in the fall of 1907.

It will be recalled that a wholly inadequate appropriation ($100,-000) had been made for a new library building by the legislature in 1905. After extended deliberation it had been decided to have plans drawn for a building that could be erected for $100,000, to which an addition could be made at a later date. A contract had been let and construction had been begun in June, 1906.

In November, 1906, the President made an itemized report to the Governor and Visiting Committee of the cost of completion of the building, which depended upon the response of the General Assembly of 1907 to the request for the $40,670 needed. Of this total, the legislature granted $25,000, the amount needed for stacks alone. So from the items required it was necessary to select those immediately needed for occupancy which could be installed for $25,000. Only 60 per cent of the stacks needed could be installed at that time.

Installation of equipment progressed satisfactorily, and by November, according to the President, it was expected

to move into the new building during the holiday vacation and to anticipate no difficulty or delay in the work. Plans have been made for the systematic removal of the books so as to minimize the risk of misplacement. As soon as the stacks are in, the locations will be finally determined and the routine of removal perfected. The building in general justifies our expectations. The light in the reading room is better than we hoped for. The basement seminar rooms are commodious and pleasant. The stack room, since plastering, is splendidly light.

The Daily Student, December 14, 1907 (p. 1), carried an article entitled "Moving Season Begins." "The first load of books is carried into new library. Heat was turned into the new library for the first time on December 12th. By the first of next week the plant will be in good working order." The Catalog for May, 1908 (p. 45), states that the new library building was completed January 1, 1908, at a cost of $140,000.[1]

In March the President had more good things to say of the way plans had worked out:

[1] W. A. Alexander gives the cost as $137,000 (Chap. XLVII). Evidently certain contemplated expenditures had been deleted.

The new library building[2] answers our expectations in every important respect. The minor inconveniences in the way of inadequate heating, leaks, etc., will doubtless be removed. It is especially satisfactory to note that the use of the Library jumped at least 25 per cent almost from the day the new building was opened. As the use is almost entirely in the field of collateral and required reading, the effect upon the substantial routine class work should be noticeable. The desk service is quicker volume for volume than in the old library and there is no reason, assuming an equally competent desk force, why it should not be as rapid with twice the number of volumes in the stacks. The great reading room is the lightest and quietest reading room of the size I know of and compares favorably in attractiveness with any similar room in the country. Already its capacity has been put to the test, over 200 readers having been seated at one time. The conversation room and lobby are in almost constant use by students engaged in preparing "syndicate lessons." The journalism room in the basement also is used for this purpose.

The third project for which the legislature of 1907 had made provision was an addition to Maxwell Hall.

With the opening of the new Library, Maxwell Hall, which had been used as a library and administrative offices, was to become the home of the School of Law. Unfortunately, the building did not provide adequate space for the law classes, even with the enrollment of that day. Therefore the addition, estimated to cost $18,125, had been planned.

Professor Foley was directed to complete plans for the addition to Maxwell Hall, take bids, and report to the board at the June meeting, 1907. This was done, and in June a contract was let for this structure.

In March, 1907, when the legislature had adjourned, appropriations had been made:

For completing and equipping the power plant $56,000.00
For stacks and other equipment for the Library 25,000.00
For an addition to Maxwell Hall 18,125.00
                                                                                          ————————
                                                                                          $99,125.00

Of the budget requests not granted the most important was that for land.

While these three objectives were receiving the attention necessary, the really absorbing interest of the University in the legislative session of 1907 and throughout the biennium was the firm establish-

[2] A $325,000 addition to this building was made in 1925–26.

ment of the Indiana University School of Medicine, the story of which is told in the next chapter.

THE FACULTY

The history of Indiana University during the Bryan administration is not merely the assembled stories of establishment of new schools and erection of new buildings. Schools had to be manned. Each year attendance at the University increased by a number approximately as great as the total student list at the beginning of the Jordan administration (January 1, 1885), which called for additions to the faculty.

Scholastic qualifications of new faculty members could be evaluated more easily than personality, and more easily than adrenal and thyroid output. Misfits, however, were few in number and quickly eliminated. The very great majority of new faculty members quickly caught the spirit of the institution and began to fill their particular niche, as in a military organization.

The ready adjustment of new faculty members and the hearty cooperation of all was due largely to the tact with which the President took the faculty into his confidence when difficulties arose. Men felt that they had a part in meeting a trying situation. The following letter (October 16, 1907) of the President to the faculty illustrates this point. It sounds a note of confidence and encouragement for those who might become alarmed, apprehensive, discouraged. Its effect was steadying.

To members of the faculty:

It is known to members of the faculty that we are in a financial situation where it becomes increasingly difficult to meet the necessary expenditures of the University with our actual income. This situation will continue and will grow more difficult until our income is enlarged. It behooves us, therefore, to govern ourselves as a wise man does under such circumstances in dealing with his private affairs—to consider scrupulously what things are most essential and what things may best be deferred.

Every item of actual or of proposed expenditure should be scrutinized in this spirit. In the purchase of supplies and books we must provide first for the necessities of undergraduate work and second for the particular lines of advanced work which have been or are about to be taken up. But where proposed purchases are not for immediate and essential uses, it is, I am sure, best to defer them.

I wish once more to call attention to the importance of economizing by eliminating undergraduate courses which parallel other undergraduate courses within the same department. I shall not repeat what I have already said upon this subject. I shall only point out that one of the most pressing difficulties is to supply a sufficient number of competent teachers for our increasing throng of students. We must not until the last extremity (which will never arrive) meet this emergency by the sacrifice of advanced productive work. But if in any case there is on the one hand a crowd of students pressing upon a department for its essential courses and, on the other hand, a supernumerary elective course which could be dispensed with without essential loss—this is plainly a case which urgently calls for a more economical use of our time and of our resources.

I have never at any time been more hopeful for the future of the University. A rapidly increasing number of scholars, lawyers, physicians, teachers, journalists, and men of other learned professions are to go out from us establishing the life of the University within and beyond the commonwealth. In considering the larger aspects of this probable future, I should take no joy in it, however large it may be, if I did not believe in the soundness of that life as it now is within our faculty. The demand for truth, as insistent as it is unpretentious, the faith in spiritual ideals without sophistication, the courage against wrong outside and inside, the loyalty to the University which should be, these are the forces which create the better State.

William L. Bryan.

THE JUNIOR PROM OF 1907

While legislative session, school difficulties, and erection of buildings in the thought of officials might be the most important interest of a period, it was not so with the student body. Their formal education involved class assignments, but they were also students in "The School of Human Relations," and both were important. The big things in their lives, the things that stirred their emotions, were the class scrap, some close game, or some social event. Such an event was the Junior Prom of 1907.

Prior to 1907, dances of student organizations of all sorts as well as those of the young faculty men's club were held in downtown halls over store rooms. The halls were unattractive places and the dances lasted beyond midnight and often were not properly chaperoned. They were, however, liquor free. The man who had been drinking was promptly escorted from the hall by his men friends.

These downtown dances of students worried the President, and in the spring of 1906 he had called a meeting of heads of departments to consider what might be done about it.

At that time I had been a member of the faculty for nearly three years and was losing some inhibition to raising my voice in that august body of department heads. At Cornell, where, like a number of other members of the faculty, I had spent some years, the women's gymnasium and the men's gymnasium were granted for use for certain dances, with closing time fixed by the university. The Student Building was nearing completion so I suggested that the problem under consideration could be solved by granting the use of the Student Building for student dances.

I argued that if the University furnished a place for dances so superior to any other available, and at no cost beyond a possible nominal charge for light and janitor service, the students would cheerfully accept chaperons and a closing time before midnight.

I can feel today, after a third of a century, the absolute silence with which my suggestion was received. Not a word was spoken. All eyes were fixed on the floor. Speak of silence being ponderable! That was crushing.

I understood the reason better later. It was a time when dancing was regarded by many churchmen as very sinful. In certain colleges where dancing was allowed, the permission extended to the so-called "square" dances only, of which there were a number, including the minuet. So-called "round" dances, such as the waltz, were taboo, or possibly only one might be allowed during the entire evening, when it might be required that men dance with men, and girls with girls.

It was about a year later that in April, 1907, the Junior class, conscious of the deep-seated prejudice of many churchmen, aware of the apprehensions of the administration, yet desiring to make this social event just as attractive as possible, petitioned the trustees for the use of the Student Building for a "class reception." The occasion for which the petition was filed was a bit camouflaged. But everyone understood that this class reception was a Junior Prom.

The Juniors had made the strongest case possible. They showed that similar promenades were held in many prominent universities.

They laid emphasis on the purpose for which the Student Building was erected. Then they awaited, anxiously, doubtfully, the decision of the board.

They were not kept long in suspense. Their pleasure at the favorable decision of the board was evidenced by a paragraph from an editorial in *The Daily Student* (April 9):

> Now that the Trustees have acted so generously in granting the Juniors the use of the Student Building for their annual promenade, it seems that the class should be able to give one of the most successful functions of the year. This time there will be plenty of room for all—it being felt that at least 200 couples can be provided for. The affair, while under the management of the Junior Class, will be University-wide in its appeal. Thus the prom will assume the importance that it should have held from the beginning. An affair of this kind will do much to unite all students of the University, for, as it is now, there are but few occasions when all students, no matter what their class, fraternity, organization, or social condition, can get together.

The Prom was held on the night of May 17, and was a great success, universally regarded as the best ever given. President Bryan was one of the chaperons, and made a short talk to the class in which he commended the spirit that had brought the class together.

Certain University officials had regarded the approaching date for the Prom with considerable apprehension. They feared unfavorable repercussions. They visualized headings in leading papers protesting the use of a building of a tax-supported institution for so sinful a pastime as dancing. When the morning following the Prom dawned and headlines were scanned, it was discovered that no one had been interested.

It is quite possible that this innovation was made without protest because of the fact that the fund for the Student Building had been contributed by alumni and Mr. Rockefeller.

It was many years later that DePauw, where opposition to dancing was more pronounced, felt she dared permit the use of her gymnasium for a like occasion. As at Indiana somewhat earlier, she discovered that the repercussions were negligible.

THE ROSE WELLHOUSE

In *The Daily Student,* October 15, 1907, we find the story of a beautiful addition to the campus of great sentimental value:

Among all the buildings which will ultimately adorn the University, there will be none so suggestive of sacred reminiscences to the old student and so pregnant of possibilities for the new as the beautiful new wellhouse which the trustees will erect on the site of the present cistern pump. In the years to come graduates of the classes of '75, '80, etc. who come back to visit the familiar scene will find on the campus old relics of their own days and old inscriptions which they know by heart.

In the spring of 1907 a committee of trustees had been appointed with Theodore F. Rose, '75, as chairman, to investigate the feasibility of securing the fronts, finials, and other ornamental stones from the "Old College Building" and incorporating them into a wellhouse. These stones were secured and brought to the present campus. Professor A. L. Foley, of the Department of Physics, drew plans for the wellhouse. Mr. Rose bore personally all expenses of this project. The Rose Wellhouse was erected at the site of the campus cistern in which pure water was stored, to be drawn by a pump for drinking purposes. It was completed in 1908 and presented to the University by Mr. Rose, in the name of the alumni.

This was a valuable gift. The portals of the Old College Building, from the site of the present Bloomington High School, tie the present campus to that original seminary-college-university campus site. It took unusual persistence to secure those old portals.

Courses in Journalism

In the spring of 1903, it will be recalled, the President had appointed committees to study and report on various lines of expansion and Professor Martin W. Sampson had submitted a plan for courses in journalism. The Press Club, of which Howard Conover was president in 1904–5, was interested in this matter and urged establishment of a school of journalism. There was no such school in the United States at that time.

In 1906 another committee consisting of Professors Will D. Howe (English), Ulysses G. Weatherly (Sociology), and Samuel B. Harding (History) had been appointed to consider this matter. The report of this committee was printed in *The Daily Student,* December 8, 1906, one paragraph of which said:

By the formation of this school it is proposed not merely to enlarge and improve the opportunities that are offered to young men for a start in life but to raise and fix the character and standard of the press itself as a moral teacher and a promoter of that publicity which makes for better government and for advancement of civilization.

The objective was worthy of this able committee. It is evident that they thought a *School of Journalism* should be established. The courses which they outlined were subsequently approved but the work was not given *School* status. Announcement of "Journalism Course" was made in the University Catalog published in May, 1907. The work outlined was under the general supervision of a committee and under the special direction of Fred Bates Johnson, who had had highly successful experience on the *Indianapolis News*.

It was planned that the work in journalism should have the closest possible connection with *The Daily Student* so that the work of the class, both reportorial and editorial, might include practical experience.

Since *The Daily Student* was to be sent to all the high schools of the state, the work of the class in journalism would have state-wide circulation.

DEFERRED FEES

Toward the close of the nineteenth century the administration desired to abolish the small contingent fee paid by students at the beginning of each term. This fee brought about $10,000 a year into the University treasury, so it was not until November 14, 1900, that it was felt this action could be taken, effective as of January 1, 1901. The fee had been retained in the School of Law, however, and a Library fee and laboratory fees were charged. With organization of the School of Medicine, heavy fees had to be charged to enable the University to provide the necessary materials for instruction. With the passing of a few years, views regarding the contingent fee changed and in November, 1907, by trustee action, it was restored, effective in the summer session of 1908.

With the resumption of this fee the President, fearing its payment might present a difficulty for some students, proposed establishment of a plan "by which a limited number of students might be allowed under certain conditions to defer for a time the payment of their fees." The plan as adopted contained certain safeguards, the most important of which was that before the student graduated or transferred to another educational institution the whole loan had to be paid in cash or a negotiable note. With development of loan funds, loans were made in worthy cases and before the end of the Bryan administration deferment of fees was discontinued.

Four Deans Needed

In the reorganization of Indiana University in conformity with a blueprint of a modern university, the President was proceeding slowly and cautiously searching for the right persons to whom responsibility might be delegated without subsequent regrets. While the initiative generally rested with the administration, the hand of the President in the spring of 1908 was being forced by legislation enacted by the Indiana General Assembly a year earlier, affecting the training of teachers. This situation was discussed by the President in June, 1908.

The University confronts no more serious immediate difficulty than the organization of the School of Education. Under the new laws we are forced to make new and better provisions for the training of teachers. So far as the high school teachers are concerned we have no choice. We must provide for their professional training and that in a first-rate way. We have a working plan with the city high school which must serve for the present, but we must develop better plans. We must also consider what, if anything, to do with the training of elementary teachers. The question is very difficult and has many sides. We are making provision for them in the summer school, and have in attendance about 280 graduates of commissioned high schools who would not otherwise be here. On the whole, I believe we should feel our way to doing the work.

Meanwhile, just at this juncture, Dr. Bergstrom goes to Stanford, leaving the School of Education without a head. We should have in his place a man with the scholarly, executive, and personal qualifications of a Dean. We should pay, if it were possible, $3,500 for such a man. We should have, besides, another strong man or woman in the department. We should have space and equipment and a practice school, all of which are beyond our present means.

Since the President, as yet, had not found a man he wished to recommend as dean, the board solved the problem by electing the President as acting dean, a position he held until 1911.

The Graduate School also needed a dean. The progress of this school up to 1908 was described by the President:

The Graduate School is not a school beside the other schools of the University. It represents the entire University on the highest level. In spite of many difficulties and particularly in spite of inadequate resources, the Graduate School of the University has had a vigorous development. We have each year a large number of graduate degrees, including this year three degrees of Doctor of Philosophy. The organization of the Graduate School is complete except the appointment of a dean. It is my judgment that this step should be taken. I recommend as Dean of the Graduate School, Professor Carl H. Eigenmann. Professor Eigenmann has made contributions to science which have given him international distinction. He is a man of great executive ability as is shown by the large sums of money which he has secured in various quarters for his scientific work. I believe that no appointment would meet with more general approval among members of the faculty than that of Dr. Eigenmann.

This recommendation that Dr. Carl H. Eigenmann be appointed dean of the Graduate School was approved June 20, 1908.

Still another deanship had been a matter of great concern to the President. Since the resignation of Professor Mary Breed as dean of women, Miss Louise Goodbody had been serving as acting dean. Her wisdom and fairness had won the confidence and cooperation of the young women students, the general commendation of the faculty, and had been observed with growing gratification by the President, who had reached the conclusion that Miss Goodbody should be made dean of women. In recommending this action, which was approved, the President said:

It is said to be impossible to find any man entirely fit to be president of a University. It is still more difficult to find a woman having all the qualifications of Dean. But Miss Goodbody does the most important things so well that the University should not be deprived of her services. I cite the fact that within the period of her service in that capacity, the records of the University show a remarkable decrease in the number of failures by women students. This is largely due to her influence in securing more reasonable hours for social affairs and also in dealing personally with girls who were not doing well. In other ways her service to the women students is no less valuable. I put my recommendation on the ground that we cannot afford not to have her service.

Within this biennium the appointment of still another dean was necessitated by the death of George L. Reinhard, Vice-President and

Dean of the School of Law, on June 13, 1906. Professor Enoch G. Hogate was promoted to the deanship.

Matters of General University Interest

Nathaniel U. Hill, Trustee and Treasurer, died on May 8, 1908. Trustee Edwin Corr succeeded him as treasurer and Attorney Ira Batman was elected by the State Board of Education to succeed Mr. Hill as trustee.

The LL.D. degree was conferred upon the beloved Hoosier poet, James Whitcomb Riley, in 1907, recommended by the faculty, and unanimously approved by the trustees.

An appropriation of $120 for stenographic service for the Schools of Law and Medicine, made on recommendation of the President, is indicative of the very modest expansion of this service beyond the University administrative offices, where, until recently, one stenographer had cared for all administrative work. The smallness of the University budget made it imperative to assume new obligations with great caution.

A very creditable performance of *The Mikado,* with Professor Henry R. Alburger, of the School of Medicine, and students Merle Bennett and Miss Florence Frazee singing leading parts, captured a large and enthusiastic audience in the spring of 1908.

Professor John S. Nollen, who had been head of the Department of German since 1903 when Professor Gustaf E. Karsten left the University, resigned in 1907 to become president of Lake Forest College. Professor Bert J. Vos succeeded him.

The need of a dormitory for girls was being pressed. The Executive Committee was directed to get full details of the condition and purchase price of Alpha Hall, a privately-owned dormitory at the corner of Forest Place and Third Street, and make recommendations regarding its purchase. It was a number of years, however, before this building was purchased.

In 1907 President Bryan and Trustee Fesler were requested to investigate and report on the feasibility of organizing a library school. Although the matter was discussed again and again, no work in this field was offered until the summer of 1930, when a course for school librarians was given.

CHAPTER VIII

ORGANIZATION OF THE SCHOOL OF MEDICINE, 1903

Scene, Legislative Hearing, Senate Chamber, 1907

Q. "If the legislature approves your bill authorizing Indiana University to conduct medical education in Marion County, will it cost the state money?"

A. "Yes, it will cost money, a lot of money. Medical education is the most expensive type of education given by any university." W. L. Bryan.

P RESIDENT BRYAN has been quoted as stating that, considering her limited resources, it was obvious that Indiana University could not do all the things that many universities with far greater income were doing, but must carefully select the things she should undertake.

"Limited resources" had handicapped Indiana University since her founding, eighty-two years earlier. The legislative act of 1838 under which the institution was given University status provided that instruction should be given in law and medicine. But no appropriation was made for maintenance of those schools. A professor of law was appointed whose compensation for a period consisted of the small fees paid by the few students of law. The University furnished a classroom and firewood.

So, decades, fourscore years and two, passed during which the University found her resources inadequate for establishment of medical education. But at the meeting of the trustees in March, 1903, though resources were still pitifully inadequate, the President had the courage to propose the establishment of a medical department. The following, he said, are the principal facts:

1. There is a general change in medical as in legal education, from schools owned and conducted by city practitioners, to endowed schools whose teachers devote their whole time to instruction. In the best cases, the medical school is not an independent institution, affiliated with the university, but is an integral part of the university.

2. In all the better medical schools the course of study requires four years. The first two years' work, however, is made up of subjects which are also

57

taught in the science departments of the universities. It has been found, accordingly, that these first two years of the medical course can be done more economically and also more satisfactorily in the Departments of Zoology, Chemistry, Botany, Physics, Psychology, etc., than in connection with the medical school proper. At Chicago University, Northwestern University, and the University of Illinois—to name our nearest neighbors, this arrangement is in force and is proving highly satisfactory.

3. For several years we have offered a number of medical courses. A student desiring these courses could take chemistry or zoology as a major and could take as part of his college course enough elementary medical subjects to receive a little more than one year's advanced standing in the best medical schools. The courses of this character offered here last year are shown on pages 139 and 154 of the University catalogue for 1901–1902.

4. In order to fill out two years' work we should have to add human anatomy and pathology and we should have to increase very considerably the amount of work offered in physiology. We should have at the outset, if possible, two additional men, a professor and an associate professor. One, or if possible both, of these men should be physicians as well as thoroughly trained scientists.

5. It is my opinion that we should, if possible, establish the medical department at once, even if we cannot equip it adequately with men and means the first year. I suggest the following plan:

a. The selection of one additional man for the first year. The title, salary, and particular work of this man might be left open until the June meeting of the Board, the determining factor upon these points to be the discovery of the best available man.

b. Professor Moenkhaus to give a large part of his time next year to Human Physiology.

c. All the science departments offering elementary medical subjects to emphasize that part of the work next year.

It would be possible in this way to offer at once nearly, if not quite, two years of a four-year medical course.

If this plan meets the approval of the Board of Trustees, I suggest that an announcement of the new department, similar in form to the announcement of the law department, be prepared for publication as soon as possible after Commencement.

Formal approval was given this plan for organization of a Department of Medicine in which the work of the first two years of the four-year medical course should be given, and President Bryan was authorized to visit the medical schools of the Atlantic coast states in search for the additional man needed.

Announcement of the new Department was made in the *Bulletin* for May, 1903, quoted in Chapter III. After this trip east, the President at Commencement time, 1903, reported to the trustees:

I have been confirmed by conversations with leaders in medical education in the wisdom of enlarging our facilities for medical education. We should, I believe, offer next year additional courses in physiology and in anatomy.

I regret to say that I am not yet able to nominate a man for the work in Anatomy. I have looked over the ground thoroughly, have conferred with the principal medical authorities of the country and with a large number of possible candidates. I shall present the whole situation orally to the board.

In response to an invitation from the Central College of Physicians and Surgeons of Indiana, Mr. Fesler and I met a committee from that institution to hear from them a proposal for amalgamation with Indiana University. This committee is present and wishes to confer with the Board of Trustees as to this proposal.

I received also a letter from Dr. Henry Jameson, Dean of the Medical College of Indiana, proposing an interview upon the interests of medical education in the state. After an extended conversation, Dr. Jameson professed himself strongly in favor of an amalgamation of the two medical colleges mentioned, with each other and with Indiana University.

I believe that an amalgamation of these institutions upon a sound basis would be very greatly to the interest of all of them and to the cause of medical education in the state. I defer further discussion of the question until after the conference with the committee from the Central College of Physicians and Surgeons.

In the discussion which followed, it was decided to ask Burton D. Myers, M.D., an associate in the Department of Anatomy of Johns Hopkins University, to come to the University at once for a conference. Dr. Myers came, met the trustees and members of the faculty, learned of and was intrigued by the prospect of developments in medical education in Indiana, was offered the headship of the Department of Anatomy, and accepted.

Courses in human anatomy and physiology were begun at the University in September, 1903. These courses, with long established courses in chemistry, microscopic anatomy, and embryology, made up all of the work of the first year and part of the work of the second year of a four-year medical course.

In November, 1903, the President reported on the work in progress and the provisions for completing the work of the first two years of the medical course which should be ready for the opening of the school year in the fall of 1904. The needs were: an associate professor of pathology, a man to give the work in pharmacology as an assistant to Dr. Moenkhaus, and an assistant professor of anatomy—all these men should be Doctors of Medicine; a laboratory for pathology and larger quarters for the Department of Physiology. Enlarged quarters and better equipment for anatomy would also have to be provided.

Incidentally, the President called attention to the necessity of establishing some legal procedure for securing cadavers for dissection and of making arrangements whereby students, on completion of the first two years in medicine being organized by the University, might get two full years' credit in four-year medical schools and thus secure the M.D. degree in a period of four years. There were at that time forty-eight students in the University who expected to be candidates for that degree.

At this same meeting Dr. Myers was elected to represent the faculty on the State Anatomical Board. Thus the legal cadaver supply referred to above was established.

By March 28, 1904, there had come a formal proposal of the Medical College of Indiana to become a part of Indiana University. It was the President's opinion that two conditions should be established if the proposition were to be accepted: (1) Unhampered ownership and control should be vested in the Board of Trustees of Indiana University. (2) The first two years of work should be maintained at Bloomington.

Councils were divided. Many thought the whole School should be established at Bloomington, as at Michigan. Today (1949) with Bloomington a city of 20,000 and with excellent roads and a growing rural population, such a plan would be feasible. But with Bloomington a small place of 4,000, with poor roads, and automobiles not regarded as yet as important means of general transportation, there were very great objections to this procedure. Others would have had the whole School at Indianapolis, in which case the tendency for it to become autonomous would have been very great.

The President proposed a wholly different plan:

I propose two years' work at Bloomington and two years' work at Indianapolis, and I propose that in the immediate future the strength of the University shall go toward making both as strong as possible.

The Bloomington end of the problem is already solved. The Indianapolis end of it is far from being so. The great medical schools are lavishing money upon their clinical work and are furnishing facilities out of all comparison with those which can be offered at present at Indianapolis by any school or combination of schools. We cannot avert the outcome simply by organizing in a new way, by giving our name to a school in Indianapolis, leaving the school in character substantially what it is at present.

If any medical school is to live in Indiana, two things are necessary, money and a modern organization. The essential thing in the organization is that it shall be controlled and directed constantly in the light of the highest ideals and methods in the medical world.

To maintain such an organization is shown by the experience of the modern medical schools to be very expensive. It is true that eminent practitioners are willing to give their services for very small salaries. But there must be also some men who are eminent chiefly as scientists, who give most of their time to the school and who are paid accordingly. There must be a large staff of expert assistants, some of whom must be paid. There must be elaborate and expensive clinical laboratories, each with its chief and his assistants. There should be a research hospital specially adapted for the investigation of diseases. These provisions are not ideal. They exist at the great schools and there the medical students will go and should go unless we are able to furnish them here.

I strongly hope that a way may be found to organize an Indiana University medical school along the lines which I have indicated. I hope that the best of the Indianapolis medical men may cooperate in such an undertaking. I recommend that a committee be appointed to confer with the Indiana Medical School in regard to their proposal.

In these proposals President Bryan indicated his grasp of the status of medical education and his vision of the development which should be brought about and indeed was brought about under the leadership of Indiana University.

The *Bulletin* for May, 1904, outlined the two-year medical course and the two years of collegiate premedical requirements. The degree Bachelor of Arts in Medicine, it was announced, would be conferred on completion of the course of premedical and medical work outlined. At that time Indiana University was the fourth school in America to require two years of college work for entrance. Harvard, Johns Hopkins, and Western Reserve had led in this innovation.

In January, 1904, a committee consisting of Messrs. Rose, Fesler, and Hill had been appointed to confer with Indianapolis physicians and surgeons concerning questions relating to a union with Indiana University. In June, 1904, the question of union with one or both of the Indianapolis schools was further considered. The school year 1903–4 ended with the strongest prospect of a desirable union being made.

In August of 1904 the medical committee of the board was requested to investigate further the question of a union with the Medical College of Indiana, the Central College of Physicians and Surgeons, or both. A conference was held with the Medical College of Indiana on November 13, 1904, and the following day the President presented to the board a written communication from Dean Henry Jameson and stated "it appears the Medical College of Indiana wishes to become a part of Indiana University on terms satisfactory to the Board."

The result of negotiations was reported on April 3, 1905:

In reply to the formal proposal for a union of the Medical College of Indiana with Indiana University referred to on November 14, two conditions were laid down by the University: First, that the University should own and control the school; second, that the laboratories of the first two years should not be permanently duplicated. . . . We discovered that the second condition specified above would not be conceded by the Medical College of Indiana. Your Committee had no further authority to proceed, and negotiations came to an end.

The question then arose as to what course to follow. Various possibilities were considered. Unhappily, a union with the Central College of Physicians and Surgeons was not pressed.

Except for the temporary failure of plans for unification of all medical educational activities in Indiana, the outlook of the Indiana University School of Medicine at the close of the school year 1904–5 was very optimistic. The School had been admitted to membership in the Association of American Medical Colleges. A number of medical students from Johns Hopkins and elsewhere had come to Indiana University for work in anatomy during the summer session. The Central College of Physicians and Surgeons had proposed, informally, to renew negotiations for a union with Indiana University. The appointment of Dr. W. H. Manwaring as associate professor of pathology gave assurance that all the work of the first two years of the medical course would be given the coming year, 1905–6. The recognition of the Indiana University School of Medicine by the Indiana State Board of Medical Registration and Examination in the summer of 1904 had removed the last obstacle to the granting of two full years of work and time credit, by leading medical schools, to students who had completed the first two years of their medical course in this School.

Thus, by the close of the second year of the School, outstanding progress had been made. The School had received wide recognition and commendation for its position of leadership in its requirement of two years of college work for entrance. Obviously it was the purpose of Indiana University not to establish just another medical school. It was clear that the University was pioneering in the solution of the difficult problem of advancement of medical education in the United States.

Believing the field of medical education was hers, the University was not rushing the union with either of the old medical schools of the state, but was hoping for the development of a basis for union with both.

Then on September 1, 1905, the Indianapolis papers carried the announcement that the Medical College of Indiana had been taken over by Purdue. This action was followed a few weeks later by the Central College of Physicians and Surgeons and the Fort Wayne College of Medicine becoming a part of the Indiana Medical College (note change of name), the school of medicine of Purdue University.

This was a staggering blow, and wholly unexpected. Now that the University had begun the development of this important field of medical education authorized by Act of February 15, 1838, it was the purpose, as rapidly as possible, to provide those who were to care for the health and lives of people with a training equal to that offered anywhere in the world. To this end, and having no thought but that the field was hers, to develop as seemed wisest, the University had been proceeding deliberately (it now appeared too deliberately).

Though a union with the Central College of Physicians and Surgeons could have been consummated at any time on terms mutually satisfactory, and though the University had the highest regard for the faculty and the sound educational organization of this school, it had seemed to the advantage of all concerned that a basis of union should be found with both of the medical schools of Indianapolis, which had been pioneering in medical education since 1869.

What should be done? Should suit be brought to set aside the agreement between Purdue and the medical schools? Should the University establish a medical school in Indianapolis, or a four-year medical course in Bloomington?[1] Should the University retaliate by establishing a school of engineering?[2] The solution of this difficult problem was found by the administration when on January 5, 1906, a favorable opportunity arose for expansion of the work in medicine to a complete four-year medical course.

The building of the former Central College of Physicians and Surgeons, an almost new, well-appointed and equipped, substantial structure, could be purchased at a reasonable figure. There was necessary something slightly in excess of $15,000 cash in addition to a mortgage which could be transferred. A meeting of Bloomington citizens was called at the home of James D. Showers. President Bryan stated the situation and these citizens, as in 1883 when a University building burned, rallied to the support of the University; the necessary fund was raised and title to this building of the Central College of Physicians and Surgeons was secured by these friends of the University. This purchase gave the University an excellent building in which to establish the work of the last two years of a medical course, and was evidence that the University had powerful friends deeply interested in her welfare.

Dr. Myers was authorized to spend the summer of 1906 in Indianapolis in charge of the transformation of laboratories of this medical building into hospital wards and private rooms for a sixty-five-bed hospital with kitchen, nursing, and all necessary auxiliaries, in organizing the clinical faculty, and in writing the Bulletin of the State College of Physicians and Surgeons, the name given the school that was being established in closest affiliation with the Indiana University School of Medicine. In this educational affiliation with the State College of Physicians and Surgeons, Indiana University was to assume no financial responsibility for the affiliated school.

Thus it came to pass that when the school year 1906–7 opened the position of Indiana University was greatly improved, with a four-

---

[1] The President studied this possibility at length. He recognized that complete medical schools had been developed in small cities. All things considered, the plan seemed to him unwise; and he then, as at all other times, reported against it.

[2] The President reported in detail on this possibility.

year medical course and a teaching hospital of her own. She had been forced to organize her own hospital when the Indiana Medical College acquired exclusive teaching privileges in the Indianapolis City Hospital. At Bloomington there were fifty-seven medical students, nearly three times as many as in the preceding year, and there was an increase of premedical students.

In October, 1906, Dr. Myers reported:

In the Medical Department, there are 37 first-year students and 20 second-year students, 27 juniors and 25 seniors, a total of 109. The work of the students shows a great improvement over last year.

I feel the state of Indiana should furnish free tuition only for students of Indiana. Accordingly, I wish to urge that a tuition of $100 per year in addition to the aforementioned fees be charged for students from other states. Or, if a tuition is unadvisable, that the fees be doubled for students outside the state of Indiana.[3]

The School of Medicine was looming large in the plans of the administration for the coming legislative session (1907). A bill was under preparation which would authorize Indiana University to conduct a medical school in Marion County. The trustees of Purdue University were preparing a bill which would give them such authority. It was obvious that the stage was being set for a great battle in the legislative session of 1907. There were dramatic legislative hearings and appeals by each institution to its friends for support. John H. Edwards, of Mitchell, had introduced the Indiana University bill in the House, and Oscar Bland, of Linton, then quite a young man, was sponsor for a companion bill in the Senate. Though the strength of the Indiana University faction was sufficient to force the Purdue bill from committee, bring it to vote, defeat it, move its reconsideration, and pass a motion to lay on the table the motion for reconsideration, its strength was not quite sufficient to pass the Indiana University measure. In the Senate, though the Bland bill had a majority, it was not a constitutional majority. So the bills of both schools failed of passage.

Judge Bland wrote reviewing the situation after adjournment:

After the fight was over, we [Indiana and Purdue] found we had the

[3] It was some years later, 1916, and again in 1924, when total enrollment of medical students taxed capacity, that a definition of an out-of-state student was established by the Board of Trustees. A higher fee had been adopted in 1910.

enmity of the non-state schools, and that they were combined against the state schools. It was realized by the Purdue men that if a fight like that continued, or if it were renewed, the legislature might withdraw its support from the state schools. Dan Simms and Will Wood came to me. They stated the enmity of the non-state schools to which I have referred and said: "Now let us stop this fight. We will not ask to teach medicine and we will surrender the exclusive right to Indiana University to teach medicine." We shook hands and were great friends afterward.

At the April board meeting the recommendation of the medical faculty of candidates for the M.D. degree was confirmed and degrees ordered conferred on May 18, 1907. The first diploma signed by President Bryan was that of Dr. Homer Woolery, who a little later ranked among the highest in the Licensure Examination conducted by the Indiana State Board of Medical Registration and Examination.

The Commencement address for the medical graduates was given by Dr. Arthur Dean Bevan, chairman of the Council on Medical Education of the American Medical Association. He presented the University fee of $75 as a prize in anatomy. President Bryan concluded his address[4] by saying:

It is a deeply satisfying fact that we have not merely organized a school of medicine, but have in fact done the things which stand approved in the supreme court of medical opinion.

Faculty members of the School were eager to have an evaluation of the effectiveness of the work of this first year of clinical medical teaching. The rival Indiana Medical College contended that some of the Indiana University School's faculty were men of little experience. This, however, did not mean that they were not good teachers. But to assure themselves that they had good teachers, the faculty had frequent meetings in which teachers of little experience gave lectures which were criticized constructively by older staff members.

The organization proved very effective. Patients could be brought by elevator to the two first-floor lecture rooms for demonstration. Students were assigned cases medical and surgical, which they visited. Specimens were carried to the first-floor clinical-pathological

---

[4] For the President's address at that first Medical School Commencement, May 18, 1907, see Myers, "History of Medical Education in Indiana" (MS).

laboratory for examination. Cases came out of textbooks and lecture rooms and became living people needing help. This was immensely stimulating to the student body.

Students and faculty had worked well. But how effective this educational effort had been was not fully realized until the report from the State Licensure Examination revealed that graduates of the Indiana University School had taken eight of the first fifteen high ranking places, twice as many as the more numerous graduates of the Indiana Medical College. A few of the first fifteen ranking places were taken by students who had gone to eastern and other medical schools. With publication of the results of this State Board examination no further question was raised anywhere regarding the inexperience of the staff.

Judge Vinson Carter, a member of the board of trustees of the State College of Physicians and Surgeons, recommended in August, 1907, that the Indiana University School of Medicine and the State College of Physicians and Surgeons should unite under the name, the Indiana University School of Medicine. A joint committee from the two schools presented the following resolution, which was adopted unanimously by Indiana University authorities:

Indiana University, as one party, and the State College of Physicians and Surgeons, as the other party, hereby unite for the purpose of conducting a school of medicine under the name and style of Indiana University School of Medicine.

Said Indiana University School of Medicine shall be the medical department of Indiana University. The organization effected by this union shall conduct a four-year school in medicine. The first two years of instruction shall be given at Bloomington, Indiana, and the last two years at Indianapolis, Indiana.

The course of study shall be prescribed and the faculty and officers thereof chosen by the trustees of Indiana University. Indiana University shall confer the degree of Doctor of Medicine upon and issue the diplomas to the graduates of this school.

Thus, without assuming any financial obligations outside of Monroe County, the position of the University was greatly strengthened.

The President in November, 1907, called the attention of the trustees to the optimistic report of Dr. Myers on the outlook for the Medical School, which, he was glad to say, was very much better than it had ever been. He also called attention to a letter from

John Edwards, House floor leader in the 1907 legislative session, concerning a proposal of union of medical schools. A committee consisting of President Bryan and Trustees Shively and Rose was appointed to consider the proposal submitted through Mr. Edwards. During the next five months, correspondence was followed by propositions, counter propositions, and mutual concessions.

On April 4, 1908, the Board of Trustees formulated a resolution embodying the conditions acceptable to the University, which, on presentation to representatives of the trustees of Purdue University and to the trustees of the Indiana Medical College, was accepted. Then a statement to be given the public concerning the consolidation of the Indiana Medical College with the Indiana University School of Medicine was agreed upon and signed by Presidents Bryan and Stone.

This statement[5] reviewed the following conditions on which mutual agreement had been reached and to which the faculties of the medical schools assented: (1) A union of the two medical schools, under direction of the trustees of Indiana University. (2) The faculty of the combined school to be selected with due regard to the members of the present faculties and to the maintenance of a complete medical school in Indianapolis as well as a two-year course in Bloomington.

The meeting of April 4, 1908, adjourned with everyone feeling assured that the pattern of medical education in Indiana had been fixed for all time.

A very delicate problem still remained, viz., the selection of the faculty of the united school. For this difficult task the President appointed the following committee: Drs. Edmund D. Clark, Alois B. Graham, Miles F. Porter, and Frank B. Wynn, from the Indiana Medical College faculty; Drs. John F. Barnhill, James H. Ford, Frank F. Hutchins, and Burton D. Myers, from the Indiana University School of Medicine faculty. President Bryan acted as chairman of this committee, which made a trip of nearly a week to visit Johns Hopkins University School of Medicine, the University of Pennsylvania School of Medicine, Columbia and Cornell in New York City, and Harvard in Boston. In intervals between visits to

---

[5] See *Indiana Medical Journal*, May, 1908, p. 457.

medical schools and dinner conferences on medical education, there were meetings of the committee in which the selection of the faculty was worked out.

Since the faculty of the Indiana Medical College was much larger than that of the State College of Physicians and Surgeons, many more men of professorial title were appointed to the new faculty from the former, fifty-five, than from the latter, twenty-nine. The report of this committee was accepted in good spirit by the respective faculties, formal appointments were made, and both Indiana University and the Indiana University School of Medicine were launched upon a new era of development.

The officers of the united faculties were: William Lowe Bryan, Ph.D., LL.D., President of the University; Allison Maxwell, A.M., M.D., Dean of the School of Medicine; Edward F. Hodges, A.M., M.D., Vice-Dean; Edmund D. Clark, M.D., Secretary at Indianapolis; Burton D. Myers, A.M., M.D., Secretary at Bloomington; John F. Barnhill, M.D., Treasurer at Indianapolis. The Executive Committee was to consist of the President of the University, Trustee Fesler, and the officers of the School of Medicine.

On May 20, 1908, the graduates of the schools now integral parts of the Indiana University School of Medicine came to Bloomington for their graduation exercises, diplomas, and medical degrees. President Bryan made the address, published in the *Indiana Medical Journal,* June, 1908, page 499.

Some non-state colleges of Indiana had feared students of Indiana University might be given advantages not enjoyed by their own students. In this Commencement address President Bryan volunteered the assurance that Indiana University students of medicine would not be permitted any unfair advantage over students of Wabash, DePauw, Purdue, Earlham, or any other school. In 1909 this assurance was incorporated in a legislative act.

In that same June issue Editor A. W. Brayton published his widely read article entitled "The Great Peace. Honor Enough for All," in which he reviewed the late controversy and the terms of agreement.

Though the University now had a complete Medical School in Indianapolis in addition to the two preclinical years in Bloomington, the administration had no authority to expend any part of University funds in support of a medical school in Marion County. Authority to make expenditures for such a school could not be secured before the meeting of the 1909 General Assembly. This body, on February 26, passed an act authorizing the University to conduct a Medical School in Marion County, Ind.

By March 29, 1909, the President could say:

Six years ago we undertook to establish an adequate medical school in connection with Indiana University. This undertaking was not taken up upon superficial grounds. The profession of medicine is one of the three or four most important ones in any civilized society. There never had been adequate provision for medical education in this state. In addition to these considerations this University differed from all other universities of standing, whether state or non-state, in the meagerness of its provision for professional education. A fundamental and permanent need of the state on the one hand and a fundamental condition of making this institution a university in fact as well as in name compelled us to enter this new field. We have had together six years of arduous labor. It is not necessary to recite the difficulties which we have met and overcome. It is a deep satisfaction that throughout the entire time we have indeed worked together, planning together for each new difficult step and standing together in dark days as well as in bright ones. This has been true not only of the Trustees, but also with very little exception of the faculty in Bloomington and Indianapolis.

At the same time Dr. Myers presented some matters for consideration by the board:

There has been great development in medical education in recent years and the evolutionary process is not yet complete. More factors than ever before are being brought to bear for the modification and improvement of the medical course. A change of course to fit the new conditions imposed by the Association of American Universities is necessary for the next catalogue after the one in press. Mr. Pritchett has announced that the Carnegie Foundation will take up the study of conditions in medical education in American Medical Schools and report in seven or eight months. The Council on Education of the American Medical Association has made an exhaustive study of the amount of time devoted to each department of the entire medical course, the sequence of courses, and the work required and elective. A fifth year is now given in all but two of the medical schools of Canada and we must come to it.

The success of our school in the past has depended in no small degree on the soundness of its organization from an educational point of view. Its future success will depend in like degree on the same factor. To this end it seems to me very vital that, though the deanship of the faculty may remain with some one of the older members of the faculty, the educational management of the school should rest with the younger members of the faculty and they should have authority in this department of the work.

Many reasons could be given for the arrangement suggested above, but I am sure they will be evident to you.

With regard to the work of the first two years, I feel that our men here at the University should be in charge, not merely nominally, but by direct trustee appointment, so no doubt could arise at Indianapolis as to the authority with which our men act. Any other arrangement will result in a compromise at each end of the line if we are to have uniformity, and we will have the stamp of independent medical school ideas put on our University courses instead of placing the University stamp in its entirety on the medical work at Indianapolis.

One of the items of the agreement leading to the union of the Indiana Medical College with the Indiana University School of Medicine was that a four-year medical course should be given at Indianapolis. This table shows how that agreement worked out:

| | Freshman | | Sophomore | |
Year	Bloom-ington	Indian-apolis	Bloom-ington	Indian-apolis
1908–09	34	35	35	42
1909–10	36	31	28	32
1910–11	20	6	23	35
1911–12	31	4	..	22
1912–13	42	..	..	34

It will be observed that for two years Freshman attendance at Bloomington and at Indianapolis was almost the same. Then in 1910–11 there was a sharp drop in Freshman matriculations, particularly marked at Indianapolis. In the fall of 1910 the requirement of two years of college work for admission to the School of Medicine, temporarily abandoned, was re-established. This requirement was rapidly becoming general throughout the United States, and uniformly had occasioned a temporary decrease in the number who could meet entrance requirements. A decrease in attendance had been anticipated, but the great disparity in attendance between Bloomington and Indianapolis was wholly unanticipated. Dr. E. D. Clark, Secretary at Indianapolis, had been in charge of matriculation at Indianapolis in the two preceding years and continued in that post.

At a meeting of the Indianapolis faculty of the School of Medicine, in Indianapolis in June, 1911, President Bryan presented for consideration the fact that there had been only six Freshmen at Indianapolis during the past year, and then withdrew in order that there might be the freest possible discussion and action. Action was taken calling for emphasis of the work of the Freshman year at Bloomington and of the Sophomore year at Indianapolis. It should be noted that this modification of the agreement between President Bryan and President Stone, signed only after approval of the Indiana Medical College, was modified by a faculty consisting largely (fifty-five out of eighty-four) of members of the former faculty of the Indiana Medical College. It was a realistic approach to a wholly unanticipated situation. In conformity with this action, the Sophomore year at Bloomington was abandoned and the full-time Sophomore faculty members transferred to Indianapolis. At Bloomington, Owen Hall, then vacant, was inexpensively remodeled for occupancy by the Departments of Anatomy and Physiology, providing greatly improved quarters for these two departments of the Freshman medical year. But the work of the Freshman medical year at Indianapolis continued to be offered.

The above table shows that during the school year 1911–12 there was an increase of 55 per cent in Freshman matriculation at Bloomington and a decrease of 33⅓ per cent in Freshman matriculation at Indianapolis, with no Sophomore medical students at Bloomington. Accordingly, the Bulletin of the School of Medicine, issued May 15, 1912, announced:

During the past year there have been but four Freshmen at Indianapolis. The per capita cost of providing instruction for so small a number has been unjustifiably great, depleting the funds available for the courses of the last two years. Under these circumstances it will be necessary next year to charge Freshmen at Indianapolis a fee approximately equal to the per capita cost. This amount will be announced later.

The amount of this fee was never determined. A few inquiries were reported over a period of years, but no student matriculated and asked for the work of the Freshman year at Indianapolis, which, however, continued to be announced in the Bulletin of the School of Medicine for many years. The work of the Freshman medical year at Bloomington continued to be emphasized as directed by the Indianapolis medical faculty.

As years passed, applications for matriculation had grown to numbers far beyond the capacity of the School. For a period of years the Freshman medical class was selected from more than a thousand applicants, and in 1937 the new Medical Building at Bloomington was completed.

In July, 1911, Dr. Charles P. Emerson, Johns Hopkins, 1899, was chosen as dean of the School of Medicine, succeeding Dr. Allison Maxwell, who in 1908 had accepted the deanship with the understanding that a successor should be appointed at an early date. Dr. Emerson had studied in the Universities of Strassburg, Basel, and Paris, 1901 to 1903. He had served as resident and as associate in medicine at Johns Hopkins, and from 1908 to 1911 had been superintendent of Clifton Springs Sanitarium (New York). During the year 1909–10 he also had served as associate professor of medicine at Cornell University School of Medicine. He had become interested in medical social service while at Hopkins and on coming to Indiana was surprised and pleased to find medical social service already provided for in a simple way in connection with the Dispensary of the School of Medicine. In 1930 Dean Emerson became ill. On July 23, 1931, Dean Emerson concurring, Dr. Willis D. Gatch was appointed acting dean. On June 11, 1932, Dr. Gatch was made dean and Dr. Emerson was appointed research professor of medicine.

In 1912 came the gift of the Robert W. Long Hospital. A site was selected on West Michigan Street adjacent to the City Hospital. The Hospital was completed in 1914. A Medical School Building was erected in 1919. The first unit of the James Whitcomb Riley Memorial Hospital for Children was completed in 1924. The Coleman Hospital was completed in 1927, and the Ball Residence for Nurses and an addition to the Medical School Building were completed in 1928, the Kiwanis Unit in 1930, the Rotary Convalescent Home in 1931, the Hydrotherapeutic Pool in 1935, and the Clinical Building in 1937. Thus over a period of twenty-three years the Medical Center arose, substantial in character and in a setting that had become a beauty spot instead of a cornfield and a dump.

Chapter IX

INDIANA UNIVERSITY, 1908 - 10

University Progress, Needs, and Appropriations

THE CHARACTER of Indiana University during these six years of the Bryan administration had very markedly changed. The Medical School was now firmly established and had an enrollment of 270. Graduate work had been organized as a Graduate School, with an active dean; fourteen teaching fellowships had been established ranging in value from $200 to $500; and the Graduate School was asking for a special budget for fellowships. Though a School of Commerce and a Department of Journalism had not been definitely established, the preliminary organization had been worked out and a course of study outlined which later led to their formal organization.

The desirability of other schools was being considered and the first faltering steps were being taken which later led to establishment of a School of Music. The appointment of a dean of a School of Education had been authorized and President Bryan had been appointed acting dean. The faculty and School of Education announcement first appeared in the 1909 Catalog.

It is obvious that substantial progress was being made in increasing opportunities for study at Indiana University and that the transition into a real University was under way.

In his report to Governor Hanly and the Visiting Committee, in the fall of 1908, President Bryan made a review, year by year, of the growth of the University beginning with 1827–28.

That review showed that it was not until the year 1866–67, forty-two years after the opening of the University in 1824, that the enrollment reached and remained continuously in excess of 100. It was thirty-one years later, 1897–98, before the enrollment reached and remained permanently above 1,000. But ten years later, 1907–8, in the sixth year of the Bryan administration, the total enrollment for the year reached and remained permanently above 2,000.[1] These figures show a definite acceleration in attendance.

The total value of grounds, buildings, equipment, and supplies had been $291,100 at the beginning of the Bryan administration. Six years later, at the beginning of the biennium 1908–10, it was reported as $839,223.99. The income of the University in the last year of the Swain administration, 1901–2, had been $129,761.01. Six years later, 1907–8, the income of the University was $236,657.64. It had almost doubled. That part of the total income derived from the state, by the educational levy, had increased from $90,200 in 1901–2 to $166,140.83 in 1907–8, an increase of about 80 per cent.

The salary roll shows that seven professors were receiving $2,500. The dean of the College of Liberal Arts received $2,600, two professors received $2,600, and the dean of the Law School, $3,000.

The President called attention to the enormous increase in attendance at colleges and universities. The enrollment at Indiana University in the fall of 1908 was 2,113. This was an increase of 30 per cent (488) over the preceding year and nearly eight times the enrollment of Indiana University in 1888 (275) twenty years earlier. The 1908 enrollment figure was larger than that of the largest University in the United States twenty years earlier (Harvard).

He called attention to the fact that Indiana was far behind surrounding states in the provision which it made, whether in state or non-state schools, for higher education. At Indiana University two chief facts confronted the administration:

1. The first is our loss of men. For the past quarter-century Indiana University has seen its most eminent men carried away year by year to universities of other states. We have lost men to Harvard, Cornell, Virginia, Dartmouth, Bryn Mawr, Chicago, Illinois, Wisconsin, Cincinnati, the Naval Academy, California, and Stanford. We have lost one this year and are in peril of losing others. These men whose eminence is vouched for by the great universities which have called them, and who make the strength and glory of institutions of other states, are not too good for Indiana. The usage in Wisconsin, to take a single illustration, is not to allow a first-rate man to go from Wisconsin except by death. Is this too high a standard for Indiana?

2. In the second place, we have reached a point where even upon the present scale of expense we cannot take in more students without more income and

[1] This does not mean there were 2,000 students on the campus at any one time but that during the year the total number of students enrolled exceeded 2,000.

room. We have been repeatedly obliged within the past few years to close certain classes after they reached certain numbers for a lack of space or of teachers or both. We have been obliged to tolerate classes which are too large. I cite from recent records classes of 75, 90, 116, and 138. We are at present obliged to deny books, laboratory facilities, and additional teachers where we know that they are badly needed. We have reached the breaking point, and see no course open to us but to announce a limit upon the number of students who can be received until relief is afforded.

The President earnestly urged an increase in income and more room. To quote:

We urge that the tax for the support of the University be doubled. When this is done, the maintenance fund of the University will still be far below that of the State Universities of Michigan, Wisconsin, or Illinois and other states. We shall not be able to multiply departments. We shall only hope to hold our own, to hold our men and to meet the young people of the State who come to us for instruction to which they are entitled.

We require immediately more room for our work. We are overcrowded in every building. The most urgent need is in the Science Departments, which are utilizing all available space including basements and attics and are still unable to receive all of the students who apply for work. We ask for one large building which will take care of several science departments and so give relief to others in the present buildings. We submit a sketch based upon plans for one of a group of buildings erected at Harvard University. The estimate on the building is $248,155.32. We earnestly urge that this appropriation be not cut so that the provision may not be inadequate from the beginning.

Instead of doubling the mill tax as requested, the legislature made a special maintenance appropriation of $35,000 for the biennium 1908–10 ($17,500 for each year). It happened that the mill tax passed in 1903 and still in force, unchanged, yielded during the biennium 1908–10, $20,000 more than during the preceding biennium. So the total increase in income for the biennium 1908–10 was $55,000, an increase of 17 per cent, but far short of the 100 per cent increase asked.

Apart from the request for a doubling of the mill tax, the budget requests made to the legislature of 1909 and, in parallel column, the appropriations granted were as follows:

	Asked	Received
Science Building	$248,155.32	$80,000.00
Addition to Library and Administration Building	37,228.00	....
Addition to Student Building	47,700.00	....

Land	$ 75,000.00	....
Grading and walks	2,400.00	1,000.00
Local telephone system	2,400.00	2,400.00
Additional boiler and equipment	5,000.00	5,000.00
Sewerage	5,000.00	5,000.00
Water supply	2,500.00	20,700.00
Improvement of Indiana Avenue	33.30	33.30
Total	$425,416.62	$114,133.30

This tabulation shows that the appropriation made was about 26 per cent of the amount asked.

Provision for more room, $80,000, was one-third of the amount requested. What could be done with $80,000? An addition to Owen Hall was first considered. But that nearly square building was not well adapted for an addition. The decision was finally made to use the $80,000 for erection of a separate small science building now called Biology Hall. The story of the erection of this building and the remodeling of Owen Hall, and the relief this little addition afforded, is told in Chapter XIII.

The next largest appropriation was $20,700 for a water supply. This appropriation was made because of an emergency which had arisen. On December 2, 1908, a water famine was announced in Bloomington newspapers. When test wells in Griffy Creek valley showed that an adequate water supply could not be secured from wells, the damming of a little side valley farther up Griffy Creek was recommended by the engineers and a request for the appropriation referred to above was made.

The seriousness of this water shortage is revealed by the anxiety of the administration to prevent water loss, however small. For illustration: It had been estimated that water waste at the power plant was costing the University $1.50 per day. Professor A. L. Foley had suggested that a cistern be built to save this waste water and use it again. Professor U. S. Hanna had estimated the cost of construction of a 2,000-barrel cistern at $785. This sum would be saved in eighteen months, so the recommendation that this cistern be built was approved.

With $20,700 available, the early steps in securing an adequate water supply for the University were taken in this biennium, 1908–

10. Most students, however, in that day, lived in the city and were subject to all the inconveniences and health hazards of Bloomington citizens in time of water famine. The University, therefore, was deeply interested in the twenty-year-long struggle for an adequate water supply for Bloomington, the story of which is told in Chapter XXIII.

Other small appropriations are indicative of campus developments during this period.

Good Work of Dean Goodbody

In November, 1909, in his report to the trustees the President included and referred specially to the report of Miss Goodbody, Dean of Women. Parts of this report revealed matters of interest in connection with young women students, rules considered proper and important for their government, and plans for their better housing. Miss Goodbody said:

The number of young women in the University this term is about 430. The number of girls is almost exactly one-third of the total enrollment. Of the 430 women, about 140 are new students here although several of them have done work in other colleges and schools before coming to Indiana. The number of Freshman girls is practically the same as the number in last Fall term.

Alpha Hall[2] houses about 75 girls this term. About 40 of these are Freshman girls. So long as conditions are not seriously unfavorable the women in Alpha Hall seem to enjoy the Dormitory life very much. Conditions are somewhat improved over last year. About 100 women are living in chapter houses and the remainder in town homes.

Before the University reopened in September, I visited all of the houses which were open to women students. The landladies were each interviewed and informed of the few regulations which are now required in connection with the student girls. Without any exception the landladies were very glad to receive me and to be assured that we wish to cooperate with them in making proper conditions for the women students. I made between sixty and seventy calls and I believe the knowledge I gained will be of help to me and I trust that beneficial effects will result to all concerned. Uniform house rules were presented to each house.

After a conference with the Faculty Advisory Committee and the Chaperons of the various Sorority Houses the following uniform house rules were presented to the Sororities and these were accepted as a matter of course:

1. That men callers may be received between the hours of 2 and 10:30 P.M.

[2] At this time the University did not own Alpha Hall. It was built and operated as a private enterprise, a dormitory for girls.

2. That each Sorority House shall have two evenings in the week when no men callers shall be received.

3. That the young women shall not drive in single carriages at night; and when driving in double carriages shall be home by nine o'clock.

4. That each Sorority House shall have the porch lighted on calling nights.

5. That the young women shall under no circumstances go to the fraternity houses or men's club houses unchaperoned, whether on a formal or informal occasion.

6. That the young women shall not be "uptown" at night after nine o'clock unless with a chaperon or an escort.

The Chapter Houses of the Sorority girls are presided over this year in most cases by desirable women. This fact makes the Sorority House problem a somewhat less serious one.

I still hope, however, that dormitories for women may be established at some future time. I have wondered if some plan might not be devised by which a dormitory for about forty girls could be erected, such a dormitory to be made as ideal as possible and entirely under University control. I believe a dormitory of this kind would be very popular and that it would further be an important factor in moulding the proper life and spirit among the women students.

Last year the Woman's League made an effort to bring two or three well-known women from away to talk to our University women. This effort was partially successful but would have been more so if we had more money at our disposal. I should like to secure two or three distinguished women to come here this year to speak before a mass meeting of the girls and would request that $100 be appropriated by the Board of Trustees for this purpose.

CONFERENCE OF INDIANA COLLEGE PRESIDENTS CALLED BY GOVERNOR MARSHALL

Thomas R. Marshall, who had succeeded J. Frank Hanly as governor of Indiana in January, 1909, issued a call the following July for a conference of state and non-state school presidents. The date October 14, 1909, was finally fixed for this meeting, which was held in the office of the Governor.

At the November, 1909, meeting of the board, President Bryan reported briefly on this conference as follows:

I went to the Conference full of concern, not knowing what the spirit or outcome of the meeting would be. It became evident that the leading Indiana college presidents and most of the members of the Conference were determined to show that there was not and should not be any revival of the old school controversy. . . . I give herewith the resolutions passed by the Conference:

(1) Ellis motion: To the effect that of the three state schools, Indiana University only be empowered to confer degree of A.B. Lost unanimously.

(2) Moved that the Conference finds that there is no essential duplication of work in the three state schools. Carried.

(3) The entire Conference votes in favor of tuition fees for all resident students.

(4) Conference votes in favor of a reasonable tuition fee to be charged non-resident students in excess of fees charged resident students.

By McConnell: That it is the consensus of the opinion of this Assembly that in the development of the State University stress be laid on graduate work and professional work. . . .

I am not supposing that we have overcome all of our troubles and that the millennium has arrived. . . . I believe further that the attitude of these gentlemen is such that our own responsibility to them has become very great and that we must seek to give them a service in return greater than any they render us.

This brief statement gives an inadequate idea of the grave concern with which President Bryan went to this meeting.[3] Governor Marshall was known to be hostile to the state-supported institutions of higher education. Ten years earlier the non-state schools had organized in opposition to the state universities and a bitter fight had been waged over the Geeting Bill. So the President's apprehension was well founded.

PUBLICITY, JOURNALISM,
AND *The Indiana Daily Student*

In his report to the trustees, November, 1909, the President introduced important considerations with reference to publicity:

The University is not getting its full share of publicity. Various committees, of the faculty and student body, are doing what they can along publicity lines, but the effort, genuine as it is, must needs be a scattered and diffused effort. This is true because there is no one man in whom all of this publicity effort centers. It is too much for one man to handle, in connection with his regular work as a professor in the University. We see literally dozens of ways by which the University could get a great deal of publicity of the right sort, but we haven't any one person who can gather up the many lines and be responsible for them.

---

[3] For a more detailed account of this meeting, particularly the statements made by President Thomas C. Howe and President Francis J. McConnell, see Chap. X, "Indiana University and the Non-State Schools," and *Thomas Riley Marshall, Hoosier Statesman,* by Charles M. Thomas, p. 102, for the attitude of Governor Marshall.

This matter did not get beyond the conference stage at this meeting, but it was far from being a dead issue. In June, 1910, the President proposed publication of a monthly bulletin on which he had secured a bid. Publication was referred to the Executive Committee, but action hung fire. Further consideration of this matter is deferred to Chapter XIV, under "The New Alumni Movement."

In June, 1910, Adolph Schmuck was selected as director of the work in journalism and served during the year 1910–11.

In the spring of 1910 the board of directors of *The Daily Student* had offered to turn over to the trustees of the University all the property of the organization with the request that the paper be conducted under the direction of the trustees by the journalism staff. The President commented on this offer:

The *Student* has been published in various forms and under various kinds of management for upwards of thirty-five years, continuously since 1883. I may venture to recall the fact that I was myself at one time the sole owner and editor of this journal. Within recent years the paper has been published by a stock company composed of students who elect a board of nine directors, including two members of the faculty and the President of the University ex officio. The paper has more than paid its way. The business manager has been able to make sometimes as much as $800 over and above the cost of publication. The *Student* stockholders finally came to the conclusion that these earnings should not go in such large amounts to a few individuals, but should go toward the development of the work in Journalism. Accordingly, without the slightest suggestion from myself, a movement developed to turn over the whole affair to the University. The stockholders desire that the earnings shall go toward the establishment of a printing press and other equipment necessary to give proper instruction in the Department of Journalism. The directors of the Association voted that stockholders should be entitled to receive the par value of their stock (fifty cents per share), but recommended that stockholders should donate their stock.

The President submitted financial statements from the Indiana University Publishing Association and *The Daily Student* and recommended acceptance of the offer. The approval of this recommendation was a boon to journalism students for it gave them a laboratory under University control. The University Catalog published in June, 1910, announced, for the next year, courses in the history and theory of journalism; the writing of newspaper stories; advertising;

the use of words ("nice discriminations") given by the Department of English; practical newspaper work.

Theoretically, the acquisition of *The Daily Student* and the establishment of a home for it under management of the journalism staff contributed in a measure to the better publicity desired by the President. But students unfamiliar with many matters could not take the place of a trained, full-time publicity man, who came later.

INDIANA UNION

During the school year 1909–10 the men students organized the Indiana Union, a club open to all men of the University. John Wittenberger was the founder. By the spring of 1910 they had 369 members, including men of all other organizations and men belonging to no other organization. The board of directors was broadly representative and the Union was in close sympathy and cooperation with the Young Men's Christian Association.

The Union was interested in securing quarters in the Student Building, and in March, 1910, John Wittenberger presented to the University trustees a request for allocation of rooms and an appropriation to supplement the fund raised by members for equipment.

In support of this request, President Bryan said:

It is my judgment that no other organization established by the students of this University has united the men so well as this club. This union of the interests and the activities of the students is of peculiar importance because most other college organizations exert more or less influence in the opposite direction. The spirit and purposes and activities of this organization meet my very hearty approval.

The club wishes, among other things, to provide for its members various forms of harmless and interesting entertainment, believing that these under good auspices are not only useful in themselves, but will keep the men from less desirable forms of amusement and from undesirable places of amusement. In this connection they desire to be authorized to install in one of the rooms of the Student Building a number of billiard tables. This request raises a legal question and a question of general policy. Mr. E. E. Stacy, Secretary of the State Y.M.C.A., has furnished me with a legal opinion by Mr. Samuel Pickens, of Indianapolis, to the effect that a clubroom such as a Y.M.C.A. clubroom, open only to members, is not a public place within the meaning of the statute which forbids the presence of minors in a public place where pool or billiards are played. I have submitted this opinion to Messrs. Corr, Batman, and Hogate for their opinion.

As to the question of policy, I have written letters to the Secretaries of Y.M.C.A. Associations in Boston, Scranton, Kansas City, New York City, Brooklyn, Milwaukee, Syracuse, Philadelphia, Omaha, St. Paul, and Detroit, and submit the replies. In general it is the view of the Y.M.C.A. leaders that the establishment of billiards in their association houses is justified by experience. It rescues an excellent and innocent game from bad associations. It leads young men to find their pleasure under good surroundings instead of under bad. I submit the request of the Union to the consideration of the Board.

The Union proposed to spend a considerable sum of money in furnishing three or four rooms in the Student Building. I recommend that, following the precedent in the cases of other organizations, the Trustees supplement the amount expended by the Union by an equal amount, not exceeding $500, the same to be expended under the direction of the Executive Committee and under the advice of the Professor of Fine Arts.

The request of the Union for rooms was granted, with the provision that the rooms should at all times be under the direction and control of the Board of Trustees. An appropriation of $500 was made for furniture and improvement of the rooms set aside in the Student Building for the Indiana Union.

With pleasant and attractive quarters available, the Union grew rapidly during the next three months, according to President Bryan:

The Indiana Union now has about five hundred members. The rooms have been refurnished as proposed at the March meeting of the Board. I trust members of the Board will visit these rooms. The billiard room has been conducted in a thoroughly satisfactory manner except to the proprietors of the billiard rooms uptown, who have suffered seriously by the movement and who have severely criticized the University for interfering with their business.

The leaders of the Union are eager to begin a campaign for the completion of the Student Building. They have hopes in various directions. They talk of the possibility of securing another subscription from Mr. Rockefeller. All are anxious to begin a campaign for subscriptions from the Alumni. I have had long conferences with them, pointing out difficulties on various sides, but at the same time cherishing the splendid enthusiasm which they have for the University. I have asked Mr. Daggett to make a sketch for an addition to the Student Building and submit this to the Trustees. I suggest that we arrange to have an informal conference between the Trustees of the University and the Directors of the Union with regard to their hopes and plans.

The Indiana Union from its beginning late in 1909 has been one of the finest organizations on the campus. Members profited from association.

RELIGIOUS ACTIVITIES

The President, at Commencement time, 1910, acquainted his Board of Trustees with certain developments and proposals having as their object the provision of religious instruction and the maintenance and development of religious activity and leadership in the student body:

1. The Christian Associations of the University within the past three months have greatly enlarged their work under the direction of the Secretary, Mr. Voris. They conducted a vigorous campaign resulting in the raising of $3,000 for the coming year. . . . They have developed various kinds of new work, including the introduction of distinguished lecturers such as Jenkin Lloyd Jones and others of his rank. The movement has apparently contributed greatly to a better spirit of friendliness, cooperation, and good life among the students.

2. Several denominations are organizing movements to place in Bloomington, in connection with their churches, college pastors who shall devote themselves to the religious instruction of their own members amongst the students. The leaders of these movements are working in harmony with each other and with the Christian Associations. They plan to have within the course of a few years a group of men of different denominations supported by voluntary contributions who together shall constitute a School of Religious Education outside the University, but working in a friendly way with it.

3. Professor Kelsey, of Michigan University, has stated to a number of state university presidents that he expects to secure a big endowment, possibly $1,000,000, the proceeds of which are to be used in sending distinguished religious leaders as lecturers to the various state universities.

4. The Catholic students of the University have a Society which has meetings in one of the rooms of the University. There is no antagonism, but, on the other hand, a friendly feeling between the Associations.

5. Mr. Kiser, a Hebrew student, tells me that Rabbi Feuerlicht has urged him to organize a religious association of the Hebrew students. He has not done so because of their small numbers at present. I hope this may be done later.

GROWTH OF THE UNIVERSITY

The President reported to the trustees in November, 1908, on enrollment in schools of the University. The enrollment in the School of Law for the current year had been maintained at 201. The enrollment in the School of Medicine was 260.

Attendance in the School of Education, of which the President was acting as dean, had greatly increased by June, 1909. There were

27 graduate students, 29 Seniors, 116 Juniors, 133 Sophomores, 52 Freshmen, and 178 special students in education. This made a total of 605 students in that School.

In 1907 arrangements were made with the Bloomington schools for practice teaching and observation work. The increase in attendance was evidence of the attractiveness of that arrangement, which had to serve until the University School of the School of Education was erected in 1938.

Indiana University had shared in the remarkable growth of institutions of higher education in the last quarter-century. Commenting on this matter in June, 1910, the President submitted impressive data:

Years	Attendance	Income
1884–5	157	$ 30,800.00
1894–5	771	93,289.99
1904–5	1,538	207,024.78
1909–10	2,562	255,900.00

I am very glad of the growth of the University in numbers and in income. It must and it will grow very much larger in both respects in order to render adequate service to the great empire which Indiana is and is coming to be. Within the past eight years we have doubled in attendance and income. Within the next ten years we shall double again in both respects. However, I am much more deeply interested in two other considerations. I am supremely interested in making the quality of what we do with Freshmen and Seniors, with graduates and professional students as good as it can be. Every poorly trained man whom we send out counts in our statistics, but injures us and the state. Every man sent out who is well trained strengthens the University and our democratic society. Secondly, I am profoundly interested in the selection by the University of the proper fields of work. If we had money, the University should turn out men for every occupation which requires a higher education. With limited resources, we must avoid undue expansion in order to do well what we undertake. We have, therefore, the always difficult problem of choosing what we shall do. In general I believe we should be guided by the need of supplying men to the greatest and most influential occupations. If the University develops satisfactorily along existing lines, we shall in larger and larger measure supply to Indiana its leaders in three great professions, education, law, and medicine. Besides this we shall supply a great many men to some technical fields though not to all. I believe that we shall in future supply an increasing number of men to the field of business. In proportion as we do this the University will become indeed a chief organ of the life of the state and the state will without doubt furnish in larger measure the means for its efficient activity.

The growth of the University was being felt in the office of the Dean of the College of Liberal Arts, Horace A. Hoffman, where the administrative work, a year-round job, was becoming too heavy for one man. This was particularly the situation at the opening of each term, and on several occasions Professor W. A. Rawles had given voluntary assistance to the hard-pressed dean. At the opening of the year 1908 Dean Hoffman had asked that Professor Rawles be appointed as his assistant, and this request had been approved in November, 1908.

There also was evidence of growth in prestige. The Carnegie Foundation had recently approved administration of entrance requirements at Indiana University, a step preliminary to eligibility of faculty members to the Carnegie Retirement Allowances.[4] Also recently the University had been elected to membership in the Association of American Universities (January 7, 1909), both of which were regarded as testimonials to the efficiency of the work of Horace A. Hoffman.[5]

There were still other matters related to the growth of the University to which the President directed attention.

There was the matter of telephones. When the buildings of the campus, Owen and Wylie, Kirkwood and Maxwell were not a stone's throw apart, telephones did not seem important and there were none except for the one in the President's office, installed after erection of Maxwell and the transfer of the office of the President to that building from Owen Hall. But with the erection of Science Hall, the Student Building, and the Library, the extremes were moving farther apart. Moreover, telephones by 1909 were coming into more general use and their absence was more felt. In June of 1909 Professor Foley had reported on various kinds of telephone systems and the selection of a satisfactory system had been left to him and the Executive Committee.

[4] This was voted by the executive committee of the Carnegie Foundation on June 9, 1910.
[5] The faculty, desiring to express publicly their appreciation of the able and efficient service of Dean Hoffman, prepared a memorial, recorded in the minutes of the trustees and presented to the Dean on the fifteenth anniversary of his appointment (June, 1909). This was the only time in the thirty-five years of the Bryan administration when the faculty made such a testimonial to a living faculty member. Professor Hoffman retired as dean emeritus in 1920.

In September, 1909, a contract for the system selected was let to the Automatic Electric Company of Chicago for $415 and the bid of a local electric company of $596 for wire and other materials and labor was accepted. Though calls were limited to the campus, though a professor could not reach his own home or anyone in or out of the city, it was a great convenience to make quick connection with different floors of one's building or other buildings. In short, the installation was a boon, but it had limitations.

Also there was the appropriation of $300 for a duplicating machine for getting out circular letters or communications to the faculty.

Of a different nature was the request of Victor M. Cook for permission to establish a lunch counter in the Student Building. While this petition was refused it helped focus attention on this need which was becoming greater with increasing enrollments and was supplied in 1917 by the University opening and operating a cafeteria in the basement of the Student Building.

The School of Law and the School of Medicine both required one year of collegiate work in 1909 and two years in 1910 for admission.

These were all part of the growing pains of a University.

UNRELATED MATTERS, 1908–10

The following unrelated matters of interest are associated with this biennium.

At Commencement time, 1908, the trustees had increased the President's salary from $5,000 to $6,000. This $1,000 increase in salary was well merited. But in November, 1908, the President, while thanking the board for this evidence of approval, refused this increase, "in view of the state of our budget." The effect on faculty morale was excellent. Salaries *were* low and departmental budgets very small. Some men were drawing on personal funds to meet living expenses. The President's action was notice that he was playing the game with the faculty for the development of Indiana University.

When Professor Robert J. Aley left the University in 1909 to become state superintendent of public instruction, the Department of

Mathematics was placed in charge of a committee consisting of Professors Schuyler C. Davisson and David A. Rothrock.

In June, 1909, the Doctor of Laws was conferred on David Starr Jordan.

In November, 1909, an appropriation of $290 was made to Sigma Xi for the purchase of the *Philosophical Transactions of the Royal Society of London.*

In March, 1910, the Executive Committee was authorized to negotiate with the Phi Gamma Delta fraternity for the purchase of the lot at the southwest corner of the campus on which their fraternity house, recently burned, had been located. This matter is considered further in Chapter XII.

The acoustics of the auditorium of the Student Building were very bad, impairing the usefulness of that audience hall. Professors Arthur L. Foley and Charles D. Campbell had been studying methods for improvement. Changes recommended by Professor Foley greatly improved the acoustic properties of the auditorium.

A special, and higher, fee scale for out-of-state students was adopted in 1910.

CHAPTER X

INDIANA UNIVERSITY AND THE NON-STATE SCHOOLS

T HE STORY of sectarian opposition to Indiana University during the Bryan administration, apart from the background of earlier periods, provides so little understanding of this interesting phenomenon that it has seemed best to tell the story as a whole, though in doing so some repetition of isolated fragments of the story, related by Banta or Woodburn, is involved. In the whole story there are the following very definite periods:

1820–1885. Development of Idea of State Universities.

1885–1902. The Geeting Bill.

1902 to date. The Marshall Conference with State and Non-State School Presidents.

1820–1885. DEVELOPMENT OF IDEA OF STATE UNIVERSITIES

The last chapter of that part of Woodburn's *History of Indiana University* written by Judge Banta is entitled "Perils from Sectarian Controversies and the Constitutional Convention." The perils from sectarian controversies appeared early in the history of Indiana University. After the one-man faculty, a Presbyterian, had conducted the work of the Indiana Seminary for three years, it became necessary, in 1827, to appoint a second professor. There were a number of candidates, most of whom had interested friends. When the trustees chose John H. Harney, who was also understood to be a Presbyterian, the cry of sectarianism at once arose.

William Lowe, a member of the first Board of Trustees of Indiana Seminary, resigned in 1826. Judge Banta says:

All the evidence at hand warrants the conclusion that Judge Lowe was preparing himself to take part in the campaign already inaugurated against the College and those having it in charge.[1]

[1] J. A. Woodburn, *History of Indiana University, 1820–1902*, p. 72.

This campaign was not launched until the 1829 session of the General Assembly when four petitions were presented calling for investigation of both professors and trustees. The object of the attack as renewed in the succeeding session was "driving sectarianism out of Indiana College."

Mr. Bassett, from the House Committee on Education to which these petitions were referred, reported that the committee had

under their consideration, the several petitions and documents referred to them, by this house, relative to the Indiana College, at Bloomington; and that they are unanimously of opinion, that the charges and complaints, as set forth in said petitions, against the trustees and faculty of said college, are wholly groundless, and without any foundation in truth or evidence, to support them.[2]

The following year, however, the General Assembly by joint resolution (approved January 25, 1830) called upon the Board of Trustees to state whether section 10 of the act establishing the College had been complied with. The reply of the board by Dr. D. H. Maxwell, its president, is very forceful:

The board do not sustain the present faculty on account of any religious opinions they may profess, but for their literary attainments, their exalted qualifications, their particular adaptation to the stations which they fill.[3]

He stated that the board would fearlessly remove any faculty member who violated the constitution of the College by teaching sectarian tenets or principles to the students. But, most convincing, a list of the trustees was given, and it was stated:

Of this Board it is believed four are Presbyterians, or at least were so educated; four Protestant Episcopalians; three Baptists; two Methodists; one Covenanter; and one a member of the Christian society or church. Out of such a mixture of religious opinion, it cannot reasonably be supposed, that a majority could be prevailed upon to establish, or in any respect to countenance a sectarian denomination.[4]

In the Senate the Committee on Education made a lengthy report on January 15, 1831, saying in part in answer to the petition of Amos Lock and others:

[2] *House Journal*, 1829, pp. 143–44.
[3] *House Journal*, 1830, p. 44.
[4] *Op. cit.*, p. 45.

Now what do the petitioners require? It is that [in] all future elections of professors, the trustees shall elect no two of the same subordinate religious sect or persuasions. How this could be effected without a violation of the Constitution under which we live, the committee cannot conceive, it would virtually compel a selection of professors without regard to their qualifications in science, but on the principles of religious tests, and could not fail to bring into disrespect, an institution founded with a sole view to education apart from sectarianism.[5]

Banta tells us that the first Methodist Conference, 1832, considered the establishment of a Methodist college, but decided "if we could receive something like an equitable share of privileges in the State University at Bloomington, that it would answer the wants of our people for several years."

In 1834 the Methodist Conference memorialized the General Assembly, saying, "one common religious creed characterizes every member of the faculty" of Indiana College.

That charges of sectarianism were continuing is revealed in the report of the trustees to the legislature of 1837–38[6], which, emphasizing the nonsectarian character of instruction and public utterances of faculty members, stated:

The public discourses and private sentiments of the President in particular, will, it is believed, shield him from any imputation of that kind [sectarian teaching], the hatred which all *bigots* bear to him, being the best testimonial in his behalf in this matter.

Sectarianism in the early days of the University is so well presented by Judge Banta that we have given only a few quotations from the period, revealing something of the character of the attack and the reply. At the constitutional convention of 1851 the very existence of the institution was threatened, and it was with great difficulty that its friends succeeded in preserving its endowment.

The fact that, with the exception of the year 1859–60 when John Lathrop was president, Methodist ministers held the office of president of Indiana University from 1855 to 1875 (William Daily, 1853–59; Cyrus Nutt, 1860–75) did not ease the situation; it merely shifted slightly the direction of the attack. People took their emotions in the superlative. Sectarianism got into politics and it was boasted that

[5] *Senate Journal,* 1930, p. 274.
[6] *Indiana Documentary Journal,* January 9, 1838, pp. 3, 4.

candidates were elected or defeated by the Amen corner of the church.

It was inconceivable to most people of that day that a minister, Presbyterian or Methodist, could occupy a professorship in the state school and be able to teach without indoctrinating his pupils. Colleges in that early day were small. The denominational colleges were established chiefly as training schools for future ministers of the founding denomination. It was the concept of the time that the education that was good for ministers was good for everyone. Education to so many meant religious education, which again was essentially synonymous with sectarian education. Presbyterian president and faculty were as alarming to Methodists as a Methodist president and faculty were to Presbyterians, and both were cause of grave concern to still other denominations.

Sectarianism was not a phenomenon peculiar to Indiana. A comparable situation in the history of the University of Michigan is related by Andrew Ten Brook.[7] The following account is condensed as much as possible.

According to the best American tradition of that day, the president should be of the clerical profession and fill the chair of mental and moral philosophy.

In anticipation of the need of the University of Michigan for a professor of philosophy at the opening of the term in September, 1844, Edward Thompson, of Ohio, a minister of the Methodist Episcopal Church, had been elected to the presidency, but in the mid-summer he declined.

Measures were taken at once to fill the place and on September 12, 1844, Schuyler Saeger, a Methodist minister, professor in a seminary of western New York, and Andrew Ten Brook, pastor of the Baptist Church of Detroit, were considered by the board and the latter was elected, the three Methodist members voting for Saeger and all the rest voting for Ten Brook.

The meeting was reported as the most exciting ever held up to that time.

Language was used by the Methodist members severely reflecting upon the motives of the other members of the board in this action, and some of the

[7] *American State Universities,* p. 189.

regents retained ever after an unfriendly feeling toward the whole Methodist denomination in Michigan, growing out of this occasion. They seemed to regard the expressions of a few men, in the board and out of it, at this time and subsequently, as a claim set up by the entire church which they represented, to a certain position in relation to the university.

To say that antagonism of church colleges to state universities was general expresses a fact, but does not give an explanation. To understand the opposition of the denominational colleges to the state universities as it manifested itself in the nineteenth century in the United States, it is necessary to turn back three hundred years to the Reformation of the sixteenth century and note the development of certain concepts during that period.

There were three major positions with reference to the relations of church, state, and education.

1. There was the position of the Roman Church, which assumed the divine authority of the church[8] over state and education.

2. There was Luther's idea, which had been gaining ground in Germany for more than half a century, that the *jus episcopale* belonged to the supreme secular authority. As stated by Thomas M. Lindsay:

All the schemes of ecclesiastical government proceed on the idea that the *jus episcopale* or right of ecclesiastical oversight belongs to the supreme territorial secular authority. All of them include within the one set of ordinances, provision for the support of the ministry, for the maintenance of schools,[9] and

---

[8] That the church had a vested right in education was recognized by an English court decision, for in 1410 the Chief Justice ruled that the education of children was a "spiritual matter, . . . one beyond the cognizance of the King's Bench." (Crump and Jacobs, *The Legacy of the Middle Ages,* p. 255.)

[9] F. V. N. Painter in *Great Pedagogical Essays, Plato to Spencer,* includes (pp. 171 ff.) Luther's "Letter to the Mayors and Aldermen of all the Cities of Germany in behalf of Christian Schools." He calls it "the first great contribution of Protestantism to the science and art of education—the beginning of the movement that has given Europe and America their public schools." The fundamental thought that underlies all of Luther's writings on education is that education is not an end of itself, but a means of more effective service in church and state.

Luther stated in this letter: "If I had children and were able, I would have them learn not only the languages and history, but also singing, instrumental music, and the whole course of mathematics."

Luther hears someone say: "Who can do without his children and bring them up in this manner, to be young gentlemen?" He replies: "My idea is that boys should spend an hour or two a day in school and the rest of the time work at home, learn some trade, and do whatever is desired, so that study and work may go on together." He had a like program for girls. (*Continued on page 94*)

for the care of the poor.[10]

Luther's conception of schools and education was very sound and very broad. The natural development of this point of view was a state church.

3. There was the point of view of the Anabaptists[11] (sometimes referred to as the radical element of the reform), who would have nothing to do with a state church. This was:

. . . the main point in their separation from the Lutherans, Zwinglians, and Calvinists. It was perhaps the *one* conception on which all parties among them were in absolute accord.[12]

Separation of church and state became the adopted policy in America. As for education, the Anabaptists were too individualistic, for the greater part, to take kindly to the idea of state-controlled education.

In December, 1520, Luther had publicly burned the Pope's bull which had been issued against him.

In 1521 the new Emperor, King Charles V of Spain, presided at the Diet of Worms. Called upon to recant, Luther expressed willingness to do so if shown to be wrong by evangelical or prophetic witnesses. He based his call for reform on the Scriptures in which he found authority for his convictions superior to that of Pope or bishops. The Emperor's condemnation of Luther was added to that

(Continued from page 93)

He says further: "But the brightest pupils, who give promise of becoming accomplished teachers, preachers, and workers, should be kept longer at school, or set apart wholly for study." He states this is an urgent necessity, not only for the sake of the young, but also for the maintenance of Christianity and civil government.

He elaborates this thought as follows: "Now the welfare of a city does not consist alone in great treasures, firm walls, beautiful houses, and munitions of war. . . . The highest welfare, safety, and power of a city consists in able, learned, wise, upright, cultivated citizens who can secure, preserve, and utilize every treasure and advantage."

In *Luther on Education in the Christian Home and School* (1940), the author, Paul E. Kretzman, has assembled 115 pages of quotations from Luther's writings bearing on education. He quotes (pp. 110–11) from a "Sermon on the Duty of Sending Children to School": "For our rulers are certainly bound to maintain the spiritual and secular offices and callings so that there may always be preachers, jurists, pastors, scribes, physicians, schoolmasters. and the like, for these cannot be dispensed with."

[10] *History of the Reformation,* Vol. I, pp. 413–14.

[11] Lindsay tells us that the Anabaptists were far more numerous than commonly had been believed. They spread throughout Europe and included in their numbers many able men. They were persecuted by the Catholics and Lutherans alike. The Baptist church of today is a descendant of this sect.

[12] Lindsay, *op. cit.,* Vol. II, p. 443.

of the Pope. Powerful German electors, however, supported Luther and no action was taken on the Emperor's edict.

In 1526 at the Diet of Spire the Emperor needed German support for war in prospect.

It was equally impracticable to withdraw the edict of Worms from the catholic states or to impose it upon the evangelical.[13]

So it was finally decided that in all matters appertaining to the Diet of Worms each state should "so live, rule, and bear itself as it thought it could answer to God and the Emperor."

Ranke further says:[14]

Had it not been for the divisions existing between the two highest powers of Europe [Pope and Emperor] the decisive resolutions of the diet of 1526 would never have passed.

Having once more established amiable relations with the Pope, the Emperor was prepared at the Diet of Spire of 1529 to repeal the action of 1526. The evangelical states had prepared, and now caused to be read aloud before the assembled states, a protest, from which they took the name their descendants still bear—Protestants.

Because of differences in interpretation of the Scriptures in which they found authority for their religious convictions, sects soon arose among Protestants. A Protestant reform in Switzerland had been led by Zwingli, whose teachings differed in certain respects from those of Luther. In 1530 and 1531 persistent efforts were made to bring about a reconciliation of these two Protestant groups. A spirit of concession was manifested by both Luther and Zwingli. It was finally realized, however, that religious differences, chiefly with reference to the sacrament, formed an insuperable obstacle to their union. Thus was laid the foundation for development of sects.[15]

To summarize, with reference to relations of church and state and education there were three major concepts:

1. That of the Latin church, dominant over the state and education.

2. That of Luther, the state dominant over church and education, i.e., a state church and state-supported schools.

[13] Leopold Ranke, *History of the Reformation in Germany,* Vol. II, p. 414.
[14] *Op. cit.,* Vol. III, p. 157.
[15] *Ibid.,* p. 390.

3. That of the Anabaptist, who could not tolerate a state church, but insisted upon separation of church and state. For the greater part, they set little value on learning.

These concepts of the period of the Reformation had an important bearing upon developments in America. Immigrants from various European countries naturally brought with them to America the religious, educational, and political concepts which they held in the mother country. In only one of those countries, the Netherlands, did the theory of separation of church and state have any considerable following. With this exception there was in Europe union of church and state under dominance of one or the other.

Relations of Church and State in the Colonies

However established, the colonies had gradually come under the domination of England. In the eighteenth century the British element of the population of the colonies in North America had increased rapidly, and small colonial groups were largely absorbed. In seven colonies the Church of England was established by law.

How it came about that the principle of a state church was abandoned is well told by Sanford H. Cobb in his interesting book, *The Rise of Religious Liberty in America.*

Though the Church of England as an established church was unsatisfactory in certain colonies to 75 per cent of the people, the principle of an established church was acceptable to a much higher per cent of the colonists, particularly to the numerous Presbyterians. Most religious groups would have been content with their particular church as the established church.

Intolerance was often extreme. Cobb (p. 125) tells that in the Carolinas in 1704 an act was passed, by a majority of one in a small House, which required that all members of the legislature should be of the Church of England. This act disfranchised Nonconformists, almost three-fourths of the population. Some dissenters living near the Pamphlico River petitioned the legislature for permission to engage and support a minister of their own faith. The petition was refused.

Cobb states (p. 362) that Maryland was

torn by continual jealousy. A foundation of Roman Catholics in the avowed interests of religious freedom, it was wrested from their grasp and made hostile to both their faith and the rights of conscience.

Cobb further says (p. 482):

With the dawn of the Revolution all the colonies were substantially ready for the adoption of measures, which should make the severance of Church from State complete. Though each had gone through an experience peculiar to itself, in some instances presenting marked contrasts to the others, all were practically together in the general desire for a religious liberty entirely untrammelled by the civil law, in which the terms *conformity* and *dissent* would become forever inapplicable.

In Virginia the controversy over an established church was not ended until some years after the Revolution. Three-fourths of the people of Virginia were outside the established church.

To quote Cobb (p. 484):

Indeed, the chief interest in all the union [of church and state] centered there [in Virginia]; there the issue was at this time more sharply drawn than elsewhere, and the answer was more clearly and positively pronounced. In the other colonies the end of establishments came as a natural consequent upon national independence, and without much discussion.

The beginning of the end of the established church in Virginia was precipitated in 1784 by introduction of a bill in the General Assembly, the purpose of which was the recognition of the Episcopal Church as the state church. Madison wrote a famous memorial in opposition to the bill, which was finally defeated by a small majority. This was followed early in 1786 by the passage of Jefferson's Act for Establishing Religious Freedom in Virginia. Hugh E. Willis[16] considers that the controversy which was waged over these two bills "a number of years before the constitutional convention and the first Congress had much to do with the origin of the guaranty of religious liberty in the First Amendment."

While the Constitution of the United States of America makes no mention of a state church, there is nothing in the Constitution which prevents the establishment of such a church at some later time. This was regarded as a defect to be remedied at the earliest opportunity. Accordingly, the First Amendment adopted in 1791 provides that

[16] *Constitutional Law*, pp. 501–2.

"Congress shall make no law respecting an establishment of religion or prohibiting the free exercise thereof."

The guaranty of the First Amendment has been thought to apply only to the Federal Government. Willis states:

The religious liberties of the people [of the several states] are not protected against state governments . . . unless the due process clause of the Fourteenth Amendment[17] includes protection against religious liberty.

As Willis observes, this federal protection against action of state legislatures is immaterial, because "all American [state] constitutions have guaranties protecting religious liberty."

Colonial Colleges

The colonial colleges were nearly all denominational. They were established chiefly for the training of ministers of the respective denominations.

Before the American Revolution nine colleges had been founded in the colonies, as follows:

Harvard University, Massachusetts, Congregational, 1636.
College of William and Mary, Virginia, Anglican, 1693.
Yale University, Connecticut, Congregational, 1701.
Princeton University, New Jersey, Presbyterian, 1746.
University of Pennsylvania, Pennsylvania, nonsectarian, 1749.
Columbia University (Kings College), New York, Anglican, 1754.
Brown University, Rhode Island, Baptist, 1764.
Rutgers University, New Jersey, Dutch Reformed, 1766.
Dartmouth College, New Hampshire, Congregational, 1769.

Though no one of these colleges is now under denominational control, they set the pattern for denominational colleges of the early nineteenth century and profoundly influenced organization of state universities.

The Tenth Amendment, declared in force on December 15, 1791, provided that "the powers not delegated to the United States by the Constitution, nor prohibited by it to the States, are reserved to the States respectively, or to the people." Since the Constitution makes

[17] The due process clause of the Fourteenth Amendment reads as follows: "No State shall make or enforce any law which shall abridge the privileges or immunities of citizens of the United States; nor shall any State deprive any person of life, liberty, or property without due process of law."

no mention of education, the Tenth Amendment clearly leaves it to the individual states to act on this important matter.

How would the states act?

In 1800 there were sixteen states in the Union. Eight of these states had adopted constitutions containing references to education, which indicated that their framers recognized education as an activity to be fostered by the state. The constitutions of New York and of Connecticut were silent on the subject of schools until well into the nineteenth century, but these states were among the earliest and most enterprising in pioneering for education.

It must not be forgotten, however, that most people were accustomed to think of education chiefly as religious education. Even in those states in which state-supported schools had been established by legislative act there were great groups of people who were profoundly distrustful of education apart from the church, and wholly intolerant of state-supported education under domination of any church other than their own. Obviously here were present the elements of inevitable conflict.

How the states would exercise their freedom of action in the matter of education was profoundly influenced by the Ordinance of July 23, 1787, in which the conditions of purchase imposed by the Ohio Company were accepted.

This story is told by Robert S. Robertson, a trustee of Indiana University, 1882 to 1894, in Theophilus Wylie's *History of Indiana University, from 1820, When Founded, to 1890.*

Rufus Putnam and other New England soldiers conceived the idea of a state in the Northwest Territory between Lake Erie and the Ohio River. Colonel Timothy Pickering in the spring of 1783 drew up a plan, presented to Congress by Putnam and his associates, with a petition for permission to form the colony. The plan provided for distribution of lands to soldiers in payment for services. Surplus lands were to be the property of the state to be used for construction of roads, bridges, public buildings, establishing schools and academies, etc. The resulting ordinance for the organization of the territory was presented by Jefferson[18] (1784) and contained no pro-

---

[18] It was two years later, early in 1786, that the Virginia Act for Establishing Religious Freedom was passed. But Jefferson's bill for the more general diffusion of knowledge had been passed in 1779. Why Jefferson did not support provision for education in Ohio is not clear.

vision for schools. Colonel Pickering protested at this omission.

A new ordinance was presented in 1785 in which there was provision for reservation in each township of one lot (section) for schools and one lot for support of the ministry. When this was modified by striking out provision of a section for ministerial support, it failed to meet the expectations and demands of the soldiers.

The Ohio Company was formed in 1786 chiefly by veterans of the Revolutionary War who wanted to make homes for themselves in Ohio. In 1787 they elected Samuel Holden Parsons, Manasseh Cutler, and Rufus Putnam as directors. They presented a memorial to Congress, which was referred to a committee. Two days later this committee presented a bill differing materially from the plan proposed by the Ohio Company. On July 13, 1787, this bill was passed and became the famous Ordinance for Government of the Northwest Territory.

Finally the Congressional Committee having in charge the sale of the lands recommended sale on terms demanded by the Ohio Company. This recommendation Congress considered too liberal and framed an ordinance reserving section 16 for schools. Dr. Cutler, for the Ohio Company, submitted another proposal containing the only conditions on which the Ohio Company would purchase. Needing the money offered, Congress unwillingly accepted the terms, and on July 23, 1787, passed an ordinance providing that lot 16 be given perpetually to the maintenance of schools, lot 29 to the purposes of religion, and two townships near the center for the support of a literary institution, to be applied to the intended object by the legislature of the state.

When in 1801 Jefferson became president of the United States, the Ordinance of July 23, 1787, providing for education had established a precedent for organization of states in the Northwest Territory. No one knew better than Jefferson the importance of education in a government of the people, for the people, and by the people. An intelligent, aggressive, and serviceable citizenship was a prerequisite for that sound public opinion, absolutely vital to the welfare of the democracy which had been established.

It is, therefore, not surprising that encouragement to consider education of first importance is found in "An act making provision for disposal of public lands in the Indiana Territory." This act provides that the sixteenth section of every township should be reserved for support of schools within that township.[19] It also provides that certain entire townships, to be located by the Secretary of the Treasury, should be reserved for the use of a seminary of learning.

This was the basic act, and it is not difficult to see in it the influence of the man who was the author of the Virginia Act for Establishing Religious Freedom and who later was to be known as the father of the University of Virginia.

Then on April 19, 1816,[20] in the administration of James Madison, a Virginian and close friend of Jefferson, who shared Jefferson's views on education, we find:

An act to enable the people of the Indiana Territory to form a constitution and a state government, and for the admission of such state into the Union on an equal footing with the original states.

Section 6 of this act provides:

And be it further enacted, That the following propositions be, and the same are hereby offered to the convention of the said territory of Indiana, when formed, for their free acceptance or rejection, which, if accepted by the convention, shall be obligatory upon the United States.

First. That the section numbered sixteen, in every township, and when such section has been sold, granted or disposed of, other lands, equivalent thereto, and most contiguous to the same, shall be granted to the inhabitants of such township for the use of schools.

Fourth. That one entire township, which shall be designated by the President of the United States, in addition to the one heretofore reserved[21] for that purpose, shall be reserved for the use of a seminary of learning, and vested in the legislature of the said state, to be appropriated solely to the use of such seminary by the said legislature.

It seems obvious, therefore, that, while the freedom of the states to act as they saw fit on the matter of education is emphasized by its repetition in section 6, above, nevertheless education was con-

---

[19] This act (*United States Statutes at Large,* Vol. II, March 26, 1804, p. 279) is reminiscent of "A Bill for the More General Diffusion of Knowledge" written by Jefferson twenty-five years earlier and reported to the Virginia Assembly by T. Jefferson and G. Wythe, June, 1779. (*Writings of Thomas Jefferson,* Ford ed., II, pp. 195, 220.)

[20] *United States Statutes at Large,* Vol. III, p. 289.

[21] That is, two entire townships. "The one heretofore reserved" refers to the Gibson County grant. James Monroe was the President who designated the township. The county was, therefore, called Monroe, and the township was named Perry, commemorating the recent victory (September, 1813) of Oliver H. Perry on Lake Erie.

sidered so vital to the general welfare that the Federal Government felt justified in extending the strongest encouragement to the states "to provide by law for a general system of education, ascending in a regular gradation from township schools to a state university."

Including the nine colleges established in the colonial period, there were forty-nine colleges in the United States, when, in 1820, the fiftieth, Indiana University, was established.[22] These fifty colleges were divided almost equally between state and nonsectarian colleges (twenty-four) and denominational colleges (twenty-six).

Five of the twelve state colleges were located in states formerly colonies (Georgia, North Carolina, Virginia, South Carolina, and Maryland). The significance of the twelve nonsectarian colleges should not be overlooked. The twenty-six denominational colleges were founded as follows: Presbyterian, 11; Congregational, 4; Baptist, 3; Anglican and Episcopal, 3; Catholic and Jesuit, 2; Methodist, 2; Dutch Reformed, 1. The fact that Presbyterian colleges so far outnumbered those of any other denomination in that early day of 1820 explains availability of men of Presbyterian faith and training for early faculty appointments.

To summarize:

1. The idea of state colleges and universities was European and old and was being widely adopted in America. There was always a minority, however, that did not approve of a state school, and this group continued to make its opposition felt.

2. Originally the state college was associated with a state church.

3. The First Amendment to the Constitution of the United States prohibited a state church.

4. With the growth of the idea of freedom of the individual in interpretation of the Scriptures, sectarianism and intolerance of religious views of others developed, which made dominance of any one church intolerable.

5. Many people were unable to conceive of state education apart from the church, and they were distrustful of education under the intimate leadership of any one denomination. Interdenominational trust and good will were as yet insufficient to make possible the

[22] For a list of colleges, 1776–1830, see Eby and Arrowood, *The Development of Modern Education in Theory, Organization, and Practice*, pp. 567–69.

presentation of fundamental Christian teachings under an inter-denominational board. The idea of instruction in religion under a Protestant, Catholic, Jewish board, as found in the University of Iowa today (1945), was quite beyond the thinking of that time.

6. The opposition of the denominational schools to state schools must be understood as merely a part of the heated controversy which had developed first in Europe, in which men were seeking religious liberty, freedom from domination of any particular church. The antagonism was not mutual. The state universities were interested in carrying into effect, against opposition if necessary, the will of the majority by which they were established. Many members of the faculties of the state universities held membership in one or another of the denominations and had sympathetic interest in, rather than antagonism for, the college supported by their denomination.

1885–1902. THE GEETING BILL

Except for the fact that during the sixty-five years from 1820 to 1885 some four hundred additional colleges were established in the United States, including most of those in Indiana, the above summary gives the background for relations of the state and denominational colleges in Indiana when in 1885 the succession of ministerial presidents was ended and David Starr Jordan was appointed president of Indiana University. This appointment proved unsatisfactory to all sectarians, and the University was dubbed "that godless institution," as Jordan tells us Cornell had been.

Jordan speaks of the University as he found it in 1879 when he was appointed professor of natural history (which then meant zoology, botany, geology, and physiology):

> While the college had from the beginning some eminent teachers, its presidents, chosen from the clergy of different religious denominations, were as a rule neither scholarly nor progressive. One of them (Dr. Daily) is said to have openly proclaimed that "the people want to be humbugged; it's our duty to give them what they want.". . . Several sectarian colleges in the state had more than once combined to try to shut off public appropriations.[23]

On becoming president of Indiana University, one of his first duties, Jordan said,

[23] *The Days of a Man*, Vol. I, p. 187.

was to secure money for new buildings from the legislature then meeting in Indianapolis. . . . But I at once encountered two distinct obstacles, the one grounded in sectarian jealousy, the other entirely personal to myself.[24]

Add to this, internal dissensions and faculty quarrels, and one gains some understanding of why it was that after sixty-one years, when in 1885 Jordan became president, there were enrolled in Indiana University only 157 college students.

In the years between the appointment of Jordan, 1885, and the appointment of Bryan, 1902, Indiana University grew very rapidly in attendance. This naturally called for an increase in faculty and also in income, in which there was a lag.

Jordan and Coulter were scientists and Swain was a mathematician. But all three were deeply religious men. Jordan's parents were Universalists with Puritan conscience and rigid as to personal conduct. As a teacher in Indianapolis, Jordan was a friend of Oscar C. McCulloch, pastor of Plymouth Congregational Church, and became a member of his church, the only religious organization he ever formally joined. McCulloch's study of hereditary poverty must have interested Jordan greatly.

Coulter was the son of a Presbyterian minister, missionary in China, and was himself an active member of the Presbyterian Church.

Joseph Swain was an active member of the Quaker Church.

All three men had the interests of religion at heart. But Jordan and Coulter were both advocates of the theory of evolution, and large numbers of ministers and members of the Christian churches in that day were much opposed to that theory on religious grounds. They were unable to believe that an evolutionist could have a religious influence on a student body and feared young people were being led astray.

During the administrations of these three presidents, new men had been appointed to the faculty without the slightest consideration of their church affiliation, the sole requirement, apart from good citizenship, being the scholastic eligibility of the appointee.

The active participation of many members of the faculty of Indiana University in the work and responsibilities of various local

[24] *Op. cit.,* Vol. I, p. 290.

churches where on Sundays they met members of the student body was gradually revealing the unfairness of the appellation "godless institution," and the antagonism of non-state schools on religious grounds was losing force.

But the rapid growth of the University referred to above constituted a new cause for alarm for certain of the denominational colleges, which were able to see this growth only in terms of their own disinterest. Furthermore, a new menace to the welfare of the non-state schools seemed to them to be rising in the growing influence and power of the State Board of Education, on which the state schools held ex officio membership.

In the legislative session of 1897 a common school bill was introduced, known as the Geeting Bill, or Senate Bill 59, the companion House Bill being H.B. 123. This bill had been prepared by a committee of the State Teachers Association, appointed in December, 1895. This committee had collaborated with D. M. Geeting, State Superintendent of Public Instruction.

This bill repealed certain features of the Act of 1865 and of the Revised Statutes of 1881. It also attempted to strengthen the weak places in the existing law. The paramount thought of the committee was the improvement of the district schools, through:

1. The provision for township high schools.
2. A minimum school term of six months.
3. Providing educational qualifications for county superintendents and making their work more professional.
4. Placing the estimate for all applicants for teachers' licenses on two distinct bases:
    (a) Scholarship, to be determined by a disinterested party and
    (b) Success, as shown by actual schoolroom work observed by the superintendent, and all licenses to be state licenses.
5. Improvement of schools of towns and cities by requiring qualifications of superintendents and making them responsible for the management of the schools and results of teachers.[25]

The attack on the bill was made by the non-state schools, whose position was explained in a Statement to Senators, published in the

[25] See the *Inland Educator*, Vol. IV, p. 141.

Indianapolis News, February 23, 1897 (p. 2), in which there were these significant paragraphs:

If the people of Indiana have become convinced that the education interests of the State demand that the student patronage which has hitherto been drawn to the non-state colleges should be gradually concentrated, through the channels and influence of the public school system, into the three higher state institutions of learning, then we cannot expect that our present contention will be regarded as valid by the members of the legislature. If the taxpayers of the state see fit to assume the financial burden of so generously equipping the state schools that, by reason of that actual superiority of the training which they afford to the youth of the state, and for no other reason, the non-state schools are placed at a disadvantage in competition, then the latter ought to submit without protest and congratulate the people on the new education regime.

The complaint of the non-state schools is that such centralization of authority in the present membership of the State Board of Education as is provided for in the Geeting Bill virtually places the censorship of the superintendents and teachers through the State in the hands of Purdue University, Indiana University, and the State Normal School. . . .

Five of the active members of the State Board are distinctly connected with the State institutions. Four are connected with the state schools, viz. the presidents of the State University, the Normal School, and Purdue, and the State Superintendent of Public Instruction, who is ex officio a trustee of State Normal. A fifth member of the Board is an alumnus of the State University and a conspicuously active promoter of her interests in the legislature, the State Teachers Association, and elsewhere.

It is understood that the Governor's connection with the Board is practically honorary. It therefore appears that only two out of seven active members of the Board are free from entangling relations with the State Schools.

This statement shows that the non-state schools were alarmed at the rapid increase in enrollment of the state schools. Throughout the United States the state universities were still small and were very generally regarded as competitors of the non-state schools in the field of education.[26] The denominational school leaders reasoned that if young people of their church were attracted to the state school instead of to their respective denominational schools, they were lost both to the school and to the denomination. They visualized dwindling school enrollment and shrinking church membership. They attributed the rapid increase in enrollment in the state schools in part to the influence of the public school system (the State Department

[26] Also in the field of athletics.

of Public Instruction) and in part to the increased support of the state schools, making superiority of equipment and training possible by reason of which "the non-state schools are placed at a disadvantage in competition."

Jordan had warned his Board of Trustees in March, 1891, that

Comparison should be made not with the small denominational colleges . . . but with the universities of our sister states, all of whom are enjoying the same remarkable growth which has taken place here.

For too long a time the idea of the state schools being competitors of the non-state schools had dominated our thinking, instead of both being collaborators in providing educational facilities of the highest quality possible for young people of Indiana. This latter point of view was definitely established in the Marshall administration, as we will show later.

A fact not stated in this communication to senators which was giving the denominational schools much concern was the decrease in denominational support some were experiencing.

A careful reading of the lengthy Geeting Bill does show that control of the state's common school system is left with the State Board of Education where by the Act of 1865 it had been placed. But this reading fails to reveal any purpose other than that of strengthening the system of public instruction, and there is not the remotest suggestion of where students should go to college.

The *Indianapolis News* and the *Indianapolis Sentinel* during February, 1897, both carried numerous accounts of meetings and a hearing, together with letters from interested school superintendents in various parts of the state. The *News* and *Journal* of February 5, 1897, carry an account of one of the most important hearings. One gets an appreciation of the capability of President Parsons in the account of his defense of the position of State Normal. One senses the wisdom of President Gobin, who urged that a bill having so much merit should not be defeated because of fancied defects.

In a House hearing reported in the *Indianapolis News*, February 2, 1897 (p. 3), President Mills, of Earlham College, had objected to the Geeting Bill because

. . . it provided that applicants for the position of county superintendent and superintendent of town schools must hold license or a certificate to be conferred by the State Board of Education on conditions to be drawn up by the State Board.

On that occasion Dr. Gobin of DePauw said that "DePauw was willing to let its students stand or fall by their examinations."

An editorial in the *Indianapolis News,* February 23, 1897, entitled "The Educational Muddle" may be regarded as a disinterested summary of the situation. Excerpts from this long editorial follow:

> The heads of our Endowed Colleges say they are not opposed to "The general features of the Geeting Bill" but they are opposed to the present composition of the State Board of Education and they fear that increased power given by the Geeting Bill to the Board, would be unfairly used against them inasmuch as the Board is so constituted that the three members connected with the State Schools control the Board though it has eight members. Just how the three get so much power we do not know and our college friends do not explain. It seems really very extraordinary that the Governor, the State Superintendent, and the superintendents of the three largest cities of the state should be complete nonentities when acting on the State Board of Education; that they should leave everything to the three other members and let them use the Board for their individual interests, and yet that seems to be what our college friends ask us to believe. . . .
>
> And we want to say that we do not believe that Messrs. Smart, Swain, and Parsons are completely dominating the board, or that they are lying in wait concocting schemes for "doing" the endowed colleges. . . .
>
> We think they are pretty decent sort of men ourselves and that they would not abuse any power or privilege that comes to them to exercise.

But the bill was amended and the amendments were declared by Superintendent Study, of Fort Wayne, to be unacceptable to the public school men of the state. The *Indianapolis News,* February 26, 1897, stated that the motion to strike out the enabling clause was made by friends of Mr. Geeting at his request.[27]

Nine months passed, then the presidents of the non-state schools held a conference in Indianapolis on December 3, 1897, in which they reaffirmed their position as to the reconstruction of the State Board of Education and appointed a committee consisting of Messrs. Mills, Stott,[28] Gobin, and Burroughs,[29] to seek a conference with

---

[27] As part of this attack see a little booklet in the Archives of Indiana University by the Reverend T. A. Goodwin, D.D., entitled: *How Indiana University a Strictly Private Corporation Became a State School.*

[28] President Stott of Franklin College.

[29] There is some question as to the personnel of this committee. On page 552 of the minutes of the State Board of Education the membership is given as above. But on page 557 the

representative men of this board in order to formulate a suitable educational bill to be presented to the next legislature. These facts were communicated to Mr. Geeting, State Superintendent of Public Instruction, in a letter dated December 10, 1897, and found on page 552 of the minutes of the board for that year.

Mr. Geeting brought this letter to the attention of the State Board of Education, which decided that, in consideration of the importance of the meeting, the entire membership, including Governor Mount, should receive the committee of the non-state schools. The meeting was held on December 20 with the non-state schools represented by Presidents Burroughs (secretary), Butler, Gobin, and Mills.

The position of the non-state school committee was presented at length by President Burroughs as secretary,[30] and taken under consideration by the State Board, which appointed a committee to formulate a reply. On February 10, 1898, the State Board in executive session considered the reply and referred it back to the committee with suggestions for revision and with direction to report back next morning. The minutes of the State Board of Education do not indicate what decision was reached, if any, at the executive session on the following day.

The minutes of November 19, 1898, contained a long statement, which was made public. This statement reviewed the legislation creating the State Board. It called attention to the fact that the board was created to have charge of public instruction, that the board did not in any way impose rulings upon the non-state schools, nor were the non-state schools in any manner bound by actions of the board. The board affirmed its conviction that, considering the duties imposed upon it, the composition of the board presented a balance of the state's school system, a composition fully justified by the commendation and high standing accorded it throughout the United States. The statement concluded, however, that in the interest of good feeling, the board had prepared a bill which would somewhat modify the composition of the board which, as proposed, would include:

names of the committee are given in full as President G. S. Burroughs, Wabash College; President Scott Butler, of Butler College; President H. A. Gobin, of DePauw; President J. J. Mills, of Earlham. Presumably the latter is correct. Stott and Scott would naturally confuse a secretary, but the college makes identity certain.

[30] See minutes of the State Board, pp. 554–57.

1. The governor of the state.
2. The state superintendent of public instruction.
3. The president of the State University.
4. The president of Purdue University.
5. The president of the State Normal School.
6. The superintendent of common schools of the three largest cities in the state, and
7. Three citizens of prominence actively engaged in educational work in the state, appointed by the governor, at least one of whom should be a county superintendent, none of whom shall be appointed from any county in which any other member of the State Board of Education resides, or from which any other member was appointed.

An act embodying these provisions is found in *Indiana Laws,* 1899, page 426.

At the meeting of the State Board of Education of May 11, 1899, Enoch G. Machan, a county school superintendent, and President Stott, of Franklin College, presented credentials signed by the Governor and took their places on the board. At the meeting of September 9, President Mills, of Earlham, presented a like communication from the Governor. Thus three men were added to the State Board of Education as provided in the Act of 1899.

Such action was, of course, wise. It gave the non-state schools place in the inner councils of this board where they could know first hand the problems encountered and the reasons for the measures taken to meet them.

Prior to this Act of 1899 the board had consisted of eight members (1 to 6 above), three of whom were state schools men. Now there were eleven members, three of whom were state schools men. The state schools never had interests other than those of the people of Indiana, which fact soon became clear to the non-state schools.

The State Board of Education was about to establish new requirements for commissioning high schools. In the inspections which were made in 1900 to 1902, with reports on inspection presented to, discussed, and acted upon by this board, and commission approved or refused, the assistance and counsels of these added men were altogether helpful.

The reader will have noted that President Burroughs, of Wabash, was a leader in this attack on the Geeting Bill. The feeling at

Wabash during that time, the late nineties, is described by Osborne and Gronert.

By the year 1898–99, nearly everybody was of the one opinion that the college was sick and would not recover except under a new president. The fall in enrollment, the prospect of a further fall, worried everybody. The students were getting out of hand with deprivation of football as their chief grievance. The Board worried about finances with no substantial increase in endowment since 1892.

It has generally been remembered, in defense of the record of Dr. Burroughs, that peculiar difficulties arose in his time.

The first of these circumstances was that in his time boys began to go to the public high schools. . . . These high school boys, graduating, found themselves still far short of the requirements for admission to Wabash—particularly the requirements in Greek and Latin. Before they could be freshmen they had still to be "preps.". . . Wabash was one of the most "classical" colleges in the West. The trustees feared, as did Dr. Burroughs, that it was quite too classical for the times.[31]

The faculty view that it was not prevailed for some time, but in the end was abandoned. The second adverse condition was the rapid rise in enrollment of near-by state universities, Indiana, Purdue, and Illinois. It was believed that:

In Indiana as elsewhere the State Institutions were in control of the State Board of Education and used the high schools with full confidence in the worthiness of their cause, to build themselves up and to displace the private institutions which had so early and so long supplied what there was in the state of higher education.

A third circumstance was the appeal of coeducation. President Burroughs and many Crawfordsville citizens were strongly in favor of coeducation, but opposition to it always accomplished its defeat. Many townspeople of Crawfordsville and alumni resented the decision against coeducation.

All these circumstances tended to limit enrollment at Wabash. They also worked to discourage donations to the endowment fund. . . . Why give money to a college so ungenerous as to exclude women from its benefits?

President Burroughs resigned in June, 1899, to take a professorship at Oberlin College. He was a sick man and died in October, 1901.

Osborne and Gronert say that while there was student, alumni, trustee, and popular opposition to Dr. Burroughs, it was faculty op-

[31] *Wabash College, The First Hundred Years*, pp. 217 ff.

position and discord which led Dr. Burroughs to resign. They state Burroughs' views of Wabash as expressed in his letter of resignation:

All such colleges are in danger and three things are absolutely necessary for their salvation. The three things are: "enlarged endowment, thorough adaptation to their environment,[32] and hearty internal cooperation." On this second need he says, "Traditions and practices in education which in one section and under fixed influences may tend to the strengthening of the life and enlargement of the influence of the college, in another section and in a changing environment may bring about weakness and arrest growth."

It is probable that this statement reveals the real cause of the difficulty at Wabash during that period. At all events it was the mature judgment of a man whose devotion to Wabash was never questioned. Burroughs' faculty was "able and willing to die in the last ditch for their educational ideals" of maintaining the New England college tradition in western Indiana, which tradition Burroughs regarded as unadapted to the environment at that time.

Recently Frank L. Jones, now (1943) of the Equitable Life, who succeeded Geeting in office, wrote of that period:

I have always thought that the dissatisfaction of the non-state school men grew unknowingly out of the large scale movement toward state-supported education-institutions together with the decreasing support of the church colleges. It was a movement, as you know, which developed in all of the states.

• • •

Only occasional references to the fight were made after the year 1899. I remember that Parsons, Swain, Goss, Smart, and I discussed the matter of the ending of the fight in such a peaceable manner by the simple expedient of adding two non-state school men and a county school superintendent, who was not committed to either, to the Board. We all enjoyed the association of Mills and Stott as members of the Board. They did their parts well and were assigned their respective duties, for the making of examination questions, and served on subcommittees without ever a thought of injury or suspicion, so far as I could see, and as I stated, that view seemed to prevail among the other men whom I mentioned above.

---

[32] A clash of educational ideals was involved. The people of Indiana through their General Assembly had established an educational system of which the State University was the crowning part, and into which high school graduates entered without much greater difficulty than they passed from one year to another in high school.

In this environment the faculty of Wabash College was endeavoring to maintain the traditions of classical education, and blaming the State Universities and the State Board of Education for their difficulties. They were unwilling to follow the wise leadership of President Burroughs, who, in his last words to the alumni, said, according to Osborne and Gronert (p. 219): " 'Here is the present problem of the college, is it not?—To find what Wabash may do to meet existing needs of this great commonwealth today. . . . Not what you and I may like the college to do is what she should do; but what the college should do you and I should like.' "

The conditions here referred to were not peculiar to Indiana, or to the Midwest. On the contrary, as stated earlier, they were present with variations in intensity and historic background throughout the United States. Reference has already been made to situations arising at the University of Michigan closely corresponding to experiences here in Indiana.

We find like situations in Virginia as related by Sadie Bell in an 800-page thesis entitled *The Church, the State, and Education in Virginia*. The author recognized three different periods in this aspect of Virginia history:

1. A period of about 200 years when Virginia, under patents granted by Queen Elizabeth (1578–84), had union of church and state. This period was brought to a close early in 1786 by the passage of Jefferson's "Act for Establishing Religious Freedom," which had been under consideration for several years.

2. A period of about 80 years in which there was separation of church and state. This period extended from 1786 to the Civil War and the constitution of 1868.

3. A period from 1868 to date, characterized by cooperation without legal alliance between church and state.

This long story cannot be told briefly, but one may get some idea of the intensity of feeling, surpassing anything that developed in Indiana, from the following illustrations:

1. If you visit Monticello you will note that on Jefferson's tomb, in the inscription that he wrote, he omits mention of his eight years as President of the United States, but he records his authorship of the Act for Establishing Religious Freedom in Virginia. The inscription reads:

Here was Buried
Thomas Jefferson
Author
of the Declaration of
American Independence
of
The Statute of Virginia
For Religious Freedom, and
Father of the University
of Virginia

Obviously his authorship of the bill for religious freedom meant more to him than the presidency, and ranked with his greatest achievements. Freedom—political, religious, educational—was the dominant motive of his life.

2. The University of Virginia (fathered by Jefferson) was established in 1819, purposefully making no provision for religious training, which was left to the home and the church. Bell tells us (pp. 378–79) that when in 1829 a typhoid fever epidemic closed the University from February to May, it "was looked upon by many as retribution for the insufficient godliness of the place." Bell further relates that on this occasion a memorial service in the rotunda of the University of Virginia was addressed by the Reverend William Meade, later Protestant Episcopal Bishop of Virginia. Mr. Meade preached to a large audience of faculty, students, visiting clergymen, and neighbors, on Amos 3:6, "Shall a trumpet be blown in the city, and the people not be afraid? shall there be evil in the city, and the Lord hath not done *it*?" The resentment at Mr. Meade's consideration of the epidemic as a visitation from God was very great.

The *Life of Thomas Jefferson* by Henry S. Randall throws much light on this particular phase of Virginia history. One gets some conception of the emotionalism of religion in that day, when Jefferson became president. He had not fought the church, but had fought union of church and state. Randall says:

> He was charged with being an active and aggressive foe of Christianity. Thousands are yet alive who recollect the furious tempest which burst on his head, on this subject, from press and pulpit, pending both his elections to the Presidency. The Christian church of our country was declared to be in danger if he succeeded. It was popularly said at the time, that in parts of New England, timid females hid their Bibles in the clefts of rocks, and enthusiastic disciples girded up their loins to encounter terrible persecutions, when it was understood that he was elected.[33]

Of another section of the United States, President Bryan relates this story. Chancellor Avery, of the University of Nebraska, was once called upon at a banquet to tell the funniest thing that had ever happened to him. It seems that Chancellor Avery was at his desk one morning when a woman came in greatly agitated and began denouncing him most vigorously. She declared he was unfit for his position and should resign and leave place for a better man. In the midst of this tirade, apparently struck by the fact that Avery

[33] Vol. I, p. 494.

had made no reply and seemed unperturbed, she suddenly paused and said, "Ain't you the President of 'So and So'" (naming a near-by church school)?

Avery answered: "No, madam, I am the president of this godless institution, the University of Nebraska. But there is an interurban a block or so from here that you can take to 'So and So College' for forty cents."

The woman replied: "No thanks, I guess I've gotten it out of my system. I guess I won't go now."

1902 TO DATE. THE MARSHALL CONFERENCE WITH STATE AND NON-STATE SCHOOL PRESIDENTS

The foregoing gives a general understanding of the relations of the state and non-state schools when, in 1902, Jordan, Coulter, and Swain were succeeded by a new type of scientist, William Lowe Bryan, as president of Indiana University.

One of the first major developments of Indiana University in the Bryan administration was the establishment of the School of Medicine. One would think that this was an objective that could not in any way disturb the non-state schools. Yet it did. Briefly, the cause of their concern was as follows:

For many years medical schools had granted advanced standing to graduates of colleges and universities, for whom the time required for the medical degree was shortened one year. In the organization of the School of Medicine two procedures were introduced which changed this custom fundamentally.

1. No advanced standing was granted in the Indiana University School of Medicine to students or graduates of arts colleges. Students of the School of Medicine might be excused from repeating certain courses completed in a fundamental way in a school of arts and sciences, but this did not shorten the time required for the four-year medical course.

2. Two years of collegiate work were required of all applicants for entrance on the study of medicine.

3. It was proposed to grant the B.S. degree to students who entered medical school with two years of specified collegiate work, on completion of the first two years of the medical course.

This procedure soon became general throughout the United States, but at that time it was an innovation.

Non-state schools, concerned about their future and believing their difficulties were due in some manner to the rapid growth of the state schools, looked upon these innovations with suspicion. They feared that the purpose was to force all premedical students into Indiana University.

In the unpleasantness which developed with Purdue (1905–8), an effort was made to fan this fear, and the *Greencastle Banner* published an article[34] which favored the Purdue plan of having the work of the medical course wholly at Indianapolis, rather than the Indiana University plan of having part or all of the preclinical work at the seat of the University at Bloomington, because of fear of the effect of the University plan on non-state school premedical enrollment.

While the *Greencastle Banner* article gained no visible following, the feeling in the background was sufficiently strong that in the bill authorizing Indiana University to conduct a medical school in Indianapolis there was included a provision

that premedical or other collegiate work done in any college or university of Indiana, which is recognized by the state board of education of Indiana as a standard college or university, shall be received and credited in the Indiana University school of medicine upon the same conditions as work of the same kind, grade and amount done in the department of liberal arts of Indiana University.

Indiana University had not the slightest objection to this provision. Students coming to Indiana University School of Medicine from non-state schools were admitted and granted the B.S. degree on completion of the work of the first two years of the medical course on exactly the same conditions as if that premedical work had been completed at Indiana University. Under University rules[35] the A.B. degree could not be granted to students of non-state schools who entered the School of Medicine with three years of collegiate work, on completion of the Freshman year of the medical course. But this matter was easily adjusted by transferring credit for the Freshman medical work, when completed, back to the non-state school, which

[34] Quoted in the *Indianapolis News* of December 27, 1906.
[35] Reference is made here to the University rule that "all candidates for the A.B. degree must do thirty semester hours of the work of the Senior year in residence at this University."

accepted it in lieu of the Senior year, and granted the A.B. degree. It was generally regarded as an advantage to have an A.B. degree from the school in which the three years of arts work had been completed and the M.D. degree from the Indiana University School of Medicine.

Gradually among the non-state schools confidence was being established in the sincere good will of the President and governing board of Indiana University. The University authorities, however, were still apprehensive regarding the attitude of the leaders of some of the non-state colleges, whose opposition was felt when University appropriations were under consideration in legislative sessions. When, in the early part of the administration of Governor Marshall (1909), the Governor called a meeting of the state and non-state school representatives, it was with grave apprehension that President Bryan left for that meeting.

It was generally understood that Governor Marshall was not sympathetic with liberal support of the state institutions of higher learning. Charles Marion Thomas,[36] telling the story of this meeting, says frankly:

> Thomas R. Marshall was not friendly to the large state universities in Indiana, nor to the state-supported normal school. He was, however, a strong advocate of education. . . . He merely thought that the state was appropriating more money than was necessary for its public universities, which were growing too rapidly, and were competing unfairly with the small privately controlled colleges in the state. The non-state-supported colleges, having to charge higher fees, were at a disadvantage.
>
> "No man would spend money for anything he could gratuitously obtain," said Marshall.
>
> He was an alumnus and trustee of Wabash College. . . . He was disturbed at the current decline in formal moral and religious training and thought that this could best be obtained at denominational schools. . . .
>
> There was considerable apprehension in the state universities when Marshall was elected governor. During previous years he had, in public addresses, made plain his views on education. In his first message to the General Assembly he warned against being "so lavish in the appropriation of money as to enable these institutions to destroy private educational institutions. . . ."

The air was clarified by a general conference which was called by the Governor. He sent letters in July, 1909, inviting the heads of both the publicly

[36] *Thomas Riley Marshall, Hoosier Statesman*, p. 102.

supported and the private colleges to meet with him in Indianapolis. Marshall hoped to end the necessity of the presidents of the state's public colleges lobbying around the legislature for funds "like railroad corporations or a lot of greedy county officials." The men were called from the non-state-supported colleges in order "to obtain a comparison of educational data in the two classes of schools." Marshall suspected the existence of duplication in work between the different state-supported schools and wished, if possible, to find a way to prevent this without injury to the institutions. The meeting assembled in October and its proceedings are reported in full in the *Indianapolis News* for October 14 and 15, 1909.

The men from the state-supported universities went to this conference with anxiety. The previous generation had witnessed the great and sudden growth to predominance of state-supported schools from small institutions comparable with the private colleges in the state. The attendance at Indiana University had increased from 190 in 1881 to 2,470 in 1909. Much antagonism remained in the minds of persons connected with the private colleges. The presidents of the state universities went to Indianapolis prepared for a severe questioning, which they received during the morning session. Marshall led the way with emphatic criticism. The president of one small college continued with repeated challenges of the practices of the state universities. He particularly objected to the rule which enabled students to obtain two degrees, such as the B.A. and the LL.B., in five years. This practice tended to discriminate against the smaller non-state schools which were not able to compete with the state universities. The questioning continued until noon, when the meeting adjourned to meet again in the afternoon.

A completely changed atmosphere existed when the meeting reassembled. The presidents of the state universities had done nothing during the noon hour. The proceedings during the afternoon were most friendly. Men from non-state-supported schools apparently organized during the noon recess, strongly defended the universities. Only one man dissented when a motion was passed asking the state to appropriate more, not less, money for the universities and normal schools. Only one vote was cast in favor of the resolution opposing the granting of two degrees in five years. President McConnell, of DePauw, a denominational college, led the arguments in support of the larger [private] schools. The explanation of this attitude is probably to be found in a frank statement by President McConnell, who explained that every time the state university got an increase in state funds he found it easier to get more money for DePauw from alumni and philanthropists. The meeting adjourned at five o'clock with the Governor saying he had got more than he had actually hoped for from the meeting and that he believed it would be of great value to him as governor in handling the state school system.

The Governor had learned that the leading educators even in the small colleges had come to see that the progress and development of one or a few schools was actually an added incentive to the development of all, that such competition was advantageous, that it tended to build up, not to destroy, private educational institutions. Marshall's own concepts were modified in this same direction. As late as March 6, 1912, he continued to speak of duplication of work in the state-supported schools, but the officers of the universities recognized that his relations "were marked by increasing friendliness as the four years went on." By 1913 he was ready to emphasize, in his message to the General Assembly, the need for a special appropriation. This money was needed to purchase land for new buildings for the Indiana University Medical School. The construction of the buildings could be financed from the Robert W. Long bequest, if the state provided the site.

The very great interest in this conference of the state and non-state school presidents with the Governor may be judged from the fact that the *Indianapolis News* reported in full the Governor's lengthy prepared statement in its issue of October 14, 1909. On the next day it gave a very full account of the discussion which followed, in addition to a half-column editorial.

In his prepared statement Marshall said:

I believe that the state has no such interest in the welfare of one child as to expend its energies upon him to the detriment and possible exclusion of other children. . . . I have not yet decided how far the State of Indiana ought to go upon the subject of higher education. . . . I do know that the state can go no farther than it has gone without increase in the tax levy.

He showed by quoting enrollments that the non-state schools were training a larger total number of students than the state schools, and asked:

If these non-state schools are doing as good work as the state schools, on what ground can higher appropriations for the state schools be approved?

We have the answer to this inquiry, made by President McConnell, of DePauw, as quoted in *Thomas Riley Marshall.*

The answer made by Thomas C. Howe, of Butler, equally noteworthy, appeared in the *Indianapolis News,* October 15, 1909:

President Howe, of Butler, led in the discussion of the question of an increased tax rate for the higher state institutions, on the ground that the state is not keeping pace with its neighbors in the matter of higher education and that its population and percentage of young men and women demanding college and university education is increasing more rapidly than the state is preparing to meet their demands. He showed that at Butler College several professors, among the best-paid men, are compelled to draw on their private resources for living expenses, and that he had been informed that like conditions existed in all the non-state as well as the state institutions. He said that the state was rapidly losing its best instructors, and that it could not afford to go on in such a course. He pledged himself to stand by the Governor in the event the executive decided to recommend an increased tax rate, and the various other non-state men hastened to pledge their support also. President Kelly, of Earlham, said it was a business matter with the state which it could not afford to disregard.

An editorial in the *Indianapolis News* of the same date closed with:

A real university in Indiana is something worth striving for. In time we ought to be able to reach this goal.

When I met President Bryan by chance as he was on his way to the afternoon session of the conference of college presidents, he suggested that I accompany him. The Governor opened the session by inquiring what the attitude of the administration should be toward state school appropriations. The morning session had been hostile. I can feel today the prolonged and, to the state schools, ominous silence with which this inquiry of the Governor was received. Each was apparently waiting for another to reply to this momentous question.

I also recall the intense relief when this silence was broken by President McConnell, of DePauw University, who said essentially this:

So far as DePauw University is concerned she will be glad to see the state-supported schools receive more liberal appropriations, because it is my experience that better support of the state schools makes it easier to get from various sources the more adequate support DePauw needs.[37]

I cannot say that this point of view of President McConnell was accepted enthusiastically. But it was accepted, and the specter of united non-state opposition to the state schools appropriations was forever laid by the broad-minded statesmanlike attitude of DePauw's president, vigorously supported by President Thomas Howe, of Butler.

[37] It happens that I have known more of the relations between Indiana and DePauw than between Indiana and some of the other non-state schools. The President, however, was making kindly contacts with all of the non-state colleges.

President McConnell, who soon afterward became Bishop McConnell, wrote of this meeting as follows (July 24, 1941):

I do not know that I can add anything to the information which you already have about the relation between the denominational schools and the state institutions during my administration at DePauw. I remember quite distinctly the meeting to which Mr. Thomas refers in his life of Marshall. I have especially in mind that Governor Marshall stated quite definitely that he believed that the course for the A.B. degree should stand for a body of relatively fixed subjects, and that it was the business of the denominational colleges to stand for such a conception of the function of the denominational schools. I took issue with him on that ground, and thought that the whole problem of education was broader than the Governor seemed to indicate. I remarked that according to my observation, the denominational schools did better when the state schools were being more generously supported, that under such a policy the increase of educational interest throughout the state helped each institution to find what it could best do. Whereupon the Governor remarked, "You evidently feel that in this educational race here in Indiana the state should spend money for its effect on the DePauw trot!" One other recollection that I have of the meeting is that President Bryan both then and afterwards showed the greatest tact and friendliness in his attempt to bring the denominational and state schools to mutual sympathy and understanding. I never have forgotten his open-mindedness and wisdom in that whole problem.

This does not mean that all denominational opposition disappeared at once, but it meant a definite change of attitude among leaders. Some men of influence continued for some years to hold a point of view acquired during student days, as the following incident illustrates.

The Methodist Area Council, a Council of the Methodist pastors and district superintendents, with Bishop Leete presiding, was meeting in Terre Haute, October 20, 1926. I had secured the permission of the Bishop to present a resolution at this Council favoring increased appropriations for Indiana University. This resolution was passed without a dissenting vote and presented to members of the legislature, meeting the following January. Andy Durham, the able representative of Putnam County, a former student of Indiana University, felt that as representative of the county in which DePauw was located he could not support our bill. I showed him, among others, this resolution adopted by the Methodist Area Council. Andy could scarcely believe his eyes and said: "Well I declare! Well I declare!"

Back of this attitude of President McConnell was a long series of kindly contacts between Indiana and DePauw, going back to the time of President Gobin, extending through the presidency of Bishop Hughes, and continuing after McConnell's retirement. It was reported that in the controversy of 1897 President Gobin took the attitude that no fight was necessary, that the non-state schools could get everything fairly due them by conference. I cannot vouch for this statement, but it is so characteristic of the broad-minded DePauw leadership that I think it very probable.

President Bryan, returning from a western trip, entered a meeting of the State Teachers Association at Indianapolis to find that, without his knowledge, he had been nominated for the presidency of the Association in opposition to some textbook slate, and President Hughes, of DePauw, had the floor and was vigorously advocating his election, which occurred. President Bryan was not at all interested in the presidency of the State Teachers Association except as an opportunity for service to the cause of education, but he valued beyond measure this voluntary support of his very able colleague.

Incidents of this sort were happening from time to time indicating the kindly attitude of non-state schools toward Indiana University. And these kindly acts were not all on one side.[38] During the years following the Governor Marshall incident nothing occurred to mar the cordial relations of state and non-state schools. They had their difficulties and we have had ours. They have known that their difficulties were regarded sympathetically by the state schools and were not in some dark way attributable to the state schools.

In those instances in which the denominational schools have been backed, not merely by the emotions, but by the purses of the denomination, the denominational schools have prospered, have increased in enrollment and usefulness, and rank among the best in the United States in the sound training given their students.

[38] I trust it will not be considered poor taste to give the following illustration.
On an occasion DePauw was closing a campaign for funds. Three days from the dead line she found herself $75,000 short of a total necessary to hold a major donation. She hit upon the plan of writing friends in the ninety-two counties of Indiana and elsewhere, explaining the situation and saying: "Will you be responsible for raising in your locality so many hundred dollars of this total?" I felt complimented as a Methodist and member of the faculty of Indiana University to receive such a letter, with Bloomington and Monroe County my territory. The time was short, but I had the pleasure of sending pledges for the requested amount before the dead line.

CHAPTER XI

INDIANA UNIVERSITY NOT A GODLESS INSTITUTION

I N THE preceding chapter the manner and degree to which sectarian opposition hampered the development of Indiana University is reviewed. Attention is called to the fact that this was not a local or midwest phenomenon but was general and had its roots in our heritage of the centuries-old European conflict of relationship of church and state and education.

In Indiana University from its founding up to 1885 its leadership was clerical. In fact, the institution was conducted essentially like a church school but free from denominational bias. Daily chapel attendance, including Saturday, was required. This continued beyond clerical administrations. There was a sermon on Sunday at which attendance was obligatory. There was a required course on evidences of Christianity. Criticism of the leadership of the University was chiefly denominational. Whatever church membership the President might hold, Presbyterian, Methodist, Baptist, the attitude of all other denominations was critical and often hostile. Church membership alone did not suffice. The President must be a cleric in accordance with the best eastern tradition.

The deeply religious nature and active church membership of Jordan, Coulter, and Swain did not meet traditional requirements for the presidency of Indiana University or relieve the University from being considered a godless institution in the thinking of many churchmen. To substitute for a clergyman president a non-cleric evolutionist, like Jordan or Coulter, was to thousands of good churchmen nothing short of blasting at the foundations of Christianity.

Though the time is long past when evolution presented a problem for pastors north of the Mason and Dixon line, the Scopes trial is sufficiently recent to emphasize the fact that it is not a dead issue in certain sections of the country. More recent efforts in certain south-

123

ern states to bar teaching of evolution by legislative act indicate the persistence of the conviction of many good people that there is irreconcilable conflict between interpretation of the Bible and the teachings of evolution.

Though Coulter, as stated earlier, was an evolutionist, yet it was in the first year of his administration that a branch of the Young Men's Christian Association was established in the University, superseding an older, less definite, organization composed of men and women students, known as the Christian Association. In this movement, Dr. Coulter took an active interest, not only in the local branch but in the State Association as well.

Professor William A. Rawles tells us[1] that:

Equally with President Coulter, President Swain encouraged the work of the Young Men's and Young Women's Christian Associations and was largely instrumental in making the organizations here the leading branches of the college associations in Indiana.

Very naturally this leadership in Christian activity among the colleges of the state left those who were accustomed to think or speak of the University as "that godless institution" in a difficult position.

It is not the purpose to give the history of the Y.M.C.A. at Indiana University, but merely to emphasize the influence of the organization as a factor in breaking down the "godless institution" idea which was held in certain quarters. When one notes the remarkably able leadership of the Y.M.C.A. during the early years of its organization at the University, one understands why it gradually took a leading place among like organizations within the colleges of the state.

For the first eight years there was no general secretary of the Y.M.C.A. at the University. The student officers provided the necessary leadership for an active and vigorous association. Among those officers we find W. H. Wylie, '97, who as the Reverend Will Wylie is known throughout the state for his lifelong Christian leadership. We find students now (1943) known as Professor George M. Howe, '94, of Cambridge, Mass.; Professor Charles T. Knipp, '94, of the University of Illinois; and Professor Whittier L. Hanson, '00, of Boston University. We find Carl E. Endicott, '97, who later served

[1] See the brief, but very excellent, "Historical Sketch" written by Professor Rawles, in *Indiana University, 1820–1904*, p. 29.

as district governor of the Indiana Kiwanis District and still later as president of Kiwanis International and came to be known throughout the United States and Canada for his Christian leadership in activities for the benefit of children and young people. We find Dr. Charles N. Combs, '00, who for many years was secretary of the Indiana State Medical Society and later became president of that body.

There was Melvin E. Haggerty, '02, who later became dean of the College of Education at the University of Minnesota. There was a student, A. Wayne Hanson, '99, who served two years as president of the campus Y.M.C.A., and after graduation became its first general secretary (1899–1900). From 1901 to 1907 Hanson was state student secretary, during which time he made frequent visits to the campus. He was assistant state secretary until 1918. From 1919 to 1923 he served in France and at Geneva as secretary of the International committee, Young Men's Christian Association, and finally as associate senior secretary for Europe. Returning to America he continued in the International Y.M.C.A. work until he retired in 1939. Since then he has been engaged in foreign travel and lecturing in the United States. There was another student, Ward E. Hanger, '01, who for two years was president of the Young Men's Christian Association (1898–1900) and whose promising career in the Y.M.C.A. field was cut short by his untimely death.

Then early in the Bryan administration there was a student of Indiana University, Jacob M. Clinton, '00, president of the Y.M.C.A., who continued in and became internationally prominent in the work of the Association. President Bryan has said of him:

Clinton was associated with Sun Yat-Sen and other founders of the Chinese Republic. He had so much to do with the formulation of the Constitution of China that Alvah Miller, later General Secretary of the Y.M.C.A. at Indiana University, said of him: "Jake Clinton[2] wrote the Constitution of China."

There were many other strong men among the officers of the organization during those early years, among whom were Howard W. Clark, '96, Frank O. Beck, '94, Joseph M. Artman, '05, Arthur H. Greenwood, '05, John K. Arnot, '07, Jacob G. Collicott, '00, Guy

[2] He was a graduate of our School of Law, and winner of the Senior law prize. He later received both the A.B. and A.M. degrees. (*Daily Student*, January 21, 1904.)

Cantwell, '03, Tom Cookson, Nicholas O. Pittenger, '11, Scott Pad-
dock, '10, Sterling Hoffman, '10, J. Herman Wylie, '10, Curtis G.
Shake, '10, Byrl R. Kirklin, '14, Paul V. McNutt, '13, and many
others.

With these men exerting leadership within this nondenomina-
tional Christian organization among the colleges of the state, it became obvious that Christian life could survive outside a denominational college and that there were potentialities for Christian leadership in the Indiana University student body which were encouraged
and stimulated even by an evolutionist president, to a degree unsurpassed in the state.

While the Y.M.C.A. was particularly fortunate in its first general
secretary, Hanson, it was also particularly fortunate in Alvah L.
Miller as general secretary. President Bryan states that:

> Miller came to Indiana after an ineffective Young Men's Christian Associa-
> tion Secretary had brought the organization to practical collapse. Miller
> resuscitated the organization with wonderful wisdom and success. Later he
> represented the Y.M.C.A. in India at Lahore, and is now [1942] at the head
> of the magnificent Young Men's Christian Association plant at Jerusalem.
> He was sent there to the most difficult Y.M.C.A. station in the world because
> he was believed to be the best possible man for the place. He has achieved
> remarkable success there in spite of the difficulties. All these men [including
> others previously named] were deeply Christian.

President Bryan says further:

> In the earlier period of the Y.M.C.A. the secretaries were students just out
> of college. I went to J. R. Mott, for years the head of international Y.M.C.A.,
> and urged that his organization should put a first-rate mature man as secretary
> in at least one state university. Mr. Mott had other plans and did not accept
> my suggestion. I talked at that time with Mr. W. W. White, who was then
> about to establish a Bible school in New York City financed by Miss Helen
> Gould. He said to me: "Your proposal appeals to me so strongly that I would
> be willing to give up this New York City project and take such a place."
> This statement from White fortifies my judgment as to the wisdom of that
> course, which unfortunately was not adopted by the national Y.M.C.A.
> At about that time we began to call the attention of the denominations to
> the importance of the state universities, if only as mission stations. We said
> that if it is worth while to send missionaries to China, it is certainly worth
> while for you to be adequately represented in the state universities. One after
> another the leading denominations began to establish work among the students

at Indiana University and other state universities. When the leaders of the national Y.M.C.A. saw the churches coming in to take a field which they felt should be left to the Y.M.C.A., a leading Y.M.C.A. man was sent to a meeting of the National Association of State Universities to read a paper entitled, "The Recrudescence of Sectarianism at State Universities." The proposal of the national Young Men's Christian Association was that the denominations should leave the field to the Y.M.C.A. However, the denominations did not withdraw, but continued to develop more and more religious work at the state universities. Jews, Protestants of leading denominations, and Catholics are all now actively and effectively at work in connection with universities. The Y.M.C.A. and Y.W.C.A. also have continued their work.

In this quotation from President Bryan is a noteworthy statement: "We began to call the attention of the denominations to the importance of the state universities at least as mission fields." Primary recognition of the opportunity for Christian leadership presented at state universities rests with Christian leaders in those universities. Excerpts from a powerful address by President Bryan before the General Assembly of the Presbyterian Church, at Chicago, 1914, follow:

Church and University

There are those who believe that the University threatens to destroy the church. There are enemies of the church who believe this and rejoice. There are churchmen who believe it with dread. Men speaking within the university, they say, are attacking every nameable faith which the church has cherished. If as churchmen we believe this, what could we do? We could not kill the university—a world-wide institution supported by all civilized peoples and governments. We could not halter the university; there is no power in the world today strong enough to suppress the freedom of teaching. We could not completely shield our children from university influences. Our children by thousands are in the universities of Europe and America. For higher professional education they must go there. They are learning to be lawyers, doctors, engineers, teachers, what not, and the philosophy of life dominant in the university is fused together with the professional knowledge by which they are to earn a living. And if the future ministers are, most of them, not in the university, but in the protected church college and the protected theological seminary, the future professors in the church college and in the university seminary are in the university. There is no alleged heresy in the university which cannot be found among the teachers in the schools established by the church. What Oxford or Berlin or Harvard or Madison is saying today is presently heard in your theological school and then in your pulpit and then from your missionary in China. If as churchmen we had the belief that the university is as dangerous to the church as some of its friends and foes think, I know of nothing we could do except *to deal with the university itself as the most important mission field in the world.* For what can it profit the church to send men and money to the ends of the uncivilized earth, if she is to be beaten at home? Ideas which have had their day and been beaten in the capitals of civilization are on the way to extinction everywhere. The old Roman religion died away first in the capitals and then in the outlying villages, so that the name "villager" became the name of a believer in the dying religion. Our religion will suffer the same fate, if it is beaten in the universities which are the capitals of our intellectual life, if it is beaten in the minds of its own children. If, therefore, as churchmen we have the belief that the life of the church is indeed threatened by the university, we must face about from China and send our strongest men to make a last desperate fight at the gates of the universities so as to rescue if possible some of our own children. For my part, however, I do not believe that the university threatens to destroy the church, or that the church must fight for its life against the university. . . .

. . .

I stand before you a moment to pray that some of you may find his mission at the gates of the university. Such a man will not come in hostility or in fear. He will come seeing what the university at bottom is and is on its way to do for mankind, as Isaiah saw what Cyrus at bottom was and was to do for mankind. He will say to the university what Isaiah said to Cyrus: "Thou art not God's enemy. Thou art God's man, appointed to marshal world-wide forces in service of His infinite charity."

The various denominations were slow to perceive the opportunity presented by state university enrollments. Churches located close to state universities were the first to become aware of the fact that many of the future leaders of the state in all walks of life were to be found within the student body of the State University. These local churches found their seating capacity taxed to the limit on Sunday morning by student and faculty attendance. They found a hundred or more students in a well-taught Bible class during the Sunday School period. The teacher might be a member of the faculty. The Christian Endeavor meeting on Sunday evening was largely attended by students. There was evidence of need for certain social activities centering in the church.

It became obvious that there were great groups of students at the State University who desired to maintain their church connections. It became clear that if these students drifted away from their church during the student days it would be largely because of neglect on the part of their churches, rather than antichurch teaching on the part of the faculty.

When a change in pastors came under consideration in churches of the city of the State University, a question sure to arise was, Will the new man under consideration not only please the church membership but will he also attract and interest the near-by body of students who held membership in, or expressed preference for, that particular denomination?

For thirty-five years I was active in such a congregation. In 1904 I brought my letter from the Universalist Church of Attica, Ohio, to the First Methodist Church of Bloomington, the church in which my wife and her family long had held membership.

The old brick church on College Avenue was only a few blocks from the old campus, but it was seven blocks from the new campus. Probably it would have served very satisfactorily for many more years. But the congregation was awake to the challenge of ever-increasing enrollments of Methodist students, so in 1909 a new site was secured only four blocks from the new campus and a beautiful new and modern church was dedicated in 1910, with a seating capacity far in excess of the needs of the congregation. And there a few hundred students came to the Sunday morning service.

In 1914 the lovable pastor, the Reverend J. W. Jones, was anxious to be near New York City where he hoped to get help for his failing hearing. So an exchange of pastors with Yonkers, N.Y., where the Reverend C. Howard Taylor was pastor, was under consideration. A major interest of the committee which met Mr. Taylor when he visited Bloomington was whether he would be liked by the student body as well as by the congregation. This question was decided in the affirmative and experience proved the decision to be correct. At that time, 1914, there were nearly 500 Methodist students in the University, 200 to 300 of whom crowded seating capacity at Sunday morning services. Special Sunday School classes were organized for students with Judge J. B. Wilson and Professor Lillian Gay Berry (Latin) as teachers.

In the autumn of 1914 First Methodist Church undertook, for the first time, organization of work for students. The official board appropriated $500 for this cause, to be used by the pastor in securing such student assistance as he might need and to defray other expenses arising in connection with the student work. In 1915 a graduate student, William Strack, was secured as assistant to the pastor and work was organized along three lines: (1) to secure church attendance on the part of Methodist students; (2) to provide a limited number of courses of study in the Sunday School affording some elements of religious training; (3) to provide a happy and wholesome social center for Methodist students.

The success of this effort in 1914–15 was pronounced and emboldened the pastor to seek assistance of the Indiana Conference, which voted one-half of one per cent of the salary of the pastor, to be paid by each church of the Indiana Conference for support of this work. By the aid of District Superintendent Storms and others, the help of the board of education of the Methodist Church was secured to the extent of $500 a year.

Mr. Strack served until the close of the school year 1916–17, when he was succeeded by another graduate student, now Dr. Frank Forry, 1917–18, and he by still another graduate student, now Dr. Edward Pitkin, 1918–19.

In 1919–20 the Reverend Walter Niles was secured to head this work as student pastor. Meanwhile support from the Indiana Conference had increased from $400 to $1,300 a year and from the board of education from $500 to $1,000. The Methodist student body had grown to 917 in the fall of 1920.

To keep the work in line with General Conference action, the Indiana Conference in the fall of 1920 ordered that the governing board of this student work should incorporate as a Wesley Foundation of Indiana University. This order was obeyed, effective as of January, 1921. Twenty-two hundred dollars were expended for this work in 1920–21.

Meanwhile like developments were taking place in other state universities. At the University of Illinois Dr. Baker put on a campaign for funds for a Wesley Foundation building. A considerable fund was raised and a beautiful structure was erected immediately adjacent to the Illinois campus. But the maintenance of this building proved burdensome.

The Wesley Foundation board at Bloomington was strongly of the opinion that it was far wiser to conduct the work of the Wesley Foundation in intimate relation with a functioning Methodist Church. It was believed that contact with the work and problems of an active church better fitted students to take their place in the work of the local church of whatever community they later made their home. Accordingly, the official board of the First Methodist Church, Bloomington, purchased the quarter-block immediately adjacent to the church at a cost of $18,000 as a site for such building as experience should prove most desirable for the center of Wesley Foundation activity. A house on this site has meanwhile been the home of the student pastor.

When a disastrous fire in 1937 leveled this beautiful church, the new structure which succeeded it (1938) was planned with special reference to problems presented by more than 1,000 Methodist students on the near-by University campus.

Just as President Bryan recognized the need for and urged provision of more mature leadership in the Young Men's Christian Association, so the need for a full-time student pastor came to be recognized by the board of trustees of the Wesley Foundation.

I have gone into the above detail since I was personally active in the work for many years and as secretary of the Wesley Foundation had recorded its development year by year. Of course, at its best, the work was never as successful as we wished it to be.

Asked what he thought the Wesley Foundation should do for Methodist students of Indiana University, the Reverend Will Wylie, a member of the Wesley Foundation board, replied: "We would like you to do for them what their home church and their parents have failed to do." We never succeeded fully in doing that. Yet this work at its best has been so good that President Grose, of DePauw, once said to me:

I do not wish to be misunderstood as in any way opposing the work of the Wesley Foundation at Indiana and Purdue, but I do wish to emphasize that a work of like character should be organized for the Methodist students of DePauw.

I trust that I have made my point, and that when the organization of Christian work among the students of the State University became a model for one of the strongest church colleges, the State University could no longer be regarded as a "godless institution" even in the most prejudiced circles.

Meanwhile other denominations had adopted variations of this Wesley Foundation plan.

The board of education of the Presbyterian Church in the U.S.A. had purchased on August 25, 1913, two houses at the Fifth Street entrance to the campus. The corner property, known as Westminster House, was the residence of the student pastor. The adjacent house, to the north, known as Westminster Inn, was the center for work among Presbyterian students. In 1931, the board, without transferring the property, entered into an arrangement with the Synod of Indiana whereby the local Presbyterian Church took over the work among Presbyterian students, and the corner house was to be used as a manse for the local pastor.

A former pastor of the Christian Church of Bloomington had secured possession of the greater part of that bit of land at the southwest corner of the campus which was not owned by the University and had made a heroic effort to found a Bible School, later called the Indiana School of Religion, in which Bible instruction should be given which would receive University credit. In spite of able and devoted leadership and sympathetic consideration by the administration, the project has not been very successful. In 1943 this site was purchased by the University.

The Catholic Church is located only a few blocks from the campus and the Newman Club is active. I was once complimented by being invited to address the Newman Club. Unhappily, I did not do so well, in that I referred to the club a couple of times as the Wesley Foundation, much to the amusement of Father Deery, the very able and efficient Catholic priest, who, fortunately, had a keen sense of humor.

The Lutheran Church has erected a beautiful little chapel and parsonage, just across Seventh Street from the campus. The number of Lutheran students is not large and this approach to the problem of providing a religious center for the students, members of their church, has seemed to be very wise and effective.

While denominationalism as such is not present on the campus and while today there are no required courses in evidences of Christianity, the activity of the denominations in making their leadership felt on the campus is very great and has received the most sympathetic support of administration and faculty.

The problem of furthering the religious interest and activity of the growing number of students of all denominations in state universities in which denominational teaching was prohibited could be solved either by interested denominations providing that instruction off, but near to, the campus, or by interfaith courses in Bible and religion on the campus.

While the first solution of this problem was the one most generally adopted, the second procedure was adopted at the University of Iowa with success considered phenomenal by President Walter E. Jessup.

After studying the problem for six years, the University of Iowa secured a grant of $35,000 from John D. Rockefeller, Jr., for a three-year experiment with an Interfaith School of Religion. It began in March, 1927, with the appointment of Dr. M. W. Lampe as administrative director, and the appointment of a Jewish professor, a Catholic professor, and a Protestant professor as a faculty.

After ten years the Rockefeller support was withdrawn and the state assumed the administrative expense, while the professorships continued to be maintained, as at the start, by Protestant, Catholic, and Jewish support. In 1938–39, 586 students were enrolled in courses in Bible, religious education, contemporary religious thought and activity, and research.

Director Lampe says that the school could not have been started without the help of Mr. Rockefeller. He summarizes the experience of nearly twenty years:

> I think we are entitled to take high hope from the fact that it has shown itself to be a vital idea, and to believe that if it continues to be fundamentally fair to all participating groups, profoundly sympathetic with the ideals of the University, and deeply concerned to be vitally religious, it will continue to attract people of insight and good intentions and to sustain the enthusiasm of those who come under its spell.

CHAPTER XII

INDIANA UNIVERSITY, 1910 - 12

THE GIFT OF DR. AND MRS. ROBERT W. LONG

LATE IN 1910 President Bryan was informed of the desire of Dr. and Mrs. Robert W. Long to make a gift to the state, of Indianapolis property valued at $200,000, for the erection of a Robert W. Long Hospital for the use and benefit of the Indiana University School of Medicine. In accordance with the wishes of the donors, Governor Marshall on January 26, 1911, sent to the Senate a message with a copy of the proposal of Dr. and Mrs. Long, and recommended acceptance of the gift. A joint committee was appointed to prepare a bill which embodied their offer and accepted the gift and conditions imposed.

This was a great event, for it marked the beginning of the Indianapolis Medical Center and was the first of a group of hospitals providing the ample clinical facilities of the Indiana University School of Medicine, to which more than one thousand students annually seek admission.

In a resolution prepared by a committee of the board,

the trustees of Indiana University recognize the philanthropic purpose of the gift, intended, as it is, to provide proper medical care and attention for worthy people of limited means in all parts of the state, and at the same time to advance the cause of medical education in Indiana.

After considering various sites and after consultation with members of the medical faculty, a site on West Michigan Street, in proximity to the Indianapolis City Hospital, at first rejected as a dump, was finally selected and purchased February 28, 1912. The wisdom of this selection is obvious today. The site of the present Medical Center is today very attractive and promises to become more so. The Long Hospital, Robert Frost Daggett, architect, was completed and dedicated on June 15, 1914.[1]

[1] For a full account see Myers, "History of Medical Education in Indiana" (MS).

134

1910 REPORT TO LEGISLATURE

Though the conference of Indiana college presidents convened by Governor Marshall in October, 1909, had been favorable to more liberal appropriations for the state institutions of higher education, the Governor, as stated by his biographer,[2] was not friendly to these institutions. In his first message to the General Assembly, referring to the state institutions of higher education, Governor Marshall had warned against being "so lavish in appropriation of money as to enable these institutions to destroy private educational institutions." The use of the word "lavish" seems remarkable to anyone acquainted with appropriations to state universities in neighboring states. The Governor's point of view, however, was shared by many in the nineteenth century. There is, therefore, reason to believe that the President had prepared his report to Governor Marshall and the Indiana General Assembly in November, 1910, with more than ordinary care.

The budgetary report and requests of the trustees were accompanied by a letter of transmittal from President Bryan, quoted below:

November 18, 1910.

Governor Thomas R. Marshall,
Indianapolis, Indiana.
Dear Sir:

Within the last year we have heard here three addresses upon the need of society for the university.

On January twentieth President McConnell, of DePauw University, said that the increasing density of population raises many new problems which must be solved and which can be solved only through the university expert in agriculture, chemistry, physics, mechanics, biology, medicine, economics, and the like.

On June twenty-second Frederick Turner, our greatest authority in American History, said that one essential factor of free democracy is free economic opportunity; that in the past this free economic opportunity has been supplied by an enormous quantity of cheap new land and a wealth of unused natural resources; that the end of the epoch of cheap land and cheap natural resources is at hand; that vast new resources can be found only through the university experts in agriculture, chemistry, and so following. Turner's doctrine is that what the university has to give is not only essential for the daily bread and other necessities of the future, but necessary to the maintenance of free democracy.

[2] Charles M. Thomas, *Thomas Riley Marshall, Hoosier Statesman*, pp. 102–3.

On October fifteenth you gave here two reasons for the existence of the university: First, the necessity for the education of experts; second, and most important of all, the need for the establishment of the right philosophy of life.

These three addresses express my faith. I devoutly hope, therefore, that Indiana will very soon deal with the University so that it may render its proper service in full measure to the people.

Before setting forth the requests made by the Trustees, I wish to call attention to two facts:

The first is that Indiana University has won a national reputation for quality. The second fact is that in income we are in the rear.

The President gave data to support each of these statements of fact and concluded:

Is not the time at hand when Indiana, which stands near the head of the states of the Union in so many ways, including wealth and population, will give a fair chance to its twin universities?

I devoutly hope that you will lend your great influence in that direction.

The trustees at this time made the following requests:

1. Increased Maintenance. (*a*) For the general maintenance of the University a 50% increase of the mill tax. In reality there ought to be an increase of 100%. (*b*) A specific appropriation of $100,000 for the Medical School at Indianapolis. Of this amount $50,000 to be used for maintenance and $50,000 for grounds. With reference to the second item we wish to urge as strongly as possible that the state which provides education in almost every subject should no longer neglect that department of education which most nearly affects the health and life of the people.

2. For University Water System. In the winter of 1909 there was a shortage of water in Bloomington. A committee of experts made an estimate for a University water system, water to be secured from wells in the Griffy Creek Valley. Their estimate of $20,700 was granted. When, however, tests were made the following summer the supply from Griffy Creek Valley was found to be insufficient. After very careful study of the whole situation, our engineers then recommended buying land and building a dam to impound water in a narrow valley opening into Griffy Creek somewhat farther away The increased distance, the higher cost of material, and the cost of land and dam make the total cost of this work greater than the estimate of two years ago. The engineers submit exact estimates for the completion of this work.

3. Additional Wing for the Library to be used for the Administrative offices. The University offices have long been too small for our needs. They are in daily use not only by the executive officers, but also by the faculty committees and by large numbers of students. They are the most used part of the Uni-

versity. Still more important is the fact that these temporary offices are not fireproof. All the documents of the University—historical, financial, and scholastic—are here unprotected. To thousands of students, past and present, their academic records are more precious than money. Our proposal and request is that the Library be completed according to the original plans of the architects. The estimated cost is $42,812.

4. New Fireproof Roof and Other Changes for Owen Hall. Owen Hall was built in 1884 with funds donated by Monroe County and presented to the University. We submit plans for changes and repairs estimated to cost $14,050. It is the judgment of the Trustees that it would be wise at the time to enlarge the building by an addition estimated to cost $26,050.

5. Completion of Student Building by a Wing to be used as [Men's] Gymnasium. The Student Building costing $100,000 is the gift of about two thousand alumni, students, and other friends of the University. It now embraces a central part devoted to the use of many student activities, and one wing used as a women's gymnasium. We propose that the State meet the gift of the people by an appropriation of $100,000 for the completion of the building.

6. Minor Repairs and Additions. The Trustees' request for minor repairs and additions such as equipment for the power house, tunnels for heat mains, equipment for the carpenter shop, a drive from Indiana Avenue to the power house for coal wagons, a greenhouse, walks, etc. amounted to $30,600.

7. Land. For many years we have urged the purchase of land adjoining the present campus. Year by year the value of this land has increased. We believe it would be a wise policy to buy more land before the value increases further. We ask that the Legislative Committee give the matter careful consideration when they visit the University. We recommend that the Trustees of state institutions be empowered to purchase land by the process of condemnation.

Summary of Requests and Appropriations

	Asked	Received
(a) Increased maintenance..............Double Mill Tax		$ 32,500.00
Graduate School		17,500.00
(b) For Medical School, Indianapolis..........$100,000.00		25,000.00
University water system...................... 25,300.00		13,800.00
Wing to Library............................ 42,812.00		....
Remodel Owen Hall........................ 26,050.00		14,000.00
Wing to Student Building..................... 100,000.00		....
Minor items 30,600.00		13,200.00
Total.............		$116,000.00

The Graduate School

The President asked the dean and the faculty of the Graduate School to make recommendations for allocation of the $17,500 appropriated by the 1911 legislature for promotion of research. After much consideration it was recommended

(1) That the amount appropriated for the Graduate School be devoted to the betterment of salaries, to fellowships, to publications, and to specific researches, the latter to include special library or laboratory equipment, traveling expenses, assistants, etc. (2) That the Graduate Council recommend to the President and Trustees special annual fellowships, as exceptional needs arise. (3) That individuals (not departments) desiring appropriations for specific researches make formal written application to the President of the University. (4) That the President and trustees select from the applications those in their estimate most meritorious. It is the sense of this Faculty that a few undertakings well provided for will, in the long run, redound to the greater credit and benefit of the University than would arise from the general apportionment of the graduate fund among the various departments.

When the faculty of the Graduate School included publications in item 1 above, they had in mind not publications in general, but publication of high quality research work. What was contemplated becomes clear if we go back about a year to July, 1910, when the first issue of an unpretentious but very important little publication appeared, entitled *University Studies*. A prefatory note explained that it was a subseries of the *Indiana University Bulletin* in which would be published, from time to time, some few of the contributions to knowledge made by instructors and advanced graduate students of Indiana University.

It was publications of this character in which the faculty of the Graduate School were interested, the further development of which will be considered later.

A year later, June, 1912, the President stated his conception of the future development of the University. He said:

It is my judgment that the larger future of the University is to be found in the development of the Graduate School and the professional schools.[3] This does not mean any neglect of our excellent College of Liberal Arts. We must, by all means, maintain and improve the essential part of the University. On

[3] This was the recommendation of the non-state school presidents at the Governor Marshall conference.

the other hand, there are many reasons which indicate that our new and larger growth must be, as I have said, in the graduate and professional schools. . . . I find that the average man believes in research because he sees in many directions the enormous advantages which it brings to the people. I am satisfied that the strongest argument which we can make before the coming Legislature and future Legislatures for appropriations is the presentation of great lines of research which the University can and should carry out. I have asked the Graduate Council to prepare a bulletin in which shall be set forth the following:
(1) The principal things which have been done by the University in the past;
(2) The principal lines of research which are now in progress;
(3) The principal things which the University ought to undertake.

I shall ask the other professional schools to set forth in a similar way their programs of research, or service to the state.

A New Dean of Women

The President wished to secure a successor to Dean Goodbody (deceased March 5, 1911) who would continue her fine influence with the young women of the campus and secure their continued cooperation. He regarded this appointment as almost the most difficult to fill, since the dean of women must have "rock-bottom integrity, sound judgment, tact, courage, and spontaneous sympathy." When he added to these requirements a fine education and extensive social experience and other desirable qualities, it becomes apparent how difficult this selection really was.

After a diligent search Miss Carrie Louise DeNise, the admirable dean of women at Iowa Wesleyan College, was recommended by the President and appointed by the board, effective as of August 1, 1911. In her first report, November, 1911, Dean DeNise repeated the recommendation of her predecessor that dormitories for young women students were their most urgent need. She supported her recommendation with reasons for her conclusion. Her study showing the need for better housing was used by the Indiana Federation of Women's Clubs in 1913 and 1914 to urge the establishment of dormitories at all state schools.

Increasing Friendliness of Non-State Colleges

In June, 1912, the President reported the increasing friendliness of Indiana colleges toward the University. He cited the fact that the president of Wabash College, in introducing him on Commencement day at Wabash, had stated publicly that Indiana University had grown in quality and power as much as in numbers, and that the secretary of the Carnegie Foundation had told him that there were no better institutions than Indiana University in the establishment and administration of high standards.

The President noted that Governor Marshall, speaking at the dinner of the medical alumni at Indianapolis in June, warmly advocated generous support by the state of the professional and graduate work of the University.

RELIGIOUS EDUCATION

At the June meeting of the trustees, 1911, the President reported on religious education[4] as follows:

There is a widespread movement among the churches of the country to establish, at the state universities, departments or schools of religious education to be supported entirely by private funds. At several state universities considerable progress has been made in this matter. Mr. Batman last year attended a Conference at Madison, Wis., upon this subject. Several churches in Indiana have begun active work along this line, looking toward such foundations at this University. The Presbyterian Church expects to have a man here within a year. The Christian Church has the same expectation. Mr. [J. C.] Todd, of the Bloomington Christian Church, has begun an active campaign to endow a Bible chair here with $50,000. He confidently expects to succeed as his church has done in several other states. These enterprises ask nothing in the way of financial support from the University. They desire, of course, to be welcomed by the trustees and faculty as independent cooperative movements. They desire to have work done under their direction receive University credit, provided the men chosen to give the work are scholars in the university sense, and provided the work done is of university quality. I recommend that the trustees extend a welcome to all religious bodies contemplating work of this kind in connection with this University.

In November, 1910, it had been ordered that

the Trustees of Indiana University approve the granting of credit for work of University quality done in departments or schools of Biblical instruction established in Bloomington by any religious body, upon the same basis as for work of like character done in other institutions of learning. The question of granting such credit and the amount of same shall in all cases be determined by the authorities of the University.

[4] Religious education is discussed in considerable detail in Chap. XI.

Some years passed without any credit being authorized. The matter of granting credit for Bible courses came formally before the faculty in April, 1917, in the application of the Bloomington Bible Chair for such an arrangement. After prolonged discussion the matter was referred to a committee for reconsideration. Partly because of opposition based on uncertainty regarding organization and stability of the chair, and partly because of pressure of many matters relating to the impending war, this committee did not report back to the faculty.

PHI GAMMA DELTA PROPERTY

The map in the front of the book shows, at the southwest corner of the campus as it was in 1902, a small area that was not part of the campus, not University property.

The west boundary of the twenty-acre campus purchased in Dunn's Woods on February 4, 1884, was 375 feet east of Indiana Avenue. It was not until March 29, 1897, that a second purchase was made of the 8⅓ acres between the campus and Indiana Avenue. But during the thirteen years between the first and second purchases certain lots on Third Street near the intersection of Third Street and Indiana Avenue had been purchased by local citizens, among whom was Joseph Swain.

When in 1893 Joseph Swain returned to Indiana University as president, he purchased a lot on Third Street just west of the campus as it was at that time and erected a house in which he lived until he resigned in June, 1902. At that time the trustees were very much interested in the purchase of land in Dunn's Meadow,[5] so the Swain home was purchased by the Phi Gamma Delta fraternity.

When this house burned on the night of February 16, 1910, the trustees decided to make a beginning at purchase of the lots at the southwest corner of the campus. On March 9, 1910, they authorized the Executive Committee to negotiate with the Phi Gamma Delta fraternity for the purchase of the lot on which their house had stood.

The correspondence with reference to the purchase of this site was considered by the President so important that it was given in full to the Board of Trustees in his report of June 14, 1912. Inasmuch

[5] For location of Dunn's Meadow, see map at front of book.

as the University has been criticized in recent years by members of the State Planning Board for not having had the foresight to gain possession of the whole of the southwest corner of the campus, it seems desirable to quote this correspondence. The President reported as follows:

In accordance with the instructions of the Board of Trustees, I wrote the following letter to the Secretary of the Phi Gamma Delta Association:

Bloomington, Indiana
May 18, 1912

Dear Sir:

The Trustees of Indiana University have instructed the Executive Committee to use every effort to purchase the lots in the corner of the campus owned by the Phi Gamma Delta fraternity. It may be said that the Trustees are far from wishing to do anything unfriendly toward the fraternity. On the other hand, the Trustees feel strongly that the larger interests of the University, which include the interests of all fraternities and all alumni as well as all others who are interested in it, require them to secure that corner, if possible, as a part of the University campus. I should be glad to have you communicate with the Executive Committee at your earliest convenience.

Very truly yours,
W. L. Bryan.

Mr. E. V. Shockley, Secretary
Phi Gamma Delta Fraternity Association,
Bloomington, Indiana

A committee of the fraternity conferred with the Executive Committee, and no agreement as to price could be reached. I then wrote the following letter to Governor Marshall:

Bloomington, Indiana
May 24, 1912

Dear Sir:

I am instructed by the Trustees of Indiana University to solicit your approval of their effort to purchase a plot of ground which now belongs to the Phi Gamma Delta fraternity, but which, in their judgment, should make a part of the campus of the University.

The Trustees believe that the campus is permanently deformed by having a little corner in a conspicuous position cut out of it. They believe that it would be possible for a fair committee to be appointed which should determine upon a just price for the lot, so that the fraternity would suffer no hardship They believe, in any event, that they can not discharge their own duty to the University without making every reasonable effort to settle the matter in a way which will commend itself to the alumni and to the people of the state.

If the question is asked why the Trustees have not acted sooner, the answer is that they did make an effort before the passage of the condemnation law,[6] and later did not have the money to proceed. They are still embarrassed on this account, but understand that it is their part to produce at the proper time the money necessary for the purchase of the lot at the price which may be fixed.

I enclose a formal description of the lot.

Very respectfully yours
W. L. Bryan.

Governor Thomas R. Marshall
Indianapolis, Indiana

Governor Marshall's reply was as follows:

May 27, 1912

My dear Doctor:

I am in receipt of your communication requesting permission to condemn what is known as the Phi Gamma Delta property. I do not know whether the erection of the building would in any wise deform the campus, but I am reliably informed by the trustees that the plans and specifications for their building have all been prepared and paid for and the contract let and that there would be no way without great loss to them for them to cancel the contract.

I have not had occasion to examine the law of condemnation and so am not certain that they could obtain payment for the damages which they would be compelled to pay by reason of the stopping of their work. It is probably the law that the University would pay only the fair value of the land and any improvements now on the same, and that the Court would not take into consideration prospective damages arising to the property.

I do not believe it would be a good thing for the University to antagonize the Fraternity and to deal with it unjustly. Many institutions of learning are anxious to have these Chapter Houses erected upon the campus as an adornment. If the University is perfectly willing to pay for the land and all damages, then I see no reason why they cannot make an agreement with the Trustees of the Fraternity without condemnation proceedings. Until I have further light upon the premises, I must refuse to grant the request for the commencement of condemnation proceedings.

Respectfully,
Thomas R. Marshall
Governor

Dr. William L. Bryan
Bloomington, Indiana

I replied to the Governor's letter as follows:

[6] The Indiana legislature enacted a law (*Indiana Laws,* 1911, p. 468) giving state benevolent and educational institutions the right to condemn property needed for building.

Bloomington, Indiana
May 29, 1912

Dear Sir:

I think it is my duty to say that the Trustees of this University have not done or thought of doing anything to antagonize the Phi Gamma Delta fraternity, or to deal with it unjustly. I am sure that many leading members of the fraternity here and elsewhere would assure you of this fact. I may add that the Trustees have been favorable to the idea of permitting the fraternities and other organizations to build on the college campus at properly selected places, if they had the legal authority to do so. Further, I am sure that the regret which the Trustees feel at a building project which they believe ill-advised is shared and will be shared by many loyal members of the Phi Gamma Delta fraternity.

Very respectfully yours,
W. L. Bryan

Governor Thomas R. Marshall,
Indianapolis, Indiana.

Professor Hogate, Professor Woodburn, and Mr. Shockley have all said to me that they hoped the University would secure the lots and that the opposition came from a very few persons, chiefly one. However, the Executive Committee has exhausted all means within its power to secure the lots, and has failed.

This story is told in some detail by Marshall's biographer,[7] from which we quote:

Marshall became a member of Phi Gamma Delta fraternity while a student at Wabash. He retained his interest in this fraternity all the rest of his life, while governor and vice-president, attended its meetings, and while he was governor came to the rescue of the brothers when harm threatened. The Phi Gamma Delta chapter house at Indiana University was on a lot forming a corner of the campus. The house burned and a contract was let for the building of a new house. Then the Board of Trustees of the University decided to acquire the lot by condemnation proceedings. This threatened financial disaster for the members of the fraternity, who were obligated by the contract for the new house. If the property was condemned before the building was erected, the state probably could pay the fraternity no more than the value of the land. But the fraternity would have to pay the contractor for his losses. Under the laws of Indiana the governor must approve condemnation proceedings which are instituted by a state university. The university officers prepared to take the proper papers to Marshall for signature.

A committee of the local brethren of Phi Gamma Delta went from Bloomington to Indianapolis and explained the situation to Brother Marshall. He

[7] Thomas, op. cit., pp. 106–7.

assured them that the lot would not be condemned so long as he was governor. He thought he could settle the matter so as to prevent condemnation proceedings for many years. The delegation returned to Bloomington, and a few days later the university officers arrived before the Governor. Marshall, it is said, rebuked them for jeopardizing instead of protecting the interests of the students, and it is certain that he wrote to President Bryan on May 27, 1912, explaining his refusal to consent to the condemnation proceedings. The stated reason was that such proceedings probably would be unfair to the boys.

Comparable situations arose later in connection with the Theta and Kappa sorority sites on Forest Place. Both sororities recognized the paramount University interest in their locations and, for a fair remuneration, transferred title to the University.

Had the University been able to secure the Phi Gam site, the purchase of the remainder of this corner of the campus would have offered little difficulty. In fact, with exception of the Professor Ramsey property, all other lots of this corner have changed hands since that date.

THE INDIANA UNION

The activities of the recently organized Indiana Union had impressed the President most favorably. He said: "Throughout the period of my connection with the University, as student, teacher, and president, I have not known any organization which has so challenged my admiration." The Union had already accomplished many things of substantial importance. The net proceeds of an entertainment given by the Union had been turned over to the University to be used for the improvement of the entrance to Jordan Field.

JOURNALISM

The work in journalism had been developing slowly during the Bryan administration. There had been pressure for organization of a school of journalism. In June, 1911, the status of this work was improved by appointment of Joseph W. Piercy as director of the Department of Journalism, beginning August 1, 1911.

The first report of Director Piercy was made a year later, June, 1912, in which he stated that during the past year courses had been given in (1) theory, (2) practice work on the *Student,* (3) publicity and advertising, and (4) short story. Forty-three students had been enrolled.

He recommended the employment of a good, full-time man who would make publicity his special business. His plans for publicity included the writing of stories for home papers and the issuance and distribution of a weekly bulletin of the principal events occurring at the University. Among other places, these bulletins should be sent to the newspapers of the state. As a further development he suggested a course in editorial writing.

Degree A.M. Privatim

In order to confer alumni status on non-alumni members of the faculty who had had long service or who held major rank, the faculty in June, 1910, recommended that the degree A.M. *privatim* be granted certain professors. This recommendation received the approval of the trustees in October, 1910. Accordingly, in June, 1911, the degree A.M. privatim was conferred upon: Joshua W. Beede, Alfred M. Brooks, Edgar R. Cumings, Warner Fite, Charles M. Hepburn, Amos S. Hershey, Enoch G. Hogate, Will D. Howe, Harold W. Johnston, Albert F. Kuersteiner, Eugene Leser, Burton D. Myers, Carl W. Osthaus, Guido H. Stempel, Henry T. Stephenson, Frank W. Tilden, and Ulysses G. Weatherly.

University Services

The first official acts of the President in 1902, we have stated in Chapter III, were simple matters of physical maintenance. There was an unending succession of these physical maintenance matters, some of which were important revelations of the economies necessary in University maintenance. For illustration, in June, 1911, inquiry was being made of officers of the Illinois Central regarding a switch from its Indianapolis Southern Railway to the campus, which would facilitate and cut expense of delivery of coal. The School of Law needed a typewriting machine. Showers were installed in the Men's Gymnasium; indeed we wonder how they had gotten along without them.

The University was essentially a service unit of the state and as such was alert to establishment of new or continuance of old services within the bounds of a limited budget. Thus at Commencement time, 1911, Professor Robert E. Lyons was authorized to offer his services, without charge, to towns and cities of the state, for inspection and analysis of artificial gas. An appropriation of $900 was repeated for cost of apparatus and assistants for the work in orthogenics conducted by Professor Elmer E. Jones. Limited provision was being made for the better housing of young women through the purchase by the Episcopal Church of the large building just east of the church, to be used as a girls' dormitory.

MATTERS OF GENERAL FACULTY INTEREST

A feature of Commencement exercises, 1911, was the ceremonial presentation to the University of the sword of Walter Q. Gresham, the Hoosier Civil War general, by his widow and son.

In March, 1911, a committee of trustees was appointed to cooperate with a faculty committee previously appointed to make provision for a suitable memorial to Dean George L. Reinhard. In the following June, President Bryan announced that the committee had accepted a bronze cast of the Judge, which was hung in the Law Library.

On the death of Dean Louise A. Goodbody, her friends, by voluntary subscriptions, founded the Louise A. Goodbody Memorial Loan Fund in her honor. This fund, the first of a number of student loan funds, is today (1944) in excess of $3,400.

On March 4, 1910, the formal application of the members of Phi Beta Kappa for a chapter of that society at Indiana University was unanimously recommended by the senate of Phi Beta Kappa. At the annual meeting of the member chapters on September 14, 1910, this recommendation was approved without dissenting voice. The organization meeting of the Indiana chapter was held on December 6, 1910. The chapter was installed by the president of the united chapters on Foundation Day, January 20, 1911. The members were: Edgar Roscoe Cumings, Charles Alfred Mosemiller, Frank William Tilden, Warner Fite, Guido H. Stempel, Bert John Vos, James Albert Woodburn, Albert F. Kuersteiner, Henry Thew Stephenson, Ulysses G. Weatherly.

On recommendation of Ulysses G. Weatherly, Professor of Sociology, an appropriation of $800 for social work in connection with the Dispensary of the School of Medicine, in Indianapolis, was made in 1911 to provide opportunity for laboratory work in sociology, particularly for those students interested in social service. It will be noted that social service work began as medical social service. Miss Edna G. Henry was placed in charge.

In July, 1911, Dr. Charles P. Emerson was chosen as dean of the School of Medicine, succeeding Dr. Allison Maxwell. (See Chapter VIII.) In his first report to the trustees in November, 1911, Dean Emerson recommended the appointment of Dr. W. D. Gatch, then in St. Louis, as assistant professor of surgery.

In the spring of 1911 Walter A. Jessup was appointed professor of education and later in the year 1911–12 he was made dean of the School of Education. When in the summer of 1912 Dean Jessup resigned to accept the deanship of the School of Education at the University of Iowa, Professor William W. Black was advanced to the deanship.

On October 31, 1910, Samuel R. Lyons was appointed by the State Board of Education as a trustee of Indiana University, succeeding James E. Watson, resigned.

On November 28, 1910, at a special session of the board called to elect a successor to Lawrence Van Buskirk as treasurer of the University, Edwin Corr was chosen to succeed him.

CHAPTER XIII

BIOLOGY HALL AND OWEN HALL, 1909 - 11

THE INDIANA legislature of 1909 had made an appropriation of $80,000 for a new science building. The grant was about one-third of the amount requested and needed and was so inadequate that consideration had been given to using it for an addition to Owen Hall. Owen Hall, however, was an almost square building and did not lend itself well to any addition.

By June, 1909, it had been decided to abandon the consideration of an addition to Owen and use the fund for construction of a separate building. A site was selected about one hundred feet from Third Street and about the same distance west of the continuation of the walk in front of Wylie, Kirkwood, and Science, southward to Third Street. Excavation for the new building was begun on September 28, 1909. It was expected that the building would be completed and ready for occupancy within the year.

This building was being called the new science building. But for what sciences was it being erected? Physics was well located in Science Hall, dedicated six years earlier. Chemistry, located in Wylie, though asking for a new building, had laboratory and lecture space about as good as could be provided in this relatively small new building. Anatomy and Physiology were located in quarters in Science Hall, never regarded as other than temporary. Zoology and Botany were in Owen Hall in quarters so poorly adapted to their needs that Anatomy and Physiology, though receptive, were making no real effort for preferment, in deference to the need of these older departments.

A faculty committee appointed to consider which departments should have space in the new building recommended that Botany be located on the first floor and Zoology on the third floor, with some of the non-science departments of Kirkwood or Wylie on the second floor. In consideration of the somewhat less than cordial relations between the Departments of Botany and Zoology, this suggested arrangement had its amusing aspect. This recommendation prevailed, and English, a large department, was selected from crowded Kirkwood to occupy the second floor.

At the opening of the fall quarter, 1910, the new building was not as yet ready for occupation. By October both Professor Mottier and Professor Eigenmann (separately) had suggested that the new building be named Biology Hall. This suggestion seemed good to the President and was accepted by the board.

The Daily Student for November 10 carried the heading: "Moving to Biology Now." English offices were already established in Biology and it was expected that moving from Kirkwood would be completed that week end. All classes occupying Owen Hall were being moved into Biology.

On June 17, 1911, the President reported

an unexpended balance in the Biology Building Fund of $6,956.91, and an unappropriated balance of $1,847.95. The latter is available for steps, telephones, sewer connection, and for additional equipment. My judgment is that most of this balance should be used for the benefit of Dr. Eigenmann's department in view of the fact that Dr. Mottier's is to have a greenhouse. I recommend that the Executive Committee be authorized to appropriate from this fund in accordance with this general plan.

This recommendation was approved.

In presenting the report of the faculty committee recommending transfer of the Departments of Zoology and Botany to Biology Hall the President observed that "it would then be possible to transfer Anatomy and Physiology to Owen Hall. This change is much desired by other departments in Science Hall."

Anatomy and Physiology were eager for this transfer. There was not a square foot of Science Hall well adapted to their needs and they were far removed from incineration. The drive was in front of the building, and everything was very public. Anatomy, located on the fourth floor, had found it necessary to have built a large storage tank. The building had not been constructed to bear so great a weight. What strain would it bear?

Owen Hall was located close to incineration in the adjacent power plant. In that day everything north of Owen was back campus. Storage could be provided in the basement on a heavy concrete floor with drainage. But Owen needed remodeling and repairs before Anatomy and Physiology could use it advantageously.

Cut deep in the stone over the entrance to Owen Hall is the date 1884. It was one of the two buildings erected for the University on the new campus in Dunn's Woods. Owen Hall was solidly built. Its massive foundation, resting on rock, would have supported a twenty-story building. Its eighteen-inch solid brick hallway walls carried out the massive construction idea.

Architecturally, viewed from the outside, the appearance was not bad. But inside the most casual examination showed great waste of space. The main feature of the second floor was a museum about forty feet square, off of which were shallow rooms, excellent private workrooms, but too small for any other purpose. Above these shallow rooms was a balcony, reached by a very narrow, steeply rising, spiral stairway, and lighted by windows about twenty-six inches square arranged in pairs at floor level. This no doubt had been designed as further museum space, but it was so difficult of access that it was practically waste space.

There was a full basement, well lighted, which at the rear of the building was a foot above ground level. The basement had a wooden creaking floor that undulated as one walked across it, and beneath the floor were the runways and nests of enormous rats.

Daggett and Company had examined the building and believed it entirely feasible to do away with the balcony of the second floor and use attic space to gain a complete third story, and to gain a usable basement by ripping out the wooden floor and substituting a heavy concrete floor. This basement floor was not won from its former occupants, however, without a contest. Before the concrete had set the rats had dug up through it from their subterranean tunnels. Plugging this opening with fresh concrete mixed with glass won the day.

An estimate of $14,050 had been made of the cost of this remodeling and in the fall of 1910 the legislature had been asked to appropriate this amount.[1] The response was an appropriation of $14,000. In March, 1911, Daggett and Company, architects, were ordered

---

[1] See Chap. XII. A larger appropriation was in fact asked, to include cost of an addition, which, on further consideration, was deemed impracticable.

to prepare plans for the remodeling of Owen Hall. A. E. Kemmerer, of Lafayette, was the successful bidder. The remodeling was completed and the building ready for occupation early in the fall of 1911.

The work of the Medical School was still sufficiently new on the campus to be viewed a bit wide-eyed by the student body. The student point of view is given in the following story of the occupation of Owen Hall by the Freshman year of the School of Medicine, published in *The Daily Student,* October 3, 1911:

SCHOOL OF MEDICINE NOW IN OWEN HALL
Medics Move From Science to New Quarters
Have Better Facilities

The Medical Department is moving from its old quarters in Science to its new and permanent home in Owen Hall. The class in dissecting did its first work in the new laboratory yesterday afternoon. The Student reporter, after searching throughout the building, found Dr. Myers in the laboratory, where a whitecoated mob of bloodthirsty young men were brandishing various sharp instruments, with long dangerous looking technical names, about the heads of the calm and unflinching "dead ones." Dr. Myers cordially invited the reporter in and told him that they were removing men's brains. Rather advanced for a beginner! But this was the initiation the reporter got to the department of medicine and he passes it on to the reader in the same order.

Owen Hall has been remodeled to suit the purposes of the new occupants. Even now, masons may be seen high on their swinging scaffolds, adding a little cement here and scratching out a little there, and on the inside painters are brightening up the woodwork with fresh paint.

The third floor is provided by using space that has never before been utilized. The great attic, where birds built their nests and bats were wont to hold their nocturnal conventions, has been converted into large, light, and airy rooms. On this floor are the lecture room, a special dissecting room, a museum, and the main dissecting laboratory. Light for this floor is furnished by three large skylights and dormer windows. Ventilation, which has been planned in a scientific manner, is obtained by a system of sidewall and ceiling ventilators, so that there is a continuous circulation of pure air. According to Dr. Myers, the essentials of a good dissecting room are light and ventilation. The whole north side of this room, which extends the full width of the building, is glass, admitting plenty of light. Here, as in the other rooms, a current of air is provided by windows at either end and ceiling ventilators.

On the second floor, formerly occupied by the botany department, are the offices of Doctors Myers and Pohlman, in which will be the cases containing the Medical Library. Here, also, is the Technician's room, where Mrs. Nichols prepares specimens for the students of histology and neurology. Just off this room two smaller ones have been prepared for advanced students doing special work. Here the student will have all his materials and will be free from interruption. The laboratory for the department of histology and neurology, which is just beneath the dissecting room, is much like it in construction, being sixty-six by twenty feet. By placing this laboratory in the rear of the building, the north light, which is best for microscopic work, is obtained.

Fewer changes have been made on the first floor, which is occupied by the department of physiology. Dr. Moenkhaus has his laboratory and lecture room on this floor.

The basement has been cemented and contains everything from rabid dogs and brainless rabbits to an electric motor for compressing air, which is used in experiments involving artificial respiration.

The medical faculty is glad to get into its permanent home and is enthusiastic over the prospect for years of successful work to come.

In addition to the facilities described by the *Student,* running water, lavatories, toilets, a seven-foot elevator, and a small incinerator were installed. This building, occupied by Anatomy and Physiology in early October, 1911, remained the home of these departments until the summer of 1937 when the new Medical Building, specially designed and equipped for these departments, was occupied, at the close of the Bryan administration. Meanwhile Freshman medical registrations had increased from 31 to 115.

Though Biology Hall was not a large building, the following statement of the relief it afforded, quoted from *The Daily Student* of November 10, 1910, will give an idea of the degree of overcrowding throughout the campus:

The rooms the English department now occupies [in Kirkwood] will be distributed among various other departments. The English office will be occupied by the Economics Department, while the present Economics office will be used by the History Department. Room 3 will be given to the German Department, and several other rooms will be given to the German Department. When Professor Moenkhaus's classes are moved to Owen, his rooms in Science will be occupied by Professor Haggerty's class in Experimental Psychology and by Professor Jones's class in Orthogenics. When the Anatomy class is moved to Owen, the Department of Geology will expand into part of the space in Science Hall now occupied by Anatomy.

CHAPTER XIV

INDIANA UNIVERSITY, 1912 - 14

LEGISLATIVE RESPONSE TO LEADERSHIP OF GOVERNOR RALSTON

SAMUEL M. RALSTON had been elected governor of Indiana in November, 1912, to succeed Thomas R. Marshall. While the annual report of President Bryan was addressed to Governor Marshall and the Visiting Committee, the fate of his budgetary requests would be determined very largely by the incoming governor. This was a situation that was repeated every four years.

The President made a remarkably forceful presentation of "What the University Does" as a preparation for his statement of "What the University Needs." He also pointed out the dire effect of what Indiana had been doing in undersupport of higher education, both public and private. His plea was for adequate support of higher education in general. The report is of historic importance:

I. The University has two chief reasons for being. The first is the discovery of truth. The second is the dissemination of truth. Society requires both. As population thickens, the necessity for both becomes more and more apparent.

As the easily available natural resources become scarce, we are compelled to look for hidden resources for food, fuel, and everything that we need in order to live. This means that we are driven by necessity to science—to the technical sciences, and back of them to the pure sciences, to the social sciences, which marshal human experiences concerning the conduct of human affairs. As this necessity becomes apparent, society sees itself compelled to establish in the universities a corps of men who are there, not to teach the elements of science to young people, but who are there to find out as thoroughly and as rapidly as possible what society must know for its own preservation and well-being.

The second duty of the university is to disseminate the truth. It does this first through the young people who attend it. But this is not enough. The millions who do not go to the university require now all that the university can give. The farmer of today requires what the agricultural college has to teach. The man who is sick today needs the benefit of the latest discovery of the university school of medicine, the most certain diagnosis from the university laboratory of pathology. Our American democracy is engaged now in a vast struggle to establish wise and just laws suited to our complex economic and social life. We cannot succeed in this by guesswork, any more than we can succeed in farming by guesswork. The whole people (since it is the whole people that vote and decide upon the laws to be established) need to study these questions with all the help possible from those who have studied them most. Beyond the purely physical and economic necessities of the people, there are higher necessities which the people do not fail to recognize. The people need, and know that they need, the great literature, the great art, the great upper life for which the lower life exists. It is the highest office of the university to minister to the spiritual hunger of men. The American university glories in its modern task of teaching the farmer who has never visited it to raise more corn in a row; but it glories also in its ancient task of teaching him some Shakespearean idea which will hearten him to hoe to the end of his row.

In sum, what society requires is the truth. It requires that the truth shall be found. It requires that the truth shall be made known to all mankind. Toward all these ends the university is able and willing to serve as minister.

II. There is a group of states where the people show their faith in the university as a social necessity. They show this by private gifts or by state appropriations or by both.

III. Indiana does not belong to the group of states given above. Indiana belongs to another group of states which have not adequately supported a university either by public or by private funds. Indiana is one of the states which has compelled most of its young men and women seeking the most advanced university training to go outside the state for it. Indiana is one of the states which has allowed most of the eminent scholars who were born in it, or who have lived temporarily in it, to find their life work in other states. *Of the thousand leading American scientists, Indiana was the birthplace of twenty-eight and is the residence of twelve. (Seven of the twelve are at Indiana University, nearly every science department having at least one of them.) The other four northwestern states have one hundred and forty-seven of these eminent scientists. No state can pursue such a policy without paying a heavy penalty. No state can continuously impoverish itself in the number of its great scholars without corresponding impoverishment of its entire civilization. Nor will the false economy which drives away these scholars make the state rich. It will instead make the state poor. The best population and the greatest wealth flow to the states which are most enlightened.*

We, therefore, plead for a revolutionary change of policy toward the two state universities. We ask that Indiana be taken out of the wrong group of states and placed in the right group of states. We ask that we be given a chance to have in Indiana at least as many eminent scholars as are born here. We ask that the vast and essential social service of the University be recognized at its true value and that we be given a chance to do in Indiana what the great universities in the adjoining states are doing for their people.

STATEMENT OF NEEDS

Income

Our greatest need is for a larger income. We ask:

(*a*) That the mill tax for maintenance be doubled. There has been no increase in this tax since 1903. Within that time the enrollment has been increased from 1,469 to 2,448, and the cost of general maintenance correspondingly increased.

(*b*) That there be levied for the support of research in the Graduate School and Medical School a graduated collateral inheritance tax. It is to be noted that there is an inheritance tax in thirty-eight states, that a collateral inheritance tax is one to which there is a minimum of objection on the part of those who pay it, that its returns vary widely from year to year so that it is not suited for the support of any work which requires a steady support, and that it is for this reason specially adapted to the support of research which may expand or contract from year to year.

(*c*) That until the above-mentioned taxes become available, specific appropriations be made as follows:

For general maintenance, annually......................$65,000
For the Graduate School and Extension Division, annually... 35,000

Buildings

(*a*) EDUCATION BUILDING: We place first the request for an Education Building to house the School of Education, which last year had 17 teachers and 506 students. We note that the School of Education hereafter should provide instruction in Domestic Economy, and that this is made especially necessary by the large number of women students (enrollment of women students this year, 900). We note further that the School of Education must hereafter train teachers and supervisors in industrial education, and that provision for such training must be made if industrial education is to be made compulsory throughout the state, as recommended by the State Commission on Industrial Education.[1]

(*b*) ADMINISTRATION BUILDING: Every legislative committee for years has recognized our pressing need for an administration building. The Trustees, the faculty, and its committees, the President, five deans, the registrar, and the bursar, and their clerical assistants carry on their business, which brings to these offices all the students of the University, in six rooms of which five are very small. All the University records are kept in the same rooms, which are not fireproof.

(*c*) AUDITORIUM: The University has no adequate auditorium. We sometimes use the old Men's Gymnasium. The student organizations some-

---

[1] On March 4, 1911, the General Assembly passed a bill providing for the appointment of a commission of seven persons to investigate the need for industrial and agricultural education. This commission was to report to the Governor. In the 1913 session of the General Assembly, provision was made for instruction in vocational education.

times rent a theater uptown. Sometimes, when the weather permits, we hold our larger gatherings upon the campus.

(*d*) MEN'S GYMNASIUM: We have no proper gymnasium for men. In view of the fact that private donors have given to the University one hundred thousand dollars for a Student Building, we believe it would be a fitting thing for the State to supplement this gift by providing an adequate men's gymnasium.

(*e*) WOMEN'S DORMITORIES: We believe that the time is at hand when the state should provide proper housing for the women students by a system of women's dormitories.

In addition to the above there were requests for:

Water	$40,500.00
Street improvements	5,549.58
Power plant	7,760.00
Renovation and repair of buildings	24,500.00
Walks and drives	8,385.00

APPROPRIATIONS

Governor Samuel M. Ralston was a great admirer of Thomas Jefferson and shared his convictions regarding support of state universities. His favorable attitude was reflected at once in more generous support of institutions of higher education in Indiana.

In 1903 the General Assembly had passed an act appropriating 2¾ cents on every $100 of taxable property in Indiana for support of the institutions of higher education. Of this tax, 4/11, that is, 1 cent, was assigned to Indiana University.

An act in 1913 provided for a tax of 7 cents on each $100 of taxable property in Indiana. Of this total, 2/5, or 2.8 cents, on each $100 was allocated to Indiana University.

While the tax rate was thus 2.8 times as great as previously, the actual income from the state was only doubled. This was because, in addition to the 1-cent tax, the session of the General Assembly of 1911 had made special appropriations, as follows:

For Indiana University maintenance	$32,500
For Graduate School	17,500
For Medical School and Hospital	25,000

This made the University income from the state in 1911 about $260,000. The 2.8-cent tax was expected to yield about $520,000, i.e., essentially double the 1911 appropriation.

Apart from the mill tax, a summary of appropriations made by the legislature of 1913 was as follows:

For waterworks $40,500.00
Third Street improvement........................... 5,549.58
Pump and heater tunnel to Biology Hall and greenhouse.. 7,100.00
Campus lights, drives, and walks...................... 5,360.00
Renovation and repair of buildings.................... 20,000.00
Furnishing and equipment of Wylie Hall.............. 3,445.00
Sewer assessment on East Third Street................. 347.96
    For Indianapolis
Purchase of additional land for the Indiana University
School of Medicine............................... 50,000.00

The General Assembly of 1913 had also made special maintenance appropriations for Indiana University as follows:

For Indiana University maintenance.................. $ 32,500.00
For Graduate School maintenance.................... 25,000.00
For Medical School and Hospital.................... 65,000.00
                                                      ————————

Total.. $122,500.00

The act providing the 7-cent tax for the educational institutions contained this sentence:

When the funds provided for by this act for said educational institutions shall become available, said funds shall constitute the total amounts to be paid out of the treasury of the state to said institutions for any purpose, thereafter, and all acts and parts of acts in conflict with this provision are hereby repealed.

This repealed the $32,500 special maintenance and the $25,000 for the Graduate School, but there was some question whether the special appropriation of $65,000 for the Medical School and Hospital was also repealed. When three years passed without payment of this appropriation, a formal demand was made in March, 1917, of the State Board of Finance for payment.

The Purchase of Land

In April, 1913, President Bryan reported that the Dunn land which the University had tried for so many years to acquire had been purchased by some persons who at this time offered to the University all of this Dunn land east of Fess Avenue, except five lots, for $130,000. Mr. Dunn still held a mortgage on such land for about $70,000.

The purchase of a tract of land (21 acres) lying between Kirkwood Avenue and Tenth Street, east of the Dunn land and adjoining the University campus on the northeast, spoken of as the Grimes land, had been approved by the Governor, and was transferred to the University, May 5, 1913. This is land on which the east end of the Stadium, and later the Auditorium, were constructed.

In June the Executive Committee was instructed to purchase the Buskirk lots adjoining the east campus at a price not larger proportionately than that paid for the Grimes land. This purchase hung fire until 1922, when these lots were acquired.

In the fall of 1913 the Executive Committee was authorized to purchase approximately 200 additional acres of land in the waterworks drainage area if the land could be secured at a satisfactory price. When this proved impossible the Committee in January, 1914, was directed to institute condemnation proceedings. At the same time the Committee was directed to purchase the east portion of the Dunn land if it could be secured on reasonable terms. This tract of 26 acres lay between Seventh and Tenth streets and between Woodlawn and the Grimes purchase and was obtained the next year. On it at a later day were built the Gymnasium, the indoor field, and the west portion of the Stadium.

SOCIAL SERVICE

Dr. Emerson had been deeply interested in social service work at Johns Hopkins. He had become convinced that in many instances there is an occupational element in the etiology of the illness of the patient, and that there is little advantage in curing the patient medically if he be permitted to drift back into his old occupation where after a little time his former symptoms would again appear. Hence a new occupation and social readjustments became parts of the necessary therapy. Dean Emerson, Professor Weatherly, and Miss Henry cooperated in developing this work.

BUDGET COMMITTEE OF THE FACULTY

With the more liberal appropriation of 1913, long-delayed salary adjustments became possible.

President Bryan on April 24, 1913, laid before the faculty[2] all the questions which arose in view of the University's larger income:

All these questions are directly connected with the immediate task of making a budget. I invite you to submit at least an outline of a budget that meets your approval. I shall be glad to furnish you with any facts in my possession that would aid you in doing this.

The budget of expenditures is divided into two parts. One part includes all the items which recur year after year, such as the salary roll or the coal contract. This may be called the regular budget. It never grows less. It grows greater every year. The additions to it grow greater every year with the enlarging areas of expenditure.

The other part of the total budget is the marginal sum which remains over after the regular budget for a year is made up. This marginal sum may be used one year for one specific purpose, another year for another specific purpose, and so on until finally it is absorbed in the regular budget.

The President suggested the regular budget be made up under the four major heads of faculty salaries, departmental appropriations, research, and overhead and other miscellaneous expenses.

In conclusion I wish to say a word about the present salary roll. I judge that it is impossible to make a salary roll which will seem entirely just to all concerned. I am certainly not satisfied with the relative justice of the present salary roll at all points, though a knowledge of the emergencies by which various salaries were determined partly explains these inequities. Meanwhile I am sincerely grateful for the charity with which members of the faculty have judged my efforts to make a just salary roll.

In response to this invitation of the President, a large and representative committee was appointed by the faculty. The President attended the organization meeting of the committee but in order to give discussion free range he thought it best not to attend the subsequent meetings.

Although the faculty heads had voted unanimously for the appointment of this committee, on second thought the opinion held both inside and outside the committee was that the authority that so successfully had guided the affairs of the University through ten lean years might with equanimity be trusted with affairs during the days of less restricted income ahead. It followed, therefore, that there

[2] The full report of the President's communication to the faculty is found in the minutes of the faculty, April, 1913, pp. 7–11.

was not 100 per cent cooperation on the part of the faculty in preparation of the budget report.

After much labor, however, a report was completed by the committee and was submitted by the President to the trustees. It was estimated that $135,000 might be allocated to the budget items suggested by the President.

The following salary scale was proposed:

Instructors . . . .$1,000 to $1,200   Without changing the status of the grades of assistants, tutors, etc.
Assistant professors . . . . . 1,300 to 1,800
Associate professors . . . . . 1,900 to 2,500
Professors. . . . . 2,600 to 3,600
Deans . . . . .A sum additional to the maximum for professors, adequate to their services.
President . . . . .Generous provisions for increase of this salary.

The appointment of a director of the summer school was recommended, and summer school salaries were estimated at about $7,000. The committee proposed an additional appropriation for the Library of $10,000, which practically doubled the Library budget. Other recommendations included $21,000 for the Extension Division, $8,530 for the annual increased needs of the School of Law, $25,000 annually for the Graduate School, and $13,200 for the School of Education. No specific recommendation was made for the College of Liberal Arts.

The total of all recommendations amounted to $132,230. It was evident therefore that the $135,000 judged available for budget increases had been nearly exhausted without making any provision whatsoever for the long-overdue needs of the College of Liberal Arts. Obviously readjustment of recommendations was necessary.

The School of Law had asked for a salary scale very much higher than that proposed by the committee, which went on record as being unable to see why the law professors rated salaries larger than those in other schools of the campus. It was the view of the chairman, Dean Eigenmann, that the Graduate School and research had made their case before the legislature.

The peculiar status of the School of Education received attention from this committee:

The present position and future plans of the so-called School of Education seem to the undersigned anomalous. On the one hand, it contains "schools" (Laboratory School of Experimental Study, School of Observation, School of Orthogenics) and requests a series of professors to round out its plans as a professional graduate school; on the other hand, it desires all of the perquisites of a department of the College of Liberal Arts and of the Graduate School.

We would recommend the consideration of the three following possibilities:

1. The retention of the organization as a school and the placing of the school in its relation to the College of Liberal Arts and the Graduate School on a par with the Law School.

2. The changing of the "School" into a Department of Education with the perquisites and limitations of a department in the College of Liberal Arts or the Graduate School.

3. The delay of action on the plans submitted until the School has been studied together with the College of Liberal Arts.[3]

The preparation of this report had features which proved helpful to the administration. Moreover, it was of great educational value to the faculty, in that the faculty came to realize the tremendous difficulty involved in making a budget, and as a result of this study the faculty was more sympathetic with the budget finally adopted by the administration.

SALARY SCALE

Recommendations made by the budget committee of the faculty had been very conservative and very general. However helpful the report of this committee may have been to the President, who was in close touch with the perils to the University of a low salary scale, it did not carry equal weight with the Board of Trustees. So we find the President in his recommendations for the annual budget of the University making the following strong presentation of the need for long-overdue increases in salaries:

The Trustees throughout the past twelve years have been so considerate of my recommendations and wishes, and even of my feelings, that I cannot be less carefully considerate of theirs. I feel, however, that I cannot do less than to restate at this time my profound conviction that nothing else is so important for the University as a higher scale of salaries.

I am doubtless not uninfluenced by the strong feeling which I know exists in the Faculty upon this subject.

[3] The full report of the committee together with certain school reports is found in the minutes of the faculty, June 12, 1913, p. 35.

I am satisfied that the Faculty as a whole, including our best men and including the men who are least self-seeking, would be thrown into profound discouragement[4] which could not but affect the entire life and activity of the University if the hope which they have entertained should be disappointed.

Aside from this consideration, which I feel profoundly, it is my conviction that we practically fix the future level of the Faculty and of the University when we fix the salary scale. Within the past year we have lost two junior men, who by no means ranked with our best men in training or ability, because two universities, neither of which is a member of the Association of American Universities, have offered them salaries higher than we pay to anyone. Furthermore, we have failed to secure two junior men from other universities, neither of whom has the rank of full professor in his own institution, though we offered them full professorships at our maximum salary. These four typical cases illustrate what has happened over and over again. We fix ourselves definitely upon a lower level when we fix upon a lower salary scale.

If it were possible, we ought to make the salaries of full professors here four thousand dollars ($4,000) per year, no matter what other sacrifices this should involve. If it were possible to do this, the result in ten years would appear in a totally different kind of university here.

President Stone tells me that the deans at Purdue are paid four thousand dollars ($4,000), and seven heads of schools are paid thirty-six hundred dollars ($3,600). Other professors are paid three thousand dollars ($3,000) and lower. Thus at Purdue there are about ten men who are paid very much more than anyone is paid here. It is certain that such a difference in salary scale maintained for ten years would make Purdue a university of distinctly higher grade than Indiana.

Passing the details, I suggest the following classification:

(1) The senior deans—Hoffman, Hogate, and Eigenmann.

(2) Professors who have taught twenty-five years in the University. At this time the only professor not mentioned above who falls under this head is Professor Woodburn.

(3) (a) Junior deans—Rawles and Black.

    (b) The following heads of departments—Lyons, Foley, Mottier, Kuersteiner, Weatherly, Lindley, Myers, Vos, Brooks, Howe, Cumings, Moenkhaus, Hershey.

---

[4] It would have been more serious than "profound discouragement." It would have meant loss of that confidence in the administration that had been responsible for maintenance of high faculty morale. The faculty was well aware of higher salary scales in neighboring states and even in the sister University within our state, but they had confidence in the sincerity of the repeated statements of the administration of the necessity for a more adequate salary scale at Indiana. They believed the administration was doing as well as possible under budget limitations and was fully prepared to do better when possible. Now that salary betterment was possible, had it not been made, the resulting loss of confidence would have led many faculty members to seek a new location where the salary scale was better. This would have hastened the day of lower-level operation which the President warned was possible.

(4) Other professors at varying amounts; associate professors and assistant professors at varying amounts.

Following the above classification, I believe that the salaries should not run lower than the following scale:

Senior deans $3,500
Head professors with more than 25 years of service 3,400
Junior deans, head professors, and a few other senior professors 3,300
Other professors $2,400– 2,700
Associate professors 1,800– 2,200
Assistant professors 1,200– 1,600

I should like before the close of the meeting of the board to present a detailed salary roll upon this basis.

The above salary scale was approved on June 13, 1913.

Extension Division

Indiana University had been mildly interested in extension work since 1891 but prior to 1912 this work had been sporadic and incidental. In June, 1912, however, extension work was definitely organized by the establishment of an Extension Division with Professor William A. Rawles as acting director.

The work began in a very simple, inexpensive way. Professor Rawles reported that in October, 1912, an appropriation of $250 was made to cover the expenses of the Extension Division, including postage, printing, paper, card indexes, and miscellaneous expenses. Enrollment fees were expected to amount to $200 or $300.

In June, 1913, Professor Rawles stated that the purpose of the Extension Division was to reach the large group of Indiana citizens who do not have access to libraries and other sources of accurate information by answering inquiries which might be made from time to time. He stated that there was the most urgent need for a secretary for the work in debating and public discussion, a field in which there was opportunity for almost unlimited service. The development of the Extension Division is told in Chapter L.

The Committee on Promotion of University Interests

Three men, Will D. Howe, John W. Cravens, and B. D. Myers, one day in 1912, in the Faculty Club, were discussing various problems confronting the University. Professor Howe asked: "Why do we not form a committee on promotion of University interests for a wider discussion and study of these matters?" At an earlier date there had been a small committee under that title, but it had not been active and for two or three years had not been reappointed. The idea of such a committee now appealed to us. The matter was presented to the President, who said: "Suggest the persons you think would work well on such a committee. I will appoint them, and you may consider yourselves authorized to study and report on any matter you regard as bearing on the interests of Indiana University."

So a large and representative committee came into existence which remained active until the appointment of the University Council nearly two decades later.

THE NEW ALUMNI MOVEMENT

During the year 1912 the faculty committee on the promotion of University interests had spent much time and thought on the organization of the alumni of the University for support of University objectives. It was their conviction that the people of Indiana would support educational objectives more liberally if they understood the educational situation better. It was realized that in the first ten years of the Bryan administration the character of the institution had greatly changed with the organization of new schools and that the alumni should be the first group to be made acquainted with the problems and needs of this changing institution which was the new Indiana University.

Carefully elaborated plans had crystallized during the year and in December of 1912 the first step was taken by the faculty and administration of the University to bring about a closer organization of graduates and former students. An informal dinner[5] meeting of alumni and former students was arranged for December 27, 1912, at the Young Women's Christian Association, Indianapolis, addressed by President Bryan and other members of the faculty. The alumni at this meeting were informed of the purpose to form a permanent organization of alumni and to publish a monthly alumni news-letter for information of alumni as to the aims, work, and needs of the University, and that the immediate objective was sup-

[5] It is of interest that this dinner was fifty cents a plate.

port of the budgetary requests of the University to be presented to the legislature meeting a few days later in January, 1913.

It is interesting to note that this movement was launched at a most auspicious time in that Governor Ralston, known to be friendly to the institutions of higher education, would succeed Governor Marshall when the new legislature convened in January.

As stated in Chapter IX, in November, 1909, the President had proposed better publicity for Indiana University. In June, 1910, he had a bid on a sixteen-page monthly bulletin, publication of which had been referred to the Executive Committee, where it hung fire. Now, nearly three years later, this ambition of the President was to be realized. The first number of the *Alumni News-Letter* appeared in January, 1913, and it was published twelve times that year. Number 1 was an appeal to alumni, bearing the signatures of forty-two senior members of the faculty.

At the annual alumni meeting in June, 1913, a new constitution of the Alumni Association was adopted, providing for election of the usual officers and for organization of an Advisory Alumni Council. Provision was made for appointment of a corresponding secretary who was to be a full-time salaried official.

With the adoption of the constitution, a resolution was presented and passed calling for the establishment by the Alumni Association of a magazine to be known as the *Indiana University Alumni Quarterly*. The first number of the *Quarterly*[6] appeared in January, 1914, and the magazine was published until 1939. With establishment of the *Alumni Quarterly,* the publication of the *Alumni News-Letter* was continued by the University as the *Indiana University News-Letter,* until 1946.

The Alumni Council was organized as follows: A ballot containing the names of forty-eight alumni was sent to the alumni. From this list twenty-one were elected as members of the Council. The Council met and organized with Jacob G. Collicott as president, Edna G. Henry, secretary, and Benjamin F. Adams, treasurer.

Search was made for an alumni secretary. The summer and fall passed without an appointment being made. As the time approached for the annual meeting of alumni on Foundation Day (January 20),

[6] The *Quarterly* was first published under an editorial committee consisting of Professors Harding and Haggerty and George M. Cook, also an alumnus.

Professor M. E. Haggerty, chairman of the committee on promotion of University interests, took over assignment of speakers and the sending out of literature on the New Alumni Movement prepared by his committee.

The search for a man to fill the post of alumni secretary continued and finally Ralph V. Sollitt, a very fortunate choice, was appointed, and began his services in January, 1915.

This New Alumni Movement, which was conceived by and set going under the leadership of the committee on promotion of University interests, marked the end of a period of purely sentimental interest in "the dear old Alma Mater" and the dawning of the conception that the alumni could and should contribute substantially to the realization of the objectives of the institution. Constructive helpfulness did not, to be sure, become at once a motivating, activating element of the lives of all alumni, but a start was made that in another decade led to great undertakings and accomplishments. The immediate effect was to give to Governor Ralston the popular support he needed to come to the relief of the institutions of higher learning in Indiana as his heart dictated.

Journalism

The report of Professor Piercy concerning a plant for *The Indiana Daily Student* submitted to the board in November, 1913, was followed by a more detailed report in March, 1914, after he had investigated the matter for some months. He secured the data on which the report was based by visiting printing plants and examining typesetting machines, office equipment, etc. The detailed estimate of cost of the plant was as follows:

Cost of No. 3½ Miehle press	$1,615.00
Cost of linotype	2,716.75
Cost of other equipment	1,510.39
	$5,842.14

He stated that he had secured a foreman at $1,000 per year, half of whose salary he thought should be paid by the University. He itemized the maintenance budget:

Foreman	$500.00
Compositor and ad man ($70 a month)	840.00

Linotype operator ($65 a month for 8 hours with 45 cents an
  hour for overtime, overtime being estimated at $100)....$ 880.00
Cost of paper ($3 an issue)..............................   540.00
Editors-in-chief 150.00
Business manager 300.00
Circulation manager 200.00
Carriers...   150.00
Ink, lead, postage and mailing, repairs, and incidentals....   250.00
                                                             ───────
                                                             $3,810.00

The purchase of equipment and the employment of the necessary
staff being approved, Professor Piercy recommended employment
of craftsmen and the appointment of Joseph A. Wright as assistant
director in the Department of Journalism for the year beginning
in August, 1914. Remodeling of the old power plant as a home for
this work was completed in the summer of 1914. The cost of remodeling was estimated at $1,570 and of equipment $7,412.14.

This was an important development. It not only made provision
for a home for *The Indiana Daily Student* with more up-to-date
equipment than ever before had been available, but it gave an additional staff for courses in journalism and a laboratory for work.

THE ROBERT W. LONG HOSPITAL

The major details of the gift of real estate to make possible the
erection of the Robert W. Long Hospital have already been presented in Chapter XII. Dr. Long had noted repeated instances of
the defeat of the will of donors, and he was determined that every
precaution should be taken to insure the disposal of his property in
accordance with his wishes. To this end his gift was made to the
state of Indiana for the use of Indiana University, and was accepted
in an act of the legislature (1911). In this manner he marshaled all
the power and resources of the state in defense of his contract. Making this gift during his lifetime, he had the pleasure of being consulted as to site and to plans and the gratification of seeing the
Hospital erected, dedicated, and in operation. He died June 18, 1915.

It was thought wisest not to sell at that time the property donated
by Dr. and Mrs. Long. Accordingly, bonds for $240,000 were issued,
secured by this property, and the money used for the construction of

the Long Hospital, which was dedicated on June 15, 1914, and opened to receive patients the next day. (For an account of the dedication, see *Alumni Quarterly,* 1914, pp. 394-410.)

While the opening of the Robert W. Long Hospital was still months in the future, Dean Emerson was looking forward to that time and in June, 1913, secured authorization for selection of four interns and two residents. The interns were to receive their living, but no salary. The residents, who were required to have at least one year's hospital experience, in addition to their living were to receive $500 per year. These six appointees were to begin their service with the opening of the Long Hospital.

OF INTEREST TO STUDENTS AND FACULTY

Loan funds, which were still very small, were given promise of some increase when, in the summer of 1913, the President entered into a contract with the Bobbs-Merrill Company to publish one of his addresses entitled "He Knew What Was in Man," in the form of a Christmas book, with the provision that the author's royalties should apply to the Indiana Union Loan Fund, which had been started by the President at an earlier date with a loan of $50. At the suggestion of William C. Bobbs, the firms that had done work on the volume contributed the amounts due them to this same fund. In March, 1914, this fund amounted to $407.22. By the close of the Bryan administration the fund amounted to $4,160.56.

The Indiana Union was authorized to install a moving picture apparatus in the Student Building, upon the condition that installation and operation should be in conformity with underwriters' rules.

In the fall of 1912 the Deans and Secretary Myers had requested clerical and stenographic assistance. The President recommended that for the current year such help be furnished through the administrative offices. This was believed at first to promise well, but it worked out poorly. It was necessary to notify the administrative office of the day and hour when help was needed. If successful in securing time, one had to leave the office, cross the campus, and meet the appointment promptly. After a few experiences of finding the stenographer's time already engaged for the desired hour, one was likely to continue to write letters longhand.

The song "Indiana, Our Indiana" by Harker and King was copyrighted in 1913.

It was in the spring of 1914 that the faculty gave approval to the plan for weekly convocations of all students for Wednesday morning. This called for four class periods and a convocation period of forty minutes each, with the usual ten-minute intermissions.

On the resignation of Dean DeNise at the close of the school year 1913–14, Miss Ruby E. C. Mason was appointed dean of women for the year beginning August 1, 1914. She had been educated in Canadian universities and in Oxford, and came from Ward-Belmont.

On August 1, 1914, Miss Ivy L. Chamness became assistant editor of publications, the first full-time appointee in this work.

Professor Amos S. Hershey, Head of the Department of Political Science, had received the signal honor of appointment as Kahn Traveling Fellow, with an honorarium of $3,300 and no duties but to travel wherever he found it most profitable to go. He spent the year 1913–14 in Europe and in the Orient, studying international politics and international law.

The Department of Home Economics was established in June, 1913. The aim of the Department was to meet the needs of two classes of students: (1) those who wish to prepare to teach the subject; (2) those who wish a general understanding of the principles and processes involved in the science and art of home-making and the care of the home. The work was placed in charge of Associate Professor Mabel T. Wellman, a graduate of Wellesley College.

Professor Selatie E. Stout, of William Jewell College, became head of the Department of Latin in the fall of 1914. Associate Professor Lillian Gay Berry had administered the Department during the preceding two years.

In the fall of 1912 alumnae of Indiana University were admitted to membership in the Association of Collegiate Alumnae (later American Association of University Women). Membership implied, among other things, graduation from an institution having high standards of scholarship, which included women among its instructors and had a dean of women of faculty rank.

Nebraska Cropsey, prominent educator of Indianapolis, received the honorary A.M. in 1913.

CHAPTER XV

INDIANA UNIVERSITY, 1914 - 16

A New Gymnasium and Other Needs

A NEW gymnasium for men was, beyond doubt, the matter of greatest student and alumni interest during the biennium 1914–16. The old wooden structure, 66 feet by 135 feet, which served as an assembly hall and a gymnasium, had been erected in 1896 when there were fewer than one thousand students. Attempts had been made to modernize the building by constructing a small swimming pool about the size of a communal bath in the dimly lighted east end of the basement and by addition of lockers and showers. But the structure was thoroughly inadequate.

The growing demand for a new gymnasium had passed from the talking stage to an organized movement when, in the spring of 1914, a committee of students called upon the trustees to urge the erection of a new gymnasium for men. The matter was taken under sympathetic consideration. In December of 1914 the trustees presented to Governor Ralston and the Visiting Committee a strong statement of the need of a new gymnasium for men:

An adequate men's gymnasium is an essential need of the University. It is needed by all the men of the University; not only by those who take part in athletics, but still more by the hundreds and thousands who do not take part in athletics. Our University physician finds that very many of the entering freshmen are distinctly defective in their physical development. He has prescribed corrective gymnastics for large numbers of them. Success in this direction means far greater success in the intellectual work of the students and also in the work which they will do after they leave the University. We have no adequate men's gymnasium at present and the trustees wish to supply this need at the earliest possible time.

In consideration of the fact that in the legislative session of 1913 the mill tax had been more than doubled, no appropriation for a gymnasium or for any other building was requested of the legislature in 1915. It followed, therefore, that no appropriation for maintenance or buildings at Indiana University was made by the legislature of 1915. Though the statement of needs presented by the president of the board to Governor Ralston began with the frank statement that it was not the purpose to ask appropriations from the legislature of 1915, yet the law required that a statement of the status of the University be made, and that involved a statement of building needs and needs of the Graduate School.

A building for education, vocational training, and domestic economy was high on the building program of Indiana University during this biennium. In his report to the Governor, Senator Shively, the president of the board, had stated:

The School of Education, which has for nearly thirty years made its contribution to the training of teachers in Indiana and which has grown from small proportion to an enrollment of many hundreds, is not at all properly housed, but is greatly hampered on every side by the lack of room. The difficulty has been greatly increased with the necessity of doing our part toward the preparation of teachers in domestic economy and vocational education. The trustees feel keenly the need of providing these departments with a proper place in which to do their work.

Other major needs of Indiana University, presented to the Governor on December 20, 1914, were: an administration building, an auditorium, an addition to the library, and a dormitory for women.

It is of considerable interest to note that the buildings, the need for which was so strongly presented by Senator Shively in December, 1914, were all built during the next twenty-seven years, as follows: 1917, the Men's Gymnasium; 1925, Women's Memorial Hall; 1926, wing to complete Library; 1936, Administration Building; 1938, Education Building; 1941, Auditorium.

These dates, however, give a very inaccurate measure of the tardy response of the state to the building needs of the University, for it was the Memorial Fund that made possible the construction of Women's Memorial Hall,[1] and federal money paid about 45 per cent of the cost of construction of the Administration, Education, and Auditorium buildings. From time to time during this period of a

---

[1] Bond issues, to be paid out of earnings, completed the financing of Memorial Hall. There was no direct state appropriation for the Administration (other than $75,000 from the Governor's Emergency Fund) and Education buildings. Bonds were issued and the state has honored the annual service charge on those issues to this time (1951). The state contributed $300,000 towards erecting the Auditorium. Additional funds were raised by a bond issue retired out of earnings and by student fees.

quarter-century, other building needs became so acute that they competed with Administration, Education, and Auditorium for priority and contributed to the delay in meeting these needs.

The 1914 report ended by calling attention to the fact that the Graduate School, the extension work of the University, the Medical School, and the Robert W. Long Hospital were being financed out of the general maintenance fund of the University, instead of by special appropriations as prior to the 1913 increase in the mill tax. The University believed that the annual appropriation of $65,000 for the Robert W. Long Hospital and the Medical School had not been repealed. (See Chapter XVIII.)

LAND AND LOTS OWNED BY THE UNIVERSITY

The President made a statement regarding University lands to the trustees in March, 1915. The campus in 1902, when the Bryan administration began, consisted of 50.82 acres. By March, 1915, this biennium, the campus had grown to 117.53 acres, for which $99,-513.50 had been paid. This was half again the sum necessary for the purchase of the whole Dunn farm at an earlier date. Though some acres were later purchased at lot prices, much of the Dunn farm was permanently lost, being occupied by residences. Chapter LIV lists land purchases from February 4, 1884, when the first 20 acres were purchased in Dunn's Woods, the present site, to June 11, 1937.

Many people had difficulty in visualizing a growing university's need for more land. Many European universities centuries old were built on sites much less than 117 acres. The University of Leipzig, for instance, was nearly as old when America was discovered as was Indiana University at the beginning of this century, yet in 1914 it had only a fraction of the Indiana University campus. But the difficulty was not altogether a lack of appreciation of the growing needs of Indiana University. Many graduates and friends of the denominational schools looked with hostile alarm at the growth of the State University and believed sincerely and honestly that that growth was a threat to the welfare of the non-state schools.

In Bloomington about a mile from the campus, the University owned the University Hospital property, of 4 11/16 acres. At Indianapolis the University owned the site of the Robert W. Long Hospital and at Winona Lake three lots occupied by the Biological Station. The University also owned the Donaldson Farm of 183.88 acres and the University waterworks site of 250.13 acres.

The President recommended that an expert forester be employed to make a survey of the University waterworks area and of the Lawrence County (Donaldson) Farm. Anton T. Boisen, alumnus and graduate of the Yale School of Forestry, was appointed and made a report in May, 1915.

Up to 1915 the general idea for development of the campus had been the formation of a quadrangle. But buildings were being considered which did not fit into that conception. In order to assure a well-considered plan for the development of the University, the services of George E. Kessler, a well-known landscape architect, were secured to make a complete and comprehensive plan for the entire campus. The plan prepared by Mr. Kessler was followed closely until there was evidence that it was being outgrown.

In addition to the lands listed above, there were isolated pieces of property, some of which came to the University as gifts. Such a piece of property was the gift of George Brackenridge, of San Antonio, Tex., of twenty acres on the Ohio River to be used toward a biological survey of the Ohio River. Dr. Eigenmann made a recommendation on its use. It is carried on the treasurer's books today (1946) at $200.

Luther Dana Waterman Gift

In May, 1915, Dr. Luther Dana Waterman, Professor Emeritus of Medicine, offered to give to Indiana University property valued at $100,000, on condition that the income from this property and an equal amount given by the University be devoted to scientific research. For the use of proceeds, see Chapter XLIX.

Robert W. Long Hospital

The President's report of October, 1915, included the report of Dean Emerson. The financial report of the Medical School is of a character with which the trustees were well acquainted. The financial report of the Robert W. Long Hospital, however, included items such as food supplies, drug supplies, laundry work, nursing supplies, nursing costs, etc., with which the trustees had little acquaintance and no background for judgment. Was the item of $2,744.70 for gauze, ether, bandages, catgut, etc. reasonable or excessive? Was $10,260 for ward nurses small or too great? These were matters concerning which it was necessary to rely almost exclusively on the judgment of the dean and the finance committee, consisting of Drs. Barnhill, Clark, Earp, and Hutchins. It was an arduous and excellent work done by these men. Patients were coming from all over the state to the Robert W. Long Hospital, which was always full.

THE INDIANA CENTENNIAL PAGEANT

In June, 1915, William Chauncy Langdon was appointed director of pageantry, with the stipulation that he should prepare a pageant for Indiana University to be given in May, 1916, in celebration of the centennial of the admission of Indiana to statehood and her place in the Union.

The first showing of the Bloomington pageant occurred on Tuesday, May 16, 1916, at 3:30 p.m., on the west part of the campus. The pageant consisted of a series of episodes following one another closely. Since the actors in each episode were costumed for that episode and inasmuch as there were from twenty to two hundred in each episode, the total number of people participating in the pageant was considerable. *The Indiana Daily Student* placed the number at one thousand.

The fact that in the audience were relatives of the characters of that early day (1816) and that, in the episodes, parts were frequently taken by descendants of those who had played them in reality one hundred years earlier added much to the interest of the audience.

We cannot here give a list of all the episodes. The Conestoga wagon used was one hundred years old. The old fiddler was present and there were old-fashioned dances in old-fashioned costumes. There were school scenes in which much emphasis was placed on "lickin' and larnin.'" There were scenes depicting the wresting of land from the Indians. The first land sale in Bloomington was reenacted. Brilliantly costumed characters livened up the old cabs and carriages which were in the procession. One episode depicted the underground railway.

The second performance was given on Wednesday, May 17. News of the success of the initial performance had spread throughout the state and by trains and automobiles people poured into Bloomington. The Governor was present. The State Historical Commission was well pleased with the performance.

Professor Charles D. Campbell had composed special music for the occasion. His Indiana song lent itself perfectly to the symbolic episode of the great community drama.

The third performance of the pageant was on May 18, and an extra performance was given on Saturday, May 20.

A very excellent account, giving a conception of the dramatic power of this pageant, is found in the *Indiana University Alumni Quarterly* (Vol. III, pp. 362–73), written by George F. Reynolds, Associate Professor of English, Indiana University. It was fortunate that a medium was at hand, the *Alumni Quarterly*, first, to stimulate the writing, and, second, to preserve the written account of this pageant.

Professor Reynolds, like most who saw it, was deeply moved by it. He describes the stage setting, the gathering of audience and actors. It is 3:30. The University clock has been stopped. There is a slight buzzing from the director's box and the orchestra begins the stirring *Hymn to Indiana* and the pageant has begun. And soon "you begin to understand what the pageant really means; it is a thing of marvelous beauty as well as of historic interest; a beauty of sound, of color, of movement."

Of the finale, Professor Reynolds says:

And here the pageant reaches its height; all around in the grandstands people of the audience join in the prayer (*America,* 4th verse, "Our Fathers' God, to Thee") and something grips your throat and tears come to your eyes.

Military Training

Following the outbreak of war in Europe in 1914 the possibility of the United States becoming involved became more and more evident. It should be recorded that the demand for establishment of military training at Indiana University came chiefly from those students who foresaw that they might be called upon to enlist and realized the desirability of training. The thought at first was to organize training as a battalion of the Indiana National Guard. When, however, it was understood that all students taking advantage of this opportunity would be required to enlist for three years in the state militia, much opposition to this plan developed and it was abandoned.

In the fall semester of 1915–16 the committee on the promotion of University interests took up an investigation of the organization of military training in the land grant universities, under an officer of the Regular Army. There was correspondence with a dozen institutions where this plan of organization was in force. Finally, at a meeting in March, 1916, the faculty adopted the report of the committee recommending this plan of organization. Further action is discussed in Chapter XVII.

TRAINING SCHOOL FOR NURSES

The Robert W. Long Hospital had been dedicated on June 15, 1914. For a time nursing service had been provided by private nurses. There was no nurses' home and one of the hospital wards was being used as a nurses' dormitory. A Training School for Nurses was announced in the Bulletin of the School of Medicine[2] published in June, 1915, and plans were under consideration for the purchase of a near-by house as a nurses' home. To expedite the acquisition of this house, Dr. Long advanced the purchase price, of which he agreed to donate $5,000. This first nurses' home, which stood on the southeast part of the open ground south of the Medical School Building, was later abandoned and removed.

Mrs. Ethel P. Clarke was appointed superintendent of nurses and director of the Training School for Nurses, to begin August 1, 1915. On assuming her duties Mrs. Clarke found on file 114 applications for admission to the Training School. Applicants were required to meet the same entrance requirements as for the College of Liberal Arts. In order to encourage young women with collegiate training to enter the nursing field, the University faculty took action permitting young women under prescribed conditions to obtain the baccalaureate and nursing degrees in a shortened period. (See Chapter XLI.)

---

[2] This publication in the Bulletin of the School of Medicine was made deliberately, with the purpose of indicating the position of the nurses as auxiliaries to the medical staff. It was a reaction to a situation which was reported in certain hospitals in which the superintendent of nurses was dictating what the medical and surgical staff might and might not do.

EDUCATION

Vocational education was coming to the fore during this period. The work seems to have begun with courses in industrial and manual training given in summer terms for elementary teachers. In 1914 there was a Department of Industrial Education which had a work agreement with the Bloomington public schools. Two years later this Department had become a Department of Vocational Education in the College of Arts and Sciences, though it remained an administrative division of the School of Education. During the summer of 1914 an Extension Center for Vocational Education was established in Indianapolis. The School of Education had been greatly strengthened by the addition of Hubert G. Childs, Melvin E. Haggerty, and Henry Lester Smith to the staff. When, in the spring of 1916, William W. Black resigned as dean of the School of Education, Professor Smith succeeded to the deanship.

EXTENSION DIVISION

A thirty-page report of the Extension Division was made in June, 1915, by Director J. J. Pettijohn, who had been appointed in 1914. He discussed the reorganization of the work of the Division under the following major heads: correspondence study, bureau of public discussion (he gave a list of several hundred topics), visual instruction, child welfare expositions, community institutes, lectures, class study, extension centers, conferences, consultation service, and field work.

There had been a substantial growth in the activities inaugurated before the last annual report, Mr. Pettijohn said, and few new lines of work had been started during 1914-15. In order to encourage debating, Theodore Thieme, of Fort Wayne, offered $250 for medals and prizes for winners in the High School Discussion League.

WATER

During this period, 1914-16, the water problem was acute. At a meeting of the Marion County Alumni Association, in Indianapolis, in June, 1914, the situation was discussed, a letter from Governor Ralston was read, and Bloomington citizens were made aware of the

growing disapproval of their failure to find a solution of this Bloomington city water problem. In June, 1915, however, the University
reservoir contained enough water to assure an abundant supply
of pure water for all the needs of the University. This, however, did
not relieve the situation for the students who roomed in Bloomington and were dependent on the city water supply. (See Chapter
XXIII.)

A New Medical Building

In the twenty years that had elapsed since the erection of the
Medical Building in Indianapolis at the corner of Senate and Market
streets, in 1896, the physical requirements for the teaching of medicine had changed so greatly that this building, though not really
old, had none the less become very inadequate and unsatisfactory.
Accordingly in June, 1916, a committee was appointed which was
headed by President Bryan and included Trustee Samuel E. Smith,
Dean Emerson, and Drs. Hutchins and Oliver, who were directed
to formulate plans for a new medical building to be located near
the Robert W. Long Hospital. This was the initial step leading to
the erection of a new medical building at Indianapolis, in 1919.

Changes in Board of Trustees

There were three changes in the Board of Trustees during this
biennium.

Samuel R. Lyons died on May 3, 1915. He was succeeded by
Benjamin F. Long, of Logansport, who was elected by the State
Board of Education on June 15, 1915, to complete the unexpired
term, fifteen days, and serve for three years beginning July 1, 1915.

Benjamin F. Shively, who was president of the board, died on
March 14, 1916. He was succeeded by Frank H. Hatfield, who was
elected by the State Board of Education on April 28, 1916, to fill the
unexpired term ending June 30, 1917.

Joseph H. Shea, alumni trustee, was appointed by President Wilson as Ambassador Extraordinary and Plenipotentiary to Chile in
the spring of 1916 and was succeeded by Dr. Samuel E. Smith by
alumni election at Commencement in June, 1916.

Student Health Service

The President had requested Dr. A. G. Pohlman, of the Department of Anatomy, to prepare and send a questionnaire to a large number of universities for the purpose of ascertaining customary procedure in care of student health. The report of Dr. Pohlman under date December 26, 1913, comprehensive and characteristically clear, was presented to the board in March, 1914. He recommended employment of a University physician, and the board, after deliberate consideration of this recommendation, appointed Dr. J. E. P. Holland to this office on December 1, 1914. On December 18 the Executive Committee ordered the purchase of $60 worth of furniture as office equipment. In this characteristically simple way was this important forward step taken in care for student health at Indiana University.

The report of the University Physician on student health in March, 1915, was considered very satisfactory. A great variety of cases was coming to his office.

As this work was organized in certain universities, Minnesota for example, the student paid a fee sufficiently large to give him the equivalent of sickness and hospital insurance during the college year. If he became ill or needed surgical care, he might go to the University hospital and receive there the care of University physicians, surgeons, and nurses.

This work at Indiana was organized and continues chiefly as a diagnostic clinic. Minor ailments are cared for. There is provision for isolation and care of students suffering from infectious diseases, smallpox, etc.

Of Particular Interest to Students

At Commencement time there were always students whose credits were short of the requirement for graduation. A high percentage of these completed all required work in the following summer session. Graduated with the class of the following year, they found themselves, as alumni, counted as members of a class with which they had few affiliations, with which they had no sense of belonging. In after years, when there had been no union there could be no reunion. To remedy this situation, a regulation was adopted providing that students who could complete the requirements for graduation in the summer should be eligible to participate in all graduation activities except conferring of diplomas and be graduated in the fall as members of the class graduated the preceding June. If, however, any of them preferred to be graduated at the next Commencement, they were to have that option. This plan, approved by the trustees in 1915, was operative for many years.

When Indiana University in 1910 adopted a fee scale for out-of-state students higher than that required of Indiana boys and girls, some out-of-state students sought to escape the extra fees, in some instances double those paid by Indiana students, by claiming Indiana residence. One man went to the length of having himself adopted by an Indiana family. To prevent such imposition a carefully worded definition of residence as applying to University fees was adopted in 1916. Each of the five paragraphs was formulated to meet a special situation. The effect was to conserve our educational facilities and special privileges for Indiana students. These rules were later revised.

Students were to profit by payment to the University of 10 per cent of the gross receipts from entertainments held in the Men's Gymnasium for which a fee was charged, the money so paid to be applied to something of general student interest.

A sorority inquired in early 1915 if it would be permitted to build a chapter house on University ground. The inquiry presented a problem of great importance as establishing a precedent for many other organizations. It was answered in the negative.

In the same year the Woman's League, cooperating with Dean Ruby Mason, provided a partial fulfilment of the long-felt need for a dormitory for women by establishing "League houses." Here girls lived together in groups of twelve to twenty-five under the care of a house mother much as in a small dormitory. One of these was cooperative. In the fall of that year the trustees approved a request of the Woman's League and the Bloomington branch of the Association of Collegiate Alumnae to undertake to raise money for a woman's dormitory on the campus. One alumna, Mrs. Josephine Pittman Scribner, suggested doing what was done almost three decades later—naming a dormitory for the first coed, Sarah P. Morrison.

In 1916 the three-year-old Alumni Council included this project when they considered raising funds for several purposes. Our entrance into World War I postponed carrying out this campaign for several years.

OF PARTICULAR INTEREST TO THE FACULTY

A matter of great importance to the faculty was the proposal of the Carnegie Foundation (March, 1916) that the University adopt a contributing retirement system for the faculty, which, for the University, would gradually amount to about 5 per cent of the salary budget, and would provide a scale of pensions equivalent to that paid by the Carnegie Foundation at that time (about $2,500). It was the opposition of the faculty which prevented the adoption of this proposal, more fully discussed in Chapter XLIV.

It would be interesting to know why the trustees adopted a motion made by Mr. Batman that it was not advisable to give keys of University buildings to the members of the faculty. This action was never interpreted as applying to faculty members of the science departments, whose experimental work made it necessary to visit their laboratories at odd hours and at week ends.

In November, 1911, the trustees had authorized a change from a year of three terms to one of two semesters, with a summer session of one-half a semester, if the faculty deemed it advisable. Fees were to be adjusted so that the total fee per student per year was unchanged. This matter was under discussion from time to time for three years. Faculty approval was voted in November, 1914. On December 1, 1914, the President concurring in the recommendation of the faculty, the change was given unconditional approval by the Board of Trustees, effective in the fall of 1915.

The recommendation of the faculty that the summer school be held for half a semester (approximately eight weeks and two days) beginning in 1915 was approved. It was decided that the rate of compensation for the half-semester in the summer should be 11⅓ per cent of the annual salary. It was, however, a missionary venture. In the late autumn of 1915 the first summer session director, J. J. Pettijohn, was appointed.

Until 1914 departmental reports varied in organization almost as much as in subject matter. In the fall of 1914, for the first time, they were called for on a common form. While the opportunity still existed for special emphasis of one or another feature of the report of each department, essential features of each report were presented in the same sequence, and facilitated compilation of the President's report based on these departmental reports.

In November, 1915, offices were rented in the Merchants Bank Building in Indianapolis for the use of Alumni Secretary Ralph V. Sollitt, J. J. Pettijohn, Director of Extension Work, and Robert J. Leonard, Director of Vocational Education.

Typewriters were not in general use in the spring of 1916, and it was a notable innovation when it was recommended that an appropriation of $70 be made for the purchase of a typewriter for the use of the Graduate School.

The Workmen's Compensation Act of 1915 applied, with certain exceptions, to every employer and employee, including state institutions. Thus it applied to faculty and other employees of Indiana University. The act was examined by the administration, and, since compensation insurance was not obligatory, the University elected to carry its own liability, under this act. See Chapter XLII for further discussion of compensation after the repeal of this act of 1915 by the Workmen's Compensation Act of 1929.

MATTERS OF GENERAL INTEREST

The new printing plant was already in need of more room in the summer of 1915, although work was confined to jobs for the University and affiliated organizations. *The Indiana Daily Student,* printed at the plant, showed a net profit of $108 in 1915–16.

In the fall of 1914 the stage of Assembly Hall was rebuilt, enlarged, and modernized to accommodate Maude Adams and her company in two performances early in December.

The indignation of the trustees was aroused by the speed and noise of autos at Commencement, 1915. The board took action limiting speed of autos on the campus to ten miles an hour and prohibiting opening the cut-out.

The perennial problem of an overloaded power plant was referred to Professor Arthur L. Foley in 1915 with the request that he prepare tentative plans and estimate of costs of enlargement.

Indiana University participated in the tercentenary of the death of William Shakespeare, April 23, 1616. A Forbes-Robertson performance of *Hamlet* on March 9, 1916, was followed on April 26 by a convocation address by Professor William Lyon Phelps, concluded by a dramatic tribute *In Honor of Shakespeare,* written by Pageantmaster William C. Langdon, incorporating tributes by Riley, Nicholson, and Ade. In June, outdoor performances of three Shakespearean plays by the Ben Greet Players, special lectures and readings brought to an end the Shakespeare week.

A bronze memorial tablet bearing the likeness of Professor Harold W. Johnston, who died in 1912 and who for many years was head of the Department of Latin, was dedicated on Alumni Day, 1916, and hung in the foyer of the Library.

Theodore C. Steele, Indiana artist whom President Bryan called "Master" of the painters in Brown County, received the LL.D. degree in 1916.

CHAPTER XVI

THE NEW GYMNASIUM, THE OLD OAKEN BUCKET, AND INDOOR FIELD, 1914 - 29

GYMNASIUMS

IN THE late eighties of the Jordan administration there was considerable agitation on the campus for the construction of a gymnasium for men. A few interested members of the faculty told the students they could have a gymnasium if they really wanted one. Thus a movement was initiated that resulted in the subscription of a small fund, used in renting and equipping a downtown hall as a gymnasium. This was a purely private affair supported by a small membership fee. It had the effect of emphasizing the widespread interest of faculty and students in such an addition to the campus.

Influenced by this obvious interest, the Board of Trustees, on August 1, 1889, instructed the Executive Committee to proceed with the erection of a Gymnasium Hall, according to plans and specifications before the board. There was some lag, however, in carrying out these instructions. Then, as now, it took more than an order of the board for a new building to materialize. The necessary appropriation had not accompanied the order to proceed with construction, and the vote had not been unanimous.

The Catalog of 1890–91 announced that early in the current year an appropriation was made for a gymnasium, for the special benefit of the young women students of the University. A large room in the basement of Wylie Hall had been equipped with apparatus adapted to the Sargent system of physical training and the Swedish system of educational gymnastics. But there was no announcement of erection of a gymnasium for men.

In March, 1891, the trustees appropriated $400 to be used in fitting up and equipping, in the basement of Owen Hall, a gymnasium for use of "the gentlemen students." Three months later (June, 1891) when it was discovered that the very definite order of March had not been executed, action was taken renewing the earlier instructions. The following day the Executive Committee reported that after a thorough investigation only one room in Owen Hall was found at all suitable for the purpose contemplated, and that was directly beneath the biology laboratory. Professor Charles H. Gilbert had protested strongly against use of this room for gymnasium purposes because of the noise and confusion disturbing his laboratory. The Committee, therefore, awaited the further instructions of the board.

Under these circumstances the board turned to construction of a separate building. At their meeting on November 7, 1891, a motion, made by Mr. Youche,[1] of Crown Point, was passed making an appropriation of $1,000 to be used for construction of a gymnasium for young men, on the campus of Indiana University, the money to be paid out of the contingent fund.

How this action was received on the campus is indicated in the following quotation from *The Indiana Student* for November, 1891: "One thousand dollars has been appropriated for a gymnasium for men to be erected and equipped immediately. The boys have reason to rejoice. We throw up our hats in appreciation of this promising act of the board." The equipment of this gymnasium, north of Owen Hall, as described in the Catalog of 1891–92, consisted of chest weights, dumbbells, Indian clubs, parallel bars, a vaulting horse, traveling rings, ladders, etc.

The Indiana Student of February, 1892 (p. 88) expressed the view that "The new Gymnasium under the efficient management of Mr. Zink[2] will add largely to our chances of success, and it is hoped we may make the spring of 1892 famous."

The baseball team of 1892 won all its games and it seemed that the optimistic outlook of *The Indiana Student* was to be realized. But in the fall of 1892, though Indiana beat Butler 11 to 10 in football, the team lost to Wabash by a lopsided score. Moreover, when it was announced in *The Indiana Student* that the University of Chicago was to build a gymnasium costing $200,000, the inadequacy of this first gymnasium began to be apparent. It was not until 1896

---

[1] For the past two years Trustee J. W. Youche had consistently led support of the gymnasium project.

[2] James L. Zink was a student at Indiana University, 1891–93, and later became proprietor of the Zink Gymnasium and Athletic Institute.

that a New Gymnasium was erected and the old Gymnasium 40 feet by 60 feet became a carpenter shop.[3]

When the first Gymnasium Hall was completed in February, 1892, there were 497 students in Indiana University. But the Catalog for 1895–96 shows that the number of students had increased to 879, an increase in four years of nearly 80 per cent. It is not surprising, therefore, that on August 6, 1896, the trustees ordered the erection of a new Gymnasium Hall. The name indicates the dual purpose of the structure. No campus auditorium was adequate for seating the student body for chapel exercises and this need was a decisive factor in hastening construction. The building was completed between August 10 and October 10, 1896.

This New Gymnasium, which stood east of Owen Hall, was a structure 66 feet by 135 feet, nearly four times as large as the first gymnasium. With the balcony on the two sides and the west end, it had a seating capacity (including balcony) of about 1,500. There was what at the time seemed to be a huge basement in which a few showers and wooden lockers had been installed. From time to time improvements were made. In September, 1910, a swimming pool was ordered constructed in the east basement. A metal roof was ordered over the pool, and 50 metal lockers were installed. In July, 1911, 100 additional lockers were ordered. Also it was ordered that a hot water heater and showers should be installed at a cost not to exceed $200.

But with the passing of years this gymnasium in its turn was becoming more and more inadequate.

On March 2, 1914, a committee of five boys (Hays Buskirk, Lester Corya, Halloway Crennan, Robert Harris, and Herbert Horne) appeared before the board in the interest of a new gymnasium. Two plans were discussed: one, a separate building to be located somewhere near Jordan Field; another, a wing to the Student Building.

Plans and costs were investigated, and on March 12, 1915, it was decided that the next building to be erected on the campus would be a Men's Gymnasium. Mr. Daggett, the architect, and a representative of the board visited a number of gymnasiums in neighboring states, with a view to getting the best ideas to incorporate in the Indiana University Gymnasium.

---

[3] This old building was located 68 feet north of Owen Hall, and three feet east of the extended west line of Owen Hall.

On the Dunn land purchased in 1914 stood the old brick Dunn residence.[4] The question of repairing this old Dunn homestead had been considered, but the expense would be prohibitive. Adjacent to the residence was an orchard. The trustees had once taken action for the preservation of the orchard. The site chosen for the new gymnasium was adjacent to the Dunn residence in part of this orchard.

At the meeting of the board in October, 1915, when the plans for the new gymnasium were approved, permission was given to the students to cut the trees on the proposed gymnasium site and pile them and all other obstacles on the site in a heap for a bonfire.

This was a joyous occasion. The students felt that they were helping clear the way for this long-desired structure. *The Indiana Daily Student* for October 25, 1915, gave an account of this event:

The celebration started at 9 o'clock in front of the Student Building with a concert by the University band and a short talk by President Bryan. Dr. Bryan and Dr. Burton D. Myers then led the march to the orchard. Once there, the men fell to work, while the band played and the women, under the leadership of Miss Luella Smith [later Mrs. Sam Hepburn], established headquarters for the commissary department in the old Dunn yard just off the northwest corner of the orchard.

The trees were cut and great piles were thrown up to be used for bonfires at pep sessions for succeeding football games with Washington and Lee, Northwestern, and Purdue. Faculty women served sandwiches and Eugene Kerr, the superintendent of buildings, brought out two barrels of water after an effort to make an old cider press function failed.

Late in December, 1915, the contract was let, and in March, 1917, on recommendation of Architect Daggett, the Gymnasium was accepted as completed. There had been a proposal that a stage and an indoor field be constructed along with the Gymnasium, but this was not done.

THE OLD OAKEN BUCKET, 1925

This history of the "Old Oaken Bucket," the now famous Indiana-Purdue football trophy, was written in the fall of 1939 by J. Frank Lindsey, of Chicago.

[4] The Dunn house stood about where the drive west of the Gymnasium is now located.

In 1925, Russell T. Gray was president of the Purdue Alumni Association of Chicago, while it was my privilege to preside over the activities of the Indiana University Alumni Club of Chicago. Wiley J. Huddle, Indiana, since deceased, suggested the informal meeting of a small group of Purdue and Indiana alumni of Chicago to discuss the possibility of undertaking worthy joint enterprises in behalf of the two schools. The suggestion was discussed with Mr. Gray, who promptly expressed favor. The following Chicago alumni committees were appointed:

For Purdue: Charles W. Morey, Macy S. Good, F. C. Haeske, Russell T. Gray. *For Indiana:* Wiley J. Huddle, Frederick E. Bryan, Clarence K. Jones, J. Frank Lindsey.

The Committee held its first meeting at the University Club of Chicago on the evening of August 31, 1925. After a general discussion of several meritorious alumni projects, Dr. C. K. Jones, Indiana, proposed the creation of a traditional football trophy to go to the winner of each annual Purdue-Indiana football game. The suggestion drew enthusiastic approval.

In order to serve the additional purposes developed in behalf of the two schools the following persons were added to the committees: *For Indiana:* John Weaver, Ben H. Drollinger. *For Purdue:* E. C. DeWolfe, Fritz Ernst.

J. Frank Lindsey, Indiana, was chosen chairman of the Joint Committee. Dr. Jones, Indiana, and R. T. Gray, Purdue, were named a committee to recommend a suitable trophy.

At a later meeting this committee "recommended an old oaken bucket as the most typically Hoosier form of trophy for the traditional Purdue-Indiana football game.

"That the old oaken bucket should be taken from some well in Indiana. That a chain should be provided for the bucket to be made of bronze block 'I' and 'P' letters, representing Indiana and Purdue. The school winning the traditional football game each year should have possession of the 'Old Oaken Bucket' until the next football game, and should attach the block letter representing the winning school to the bucket bail with the score engraved on the letter link. As the years go by there shall be a chain of 'P' and 'I' links attached to the bucket." The report was unanimously and enthusiastically approved.

Fritz Ernst, Purdue, and Wiley J. Huddle, Indiana, were charged with securing the old oaken bucket.

F. E. Bryan, Indiana, and Macy Good, Purdue, had the responsibility of getting the block "P" and "I" links.

F. C. Haeske, Purdue, and Ben H. Drollinger, Indiana, were named to engrave the presentation message appearing upon the plate on the outside of the bucket.

At the powwow preceding the Purdue-Indiana football game at Bloomington in 1925, Dr. Jones, as the father of the trophy idea, presented the story of the "Old Oaken Bucket" over a state-wide radio hookup.

The next day (November 21, 1925), as a part of the dedication ceremonies of Indiana Memorial Football Stadium, George Ade, Purdue, and Harry R. Kurrie, Indiana, carried the bucket between them to the center of the football field, and there jointly presented it to President Bryan, Indiana University, and President Elliott, Purdue University, as the future annual football trophy for the winner of the Purdue-Indiana football game.

As all will remember, the game that day resulted in a scoreless tie, with a block "IP" becoming the first link to go on the "Old Oaken Bucket's" bail.

These facts are taken from the minutes of the various meetings to which I have referred.

It will be remembered that out of this joint Indiana-Purdue Committee of Chicago Alumni came the State Schools Committee, which did very effective work before the Indiana General Assembly in behalf of the state schools in Indiana.

THE INDOOR FIELD, 1925–28

Back in 1915 when contracts were being let for the New Gymnasium an indoor field was considered, but the cost of both buildings was too great for the indoor field to receive favorable action at that time. Ten years later, however, the project was revived.

Professor William J. Moenkhaus, chairman of the athletics committee, appeared before the trustees, June, 1925, to present the idea of an indoor field adjoining the Gymnasium. Again in November, Dr. Moenkhaus presented the desirability of such an indoor field, the probable income, seating capacity, etc.

Judge Ora L. Wildermuth, who had taken his place on the board by alumni election in June, 1925, had become interested in a Fieldhouse, as the indoor field was now being called. The Judge visited the University of Michigan, the University of Illinois, and the University of Iowa to gather information regarding indoor fields.

The indoor field was an obvious need of which many had been aware. It was, of course, a perfectly logical companion structure to the Gymnasium and the Stadium which in the meantime had been dedicated (November 21, 1925). As in 1915, however, no money was available for this project.

During the Memorial Fund campaign of 1922, pressure groups had developed. The women constituted a group which urged insistently the construction of the women's dormitory. Another pressure group was urging the raising of a substantial fund for the erection of a Don Mellett Memorial building for the Department of Journalism. Among others a pressure group had developed in connection with the indoor field. As a result of the Memorial Campaign the alumni were becoming constructively articulate. Whoever first advanced the idea of a Fieldhouse, it is certain that the idea was taken up and vigorously pressed by the Chicago alumni group during the presidency of J. Frank Lindsey, who at that time was also a member of the Alumni Council.

Judge Wildermuth presented a plan for financing such a structure in July, 1926. Arthur Stonex, John Weaver, and J. Frank Lindsey were present at the board meeting and took part in the discussion as did also Director Z. G. Clevenger, Professors William J. Moenkhaus and Charles J. Sembower, and Bursar U. H. Smith.

There was no fund available for the erection of a Fieldhouse. When the women's dormitory was built, and supplementary funds were needed, the board ordered a bond issue which, however, covered only a small fraction of the total cost. The income from Memorial Hall assured the ready retirement of that comparatively small issue, and the bonds had a ready sale. For construction of an indoor field, the bond issue would have to cover the entire cost. The Indianapolis bankers at first could see no way of financing construction of a Fieldhouse, and the board at their July, 1926, meeting decided not to undertake this construction at that time. But the committee of the board heretofore appointed to consider plans and financing of the Fieldhouse was continued.

When in April, 1927, Judge Wildermuth presented general plans for a Fieldhouse and submitted a tentative proposition from one of Chicago's financial houses, interested by the Chicago alumni in financing its construction and equipment, Indianapolis bankers sharpened their pencils and developed increased cerebration.

As a consequence, on May 20, 1927, Judge Wildermuth, as ordered at the April meeting, presented tentative blueprints for a Fieldhouse as prepared by Architect Robert Frost Daggett; and Earl H. Richardson, on behalf of the City Trust Company, Indianapolis, submitted a proposition to furnish funds for its construction. The following day two other banking firms submitted propositions for financing the construction of the Fieldhouse and Judge Wildermuth and Provost Samuel E. Smith were appointed to investigate the three propositions and make recommendation to the board. Robert Frost Daggett was employed as architect and erection of the Fieldhouse was ordered.

On July 9 Judge Wildermuth made his report, and Mr. Daggett was ordered to complete detailed plans and specifications at the earliest date possible. On November 18, 1927, Mr. Daggett presented blueprints, which, with minor changes, were adopted. On January 25, 1928, detailed plans and specifications were approved and ordered advertised for bids. On February 1 the contract was awarded to Charles A. Pike, for $259,380. Judges Wildermuth and Batman were appointed to draw up the contract.

A number of responsible companies were on hand with propositions for financing this construction. Of these, the proposal of the Fletcher American Company of Indianapolis was accepted, and resolutions were adopted by the trustees setting forth the reasons for the issue of $300,000 of 4½ per cent bonds and the pledge of income of the Athletic Association.

On July 8, 1927, the board had approved the levying of a contingent fee of $2 a student, the proceeds to be set aside for payment on the Fieldhouse. In the resolutions adopted by the board this fee and a tax of 25 cents for each admission ticket (other than student tickets) were pledged irrevocably to the payment of the bonds. Furthermore, such part of gross receipts derived from athletics as might be necessary for retirement of the bonds was pledged for that purpose. These conditions the Fletcher American Company accepted.

On July 27, 1928, Mr. Daggett reported that work on the Fieldhouse was progressing satisfactorily and he believed that the job would be completed on time.

The Fieldhouse was dedicated on December 13, 1928. A dinner was served in the Men's Gymnasium at which President Bryan, in a powerful address, lauded contributors who had made possible approximately half of the buildings at Indiana University without cost to the state. He urged immediate favorable action in full on the University's appropriation bill in the 1929 legislature.

Judge Ora L. Wildermuth, Major John L. Griffith, Big Ten Athletic Commissioner, and Harry G. Leslie, Governor of Indiana, were among the speakers introduced by Athletic Director Clevenger, who acted as master of ceremonies. That Judge Wildermuth was chosen to represent the Board of Trustees on this occasion was a fitting recognition of his unfailing championship of the Fieldhouse throughout the three years of his membership on the board.

The diners adjourned to the Fieldhouse where a crowd of eight thousand had assembled to see the Crimson net men, co-champions of the West, play the dedicatory game against Pennsylvania, the eastern basketball champions. The Crimson won 34 to 26.

The minutes of the board actions taken on June 7, 1929, contain this paragraph:

In view of the strong and repeated assurances of the Athletic Board of Control and associated alumni that the athletic receipts would provide for the payment of the cost of the Fieldhouse, and in view of the fact that the Trustees upon those assurances have assumed the financial responsibility for the same, the Athletic Board of Control is asked to set aside from its gross receipts for the coming year the sum of $15,000 to be paid upon the Fieldhouse debt, and to make a budget for the athletic program which will be provided for within the balance of such receipts.[5]

The last of the Fieldhouse bonds were due and paid on April 1, 1942, thus vindicating in every detail the courageous action taken by the Board of Trustees fifteen years earlier.

The minutes of the Board of Trustees are records of actions taken by the board. The discussion leading up to action may have been long and spirited, but the minutes give no hint of tense situations that may have arisen or the humorous incidents that may have occurred. It is only by chance and on rare occasions that "off the record" matter becomes available. We have such a glimpse of the board in session, in the development of the plans for the Fieldhouse. We have stated that Judge Wildermuth was an enthusiastic advocate of the erection of a Fieldhouse, though no funds were available for that purpose. The Judge had worked hard on the project and had committed himself as to the cost of the building. When the bids were opened, however, it was learned that they were many thousands of dollars in excess of the Judge's estimate, whereupon Trustee Charles M. Niezer glanced at the Judge and raised a quizzical eyebrow.

[5] See Chap. XXXIV.

The Judge, however, was still confident. Leslie Colvin, a contractor of wide experience who had won the confidence of the board by the integrity of his construction, was present and was drawn into conference by the Judge. Together they worked out changes in plans which did not sacrifice utility, which did not detract from the appearance of the structure, but would greatly reduce construction costs.

When bids were again submitted on the architect's revised plans they were found to be within a few hundred dollars of the Judge's estimate, whereupon Trustee Niezer, in mock criticism, exclaimed: "I thought you posed as having some prestige in estimating costs of construction! Here you have missed it by $700!"

CHAPTER XVII

INDIANA UNIVERSITY, 1916 - 18

MILITARY TRAINING

ILITARY TRAINING at Indiana University, the most note-worthy development of the biennium 1916–18, was authorized reluctantly by the Board of Trustees in response to repeated petitions of the student body and recommendations of the faculty, based on the conviction that the involvement of the United States in the war that had broken out in Europe in August, 1914, was unavoidable.

At first the war had seemed so far away, and few, if any, of the millions of our people had any thought of our becoming involved. There were thousands of citizens of English descent in the United States, and other thousands, particularly in the Midwest, of German descent, but few of either group were war-minded. It is probable that a Gallup poll of the United States would have shown that sympathies were very evenly divided.

It was not long, however, until provocative incidents began to occur which led to our protest to both England and Germany. When the English Navy began to stop and search our ships we found it reminiscent of 1812, and lodged a vigorous protest. But when the German submarines began sinking our ships we were deeply angered and a remarkable shift in our sympathies began to take place. This shift continued as the American people were goaded by other and graver incidents until the student body was eager to join in helping stamp out the evil thing loose in Europe. Woodrow Wilson, however, kept the ship of state on an even keel, and on November 7, 1916, won his election to a second term as president of the United States, helped no doubt by the slogan: "He kept us out of war."

German submarine warfare had been begun early in 1915. People in America were shocked when in May, 1915, the *Lusitania* was sunk with hundreds of passengers, more than one hundred of whom were Americans.

As the school year 1915–16 got under way at Indiana University an occasional student dropped out, and later it was learned that he had crossed our northern border to join some Canadian unit in training. Within the faculty there were a number of men who had taken advanced degrees in German universities and had a high regard for German institutions and the German people. But some also had seen arrogant Prussian army officers and had misgivings at the thought of the Prussians running the German attack.

As the year 1916 began the conviction was growing among faculty and students that this European war was coming closer to our shores. They were coming to believe that our involvement was inevitable, and that their self-interest necessitated knowing as much as possible of military drill. By the time of the March, 1916, meeting of the trustees the call for military training had become so insistent that the President proposed consideration of the matter. Military training had been an elective in Indiana University in charge of Colonel James Thompson, Professor of Military Tactics and Civil Engineering, 1870–76. But now it was long forgotten. The trustees postponed consideration of the matter until the June meeting, when a resolution of the faculty that military training with a schedule of hours should be established at Indiana University was disapproved by a vote of 5 to 3.

In this and succeeding actions the trustees exercised the authority definitely assigned them in the legislative act establishing the University, nearly one hundred years earlier. They had concurred so often in recommendations of the faculty relating to curriculum that some had forgotten that final authority on course of study lay with the trustees.

The following day, June 13, the President inquired if a program of military training, calling for less time, would meet the approval of the board. Whereupon Mr. Corr moved to amend the faculty recommendation by striking out certain words and that when so amended the recommendation be approved. After full discussion this motion was carried 7 to 1. The board was never unanimously in favor of this innovation.

Though every effort was made for organization of the training now authorized by the trustees, there were incredible delays. The appointment of an Army officer to be in charge of drill had been promised readily enough, but the fall semester of 1916–17 slowly passed without any appointment being made for this important work.

With the beginning of the year 1917 the war situation grew rapidly more serious and on February 3 diplomatic relations with Germany were severed, whereupon President Bryan was notified that the arrangement for appointment of an Army officer in charge of military training at Indiana University of necessity would have to be canceled.

It was known that German spies were in America sending out information to U-boats regarding sailing dates of vessels and doing many acts of sabotage. Then on March 1, 1917, a message from the German government to its minister in Mexico, which had been intercepted, was published. The minister was instructed to ask Mexico to make an alliance with Germany promising in return that Germany would help Mexico in an invasion of the United States for recovery of Texas.

This confirmed the widespread view that in helping England and her allies we were helping ourselves avoid a future war with Germany. Millions were ready to fight and troops, for a time, were sent to the Rio Grande.

On March 5 *The Indiana Daily Student* quoted opinions of officers of organizations, class presidents, and representative men who urged immediate establishment of military training at Indiana University. Though war had not been declared, there was the growing conviction that the United States would be forced to enter the conflict in a short time.

Students and faculty were becoming very impatient with delays. On March 6 at a meeting of the faculty a plan was presented and approved for the immediate establishment of military training under drillmasters chosen chiefly from faculty and students. In the preparation and promotion of this plan, Professors Morton C. Campbell and Warren A. Seavey, of the School of Law, and H. Lester Smith, Dean of the School of Education, were particularly helpful. On the evening of that day a mass meeting, described by *The Indiana Daily Student* as the greatest in the history of the University, was held, in which loyalty to the nation and support of President

Wilson in this grave crisis were pledged, and approval of his policy of armed neutrality was expressed.

Resolutions were read by Lieutenant Kenneth P. Williams, of the Department of Mathematics, recently returned from the Mexican border. A storm of applause met the reading of these resolutions which, among other things, provided that the University should take such steps as might be necessary to prepare students for any eventuality which might arise.

The following day a recruiting office was opened and soon 350 students were enrolled. Four companies were formed under direction of Lieutenant Williams and began drilling five hours a week.

The Indiana Daily Student of March 20 carried the announcement that the government had detailed an officer, Captain Campbell King, to take charge of military science and tactics. Rifles and ammunition were requisitioned for the student companies.

When Captain King took command, Lieutenant Williams continued as officer of one of the four companies. Lieutenant Lewis B. Hershey, who, like Lieutenant Williams, had been on the Mexican border, matriculated in Indiana University during the second semester of 1916–17, and was placed in charge of another of the four companies. Lieutenant Hershey, three months later, like Captain King, was sent over to France. Both rose rapidly in the service. Captain King became a brigadier general and Lieutenant Hershey became Major General Hershey and in 1940 was placed in charge of selective service.

On the evening of April 2, 1917, a mass meeting was held in Assembly Hall for the organization of a battery of the First Indiana Field Artillery. Major Robert Tyndall and President Bryan addressed the student body. It was known that on that same evening President Wilson would address Congress and it was believed he would ask for a declaration of war against Germany. Therefore, after adjournment of the meeting in Assembly Hall, a considerable number of students and a few faculty men remained expecting any moment a report on the President's message.

Baker's *Woodrow Wilson, Life and Letters*[1] states that at about 8:30 p.m. President Wilson began his address before Congress in

[1] Vol. VI, p. 509.

which he asked for a declaration of war against Germany. But it was about 10 p.m. Central Standard Time when a report of the President's recommendation reached Assembly Hall. Immediately a line was formed by students marching up to the stage for preliminary enrollment for enlistment. It was four days later, April 6, that, by act of Congress, the declaration of war against Germany was made.

Two illustrations of the eagerness of the student body to enlist come to mind.

1. A student who had added strength to Indiana's line throughout the preceding football season came before the examining board for enlistment and was rejected under rules then in force, because he had an inguinal hernia. He left at once for an operation and in twelve days was back with a scar barely healed but technically eligible. His name was very German but his heart was unhesitatingly and wholly American.

2. Medical students were urged by Washington authorities to complete their medical course and qualify for medical service. But many withdrew from medical school and enlisted. Similar cases were numerous.

During the months following the declaration of war, equipment was gradually supplied and the military aspects of the campus multiplied. The following is a mere catalog of military developments up to June, 1918.

On April 10, 1917, a mass meeting was held for the purpose of encouraging enlistment in the Coast Guard Reserve and in the Regular Navy. A few weeks later (April 30) one hundred students and faculty members applied for admission to a reserve officers' training camp that was being organized at Fort Benjamin Harrison, and on May 10 eight students and two members of the faculty were accepted. Others were sent at a later day.

On May 3 *The Indiana Daily Student* printed the formal offer of all the resources of the University for the aid of the United States Government. These resources were classified as (1) personal services; (2) instruction applying to war conditions; (3) research; and (4) publicity.

There was the announcement on May 16 that fifty students had responded to the call for volunteers for immediate service in the ambulance corps in France. Enlistment of a second unit was called for through the office of Alumni Secretary Sollitt on May 22.

When in June, 1917, Captain King was sent over to France, the command of the one company on the campus during the summer session of 1917 reverted to Lieutenant Williams. Rifles, the first equipment received, were available for that summer session drill.

In June, 1917, the recommendation that Freshman and Sophomore men students be required to take military training at least three hours a week beginning September, 1917, was approved by the trustees, who were authorized to give bond for the arms and other equipment supplied by the government for military training.

The final War Department inspection of Battery F, First Indiana Field Artillery, formed on April 2, was held on the evening of June 25, and the unit was to be reported immediately to Washington. The battery received a mess fund of more than $500 from the women of the University and the town at a patriotic service held on Jordan Field on August 4, and was given a rousing send-off when they left on August 5 for Fort Benjamin Harrison. The battery sailed with the Rainbow Division on October 18.

At the same August 4 service a Red Cross and a University flag were presented to the University ambulance unit, then stationed at Allentown, Pa.

With the opening of the school year 1917–18 the military program was gathering momentum. The draft was on and drafted troops left for Camp Taylor (October 8). Military drill began on the campus the following week.

Leave of absence was granted (October, 1917) the following twenty-eight doctor members of the medical faculty[2] who had entered the service of the Army or Navy:

Edmund D. Clark, Frank F. Hutchins, Orange G. Pfaff, Alois G. Graham, Lafayette Page, Ernest DeW. Wales, John W. Sluss, Jewett V. Reed, Paul B. Coble, Charles E. Cottingham, Harrison S. Thurston, Frank A. Brayton, Lehman M. Dunning, Leonard A. Ensminger, Larue D. Carter, Elmer Funk-

[2] Eleven of these twenty-eight doctors went over with the Eli Lilly Base Hospital No. 32. The other seventeen went with other units. Still other members of the faculty of the School of Medicine who are not included here enlisted and served.

houser, Arthur E. Guedel, Charles D. Humes, Bernard J. Larkin, Leslie H. Maxwell, Robert M. Moore, Eugene B. Mumford, Joseph W. Ricketts, Louis H. Segar, Walter M. Stout, Frederick C. Warfel, Arthur F. Weyerbacher, J. Kent Worthington.

From the Bloomington campus fourteen faculty members went into service:

Morton C. Campbell, Warren A. Seavey, Paul V. McNutt, Kenneth P. Williams, Joseph A. Wright, Georgia E. Finley, Charles W. Snow, S. Frank Davidson, Arthur C. Krause, Michael J. Blew, George C. Hale, George R. Havens, Claude M. Bolser, J. E. P. Holland.

Courses in wireless telegraphy were begun on October 15. The second Liberty Loan drive went over the top on the campus. On November 22, 1917, the trainees on the campus toted guns for the first time. On December 7 orders were received requiring all medical students to enlist in the medical reserve corps and continue their medical course in preparation for service as physicians.

To provide time for drill at 9:30 a.m., hours for classes were changed to begin at 7:30. Captain King had been succeeded by Lieutenant Colonel Edwin J. Nowlen, and on January 11, 1918, he was succeeded by Captain Arthur T. Dalton. New uniforms were distributed to the trainees on March 27, 1918. As the close of the year drew near, speeded-up courses were announced (April 24) for the summer for medical students. On May 14 it was announced that enrollment in military instruction in the school year 1918–19 would constitute enlistment.

In June, 1918, President Bryan reported receipt of an order from the War Department to the effect that military instruction under officers and noncommissioned officers of the Army was to be provided in every institution of college grade which enrolled for this instruction one hundred or more able-bodied students over the age of eighteen. The necessary military equipment so far as possible was to be furnished by the government. In brief, this meant that military training authorized by the Board of Trustees in June, 1916, was now adopted by the Federal Government for all colleges.

Miss Georgia E. Finley, of the Department of Home Economics, was the first Indiana University woman to receive an appointment to service. She went as dietitian to Base Hospital No. 32, and was honored in the ceremonies for Battery F on August 4.

The effect of the war was being felt in many ways having no connection with military drill. The Library was finding it increasingly difficult to secure publications of German origin, which were about 40 per cent of its continuations. Evidence of the height of anti-German feeling is the protest which the war mothers of Bloomington filed in June, 1918, against the teaching of German in the University. The students themselves had gone far toward that end, for, although German had formerly been the foreign language chosen by a majority of students, enrollment in these courses had decreased to such a degree that although Professor Bert J. Vos, the Head of the Department, and Professor Carl W. F. Osthaus, the oldest member of the Department whose service was longest, were elected as members of the faculty for the year beginning August 1, 1918, it was with the provision that the election held only if the President judged that enough students had applied for German courses.

LEGISLATIVE SESSION OF 1917

In October, 1916, President Bryan submitted to the trustees matters for consideration in formulating their report to the Governor and Visiting Committee. A new governor would be elected in November to succeed Governor Ralston and take his seat early in January, 1917. The fundamental needs of the University were set forth as follows:

The Trustees are required by Law to make a report to the Legislature at this time, including a statement of requests: Following is a statement of the *needs* of the University which have been considered by the Trustees at former meetings:

I. BUILDINGS:
1. Building for education, vocational education, and home economics.
2. Auditorium.
3. Administration Building.
4. Nurses' home, power plant, and laundry at Robert W. Long Hospital.
5. New Medical Building. (The cost of this would be met in large part if the present medical building were sold.)
6. New power plant.
   Estimated cost—$1,000,000 to $1,250,000.

II. ADDITIONS TO BUILDINGS *ASKED FOR:*
  1. Addition to Wylie Hall.
  2. Addition to Owen Hall and animal house.
  3. Addition to printing plant.
  4. Wing to Library.
  5. Completion of Men's Gymnasium.
  6. Modification of Student Building auditorium to cure its acoustic defect.   Estimated cost—$182,000.

III. OTHER IMPROVEMENTS:
  1. Better seats in auditoriums.
  2. Grading for new athletic field and tennis courts.
  3. Telephone system.
  4. Equipment of cottage for home economics.
  5. Commons.
      Estimated cost—$16,000.

IV. EXPANSIONS *ASKED FOR:*
  1. School of commerce or professor of commerce.
  2. Professor of orthogenics.
  3. Professor of economic geology.
  4. Expansion of social service at Indianapolis.
  5. Expansion of Extension Division.
  6. Expansion of summer school budget.
  7. Expansion of stenographic service.
  8. Increase of Library funds.
  9. Expansion of medical service for students.
      Estimated cost a year—$43,500.

V. *REQUESTED* INCREASE OF SALARIES:
      Estimated at $23,600 plus some requests for increases without specified amounts.

No special appropriations were made by the 1917 General Assembly for the State Universities.

FIFTEENTH ANNIVERSARY OF PRESIDENCY OF WILLIAM L. BRYAN

The following tribute to William Lowe Bryan was prepared by a committee of the trustees and faculties of the University on the occasion of his fifteenth anniversary as President:

The Trustees and Faculties of the Schools of Indiana University desire to record their appreciation of the service of William Lowe Bryan as President of Indiana University, a service marked by unselfish devotion to the cause of education, sympathetic tolerance of the opinions of others, unfaltering loyalty to high ideals of citizenship, and a discerning vision of a true University.

As a further tribute a Memorial Fund—The Bryan Memorial Fund for War Relief of Enlisted Indiana University Men—was established by members of the board and of the faculties, and described in the board records as follows:

This fund has been started and now amounts to about $600, and it is the hope that it will exceed $1,000; the purpose is expressed in the title. Several things were considered in the way of a testimonial to President Bryan but it was the feeling of the Faculties that at this particular time this "War Relief Fund" would appeal to him more than anything else could do.

LIBRARY OF CONGRESS CLASSIFICATION

The Library of Congress classification for the University Library was adopted in June, 1918, for the following reasons advanced by President Bryan:

About twenty years ago the Library changed its classification from a standard classification, the Dewey Decimal, to the local system now in use. In doing so it gained certain minor advantages but on the total account lost very considerably through the adoption of a system that is nowhere else in use, that has a very inferior notation, and that is not closely subdivided. The case against it is set forth in Miss [Ida] Wolf's memorandum appended. These disadvantages have been felt for many years but I have hesitated to recommend a change because of the lack of a consensus among librarians as to a system that could be regarded as practically final. The development of the Library of Congress classification supplies us with such a system.

The President continued his argument for this change. He stated that the Library was feeling the handicap of a local and inferior classification. Some day a change would have to be made. The cost was estimated at $5,000, but the longer the change was put off the greater the cost would be.

THE FRESHMAN-SOPHOMORE CLASS SCRAP

The traditional rivalry between Freshmen and Sophomores had become an annual class scrap by the early part of the twentieth century. It began with pre-scrap activities such as hair cutting, ducking in Jordan River, etc. On scrap day the Freshmen were frequently victorious because of their greater numbers. In the excitement of the scrap, tempers rose and personal encounters were numerous. The administration had become much concerned over the possibility of serious personal injury of participants. After thoughtful consideration, it seemed desirable to retain the competitive feature of the scrap but to direct it into less dangerous but possibly more attractive forms.

Accordingly in 1916, in order to equalize the chances of the two classes, 176 able-bodied representatives were chosen from each class. The scrap consisted of six events: a shuttle race, a tug-of-war, two wrestling matches, and two pushball contests. For the last events, John W. Cravens and Burton D. Myers were umpires. A picture near page 160 gives an idea of the second pushball contest, in 1917.

Matters of Interest to Faculty and Students

Though the war in Europe was occupying the attention of administration, faculty, and students during this biennium, 1916–18, and though military training had been established and a new building for the School of Medicine was under consideration to meet the demands of the War Department for more doctors, miscellaneous matters of importance to the normal life of the University were receiving due consideration.

As a measure of the expansion of the medical social service work, Miss Henry reported (October, 1916) a list of 66 Indiana towns that had been visited during the past year. The social service workers had made 477 visits outside Indianapolis. Dean Ruby Mason reported the enrollment of 567 women in the fall of 1916.

Mr. Kessler, landscape architect, submitted a comprehensive plan for the campus.

The walls of the auditorium of the Student Building were treated for the purpose of curing acoustic defects of that much-used audience room.

Professor Van Hook, of the Department of Botany, who had been placed in charge of reforestation of the waterworks drainage area, reported in the fall of 1916 that 20,000 black cherry seedlings had been planted in the nursery and that 1,000 white ash would be transplanted to the waterworks area. Black walnut, hickory, and oak would be set out in the fall. In the spring, yellow poplar seedlings would be planted. The evergreen seedlings set out the previous spring were in excellent condition.

By March, 1917, 32,000 trees had been ordered as follows: 25,000 yellow poplar seedlings; 2,000 hard maple; 2,000 red oak; 3,000 pine, spruce, and fir.

A primitive six-hole golf course had been located on land later occupied by the Stadium and the parade ground which in 1945 became a trailer camp. Faculty members were charged $5 and students $1.50, the money to be used for maintenance of the course. Little work had been done toward transforming fields into fairways, but it served to stimulate an interest in the game, which led a bit later to the development of the beautiful 9-hole Country Club course south of Bloomington and to the 18-hole municipal course.

In June, 1917, Howard Sandison succeeded Robert I. Hamilton as trustee.

On the recommendation of Architect Daggett, the Men's Gymnasium was accepted as completed (March, 1917).

The first mass meeting in the new Gymnasium was held on October 5, 1917.

Professor Albert F. Kuersteiner died in June, 1917, and George D. Morris, Associate Professor of French, served during the following year as acting head of the Department of Romance Languages, in which capacity he also served in 1924–26.

Enoch G. Hogate, Dean of the School of Law, had become seriously ill and Professor Charles M. Hepburn was asked to serve as acting dean (March, 1917). At the same time Paul V. McNutt was selected as an instructor in law. When in June, 1918, Dean Hogate submitted his resignation, Professor Hepburn, the senior professor, was elected dean.

Mitchell Hall in 1918 was occupied by the Department of Music headed by Professor Charles D. Campbell, and was badly in need of repair. It was remodeled and rehabilitated at a cost of $800.

In June, 1917, plans and estimates were submitted by Miss Colburn, of the University of Chicago, for a cafeteria, which had been under consideration for some time. The changes in the Student Building, minor in character, suggested by Miss Colburn were made, and installation of a cafeteria was completed and ready for opening in the fall under the management of Miss Nola Treat.

In June, 1918, it was decided to rent a furnished house at an expense to the University of approximately $300 to be used as a practice house for students in domestic science.

At Commencement in June, 1918, Colonel Theodore Roosevelt gave the address. His subject was "Straightout Americanism." His powerful war address cannot be reproduced here but we may quote two sentences: "I love peace. I ask for preparedness, not because I wish war, but because I wish to avoid war."

Dean Carl H. Eigenmann in the middle of June, 1918, started on his third scientific expedition to South America to determine the origin of its fresh-water fishes, a problem that had intrigued him since his student days under Jordan in the early eighties. The American Association for the Advancement of Science and the National Academy of Sciences made grants-in-aid. Indiana University supported the expedition in various ways. The University of Illinois sent along a research fellow. On the recommendation of Theodore Roosevelt, Will Irwin of Columbus, Ind., underwrote the expedition so substantially that it was known as the Irwin Expedition. The very interesting report of this trip is found in the *Alumni Quarterly,* Volume VII, page 1.

William F. Book, who served as professor of educational psychology in 1912–13, returned in 1917 to head the Department of Philosophy and direct the psychological clinic. Professor Ernest H. Lindley resigned the headship of the Department of Philosophy that year to become president of the University of Idaho.

Chapter XVIII

INDIANA UNIVERSITY, 1918–20

Military Training

THE PRECEDING chapter tells the story of the organization of military training at Indiana University. The idea and procedure were not to be found in any book of rules of the War Department and the appointment of an Army officer to take charge of military drill was made only after a delay of eight months. But, once accepted, the idea developed rapidly.

At Indiana University interest in military training in the summer of 1918 centered to a considerable extent on the Reserve Officers' Training Camp being conducted at Fort Sheridan, to which men from many midwest colleges were sent. At the end of this camp, about the middle of July, the government decided to assemble a second camp (July 18 to September 16) to which sixty students and eight faculty members were sent. This second camp was called the S.A.T.C., the Student Army Training Corps, and it differed from the first camp, the R.O.T.C., in certain important respects, perhaps most important of which was that members of the first camp were not given commissions but were expected to assist in drill at their home colleges during the following year. Men who completed the work of the second camp successfully were given commissions. Among those were twenty-three Indiana University men, commissioned second lieutenants.

This work fortunately had come under the charge of Lieutenant Colonel Robert I. Rees, a very superior man who comprehended the potentialities of this S.A.T.C. With the experience gained at Fort Sheridan, the government announced a change which involved carrying this S.A.T.C. organization to every college that enrolled one hundred or more able-bodied men. Participation on the part of the college was to be voluntary. The colleges were to provide barracks and subsistence and were to be reimbursed at a rate to be agreed upon and made of record in a contract.

So the stage was set for military training at Indiana University in the fall of 1918. The opening of the fall session had been postponed from September 16 to September 23 to give the University opportunity to get barracks in readiness. Barracks were not just fraternity houses under a different name with a big banner carrying the number of the barracks. For illustration, the Phi Psi House, Barracks No. 2, had 111 soldiers, a number greatly in excess of normal occupancy.

The purpose of S.A.T.C., it was announced, was to give students the benefit of thorough military instruction under direction of the government and to prevent promiscuous enlistment of men under draft age, which threatened to deplete the colleges and universities of the country of great numbers of young men who, if they remained in school and received military training, would be fitted on graduation to enter officers' training camps and try for a commission, or go into the Regular Army as noncommissioned officers.

The procedure prescribed for the opening of the school year 1918–19, which, after three years on the semester plan, was changed to the term plan at the recommendation of the government, was as follows for men students: They were to register and enroll in fourteen hours of University courses approved by the government. Then all were given a physical examination. If they passed, their home induction board was requested to transfer papers and jurisdiction to the Monroe County board from which the student received his induction papers. These papers were filed with the commanding officer of the S.A.T.C. unit at Indiana University and the student became an enlisted soldier.

The ceremonial induction of the S.A.T.C. at Indiana University took place on October 1, when 1,2000 Indiana University students took the oath of allegiance to the United States flag. Men were assigned to barracks and the next morning they had their first mess. In addition to housing and food the soldiers received $30 a month. Thus to all intents and purposes Indiana University was an Army training camp.

The S.A.T.C. at Indiana University[1] consisted of three groups of students. There was the vocational group of 280 men (the numbers varied), who had come earlier, were fully equipped, and started on

[1] The 128 medical reserves and 8 sailors at Indianapolis were included in this unit.

their program. There was a naval unit of 80 plus, all in one barracks and under a naval instructor. Then there was the University unit of more than 900 men, who, in addition to the fourteen credit hours of University work, took eleven hours a week of military training.

Had the faculty been authorized to name the hours for military drill, the hours from 4 to 6 might have been assigned for that purpose. But the Army wanted and got the morning hours from 7 to 9 and the faculty made such adjustments as were necessary. For evening study period, companies were marched from barracks to some assigned lecture room where students made preparation for classes under supervision of a noncommissioned officer.

These men of the S.A.T.C. were not a deferred group but were subject to active duty as others of the same age. They were, however, a special group from an educational point of view and from their number selections were made for special training. Early in the fall forty-eight men had applied for entrance to officers' training camp. To be eligible to Infantry officers' training, the applicant must have had a high school education and be physically fit. To enter the Artillery a college education and a thorough knowledge of mathematics were required.

War Aims classes were begun. This course dealt with the remote and immediate causes of the war and the underlying conflicts of points of view as expressed in the governments, philosophies, and literatures of the warring countries on each side of the struggle.

The story of the influenza epidemic, October 10 to November 4, in which 350 were hospitalized, is told in Chapter XXXII.

The men who were to be sent to officers' training camp on November 13 were immunized for typhoid and smallpox. Additional clothing and overcoats were issued to all men sent to various training camps. Forty men were transferred to aviation school. Twenty were sent to Camp Gordon in Georgia for Infantry officers' training school, etc.

Then on November 11 came the Armistice. The ringing of the old Bloomington fire bell early in the morning of November 11 was the signal (prearranged) that the Armistice with Germany had been signed. Within a few minutes the streets were thronged with citizens and University students, including all the S.A.T.C. men, who marched under the orders of Captain Dalton. This celebrating in the wee sma' hours naturally subsided after a time, but was resumed early in the forenoon. University classes were dismissed and a holiday spirit prevailed. The S.A.T.C. of Indiana University joined in the coast-to-coast rejoicing which followed. There was a great parade of the entire S.A.T.C. and student body—with speeches by prominent men. Though firing had ceased, there was no certainty that it would not begin again, so training in all its details continued. Rifles were issued to Companies A and B, and to other companies later. New uniforms had been received and were issued. On November 12 men left for special training camp. With surrender of Germany came rumors of disbandment of S.A.T.C. and the well disciplined organization began to slow down. Transfer of soldiers was canceled except for aviation candidates. On November 15 the influenza ban was lifted for the S.A.T.C.

As chill crept into the mid-November air, overcoats and sweaters were requisitioned. Then under orders from Washington some S.A.T.C. camps were closed. Cases of influenza again developed. On November 22 the ban was again imposed, and on November 23, because of threat of another influenza epidemic, all week-end passes were canceled. Prophylactic vaccination was made available.

On November 27 notice was given that S.A.T.C. would disband December 21, until which date military classes were to continue. On November 30 demobilization was getting under way. On December 3 the influenza ban was lifted. Men were returning from camp. On December 6 it was announced that demobilization plans were completed and one hundred would be discharged each day.

With disbandment of S.A.T.C., the University authorities again took over the campus and student body. Athletics returned to the prewar basis. The R.O.T.C. was restored and announcement was made that there would be four hours of compulsory training under requirements of R.O.T.C. in the next semester.

It would take pages to record the services of various sorts rendered by the University with the help of the people of Bloomington during these months and the many services performed by members of the faculty, on and off the campus. The University received special commendation for its gardening projects. Acres of corn and potatoes had been planted on University land and tended by students and faculty. Hundreds of socks and sweaters were knit by University and town women, Liberty loan drives went over the top, French war orphans were adopted, etc. All told, it was a record of which Indiana University could be proud, made by the men who went across and those who stayed at home. And everyone hoped it would never have to be done again, that the world had been made safe for democracy.

The Indiana University Roll of Honor in World War I is found in the *Alumni Quarterly,* Volume VII, pages 145–55.

REPORT TO GOVERNOR AND VISITING COMMITTEE

At the meeting of the trustees in November, 1918, after full discussion of the needs of the University for the coming year, a committee consisting of Mr. Rose, Dr. Bryan, Mr. Fesler, Dr. Smith, and Dr. Emerson was appointed to confer with Governor James P. Goodrich with a view to getting his ideas concerning the requests that should be made to the legislature. It was the opinion of the board that among the needs of the institution which should be enumerated in the report to the legislature and the Governor should be the following:

1. Reimbursement to the University on account of certain added expenses due to the war situation.
2. Completion of the Medical Building ($150,000 on present building and $200,000 for its completion).[2]
3. Maintenance for the Hospital and Medical School.
4. Women's dormitories.

For information of Governor Goodrich, Visiting Committee, and the General Assembly, the President and Board of Trustees reported (in part) as follows:

We judge it proper to call attention to the extraordinary expenditures of the University for war service. A large part of all the activities of the University during the period of the war has been directly or indirectly in the service of the Government.

The following named members of the Faculty have given part or all of their time to war service in Indianapolis, Washington, or elsewhere:

[2] The entire building as planned called for $350,000. It was proposed to ask the legislature for this amount, $150,000 of which would be used to pay back money advanced by public-spirited citizens for the part of the building under construction.

J. J. Pettijohn . . . . Speakers' Bureau
R. E. Cavanaugh . . . . Assistant Secretary, Educational Section of State
Council of Defense
S. B. Harding . . . . Work in Washington
A. S. Hershey . . . . Work in Washington
L. S. Davis . . . . Publicity work in Indiana
Tobias Dantzig . . . . Experimental work on engine
H. L. Smith . . . . Work in Washington
B. J. Vos . . . . Special mission in connection with the United
States Embassy at The Hague
Logan Esarey . . . . Military training at Fort Sheridan
J. W. Piercy . . . . Military training at Fort Sheridan
C. M. Bolser . . . . Military training at Fort Sheridan
R. W. VanValer . . . . Military training at Fort Sheridan
G. G. Greever . . . . Military training at Fort Sheridan

The proportions of the salaries of the above named men paid during such absence in war service amounted to $11,673.73 for the past year.

Like all individuals and institutions, the University has had a very large increase in expenditures on account of war prices.

BUILDINGS

A new medical building was the first consideration of the President and trustees during the first half of this biennium. Other needs included in this report were the following:

1. *Power Plant:* The University has outgrown its present Power Plant. It will be absolutely necessary in the near future to begin erection of a new Power Plant. The Trustees contemplate a plan which will permit the construction of successive units which may be added to as the needs of the University require.

2. *A Building for Education, Vocational Training, and Domestic Economy:* The School of Education, which has for nearly thirty years made its contribution to the training of teachers in Indiana and which has grown from small proportions to an enrollment of many hundreds, is not at all properly housed, but is greatly hampered on every side by the lack of room. The difficulty has been greatly increased with the necessity of doing our part toward the preparation of teachers in Domestic Economy and Vocational Education. The Trustees feel keenly the need of providing these Departments with a proper place in which to do their work.

3. *An Administration Building:* The need for an Administration Building large enough to carry on the administrative work of the University has been recognized for many years and has been stated repeatedly to successive legislative committees. One has only to walk through the administrative offices on

any working day to see the extreme need for relief by the erection of a proper building.

4. *An Auditorium:* The University has not had for many years an Auditorium large enough to hold the entire student body, to say nothing of the larger audiences which assemble from time to time. The only place which we have for this purpose is the wooden building which formerly served as a men's gymnasium.

5. *The Library* is now used to its capacity. We should, as soon as possible, add a wing to complete the building.

6. *Women's Dormitories:* This is one of our most urgent needs.

7. *Nurses' Home at Indianapolis and Laundry in connection with the Robert W. Long Hospital:* The State Accounting Board two years ago recommended that the State appropriate money for these necessary additions to the Robert W. Long Hospital.

No appropriation was made for items 1 to 7. How money was made available for a new medical building is explained later.

A state tax levy of 7 cents on each $100 of taxable property of the state for the benefit of the state educational institutions was changed by action of the legislature of 1919 to 2.8 cents. Of this income, Indiana University received two-fifths. Any unexpended balance at the close of the fiscal year was available for building and other purposes subject to approval of the State Finance Board. This reduced tax rate still yielded a little more than the 7-cent tax had yielded a year earlier, for property values had been raised. This act of 1919 repealed everything in conflict with it and was so comprehensive that a special committee of the board was appointed to ascertain at once its effect on the University.

THE NEW MEDICAL SCHOOL BUILDING

Since the union of all the old medical schools of the state in 1908, the Indiana University School of Medicine at Indianapolis had occupied the building of the former Indiana Medical College at the northwest corner of Senate and Market streets. This was a large, four-story building erected in the middle nineties, just before the remarkable development in medical education which began in the first years of the twentieth century. The building, though of recent construction, could not have been more out of date if one hundred years old. The north elevation was an almost unbroken brick wall. Rooms were lighted from the east, south, and west. The anatomy laboratory was the only one for which special provision had been made. To modernize the structure would have been expensive and unsatisfactory in the end.

The educational committee of the Medical School, consisting of Drs. Emerson, Barnhill, Burckhardt, Clark, Gatch, Hurty, Hutchins, Lyons, Moenkhaus, Moon, Morrison, Myers, Oliver, Turner, Wishard, and Wynn, meeting with President Bryan at the opening of the fall semester, 1916, discussed the need of a new building and considered whether to ask the legislature for an appropriation. It was reported that the doctors of the state were taking the initiative in urging legislators to make an appropriation for a new medical building. So this committee recommended that the need of the University for this new building should be presented to the State Medical Association. This idea was approved by the Board of Trustees, and Dr. Edmund D. Clark was chosen as chairman of a legislative committee, with full power to select the other members.

Dr. Clark's committee presented a strong resolution to the House of Delegates at the annual meeting of the Association at Fort Wayne, September 28, 29, 1916. The result was this statement by the organization:

We favor the adequate equipment of the Department of Medicine and Surgery at Indiana University both as to buildings and other equipment, so as to render it as efficient as similar institutions in other states. We recommend that the members of this association urge upon their legislators the necessity for the appropriation of such money as may be necessary for this purpose.

Dr. John Oliver, Professor of Surgery, was elected president of the State Medical Association for 1917, so the continued active support of that body was assured.

Since there were, within a five-hour railway trip of Indianapolis, six medical schools having physical facilities much better than those of Indiana University, the comparison of physical plants was made by many students to the disadvantage of this institution. But what had been poor soon became still more inadequate when a fire on December 7, 1916, which had caught from an incubator in the pathology laboratory, destroyed most of the fourth floor of the old building at the corner of Senate and Market. All things considered, the trustees in December, 1916, were of the opinion that $400,000 should be asked of the legislature for a new medical building at Indianapolis. But after repeated conferences with the Governor it was decided to introduce a bill making provision for only $350,000 for this purpose.

Their bill, thus drawn, was reported favorably from committee and passed to second reading, where it was held up until near the close of the session (1917). This bill had the support of the Indiana State Medical Association. The legislature of 1917 was favorably disposed, as will appear later. On February 3, 1917, diplomatic relations with Germany were severed and the need of physicians for the Army if the United States became involved in the European war would be very great. The trustees were worried and ten days after diplomatic relations with Germany were severed a meeting of the board (February 10, 1917) was called in Indianapolis. On the afternoon of that day the entire board went to the Statehouse for a conference with Governor Goodrich to urge the need of the new medical building. The influence of the Governor was sought in expediting the passage of this measure through an assembly known to be favorable. Even the *Indianapolis News,* one of the most conservative papers in matters involving appropriations and tax increase, joined in asking for more adequate quarters for the School of Medicine.

Three days before the close of the legislative session the bill passed the House by a vote of 86 to 5 and under suspension of rules it passed the Senate by a vote of 40 to 1. But the Governor exercised his right not to receive the bill on the excuse that the state of the treasury did not justify his signature.

On April 6, 1917, the United States declared war on Germany. As the year wore on and enlistment of medical personnel grew, the need for an increasing number of physicians and the desirability of speeding up medical courses was emphasized by the War Department. The need for an adequate medical plant was therefore no longer merely a matter of University and state interest, but had come to be a part of the problem of national defense. In order that the Medical School and the state of Indiana might fulfil their obligation to provide their full quota of doctors, a new medical building became a necessity. The problem of financing construction of such a building was considered from every angle in every meeting of the trustees.

With a favorably disposed General Assembly in 1917, the likelihood of passage of a bill providing for a new medical building had seemed so great that with a need so imperative the trustees had authorized Architect Robert F. Daggett to prepare plans. In June, 1917, the tentative plans were adopted and construction was to proceed to the extent of available funds. Since available funds were wholly inadequate, this action merely gave the "go sign" when adequate funds should be available. There was an abiding faith that the necessity would open a way. Mr. Daggett was instructed also to prepare plans for power plant, laundry, and cold storage as part of the Medical School plans to be submitted to the Governor by the educational committee of the School.

Governor Goodrich had finally realized that it was not merely a need of Indiana University that was at stake. He had written President Bryan stating that the Finance Committee appointed by the last legislature had decided that they could appropriate $130,000 to the State University for use in erecting a Medical School building and he hoped to increase this total to $150,000 from his contingent fund. A few days later, on March 7, 1918, the Governor again wrote to President Bryan stating that he had overlooked certain items authorized for other institutions and that this would reduce the amount available for a Medical School building to $125,000.

After a general discussion of the proposition in the letters of Governor Goodrich, it was decided that the board should agree to accept the proposal of the Governor to furnish funds to erect the building, providing that the Governor accepted certain modifications of the conditions named in his letter, as might be suggested by the trustees.

The sum of $125,000 was far from sufficient for the construction and equipment of an adequate Medical School building. The trustees, with the approval of the Governor, had prepared plans for a medical building. The best bid for this building was $386,519. Bids were also taken on a part of the building, the best bid being $238,-574.75. In order that construction might proceed as a public necessity and as a war necessity, Governor Goodrich in June, 1918, proposed to the trustees that he ask a number of other public-spirited citizens to join him in advancing credit of $175,000, stating that he would ask the legislature at their next session (1919) to purchase the present Medical School building. This was done and the trustees accordingly let the contract for the part of the building at $238,574.75, on June 8, 1918.[3] Construction was begun without delay.

The twenty-two men who joined with the Governor in financing construction of the Medical School building did so on condition that the Governor should lend his support to a bill, to be introduced in the next meeting of the General Assembly, January, 1919, which would provide a state appropriation for this building and thus release the guarantors. In his message to the legislature of 1919 Governor Goodrich recommended that the state purchase the old Medical School Building at the corner of Market Street and Senate Avenue, immediately west of the Statehouse, for $200,000, this sum to be applied to the fund for a new building for the School of Medicine at Indianapolis.

While this recommendation was under consideration the Supreme Court of the state handed down a decision which caused a change in the situation. This decision was to the effect that Purdue University was entitled to special annual appropriations amounting to $121,000 which had been paid previous to the year 1913 and which had not been paid under the law of 1913, which provided seven cents on the hundred dollars for the benefit of Indiana University, Purdue University, and the Indiana State Normal School. The trustees of the University did not bring suit at the time Purdue started legal proceedings, since they were assured that any final action taken with reference to Purdue University would be taken with reference to Indiana University also. Eminent legal counsel, as well as the general public, felt that the appropriation of $65,000 annually to the Medical School and the Robert W. Long Hospital as provided by the legislature of 1913 was of the same character as the special appropriations for Purdue University. This view was confirmed by the Indiana Supreme Court decision.

In view of these facts, Governor Goodrich and the trustees of both institutions agreed upon a compromise. By the terms of this compromise Indiana University was to receive $165,000 and the annual appropriation of $65,000 was to continue. The legislature in its closing days approved this compromise and made an appropriation for Indiana University of $230,000 ($165,000 and $65,000).

[3] The contract for the building was let to Leslie Colvin.

By this action the men who came to the rescue of the Medical School were reimbursed and relieved of any further financial responsibility. Their public-spirited action is worthy of special record. Of the twenty-three men the following were from Indianapolis: Governor James P. Goodrich, James A. Allison, Arthur V. Brown, H. F. Campbell, Eugene H. Darrach, Thomas C. Day, Fred C. Gardner, Edgar H. Evans, Fred C. Dickson, John H. Holliday, J. I. Holcomb, L. D. Huesmann, Hugh McK. Landon, Josiah K. Lilly, Sr., James W. Lilly, W. C. Marmon, and S. E. Rauh. Those from other parts of the state were: George Ade, Brook; F. C. Ball and Theodore F. Rose, Muncie; A. V. Conradt, Kokomo; Winfield T. Durbin, Anderson; and William G. Irwin, Columbus.

Contracts for about $240,000 had been let for the first unit of the building and its equipment. The structure was located about two hundred feet northeast of the Robert W. Long Hospital. The building was completed in the summer of 1919 and ready for occupancy at the opening of the fall semester.

The entire contract for the Medical School Building amounted to $257,699.32. The final payment on the building was made in October, 1919.

A Girls' Dormitory and a Practice House

In the fall of 1919 a contract was made with Colonel Theodore J. Louden for the rental of what was henceforth known as Residence Hall, corner of Forest Place and Third Street, to be used as a dormitory for women. Miss Florence M. Bond, Social Director in charge of the Hall, proved to be a most valuable addition to the life of the young women at the University.

Residence Hall Annex, 411 Henderson Street, was also leased and put in repair with the privilege of renewal of lease for four additional years.

Dean Agnes Wells reported in March, 1920, that Residence Hall had been a great success, but that the Annex had not been so successful. The Annex building was old and out of repair. Its use was discontinued after two years. Dean Wells recommended the securing of four houses to be used as additional dormitories for women students.

It was necessary to spend $4,000 to put Residence Hall in shape to meet the requirements of the state building inspector and state fire marshal.

For several years the Department of Home Economics had recommended securing a house to be used as a practice house. In November, 1918, $600 was appropriated for maintenance of a house (815 East Seventh Street) which had been secured for this purpose in accordance with board action taken in June.

The Centennial

As the centennial year of the University approached, William C. Langdon, author of the successful 1916 pageant, was invited to prepare a pageant. In March a budget of $6,000 was approved for this purpose.

This pageant was given first on Wednesday, June 1, 1920, and *The Indiana Daily Student* of June 2 stated that it was pronounced a great success by all who witnessed it. The whole performance lasted about an hour and forty minutes. The second performance was given on June 2, at 4 p.m.

In March, 1920, the trustees considered whether or not the centennial program should include a drive for money. It was ordered that a letter be sent to a large group of graduates to get their ideas upon this point. The letter was to be prepared by President Bryan and Alumni Secretary Humphrey M. Barbour.

The Alumni Association in 1920 revived a movement for a Memorial Fund campaign and set the goal at $250,000, a goal which was later raised to a much higher figure.

Foundation Day meetings, January 20, 1920, in the centennial year, were of unusual interest. The Foundation Day address at the University was delivered by Jacob Gould Schurman, President of Cornell University. The exercises opened with the Foundation Day Ceremonial, first used in 1916, written by William C. Langdon with music composed by Charles D. Campbell, Head of the Department of Music.[4]

A remarkable feature of Commencement in the centennial year

---

[4] The story of the writing of the music for the "Hymn to Indiana" is found in the *Alumni Quarterly*, Vol. VII, p. 366.

was the presence and participation in the program of the four Presidents of the past forty-five years, 1885–1920. They were: David Starr Jordan, 1885–1891; John M. Coulter, 1891–1893; Joseph Swain, 1893–1902; William Lowe Bryan, 1902–1920. Their addresses are found in the *Alumni Quarterly* for July, 1920, as a part of the Centennial Commencement article.

The degree Doctor of Laws was conferred upon President Joseph Swain, Professor John M. Coulter, Dean Horace A. Hoffman, and Enoch Albert Bryan, Commissioner of Education in Idaho, at this Commencement.

A SCHOOL OF COMMERCE AND FINANCE

Since the first year of his presidency, Dr. Bryan had in mind the establishment of a school of commerce and finance. Courses were added from time to time to the Department of Economics and Sociology. In 1919 this work was expanded and in March, 1920, the trustees decided to increase the number of courses, coordinate and organize them as a separate school. William A. Rawles was appointed dean of this School of Commerce and Finance. The story of the development of the School of Business, as it is now called, is told in Chapter XXXVIII.

COUNTY SCHOLARSHIPS

At the legislative session of 1919 a law[5] was enacted amending earlier legislation providing for admission of two students from each county, fee free. The trustees at their meeting in June ordered that the University admit students under the provisions of this law, and the Bursar was requested to have a conference with the State Board of Accounts to get their opinion as to the best method of administering the law. This law, at start, did not operate in a desirable manner. The appointments were at first political and were often issued to students of low ability and accomplishment and no financial need. Later (1935) this law was amended[6] and appointments were made on a scholarship basis, by the trustees and faculty of Indiana University.

[5] *Indiana Laws,* 1919, pp. 735, 736.
[6] *Indiana Laws,* 1935, p. 131.

FACULTY SALARIES

The increase in the cost of living which followed World War I had practically wiped out the small increases in salaries that had been made a few years earlier and had created a problem in educational institutions throughout the United States.

The President in June, 1919, addressing his Board of Trustees, cited an example of an instructor at Indiana University who had been receiving $1,700 and had left to take a nonacademic position at a salary of $3,000, and had later been raised to $3,600. He cited the case of an instructor at the University of Chicago who was being considered for a $3,000 professorship at Indiana University but who had been offered a $10,000 position as an efficiency expert in a great printing establishment in Chicago. The President called attention to the fact that all schools of every grade in the country confront the same difficulty. In concluding he made a strong case for a substantial increase in salaries for the faculty:

> The men whose salaries are highest are by reason of the high cost of living in the same position they would have been ten years ago with salaries one-half the present amount. Owing to the high cost of living those receiving lower salaries, especially the married men, are suffering great hardships in many cases. The country over, brilliant young men who could make the strength of the faculty of the future are being drawn into other pursuits.

MATTERS RELATING TO FACULTY

The biennium 1918–20 includes the period immediately following the close of World War I during which there were many board actions of great importance to the faculty and the University, some of which are the following:

The trustees in January, 1919, approved the recommendation of the law faculty that discharged soldiers of six months of service in the Army or Navy, with four years of high school but less than two years of college work, should be admitted to Law School on probation. If at the end of the first year they had attained an average grade of "C" they were to be considered eligible to become candidates for the LL.B. degree.

Miss Agnes E. Wells, of the University of Michigan, on September 16, 1918, was elected dean of women to succeed Dean Ruby E. C.

Mason, who resigned to accept a similar position in the University of Illinois. Miss Wells served with rare good judgment and tact for nearly two decades.

Amos S. Hershey, Head of the Department of Political Science and well-known authority on international law, was chosen as technical adviser in the Peace Conference, 1919.

In the early fall of 1919 Captain Dalton was succeeded by Major Robert E. O'Brien, who assumed charge of military science and tactics with the title of professor.

B. Winfred Merrill was appointed to succeed Charles D. Campbell, who died March 29, 1919, as professor of music and director of the Department of Music, for the year beginning August 1, 1919.

Of the many faculty members, alumni, and students who went "over there" during the war, one faculty member, Dr. Paul Coble, and fifty-four alumni and students did not come back. A memorial tablet in honor of Dr. Coble was placed on the wall of the main hallway of the School of Medicine Building at Indianapolis, and a tablet containing the names of alumni and students, the gift of the class of 1919, was placed in the main hallway of the University Library.

The United States Interdepartmental Social Hygiene Board had made a proposition (July, 1919) to Indiana University, offering to establish a Department of Hygiene here, for which an appropriation of $6,200 annually for two years would be furnished by the government. The board accepted the offer, and Clarence E. Edmondson was appointed director.

Governor Goodrich in September, 1918, appointed Professor William N. Logan as chief of the Division of Geology in the newly created Conservation Commission.

In October, 1919, Dean H. Lester Smith was appointed director of the summer session, succeeding in that post Will D. Howe, Head of the Department of English, who had resigned. The summer session had grown to be a feature of the school year of great importance, largely attended. The appropriation for 1920 was fixed at $42,500.

Clarence E. Edmondson was appointed dean of men. He handled many difficult situations with great tact.

On October 28, 1919, Horace A. Hoffman was appointed vice-president of the University, becoming the first vice-president to be appointed since the death of George L. Reinhard. In March, 1920, the President submitted to the trustees the resignation of Dean Hoffman to take effect August 1, 1920, and said:

The departure of Dean Hoffman is a great calamity for the University. We have no choice but to accept the resignation.

I recommend that a letter be sent to Dean Hoffman expressing the thanks of the University for his many years of devoted service.

An appropriate resolution to Dean Hoffman was recorded in the minutes of the trustees.

When Professor Will D. Howe, Head of the Department of English, resigned in 1919, Professor Henry T. Stephenson was appointed to fill the post. Professor Elijah C. Hills, Head of the Department of Romance languages since the fall of 1918, received appointment as corresponding member of the Royal Spanish Academy, regarded as one of the highest honors ever paid to a member of the Indiana University faculty. There were only two foreign members of this society, and only thirty-six members of the Academy in Spain.

In March, 1920, Amos Butler, Secretary of the State Board of Charities, was appointed nonresident lecturer in applied sociology.

Professors Selatie E. Stout and David A. Rothrock (June, 1920) were elected deans of the College of Liberal Arts, Professor Stout to have seniority. At the same time Dr. Burton D. Myers was appointed assistant dean of the School of Medicine.

RELATING TO THE BOARD OF TRUSTEES

President Bryan reported (July, 1919) the death of Trustee Sandison on July 1, after an illness of several months, and the election of Charles M. Niezer by the State Board of Education for the unexpired term.

Theodore F. Rose, who had been president of the board since 1916, died suddenly in his home in Muncie, September 6, 1919. George Ball, of Muncie, was elected by the State Board of Education to succeed him.

At the October, 1919, meeting of the trustees, James W. Fesler was unanimously elected president of the board to succeed Mr. Rose. Dr. Samuel E. Smith was elected vice-president.

MISCELLANEOUS

The American Council on Education had been organized as a war measure, as a coordinating body for educational institutions and associations of every sort. The recommendation of President Bryan (October, 1919) that $500 be appropriated for the American Council on Education was approved. Dr. B. D. Myers, of the School of Medicine, represented the Association of American Medical Colleges on this Council for a term of years.

Miss Jane Addams was a special Convocation speaker at the University, March 1, 1920.[7]

It was decided to admit five Latin-American students to the College of Liberal Arts of Indiana University without payment of any fees except laboratory and other similar fees.

On request of Professor James M. Van Hook, an appropriation of $157.75 was made to purchase young trees for the reforestation of the waterworks area. Professor Van Hook was authorized to employ two men in the fall and two men in the spring to aid in the planting of trees.

At the June, 1919, meeting of the trustees, the block of land immediately west of the Men's Gymnasium was purchased.

[7] See editorial, *The Indiana Daily Student,* March 2, 1920.

CHAPTER XIX

ESTABLISHMENT OF THE SCHOOL OF MUSIC, 1921

By Barzille Winfred Merrill

MUSIC AT INDIANA UNIVERSITY IN EARLY DAYS

NOTWITHSTANDING the fact that music is the last of the arts to appear in the culture of a people, and that musical understanding is given to the very few, it seemed to me that any man of broad enough culture to be chosen as head of a university would be one who would know that music has a most important place in education. Therefore in preparation of the story of the development of music at Indiana University I first made a most exhaustive (and exhausting, yet highly instructive) study of the lives and writings of Indiana's presidents and a few faculty members to get at their thoughts on the subject and to find the reason why music was so late in coming to this university as a recognized and authorized subject of the curriculum.

Baynard R. Hall in *The New Purchase*[1] tells us that shortly after being elected as the first professor and sole faculty member of the Indiana Seminary he

set out for Louisville to lay in goods, and also to bring out for our school purposes, a piano. Now this was the very first that "was ever heern tell of in the Purchus!" and hence no small sensation was created, even by the bare report of our intention. Nay, from that moment, till the instrument was backed up to our door to be removed from the wagon, expectation was on tiptoe, and conjecture never weary. "A pianne! What could it be? Was it a sort a fiddle-like—only bigger, and with a powerful heap of wire strings? What makes them call it a forty pianne?—forty—forty—ah! yes, that's it—it plays forty tunes!"

Some at Woodville [Bloomington] knew well enough what a piano was, for there, as elsewhere, in the far west, were oddly congregated, a few intelligent persons from all ends of the earth: but these did all in their power to

[1] Pp. 260, 261, 276.

mislead conjecture, enjoying their neighbor's mistakes. After a narrow escape of being backed, wagon and all, into the creek, . . . and notwithstanding the roughness, or as my friend, Lawyer Cutswell used to say, "the asperities" of the road, the instrument reached us, *and* in tune,—unless our ears were lower than concert pitch. At all events, we played tunes on it, and vastly to the amazement and delight of our native visitors; who, considering the notes of the piano as those of invitation, came by day or night, not only around the window, but into the entry, and even into the parlour itself, and in hosts; Nor did such ever dream of being troublesome, as usually it was a "sorter wantin' to hear that powerful pianne tune agin!" but often the more curious "a sort o' wanted the lid tuk up like to see the tune aplayin,' and them little jumpers (dampers) dance the wires so most mighty darn'd powerful smart!"

All this was, indeed, annoying, yet it was amusing. Beside, we might as well have bolted the store, and left the Purchase, as to bolt our door, or quit playing; and beyond the ill-savor of such conduct in a backwoods republic, it would have been cynical not to afford so many simple people a great pleasure at the cost of a little inconvenience and some rusting of wires from the touches of perspiring fingers.

This piano, now in the museum of Indiana University School of Music, is one of the earliest pianos made in America. Nine years after it was bought by Professor Hall it was acquired by Joshua O. Howe, one of the University's first trustees, and for eighty-nine years it remained in the Howe family. In 1851 it passed to James Howe, the oldest son. After his death in 1902 it was shipped to Vicksburg, Miss., by Mrs. Ellis Polk and given to her daughter, Mrs. George Roberts, who bequeathed it to the University on her death. It was made in 1820 by Geib and Walker, No. 23, Maiden Lane, N.Y.

Professor Hall has also much to say in his book about the violin, or fiddle, as it was commonly called (is still called, and always will be called by those who love their instruments) and relates a story showing one of the superstitions surrounding it:

Mr. Cutswell, among other matters, was no mean performer on the violin; and on one occasion, at a private concert at my house, forgetting his usual caution, he entertained me with an anecdote about his fiddle and his bishop. For be it known, that like other politicians, Mr. C. was a theoretical member of a religious people, who looked on fiddle playing as on the sin of witchcraft— although I do not know whether he had ever received the rite of confirmation; yet nothing but his high standing saved him from an excommunication, that out there would speedily have been visited on a *poor* player. Still his Bishop was a faithful shepherd's dog, and hesitated not to growl and bark, if he did to bite; being, also, one who prayed *for* men sometimes by name, and *at* them often by description. And so he contrived once to pray *at* Mr. Cutswell's fiddling or rather *against* his *fiddle;* and nothing could ever so belittle that instrument as this preacher's periphrastic abuse of that curious compound of catgut, rosin, and horsehair.

"I was present," said Mr. Cutswell, laying down his fiddle and bow upon our piano,—"some few evenings since, after the discharge of my legal duties at the courthouse—present, Mr. Carlton [Hall], in the prayer-room of our chapel, a large concourse of members being congregated for the customary weekly devotions. Among others in the apartment, was our venerable Bishop. He is a good and worthy man, sir; but *sub rosa* not wholly exempt from prejudice. Indeed, as to music generally, but more especially that of the violin, he entertains the most erroneous sentiments; and I fear that he regards both myself and my instrument with feelings of acerbity. In the course of his prayer this evening, he contrived to administer to myself in particular; but also to you, Mr. Carlton, and all other gentlemen that handle the bow, the following very severe and appropriate admonition and in the exact words I now quote:

"'Oh! Lord! ah—I beseech thee to have marcy on all them there poor sinners what plays on that instrumint, whose sounds is like the dying screech of that there animal out of whose intrils its strings is made!'"[2]

Of music during Andrew Wylie's administration as first president of Indiana College little information is available. Dean David D. Banta[3] tells us that at the reception for President Wylie:

Between the speeches the flutist and the fiddler played their most enlivening airs, such as "White River," "Fire in the Mountain," "Jay Bird," and "Bonaparte Crossing the Alps," the fiddler keeping the time by the pat of his foot, in which exercise all the boys and a good many of the citizens gleefully joined.

Of the June exhibition of 1832, held in the newly built Presbyterian Church, he says:

One grim old carpenter engaged upon the work, who was a Presbyterian as well and held that the fiddle in the church was an abomination, declared his unwillingness to lose his day's work. The exhibition could go on if its promoters chose, but he was going on also; and so he planed away. . . . Presently the procession from the college, composed of musicians, faculty, officers, students, and citizens came filing in. There was a triangle, a fiddle, a bass viol, a drum, and a clarinet. James Whitcomb, a brilliant young lawyer of the town and subsequently a governor, a United States senator, and commissioner of the General Land Office at Washington, played the fiddle. John Orchard, one

---

[2] Hall, *op. cit.*, p. 276.
[3] J. A. Woodburn, *History of Indiana University, 1820–1902*, pp. 53, 86.

of the proprietors of the Orchard House and a pillar in the church, played the bass viol; and Austin Seward blew on the wind instrument. Who struck the triangle and who the drum, the muse of history does not record.[4]

Professor Ebenezer N. Elliott wrote of this same year:

Our trustees . . . found the College . . . flourishing, the new building finished, the chapel complete with rostrum and orchestra, a fine brass band, two society Halls, and (best of all) a large increase of students.[5]

This is the first mention of a band in the archives of the University. Of the Commencement of 1833 Professor Elliott says:

The Commencement of 1833 that year was held in the new chapel, and the orchestra was composed of two flutes, one of them cracked. Imagine the discord. Dr. Wylie whispers to a professor, "What makes more noise than a pig in a gate?" Reply, "I give it up." The doctor, turning his thumb towards the orchestra, says, "Two of them."[6]

In a "Discourse on Education," delivered before the state legislature in 1850, President Wylie said:

Except the grace of God, nothing tends more to soften the asperities of human character, to sweeten the temper, refine the manners, and even purify the heart, than a judicious attention to the several fine arts. This tendency was beautifully set forth by the ancients in those fables of mythology, which represented the power that music and poetry, for instance, are capable of exerting over the hardest and most intractable natures.

Unluckily, a musician would have starved in Bloomington, for even after Dr. Wylie's death in 1851 there were but fourteen people listed as musicians in the whole state of Indiana.

On March 26, 1849, the program of the Philomathean Society shows the following numbers played by the University band: "Bealoth," "Washington's March," "Santa Anna's March," "Kenmuir's Awa,'" "Schumacher's Waltz," "Union," "Star Spangled Banner."

Since the Philomathean Society was one of the two most important student organizations of Indiana University for a considerable period of years, this program may be considered as representing

[4] *Ibid.*, p. 86.
[5] *Ibid.*, p. 101.
[6] *Ibid.*, p. 106.

music at its best at Indiana University in the middle of the nineteenth century.

On conferring the LL.D. on Artist T. C. Steele in 1916 President
Bryan said:

> They had music. They had the pioneer melodies that Riley loved to hear the
> Old Band play. We are not ashamed of the melody nor of the Band. But the
> great music was not there. The empire of Beethoven was as far from our
> people generally as the empire of Genghis Khan.

These anecdotes took me back into another world and I asked
myself, "Could these things have been?" And yet, when, in 1920,
contemplating bringing an orchestra to the University, I asked a
Convocation audience of faculty and students for a show of hands
of those who had ever heard a symphony orchestra, there were only
seven students who responded out of an audience of more than a
thousand. Remembering this, I looked back over the old times.

The slowness with which music came to Indiana University was
not a phenomenon peculiar to the Midwest. Harvard, founded two
centuries before Indiana, during its first 216 years had twenty presidents, seventeen of whom were preachers. In all these years *no mention* of music is made in the Catalog. Officially there was no such
thing, until the Bulletin of 1856–57, which announces:

> Instruction in Music, with especial reference to devotional services in the
> Chapel, is open to Undergraduates. The course will extend to the higher
> branches of part-singing. Separate classes for Graduates will be formed if
> desired.

Music to be studied and practiced as a serious subject in a university curriculum was not considered, although at times used as an
adjunct to religious meetings in "psalms and hymns and spiritual
songs."

Of the next three presidents, Thomas Hill, Charles W. Eliot, and
A. Lawrence Lowell, Walter Raymond Spalding says: "Harvard
had indeed been fortunate and probably unique for having three
presidents in succession over many years—1862 to 1933—who endorsed and furthered the cause of music in every way in their
power." And yet, the name of J. K. Paine, first musician to be mentioned in the Harvard Catalog (1862–63), was at the bottom of the
list of college officers.

Charles W. Eliot became president of Harvard May 29, 1869, and in his inaugural address said, "We cannot afford to neglect the fine arts. We must try to satisfy the cravings of the few as well as the needs of the average many." In all of his writings this thought comes as a *melodia ostinato*. In *Changes Needed in Education* (1915) he says:

Drawing and music, like other fine-art studies, were regarded by the Puritan settlers of New England and by all their social and religious kindred as superfluities, which, if not positively evil, were still of wasteful or harmful tendency, and were, therefore, to be kept out of every course of education. By many teachers and educational administrators music and drawing are still regarded as fads or trivial accomplishments not worthy to rank as substantial educational material. . . .

As far as I can find out, this is the first time any university president came out into the open on the side of music as a university subject.

John Tasker Howard in *Our American Music* says:

Of instrumental music there was practically none in early New England. Organs were not introduced into churches until the next century, and then only after bitter opposition. In 1675 one of the states enacted a law "that no one should play on any kind of musical instrument except the drum, the trumpet and the jewsharp."

How long this law was in force is not stated but among the instruments consigned to the Devil was the violin, which had just been brought to a marvelous state of perfection by Nicola Amati, Antonius Stradivarius, and Joseph Guarnerius del Jesu, a perfection never since surpassed, scarcely equaled.

Vocal music was announced in the Indiana University Catalog for a few years, 1854–57, as one of the courses of the Normal Department in which the passing of an examination was required to secure the University diploma as a professional teacher.

Yes, the University had music, lots of it. It is interesting to note how much it had during the Civil War period. While on the Commencement program for 1859 there were only two pieces of music, it was the lull before the storm.

The war period programs had music as follows: 1860, 17 pieces; 1861, 25 pieces; 1862, 18 pieces; 1863, none; 1864, 13 pieces, which was about the normal number of musical selections on each graduate program up to 1891, when 3 pieces became the average until 1902.

The Commencement and other programs record neither the names of the pieces performed nor those of the performers. In 1845–46 the Monroe County Band furnished the music and in 1854–59 the Bloomington Saxe-horn band. In all these programs the word "Music" filled an interlude between the graduation speeches and the other numbers of the programs. In 1881, at the fifty-third Commencement, among the three orchestral numbers were, "Lustspiel Overture," by Keler Bela, "Boccaccio March," by von Suppe, and "Le Diadem Overture," by Hermann; in 1889, a song entitled "Lo, Hear the Gentle Lark" (composer's name omitted); in 1889, nine "Music" and one song, the "Trinklied," Donizetti, sung by Miss Nutt. Further the records do not go. The instrumentation may have been anything since any combinations of three or more instruments seem to have been called an orchestra.

But at no time during the nineteenth century was music a subject for which University credit was given.

DEVELOPMENT OF DEPARTMENT AND SCHOOL[7]

In the Catalog of 1893–94, under the heading "Miscellaneous Information," we read:

Mr. M. B. Griffith is the director of the college choir and the University Glee Club, and, also, by the authority of the University, teaches private classes in vocal music in the University buildings.

This announcement was not repeated in the Catalog of 1894–95, but in 1895–96 there was the announcement that Mr. Griffith had been engaged to give instruction in elementary sight reading. Classes met three times a week. No fee was charged and no credit was given.

From 1896 to 1899 instruction was given in vocal music and chorus by Charles N. Hassler. He was succeeded in 1899 by Lucius M. Hiatt, who served until 1910 and whose instruction included chorus singing and sight reading. He organized the first band and orchestra and instructed the glee club.

From 1906 to 1910 piano lessons were also given by Edward Ebert-Buchheim.

[7] This section was written by Dr. Myers, with the collaboration of Miss Winifred Merrill, who furnished many details of her father's administration.

During these seventeen years, 1893–1910, instruction in music at Indiana University was on a no-credit basis.

I was present at Commencement at Indiana University in 1903 when I saw the University for the first time and heard the orchestra, which was the one sour, discordant note of the occasion. A few decades later one could find in Indiana a hundred high school orchestras vastly superior to that University orchestra of 1903.

A School of Music was one of a number of projects the President had in mind for the development of Indiana University. On November 18, 1904, the establishment of such a school was discussed at length by the trustees, who directed the President to secure information concerning available candidates for the position of "Professor or Dean of Music."

The President did not find this an easy assignment. He reported that "out of a score whose credentials I have considered there are four who appear to deserve further consideration." He added: "It is extremely difficult to find a man whose musical training is quite first-rate and who has also the good sense and executive ability required."

Other matters of critical importance delayed promotion of music, but on January 4, 1906, the President recommended that Edward Ebert-Buchheim be engaged to give a series of piano recitals during the winter and spring terms. The attention of the President had been directed by Professor Guido H. Stempel, a music lover and able music critic, to the occasional presence in Bloomington and on the campus of Mr. Ebert-Buchheim, a really remarkable and highly trained pianist, who, since March, 1903, had occasionally given recitals at chapel. He had been educated in Berlin and Leipsic and had taught music in Europe for seventeen years before coming to America.

There is no record of the agreement entered into with Mr. Buchheim, which was probably very informal. But it becomes obvious that the agreement involved giving recitals at chapel and giving piano lessons, for in November of 1906 the President reported to his board that the work of Professor Buchheim was progressing though the number of pupils enrolled was still small. The University had two pianos on trial. Professor Buchheim's recitals were well attended and were "a very valuable educational agency."

Up to midyear 1907, Mr. Buchheim had lived at Danville, Ind., where he was professor of piano in Central Normal College, later Canterbury College. But in June, 1907, President Bryan submitted to the trustees a proposal under which it would be possible for Professor Ebert-Buchheim to take up his residence in connection with Indiana University.

Indiana University agreed:

1. To insure 25 lessons per week for 36 weeks of the College year, at $1 per lesson—$900.
2. To pay for 15 recitals at $15—$225.
3. To furnish a studio with heat and light, piano and chairs.
4. To turn over all fees in excess of $900 for the College year, and fees for the summer work.

Mr. Buchheim agreed:

1. To accept all pupils as he had been doing.
2. To give no lessons in Bloomington except under the agreement herein contemplated.
3. To be in residence at least four days of every week during the College year.

The announcement of the Buchheim recitals appeared in *The Daily Student*, October 19, 1907:

FIRST BUCHHEIM RECITAL
WELL-KNOWN ARTIST WILL BEGIN ANNUAL SERIES, MONDAY

Monday evening at seven in the Student Building, Mr. Ebert-Buchheim will give the first of his annual series of recitals. The program will consist of Beethoven's first three sonatas, dedicated to Haydn, and of the variations in F minor. The series will be one of unusual interest. The composers represented will be Beethoven, Bach, Schubert, Schumann, Chopin, Liszt (died September 4 of the present year)—the great masters of harmony. But the chief interest will be in the fact that Mrs. Ebert-Buchheim will accompany her husband in some four-handed arrangements and will sing two songs at the Grieg memorial November 4. Dr. Myers and Dr. Alburger have also promised to appear on the programs and will sing Schubert, Schumann, and Liszt songs. With the same broad musical foundation as in former years, the series this year will have the added charm of variety. The recitals are under the auspices of the University and are free to all.

These recitals were well attended by students and faculty and had educational value in acquainting students with some of the compositions of the great masters. To audiences little accustomed to the performances of artists, it seemed remarkable that these recitals were played entirely without music. They were to the great composers what the Ben Greet Players at a later date were to Shakespeare.

Though music had now moved closer to the campus, it was not there as yet in courses receiving University credit. The continuance of Mr. Buchheim's work was seriously threatened in the summer of 1908 when he suffered a right-sided hemiplegia, which for a time necessitated discontinuance of his recitals. With great courage, we are told by Professor Stempel, Mr. Buchheim by 1909 "had recovered sufficiently to play a remarkable series of compositions for the left hand." Though he carried on heroically, he was a stricken man unable to exert leadership in the expansion of the work for which the time was ripe.

In June, 1910, the President reported to the trustees as follows:

It is well known to the Board that we have had a very unsatisfactory and inadequate provision for Music and that we have delayed making a change for lack of means. We have had with us in the Department of German for a number of years Dr. Charles D. Campbell, who took his doctor's degree at Strassburg in German and Music. He has a very considerable proficiency in the most difficult work of the musician, namely the conducting of an orchestra. The Trustees will have an opportunity to see the character of his work on the night before Commencement when he will conduct a large chorus, orchestra, and soloists in the production of *Robin Hood*. I have asked Dr. Campbell to submit plans for some courses in music as part of the Department of Liberal Arts, and also to submit plans for some enlargement of the work in applied Music. I ask that his report be read.

Upon the President's recommendation that Dr. Campbell be placed in charge of the Department of Music and that he be paid $250 for his services in this Department, official approval was given along with his title, associate professor of music.

It will be noted that music now had become a Department, and, in the fall of 1910, students taking certain courses such as the history of music, etc. were given credit in the College of Liberal Arts.

The new associate professor of music announced the following courses beginning with the fall term of 1910: "Music I, History of Music; Music II, Elements of Music; Music III, Musical Form; Music IV, Chorus Singing, and Sight Reading; Music V, Orchestra."

During the school year 1910–11 Mr. Ebert-Buchheim continued instruction in piano. One of the assistants, John Geiger, continued as a member of the department until 1938, teaching voice.

In November, 1911, Professor Campbell reported:

> The past year has been the first in the history of the University with regular courses on the History and Theory of Music. In conducting these courses the general policy has been to give the work as far as possible the same treatment that the study of Literature and the Fine Arts receives. An endeavor is made in all the courses to give to the student such acquaintance with the names and work of the great composers as is generally expected in the world at large of an educated and cultured man, and to lead him to an appreciation of the great works in the art of Music.
>
> Although, under the difficulties existing in the unknown character of the work, in the peculiar attitude of the general student body towards Music, as well as in the lack of much needed scores, music rolls, and books, the ideal has not been attained, the progress has been far greater than was expected.

This report showed a steady increase in enrollment. "There are now about 120 students each term." Dr. Campbell itemized equipment needed, totaling $1,000, and explained the need for a victrola, pianola piano, music, etc.

There are two phases of instruction in music as a cultural subject, he said: first, that leading to a knowledge about music, and, second, that leading to a knowledge of music. As far as possible he had sought a balance of these two phases.

The first phase is covered in courses in the general history and development of music, as well as in the more detailed study of particular periods, kinds of music, and composers, giving an acquaintance with such facts as will aid in the appreciation of music itself.

The second phase seeks to give an intimate acquaintance with some of the great masterpieces of music on which the appreciation of them largely depends. This presents the more difficult problem. Campbell considered that the player piano and victrola had done much toward the solution of the difficulty of this phase of the work. How interested he would have been in the radio!

He believed that the establishment of music reading rooms, small and if possible soundproof, equipped with instruments and a full collection of rolls, records, and music scores would be very helpful. It was his conviction that participation in the work of the chorus and the orchestra was a very good way to obtain a knowledge of music.

His report is too long to abstract briefly. Reading it, one gains the conviction that the University was fortunate in having his leadership in this work.

Campbell objected strenuously to dismissing students from regular work of the chorus, orchestra, etc. for the purpose of discipline or punishment, though he agreed that no student on probation for any reason should be permitted to become a regular member of the glee club.

Reporting to the trustees (June, 1915) Professor Campbell said:

I have before this commented on the two great fields of music instruction, the appreciative and theoretical on one hand, and the applied on the other. The former has its rightful place along with such subjects as literature, the fine arts, history, etc., in the college of liberal arts. Its purpose is broadly cultural, its point of view that of the intelligent understanding of a work of art, and hence the appreciation of it as an expression of the inner emotional and intellectual human progress and development. The latter field may be compared to such specialized professional courses as those in law or in medicine. Its purpose is the acquiring of the specialized knowledge and technique of a profession; its point of view that of the intelligent interpretation or reproduction, both physically and intellectually, of a work of art. The former gives us the broad-minded, cultured audience, the latter the skillful, intelligent performer. The two fields merge into each other so gradually that the drawing of a definite line between them is difficult, and must, for the most part, be purely arbitrary.

Dr. Charles Campbell had composed special music for the centennial pageant, May, 1916. He was Hoosier born and his very meritorious song, "Indiana," lent itself perfectly to the symbolic episode of the great community drama. "Indiana" was a processional song and should be judged as such. The story of the writing of this song is found in the *Alumni Quarterly,* Volume VII, page 366.

Instruction in violin had been added to the work of the Department of Music in 1913–14.

Dr. Campbell's unfortunate and untimely death occurred on March 29, 1919. He was taking his daughter for a ride in her baby buggy. Something happened to one of the wheels. In attempting to repair it he skinned his finger. Septicemia became septic pneumonia. He was dead in a week.

Charles Campbell was a lovable character, a hard worker, an effective head of the Department of Music. He was of a cheerful disposition with a fine sense of humor. The Department of Music had been assigned quarters in Mitchell Hall, which was badly in need of repair. Campbell reported that "the roof lets in the sunshine and the rain."

It would have been difficult to have found anyone possessing the fine personal qualities of Charles Campbell to a higher degree than the man appointed to succeed him as head of the Department of Music, Barzille Winfred Merrill. There was this difference, however. When Professor Campbell was appointed head of the newly created Department of Music he was assistant professor of German in Indiana University, his Alma Mater, and had been a member of that Department for four years. Music had been his second major in Heidelberg and Strassburg. In 1910 he was beginning his successful career as a teacher of music at the age of thirty-three.

With Professor Merrill, however, music had been his major since his youth. After an extensive private training under leading teachers of America, he had conducted the Merrill School of Music and the Atlanta Symphony Orchestra from 1895 to 1900. The years 1900 to 1903 he spent as a student of music in Berlin, where he learned to know many of the musicians of Europe. From 1903 to 1919 he was professor and head of the Department of Music in Iowa State Teachers College. He came to Indiana University in 1919, with nearly a quarter-century of experience as a teacher, conductor, and department head. Two years after his coming to Indiana University the Department of Music was made the School of Music with Professor Merrill as dean.

As dean of the School of Music, Professor Merrill began building up his faculty. In the fall of 1919 Archibald Warner, who had been band conductor since 1916, had been added to the staff in the Department of Music, Adolph Schellschmidt became instructor in cello, and Mrs. Ruby Mosemiller was appointed instructor in piano. In the early years Indiana musicians on the instructional staff received their fees for their services. It was Dean Merrill's desire to substitute for this arrangement a resident faculty with guaranteed salaries. In 1921–22 Professor Edward B. Birge was added to the staff in charge of public school music. In 1925–26 Douglas Nye (voice), Axel Skjerne (piano), and Miss Montana Grinstead (piano) joined the faculty, and in 1926–27 Miss Winifred Merrill (violin). In 1927–28 Ernest Hoffzimmer, of Berlin, succeeded Professor Axel Skjerne in piano.

When, in 1928–29, the Finnish cellist, Lennart von Zweygberg, became a member of the faculty, the International Trio was formed. Its members were, besides Mr. von Zweygberg, Mr. Hoffzimmer, pianist, and Miss Merrill, violinist. This trio made its Indianapolis debut at the Maennerchor on January 27, 1929. Thus the first chamber music ensemble "in residence" was brought to the University. This practice was to become more general in music schools all over the country a decade later.

In 1921–22 the trustees approved the following degrees to be granted by the School of Music: Bachelor of Music with practical theory and composition, voice, piano, or orchestral instrument as major; Master of Music, graduate degree in the same field; Bachelor of Public School Music. Later were added: Bachelor of Arts with music major; Master of Arts with music major; a five-year course, Bachelor of Music with teacher's license. This combined a Bachelor of Music with the additional courses in education necessary for a teacher's license.

In June, 1923, the first "class" was graduated. There were two graduates, one a Bachelor of Public School Music, the other a Bachelor of Arts with music as major.

One of the most important contributions to the musical life of the state in general and the town and gown of Bloomington in particular was the establishment by Dean Merrill of the Music Series of world-famous artists in 1923–24. Prior to that time there had been occasional concerts, but the deficit had usually to be met by community-minded citizens. The dean also conceived the idea of inviting townspeople, faculty, and students to send in a list of the artists they wished to hear the following season. From these lists a ballot was made and at a later date given out to be voted on. Ballots had to be signed to be valid. Each year, as far as was humanly possible, the artists receiving the largest number of votes were engaged. The joker was, of course, that the only place with adequate seating capacity was the Men's Gymnasium. It was necessary, therefore, to wait to find out the athletics schedule before concert dates could be confirmed. One dollar and a half of the $5 activities fee was available for the Music Series. This gave a definite amount of money to be spent in bringing fine artists to the campus. Among these were Madam Louise Homer, Roland Hayes, Edward Johnson, Giovanni Martinelli, Mary Garden, Gladys Swarthout, Rosa Ponselle, singers; Bauer, Gieseking, Iturbi, Hoffmann, Paderewski, Rachmaninoff, pianists; Hubermann, Kreisler, Maud Powell, Spalding, Szigeti, Zimbalist, violinists; Flonzaley, Lener, Kolisch, Budapest, string quartets; Minneapolis, Cincinnati, Cleveland, Indianapolis, orchestras; Charles Humphreys and Doris Weidman with their dance group, Georgi and Kreutzberg, Nini and Theilade, Trudi Schoop Comic Ballet, dancers; the Abby Irish Players, Mrs. Fiske in *Becky Sharp*, theaters. Mozart's opera, *The Marriage of Figaro,* was given in Assembly Hall two evenings with matinee, on November 30 and December 1, 1925.

With the coming of the Minneapolis Symphony Orchestra, an invitation was extended to Miss Winifred Merrill to play as soloist with the orchestra. In 1930 Professor von Zweygberg and Miss Merrill were invited to play with the same orchestra.

An annex to Mitchell Hall costing $3,500 had been built in 1921, and in 1922 Dean Merrill began his long struggle for an adequate building for the School of Music. In the meantime the School was doing, with all the enthusiasm and zest of pioneers, things that had never been done before in southern Indiana.

The Juilliard Foundation was going about the country, scouting for talent. A talented voice student of the School of Music was awarded one of the fellowships for three years of study in New York City.

Annual composition recitals had been established in 1923–24. By 1930 composition students began to win national prizes. The *Bulletin of Indiana Composers, Native and Adopted,* published by the Indiana Federation of Music Clubs in 1936, lists no fewer than eight composition students of the School.

There were times, as in 1926, when President Bryan suggested a talk with the bursar, and again in 1927 when the Presser Foundation was approached, that a building seemed imminent. Other, larger quarters on the campus were offered, but the specialized quality necessary for suitable housing resulted in the refusal of these offers.

Resting the matter for the time being, in 1929 the dean made plans to further the education of the music students by taking them abroad with certain of the artist faculty as teachers. He obtained offers of the Palace at Charlottenburg from the German government at Berlin. There was also an invitation from the government of Bavaria to occupy the Odeon, the finely equipped building of the State Academy of Music at Munich. The latter offer was accepted. Six weeks were devoted to European travel and six weeks to intensive music study in Munich, during which time the students attended all of the Mozart and Wagner operas. This summer school in Europe proved so successful that it was repeated in 1930. Plans were being made for 1931, but the depression following World War I had reached the Middle West, and the plans had to be abandoned.

The year 1936 was a banner year. Music contests, judged by School of Music faculty, had been held with the cooperation of the Extension Division in key cities of the state since 1929. Winners were invited to compete at the School. These contests had grown in quality and size until 1936, when Indiana University held a music festival from April 16 to 18, which attracted 1,990 high school students from 102 Indiana schools competing in contests of choruses, glee clubs, bands, and orchestras. The state finalists in vocal and instrumental contests numbered 332, 180 of these being soloists only, the others taking part in group performances. The winners in voice, piano, violin, cello, wood wind, and brass received scholarships to the School of Music.

The Hoosier Music competitions in strings, wind, voice, and piano were held annually at the State Fair, where the winners were awarded scholarships.

Dean Merrill again submitted his plans for a School of Music building, with the able assistance of members of the Board of Trustees, supported by petitions from music students and many other friends of the School, and the project was finally approved. Robert Frost Daggett, of Indianapolis, was the architect. The cost was $384,-569 for a building representing the finest artistic quality.

It contained a recital hall seating 435 with a stage for large choruses and orchestra pit accommodating a full opera orchestra. Forty-eight practice rooms, twelve studios, five classrooms, a large rehearsal room, a radio and recording room, offices, etc. are provided in this excellent building.

Although the building was first planned with six organ practice rooms, twenty-four teaching studios, and ninety-eight practice rooms, these figures were cut in half. A scant ten years later, at great cost, temporary buildings had to be erected to meet the need which Dean Merrill had originally foreseen.

The laying of the cornerstone was an impressive ceremony on May 16, 1936.

"The Last Serenade in the Court of old Mitchell" was given by the summer school orchestra, Dean Merrill conducting, August 5, 1936, the second program of the eighteenth series of the School of Music. On January 15, 1937, the first program in Recital Hall of the new building was given by the University symphony orchestra, now numbering some sixty players.

Through all the years, Professor Guido H. Stempel, of the Department of Comparative Philology, musical amateur of the highest type, had aided and abetted the School with his able and inspiring criticism in his fine columns in both *The Indiana Daily Student* and the *Bloomington Star*. He also gave a course in writing music criticism, which held the standard of student writing exceptionally high.

The first performance of light opera was given in the Recital Hall of the Music Building on the evening of April 29, 1937, and repeated the following night. The opera was *H.M.S. Pinafore* by Gilbert and Sullivan, followed in 1938 by *The Mikado,* sponsored by the Pro Music Club of the School of Music.

In the spring of 1937 Dean Merrill was elected president of the Association of Executive Heads of Departments and Schools of Music in State Universities. The organization met in the new Music Building in the fall. In this year he also published his book on orchestration, the fruit of many years of teaching. The Music Building was formally dedicated on June 13, 1937.

At the end of Dean Merrill's nineteen years of service, the School of Music had twelve full-time instructors, a library of 15,000 carefully chosen volumes, a small but good library of music for chorus, orchestra, and chamber music. It showed an increase of 600 per cent in students graduating, 603 students enrolled in music courses, one of the finest music buildings in the country.

Dean Merrill retired in 1938 and was succeeded by Dean Sanders. Since this history is to end with the close of the Bryan administration, the development of this School under Dean Sanders and the remarkable increase in equipment and facilities of the School of Music brought about by erection of the beautiful Auditorium, Music Hall, must be left to a later history of Indiana University.

Few developments in Indiana in the past forty years have been more remarkable than that which has occurred in music. The contrast between Indiana University in 1938 and Indiana University at the beginning of the Bryan administration, the contrast in roads of 1903 and 1938, the contrast in transportation or anything else that existed in 1903 with that same thing in 1938 is not greater than the development which has occurred in music.

CHAPTER XX

INDIANA UNIVERSITY, 1920 - 22

"The State of Indiana should awaken to the fact that it must take a long step in advance unless it would see its higher educational institutions fall hopelessly in arrears of those in surrounding states." President Bryan to Board of Trustees, October, 1920.

Two Great Fund-Raising Campaigns

THE BIENNIUM 1920–22 was a period of very unusual interest. Two great fund-raising campaigns of major importance to the University were being organized.

One of these was the campaign of the James Whitcomb Riley Memorial Association for $1,000,000 with which to build a James Whitcomb Riley Hospital for Children. The Association had initiated and continued to have full responsibility for this project. Wisely they were much concerned for the permanency of the memorial. After thorough investigation they had turned to Indiana University convinced that in the State University they found the highest degree of permanency possible. Moved by a desire to promote the tribute to the Hoosier poet, and glad for the unexcelled clinical facilities the hospital would afford students of medicine, the University had accepted responsibility for the Hospital.

A subcommittee of the trustees was appointed on January 27, 1921, to draft a bill which would provide for such a hospital. This bill, carrying an appropriation of $125,000 for construction and also carrying provision for maintenance, received the signature of the Governor on March 11, 1921. It established the legal status of the Riley Hospital as a part of Indiana University.

The $125,000 was in the nature of a friendly gesture, since it was only five or six per cent of the ultimate cost of the project. But the provision for maintenance was of major importance, assuring the permanency so much desired by the Riley Association. Chapter XXVI contains the story of this great project.

The other fund-raising campaign, the Indiana University Memorial Fund drive, for $1,000,000 was being organized in the spring of 1921. In June, 1921, William A. Alexander was appointed librarian of Indiana University effective as of August 1 and was charged with responsibility for organization of the Alumni Memorial drive. As this drive progressed it included students, faculty, and friends of the University, in addition to alumni.

In October, 1921, Mr. Alexander explained that there were three major objectives for which this fund was being raised: (1) a University building having a large auditorium (this soon became the Union Building), (2) a stadium, (3) a dormitory for women.

In November he was authorized by the trustees to enter into a contract with Lowe and Bollenbacher, of Chicago, for preliminary plans for these three structures. The first pledge to this fund was made by former President Joseph Swain and wife. By April 5, 1922, the total subscribed was in excess of half a million dollars. This campaign is discussed further in the next chapter.

REPORT TO GOVERNOR AND VISITING COMMITTEE

The needs of Indiana, Purdue, and State Normal differed so greatly that it was very unusual for them to join in any request of the legislature. In the fall of 1920, however, all three were feeling the need for greater income. Accordingly, in November the trustees of the three institutions met at Indianapolis, in joint session, to discuss their needs and to plan a united effort for restoration of the 7-cent maintenance tax.

In the report submitted by Indiana University to the Governor and the Visiting Committee for the legislature meeting early in January, 1921, two major needs were stressed, namely the need for greater income and the need for a number of new buildings. In support of the need for increased income the President said:

It is a painfully evident fact that we are not able to pay salaries to fill vacancies as they occur, with men as good as the men we now have; and that it will not be possible to retain the best men that we have against the competition of surrounding states which pay much larger salaries. It is, for example, impossible at the present moment to secure an adequate head for the Department of English because the men whom we would like to have are beyond our reach. The same problem will soon recur as to the headship of the Department of History and a similar problem recurs in almost every department as fast as vacancies take place.

I may note that the Director of our School of Education, whose salary is $4,000, recently asked a young man who had not yet taken his doctor's degree at Columbia whether he would come here for a salary of $3,600. The young man replied that he was already receiving over $5,000.

I have already written the Board concerning the larger salaries offered to three of our young men, who have, nevertheless, decided to remain with us during the present year.

It is certain that, unless substantial relief is obtained, we must suffer a grave deterioration in the level of our Faculty within the near future.

The legislature of 1921 did not restore the 7-cent tax, but the tax levy was increased from 2.8 cents to 5 cents on each $100 of taxable property in the state of Indiana. The act provided that the unexpended balance of the fund derived from the maintenance tax should be held as a building fund. The amount of this fund credited to Indiana University on September 30, 1921, was $2,674.12. Under the 5-cent tax this balance would be larger for a short time, until imperative maintenance needs again reduced it to the vanishing point.

It was the view of the President that larger salaries should be paid men of first-rate value and relatively small increases voted to men whose ability was not yet determined. Though the income from the educational tax in 1921–22 was a quarter of a million dollars in excess of that of 1920–21, the President's reiteration of the major importance of salary increases elicited no favorable action from the Board of Trustees.

As for buildings, it should be recalled that, although the Gymnasium for Men had been completed in 1917, no classroom building had been erected on the Bloomington campus since the completion of Biology Hall in November, 1910. Meanwhile enrollment had increased 52 per cent, and the President stated regretfully:

We are turning away students from several of the laboratories, which are used throughout the entire day to capacity.

It is almost impossible to provide recitation rooms enough to take care of classes which we now have and students are turned from departments because classroom capacity has been reached.

The working space in the Library is now inadequate to meet the demands of daily use. The head of the Department of Romance Languages with 1,800 students had to have his office in the hallway of Kirkwood, the students meeting three senior Professors in the Department at three points in the hallway.

It was not merely classroom space that was needed. The University in the fall of 1920 was in need of living quarters, particularly for the young women students.

The Residence Hall for women, formerly Alpha Hall, is now conducted in a first-rate manner and proves a most desirable place to reside for something more than 100 girls. Miss Wells has also established an annex dormitory and a cooperative house where girls can in part work their way. The sorority houses furnish dormitories for another considerable group of girls. Many more girls are housed in private residences, some of which are very desirable and some of which are very undesirable. It is especially undesirable that so many of the girls should be scattered about in places where there can be no adequate supervision.

It is within our knowledge that a very considerable number of girls have not come to the University or have gone away after coming here because they could not find adequate places in which to room and board.

All these considerations lead us to realize the urgent necessity for a first-rate modern dormitory for girls.

Among the building needs the President stressed the urgent need for enlarged quarters for the School of Law, the importance of completing the Medical Building together with a new power plant, laundry, and nurses' home at Indianapolis. At Bloomington the perennially inadequate power plant would either have to be overhauled and enlarged or a new power plant would have to be built.

With adjournment of the 1921 legislature and the increase of the mill tax, the trustees of the University had to make a difficult decision between increasing salaries and erecting buildings. With three major professors of the Department of Romance Languages meeting students for conferences at three different points in a hall in Kirkwood, the trustees no doubt felt that this situation was approximating that of Mark Hopkins on his log and decided in favor of a new building to give needed classroom and office space.

SCHOOL OF COMMERCE AND FINANCE BUILDING

This building project of 1920–22 would have ranked as the most important event of an ordinary biennium. The unique procedure adopted for financing construction is of particular interest and is described in Chapter XXXVIII. Construction was completed and the building dedicated April 25 and 26, 1923.

THE POWER PLANT

The power plant was an ever-present problem of the administration because funds had never been made available to do more than boost capacity to meet present needs. Now construction was being considered with an eye to the future. The plant was carrying a maximum load. With erection of a School of Commerce and Finance building, the power plant would be entirely inadequate.

On June 4 the engineering firm of Ammerman and McCool was authorized to prepare plans and specifications for "repair and rebuilding" the power plant, and August 13 a contract was awarded the Hayes Brothers. The project involved the expenditure of about $45,000.

RESIDENCES FOR GIRLS

In October, 1920, the President reviewed certain substitute measures adopted by the administration in meeting the need for dormitories for girls. The Executive Committee had leased, as residences for girls, in addition to Alpha Hall and the Annex, the Siebenthal residence at 701 East Tenth Street at $80 a month for five years, the Cooperative House; the Ritter residence at Kirkwood and Lincoln at $1,000 a year for five years, the Freshman House. They had authorized the purchase for the Ritter house of $1,500 worth of furniture to be paid for as far as possible from proceeds of the house, the furniture to become the property of the University. It was expected that the running expenses of both houses would be met by room rent charges. An appropriation of $500 was made for furnishings for the Annex and $200 for the Cooperative House.

This made a total of $2,200 for furnishings. In addition, an appropriation of $450 was made for the Practice House. This total was not large, but, under the persistent urging of Dean Wells, it showed a determined effort for, and a definite trend toward, better housing for young women.

Dean Wells stated that Alpha Hall (Residence Hall) had been run successfully in every respect during the year 1919–20. There had been enough applications for the year 1920–21 to fill it twice.

The Indiana University Annex, 411 South Henderson Street, had been opened again for 1920–21, but it had not been so successful during the past year. They had not had money to make it attractive. The house was old and they had had a great deal of trouble with bedbugs. The furnace was hard to regulate and expensive to run.

At the June, 1921, meeting of the board, a conference with Bloomington citizens was authorized to consider the building of a dormitory for girls. The meeting took place on the morning of June 6, the board meeting with the Bloomington Chamber of Commerce. Mr. Niezer presented the need of the University for a dormitory for women and raised the question of the possibility of Bloomington citizens assuming responsibility for this project. Messrs. Bryan, Batman, and Fesler also spoke for the board. A joint committee was appointed. This was an interesting approach to the problem of providing dormitories for women, from which some help might have come, but for the organization of the Memorial Fund campaign. Dean Wells, with other interested women, was losing no time in urging the inclusion of a woman's dormitory as one of the objectives of this drive.

In October, 1921, the President reported that the four houses maintained by the University for the benefit of girl students had involved a budget in 1920–21 in excess of $50,000. The enterprises had been so well managed that they had a little more than paid for themselves.

Death of President Stone

An appropriate resolution was adopted on the tragic death of Winthrop Ellsworth Stone, President of Purdue University, who lost his life in a fall while mountain climbing. This resolution, emphasizing the long maintenance by President Stone of the least possible duplication of work between Indiana University and Purdue and the greatest possible cooperation between the two institutions, was inscribed in the records of the trustees of Indiana University and a copy was sent to Henry W. Marshall, Acting President of Purdue University.

The following letter presents the fine attitude of Acting President Marshall, continuing a policy maintained for many years by President Stone. Because of its importance, it is quoted in full.

January 9, 1922

My dear Dr. Bryan:

Referring to our telephone conversation regarding the request of Professor Roberts of the Department of Education that the Department be permitted to give Adjunct or Extension Courses in Teacher-Training for which University credits would be given, wish to advise you that the matter was given consideration by the Board of Trustees, and after a thorough discussion the following resolution was adopted:

"Resolved that the Board of Trustees decline to sanction any adjunct or extension work or the giving directly of University credits which would violate in any letter or spirit the agreement now existing between the late Dr. Stone and Dr. Bryan, that the institutions should not engage in extension work which would constitute duplication of work or trespass upon the proper field of work of each other."

> With kindest personal regards, I am,
> Sincerely yours,
> Signed: Henry W. Marshall,
> Vice-President and Acting President

MATTERS OF GENERAL UNIVERSITY INTEREST

Dean Wells in 1920 arranged a centennial breakfast, at which $1,970 was pledged for scholarships, student loan funds, and for furnishing the Cooperative House. Dean Wells had a way of getting things done. A self-government constitution for women had been adopted. With a strong girl president, there was good prospect that the system was going to work. During the year, Dean Wells had arranged for a meeting of the fourteen deans of women in the state of Indiana. The Woman's League had planned a centennial thank offering. With the help of alumnae organizations they raised $1,050, which was used to buy three Steele paintings.

Frank H. Levell was appointed alumni secretary in October, 1920, on the resignation of Humphrey M. Barbour.

Dean Joseph C. Todd, of the Indiana School of Religion, had recently purchased two pieces of property at the southwest corner of the campus, which he was prepared to sell (January, 1921) to the University at cost plus interest. The University, however, did not take advantage of this opportunity.

About $60,000 of improvements were under construction in October, 1921, as follows:

Power plant $43,318.13
Kirkwood Hall stairs, wiring, fixtures........................ 12,716.00
Commons-refrigerator 3,965.00

The Commons was proving a great success. In 1920–21, 332,240 persons were served.

Architect Robert F. Daggett was asked in October, 1921, to proceed at once with completion of plans and specifications for a President's House, to be built of brick, according to the wishes of President and Mrs. Bryan. A site had been selected in June, 1915.

Land one block deep, lying east of Sluss Street and between Eighth and Tenth streets, was purchased in 1921.

Frank R. Elliott was appointed as the first full-time publicity director in the summer of 1921.

The board requested, in April, 1922, the establishment of a post office substation at the University.

A committee consisting of Trustees Smith, Niezer, and Long was appointed in June, 1922, to consider the question of group insurance.

At Commencement, 1921, the honorary LL.D. was conferred upon Willis Stanley Blatchley. At Commencement, 1922, this degree was conferred upon Amos W. Butler, Lotus D. Coffman, Ernest H. Lindley, General John T. Thompson, and Elwood Haynes.

The Indianapolis visit of the great Marshal Foch on November 4, 1921, is commemorated in this *History of Indiana University* for two reasons: the Indiana University band marched in the parade in honor of this hero of World War I; and President Bryan secured from the Marshal a copy of his historic telegram which, translated, read: "My left is giving way, my right is falling back; I am ordering a general offensive, a decisive attack by the center.

F. Foch."

The autographed copy of this telegram of September, 1914, is in the Union Building.

Matters of Faculty Interest

Robert E. Cavanaugh was appointed (December, 1920) as acting director of the Extension Division until July, 1921, succeeding Professor Pettijohn, who had gone to Minnesota. On August 1, 1921, Mr. Cavanaugh became director.

Charles J. Sembower, who was to return to the University after two years' absence, was appointed dean of men and professor of English for the year beginning August 1, 1921. As dean of men, his work was coordinated with that of Dean Edmondson.

Professor Woodburn was made research professor of history for the year 1921–22, an appointment continued until the close of the year 1923–24, when he retired.

The trustees, in June, 1921, ordered that no drive or request for money be made by the University for any school or department except upon authorization of the board.

Associate Professor Robert E. Burke became head of the Department of Fine Arts in 1922, on the resignation of Professor Alfred M. Brooks, who went to Swarthmore.

Compensation for teaching in the summer school was fixed in June, 1921, at 15 to 17 per cent of the annual salary, for eight and a half weeks' work, and 22⅔ per cent of the annual salary for twelve weeks' work.

In the fall of 1922 Artist Theodore C. Steele, appointed as honorary professor of painting, took up residence on the campus. He established a studio on the top floor of the Library. Prior to this time at least two poets and a composer had had similar connections with colleges, but it is believed that Indiana University was the first institution to invite a painter to accept such a post.

It was announced (April, 1922) that Professor Ulysses G. Weatherly had been elected to Associé de l'Institut International de Sociologie.

Bert E. Young, of Vanderbilt University, was made head of the Department of Romance Languages in June, 1922, to succeed Professor E. C. Hills, resigned.

Matters of Student Interest

On recommendation of Professor Hills, two scholarships for Mexican students were established, the students to be selected by their committees, subject to University approval. A graduate scholarship for Spanish and Spanish-American students was authorized with a value of $750 and fees. S. P. Capen, Director of the American Council of Education, offered his assistance in the selection of a French teaching fellow with the same stipend.

The President reported, October, 1921, that there were now ten loan funds for students, totaling $9,743.78. This total, of course, was small, but growing.

Military training under the competent leadership of Major O'Brien was making a fine record. Reporting at President Bryan's request, Major O'Brien stated that Indiana University for the years 1920 and 1921 was given the rating "Distinguished College" by the Secretary of War. At the R.O.T.C. camp at Fort Knox, 1921, the advanced course students of Indiana University were the best in the Fifth Army Corps, winning the Roosevelt Cup as a permanent possession. Twenty-five colleges and universities were represented.

Chapter XXI

INDIANA UNIVERSITY, 1922 - 24

A Great Building Program Insecurely Financed

THE YEARS 1922–24 were a strenuous period for the trustees of Indiana University. A great building program, the James Whitcomb Riley Hospital for Children, was under way at Indianapolis. Considerable optimism had characterized the embarkation on this program involving expenditures far in excess of funds immediately available. All would be well if the financial response of the people of Indiana was as generous as its promoters anticipated.

In recognition of the dual interest of the Riley Association and the University in this project, a joint committee had been appointed consisting of five members of the Riley Association and five members of the Board of Trustees of Indiana University. Thus, either directly or indirectly, the board shared in all the anxiety over this project, considered in Chapter XXVI.

At Bloomington, the Memorial Fund drive was still under way, and a great building program was being underwritten.

The Indiana University Memorial Fund Drive, 1922–24

As the biennium 1922–24 opened, William A. Alexander, who in 1921 had been placed in charge of the Memorial Fund campaign of Indiana University, was ordered to keep interest on subscriptions as a separate fund, to be used to pay expenses of the campaign.

On September 15, 1923, the subscription to the Fund totaled $1,118,308.75, of which $216,732.56 had been paid.

The total Memorial subscription to June 6, 1924, was $1,392,249.14. Of this total, about one-third, or $400,000, was due, and, of this amount due, about 10 per cent was more than six months overdue.

In May, 1925, the total was reported as $1,444,304.08, and on May 21, 1926, as $1,632,810.52, of which $583,471.39 had been paid. President Bryan reported on June 5, 1926, that the campaign under Mr. Alexander to raise $1,600,000 had been completed and oversubscribed.

The above is a very inadequate statement of this drive. Mr. Alexander perfected a very effective organization of students, alumni, and officers of the University. Great enthusiasm was aroused and the total subscription was very gratifying.

Though there was shrinkage in collections, the administration supplemented the fund in such manner that the Union Building, Stadium, and women's dormitory ultimately were erected.

I one day encountered in the Union Building a man who had been opulent in the early twenties and had subscribed accordingly. Now he was broken financially and physically. He said, "Well, sir, I contributed $1,000 to this building, and, hard up as I am today, I don't begrudge a penny of it." That, I think, was the general attitude of donors.

MEMORIAL BUILDINGS

In midyear of 1923, when the Memorial Fund drive was still some years short of completion, when the total subscription was only $1,000,000, with only $200,000 paid in, the administration was being urged with much insistence and from many sides by interested pressure groups to get started at once on erection of one or another, or all, of the three major structures, the Union Building, the Stadium, and the women's dormitory, for which subscriptions had been made.

Dared the administration initiate a million-dollar building program with approximately $200,000 in cash and $800,000 in promises? It was well known that in all such campaigns for funds there was a shrinkage in collections when the emotional enthusiasm of the subscription period was succeeded by the very different emotion attendant on parting with, and paying over, real money. Furthermore, subscriptions had been made on the basis of five annual payments, and it would be some years before the whole subscription would be due.

The problems created by the whole situation were harassing the President and his Board of Trustees. Lowe and Bollenbacher, architects of Chicago, had been under consideration as architects for the

Union Building and the dormitory for women. On June 4, 1923, J. C. Bollenbacher presented tentative plans for these buildings and a contract was signed with this firm.

It was decided August 1, 1923, that Lowe and Bollenbacher should be required to furnish an estimate as accurate as possible showing whether the women's dormitory could be erected within the appropriation for that purpose, $250,000. On December 20, 1923, plans for the dormitory were approved and ordered advertised for bids to be considered by the board at their meeting to be held January 30, 1924. On that date bids were opened, fully discussed, and rejected.

The minutes of the board, with rare exceptions, merely record board actions. The result is that one who reads the minutes of the meetings is sometimes at a loss to understand the action taken. A case in point is the rejection of all bids on the dormitory at this January, 1924, meeting. Nine weeks later, April 7, 1924, comes the explanation of this action.

It will be recalled that $250,000 had been allocated from the Memorial Fund drive for the construction of the women's dormitory. The board now realized that this amount was not sufficient for construction of the dormitory which everyone wished to see erected. Accordingly, on April 7, a committee consisting of President Fesler and Provost Smith was appointed to make an effort to secure a loan of $150,000 to supplement the $250,000 from the Memorial Fund, to be used in the construction of the dormitory. The architect was to proceed with his Plan C if the additional funds were secured. If the committee failed to make arrangements for the additional $150,000, then the architect was to proceed with Plan B, a $250,000 dormitory.

The committee was successful in securing the additional $150,000. On June 11, when plans were discussed, it was particularly emphasized by the board that the cost of the building proposed must not be in excess of $350,000. There would then be $50,000 for equipment.

After changes of plans and revisions of estimates and specifications were approved, they were ordered advertised for bids to be opened July 21. In October of 1924 the building was named Women's Memorial Hall.

The Stadium construction story is told in Chapter XXIV. It will be noted at this time that in the spring of 1924 the building of the Stadium was becoming a major problem. It is not surprising that the trustees felt, on letting the contract for the women's dormitory (July, 1924), that they had drawn on the slowly accumulating paid-in subscriptions to the Memorial Fund as fully as they dared. The construction of the Union Building, therefore, drops out of the picture temporarily to reappear five years later, June, 1929.

THE BUDGET

While these two building programs, one at Indianapolis and the other at Bloomington, with the problems of two fund-raising campaigns, were major interests of this period, the report to the General Assembly of 1923 was receiving due consideration.

In October, 1922, the budget prepared for submission to Governor Warren T. McCray and the General Assembly was approximately $1,400,000 and $1,415,000 for the years 1923–24 and 1924–25, respectively. These estimates were exclusive of these building programs and of such support of the Medical School and Hospitals as the board might see fit to propose. Emphasis was laid chiefly on the need of a service building for the University Hospitals and Medical School. The old plant had become entirely inadequate and a new service unit providing heat, light, power with the necessary tunnel system and an adequate laundry was an obvious necessity prior to opening the Riley.

The University budget for the year 1922–23, as adopted on October 31, was based on an estimated income of $1,503,555.93, with disbursement estimates leaving a working margin of $84,546.05 unassigned. The financial report to the Governor was made on December 12, 1922.

IMPORTANT ACTS OF THE GENERAL ASSEMBLY, 1923

Certain legislation important to the University was enacted by the General Assembly of 1923.

One act authorized the trustees to refund the Long Hospital bonds issued for construction of the building. Enough property and more had been turned over to the board by Dr. Long to pay off these

$200,000 worth of bonds. The property, located in Indianapolis, was increasing in value and it was thought wiser to refund the bonds than to sell the property.

In the appropriation bill Indiana University was granted $275,000 for construction of a heat, light, and power plant to serve the Riley and Long Hospitals and the School of Medicine.

But more important than any of these acts of the legislature of 1923, in the estimation of the late John W. Cravens, for many years registrar of Indiana University, was the bill "which insured success of the proposed plan to furnish an adequate water supply for Bloomington—a water supply that absolutely can be depended upon twelve months in the year." [1] This was House Bill 199, which "provided that the common council of any city of the fourth class may, by ordinance duly passed, abolish the Board of Public Works and provide that the common council of such city shall perform the duties of the Board of Public Works." The importance of this legislation lay in the conviction that the mayor of Bloomington planned the appointment of a Board of Public Works hostile to the Griffy Creek project, for a water supply for the city of Bloomington. [2]

Twenty-First Anniversary of Dr. Bryan's Presidency

The following communication from President Bryan was ordered placed in the minutes of the board August 1, 1923:

Today is the twenty-first anniversary of my entrance upon the presidency of Indiana University. During that time eighteen men have served upon the Board of Trustees. Of these, six have passed from life. Four others have retired from the Board. Two—Mr. Fesler and Mr. Corr—have served throughout the twenty-one years.

Isaac Jenkinson, 1866–70, 1875–1906, has the distinction of having served upon the Board longer than any one else has served. He was especially proud of his efforts to make Indiana coeducational, and of his vote to locate the University in Dunn's Woods where it now is.

Nat U. Hill, 1898–1908, loved the University almost as he loved his family. He gave without stint and asked nothing in return but the welfare of his beloved school.

Benjamin F. Shively, 1893–1916. Those who served on the Board with Senator Shively will never forget the wisdom and geniality with which he

---

[1] *Indiana University Alumni Quarterly*, Vol. X, p. 318.
[2] The full story of a water supply for Bloomington is in Chap. XXIII.

joined with his colleagues in meeting the problems of the University. It was a joy to work with him. Nor can we easily measure the importance of his great influence in many a crisis.

Howard Sandison, 1917–19, for a generation had more influence than any other man upon the public schools of Indiana. His service as a member of our Board was all too short.

Samuel R. Lyons, 1893–98, 1910–15. A man whose goodness and wisdom won for him abounding admiration and affection.

Theodore F. Rose, 1903–19. A University can have no greater riches than the devotion of such a man as Theodore Rose. A man successful in business, he could not have given to his business more of his mind and heart than he gave to his University.

I shall not now speak of the twelve who are yet living, four of whom (Messrs. Henry, Shea, Watson, and Hamilton) have retired from the Board. I will only say that to work through a score of years and more with these men, the living and the dead, has been one of the greatest satisfactions of my life.

Election of Alumni Trustee, 1924

The election of a trustee by the alumni of Indiana University was often uncontested, but in June, 1924, there were four candidates, three men (Edwin Corr, Roy O. Pike, and James A. Price) and one woman, Nellie Showers Teter (Mrs. Sanford Teter).

The term of Edwin Corr expired on July 1. For eleven successive terms (1891 to 1924) he had served as a trustee. He had been graduated in 1883 under President Lemuel Moss, when the University was located on the old campus. He was one of three trustees elected by alumni in 1891 under the new act which gave alumni of Indiana University the privilege of electing three of the eight trustees of the institution. In June, 1924, not only was his re-election being contested by two men candidates, but the women graduates for the first time had entered a candidate and were successful in her election. Thus Nellie Showers Teter became the first woman trustee of Indiana University.

Mrs. Teter had been graduated in 1893. For some years she had been active in civic affairs of Bloomington. She had been a member of the Local Council of Women, of the Bloomington Hospital board, and had served as president of the Bloomington branch of the American Association of University Women.

THE PRESIDENT'S HOUSE

From time to time during a period of eight years (1915–23), the trustees had considered the desirability of erecting a President's House on the campus. During that time the President occupied a large, comfortable house on North College Avenue, next to the Illinois Central depot, more than a mile and a half from the campus. The trustees had gone so far as to have Architect Robert F. Daggett prepare plans and specifications for this residence, and twice bids had been taken for its construction. Other University needs, however, were always so great that the President could not bring himself to join with the trustees in approving this outlay.

Consideration of this matter continued to be urged from time to time from various quarters. The University Men's Faculty Club voted unanimously recommending early consideration of erection of an adequate residence for the President, October, 1921.

On April 7, 1923, Charles Mundy, a contractor of Bloomington, submitted estimates as to what this proposed house would cost constructed in accordance with revised plans of Mr. Daggett and was engaged as superintendent.

The house was completed in July, 1924. *The Indiana Daily Student* of July 8, 1924 announced, "The Bryans will move into new house last of week."

As an expression of his personal interest, President Bryan insisted on contributing $10,000 to the expense of construction of this well-built, durable building comparable with some of the fine old antebellum homes in the neighborhood of Columbia, Tenn., which have stood more than a century without a crack in outer or inner walls.

NURSES' HOME

Henry Ostrom, of Indianapolis, presented plans, June 23, 1923, for a temporary home for nurses, to be erected on the Robert W. Long Hospital grounds. The Peoples State Bank was prepared to finance the construction by notes of $1,000 denomination payable over a period of about nine years, and a contract was accordingly signed with the Ostrom Realty Company. This home, with accommodations for fifty-nine nurses, was reported completed on September 15, 1923.

THE CENTENNIAL OF THE OPENING OF INDIANA UNIVERSITY

For many years January 20 had been celebrated as Foundation Day, the day of the passage of the act in 1820 creating Indiana University. Because of the inclement weather in January which often made it difficult for alumni to assemble and for faculty representatives to travel to meetings, it was recommended to the Alumni Association in 1924 that May 1, the date on which the University was opened for instruction, should hereafter be celebrated as Foundation Day.

Inasmuch as Foundation Day, 1924, was the centennial of the opening of the University it was proposed that the first Wednesday in May, 1924, be celebrated appropriately.

Accordingly, on May 7, 1924, the University celebrated with impressive pageantry the one-hundredth anniversary of the opening of the University for enrollment of students. Mr. Fesler, President of the board, contrasting 1824 with 1924, said: "In 1824 there was one building, one professor, and ten students. Today [1924] there is a faculty of 217 and a student body of 5,100."

A tablet was unveiled that day on the site of the first building on the old campus.

MEN'S DORMITORY (SOUTH HALL)

The architectural plans of a proposed men's dormitory and a financial scheme for erecting it presented by representatives of the Ostrom Realty Company and the Peoples State Bank of Indianapolis on February 16, 1924, were adopted, and a dormitory committee consisting of Trustees Smith, Fesler, and Batman was instructed to perfect a proper execution of these plans. Robert Frost Daggett was retained as consulting architect.

Rumors that the men's dormitory would not be ready for occupancy by the opening of the school year were refuted by *The Indiana Daily Student,* September 16, 1924, which quoted Miss Alice McDonald, the business manager, who said that all who had applied for rooms would be accommodated and that it was likely that accommodation could be assigned all others who applied within the next few days.

The floors are being covered with a special, sound-preventive preparation, and the furniture is being moved in. Kitchen furnishings are already in and the larder well supplied. Breakfast was served this morning for the first time.

Sixty-seven applications had been received by Saturday night and several of the men had moved in. The flooring will be finished next Wednesday, Miss McDonald announced, and the first two floors will be ready shortly afterwards.

All modern comforts and conveniences are promised the students. The large kitchens are all that modern electrical appliances can make them. In every possible way the comfort of the students will be cared for, according to Miss McDonald.

The total cost of the dormitory housing 112 students was $155,000, and 310 $500 coupon bonds maturing over a period of twenty-four years were issued to be paid from University income. It was believed, however, that these bonds could be paid from income from the dormitory; with good management this proved true.

The building was first named Washington Hall, but the next year the name was changed to South Hall, in anticipation of the day when West and North Halls would be erected.

MISCELLANEOUS MATTERS

At rare intervals in the history of the University it became necessary to dismiss a faculty member. Such a case arose in the summer of 1922 when it was discovered that a member of the faculty had mutilated library books. If he wanted a paragraph or a page, he simply cut it out. The action of the Executive Committee dismissing this man was approved at the October meeting of the Board of Trustees.

A letter from Indianapolis alumni asked that the practice football field be moved from Jordan Field to the higher ground east of the Gymnasium. An engineer employed to get data on the subject reported on February 17, and the board ordered Professor Ulysses S. Hanna and Superintendent Eugene Kerr to proceed at once with the preparation of this new athletic field.

A committee of students appeared before the board in April, 1923, and presented a plea for authorization of an additional fee of $3.50 a semester for each student, this additional fee to provide admission to all athletic games. After consideration of the matter, a fee of $5 a semester to be known as the activities fee[3] was authorized. Of

[3] This fee was discontinued in June, 1933.

this amount, $3.50 provided free admission to all athletic games and $1.50 was for admission to all other activities such as music, lecture courses, etc.

Professor Henry Holland Carter, who had joined the faculty in 1922, was made head of the Department of English for the academic year beginning August 1, 1923, succeeding John D. Rea, who had resigned after serving for two years in that post.

Professor Bert E. Young received from President Millerand the distinction of Chevalier de la Legion d'Honneur.

The property at the southwest corner of the campus was again offered to the University by the Indiana School of Religion, this time for $120,000. The offer was again refused.

The five-acre tract owned by Henry B. Gentry, lying east of the Mayfield addition at the southeast corner of the campus, was purchased June 22, 1923. This was the land one-half block from Jordan Avenue on which the University School is located.

An appropriation of $4,000 was made to cover the cost of sending nurses over the state to instruct school nurses and community nurses in connection with the Extension Division.

In the spring of 1923 the School of Education was authorized to reorganize on a basis comparable with that of the other schools in the University.

On recommendation of the Alumni Council, Edward Von Tress was selected as alumni secretary for the year beginning August 1, 1923.

Professor Carl H. Eigenmann was elected to the National Academy of Science.

The class of 1923 gave a bronze memorial tablet dedicated to President Bryan. It hangs in the Administration Building.

Z. G. Clevenger was elected director of physical education (June, 1923) succeeding Ewald O. Stiehm.

Ward G. Biddle was elected manager of the University Bookstore in July, 1923.

On October 8, 1923, Dr. S. E. Smith was appointed provost of Indiana University with the provision that he should have his residence in Indianapolis and should be the ranking executive officer of the University in Indianapolis, i.e., the ranking officer of the School of Medicine, the Training School for Nurses, and of the hospitals of the University, together with the School of Dentistry, should it be established.

The minutes of the Board of Trustees for the first hundred years were written in longhand. For some time the board had considered a loose-leaf record book, the pages of which could be typed in a special machine. Typewritten minutes were begun April 8, 1924.

On April 21, 1924, the trustees redefined the terms *resident* and *residence* as applied to registrants of the University.

The ceremonial induction of Seniors into the alumni body of Indiana University which has now become a tradition was introduced at Commencement, 1924. The text for this ceremony was written by Paul V. McNutt and Dean and Mrs. Charles J. Sembower.

The honorary degree LL.D. was conferred on Ernest P. Bicknell '87, and William Niles Wishard, M.D., at Commencement, 1924.

In 1923 Major Harry B. Crea was assigned to take over the work in military training and tactics when Major Robert E. O'Brien was ordered to Fort Leavenworth to attend the staff school.

Chapter XXII

ESTABLISHMENT OF THE SCHOOL OF DENTISTRY, 1925

For a number of years Indiana University had been approached from various quarters with proposals that the University take over the Indiana Dental College, Indianapolis. While the desirability of this action was obvious, the University up to 1923 had not found it feasible to do this.

The faculty of the Indiana Dental College and the members of the Indiana State Dental Society, observing the advancement of medical education under the leadership of Indiana University, were anxious to place dental education under that same leadership, and, in the school year 1923–24, although the administration was nearly submerged by the Riley and University Memorial building programs, the Dental Society and the faculty were urging this step.

The State Board of Dental Examiners and the dental department of the Carnegie Foundation had become interested and had joined in the promotion of dental education in Indiana, which involved purchase of equipment of the Indiana Dental College and taking over that school as the Indiana University School of Dentistry. On September 15, 1923, a very important conference was held by the trustees with the Dental Educational Council of America.

The Dental College property, privately owned, had been offered to Indiana University for $60,000. The University made a counter proposition of about half that amount, which was refused.

A committee of the board, consisting of Messrs. Batman, Hatfield, and S. E. Smith, had been appointed to negotiate for purchase of the equipment of the Indiana Dental College. On January 30, 1924, the report of this committee was discussed at length by the board, and an evaluation of property at $40,000 to $45,000, subject to itemization by appraisers, was considered approximately correct. A bill to authorize purchase of this property passed both houses of the legislature of 1925 by large majorities.

On March 9, 1925, the Governor signed this bill providing for the purchase of the equipment of the Indiana Dental College, which was to be incorporated into Indiana University, making appropriation therefor, and declaring an emergency. Sections 3 and 4 read as follows:

Section 3. The board of trustees of Indiana University is hereby authorized and directed to operate and maintain the dental college as a department of Indiana University, to be known as the Indiana University School of Dentistry.

Section 4. The transfer of assets herein provided shall take place as of June 1, 1925.

For purchase of the property, $40,000 was made available, the price to be determined by appraisal and approved by the Governor. Unexpended balance was to revert to the state treasury.

The dental class graduating June 9, 1925, received their degrees on the Bloomington campus.

It was stipulated in the negotiations involved in taking over the Indiana Dental College that the building on North Pennsylvania Street which had been occupied by the Indiana Dental College should be leased by the trustees year after year for a period of five years with the privilege of terminating the lease on six months' notice by the trustees. This agreement made provision for housing the School until a modern dental building could be erected.

The first state conference on dental education was held June 8, 1926, in Memorial Hall in connection with the annual Commencement exercises of the University. Visiting dentists from all parts of the state were in attendance at this conference, which constituted a splendid opportunity for the dentists and the University authorities to know each other better and make their aims mutual.

In May, 1929, the board decided that a building for the School of Dentistry should be the next new structure erected at Indianapolis, and in December, 1931, appointed Robert Frost Daggett architect for a new building to cost $250,000. In the following February Dean Henshaw and Architect Daggett presented tentative plans. Since a site for the new building had not been secured, final decision was deferred to a later meeting. In September, 1932, the purchase of the present site for the School of Dentistry was authorized at $17,500, of which $12,300 was paid from the Educational Improvement fund and $5,150 was contributed by an anonymous donor.

So far as records are concerned, the account of the purchase of this site is now ended. Yet the story back of these brief records is very interesting and illustrative of the months of discussion sometimes necessary in finding a satisfactory solution of some difficult problem. The story runs as follows:

The selection of a site for the new building was presenting difficulties for all concerned. Dean Henshaw and Dr. Gerald D. Timmons, Secretary to the faculty, were very desirous of having the building located near the Medical School, preferably on the Medical School campus. The Medical School Council was none too hospitable to this idea. A certain relationship of medical buildings, existing and projected, had been established, and, while there was much ground unoccupied by any building, it was difficult to find a site where a dental building would not appear as an intruder. A site to the west of the Ball Nurses' Home was suggested but almost at once rejected, partly because the ground was very low, and partly because the location of the School of Dentistry with its necessary traffic adjacent to the Ball Nurses' Home seemed a threat to the restful quiet of that home.

This was the situation when, at the meeting of the board in May, 1932, Dean Henshaw, Dr. Timmons, and Mr. Daggett presented the advantages of the present site on West Michigan Street just opposite the School of Medicine. This site seemed a happy answer to the question as to where the Dental School building should be located. It had the desired advantage of proximity to the medical campus without any of the undesirable features of a location on the Medical School grounds. But when the price at which the site was held was stated, purchase of the site was regarded as entirely impossible. Within the board there was strong opposition to paying any considerable sum of money, badly needed elsewhere, for a site for this medical specialty, dentistry, when so many adequate sites seemed available on the Medical School campus. So the matter seemed to be right back where it started.

Dean Henshaw, however, was an aggressive man, and a golf player. He had a club for every possible lie of the ball, and he knew when to use a niblick. As the summer of 1932 wore on he returned again and again with the owner to present some improved proposition to Mr. Fesler, who, as the trustee from Marion County, was closest to the situation and sympathetic with the purchase of this site if priced reasonably.

Though the price asked for this site was now about 40 per cent of the original, $17,450 was still a sum so large for this small, unproductive bit of ground, 4.03 acres, that it seemed almost certain that the trustees would reject the purchase.

In this emergency an anonymous donor, to whom Mr. Fesler had confided the various angles of the situation, handed him a check for $5,000 to be applied to the purchase of this West Michigan Street site, and with this check in his pocket Mr. Fesler went to the September board meeting.

As the business of the session progressed the matter of a site for the School of Dentistry finally came up for discussion, whereupon this is what happened:

1. Mr. Fesler informed the board of the check for $5,000 in his pocket to be applied to the purchase of this West Michigan Street site.

2. President Bryan handed Mr. Fesler a telegram to be read to the board from Mr. Ball,[1] who had not been able to be present but had wired, strongly urging this purchase.

3. President Bryan, who, in a controversial matter, usually let the board work out their own solution, now threw the weight of his judgment in favor of this West Michigan Street site.

4. Whereupon Judge Batman, a most conscientious and fair-minded member, who had led the opposition, said: "Well, I could be mistaken; I will not stand in the way of the purchase."

5. Other opponents embracing this view, the purchase was approved.

It was a particularly happy solution of a difficult problem in which the anonymous donor was largely responsible.

Mr. Daggett was directed to submit final plans and specifications, which were approved in October, 1932. The general contract was

[1] Mr. Ball, a resident of Muncie, was very conscientious regarding attendance at meetings of the Board of Trustees. There were times when he came on from New York City for a meeting and then returned to New York City following the meeting.

awarded to William P. Jungclaus, for $165,100, and subcontracts amounted to $54,779.30, to bring the total cost to $219,879.30.

Excavation for the building began November 29, 1932. The cornerstone was laid on May 15, 1933. The Dental School was moved from its former location on North Pennsylvania Street at the opening of the fall semester, 1933.

The dedication ceremonies were held on January 8, 1934. President Bryan spoke for the University, J. W. Fesler for the Board of Trustees, Dean W. D. Gatch for the School of Medicine, and Dean Frederic R. Henshaw for the Dental School. The principal dedication address was made by Dr. C. N. Johnson, of Indianapolis, termed "the Dean of American Dentists." The program was climaxed by an alumni dinner.

Perhaps the most impressive part of this fine building was the operative clinic. It is beautifully lighted, facing north, two stories (40 feet) high with provision for enlargement.

Great credit was due and granted Dean Henshaw and the efficient secretary, Dr. Timmons, for their persistence in urging state support for dental education, for their recognition of the optimum site for the School of Dentistry, and for their continued pressure for a building so admirably adapted to their needs. These two men, and, indeed, the entire faculty were most enthusiastic over the achievement and with difficulty were restrained from organizing the entire dental profession of the state in support of a bill to be presented to the legislature making provision for a separate Dental School budget.

In June, 1935, a great forward step was taken in requiring two years of predental collegiate work for admission to the Indiana University School of Dentistry.

Dean Henshaw had the satisfaction of seeing the conclusion of his persistent endeavors of more than a decade. He was ill in the summer of 1937 but had recovered sufficiently to be at his post for the opening of the school year, 1937–38. On January 15, 1938, the Board of Trustees gave him a leave of absence for the second semester and appointed Dr. Timmons as assistant to the dean. Dean Henshaw did not improve as hoped, but died on May 27, 1938, leaving his estate for the sole use and benefit of the Indiana University School of Dentistry which he had piloted so successfully.

Chapter XXIII

WATER, 1903 - 26

Water had been a consideration in the selection of a site in Perry Township for location of Indiana Seminary. The site chosen in July, 1820, was "convenient to an excellent spring of water, the only one on the section selected that could with convenience answer the purposes of a seminary."[1] This spring had dried up and had been forgotten, and for many years the University had depended on cisterns for water. When, in 1885, the institution was moved to the present site, cisterns and wells furnished water for a time. But as the institution grew and water consumption increased, it came to depend upon the water supply of the city of Bloomington.

The problem of an adequate supply of water for Bloomington was proving particularly difficult around the turn of the century. First of all, the city was not located near a lake or river, but on a watershed between the two forks of White River. The site had been chosen because of that fact and was regarded as especially healthful. As population increased and wells and cisterns became inadequate, it was necessary to build a dam and form an artificial lake.

Here the second difficulty presented itself. The region to the south of the watershed was limestone country, full of sinkholes and underground streams, and it was in this region that, in 1894, the first effort to provide a water supply for Bloomington was made. When the promoters of this project failed with heavy loss, the city took over the plant, which can be seen today from Road 45, running between the two small lakes about three and one-half miles west of Bloomington. The plant, however, never was adequate in a dry season. There was a water famine in 1899 and another in 1901, necessitating a temporary shutdown of the plant.

In 1902 when William Lowe Bryan became president, except for a cistern from which thirsty faculty members and students drank,

[1] Report of meeting of the Board of Trustees of Indiana Seminary, July, 1820.

the University was getting its water from the city, which was depending on this small water plant. With growth of the city, the population of which was about 3,500, and with increase in the number of homes using city water, it was obvious that the plant would become increasingly inadequate.

This situation was proving of growing concern to the administration. In December, 1903, it was feared that the University would have to be closed for lack of water. In March, 1904, the President, with Trustees Rose and Shively, was appointed to confer with city authorities on the water situation and to urge immediate action. The minutes of every meeting of the Board of Trustees show their growing uneasiness. Professor Foley was requested to report on construction of a catchment basin on the campus to provide water, not for drinking, but for toilets, lavatories, and for boilers of the heating plant. The Executive Committee ordered two wells dug on the campus. One of these wells gave six barrels of water an hour; the other, less. In June, 1906, an additional cistern was ordered to be dug at the west side of the Student Building.

The *Bloomington Daily Telephone* for December 2, 1908, carried the headings: "Water Famine at Last; plant closes down to await heavy rains." What had long been an inconvenience and annoyance now had become a great menace. Since there was little hope of an early solution of the problem of a dependable water supply for Bloomington, the administration concluded that the University must have its own independent supply. Accordingly, a request was presented to the legislature of 1909 for an appropriation for that purpose. Meantime, as an emergency measure, pipes were laid to the Illinois Central Railroad where tanks of water had been shipped in, which was then piped to the campus and stored in cisterns.

The legislature of 1909 made an appropriation of $20,700 for a water supply for the University. The wording of the act was so general that the administration was free to use its best judgment in the development. It had been thought that wells in Griffy Creek valley would furnish an adequate supply, but test wells showed this view mistaken.

The University then adopted a second recommendation of the engineers. Farther up Griffy Creek valley a narrow gorge opened into the valley, the damming of which would impound a consider-able supply of water. This land was purchased or optioned, a low dam was constructed, and pipes were purchased and laid to the campus.

In the fall of 1910 the trustees presented to the Visiting Committee a request for $25,300 for a more adequate installation. Of the $13,800 appropriated, part was used on the dam and part to buy additional land, the object being to own and control the watershed.

In June, 1912, the question of a lake on the north side of the cam-pus was referred to a committee consisting of Professors Foley, Cumings, Beede, and Hanna, whose report was presented in October. Such a lake could be formed, they said, by running a dam across Jordan valley from the walk west of the Student Building, to Seventh Street. The lake would extend almost to the power house.[2] The flow of Jordan River would keep the dam overflowing most of the year. During the winter season almost half of the water used by the Uni-versity was used by the boilers. From the University waterworks lake the water had to be pumped up a 220-foot hill. The campus lake could be built for $3,500, the interest on which would be much less than the cost of pumping.

In the fall of 1912, reporting to the Governor and the Visiting Committee, the President said:

Two years ago doubt was expressed whether plans proposed by our engineers would work. It was doubted whether there would be enough water within the drainage area and also whether the dam and the bottom and sides of the reservoir would hold. It is now clear that there is an abundance of water to be caught, and that the reservoir and dam hold.

The legislature of 1913 appropriated, for the completion of the plant, $40,500, available after October 1, 1913. The height of the dam was increased twelve feet, additional land of the drainage area was purchased to protect the water from contamination, duplicate ma-chinery was installed, and the plant was completed in 1914.

Governor Ralston had become irritated at the failure of Bloom-ington to solve its water problem. In June, 1914, *The Indiana Daily Student* quoted a letter from him in which he said:

[2] The coal road, the extension of Woodlawn south of Seventh Street, had not been built at that time.

I do not wish to be harsh in what I say, but it seems to me that they [the people of Bloomington] do not fully appreciate the serious consequences that may result to the student body growing out of a water famine.

The Marion County alumni held a meeting in the Claypool Hotel, on June 15, 1914, at which Judge James B. Wilson spoke for the city of Bloomington, Mayor John Harris for the city administration, and President Bryan for the University. A recent statement of Governor Ralston was read in which he had said:

The water situation in Bloomington is very serious. I have about made up my mind as Governor to ask the legislature to take account of the situation and, if necessary, to remove the University from its present site.

George M. Cook, president of the Alumni Association, said:

There have been water famines in Bloomington (i.e., a shortage of water necessitating a temporary shutdown of the plant) in the years 1899, 1901, 1904, 1908, and 1913. There were serious shortages, with prohibition of lawn and street sprinkling, notably in 1911 and 1912.

In March, 1915, the President reported to the Board of Trustees:

As a matter of record I note the fact that there were brought before the legislature two proposals for removal of the University. The matter came to a public hearing largely attended by citizens of Lafayette and Bloomington. Some efforts were made looking to a reduction of University income.

The people of Bloomington had not been insensible of the rising criticism of alumni and parents of students throughout the state relative to their water situation. They finally realized that expansion of the water plant was necessary. It was natural that they should seek to salvage as much of the old plant as possible, and that could be accomplished if the new lake were constructed near the old plant. A few miles south was Leonard's Spring. It was really an opening of a small underground stream, the flow of which had been utilized at an earlier day as power for Leonard's Mill. Unfortunately, the Leonard's Spring site was deeper in the cave, sinkhole, limestone formation. Campus experts had stated that a lake constructed at that site would almost certainly leak, and the advantages of the nearer Griffy Creek valley were pointed out.

But the Leonard's Spring site was purchased and the dam built in the summer of 1915. For a few seasons the rainfall was good, and everyone was hopeful, but the water under pressure was searching out every fault in the lake bed. In the fall of 1919 the city water supply was alarmingly low. In May, 1920, President Bryan wrote Mayor Harris as follows:

The authorities of the University have no desire to interfere with local matters. On the other hand, they feel they have a responsibility for the health and well-being of the young people from all parts of the state who are under their charge. The University has been greatly injured three times by water famines. Last fall the University could not have opened at all except for the fact that the University had provided a supply of water for its own use, which, however, did not make provision for the students at their places of residence. Those who are charged by the state with responsibility for the University wish to know definitely what the prospects are for a water supply during the coming summer and fall, and what assurance can be given to the state for an adequate supply in the future.

To this Mayor Harris replied:

We all feel our responsibility in regard to the water situation and hope soon to devise ways and means for an immediate as well as permanent supply of water for the city.

But month after month passed without anything being done.

Although the University now had its own water supply for the campus, this did not ease the situation for the students, who, in times of drought, were subjected to all the inconveniences Bloomington citizens endured. In such times water might be pumped into the city mains once or twice a week. Overdue baths were taken hastily, then bathtubs and other vessels were filled, from which water was dipped for washing hands and faces and flushing toilets. The tale of these inconveniences carried by students to all sections of the state was cutting normal increase in attendance. University authorities and many Bloomington citizens felt that the future of the city, of its industries, and of the University depended upon securing for Bloomington an adequate and dependable water supply.

In the winter of 1921–22 it had become apparent to about 98 per cent of the Bloomington citizens that the Leonard's Spring site was inadequate. They had been patient with the seven-year trial of Leonard's Spring, but were now convinced that a new and adequate supply must be found. Where, they did not care. They wanted water. A small minority of Bloomington citizens still proclaimed the adequacy of the Leonard's Spring site, and for them the vindication of their opinion was becoming the major issue.

The files of the Bloomington papers tell the story of the steps leading to the final establishment of a dependable water supply for Bloomington.

1922

The crucial drama opened with the announcement on February 27, 1922, that the mayor and City Council, by a 5 to 4 vote, had contracted for purchase of land adjacent to Leonard's Spring and proposed to build a second dam 1,100 feet below the old one, at a cost of about $150,000, later reduced to $100,000. This announcement was supposed to end the controversy as to whether a permanent solution of our water problem would be found at White River or at Griffy Creek. Instead of the end, it proved the beginning of a struggle which dragged on nearly four and one-half years.

Fortunately, at this time an agency had been organized, the Bloomington Chamber of Commerce, through which the wishes of Bloomington citizens could find expression. Dr. J. E. P. Holland, the active president of the Chamber, was supported by an able and influential board of twelve directors. On May 24 the Chamber of Commerce held a banquet at which a movement was launched, not for a stopgap, but for a real solution of Bloomington's water problem. The Monon Railway was an interested water-user and Harry R. Kurrie, the president of the Monon, was present and one of the speakers.

Disregarding the action of this body of several hundred leading citizens, the City Council on June 6 again affirmed its purpose to develop a site immediately downstream from Leonard's Spring.

On June 8 the Chamber of Commerce went on record as unanimously and unalterably opposed to the Leonard's Spring development and protested further waste of city funds. Two days later the *Daily Telephone* carried a full-page editorial supporting the position of the Chamber of Commerce.

On July 21, 1922, the Chamber of Commerce elected new officers. Dr. Burton D. Myers was chosen president. The new directors, elected for a period of three years, were: George Talbot, Dr. G. F. Holland, Professor U. S. Hanna, and Oscar H. Cravens. The holdover directors were: William Graham, B. G. Hoadley, L. W. Hughes, Wood Wiles, Rev. William Burroughs, Dean H. L. Smith, Dr. A. M. Snyder, and Dr. J. E. P. Holland. An adequate water supply for Bloomington was the major objective of the Chamber.

Though the mayor had won every round in the contest up to this time, there was a final hurdle to be negotiated, namely, approval by the State Tax Board of the necessary bond issue. It was to this board that the Chamber of Commerce now appealed for a hearing, which was granted, to be held in September.

On August 4 a ban was placed on the use of water for sprinkling. This was the beginning of an unusually dry period which was to tax the water resources of many communities, while our supply was to diminish to an intermittent trickle.

The hearing before the State Tax Board, protesting the $100,000 bond issue proposed by the City Council, was held in the Monroe County Courthouse on September 1, 1922. Attorney Robert G. Miller and Judge James B. Wilson spoke for the position of the Chamber of Commerce.

An amusing incident occurred. One of the advocates of the Leonard's Spring development was making an impassioned speech. He said: "They say that lake out there (Leonard's) leaks. I was out there a few days ago and walked across that lake bed from side to side, and you couldn't see a sign of a leak." The crowd burst into a roar of laughter and the speaker, startled and resentful, did not at once understand that the fact he could walk across the lake bed was the best possible evidence that all the water had leaked away.

The Bloomington papers of September 8, 1922, and following carried the headings, "City Gripped by Drought," "Nearly 90 Days Without a Good Rain," "Temperature 102 degrees."

On September 9 the State Tax Board handed down its decision, disapproving the bond issue of $100,000, saying:

1. A bond issue of $100,000 would not give Bloomington the water supply contemplated.

2. Citizens and taxpayers of Bloomington were entitled to know the full amount necessary to give the relief desired.

3. The amount proposed to be paid for the land ($35,000) was greatly in excess of its value (about $5,000).

On September 21 Councilman Lynn Lewis, who had been voting with the city administration, introduced a resolution at the Council meeting to rescind all action on the Leonard's Spring site and employ competent engineers to search out the location which would give Bloomington a dependable water supply. Lewis and Samuel Franklin, voting with the four men who had constituted the minority, carried this resolution 6 to 3. The engineering firm of Pearce, Greeley, and Hansen, of Chicago, was employed to make the survey.

Here appears the fundamental difference in the basic thinking of the two groups. The one group in this crisis turned to experts, specialists, for help. The other group ignored the expert and placed confidence in lay observation. It was not wholly a matter of good, public-spirited men in conflict with selfish elements of the community. The Leonard's Spring advocates included some of the most influential, public-spirited citizens of Bloomington. But this group also included those men interested in selling land to the city at a price ($35,000) which the State Tax Board declared was greatly in excess of its value as everyone knew. Some of these influential citizens had seen quarry holes hold water for years, and from this observation they made the generalization, "Limestone land will hold water." In making this generalization they closed their eyes to all they knew of sinkholes filling with water which rapidly sank away; they stopped their ears to the hearing of caves and underground streams found in a territory extending from Bloomington southward to Indian Springs, Lost River, Marengo Cave, Wyandotte Cave, and on down to Mammoth Cave in Kentucky.

On October 6 an inspection was made of Bloomington by state officers to determine the effect of the city's water famine on fire hazards and its bearing on insurance risks and rates. On October 25 a greatly increased insurance rate was announced for Bloomington. In one instance, a 42 per cent increase was reported. The officers of the Chamber of Commerce made a personal study of fire hazards in the business district, visiting and inspecting basements for accumulations of inflammable material. The Bloomington papers were carrying two-column and three-column editorials.

Reporting to the Board of Trustees in October, 1922, President Bryan said:

The Trustees are already aware of the existence of another water famine in Bloomington. The hopeful fact in the situation is that six of the nine members of the Council have resolved to abandon the hopeless situation southwest of town; have employed competent engineers to investigate Griffy Creek and White River locations, and have expressed the determination to provide an adequate water supply for Bloomington.

Meanwhile, the University has taken every possible means to alleviate the situation so far as the students are concerned. Water is taken daily in tanks to all houses where students room. I am advised that so far there is no apparent danger from a sanitary standpoint.

Having been informed by Mayor Shank that Indianapolis was too short of fire equipment to lend any to Bloomington, Dr. Myers, the president of the Chamber of Commerce, on October 29 took Henry Gentry, John Cravens, and two other interested persons to Indianapolis to the Stutz factory, where they saw demonstrated a $10,000 fire fighting truck, built for San Francisco, which they were able to secure for Bloomington in its emergency until the City Council could take action. A meeting of citizens held at the Chamber of Commerce passed a resolution asking the Council to organize a force of watchmen for night patrol of the business district. Showers Brothers furniture factory was shipping in water in order to keep running.

By November 10 the engineers studying the water problem had narrowed it to two sites, Griffy Creek and White River. On November 22 their report reached Bloomington and proved to be in favor of Griffy Creek. The report stated that Bloomington would need to be a city of forty or fifty thousand to bear the expense of construction and maintenance of the White River site.

On December 18 a barrel of alcohol in a garage on West Sixth Street exploded and the fire threatened the west side of the square. It was held in check by the new pumper. Escaping a disastrous fire did not end the opposition of the city administration. The mayor vetoed the Griffy Creek development. The Council overrode his veto. A petition for a referendum to popular vote was presented by certain obstructionists. The Council tabled the motion.

Bloomington, at that time, had a bonded indebtedness limit of $150,000. This fact gave rise to a problem in development of the Griffy Creek site, which would cost $300,000 or more. Therefore, a holding company was formed to finance the project locally. The board of directors of the holding company was announced on December 23. The banks and citizens were prepared to finance the construction and lease the plant to the city. Plans were made to begin work on the dam at an early date.

1923

On January 5, 1923, a charter of incorporation of the Bloomington Water Company was received from the Secretary of State.

February 16 was known as Bloomington Day in the legislature. The House unanimously adopted a minority report and passed H.B. 199 giving cities of the fourth class authority to abolish the board of public works. This legislation prevented the mayor of Bloomington from appointing a board of public works hostile to the Griffy Creek project, and was regarded by Registrar Cravens as the most important act of the General Assembly of 1923, affecting Indiana University, although another bill appropriated to Indiana University $275,-000 for a power plant for the School of Medicine.

On February 23 the progress of this movement for a dependable water supply for Bloomington was interrupted by the Public Service Commission, which raised the question as to whether Bloomington needed a second utility. The attorneys for the new water company held that this was not a second utility, and in this view, after deliberating four weeks, the Commission finally concurred. This cleared the way for the construction of the Griffy Creek system and preparations were made to rush the work.

On June 1 the City Council, over the protest of the mayor, voted that the city should take $150,000 of common stock in the new holding company, which would give the city control of the company. This $150,000 was to be raised by a bond issue.

On July 5 twenty-five Bloomington citizens filed a remonstrance with the State Tax Board against the $150,000 bond issue authorized by the City Council. This remonstrance called for a hearing before the State Tax Board, which was held in Bloomington on July 20. President Bryan was one of the chief witnesses. He told of the demand over Indiana for action to end the local water "crime." He asserted that the University dam, forty feet high, in the Griffy

Creek valley, held water like a jug. Asked about injury to the University caused by droughts, the President said that during the water famine in 1922, 175 students left the University and that at the next term 450 old students did not return. He stated that in 1922 the University spent $4,400 on account of the drought in Bloomington. The tax commissioners took a standing vote of the people in the courtroom. About 90 per cent were in favor of the Griffy Creek project. It was asserted that followers of the mayor had stated that they would fight the proposed water solution through the Supreme Court if necessary.

On July 30, 1923, in Indianapolis, the Public Service Commission held a hearing on two petitions relating to the Bloomington water question: (1) the petition to ratify the contract between the city of Bloomington and the new Bloomington Water Company; (2) the petition to issue $150,000 of common stock and $300,000 of preferred stock. The decision of the Public Service Commission handed down on August 31 was in favor of both of these petitions.

On September 4, 1923, a hearing was held in Indianapolis by the State Tax Board in which oral arguments in the Bloomington water case were presented. Attorney Walker, for the mayor and his supporters, contended that the procedure whereby the Griffy Creek system was to be built was an evasion of the debt limitation of the city of Bloomington. The attorneys for the City Council and the new company claimed that the city would assume no debt beyond its legal limit but only contracted to take water of the new company. The decision was in favor of the water company.

On September 4 a tax levy of $1.54 including 38 cents toward carrying out the waterworks plan was passed by the City Council. It was promptly vetoed by the mayor. The issue was passed over the mayor's head by a 6 to 3 vote.

On September 18 the Public Service Commission refused to grant a rehearing of the Bloomington waterworks case requested by the "wrecking crew," so called because of the obstructionist, delaying tactics they had adopted.

On September 21 fourteen citizens filed a remonstrance with the county auditor of Monroe County against the $1.54 tax levy. This found its way before the State Tax Board for a hearing. On October

24 the State Tax Board handed down its decision cutting the Bloomington tax rate 32 cents. This was believed to have no serious effect on the water situation because the fund yielded by this 32-cent tax was not needed at once.

On October 13, 1923, a complaint was filed in the Monroe County Court by Will H. Adams against the Public Service Commission seeking reversal of its action on the Bloomington water contract. It was expected that the complaint would not be heard until the December term of the Monroe County Circuit Court. In reality the case was not heard until March 20, 1924, and it was heard then only because Judge Rundell on March 15 ordered the case brought to trial without further delay. The action of the Commission was sustained.

The State Tax Board held a hearing in Bloomington on October 30. This was really a continuation of the hearing of September 4 and related to all unanswered questions before the board on the Bloomington water problem. The daily papers carried announcements, "Tax Board Settles Water Fight." The hearing began at 10 a.m. and for an hour the hearing progressed peacefully. Fireworks were introduced at the hearing when Roy O. Pike, impatient at the many hearings without a conclusive decision being reached, took the floor and demanded that the Tax Board show a proper amount of backbone and bring about at once a settlement of the water fight.

The Tax Board aimed to do this in the following decision:

1. The ultimate water supply for the city of Bloomington was to be located in the Griffy Creek valley.

2. The first expenditure at Griffy Creek must be limited to from $280,000 to $300,000 and a thirty-foot dam.

3. The Leonard's Spring plant was not to be junked but was to be continued in operation as long as the present machinery and mains leading into the city last. No new equipment was to be installed at Leonard's Spring.

4. The waterworks must support itself and the citizens of Bloomington must not be called upon to support it by taxes.

5. A special committee of four local men, with the engineer of the Tax Board and the Public Service Commission acting as the fifth vote in case of disagreements, was to have the Griffy Creek

valley core-drilled in the next thirty days so the contractors could make definite bids on the construction work for the new dam. The committee was composed of W. E. Showers, Professor U. S. Hanna, Mayor John Harris, and W. H. Adams. This committee must finish its work inside of thirty days.

Some thought that this committee as named would not be able to agree on anything. But it was pointed out by Mr. Showers that they did not have to agree on anything; they had merely to employ experts to core-drill the land.

The committee acted without delay. The landowners were given a bond guaranteeing payment for any damage and the core-drillers were ordered on the site. This harmonious action was hoped to clear the way for a solution of the Bloomington water problem. It was generally hoped that personalities and politics would be put aside and all would work in harmony for the good of Bloomington and Bloomington institutions.

By November 24 the core-drilling was completed. Nine test holes and two trenches were put down and knobstone was struck at depths from 15 to 27 feet. This gave the definite information insisted upon by the State Tax Board as necessary for contractors in bidding on the work.

1924

On February 19 bids were opened for the construction of the new Bloomington waterworks. It was found that the bids were low enough to assure the building of the Griffy Creek project under the $300,000 limit imposed by the State Tax Board and the Public Service Commission. The contract was awarded to the Phelps Construction Company of Iowa on February 21, the work to be completed by December 1, 1924. It was provided in the contract that it was not good if the State Tax Board failed to O.K. the plans, if the bonds could not be sold, or if the construction was stopped by legal action of the citizens.

On February 27 in Indianapolis at a hearing of the State Tax Board, the board signified its intention of approving the $150,000 bond issue of the city of Bloomington for the Griffy Creek water project, and it was expected that formal approval would be made by

February 29. The "wrecking crew," however, gave notice that favorable action of the board would be contested and carried to the Supreme Court of Indiana if necessary. Thus ended the hope which was raised of all working together for the best interests of Bloomington institutions and Bloomington people.

On February 29 a petition to reopen the Bloomington water case was filed before the State Public Service Commission by Mr. Walker, the attorney for the mayor, and W. H. Adams.

Early in March, the Tax Board cut the city bond issue to $125,000. So another hearing was scheduled at Indianapolis before the Indiana Public Service Commission for March 12 to hear the petition to make the bond issue $125,000 instead of $150,000. This meeting was duly held and arguments were made by Attorney Walker, of Indianapolis, against the bond issue, and by Attorneys Matson and McCord speaking for the new water company. Attorney Walker said that there should be some available evidence that the bonds could be sold. To provide this evidence, friends of the Griffy Creek project subscribed for $863,500 worth of bonds in a few hours.

As resentment at delay and obstruction rose, the women of Bloomington entered the fight. The Local Council of Women carried a petition and secured the signatures of 1,900 women within ten hours. Only one out of fifty refused to sign.

That the interest of Bloomington and the welfare of her citizens had been lost sight of by the city administration is indicated in a statement of the mayor, quoted in the *Telephone* on March 15, 1924, as follows:

If they build their waterworks, they cannot run their pipe lines in Bloomington without the consent of the Administration.

On Monday, March 17, 1924, a vast multitude turned out for a meeting which it was hoped was to mark the end of the long water fight and the beginning of a greater Bloomington. The mass meeting which assembled on the south side of the square was one of the greatest and most enthusiastic crowds ever seen in southern Indiana. Factories, mills, stores, and schools closed down for the hour of the celebration from 10 to 11 in the morning, when thousands were packed in front of the speakers' stand. A photograph of the meeting near page 400 gives evidence of the accuracy of this statement. Roy O. Pike acted as chairman. President W. L. Bryan was one of the principal speakers. The meeting demonstrated the support of the new waterworks program by an overwhelming majority of Bloomington citizens.

On March 18 the following box notice appeared in the *Bloomington Telephone*:

In consideration that A. Phelps and Sons will proceed with the construction of the Griffy Creek water improvement without waiting for the sale of municipal bonds of the city of Bloomington, Indiana, and the purchase of common stock of Bloomington Water Company by said city, and the sale of the Preferred Stock of said Bloomington Water Co., the undersigned agree with A. Phelps and Sons that the undersigned will loan to Bloomington Water Company sufficient funds and at such times so that said Bloomington Water Company can perform punctually all its obligations to A. Phelps and Sons under the contract between said Bloomington Water Company and A. Phelps and Sons, dated March Seventeen, 1924.

Citizens Loan and Trust Co.
    by Roy O. Pike, Cashier.
Showers Bros. Savings Co.
    by Edward Showers.
First National Bank
    by Chas. S. Small, V.-President.
The Monroe Co. State Bank
    by C. L. Rawles, Cashier.

On this same day, March 18, the city bond issue of $125,000 for the Griffy Creek site, which had been vetoed by the mayor, was passed over his veto by the Council by a vote of 6 to 2.

The Public Service Commission stated that the matter of an adequate water supply was vital for Bloomington and it would not act in any way which would allow more delay. The wisdom of this attitude of the Public Service Commission was to be recalled in February, 1925, when water back of the dam Bloomington citizens were fighting to build was used to break Bloomington's last water famine.

It had been hoped that the necessary land could be secured without condemnation. About half of this land was owned by Charles Matlock and the remainder by four or five other men. Appraisers had been appointed by Judge Rundell to determine the value of the land. On May 8 these men reported that they had agreed upon a price of $25,025 as the value of the 241½ acres owned by Matlock, and a check for that amount was deposited with the County to be accepted or refused by Matlock. If he refused, his procedure would be an appeal. Most people regarded this finding as very favorable for Matlock. The average price of land in Monroe County at that time was $35 per acre. This legal procedure made it possible to begin construction of the dam at once, and a week later work was under way.

But on July 3, 1924, a new attack on the city's water supply had to be met when an injunction suit by William P. Bollenbacher to prevent the mayor from signing the bonds was tried before Judge Cyrus Davis at Bloomfield and lost.

The right of way for the pipe line was completed by mid-July and construction was proceeding in a most satisfactory way, and promised completion by December 1, according to the contract.

The mayor was still refusing to sign the bonds. The question of his legal right to sign these bonds was tried before Judge Davis. On September 25 came the decision of Judge Davis mandating Mayor Harris to sign the waterworks bonds. Earlier the mayor had stated that he would sign the bonds if the courts assured him that doing so was legal. Now, however, he delayed. On the morning of November 14, 1924, the mayor was to appear before Judge Rundell at Spencer, Owen County, to answer for contempt of court and to receive his punishment for failure to sign the waterworks bonds issue. A restraining order was issued by Judge Myers, of Indianapolis, delaying further action in the waterworks fight until November 21, 1924. The mayor died without signing the bonds and without appearing in court.

The list of guarantors was lost in the great fire which destroyed the Bradfute Building and most of the southwest corner of the square. A new list of guarantors was quickly signed up (see *Bloomington Star,* November 21, 1924). On December 5, 25 per cent of pledges was called for, to pay waterworks bills. In a short time $200,-000 was made available.

It was becoming evident that instead of the city owning control of the Water Company as planned, the refusal of the mayor to sign the bonds would result in the guarantors being the owners of the waterworks. The matter of signing the bonds was now in the Supreme Court. Mayor Harris had until January 5 to file briefs. The Water Company would then be given thirty days in which to file an answer. Fifteen days would then be allowed the mayor for a reply. So a decision in this important matter could not be expected before sometime in March.

The dam and lake were completed November 24, about a week ahead of contract. On December 19 it was announced that thirty more acres had been added to the water site. With a temporary shut-off of the water supply from Leonard's Spring, announced for January 9, 1925, officials of the new water company, meeting with contractors, brought about a promise of speedy action in the finishing touches which would give the city first service from the new system at Griffy Creek.

1925

It was planned to connect the new water mains from Griffy at once with the big main of the old system on the north side of the square (*Bloomington Star*—January 9, 1925). At the new lake, the gates were to be closed and the impounding of water begun. Meanwhile the city would go on water rationing as Bloomington faced her last water famine. The University, as in former droughts, again took steps to haul water from the University supply to all houses where students roomed. The student health committee issued instructions to the student body and cautioned house managers particularly against delay in calling a plumber to remove furnace coils. Lavatories and showers in the gymnasiums were to be open from 6:30 a.m. to 10 p.m.

On Monday evening, February 2, 1925, the pumping of water from the Griffy Creek lake was begun, and all during the following week this source supplied the city of Bloomington, and during all that week the water level was rising in Griffy Creek lake.

The *Bloomington Star* of January 30, 1925, stated that there had been prepared and would soon be introduced in the General Assembly a bill with the following title: "A bill for an act to ratify, confirm, and legalize all ordinances, bonds, and contracts entered into by the City of Bloomington or on its behalf for the purpose of securing a supplemental water supply for the City of Bloomington, and also to ratify and confirm all acts of the State Tax Board, and Public Service Commission relating thereto."

On February 13 this bill passed the house 87 to 0, and on February 27 it passed the Senate and in due time was signed by the Governor.

On March 2, 1925, Mayor Harris died.

On March 19 Lynn Lewis was elected mayor of Bloomington by the City Council. Lewis was a loyal party man, but he was also loyal to the best interests of Bloomington. It was Lewis who, on September 21, 1922, had broken the administration majority by introducing a resolution rescinding all action of the Council with reference to Leonard's Spring. Great credit was due Lynn Lewis, and he was now put in a position where he could do much to end the long-drawn-out fight.

On March 19 another legal obstacle was removed by a Supreme Court decision. Matlock had brought suit in the Monroe County Circuit Court claiming that the Water Company had no legal right to condemn land in the Griffy Creek valley, needed for the erection of the new water plant. The court found for the Water Company. Matlock then appealed to the Supreme Court and that court affirmed the decision of the local court.

Only two cases still remained:

1. One filed by William Bollenbacher against the City of Bloomington and the Bloomington Water Company challenging the legality of the Griffy Creek bond issue was now pending in the State Supreme Court.

2. The case filed by Charles Matlock against the Bloomington Water Company protesting the amount paid by the company for land under condemnation proceedings. This case was pending in the Owen County Court.

On June 25, 1925, the Supreme Court handed down a decision against William Bollenbacher. On August 25, 1925, Bollenbacher filed a motion for a new trial. Commenting on this the *Evening World* said:

Those who have been opposing the City in its effort to provide Bloomington with an adequate water supply have contended all along that they merely wanted to test the legality of all proceedings. Matters have progressed until it now seems there is something more back of the effort. If Bollenbacher is merely the goat, citizens would like to know who are really behind the project.

On November 5, 1925, the Supreme Court of Indiana denied a rehearing. There was some indication Bollenbacher planned an appeal to the Supreme Court of the United States. The *Bloomington Star* for November 13, 1925, carried the subheading: "Citizens would sue Bollenbacher for malicious prosecution."

Bloomington citizens had become thoroughly exasperated after nearly four years of continued opposition on the part of a small group of wilful men, who had cost the city thousands of dollars of needless expense in fighting cases through the courts. Had Bollenbacher appealed to the Supreme Court of the United States, it is probable that he would have been called to file bond for cost. Since the opposition had lost every suit, the bondsmen were probably shy. Whatever the restraining factor may have been, the case was dropped and that fight was at an end.

With the election of Lynn Lewis as mayor, March 19, 1925, the stage was set for the signing of the waterworks bonds. But where were the bonds? The most exhaustive search failed to locate them. In fact, they never were found and a second printing had to be arranged.

Since the Bollenbacher suit had been a cloud on the $125,000 bond issue, it had been decided not to sell the bonds until the Supreme Court handed down its decision. The Supreme Court decision adverse to Bollenbacher had come on June 25; this petition for a rehearing was denied November 5. This was looked upon as the final chapter in the long-drawn-out obstructionist proceedings.

On November 10, 1925, the *Bloomington Evening World* carried a statement that the City Clerk had delivered the bonds to two Indianapolis banking houses. The bonds were sold at a premium.

The ending of the Bollenbacher suit left pending only the Matlock suit for more money for his land than had been agreed upon by the appraisers ($25,025). Matlock's land (241½ acres) consisted of a valley with bounding hills on the north and south sides, into which were anchored the ends of the dam built across the valley. Matlock contended that his land was something more than merely farm land, that it was a natural water site, and that he should be paid what it would have cost the water company to construct these anchorages of the dam.

Matlock had taken a change of venue from Monroe County Circuit Court to the Owen County Court at Spencer. On June 8, 1925, he filed a motion for change of judge, which was sustained. Homer Elliott was appointed. He accepted and qualified and on June 22 heard arguments on plaintiff's motion to strike out certain exceptions. On July 3[3] Judge Elliott ruled that the farm value of Matlock's land determined its price. What happened that made Judge Elliott unwilling to try the cause of action is not a matter of record. But it is a matter of record that on October 27, 1925, he filed a written declination to do so.

After several appointees declined to serve, Robert R. Mellen, on April 24, was appointed special judge and accepted. The case came to trial on July 19, 1926. The jury was selected and the evidence introduced. The case was concluded on July 26 and the jury instructed. On July 28 the jury reported for the defendant, Matlock, $44,000 as of April 16, 1924, not including interest.[4] The court rendered a judgment for $50,028 and costs. An appeal was considered but a compromise of approximately $45,000 was agreed upon.

Thus ended the opposition to the sustained purpose of Bloomington citizens to establish for the city a dependable water supply.

The beneficent results of this successful effort to secure a dependable and adequate water supply for Bloomington had begun when water from Griffy Creek broke the last water famine in Bloomington in February, 1925. University enrollments increased, factories expanded, a great building program in Bloomington was begun, the assessed value of new houses on a single street was in excess of half a million dollars, the number of water-users greatly increased, and, from the completion of the Griffy Creek plant, there never has been an hour when water was not available at every tap in Bloomington.

The above is the unhappy story of a conflict which never should have occurred. But it did. In addition to health and fire hazards of water famines, cost of shipping in and distributing water, cost of increased insurance rates, cost of needless litigation[5] amounting to more than $18,000, there had been the blighting effect of undesirable publicity on normal growth of the city, its industries, and the Uni-

[3] Owen County Clerk's Record Book, p. 119.
[4] Owen County Clerk's Record Book, p. 368.
[5] All told, there were eleven law suits, three of which reached the Indiana Supreme Court.

versity. When the fight was ended the people of the state had ceased blaming Bloomington for the intolerable water situation and understood that it was just another of those unhappy instances in which a city administration ceases to represent the interests of its citizens.

Credit has been given the Chamber of Commerce for staging the initial hearing before the State Tax Board which disallowed the bond issue for further development at Leonard's Spring, and for leadership of officers of the Chamber, the directorate, and membership throughout four long years.

Credit has been given Lynn Lewis for the pivotal part he played in breaking the administration majority and making employment of experts possible. Lewis was encouraged in this radical procedure by the fact that about 90 per cent of Bloomington people were in favor of the Griffy Creek site.

Credit must be given all three Bloomington newspapers for their unfailing advocacy of the Griffy Creek development in editorials and news items. The wide publicity given the various episodes of this four-year battle went far toward building up that sound public opinion supporting the project.

While many individuals played important roles in the unfolding drama, a review of the various incidents of the contest seems to show that one man in particular was always in the forefront of the conflict, a sort of unofficial captain of the team, a director of the various episodes of the pageant. That man was Roy O. Pike. If he had been officially assigned the task of leading the campaign for Griffy Creek, he could not have devoted himself more continuously and unselfishly to the job.

CHAPTER XXIV

THE BUILDING OF THE STADIUM, 1923 - 31

For a considerable group of alumni in the early twenties, a stadium was a major interest. As stated elsewhere, the campaign for a memorial fund was not yet completed when pressure groups began urging the erection of this particular structure.

Professors William J. Moenkhaus and Ulysses S. Hanna were sent on a journey of inspection and investigation to the University of Iowa, the University of Illinois, and other institutions where they secured information concerning the best material and methods for constructing a stadium. On April 5, 1923, they reported to the trustees.

On May 11, 1923, the vice-president of the Osborn Engineering Company, of Cleveland, presented to the board his views concerning materials and site for the Stadium. That company was retained as engineers.

The board on April 23 had approved steel construction for the Stadium. But on May 12, after hearing the report of the engineering company, the board reconsidered this action and ordered that the Stadium be constructed of concrete and located in the little valley northeast of the Men's Gymnasium.

On June 4 Mr. Evans, of the Osborn Engineering Company, presented tentative plans for the Stadium. Plans and specifications were advertised for bids, and on July 10 bids for construction of the Stadium were opened and tabulated. It was found that the Bedford Steel and Construction Company was low bidder by $20,000. This low bid might have seemed a bit ominous. Mr. Haynes, a representative of this company, was interrogated concerning the financial responsibility of his company.

The matter of awarding the general contract was taken under advisement by the trustees, but with instruction to the Executive Committee to award the contract to the lowest bidder upon execution of a bond for $50,000, approved by this Committee.

The work of construction of the Stadium was promptly begun and seemed to be progressing satisfactorily. On September 15, 1923, a report of progress was made. On January 30, 1924, the trustees considered width of seats. On February 16 the Executive Committee was ordered to let the contract for the facades to the Bedford Steel and Construction Company.

Then in March, 1924, alarming cracks were discovered in the concrete of the completed structure. Careful examination revealed evidences of disintegration.

On April 8, 1924, Leslie Colvin, a building expert of Indianapolis, who had done very satisfactory work as a contractor and builder for Indiana University, was present on the invitation of the Board of Trustees and, with the board, made an inspection of the Stadium, following which Mr. Colvin made a statement to the board concerning the construction they had carefully examined. A committee[1] consisting of Professors William N. Logan, Arthur L. Foley, and Robert E. Lyons, Bernard Green, of the Osborn Engineering Company, and Mr. Colvin made a further inspection and then in conference formulated a report to the Board of Trustees which recommended:

1. That a loading test be applied to the columns and beams, such load to be at least 200 pounds per square foot of surface. If this test proved satisfactory, then,

2. That all disintegrated concrete of all parts of the Stadium be removed and replaced.

3. That a new reinforced concrete deck of sufficient thickness be placed over the entire existing deck, after the latter has been coated with coal tar pitch. The new deck to be entirely self-supporting. The surface of the deck to be finished with a 1:3 finish, not less than ½ inch thick and finished with a trowel.

4. That waterproofing be applied to all exposed surfaces of concrete in columns, beams, parapet wall, and other exposed concrete surfaces.

5. All aggregates used in concrete shall be clean washed sand and gravel. The proper provisions shall be made for the curing and the protection of the concrete from the time it is poured until it has properly cured.

On receipt of this report the board ordered that the contractor and his surety for the construction of the Stadium be notified that the condition of the work was unsatisfactory and that immediate steps

---

[1] This committee is referred to hereafter as the Stadium repair committee.

should be taken to make the work conform to the specifications. It was insisted that a conference be held with the University's engineers at once.

Statements from President Bryan and Registrar Cravens were printed in *The Indiana Daily Student* on April 9 assuring students and alumni that the University was protected from loss due to faulty work by its $50,000 bond with the Detroit Fidelity and Surety Company. President Bryan's statement follows:

April 8, 1924

The trustees of Indiana University find that the concrete work on the part of the Stadium which was done last season is unsatisfactory. The trustees have called into counsel four of the best scientific and practical experts to determine the cause and extent of the defects and to advise the remedy. It is fortunate that the Stadium was not completed last fall. The intervening winter has brought the defects to light. The University and the Memorial Fund are protected financially on the contract. The work of construction will proceed promptly on thoroughly sound lines and will be completed in good time for the opening in the fall.

Board of Trustees of Indiana University
By William Lowe Bryan

At the board meeting on April 10, Mr. Haynes, speaking for the contractors, stated his willingness to go ahead with repair and completion of the Stadium along lines indicated in the committee report quoted above. Likewise, Glen B. Woodward, speaking for the Detroit Fidelity and Surety Company, stated that he had had a conference with the company and that their attitude was one of cooperation.

On April 12 the Stadium repair committee made its report to the Executive Committee on the loading test. This test showed a slight settling. It was the judgment of the committee that dead load tests should be made on the south side and that the portion of the structure in contact with the earth would deteriorate. Mr. Anthony, president of the State Board of Engineers, was present and stated that his board stood ready to give any assistance in its power in working out the difficulties in the construction of the Stadium.

At this time it was believed that a repair and resurfacing job would render the Stadium acceptable. Accordingly, on May 7, the board authorized its president, Mr. Fesler, Dr. Smith, and Judge Batman to negotiate with the Bedford Steel and Construction Company, the contractors, and the Detroit Fidelity and Surety Company, the bonding company, and make such contract and agreement with them for repair and completion of the Stadium as the committee might deem proper.

On May 19 the Stadium repair committee reported that additional tests of the concrete in the columns and beams of the Stadium should be made before they reached a final conclusion in regard to a plan of making the Stadium construction satisfactory.

In the midst of these difficulties in which haste was dangerous, there were groups of students and alumni urging haste. Such a group of students appeared before the board on June 9, 1924, making a plea that the Stadium be completed in time for the home-coming game with Ohio State University on November 8, 1924.

Though the Bedford Steel and Construction Company had expressed willingness to proceed in accordance with the recommendations of the Stadium repair committee, time dragged along and they did nothing.

On June 11 the president of the board was ordered to execute and send to the contractor on the Stadium, proper notice of failure to comply with contract upon certification of engineer. A committee of the Board of Trustees was authorized to take such steps as might be necessary to protect the rights of the University under the Stadium contract.

On June 20, 1924, William J. Titus, State Highway Department bridge engineer, and Fred Kellam, testing engineer, made a report to Mr. Fesler alleging deficiency in construction of the Stadium and, according to *The Indiana Daily Student,* July 18, 1924, condemned the work already done.

Under date of July 2, 1924, Bernard L. Green, president of the Osborn Engineering Company, sent to the Board of Trustees a communication which ended by quoting the notice sent the Bedford Steel and Construction Company:

TO THE BEDFORD STEEL AND CONSTRUCTION COMPANY, BEDFORD, INDIANA

You are hereby notified that all of the work done by you for the stadium at Indiana University, Bloomington, Indiana is condemned by us as unsound and improper, and the same wholly fails to conform to the drawings and specifications of a certain contract of July 10, 1923, between the Trustees of Indiana University and yourselves; and the structure erected by you for said stadium should be in its entirety destroyed and removed.

Dated at Cleveland, Ohio, July 2, 1924
Signed: The Osborn Engineering Company
of Cleveland, Ohio,
By Bernard L. Green,
President.

One week later on July 9, 1924, the trustees received from the Osborn Engineering Company, by Bernard L. Green, president, a certification with reference to the contract with the Bedford Steel and Construction Company, as follows:

That the contractor has failed in the performance of the agreement contained in said written contract, and said Osborn Engineering Company, of Cleveland, Ohio, further certifies that such failure is sufficient ground for the owner to terminate the employment of the contractor for said work, and to enter upon the premises and take possession, for the purpose of completing the work included under said contract, of all materials, tools, and appliances thereon, and to employ any other person or persons to finish the work and to provide the materials thereof.

On July 15, 1924, the board took this action:

Be it further resolved that unless the Bedford Steel and Construction Company has entered upon the work of removing the structure erected by it in an attempt to comply with the contract for the construction of a stadium on the campus at Bloomington, Indiana, with a view of reconstructing the same in accordance with such contract, by the close of this 15th day of July, 1924, in compliance with the notice heretofore served on it, that steps be taken at once to have such structure removed and a proper stadium constructed in its stead.

On this same day the board entered into a contract with Leslie Colvin for construction of the Stadium, conditioned that the Bedford Steel and Construction Company had not complied with the notice served on it and that the president of the Board of Trustees be authorized to execute the contract on behalf of the trustees.

On July 21 Colvin began the work of demolishing the construction of the Bedford company. Lumber, glass, and tile were salvaged.[2]

Dr. S. E. Smith was appointed to represent the trustees under the

[2] *The Indiana Daily Student,* July 22, 1924.

provisions of the contract with Mr. Colvin, with reference to purchase of materials and employment of labor.

A committee consisting of R. E. Lyons, chairman, and Z. G. Clevenger, A. L. Foley, Wiley J. Huddle (representing alumni), W. N. Logan, and William J. Titus was appointed to act in a consulting and supervisory capacity in all matters relating to the Stadium.

Albert Rabb, representing the firm of Miller, Dailey, and Thompson, conferred with the Board of Trustees on October 6, 1924, concerning the time and the kind of suit to be filed in connection with the defective Stadium erected by the Bedford Steel and Construction Company.

Impressive and appropriate ceremonies of laying the cornerstone at the southwest end of the Stadium had been announced for November 15, 1924. A copper box containing a history of the Memorial drive was placed in the cornerstone by President Bryan, who wielded the trowel. Mr. Fesler, faculty members, and student representatives gave three-minute speeches. These exercises were followed by the Wabash-Indiana game.

In May, 1925, the suit of the trustees against the Detroit Fidelity and Surety Company came to trial. *The Indiana Daily Student* of May 23, 1925, carried the following account:

DEFENSE TESTIFIES IN STADIUM SUIT

Detroit Surety Company Alleges Blasting Caused Disintegration

Presentation of the testimony of the defense in the $50,000 damage suit of the University trustees against the Detroit Fidelity and Surety Company will be continued Monday in the Federal Court at Indianapolis before Judge Robert C. Baltzell and a jury. The case grew out of alleged faulty construction of the concrete stands of the old Memorial Stadium.

The defense, through its witnesses Saturday, attempted to prove that the disintegration of the concrete might have been caused by the blasting of rocks in the site of the Stadium bowl by engineers of the University at the time when the concrete had not yet "set."

The bonding company also tried to show, through the testimony of Theodore L. Condren, a civil engineer of Chicago, that the concrete was of good quality. Condren also stated that the alleged blasting at the time stated would result in the disintegrating of the material.

Four days later *The Indiana Daily Student* announced the outcome:

I. U. MAY CONTINUE FIGHT IN STADIUM DAMAGE SUIT CASE
Decision for the Detroit Fidelity and Surety Company Given Tuesday

JURY WAS OUT 5 HOURS
*Counsel for Plaintiff Uses Three Witnesses to
Prove Blasting Did Not Hurt Cement*

INDIANAPOLIS, May 26—Following the jury's verdict for the defendant in the $50,000 damage suit of the trustees of Indiana University against the Detroit Fidelity and Surety Company in the federal court here Tuesday, the attorneys for the University announced that they would consider continuing action in the case.

The claim was brought by the trustees of the University, who charged that the bonding company of the Bedford Steel and Construction Company had not paid the amount stipulated in the bond which insured satisfactory completion of the construction work. The plaintiff charged that this money was due it, since the Stadium had crumbled after the job was supposed to have been completed.

The verdict in the case was reached Monday night after more than five hours deliberation, and was read in court Tuesday morning. Following the reading of the jury's verdict, which was a surprise to many, because the instructions of Judge Robert C. Baltzell seemed favorable to the plaintiff, attorneys for the University made no comment only that they would carry the suit farther.

Say Concrete was Faulty

Attorneys for the plaintiff denounced the type of cement used in building the Stadium, and argued that the work done was so unsound that the entire structure had to be condemned. The counsel for the plaintiff used three witnesses in its argument in the morning session, who testified that the blasting done around the Stadium had not, to their observation, caused any injury to the cement work. The witnesses testifying for the plaintiff were: W. J. Titus, of the state highway commission; Dr. W. A. Hatt, of Purdue University, and Fred Kellam. Their testimony was in rebuttal of that of the seven witnesses for the defense who told the jury that, according to their observations, the blasting had caused the cement to crumble.

Hearing of evidence in the case was begun last week. Frank C. Dailey, of the Miller, Dailey, and Thompson law firm, of Indianapolis, was the attorney for the plaintiff, and Cassius C. Shirley, of Indianapolis, was the counsel for the defense. Perry O'Neal, Indianapolis attorney, also acted for the University.

The Indiana Daily Student of October 28, 1925, carried a brief announcement that "a motion of the Indiana University Trustees for a new trial in their $55,000 damage suit against the Detroit Fidelity and Surety Company was overruled by Judge Robert C. Baltzell in the United States District Court" in Indianapolis.

A very impressive ceremony marked the dedication[3] of the $250,000 Indiana University Stadium, November 21, 1925. Major General Hanson E. Ely, Commandant of the United States Army College, Washington, D.C., had come to Bloomington to make an address appropriate to the occasion. Prominent men of the state and nation had assembled for the ceremony and to see the Purdue-Indiana game, which followed the dedication.[4] The Old Oaken Bucket, the presentation of which had been a part of the dedication ceremony, hung in the Indiana University Gymnasium following the o–o score.

At the meeting of the trustees on December 16, 1925, Frank C. Dailey made a statement as to an appeal in the Stadium suit. An appeal was under consideration for some time. But on June 5, 1926, the board decided that, on the advice of the attorneys in the case, they would not take an appeal.

But this did not end the difficulty of the trustees in connection with the construction of the Stadium. In the fall of 1927 the Bedford Steel and Construction Company brought suit for $22,730 which they claimed was still due them. On November 19 Edwin Corr, attorney for the board, met with the board on matters relating to this suit. At the board meeting of January 4, 1928, Attorney S. C. Kivett, of Martinsville, Contractor Leslie Colvin, and Bernard L. Green, of the Osborn Engineering Company, gave information concerning the facts that were to be presented in the suit of the Bedford Steel and Construction Company against the trustees of Indiana University then pending in the Monroe County Circuit Court in relation to the erection of the Stadium.

The University trustees filed a counterclaim. According to *The Indiana Daily Student* of February 17, 1928:

Alleging that the materials used in building the Memorial Stadium prior to July 2, 1924, were of inferior quality and that the work was done unskillfully, the university trustees, through their attorneys, Miers and Corr, and S. C. Kivett, of Martinsville, have filed a counterclaim and cross complaint in circuit court against the Bedford Steel and Construction Company, asking for $100,000.

[3] Formal dedication was reserved for the Purdue-Indiana game. The first game played in the new Stadium was that with Indiana State Normal on October 3, 1925.
[4] *The Indiana Daily Student*, November 21, 1925.

This case dragged along for some years. The case finally came to trial on October 12, 1931, at Bloomfield, Greene County, Ind.

On October 20 *The Indiana Daily Student* published the following statement of compromise:

Decision of the involved parties Monday to resort to a three-way[5] compromise to settle their grievances without the trial by jury, brought hope that the Indiana University Stadium trial which has been dragging along and reappearing at intervals for the past six years, may be settled by Wednesday. . . .

The jury was dismissed from Thursday until Monday because of the death of the mother of one of the jurors. When the jury reconvened Monday the three principals announced that they were ready to compromise, and the jury was dismissed.

Thus, after eight years, the last chapter in the construction of the Stadium was ended.

[5] Indiana University, the Bedford Steel and Construction Company, and the Detroit Fidelity and Surety Company (original bonding firm of the Bedford Company).

CHAPTER XXV

INDIANA UNIVERSITY, 1924 - 26

THE TEN-YEAR BUILDING PROGRAM

THE COMMITTEE on promotion of University interests, organized in 1912, had devoted considerable time in the school year 1923–24 to the development of a ten-year building program for the University. It should be recalled that this was a large committee on which the various schools of the University were represented. In the preparation of a ten-year building program the finest spirit characterized the meetings. Though every possible special interest was represented on the committee, a plea was made for consideration of special needs on a University basis, and, after full discussion, a nearly unanimous vote was accepted as establishing the validity of the special need as part of the building program.

The need of the Department of Home Economics in Wylie Hall made a remodeling of that building at an early date very desirable. The need for an addition to the Library was recognized as one of the immediate needs of the University. The quarters for the School of Medicine in Owen Hall were generally recognized as being wholly inadequate for the accommodation of the increasing number of students selected annually from the hundreds (500 to 1,000) who were applying for admission to that School. In 1924 it was the opinion among the science men of the campus that there should be a great science building that would house the Departments of Geology, Zoology, and Botany, with museum space for all. The pressing need for an auditorium, an administration building, a new building for the School of Music, and expanded quarters for journalism was fully recognized, and each building was given its place in the program by committee vote.

The building program for the next ten years at Bloomington and at Indianapolis proposed in 1924 was the following:

At Bloomington:

Power plant, equipment, and tunnel extension		$ 500,000
Addition to Wylie Hall	$132,500	
Equipment	17,500	150,000
Addition to Library		226,000
Building for School of Education		582,100
Addition to Owen Hall plus equipment		150,000
Building for Geology, Zoology, Botany, and Museum		692,160
Group of small buildings, the most important being an addition to Science Hall for use in Physics		148,000
Auditorium and Administration Building		650,000
Building for School of Music		250,000
Building for Journalism		150,000
Bloomington total		$3,498,260

At Indianapolis:

Nurses' home	$ 250,000
Additional wards for the Long Hospital	500,000
Psychiatric clinic	350,000
Outpatient building	150,000
Gynecology and Obstetrics	400,000
Therapeutics building	400,000
Environmental Medicine	350,000
Clinical building	250,000
Indianapolis total	$2,650,000
Grand total	$6,148,260

Provision for most of these building needs was made not in the next decade, but in a fifteen-year period following 1924. Very naturally plans changed somewhat as years passed. The building for the School of Education was ultimately given a far better setting than that considered in 1924. Instead of an addition to Owen Hall to meet the growing demand for matriculation in the School of Medicine, a new medical building was erected. Instead of a single large building for the Departments of Geology, Zoology, and Botany, temporary adjustments were made by which all three of these departments were given more adequate quarters: Zoology and Botany, by the removal of English from Biology Hall; and Geology, by its transfer from Science Hall to Owen Hall where excellent quarters were found available and where this old, solidly constructed building, which once housed all of the science of the campus except chemistry, carried forward that early tradition by becoming the home of one of the major sciences.

SUMMARY OF UNIVERSITY NEEDS AND LEGISLATIVE RESPONSE

The needs of Indiana University for the years 1925–26 and 1926–27 as presented to Governor Emmett F. Branch were as follows:

	1925–26	1926–27
Buildings	$ 450,000	$ 500,000
Lands	50,000	
Deferred repairs and improvements, including walks, drives, drill and play grounds, and grading	115,000	110,000
Additions to Library—books and periodicals	60,000	60,000
Additional equipment—all schools and departments	150,000	155,000
Salaries and wages, including additions to staff	125,000	130,000
Supplies—all departments	50,000	55,000
Totals	$1,000,000	$1,010,000

As the 1925 session of the General Assembly got under way and the legislative program began to unfold, the conviction grew that it would be the part of wisdom to concentrate on a request for an adequate appropriation for an addition to the Library instead of the general request for buildings originally made.

It will be recalled that for many years, in fact from 1895, a time antedating the elevation of W. L. Bryan to the presidency, the University had been operating on a state mill tax income. Provision of such an income had a certain advantage if assessed values were gradually increasing, in which case an increasing income was provided automatically. There were, however, grave disadvantages. Assessed values might be stabilized, or might shrink. Moreover, under a mill tax system the institution was less likely to analyze her needs at frequent intervals, and, even more important, the institution was less likely to present its program of pressing needs to the people of Indiana each biennium, in solicitation of their support.

With these latter considerations in mind, the administration welcomed the proposal of the General Assembly to repeal the mill tax law and substitute therefor a budget[1] based on a searching inventory of University assets and needs.

Accordingly, the 1925 legislature appropriated for the University

1. At Bloomington:
   For operating expenses, $1,050,000 in lieu of the mill tax.
   For capital outlay, $325,000 for construction and equipment of an addition to the library.
2. At Indianapolis:
   For the James Whitcomb Riley Hospital $75,000 for equipment and maintenance for the year October 1, 1925, to October 1, 1926, and $50,000 annually thereafter.
   For operating expenses of the School of Medicine and the Robert W. Long Hospital, $65,000 annually.

ADDITION TO LIBRARY, 1925–26

We have noted above that the legislature of 1925 appropriated $325,000 for construction and equipment of an addition to the Library. This addition may be identified as the east wing of that building. It was greatly needed, and the legislature had barely adjourned when on March 14, 1925, Robert Frost Daggett was selected as architect and was ordered to prepare plans and specifications, cost not to exceed $225,000.

Preliminary sketches of this addition were presented June 6, 1925. When bids were opened on September 8, 1925, it was found that Leslie Colvin was the low bidder, and his bid was accepted by the trustees. The Governor and the Budget Committee, after receiving a report of the amount covered by the contract for construction and necessary equipment, agreed that any balance would be made available to the trustees for repairs and equipment of other buildings on the campus.

It was hoped that this balance would be sufficient to cover the cost of installation of a new boiler and to make the contemplated changes and improvements in Wylie Hall. On October 26, 1925, Provost Smith reported the following allocation of the $325,000:

Library building and equipment..........................$290,000
New boiler and accessories.................................. 25,000
Repairs, chemical laboratories.............................. 10,000

[1] The State Budget Committee was created by the 1925 legislature.

This addition to the Library, which nearly doubled the reading room capacity, was completed in the early fall of 1926.

Women's Dormitory, 1924–26

It will be recalled (Chap. XXI) that plans and specifications for the women's dormitory were advertised for bids to be opened July 21, 1924. Of the eight bids received, all were rejected except those of E. A. Carson, of Logansport, and the Great Lakes Construction Company, of Chicago, whose bids were tabulated and held for further consideration at the next meeting of the board. On August 1, 1924, a contract for construction of the dormitory was let to Mr. Carson on his bid of $333,345.

In the minutes of August 6, 1924, the trustees set forth, in a resolution, the conditions which they faced in the ever-growing need for living accommodations for students, particularly for young women. All of this led up to the resolution which they adopted calling for the issuance of coupon bonds to a total of $175,000 to be made available in addition to the $250,000 previously allocated for this building. These bonds were made payable to the Peoples State Bank of Indianapolis, which came to the aid of the trustees in solving this financial difficulty.

The wisdom of this procedure has been abundantly demonstrated. A substantial and beautiful building was erected providing excellent living quarters for young women. The financial plan was sound. The bonds were retired as they matured, and this was accomplished over a period of twelve years from the earnings of the building, without rates for rooms being excessive.

The cornerstone of the women's dormitory was laid October 20, 1924, and the building completed in 1925.

Temporary Quarters for the Bookstore

For a considerable number of years the Bookstore had been in the basement of the Library. With the construction of the new wing to the Library, it became necessary to find other quarters. In June, 1925, bids for a temporary wooden building for use of the Bookstore were submitted. The temporary structure was erected between Owen Hall and Maxwell Hall and was occupied until the splendid new quarters were available in the Union Building.

The Sale of the Indiana Medical College Building

In the spring of 1925 Governor Ed Jackson was desirous of having the state purchase the old Medical College Building at the corner of Market and Senate to be used as an overflow building for state departments.

It was the belief of the Board of Trustees that they could not, under the terms of the deed, relinquish their rights, because the property was deeded to the state with the definite understanding that it should be used by the University for Medical School purposes only.

On June 4, 1925, Trustee Fesler, accompanied by Dr. William N. Wishard, representing the trustees of the former Medical College of Indiana,[2] called upon Governor Jackson and took up with him the subject of the use of this building for state offices. The Governor expressed the hope and belief that under terms of the deed transferring this property to Indiana University the state might purchase this property and authorize the trustees to use the proceeds from the sale for additional construction and equipment in connection with the Indiana University School of Medicine on West Michigan Street. The board fixed the price of $100,000 on the old Medical School Building. After consulting with the Budget Committee, the Governor promised to support a bill to be submitted to the next General Assembly appropriating $100,000 for this purpose.

House Mothers

On May 5, 1925, the board approved the idea of having house mothers in the fraternity and sorority and other organization houses. The dean of men and the dean of women were asked to submit a report in regard to the requirements and means of establishing this rule.

On June 25 a committee from the fraternities appeared before the board and asked a postponement of the inauguration of this plan

[2] Known after the merger as Indiana Medical College, the School of Medicine of Purdue University.

since the plan would require certain house rearrangements to accommodate a house mother. It was stated that not enough representatives of each organization were present to take the necessary action. The request was signed by representatives of eighteen fraternities. In response to this request, the board postponed the time of taking effect of this rule until the beginning of the second semester of 1925–26.

On October 27 a committee representing the Pan-Hellenic Council protested the idea of establishing a system of house mothers for fraternities. The Aeons[3] joined in this protest. The trustees then directed that action in the matter be deferred pending further conferences.

THE PURNELL BILL

There had been an exchange of letters between President Bryan and Edward C. Elliott, President of Purdue University, in the spring of 1925 regarding duplication by Purdue of work being conducted by Indiana University in its School of Commerce and Finance.

The occasion for this correspondence was a bill introduced by Fred S. Purnell and passed by Congress, which President Bryan feared was intended to develop the field of commerce and finance at Purdue under federal support. Mr. Purnell had assured Dr. Bryan that his interpretation of the bill was incorrect.

President Elliott's most definite statement was the following:

Personally, I have no apprehension as to the abilities of the representatives of Indiana University and Purdue University to arrive at a common-sense, effective, and harmonious understanding concerning the work to be done. The untilled area of education is altogether too large for us to waste any time and strength in disputing over petty-paced areas.

On September 9, 1925, Trustee Wildermuth made an interesting report concerning the Purnell Act which made appropriations for research work to land grant colleges. The final paragraph of this report addressed to President Bryan read:

The Secretary of Agriculture has stated that it is his understanding that research in commerce and finance may be carried on under this act, but only

---

[3] The Aeons were a group of not to exceed twelve men, of at least Junior standing, appointed by the President on the basis of exceptional leadership or scholarship. Their object was to further University interests.

as such investigations have to do with the production, manufacture, preparation, use, distribution, and marketing of agricultural products; and scientific researches concerning the agricultural industry and the development and improvement of the rural home. The trustees of Purdue, with whom I have conferred, assure me that it is not their purpose at Purdue to undertake to duplicate our School of Finance and Commerce and they cannot possibly hope to do so under the provisions of this Act.

THE INDIANA-PURDUE COMMITTEE

In the fall of 1924 Indiana University, Purdue University, and Indiana State Normal had endeavored to prepare a joint statement of needs, a common legislative program for presentation to the General Assembly of 1925.

On October 20, 1925, a joint meeting of Indiana and Purdue alumni was held in Chicago at which a resolution was adopted reciting the fact that:

Whereas, Indiana University and Purdue University are both institutions of higher education in the State of Indiana, each serving separate and distinct fields of learning and scientific research, both dependent upon growth and maintenance, most largely through funds from legislative appropriation and taxation in the State of Indiana, etc., etc.

Therefore it was resolved: First, that a committee be created to be known as the Indiana-Purdue committee, etc. Second, the committee was to be composed of the President, a member of the Board of Trustees, and three alumni of each institution. Third, that the function of the committee shall be to cooperate in preserving and promoting the welfare of the two universities. This was signed by six Purdue and six Indiana alumni. Copies were sent to the presidents of the two institutions.

President Bryan presented this communication to the trustees at their November (1925) meeting.

It was not until June 7, 1926, that the Board of Trustees made its decision.

The board expressed its approval of the appointment of a committee to be known as the Indiana University-Purdue University committee. . . . Judge Ora L. Wildermuth was elected to represent the Board of Trustees on said committee and Secretary John W. Cravens was directed to notify the President of Indiana University Alumni Association of this action in order that three alumni members might be appointed.

On July 1, 1926, it was announced that three alumni members of this committee had been appointed: Arthur Stonex, of Goshen, John Weaver, of Chicago, and Allen G. Messick, of Marion.

This was a laudable effort. Conversations were held but no decisions were reached. Emphasis on institutional requests of the legislature sometimes changed after the legislative session had begun, because of some preference or opposition of legislators. Apart from maintenance, the needs of the different institutions were so unlike that they found united action difficult.

THE POWELL PROFESSORSHIP

The Mahlon Powell Professorship in Philosophy was established by a bequest of property valued at $65,000, made by Mahlon Powell, of Wabash, Ind. Litigation following his death in 1928 reduced this bequest to $31,622.32. The Powell Lectures were given first in 1936 by Professor W. E. Hocking, of Harvard.

MISCELLANEOUS

In June, 1925, Ora L. Wildermuth became a trustee of Indiana University, by alumni election, succeeding Dr. Samuel E. Smith.

Paul V. McNutt was made dean of the School of Law, assuming his duties August 1.

George F. Heighway, on the recommendation of the Alumni Council, was appointed alumni secretary beginning November 1, 1925, succeeding Edward C. Von Tress.

The Memorial Fund campaign was brought to a close on May 5, 1926, with a student campaign which put the total subscription over the $1,600,000 mark set in June, 1922.

In the winter of 1925–26 President and Mrs. Bryan made an extensive western trip in which they followed a work program which made sight-seeing incidental. They met and addressed alumni groups in Mitchell, S.D., San Francisco, Oakland, Palo Alto, Los Angeles, Glendale, Pasadena, Riverside, San Diego, Phoenix, Tucson, El Paso, San Antonio, and Houston. They had the deep satisfaction of seeing Indiana University graduates playing a worthy and sometimes a distinguished part in the life of these communities.[4]

[4] For more detailed account see *Alumni Quarterly*, Vol. XV, p. 137.

Chapter XXVI

THE JAMES WHITCOMB RILEY HOSPITAL
FOR CHILDREN, 1921 - 26

THE YEAR 1921 is memorable in the annals of Indiana University because preparations were being made for the launching of two great fund-raising campaigns, the one for the Memorial Fund and the other for the Riley Hospital for Children. The first of these campaigns was launched by the alumni of the University, and from it came the Memorial Stadium (1925), Memorial Hall (women's dormitory, 1925), and the Memorial Union Building (1932). The second of these campaigns was sponsored by the Riley Memorial Association and from it came the James Whitcomb Riley Hospital for Children (1924).

The story of the development of the idea of a hospital for children as a memorial to Riley has been related by Frederick E. Schortemeier, first secretary of the Riley Memorial Association (see Archives) and his version is here followed.

Shortly after Riley's death on July 22, 1916, William C. Bobbs, Indianapolis publisher, called a meeting of a score or more of the poet's personal and intimate friends for the purpose of developing a suitable memorial. After several meetings were held and various suggestions had been made and discussed, Dr. Lafayette Page, at a meeting at his home in late summer, presented the need of a hospital for children in Indiana.

The idea of a hospital for children as a memorial to the man who had sung of the "Happy Little Cripple" had so much to commend it, the need was so obvious, and the appeal so great that it became the adopted objective of this group. But war clouds were gathering and our entry into the war made the time inauspicious for launching a campaign for funds for this project.

Meantime the question of permanency presented itself. How could a hospital for children be organized so that, centuries after the passing of those personal friends of Riley, the institution would

309

continue to function as projected? The idea of a state charter or a national charter was discussed and discarded.

The war over, these same men met again on December 11, 1920, at the Indianapolis University Club and formed the James Whitcomb Riley Memorial Association. A committee[1] on establishment of a children's hospital was created. It was found that the Board of Trustees of Indiana University and the Indiana Child Welfare Association, in addition to the Riley Memorial Association, were interested in establishment of a hospital for children.

The collaboration of Indiana University and the Riley Association in the joint project of a hospital for children as a memorial to Riley came about very informally. On November 29, 1920, there had been an educational dinner in Indianapolis at which a drive was launched by Indiana, Purdue, and State Normal for the restoration of the 7-cent tax. Louis C. Huesmann, one of the speakers, and President Bryan talked about a hospital for children. On December 2 President Bryan wrote Mr. Huesmann expressing his indebtedness for Mr. Huesmann's presence and speech and added, "We ought by all means to have an orthopaedic hospital where the crooked children of Indiana might be made straight." Mr. Huesmann in his reply of December 5 related successive steps in the thinking of the Riley Memorial Association, and added, referring to the hospital, "I would like to see it located on the ground of the Long Hospital and have it under the charge of Indiana University."

It became obvious to members of the Riley Memorial Association that in Indiana University, founded by the state with the aid of a federal grant of land, there was that permanency which the Riley Association had been seeking. Furthermore, the establishment of a Riley Hospital for Children as a part of the University would make its facilities available for instruction of successive classes of medical students and would thus greatly augment the beneficent service of this hospital.

After informal conversations in which James W. Fesler, who was president of the Board of Trustees, took an active part, the matter was discussed by the board at its meeting in Indianapolis on January 13, 1921.

[1] This committee consisted of Hugh McK. Landon, J. K. Lilly, Sr., Louis C. Huesmann, Lafayette Page, and Carleton B. McCulloch.

The Riley Memorial committee met at the University Club on January 26, 1921, at the call of Mr. Bobbs, acting chairman, and tentative articles of association were read. The committee on the Riley Homestead site reported that the Indianapolis Park Board was favorable to the preservation of this site. Hugh McK. Landon reported that his investigation showed a great need for a children's hospital, and that Indiana University and the Governor, together with the Indiana Child Welfare Association, were interested in the undertaking. Mr. Schortemeier was directed to make an appointment with Governor McCray in order that the hospital project might be further considered with a view toward legislative action. The following day the revised articles of association were adopted as the articles of incorporation. The twenty-one incorporators were: Henry W. Bennett, Arthur V. Brown, James W. Fesler, George C. Hitt, Louis C. Huesmann, Hugh McK. Landon, Dr. Carleton B. McCulloch, Meredith Nicholson, Fred Dickson, Frank D. Stalnaker, N. Booth Tarkington, Evans Woollen, H. H. Howland, George Ade, J. K. Lilly, Sr., Dr. Lafayette Page, William E. Fortune, Charles E. Coffin, William C. Bobbs, Frank C. Ball, and William Pirtle Herod.

At the meeting of the trustees, January 27, 1921, the prospect of securing funds from private sources for a children's hospital was discussed at length. On January 30 President Bryan, Dr. Samuel E. Smith, and a committee of the Riley Memorial Association met and decided that the state legislative drafting board should be requested to draw a bill which would provide for a children's hospital. This bill was drafted, submitted, passed, and on March 11, 1921, approved.

The bill was very wisely drawn. It authorized the trustees of Indiana University to establish and maintain a hospital in Indianapolis as a department of the University, to be known as the James Whitcomb Riley Hospital for Children. It was to be located in convenient proximity to the Long Hospital. Section 3 provided:

Any child under sixteen (16) years of age, having a legal settlement in any county of the state, and afflicted with a defect, disease or deformity, presumably curable or improvable by skilled medical and surgical treatment, or needing special study for diagnosis, may be admitted to the said hospital, treated therein and discharged therefrom, under such rules and regulations as may be adopted by the management of the same, and approved by the board of trustees of said university.

Section 4 made detailed provision for the payment of the cost of care by the state treasurer, who then was directed to collect that cost from the county from which the patient was sent to the hospital.

The University was authorized to receive donations and bequests for the purpose of assisting in construction, extension, equipment, and maintenance of the Hospital. There was provision that the University's trustees should receive and consider such suggestions and advice as might be rendered by the James Whitcomb Riley Memorial Association. The trustees were authorized to establish and maintain, in connection with this hospital, a training school for child nursing.

An appropriation of $125,000 was made for construction and equipment of the building. An additional appropriation of $75,000 a year for two years was included for equipment and maintenance, with $50,000 annually thereafter for maintenance.

This bill was very important, for it established the fundamental status of the Hospital and the conditions under which it has operated, under which it has had its splendid development and has rendered its unsurpassed service.

On March 27, 1921, the trustees were informed that a number of citizens had agreed to give a considerable sum of money for the use and benefit of a James Whitcomb Riley Hospital for Children. To facilitate collaboration in this project the board passed the following resolution:

WHEREAS, The General Assembly of the State of Indiana, by an act approved March 11, 1921, provided for the establishment of a hospital in the City of Indianapolis, to be known as the James Whitcomb Riley Hospital for Children, and

WHEREAS, By the provisions of said Act, said hospital is made a department of Indiana University, and its establishment and management is placed in the hands of its Board of Trustees, with an express stipulation, as found in section seven thereof; that "in the construction, equipment, and direction of said hospital, the Board of Trustees of said University shall receive and consider such suggestions and advice as may be rendered by the James Whitcomb Riley Memorial Association," and

WHEREAS, Said Association has proposed to secure a large sum of money, with which to supplement the amount appropriated by said Act for the construction and equipment of said hospital, in order that adequate relief may be given to the afflicted children of this State, and a worthy memorial to one of Indiana's most distinguished citizens may be established. Now, therefore be it

Resolved, That the Board of Trustees of Indiana University, in keeping with the spirit of said act, and in order to more effectually accomplish the purpose thereof, appoint an Executive Committee of ten persons, five of whom shall be members of the Board of Trustees of said University, and the remaining five to be from the members of said James Whitcomb Riley Memorial Association, who shall be nominated by it, and which committee shall have charge of the construction, equipment and direction of said hospital, under the supervision of the Board of Trustees of said University, and subject to its approval. Be it further

Resolved, That the President of the Board of Trustees of said University, in its name, and for and on its behalf, present to said Memorial Association, duplicate copies of this resolution, duly certified by him, as evidence of its plan for executing the trust conferred upon it, and that an acceptance thereof by said Association, duly endorsed thereon shall constitute a contract between the Board of Trustees of said University and said James Whitcomb Riley Memorial Association, for their mutual cooperation in the accomplishment of the worthy enterprise contemplated by said Act.

The James Whitcomb Riley Memorial Association on March 31, 1921, took formal action "approving, accepting, and in all things ratifying" the above resolution, and Hugh McK. Landon, William C. Bobbs, Louis C. Huesmann, Dr. Lafayette Page, and Dr. Carleton B. McCulloch were chosen to represent the Riley Association on the proposed Joint Executive Committee. President Bryan and Trustees Fesler, Smith, Ball, and Batman had been appointed by the Board of Trustees to represent Indiana University on this committee.

A conference of these two groups was held on April 2, 1921, and the Joint Executive Committee of the James Whitcomb Riley Memorial Association was organized with William L. Bryan as chairman, Hugh McK. Landon as vice-chairman, and Frederick E. Schortemeier as secretary-treasurer. On and after September 6, 1922, James W. Carr was executive secretary of this committee. When, in the early nineteen thirties, Mr. Schortemeier retired as secretary of the Riley Memorial Association, Mr. Carr succeeded him but continued to serve as executive secretary of the committee.

The President gave to the trustees in June, 1921, a brief historical review of the Riley Hospital movement and a summary of activities of the Riley Hospital Joint Executive Committee created under the resolution quoted above.

As an immediate objective, arrangements were completed by the Riley Association to raise a fund of at least $250,000, and it was understood that the Hospital was to be located on a site adjoining the Robert W. Long Hospital on the north. The plan contemplated a million-dollar structure in the next ten years. Robert Frost Daggett was engaged to prepare plans.

A committee appointed by the Joint Executive Committee, including Architect Daggett, visited numerous children's hospitals throughout the United States. By April, 1922, Mr. Daggett had practically completed preliminary plans for the Hospital and was working on drawings for the main building and such other buildings as would be necessary.

The committee expected to be able to call for bids by June 1. It was thought that the first unit, which would include the main building and the power plant, would cost about $700,000, of which about $225,000 would be required for the power plant alone. The School of Medicine power plant then in use, supplying the Long Hospital and the Medical School with heat and light, was looked upon as a temporary structure since it would be wholly inadequate when the Riley unit was added.

The new power plant presented a difficult problem since it would supply not only the Riley but the Long Hospital and the Medical School as well. It was thought that perhaps a special appropriation should be asked of the next legislature for this purpose. At all events, it was believed that a general conference on the matter was desirable.

Steps had been taken several months earlier to acquire the real estate immediately north of the Long Hospital as a site for the Riley Hospital. The committee had successfully approached the city of Indianapolis, which had agreed to establish, immediately east of the Riley Hospital site, a convalescent park, greatly improving the setting of the contemplated hospital.

The task which this committee had undertaken was arduous, and called for unusual vision and optimism. The site chosen was in an unattractive portion of the city, bordered on the east by small rental properties. Moreover, with $225,000 available, the committee was making plans for a $700,000 building program which might easily grow into a program of twice that size. They had reason for encouragement, however. The school children of Indiana had already contributed $17,000. The Indiana Child Welfare Association, the Rotary Clubs of Indiana, the Junior League, and the Tri Kappa sorority of Indiana had given assurance of their official cooperation and there was a probability that other organizations would follow their lead. In the meantime, the Riley Homestead on Lockerbie Street, Indianapolis, had been purchased.

On June 23, 1922, the bids for construction of the Riley Hospital were opened, tabulated, and studied by the trustees. A committee consisting of Dr. Smith, Mr. Huesmann, and Mr. Daggett was appointed to present the plans to the State Board of Accounts. On approval by that body it was ordered that a contract be let to the lowest bidder. Mr. Huesmann assured the trustees that as construction advanced and the fund provided by the state was exhausted, the Riley Memorial Association would provide additional funds to meet bills as they came due.

On April 7, 1923, it was ordered that the Joint Executive Committee of the Hospital be asked to have plans and specifications prepared for a service unit and power plant, to be submitted to the University board at the earliest possible date.

On April 26, after consultation with the James Whitcomb Riley Committee, the Joint Executive Committee let contracts for the chimney, boilers, and mechanical stokers of the power plant and for elevators in the Hospital. The contract for the power plant at Indianapolis was let to the Cornell Engineering Company on July 2. Subscriptions amounting to $879,000 were reported to date.

On August 1, 1923, Mr. Fesler reported to the board that the following bids were recommended to them for acceptance:

1. A tunnel system connecting the Riley, the Long,
   and the Medical School.................................$ 43,790
2. For water supply and drainage system......................... 58,173
3. For switchboard and electric distribution system............... 27,795
4. For miscellaneous steam equipment and piping
   systems for power and heating plant......................... 115,909
                                                              ──────────
                                              Total........$245,667

Contracts were awarded the successful bidders on the above items.

By September 15, 1923, subscriptions to the Riley building fund were $911,518, of which $638,000 was yet due.

The formal exercises of laying the cornerstone of the Riley Hospital took place on October 7, 1922 (Riley's birthday). It was a red letter day in the history of medical education in Indiana and carried the promise of a new and very great service for indigent crippled children of the state. The following day (October 8) a contract for the kitchen, laundry, and service plant of the Riley was let to Leslie Colvin, the lowest bidder ($94,181). Very much more was involved in the construction of the Riley Hospital than the Riley Hospital building proper. Add the cost of the service unit and a nurses' home, made necessary by this Riley Hospital, and it will be understood that the ground plan for a great Medical Center was being laid.

The Riley spirit was high.

Among the best things written at the time were a few verses appearing in the *Indianapolis News,* written by Charles R. Williams, at that time editor of the *News,* paraphrasing Riley's "A Monument for the Soldier." We quote:

> A monument to Riley!
>   And what will ye build it of?
> Can ye build it of marble, or brass or bronze
>   Outlasting Riley's love?
> Can ye glorify it with fancies
>   As glad as his soul gave birth
> Which stir and thrill the heart they fill
>   To the outermost verge of earth?
>
> A monument to Riley!
>   Build it of people's love,
> And blazoned and decked and panoplied
>   With the hearts ye build it of!
> And see that ye build it stately
>   In pillar and niche, and gate,
> And great in plan as the soul of the man
>   Ye would commemorate.

In those early years of this project comparatively few persons had an appreciation of the need of this Riley Hospital for Children. For example, the statement was made repeatedly that there were ten thousand children in the state needing the care such a hospital could give, children who but for the service of such a hospital would grow up physically handicapped in various degrees, and also suffer an economic and probably a social handicap throughout their lives. Many people regarded this and like statements as exaggerations entirely justified by enthusiasm for a very worthy project. Later these statements were shown to be, in fact, understatements.

In undertaking and completing a project calling ultimately for more than $2,000,000[2], serious difficulties, some psychological, some financial, were encountered. Areas far distant from Indianapolis like the Calumet, or Posey County, feared Marion County would fill all the beds, that they were being solicited for funds for construction of an institution of benefit to Marion County only. So quotas were established.

Subscriptions were made on a five-annual-payments plan. But many were impatient to see walls begin to rise at once. And when, prudently, they did not rise immediately, then many said they never would, that the project was so huge it would not be underwritten, or people would subscribe and then not pay.

The psychology of the situation led the committee to press construction far beyond income and it became necessary for the Riley Association to borrow money secured personally.

On October 7, 1924, the Riley Hospital was dedicated; and the deed conveying it to the state of Indiana, for the use and benefit of the Indiana University, was formally delivered to the President of Indiana University, to be controlled, as provided by statute, by the Board of Trustees of Indiana University with the cooperation and advice of the James Whitcomb Riley Memorial Association.

At this dedication Dr. John H. Finley, editor of the *New York Times,* made the principal address. An introductory speech was made by Hugh McK. Landon, who was president of the Riley Memorial Association and chairman of the building committee. Louis C. Huesmann, chairman of the finance committee, made the presentation address. Dr. Walter Jessup, President of the University of Iowa, spoke briefly. It was stated by Mr. Landon that the campaign for

[2] $2,300,000 as of April 25, 1945.

funds was still on and that more than $700,000 had already been put into building. The Hospital as dedicated included the service unit, which was ready for use, and provided heat, light, power, laundry, kitchens, refrigeration, storage, and dining room. Mr. Landon did not state how much of the $700,000 already spent in construction of the Riley had been borrowed with the personal endorsement of four members[3] of the committee on the conviction that pledges made by Indiana citizens would not shrink seriously.

After the dedication, essential equipment was completed, medical, surgical, nursing, and service staffs were organized, and on November 12, 1924, the first patient, a polio case, was admitted.

In the late fall of 1924 it became evident that $165,000 would be needed in the near future. On December 9, after careful consideration, the board decided to issue notes to all contractors for material, labor, and equipment on the Hospital for balances due them, to a maximum of $165,000, bearing interest at six per cent per annum, due in three, six, nine, and twelve months, the notes to be endorsed by the Riley Memorial Association and the president of the Board of Trustees.

Though the Riley Hospital had been dedicated in October, 1924, it was not fully equipped and much construction was still necessary in completion of the plans of the Riley Association. Some hundreds of thousands of dollars had been borrowed, but it became necessary to borrow still more. At the meeting of the Joint Executive Committee on November 26, 1924, Mr. Landon reported that in order to borrow $75,000 Mr. Huesmann had offered the Union Trust Company collateral in excess of $100,000. On June 21, 1925, this Committee was informed that approximately $185,000 had been expended for equipment.

The year 1925 was a year of much worry for the Riley Association. It was, of course, quite natural that after the first enthusiasm for the erection of the great memorial to James Whitcomb Riley had spent itself, there should be a diminution in the number and size of subscriptions. Moreover, the general economic condition of many was not as good in 1925 as it had been back in 1922 and 1923. The

[3] These four members who personally endorsed Riley Association notes, thus pledging their personal estates, were Messrs. Hugh McK. Landon, Louis Huesmann, William Bobbs, and James W. Fesler.

Joint Executive Committee was uneasy over the fact that the Riley Association notes at the Union Trust Company totaled in excess of $700,000. The interest on these notes was a formidable sum. The endorsers of notes were, of course, particularly concerned. Then, when the hour was darkest, a great good fortune befell the enterprise. At the meeting of the trustees on December 16, 1925, the vice-president of the board, George A. Ball, stated that his firm, the Ball Brothers of Muncie, had offered to give $500,000 to the Riley Hospital.

In his address at the dedication of the Ball Residence for Nurses, Mr. Landon told most effectively the story of the announcement of this offer of Ball Brothers to himself and Mr. Huesmann. With assurance of this generous gift, a plan for a new campaign for funds was inaugurated and by May 21, 1926, this new campaign for the Riley Hospital had resulted in subscriptions of $1,800,000. With the successful completion of this campaign the Ball Brothers paid in the whole of their offer, thus stopping interest on half a million dollars. The trustees expressed appreciation of this gift (June 5, 1926):

The Trustees of Indiana University wish to express heartfelt appreciation of the great gift which you have made to the James Whitcomb Riley Hospital for Children. You have had the wisdom to do this splendid act of beneficence while yet in life and able to join in counsel as to its use. You will therefore have the satisfaction of seeing the work of your hands. You will see afflicted children growing toward health through your help. At the same time you have set an example which others will follow. The good that men do is catching.

To create a great business and fortune as you have done satisfies the ambition of many men. Your ambition is satisfied only as you transmute fortune into human well being and happiness. You have learned and by your acts you teach the supreme truth that Charity alone is eternal.

The natural sympathy of thousands of Hoosier citizens had been deeply stirred. I give two illustrations:

A student nurse, Ruth Firestone, who had begun her training with the opening of the Riley, wrote the following verses which give a measure of the impress made by this hospital:

In a Children's Hospital
Slim beds, straight beds,
And toys piled high,
Small hands aweaving
While others idle lie.

Bare walls, white walls,
  Ceiling stark and high,
Rows and rows of slim straight beds,
  On which the small folk lie—
Some who are coming back to health
  And some who wait to die.

Nurses here, nurses there,
  Soft-faced and wise,
Lips curved to laughter
  But with understanding eyes.

Faint scents, strange scents
  The corridors fill.
Outside the closed doors
  A mother crouching still
While a surgeon with the hands of God
  Works his miracle.

I was a guest at the noon luncheon of a Kiwanis Club in the Calumet. The club had raised a small fund to pay transportation of a
little newspaper boy to the Riley, a boy whom no one had ever seen
walk. At this noon luncheon it was expected that the boy would be
present. At a time arranged by the president, the door opened and in
walked the boy, holding the hand of a nurse, walking a bit wobbly,
but walking. The club collected about 10,000 per cent dividend on its
investment.

Section 3 of the Act of 1921 provided for admission of patients
under rules approved by the trustees of Indiana University. The need
of indigent children for the facilities of the Riley Hospital grew so
rapidly, however, that for a few years rules and regulations were not
formulated and pay patients and part-pay patients were admitted
only as emergency cases. An emergency case, for example, was admitted at once and the financial status of the patient determined
later. If it chanced that the patient was able to pay, he did so. It was
not until December, 1925, that a resolution was adopted by the board
establishing rules as follows:

WHEREAS, The daily average number of patients in the Riley Hospital
during the past two months has been less than the capacity of the hospital, and
  WHEREAS, Under the existing rules and regulations of the hospital only such

ALLISON MAXWELL   CHARLES PHILLIPS EMERSON

WILLIS DEW GATCH   BURTON DORR MYERS

DEANS OF THE SCHOOL OF MEDICINE

College Hospital and the State College of
Physicians and Surgeons

The Medical Center, now "a beauty spot instead of a cornfield and a dump." It all began with the gift of the Long Hospital.

The Medical College of Indiana

DEAN FREDERIC HENSHAW

The Dental School building acquired in 1925. (The new Dental School Building is in the foreground of the Medical Center.)

Owen Hall was the home of the School of Medicine at Bloomington from 1911 until the new building was completed in 1937.

THE COMMERCE BUILDING

WILLIAM A. RAWLES

HERMAN B WELLS

DEANS OF THE SCHOOL OF COMMERCE

ENOCH GEORGE HOGATE

Seven deans have served the School of Law, the oldest professional school in the University.

GEORGE LOUIS REINHARD

BERNARD CAMPBELL GAVIT

WILLIAM PERRY ROGERS

PAUL VORIES MCNUTT

DAVID DEMAREE BANTA

CHARLES MCGUFFEY HEPBURN

JOHN J. PETTIJOHN

WALTON SIMON BITTNER

ROBERT EMMET CAVANAUGH

These men have directed the Extension Division during 1914–37.

Extension Building at Indianapolis

WILLIAM LOWE BRYAN

WALTER ALBERT JESSUP

WILLIAM WESLEY BLACK

HENRY LESTER SMITH

The four deans who have guided the School of Education and the building
for which they waited long years.

patients are now admissible to the hospital as are committed to it by the judges of the courts as indigent and unable to pay for proper care and treatment; therefore,

Resolved, That hereafter both pay and part-pay patients be admitted to the Riley Hospital under such rules and regulations as the trustees may hereafter adopt.

With the establishment of county boards of public welfare, the eighty-fourth session of the General Assembly considered it desirable to define the relation of these boards to the indigent and part-pay patients sent to the Riley. Accordingly, an act was passed and approved March 7, 1945, amending section 4 of the Act of 1921 under which the Riley Hospital was organized, and providing, in detail, procedure in admission of indigent and part-pay patients.

One of the factors of great strength of the Riley Hospital for Children is the number of people and organizations interested in its work and welfare. The Kiwanis and Rotary Clubs made additions to the physical plant of the hospital (described in Chapter XXVII) and many other organizations have made important contributions to the Riley. Two of these organizations are the Indianapolis Junior League and the Riley Hospital Cheer Guild.

OCCUPATIONAL THERAPY

At the first meeting of the Indianapolis Junior League in the spring of 1922 they voted to undertake the equipment and maintenance of an occupational therapy department in the proposed Riley Hospital. An annual budget in excess of $10,000 was met by temporary money-raising projects and proceeds from the operation of a gift and a salvage shop until 1948, when the League discontinued support of this work.

Mrs. Winifred Conrick Kahmann, a graduate of Devereaux Mansion, came to the department when the hospital opened in 1924. She has since assumed the responsibility for the physical therapy department as well and directs the work of both departments at the Medical Center. The success and reputation of the occupational therapy department is in no small measure the reflection of Mrs. Kahmann's administrative ability and her qualities of leadership. She is recognized nationally and internationally as a pioneer in her field.

Volunteers of the Junior League, while sponsoring occupational therapy, always worked under graduate therapists at Riley, on the wards, and in the Rotary Convalescent Home as well as at Long and Coleman hospitals upon request. Mrs. Kahmann trained these volunteers, not only in occupational therapy, but in the fundamentals of volunteer service. Many leaders in the community today received their first training and experience under her.

Since the University hospitals are teaching hospitals, students from occupational therapy schools all over the country come to these hospitals for their practice training under Mrs. Kahmann.

The Riley Hospital Cheer Guild

The Riley Hospital Cheer Guild, an auxiliary serving the Medical Center, was organized April 2, 1924, seven months before the doors of the Hospital were opened, and has grown from a group of 12 women to nearly 12,000 in this time. At present (1947) there are 2,509 members in Indianapolis and 8,869 members out in the state. The leaders of the Guild have organized their membership in chapters and almost every county in the state has at least one chapter.

The motto of the Guild is "Inasmuch as ye have done it unto one of the least of these, ye have done it unto Me."

When the doors of the Hospital were first opened, the first patient, a little lad who had been stricken six years prior to his admission with polio, was served by the Guild with flowers, and this gesture on the part of the Guild made his stay just a bit pleasanter. In various ways, some of them of vital importance, the Guild has served every little patient that has ever entered the Riley Hospital.

Limited space permits mention of only a few of the many, many things done by the Guild. It maintains solely the bronchoscopic department. The visitor to this department sees many glass-covered trays containing objects, safety pins, peanuts, coins, etc. taken from the bronchi of patients. The Guild also serves in the Arthur Newby Clinic of the Riley Hospital, the waiting room of which they have furnished, where they act as receptionists and help, wherever needed, those who are waiting their turn for medical attention.

Every patient in the Hospital on his or her birthday and also on all holidays is made happy with gifts from the Guild. It has presented many books to the Riley Hospital Library for children and thousands of needed articles. The Guild maintains a sewing room in the Hospital where members come to help in making bandages and in doing all types of necessary sewing.

The Guild also maintains a toy room, has purchased many types of equipment, and has been instrumental in having a number of the hospital wards soundproofed. It has purchased radios, record players, projectors, and projector books and films. Music in therapy is foreseen by the Guild, and recently it purchased a piano and vibraharp to bring this music in therapy to the patients.

The Guild extends its cheer to the Rotary Convalescent Home patients. At the suggestion of the director of the University Hospitals, the Riley Hospital Cheer Guild undertook the work of bringing cheer and comfort to the patients in the Long hospital. This work is no longer on an experimental basis but is a part of the regular activities of the Guild. It takes much money to maintain the work of the Guild in all its branches but the work has always been taken care of because "thousands of worth-while women in our state have at heart the interest of one of the finest university schools in the country."

All members of the Guild pay into their treasury ten cents annually as dues and also make one annual contribution of toys, wool for the polio treatment, clothing, etc. It is not what one individual does but it is the combined efforts of all of the Guild members in the state of Indiana that has distinguished their service.

All of the members of the Guild are volunteer workers. The Guild maintains an office for its business transactions in the Hospital, Room 111, and it is indeed a very busy place.

"The Prayer Perfect," written by our beloved Hoosier poet, James Whitcomb Riley, is always uppermost in the minds of the women of this organization:

> Dear Lord! kind Lord!
>   Gracious Lord! I pray
> Thou wilt look on all I love,
>   Tenderly today!
> Weed their hearts of weariness;
>   Scatter every care

Down a wake of angel-wings
  Winnowing the air.

Bring unto the sorrowing
  All release from pain;
Let the lips of laughter
  Overflow again;
And with all the needy
  O divide, I pray,
This vast treasure of content
  That is mine today!

BACKING THE PROJECT

Great credit is due those who had the vision and broad conception of this Riley Hospital project and the patience and courage to carry it to completion. How unstinted was the devotion of the leaders of this project may be understood from a single sentence of a resolution passed by the Riley Association following the death of Mr. Landon on April 2, 1947: "He was personally present at more than 600 meetings of the Association." Not only will this great hospital serve the underprivileged of Indiana through coming centuries, but through the better training of medical students provided by its facilities its blessings are carried throughout the state and nation.

After the death of Mr. Landon, Perry W. Lesh was elected president of the James Whitcomb Riley Memorial Association and chairman of the Board of Governors, the successor to the Joint Executive Committee.

The work of the Riley Memorial Association has not ended after a quarter-century of distinguished service. The Board of Governors functions actively in increasing endowment for research. This endowment is already of sufficient size to yield important income for investigative work and gives promise of making the Riley one of the outstanding research centers in America in children's diseases.

On entering the Riley Hospital one sees at the right an alcove. Under the portrait of James Whitcomb Riley stands a cabinet in which are filed the names of the 45,000 persons who contributed to the fund necessary for erection of this memorial to our beloved Hoosier poet, a memorial in which many a "Happy Little Cripple" is relieved of his handicap.

Chapter XXVII

ADDITIONS TO THE RILEY HOSPITAL

The Kiwanis Unit

As evidence of the seriousness with which members of the Riley Memorial Association were taking their connection with the Riley Hospital project, I cite the trip to Anderson in September, 1922, taken by two members of the Joint Executive Committee, James W. Fesler and Louis C. Huesmann.

The annual convention of the Indiana Kiwanis District was meeting in Anderson at that time and these men secured a hearing before the trustees of that body to whom they explained the Riley Hospital project, the campaign for which was just beginning to get under way, and they expressed the hope that inasmuch as service to the underprivileged child was a major objective of Kiwanis, the Indiana Kiwanis District might be interested in undertaking to raise $150,000 for an orthopaedic ward of the projected hospital, to be known as Ward K, the Kiwanis ward.

This was, of course, a major undertaking calling for a subscription of approximately $40 from each of the 4,000 members of Kiwanis in Indiana. The appeal of the project, however, was so great that it was presented at the business session of the convention with the unanimous approval of the trustees and was adopted.

Since it had been explained that the Riley Hospital was to be erected on the campus of the School of Medicine and be under the management and control of Indiana University, Indiana Kiwanians chose Dean Burton D. Myers as district governor for the ensuing year, 1923, and thus assured interested leadership in the campaign for funds for this project.

The immediate effect of the adoption of the project of attempting to raise $150,000 for an orthopaedic ward of a Riley Hospital for Children was that soon there were, in 65 cities of Indiana in which there were Kiwanis Clubs, from 50 to 150 leading citizens who were informed about and boosters of the Riley project. This project of a

Riley Hospital for Children was so big that many believed it would never be completed. Not all groups or communities could have the personal presentation of the project by Messrs. Fesler and Huesmann. The next best thing was to know that fellow-citizens who had caught something of the vision and devotion of these leaders of this great objective had confidence in it and were supporting it. During the year 1923 every Kiwanis Club in Indiana was visited and solicited with the result that on January 1, 1924, subscriptions totaling $103,-961.50 had been received at Riley headquarters as reported by the Riley executive office.

Subscriptions to the Riley, in general, were on a five-year basis, one-fifth payable each year. By 1929 the accumulation of paid-in subscriptions amounted to a total sufficient to warrant preparation for construction. Accordingly, on March 25, the trustees of Indiana University, meeting in Indianapolis, invited the Kiwanis building committee to a conference at which plans prepared by Architect Daggett were discussed. With the acceptance of the suggestion that the cornerstone should bear a large K, the plans were approved. It was decided that this wing should be known permanently as the Kiwanis Unit of the James Whitcomb Riley Hospital for Children.

The exercises of laying the cornerstone took place on August 1, 1929, with international officers of Kiwanis present. As construction progressed the connection with the main hospital, which in the approved plans was to be one story, was changed to two stories in height, and the extra expense was borne by the Riley Association. This second story became the home of the occupational therapy work, which was conducted for many years so successfully by the Junior League.

The dedication ceremonies took place on January 7, 1930, beginning with an inspection of the hospital and the Kiwanis ward. This was followed by a banquet at which the president and secretary of Kiwanis International, Horace W. Davis and Fred C. W. Parker, were guests. The presentation of the Kiwanis Unit was made by J. Raymond Schutz, the Indiana Kiwanis district governor, and the acceptance address by Hugh McK. Landon, the president of the Riley Association.

President Bryan, in his address of appreciation, said:

The cooperation of individuals and organizations with the state in one beneficent enterprise is nowhere better illustrated than on this ground. Here Kiwanis has built a brick structure which year after year will help build a living structure of better men and women. In our attempts to better humanity we make many costly, well-meant failures. But if anything in this world is worth doing it is worth while to lift from a child an intolerable burden of illness or deformity so that it may have an efficient and happy life.

The president of the Board of Trustees, James W. Fesler, also spoke in appreciation of the gift:

I recall with some pride a trip to the city of Anderson a few years ago with Mr. Louis C. Huesmann, in the early months of the Riley Memorial Association, for the purpose of inviting the District Council of Kiwanis then in session there to join in the plans for the Riley Hospital then taking form. . . . I shall not forget the encouragement that group of men gave us, nor its importance in the future development of our building plans.

I see in this ceremony, therefore, the completion of a notable achievement undertaken by the Indiana District of Kiwanis at its Anderson meeting. . . .

So the Trustees of Indiana University desire to offer their very sincere congratulations to those who as officers have so successfully directed this undertaking and to every individual member of Kiwanis who has had a part in this most creditable achievement, even now so necessary in the important work of the Riley Hospital. . . .

May I also, Mr. Chairman, take the opportunity at this time to bespeak from Kiwanis its continued interest in the work of this hospital and to urge upon its membership the importance of bringing the Riley Hospital to the knowledge of parents whose children may be benefited and made over here.

Shortly after the dedication, patients were transferred from the temporary orthopaedic ward to Ward K, the Kiwanis ward, which became and has remained the orthopaedic ward of the Riley.

The Kiwanis Unit was built to accommodate 50 children, but frequently 65 have been crowded in. It is 186 feet long and 47 feet wide, with a 10-foot terrace on three sides. The floor space is divided into eight cubicles each containing six beds. Each cubicle has an outside door opening directly upon the terrace, permitting the moving of patients out of doors and into the sunlight. At times ten or a dozen additional beds are crowded into this ward. Between the cubicles are glass partitions. The supervisor at her centrally located desk can see every one of these beds. Up to December 31, 1945, there were 10,529 admissions to Ward K.

The Rotary Convalescent Home

In the early days of the campaign for subscriptions for building the Riley Hospital, the Rotary Clubs of Indiana undertook to raise a fund of $250,000 for a convalescent home. This is the unit in which those children who are not bed cases, but who require occasional check, or brace adjustment, etc., live and go to school, during the often long period of convalescence.

On July 29, 1930, Hugh McK. Landon, president of the Riley Memorial Association, and Robert E. Heun, of Richmond, chairman of a special Rotary committee on the Riley Hospital, announced that the tentative plans for immediate construction of a convalescent unit had been approved by the proper committees. Mr. Landon said:

> This marks an achievement in Rotary, so I am told, which has no parallel in the history of the organization. It marks another great step forward in the Riley Hospital program and fills a gap which has given us great concern.

It was the expectation that this unit would be a building more than 150 feet in length and more than half as deep, located on a ten-acre tract set aside by the Riley board and the trustees of Indiana University for convalescent uses.

On November 5, 1930, the trustees, in session in Indianapolis, met with the Riley Memorial Association committee (Hugh McK. Landon, Arthur Baxter, and Dr. C. B. McCulloch, and the secretary of the Association, J. W. Carr), and with a committee of the Indiana State Rotary (Charles Grafton, Muncie; Robert Heun, Richmond; Ben Sherwood, Bedford; and Obie J. Smith, Indianapolis). Mr. Daggett presented the final plans for the Rotary Convalescent Home, which were approved. When bids were opened Leslie Colvin received the general contract for the unit.

Construction progressed rapidly. On April 28, 1931, at the formal exercises of laying the cornerstone, the speakers were District Governor William F. Hodges, of the Gary Rotary Club, and Obie J. Smith, president of the Indianapolis Rotary Club. Robert Heun, of Richmond, was toastmaster at the accompanying dinner.

The formal dedication of the Rotary Convalescent Home was held on November 17, 1931. According to the governor's[1] monthly letter:

[1] Governor of Rotary.

The Indiana Rotary Convalescent Home was built by a freewill offering from Hoosier Rotarians. It is a three-story structure with an exterior of brick and Indiana limestone, faces south from a terrace immediately west of the present hospital. It will accommodate sixty children ranging in age from infants to those sixteen years old. It will have two schoolrooms accommodating twenty children each, a kindergarten, a library, a dining room, an assembly room, a therapeutic pool in the basement, and quarters for the staff on the third floor.

The interest of Rotary in subscriptions for and construction of this convalescent home had importance for and influence on the general campaign for funds for the Riley. There were at that time fifty-seven Rotary Clubs in fifty-seven cities of Indiana. There were, therefore, fifty-seven centers of special interest in the Riley Memorial Hospital which helped impress upon whole communities the importance and great merit of the Riley Hospital project.

THE HYDROTHERAPEUTIC POOL

This new unit of the Riley Hospital designed to furnish up-to-date facilities for treatment of infantile paralysis, spastic paralysis, spinal curvatures, and all other deformities requiring development of muscles was built jointly by Indiana University, the James Whitcomb Riley Memorial Association, and the Governor's Unemployment Relief Commission of Indiana at a cost in excess of $72,500. The pool is the outgrowth of very definitely improved results obtained in treatment of both children and adults by exercises in water, as demonstrated at Warm Springs, Ga., and similar institutions.

The pool itself is 18 by 35 feet and has a depth from 2½ feet to 4½ feet. It is lined with ceramic tile. It is housed in a building 35 by 60 feet with a dressing room 28 by 48 feet joining it to the Riley proper. There is special equipment under thermostatic control for maintaining the water at a given temperature, and provision for purification of the water. The pool was dedicated October 7, 1935.[2]

These three additions to the Riley—the Kiwanis Unit for orthopaedic cases, the Rotary Convalescent Home, and the hydrotherapeutic pool—represent a capital investment of about $500,000.

---

[2] For a full account of the hydrotherapeutic pool, see chapter on Capital Investment, in Myers, "Medical Education in Indiana" (MS).

CHAPTER XXVIII

THE BALL RESIDENCE FOR NURSES, 1927 - 28

THE TIMELY and fine-spirited gift of $500,000 by the Ball Brothers announced at a most critical time (December, 1925) in the financing of the Riley Hospital had been made without restricting conditions or stipulations as to its use. With the financial difficulty of the Riley relieved by the generous response of the people of Indiana to the campaign for additional subscriptions, headed by the Ball gift, the attention of the Joint Committee turned to a home for nurses, which, from the beginning, it had been foreseen would be needed for the Riley Hospital.

The Joint Committee believed the Ball gift should not lose its identity by being applied as part payment for the Riley, but that it should be used for some needed special construction in which identity would be preserved, and a residence for nurses seemed to afford this opportunity in an ideal way. Since this proved to be an objective in which the Ball Brothers were interested, the project was "given the green light," and on May 2, 1927, plans and specifications for this building were submitted by Architect Daggett and approved by the trustees and the Joint Executive Committee. Thereupon the vice-president of the board, George A. Ball, was authorized to sign the contract with Leslie Colvin for construction of the Ball Residence for Nurses.

Fourteen months later, on July 27, 1928, the board made a complete inspection and expressed their pleasure and appreciation of the building and especially of the spirit of the donors in providing such a valuable and practical home for nurses, embodying all the comforts and conveniences of the dormitory for girls recently erected on the University campus. The home contained well-equipped offices, lecture rooms, laboratories, and a gymnasium. There was a very attractive reception room and there were living quarters for 165 nurses.

The formal dedication took place on October 7, 1928, with approximately two thousand in attendance. Dr. Bryan paid high trib-

ute to the Ball family of Muncie, through whose generosity the
$500,000 allocated for construction of this beautifully appointed
building was made available. This was the largest single contribution ever made to a state institution of Indiana up to that time.

President Bryan cited as two immediate needs of the School of
Medicine: a hospital for psychiatry and provision for research work.
He summarized gifts for the Medical Center as follows:

The gift of Dr. and Mrs. Long, for the Robert W. Long Hospital	$ 245,000
The Coleman Hospital for Women, the gift of Mr. and Mrs. William H. Coleman	346,425
The James Whitcomb Riley Memorial Hospital for Children with adjacent land	1,288,370
The Huesmann Foundation for Research	60,000
The Ball Residence for Nurses	500,000
Total	$2,439,795

Add to these an appropriation of $550,000 and other gifts, not in-
cluding bequests, and it makes up a total of $3,550,000, invested in
the Medical Center at Indianapolis at that time.

With reference to the future of the Medical School, *The Indiana
Daily Student* quoted President Bryan as follows:

There is need of a hospital for psychiatry. Heads of our asylums for the
insane and other physicians have for years urged the establishment of such a
hospital here. They show from the results in other states that such a hospital
is effective in curing thousands of borderland cases, which, without such
service, go to asylums. They show that such a hospital soon saves a large proportion of the great and growing cost of our insane asylums. We have no
provision in prospect for a psychiatric hospital. Here is a fine opportunity for
a great service and an enduring monument such as we now in the three great
hospitals already have.

Reference has been made to the fact that this gift of $500,000 by
the Ball Brothers came at a particularly dark hour. This fact deserves
elaboration, and no one could tell the story so well as the president
of the James Whitcomb Riley Memorial Association, Hugh McK.
Landon, who had lived through those dark hours and now, following Dr. Bryan on this program, spoke as follows:

Speaking on behalf of the James Whitcomb Riley Memorial Association in acknowledgment of this beautiful and generous benefaction, I am mindful first of its timeliness, secondly of the spirit in which it was made, and finally of its significant quality.

As president of the Riley Memorial Association, conscious of the primary responsibility that rests upon me for what is done in connection with this hospital enterprise, I suppose it is natural that I think first of the timeliness of this gift of the Ball family. For it was made at the very moment when it meant most, at a time when the officers of the Association were beset by darkest discouragement and foreboding concerning the ultimate outcome of this undertaking. All of you who have been connected with large enterprises of any character know the terrific depression which comes when that moment of black doubt settles down on your spirit.

The people of Indiana had been so generous in their response to our first appeal for funds to make the dream of the Riley Hospital a reality that it was perhaps excusable that the Association should conceive the hospital on a generous scale. Other conditions—in particular the needs of the entire medical plant of the University, combined with our own buoyant spirit—led to the development of a very large project.

Knowing the urgent need of the hospital, the Association did not wait for the collection of the pledges made but drove ahead with utmost vigor to convert plans into actual structures. The result was that when we had completed the main hospital building, the service wing, the power plant, and equipped them so that we could begin serving the children of our state, the Association found that it had outrun the collection of pledges more than $800,000 and was in debt to the banks for that sum.

Through the dedication and opening of the hospital our enthusiasm sustained us. Then we settled down to the slow and always discouraging job of liquidation of obligations so cheerfully incurred when fires of enthusiasm burn brightly.

In the expenditures made we had not gone the limit of funds pledged to us. But in the slow months which followed we began to learn that pledges are often made in sanguinity not matched by willingness, or perhaps ability to meet them. A discouraging shrinkage began to be apparent. If we had told how discouraging, our bankers would have been seriously alarmed. Meanwhile that interest charge of $50,000 a year was rolling up to make the situation darker. The inevitable reaction which always follows the cessation of active driving efforts such as characterized the building of the hospital settled upon us. Within a year after the opening of the plant it had become evident that to complete the hospital in accordance with the plans published another appeal to the people of the state would be necessary.

I say frankly that few of us had the stomach to contemplate such an appeal with equanimity. It meant tightening the belt when energy was already pretty well spent and enthusiasm at low ebb. It was like the tired runner challenged at the turn into the homestretch and under necessity to whip up his spirit for the final drive to the finish. I cannot forbear a tribute here to him who was then chairman of our finance committee, Louis C. Huesmann. What a glorious figure of a man he was! Handsome, lovable, gallant, indomitable! We were pledged to the completion of this enterprise and he at least never had a doubt of our success.

I sometimes think that the Lord has a sense of the dramatic. I know He loves the man of courage in a worthy cause. For it was while Louis Huesmann was sitting at my desk discussing with me this very situation which I have outlined, and while we were searching our minds and hearts for the most effective basis for another appeal to the good people who had already been so generous to the Riley Memorial Association—it was at this moment, I repeat, that George Ball walked up and gave the answer. He evidently surmised that we were discussing hospital affairs, and asked what the situation was. We put the figures down on paper for him. After studying them for a few minutes he said, "It looks as if you are going to have to find another million." We agreed with his analysis of the figures and told him that we had just been cudgeling our brains for the best basis for making the appeal. He sat quietly for a moment and then in a modest, almost deprecatory way, he asked, "Do you suppose it would help you to get the rest of it if we gave you half?"

As long as I live I shall be grateful that Louis Huesmann had the satisfaction of hearing and answering that question, for he, more than any other man in our organization, deserved that most timely justification of his faith and devotion.

In speaking thus at length of the timeliness of the gift I have indicated also something of the spirit in which it was made. This was not the first occasion which the Riley Memorial Association had had for gratitude to the Ball family. Indeed they were among the earliest to give the hospital project impetus by substantial financial support, support which was increased whenever it would do the most good in helping to win pledges from others. The Ball gymnasium wing of the main hospital building is so named in recognition by the Association of this generous helpfulness. Mr. George Ball, one of the busiest men I know anywhere, accepted a position on the Executive Committee which was constituted to plan and construct the hospital and supervise its operation. And in spite of the many demands on him in other directions he made time to participate actively in the work of that committee; and I need not elaborate on the value of his service. Those of you who have had experience in similar undertakings know it is those who are really busiest who render most efficient service in purely voluntary work of this sort.

The sincerity of the purpose of the members of this family to be really helpful was never better illustrated than when they handed the Executive Committee a check for the full amount of this $500,000 gift more than a year before the money was needed to meet the construction bills. They realized that one of the most serious embarrassments under which the committee was laboring was that interest charge of $50,000 a year. By paying their pledge in full ahead of our need of the money they enabled us to put the money at interest and to receive $30,045.48 toward meeting our interest burden. So that their actual gift to the Association was just that much more than the $500,000 publicly announced.

But even more important than its timeliness and the actuating spirit of the gift, it seems to me, was the purpose to which they asked that it be devoted. That was the only condition attached to the gift and it was suggested rather than imposed. Mr. George Ball said that the family was interested particularly in the educational aspect of the hospital and that they would like to see the money used for the construction of a nurses' home and training school. In this suggestion he showed how truly they apprehended the essential purpose back of this whole effort. From the very inception of the idea the emphasis has been on making the hospital a teaching institution. The reason for that emphasis is that the work done here for the children of Indiana shall be done in the best possible way. And to that end nothing shall be left undone to qualify those directly engaged in the work to carry on with the finest possible equipment that training can provide. To give the fullest efficiency workers must not only have their minds and hands trained to the utmost, but their bodies must be built up by the opportunity to live and work under favorable conditions. Certainly the nurses of these allied institutions will be trained and will live under ideal conditions, thanks to this generous family, and should always be ready to render the maximum of service to those under their care.

And so I say that I can recall no gift to the people of Indiana which surpasses this in the three respects I have emphasized: its timeliness, the spirit in which it was made, and the significant quality which characterized its purpose.

In response, George A. Ball, substituting for his brother, Frank C. Ball, who, because of illness, was unable to be present, said:

If the new building serves to make happier the lives of the nurses it houses; if it makes their lives any more tender and beautiful, our purpose will have been accomplished.

Grading and beautification of grounds about the Ball Residence for Nurses could not be carried out at once. The Association of American Medical Colleges met at the School of Medicine in October, 1928. The most desirable place for the program of the sessions at Indianapolis was the reception room of the Ball Residence. Some deans got their shoes muddy in reaching this meeting place and remembered it. They should see it now.

Again George Ball came to the relief of the University, hard pressed for funds, by giving (March 21, 1929) $10,000 for the construction and improvement of walks and drives on the campus of the Medical Center at Indianapolis. It was eleven months later, February, 1930, that, with concurrence of the Joint Executive Committee, the trustees began grading and beautification of the grounds about the Ball Residence for Nurses.

Still again on May 17, 1929, George Ball generously supplemented an inadequate appropriation. An extension of the power plant at Indianapolis was necessary. The sum of $160,000 was needed, and $80,000 had been voted by the legislature. When every possible cut had been made it still required a minimum of $103,000 to complete the job. In this extremity Mr. Ball informed the board that he would make a gift of $25,000 in order that the absolutely necessary items might be provided.

In succeeding years the whole Medical Center campus has been made attractive. Adjacent property has been purchased by the Riley Association, old shacks have been removed, and the grounds parked. To the west toward White River the city of Indianapolis is making a park of adjacent land, while to the north the grounds of the Medical Center merge with those of the Indianapolis City Hospital.

CHAPTER XXIX

THE WILLIAM H. COLEMAN HOSPITAL FOR WOMEN; ENDOWMENT OF THREE CLINICAL CHAIRS, 1924 - 27

ON JUNE 15, 1924, Provost Samuel E. Smith reported to the University trustees a gift of real estate valued at approximately $75,000 by Mr. and Mrs. William H. Coleman, of Indianapolis, to be held in trust by the trustees for the endowment of the following chairs in the School of Medicine: Ophthalmology, under Dr. Frank A. Morrison; Surgery, under Dr. John H. Oliver; Gynecology, under Dr. Orange G. Pfaff. The income of the gift was to be divided equally among the three men during their lifetime. At the death of these men (or either of them) the income or principal, in the judgment of the trustees, was to be applied for the benefit of these three chairs.

This gift was a definite innovation in the history of the School of Medicine. Mr. and Mrs. Coleman had suffered a grievous loss in the death of their daughter, Suemma Coleman Atkins, April 16, 1924, in whose name the gift was made. During her life she had been much interested in sick and suffering people, and had been a director of the Florence Crittenton Home.

When informed of the gift Dr. Frank Morrison said: "My share of the endowment provided by the generosity of Mr. and Mrs. Coleman shall revert to Indiana University."

But Mr. and Mrs. Coleman had been considering a still greater memorial to their loved daughter in the form of a hospital for women. They had discussed this project with Provost Smith and on December 16, 1924, Mr. Coleman submitted his formal proposal:

I propose to give for the benefit of Indiana University School of Medicine, at Indianapolis, real estate located at the corner of Illinois and Vermont Streets in the city of Indianapolis, valued at $175,000, which will be under ninety-nine years' lease, bearing five per cent interest on that amount, with an increased rental each five years for three periods. I, also, will give property and securities to the amount of $75,000 additional, making $250,000 in all, for the purpose of building [a hospital] on the State's property at Indianapolis (near the Robert W. Long Hospital), and to be used chiefly for lying-in patients and a smaller number of gynecological cases; provided that the trustees shall have authority, when all beds are not occupied for the above purpose, to use them for other classes of female cases according to their best judgment.

The proposed hospital is to be known as *William H. Coleman Hospital for Women* and is to be supported by the State of Indiana and to receive for care and treatment both patients who are not able to pay and patients who are able to pay part or all of the expense of their care at such an institution.

The property included in this proposition will be subject to the taxes of 1924 and the income on the gift is to begin April 1, 1925.

The proposed hospital building is to be erected in 1925 if possible.

President Bryan wrote Mr. Coleman with reference to the proposal as follows:

My dear Mr. Coleman:
I have heard with deepest appreciation of the additional gift from you and Mrs. Coleman to Indiana University to be used for hospital purposes in memory of your daughter. What a wonderful thing it is for humanity that we have men and women who are willing to transform their visions into agencies that will bring hope and joy to countless numbers.

In 1825 Thomas Campbell in his poem "Hallowed Ground" expressed this beautiful thought which is particularly appropriate now—
"To live in hearts we leave behind
Is not to die."

On January 30, 1925, the trustees accepted this gift on the condition that the legislature provide the necessary maintenance.

Governor Ed Jackson and the Budget Advisory Committee promised in a letter of June 25, 1925, that a recommendation would be properly presented to the next session of the General Assembly for an appropriation not to exceed $50,000 annually for maintenance.

Since the real estate given by Mr. Coleman was under a 99-year lease at advantageous rental it seemed wisest for the trustees to issue $175,000 of 5 per cent bonds for money with which to build this hospital rather than to sell the property at that time. This plan was implemented on February 19, 1926, by a resolution adopted by the Board of Trustees.

On August 17, 1926, a site for the William H. Coleman Hospital for Women was chosen west of the temporary nurses' home, fronting on Michigan Street. A contract heretofore approved by Mr. Coleman was awarded to Leslie Colvin for construction according to plans prepared by Architect Daggett.

In addition to gifts already made, Mr. Coleman generously agreed to provide an additional $125,000 when it might be required for the completion of the Hospital, making a total of $300,000 available for this project. This brought the total given by Mr. and Mrs. Coleman for the three clinical departments and the Hospital to $375,000.

The Coleman Hospital was dedicated on October 20, 1927, in the presence of some three hundred guests. The exercises were held in the large lecture room of the School of Medicine with the president of the Board of Trustees, James W. Fesler, presiding.

At the request of Mr. and Mrs. Coleman the presentation of the Hospital was made by Provost Smith, who stated:

The Hospital was designed as a maternity hospital with provision for the surgical and medical treatment of women suffering from those diseases and accidents incident to childbirth. In addition it will maintain a limited prenatal clinic for the study and care of obstetrical cases with a view to the prevention of complications.

Mr. and Mrs. Coleman desired Provost Smith to add that Indiana University was selected by them to administer this gift in memory of their daughter Suemma Coleman Atkins, because as a part of the School of Medicine it would be a teaching hospital, helpful in the training of physicians and nurses who would carry the beneficent influence of the Hospital throughout the state and nation. Also in this trusteeship of the Hospital it was assured perpetuity.

Mr. Fesler accepted the gift on behalf of the University. Charles E. Ferguson and Dr. Louis Burckhardt, both Professors Emeritus of Obstetrics, spoke briefly of the work of their Department in the School of Medicine. Dr. Palmer Findley, of Omaha, Neb., president of the American Association of Obstetricians, delivered an interesting address on the history of obstetrics.

The meeting then adjourned to the Coleman Hospital where the excellent equipment was inspected and a bronze tablet was unveiled bearing the inscription:

This Hospital was given by Mr. and Mrs. William H. Coleman in loving memory of their daughter Suemma Vajen Coleman Atkins, A.D. 1927.

CHAPTER XXX

INDIANA UNIVERSITY, 1926 - 28

LEGISLATIVE PROGRAM UNDER BUDGET SYSTEM

T HE PREPARATION of the University for the legislative session of 1927 was unusual in two respects: (1) the University organized an extensive educational program throughout the state in which it was sought, by pamphlets and speeches, to inform the people of the state of the needs of the University, and (2) an effort was again made to interest Purdue University, Indiana State Normal, and its Eastern Division at Muncie in uniting with Indiana University in a joint effort to secure, from the General Assembly of 1927, more adequate appropriations for the state institutions of higher education.

To understand the motive for these unusual procedures it is necessary to recall that in the legislative session of 1925 the mill tax method of providing for maintenance of the state institutions of higher education had been abandoned in favor of a budget system. Indiana University had welcomed this change for it was believed that the budget system would provide at two-year intervals the opportunity of presenting the needs of the University to the people of the state. The administration believed that, as people understood better what the University needed in order to provide for their children the opportunities being offered in other midwest states, this informed public opinion would encourage the 150 members of the General Assembly, who aimed to represent their constituents, to vote more adequate support of Indiana University.

On June 7, 1926, months earlier than customary, the trustees forecast the major request to be presented to Governor Ed Jackson and the legislature of 1927 by recording their conviction that more money for maintenance, "especially to be able to secure and keep the best men of the faculty," was the greatest need of the University. At the board meeting on July 1 there was a long discussion of the prospect of increasing support for the educational institutions. Again in October an entire evening was spent in discussing this matter.

The committee on promotion of University interests had gathered data relating to budgets of neighboring state universities to be used in addressing various groups throughout the state. It was shown that attendance at the University had increased out of all proportion to increase in University budget and teaching staff. Funds appropriated by neighboring states for their state universities in 1925 were as follows:

Michigan	$7,628,501
Illinois	6,205,782
Iowa	6,045,789
Ohio	5,130,510
Minnesota	4,063,047
Wisconsin	4,025,173
Indiana	2,598,173
(Indiana and Purdue)	

It was stated:

Indiana University needs an additional appropriation of $1,500,000, i.e., a total $2,805,000, and Purdue a like amount, in order that the income of these two institutions may approximate the income of neighboring state universities.

It was then shown that, counting assessed valuations of property in Indiana at $5,400,000,000, a tax of .28 of a mill would yield the needed additional $1,500,000. That is, a man who paid taxes on $10,000 would pay $2.80 to this needed increased income for Indiana University.

Faculty members addressed civic groups on the needs of the University. One of these men, for example, said:

Seven hundred years ago, about 1224, the University of Naples, one of the first universities, was founded solely by the fiat of Frederick II, as a school of theology, jurisprudence, arts, and medicine, his design being that his subjects should find accurate instruction in every branch of learning and "not be compelled in pursuit of knowledge to have recourse to foreign nations or to beg in other lands."

Shall we have a vision for the boys and girls of Indiana less than that of Frederick II, 700 years ago, or shall we with pride bring the educational facilities of our state university fully up to those of neighboring state universities?

President Bryan, addressing a group of Indiana citizens, said:

The excellence of a university is in its men. The excellence of the men of Indiana is indicated by the fact that they have been called away to every great university in the United States and year by year still are called.

The administration of Indiana University was making a vigorous and persistent effort to effect a joint report of the needs of the state institutions of higher education for presentation to the General Assembly of 1927. Accordingly, the following statement prepared and presented by President Bryan was read and approved by the board, July 1, 1926:

To the Joint Committee representing the interests of the State Normal School, the Ball Teachers College, Purdue University, and Indiana University:

The Trustees of Indiana University earnestly desire to join with sister institutions in providing for the people of this state an adequate system of higher education.

Since the state requires thorough training of teachers of all grades, adequate provision should be made for that training. This means buildings, equipment, and books far beyond the present provision and, above all, money to secure and hold faculties at Terre Haute and Muncie second to none in the country.

Purdue University touches the industrial life of the state at many vital points. The interests involved require nothing less than a plant in every respect first-rate and men in every department who are unexcelled in their several fields. It is recognized that the activities of the Agricultural Extension and Experiment Station should as in the past be provided for without being a charge upon the budget of Purdue University *per se*.

In like manner it is essential that the needs of the institutions associated with Indiana University at Indianapolis should be provided for without being a charge upon the budget of the University at Bloomington.

In all the educational institutions of the state there is urgent need of far larger appropriations for building, equipment, and, above all, men. The young people of Indiana are wronged and all of the people of Indiana are wronged when the training of youth and the demands of industry for counsel are met in a way that falls far below what is found necessary and actually done in all other middle western states.

The Trustees send herewith pamphlets representing in considerable detail the immediate needs of Indiana University. In connection with all this publicity, we constantly call attention to the corresponding needs of other state educational institutions.

On invitation of President Bryan, Ex-Lieutenant Governor Edgar D. Bush and Guy Cantwell, of the State Farm Bureau, appeared before the board in January, 1927, and discussed matters relating to methods of raising additional funds for the state educational institutions. Representative Lemuel A. Pittenger also spent some time with the board reviewing the legislative program of the state institutions of higher education.

The revised ten-year building program of Indiana University presented to the General Assembly in January, 1927 follows:

BUILDINGS REQUESTED FROM LEGISLATURE IN 1927:

At Bloomington:

Power plant, equipment, and tunnel extension	$ 500,000
Addition to Wylie Hall	200,000
Building for School of Education	582,100
Addition to Owen Hall plus equipment	200,000
Building for Geology, Zoology, Botany, and Museum	692,160
Group of small buildings, the most important of which is an addition to Science Hall for the use of Physics	148,000
Auditorium	800,000
Administration Building	350,000
Building for School of Music	350,000
Building for Journalism	150,000
Bloomington total	$3,972,260

At Indianapolis:

Completing Medical School Building	$ 200,000
Additional wards for the Robert W. Long Hospital	500,000
Psychiatric clinic	350,000
Outpatient building	150,000
Therapeutics building	400,000
Environmental medicine	350,000
Clinical building	250,000
Indianapolis total	$2,200,000
Grand total	$6,172,260

How did the General Assembly of 1927 respond to the vigorous campaign conducted for the purpose of acquainting the people of Indiana with the needs of her institutions of higher education?

Figures for Indiana University for each year of the coming biennium show the response.

At Bloomington:

Equipment and Library....................................$ 50,000
Structures   150,000
Repairs to buildings and grounds............................   50,000
Operating expenses 1,175,000

At Indianapolis:

Maintenance, James Whitcomb Riley Hospital.................$ 50,000
Maintenance, Medical School and Robert W. Long Hospital....   75,000
Equipment for new wing of Medical School Building...........   25,000
Medical School Library   20,000
Dental School operating expenses............................   15,000

The state appropriation for Indiana University as a whole (Bloomington and Indianapolis) in 1927 was about one-fourth of the increase needed.

But in addition to the appropriations tabulated above, a 2-cent tax for buildings for the four state educational institutions was passed by the General Assembly of 1927. It was estimated that this tax would yield for Indiana University in the next ten years $3,500,-000, which would provide for about 56 per cent of the ten-year building program. It was a great fortune to secure this 2-cent building tax for it made possible a planned building program.

While the response of the General Assembly was far short of the $1,500,000 increase needed, yet, all things considered, there was promise of better days. There was a conviction that the response of Indiana citizens to the campaign of information regarding the needs of Indiana University had helped and would help still more in the future.

THE INDIANA UNIVERSITY SURVEY

In the fall of 1926 a survey of institutions of higher learning in Indiana was made by a committee appointed by Governor Ed Jackson, consisting of Charles H. Judd, Dean of the School of Education, the University of Chicago; John A. Keith, President of the State Normal School at Indiana, Pa.; Frank L. McVey, President of the University of Kentucky; George A. Works, Professor of Rural Education, Cornell University; and Floyd W. Reeves, Professor of Education, University of Kentucky. The report of this committee was submitted in December, 1926, and published by the state printer, a volume of more than two hundred pages.

In the summary of findings, twelve questions were asked and answered. The questions are easily deduced from these answers.

1. The State of Indiana at present does not provide financial support to Indiana University, Purdue University, and the two State Normal Schools to a degree comparable to that provided similar institutions in neighboring states.

2. The present budgetary methods of the state are in the main such as to enable the state's higher educational institutions to secure legislative attention to their needs for funds.

3. The present physical facilities in the forms of land, buildings, service utilities, scientific and industrial equipment, and libraries are not adequate to permit these institutions of higher learning effectively and economically to carry on their work.

4. The Survey Commission recommends that the inadequacy of equipment be cared for by the establishment in the budget of each institution of an item for obsolescence. Provision should be made for enlarged physical facilities to care for deterioration of present plants and equipment, unmet needs, and recent expansions.

5. The salaries paid and the conditions and facilities for service at Indiana state institutions of higher learning are not such as to enable these institutions to secure and to retain teaching or scientific staffs professionally comparable to those of the institutions of other states.

6. The tax-supported institutions of higher education are handicapped in their work and in the maintenance of their standing by present large annual replacement of teachers in certain departments.

7. The absence of adequate provision for age or disability retirement of members of the staffs of the institutions of higher education of the state results in an unduly large annual replacement of staff members, difficulty in securing competent instructors to replace those who leave, and the retention of staff members who have reached the normal age of retirement. A number of neighboring states have retirement provisions for staff members.

8. A greater per cent of high school graduates enter institutions of higher learning in Indiana than in the states of the North Central group; however, the Indiana institutions of higher learning as a group do not retain the students who enter as well as do the institutions of other North Central States.

9. The Survey Commission believes that at an early date agencies should be set up in the state for the purpose of assembling data from year to year upon the basis of which a satisfactory answer can be given to the problems stated above. Plans for the accomplishment of this purpose are suggested (Chapter VI) by the Commission.

10. The extent to which funds are wasted as a result of faulty institutional organization or administration, needless duplication of the offerings of departments or colleges within each institution, or in courses offered among state institutions, is commendably small.

11. The average instructional load, as well as the average total service load of members of the staffs of Indiana institutions, is greater than loads reported by institutions of other states where similar investigations have been made.

12. Unless the state is willing to spend a much larger amount upon its two universities than the amount expended during recent years, substantial increase will have to be made in the fees collected from the University students. No student need be deprived of the opportunity for an education by increases made in fees charged if, accompanying these increases, ample provision is made for free scholarships and loan funds for worthy students of limited financial resources.

With reference to the School of Medicine the committee stated:

The need for staff increases at the School of Medicine at Indianapolis is so great as to warrant a separate discussion. Only four persons are employed for full-time instructional purposes. The remainder of the staff consists of volunteers or of persons employed for part-time at low compensation. The situation as it now stands is well-nigh impossible. No school can do justice to great hospital facilities with a budget as small as the one now provided. In order to meet the situation adequately and to grasp the opportunity which is before the Medical School of Indianapolis, it will be necessary materially to increase the expenditure now made for salaries. Certainly not less than ten full-time men should be employed, and the budget of the school ought to be increased materially without drawing upon the funds available for the work at Bloomington.

In general, one may say that the effect of this report was to support the educational campaign of Indiana University, the purpose of which was to show the need for a greatly increased budget. The special discussion of the situation in the School of Medicine likewise supported the contention of the University that the state should provide increased support for the Medical School without drawing upon the funds allocated for University work at Bloomington.

PRESIDENT'S REPORT TO THE TRUSTEES, NOVEMBER, 1927

While the president of the Board of Trustees, as required by legislative act, submitted to the Governor and Visiting Committee, every two years, a report on the needs of the University and requests made of the General Assembly, President Bryan submitted to the trustees annually (or more frequently) a report on the status of the University.

This annual report submitted in November, 1927, was very detailed. For instance, it included a report on the University Commons, which showed that during the past year the income had been $89,368.23. It had been run at a profit of $6,429.54. There had been 277,883 meals served at a profit of 2.31 cents per meal. It is obvious that they were succeeding in their objective of serving good food at near cost.

Separate accounts were kept as usual with the University Printing Plant, *The Indiana Daily Student,* with each of the different loan funds, with each residence hall, with the Bookstore, with each school of the University, etc., and reports on each were included.

These reports were made in a manner so simple yet clear that a layman could understand them. It could be seen that these University activities, such as Commons, University Printing Plant, etc., not parts of the educational program of the University, but projects for the advantage, convenience, or welfare of the student body, were so carefully managed that they paid for themselves, were not a charge on the educational budget, yet yielded a profit so small that no one could feel that the student body was being exploited.

Communication from Faculty

Among items on the agenda for the meeting of the trustees in May, 1928, there was a communication from the faculty concerning the first building for academic purposes to be erected, after the erection of the Chemistry Building.

This was an interesting communication. It expressed the conviction of those signing that the interests of Indiana University would be best served if the next building after Chemistry were a "building for the biological and earth sciences," namely, botany, geology, zoology, and psychology. The communication was signed mainly by members of these four departments.

Since the 2-cent building tax would provide for only part of the ten-year building program of the University, it was evident that selection would have to be made from the proposed building program. This signed statement was, therefore, entirely in order. It is probable that the judgment expressed in this communication was not wholly impersonal. But it is likely that another factor also was involved. In the ten-year building program, which, on recommendation of the committee on promotion of University interests, had been adopted and given wide publicity, the next structure following Chemistry was a building for the School of Education.

The President's long-standing conviction that the future of Indiana University depended on establishment of new schools and new opportunity for study had not had full faculty support. Not a few believed that new schools would be established at the expense of the College of Liberal Arts. The establishment of the School of Education in particular had been regarded by some faculty members with bitter hostility, by others as a procedure of very questionable wisdom.

The opinion generally prevailed that a Ph.D. with a major, two minors, and a thesis representing concentration in a very circumscribed field was prepared to teach. By many the idea that there might be a technique to be advantageously acquired by those who would teach was not hospitably entertained. It is probable that this lack of sympathy with the aims and objectives of the School of Education influenced judgments more than self-interest, though the leader, a very superior man, rarely saw a University problem other than subjectively.

POWER PLANT

On February 1, 1928, President Bryan suggested the desirability of a survey of the heating plant at the University to see whether it was adequate to meet the additional load of the building program of the immediate future.

This survey was made by Charles R. Ammerman, of Indianapolis, who, on March 22, made a report and suggested methods of remodeling with estimates of cost. The trustees ordered that steps be taken to remodel the present plant rather than build a new one. The matter of examining plans and specifications, advertising for and receiving bids, was referred to Trustees Fesler and Batman.

All told, there were a dozen different contracts totaling approximately $125,000. This meant a fundamental remodeling of the power plant in the ever-recurring problem of keeping it adequate for the ever-increasing load imposed by erection of new buildings.

NEW ADDITION TO THE MEDICAL SCHOOL BUILDING, INDIANAPOLIS

When the General Assembly of 1927 convened, a bill making an appropriation of $100,000 for purchase of the old Indiana Medical

College building was introduced and passed, and the appropriation made available on April 1, 1927, for construction of an addition to the building of the School of Medicine on West Michigan Street. This was in accordance with an agreement reached with Governor Jackson in June, 1925.

Tentative plans for this addition had been prepared by Robert Frost Daggett, and were approved by the board on April 19, 1927. A contract was made with Leslie Colvin to supervise construction of this addition. The plans for the building provided for administrative offices and a small lecture room on the first floor, a fine auditorium seating about four hundred, with facilities for projection equipment on the second floor, a third floor balcony of the auditorium, and valuable laboratory space in the basement. The initial meeting in the auditorium of this new addition to the Medical Building was a seminar held on Wednesday evening, January 18, 1928. The administrative offices were occupied about the same time.

THE PURCHASE OF THE BOBBS-MERRILL BUILDING

The Extension Division at Indianapolis had occupied rented quarters, but the desirability of owning quarters adapted or adaptable for extension work had been discussed by the trustees. When, in December, 1927, there was an opportunity to purchase the Bobbs-Merrill building, the board was called in session to consider the matter.

R. E. Cavanaugh, Director of the Extension Division, made a written report concerning the need of more room, which would be provided by the Bobbs-Merrill building. After considering the cost of construction of a satisfactory building the board decided to purchase this Bobbs-Merrill building on East Michigan Street, Indianapolis, at a cost of $125,000 subject to the approval of the Governor and Budget Committee. This was the first of a number of buildings purchased for extension work in different cities of Indiana.

JAMES W. FESLER AND WILLIAM LOWE BRYAN

On May 21, 1927, the Board of Trustees, with Judge Batman acting as president pro tem in the absence of Mr. Fesler, fixed the salary of Mr. Fesler as president of the board at $1,200 a year. At the June 3 meeting, the secretary of the board reported receipt of a letter from

Mr. Fesler thanking the board for their action but stating that he could not accept any salary.

A letter from President Bryan appears in the board minutes of the same date in which he refused an increase in salary voted him on May 21, 1927.

On June 6, 1927, the board passed a long resolution on the twenty-fifth anniversary of Dr. Bryan's election to the presidency of the University. This resolution said, in part:

On the occasion of the silver anniversary of the unanimous election of William Lowe Bryan as President of Indiana University, the Board of Trustees desire to express to him and to the institution their congratulations on the wonderful success that has come under his administration to the head of the state's educational system.

Under the leadership of President Bryan, Indiana University enrollment has increased from 1,334 in 1902[1] to 5,742 in 1927; the faculty has increased from 61 to 310; new buildings have gone up here and at Indianapolis and others will follow; the campus has grown, and on every side are evidences of substantial growth.

OF INTEREST TO FACULTY AND STAFF

The title of Dr. Burton D. Myers was changed from assistant dean to dean of the School of Medicine in Bloomington on May 21, 1927.

On January 21, 1928, Dr. Willis D. Gatch was appointed head of the Department of Surgery, including gynecology and orthopaedic surgery, succeeding Dr. John Oliver, deceased.

On April 20, 1928, Dr. Edward T. Thompson was appointed administrator of the Medical School and Hospitals and Superintendent of the Hospitals, succeeding Robert E. Neff, who had resigned to accept a like position at the University of Iowa School of Medicine.

Fernandus Payne, Assistant Dean of the Graduate School since 1925, was appointed dean, on May 20, 1928, succeeding Dr. Carl H. Eigenmann, who had died April 24, 1927.

The degree A.M. *privatim* was conferred upon Frederick Dodds Rose, of Muncie, son of Theodore F. Rose, a former trustee, at the 1928 Commencement.

At the same Commencement the LL.D. was conferred upon three alumni eminent in science: Barton Warren Evermann, John

[1] In the fall of 1902.

Anthony Miller, Aldred Scott Warthin; upon one university president, Walter A. Jessup; and upon three eminent authors, George Ade, Meredith Nicholson, and Booth Tarkington.

Professor Juliette Maxwell, long the director of work in physical education for women, retired in 1928 and was succeeded by Associate Professor Edna F. Munro, a graduate of Oberlin and Columbia.

OF INTEREST TO STUDENTS

In May, 1927, the trustees called the attention of the student body to the following rules which had been adopted to protect students and the good name of the University:

When a class or other organization bearing the name and credit of the University desires to arrange for a dance or other function involving expense, there must be filed in advance at the office of the Bursar a list of members who agree to be responsible for the payment of all just debts incurred in connection with the affair. The principle involved is that students are not required to have such functions but, if they have them, must not leave unpaid debts to the discredit of the University.

Students who in no way assume responsibility for the function either by consenting to it in advance or by attending the same may not be assessed to cover deficit.

All financial transactions connected with such affairs shall be subject to the supervision and audit of the appropriate departments of the Bursar's office.

At the same meeting of the board, the following resolution was introduced and adopted:

WHEREAS, It is a paramount duty of the University to stand for the Constitution and laws of the State and of the United States, and,

WHEREAS, It is also the duty of the University to strive constantly for the best possible moral environment about the Institution; therefore be it

RESOLVED, That the thanks of the Board of Trustees are extended to all members of the University who have recently aided in the successful prosecution of a liquor nuisance case, and that a special vote of thanks be given to Professor James J. Robinson for his professional services in this essential work.

A fee of fifty cents a semester and twenty-five cents for the summer session was ordered assessed and appropriated by the Executive Committee to the Indiana Union.

CAPITAL INVESTMENT, MADE OR PROPOSED

In 1926 there was a local telephone system in use in University buildings which, however, provided no direct communication with the city. In August of 1926 an installation was authorized that would provide direct connection with the city system.

A committee of students presented a plea to the Board of Trustees at their October meeting that one or two additions to South Hall be erected to furnish dormitory accommodations for a still larger number of students. The trustees observed with pleasure the success of South Hall and the expression of satisfaction of the men who lived there. Before new commitments were assumed, however, it was the judgment of the trustees that they should await the further financial showing of South Hall.

For some time there had been an effort to get a campaign under way for a Don Mellett Memorial Fund for a Journalism Building. The University Memorial Fund campaign had been completed so recently that this laudable but very special campaign was slow in gathering momentum. Despairing of the success of this movement, the trustees on June 3, 1927, ordered that the Journalism Building be remodeled at a cost of approximately $2,800 to provide emergency relief for this Department.

On May 17, 1928, the board concurred in the recommendation of Ward G. Biddle that the north end of the temporary Bookstore building be extended fifteen feet at an estimated cost of $785.

In the spring of 1927 the University purchased the Johnston house on East Third Street for a Home Economics Practice House.

CHAPTER XXXI

THE DONALDSON FARM, 1903 - 28

THE DONALDSON Farm, in Lawrence County, was under the control or ownership of Indiana University for twenty-five years (1903–28). During that time it came before the Board of Trustees again and again for consideration. It is the purpose here to explain this long-sustained interest in this quarter-section of Lawrence County hills, the monetary value of which was not great.

This Donaldson Farm of 183.88 acres was very much more than a mere piece of wooded hill land. The hills were covered with virgin forest, one of the very few tracts remaining in the state, and, therefore, very definitely worth preserving. Concealed within the hills were caves and underground streams with blind fauna offering opportunity for important research. These values explain the long-sustained interest of the trustees in this Donaldson Farm, an interest defended in long-continued litigation, much of it in the Indiana Supreme Court, an interest the scientific aspects of which were retained, when, in 1928, the land was deeded back to the state of Indiana to become a part of Spring Mill Park, and to be made accessible to successive generations of citizens[1] through centuries to come.

The story of the Donaldson Farm begins with an immigrant, George Donaldson, a Scotsman, as the name suggests, who, coming to Indiana, became the owner of a tract of land in Lawrence County, Ind., about two miles east of Mitchell. Donaldson had returned to Scotland and died there on September 15, 1898. Under Indiana law, he was not able to transfer the property by descent. The property escheated to the state and was subject to sale by Lawrence County.

Litigation in connection with this land had been started in 1900 by the Scotch heirs of Donaldson in an effort to gain possession of his estate.

[1] The word "citizens," of course, includes children since people of all ages, the newborn babe and the nonagenarian, are in equal measure citizens of Indiana and of the United States.

In 1903 the Indiana General Assembly had passed an act concerning escheated estates[2] which provided that:

> . . . . in all cases when lands located in Lawrence or Monroe Counties have escheated, or hereafter shall escheat to the State for want of heirs or kindred entitled to the inheritance, such lands shall not be sold by the Board of Commissioners of the County where such estate is situated, but the title to all such lands shall be and remain in the State of Indiana and such lands shall be devoted to educational purposes.
>
> The control and management of all such lands shall be vested in the trustees of Indiana University and such lands may be used by said trustees for any proper educational purpose.

The Donaldson Farm, in Lawrence County, had come under control of Indiana University under this act. University control of this property was only a few weeks old when in March, 1903, Dr. Carl H. Eigenmann made a seven-page report to the trustees regarding this farm, which he had visited repeatedly and in practically every month of the year. In his report Dr. Eigenmann spoke of the flora which made this virgin forest of interest to botanists. But the cave fauna gave it unique value. The cave and "the underground stream, which could be followed for about two miles, was rich in blind fish, crayfish, beetles, spiders, and other cave animals, in numbers sufficient to insure that both the stream and the dry portion of the cave were suitable for raising cave animals."

In March, 1903, Dr. Eigenmann wrote to the Forestry Service of the Department of Agriculture, Washington, D.C., asking the cooperation of the Bureau in the management of the Donaldson Farm. Cooperation was immediately assured.

In 1906 President Bryan wrote to the Forestry Service asking that an agent of the service make a survey of the property. This survey was made and a report submitted by Samuel J. Record, Forest Assistant, Forestry Service, March, 1906.

Thomas J. Brooks (Brooks and Brooks, of Bedford) in a letter to E. B. Stotsenberg, under date March 17, 1916, throws light upon the activity of claimants to this property. Mr. Brooks states that:

> About 1901 I was employed by the then Attorney General, William L. Taylor, to prosecute the suit in the Circuit Court of this county [Lawrence] for the escheat of said land [the Donaldson Farm] to the state. . . .

[2] See *Indiana Laws*, 1903, p. 152.

There were three sets of claimants to the property. One set under the will which was invalid in Indiana because of lack of due execution. A second set of heirs in Scotland, and a third set of heirs in America, of whom two were named James Frazer and Thomas McAuley. The last set were residents of America, and they thought they were entitled to the property because of the other parties being aliens.

One of these sets of claimants had succeeded in having a receivership appointed.

The President reported to the trustees on June 14, 1906, that

> On May 7 the State filed motion in the Lawrence Circuit Court to discharge the receiver of the Donaldson Farm and to end the receivership. On May 18 the motion was argued before Judge Wilson, who sustained it, leaving the farm in possession of the University as provided by Act of the Legislature of 1903.
>
> On June 8 [1906], a petition for a rehearing of the original case was granted and, the Supreme Court reversed judgment ordering a new trial, with leave to amend pleadings if desired.[3] The point on which the case is made to turn is that the special findings do not show that Donaldson intended a permanent removal from this country when he returned to Scotland.

Rehearing was denied December 20, 1906.

On April 2, 1907, a committee of the board consisting of Messrs. Corr, Fesler, and Shea was appointed to confer with Merrill Moores, of Indianapolis, concerning the legal questions relating to the Donaldson Farm. On June 13, 1907, the President reported to the trustees that "Mr. Corr had visited Alabama and Scotland in search of evidence bearing on the Donaldson case." In the fall of 1907 President Bryan said:

> I have made some effort to secure from the outside an amount sufficient to purchase the equity of ———— and quiet our title in the Donaldson Farm. So far I have had no success. Mr. Scott[4] is in charge of the place at a salary of $500 for the full year. He will make physical records, look after the farm in general, and do some work on his own account. I have had some small pools built that will enable us to begin experiments with cave animals in the light, or at least determine the conditions under which they may be made.

On January 20, 1908, Trustee Corr made a statement concerning the legal status of the Donaldson Farm case. In June, 1909, Mr. Corr again reported:

[3] Donaldson vs. State, 167 Indiana 553.
[4] This was Will Scott, later professor of zoology.

The Donaldson case is in *status quo*. Mr. Moores until recently has said that the best policy for us to pursue, being in possession, is not to hurry a decision in the case. However, the last time I talked with him he said he thought the case ought to be tried. The other side have taken no steps to urge a speedy trial of the case. Mr. Moores, some time last winter, suggested that we ought to have Mr. Thomas J. Brooks, of Bedford, assist in the trial of the case without fail. President Bryan and I talked the matter over and agreed that Mr. Brooks ought to help try the case as he assisted in the first trial and is familiar with the case. I believe the case ought to be tried at an early date after the filing of amended pleadings.

The minutes of the board show that on June 20, 1909, March 14, 1911, June 17, 1911, October 31, 1912, and November 13, 1913, Mr. Corr made further statements on the Donaldson Farm case.

On June 16, 1911, the President stated that the trial concerning the Mitchell farm was in progress in the Lawrence County Court. This was the retrial in the Circuit Court of Lawrence County authorized by the Supreme Court of Indiana in which the state again recovered judgment.

The case again came to the Supreme Court, April, 1913. A decision was handed down[5] in which the court reviewed the fact that under the Constitution, Article 8, Section 2, it is provided that the common school fund shall consist, among other things, of "all lands and other estates which shall escheat to the state." In the decision it was "ordered that the clause 'and that the possession and control of the same is vested in the trustees of Indiana University' be stricken from the judgment, and, so modified, the judgment is affirmed."

Retrial was denied on January 19, 1915.

To correct this situation, in which possession and control of the Donaldson Farm was withdrawn from Indiana University, on February 25, 1915, H.B. 148 was approved[6] by the 1915 General Assembly:

AN ACT providing for the sale and manner of conveyance by the State of Indiana of certain escheated real estate in Lawrence County, Indiana, and authorizing the trustees of Indiana University to purchase the same, and providing for the payment of the same, and declaring an emergency.

Preamble.

WHEREAS: After litigation, extending over many years, the following described real estate, located in Lawrence County, Indiana, to-wit: . . . was

[5] Donaldson vs. State, 182 Indiana 615.
[6] *Laws of Indiana,* 1915, pp. 45–47.

adjudged to have escheated to the State of Indiana for lack of persons entitled to inherit such real estate; and

WHEREAS: The kindred of the owner of said real estate at the time of his decease, agreed to sell said real estate for the price of four thousand dollars on condition that they should be decreed to be the owners thereof; and

WHEREAS: A large part of said real estate consists of primeval forest; and

WHEREAS: It is desirous to preserve said forest and to use said real estate for educational purposes; and

WHEREAS: The general assembly of Indiana in 1903 manifested a desire that the control and management of said real estate be vested in the trustees of Indiana University; therefore:

Section 1. *Be it enacted by the general assembly of the State of Indiana:* That the auditor of state of the State of Indiana, is authorized and directed to sell said real estate to the trustees of Indiana University, at private sale without notice for said sum of four thousand dollars. Upon the sale of said real estate to the trustees of Indiana University and the payment of said sum of four thousand dollars said auditor of state is authorized and directed to execute in the name of the State of Indiana a deed of conveyance conveying all the title of said real estate to said trustees of Indiana University, for the use and benefit of Indiana University.

Emergency.

SECTION 2. WHEREAS: An emergency exists for the immediate taking effect of this act, the same shall be in full force and effect from and after its passage.

The Executive Committee was authorized on March 12, 1915, to close the deal for the Donaldson Farm in accordance with the bill passed by the last legislature. By this act the value of this property, $4,000 (see the second "WHEREAS" above) was paid by Indiana University into the common school fund as provided in the Constitution and control and management again was vested in the trustees of Indiana University. The following May, Anton T. Boisen made a survey and recommendation for treatment of the forest.

The deed of the state of Indiana to the trustees of Indiana University conveying the Donaldson Farm in Lawrence County was accepted and recorded, December 18, 1915.

A letter from Brooks and Brooks, attorneys of Bedford, stated that James Frazer and Thomas McAuley had a lien and claim against the Donaldson Farm for taxes and that this should be paid. It was ordered (June 12, 1916) that the University pay this claim and that the Governor be informed of the action and be asked whether or not the University should be reimbursed from the general contingent fund.

The active and efficient State Park Board of Indiana had become interested in the many attractive features of the Donaldson Farm. As a consequence, on June 12, 1917, it was ordered that a committee of the Board of Trustees, of which President Bryan should be a member, should confer with the State Park Board in regard to leasing a part of the Donaldson Farm for State Park purposes.

Governor Warren T. McCray and W. A. Guthrie suggested to the University in October, 1922, that the Donaldson Farm be transferred to the Forestry Division of the Department of Conservation. The trustees expressed the opinion that they did not see their way clear for the University as one part of the state to transfer this farm to another part or division of the state, and President Bryan was authorized to write Governor McCray and Mr. Guthrie accordingly.

On April 21, 1924, a committee consisting of Professor David M. Mottier, Secretary John W. Cravens, and Bursar Ulysses H. Smith reported to the President and trustees as follows:

> Your committee would recommend that a modest beginning be made this spring in establishing an auto-rest camp at the Donaldson Farm, and in taking certain inexpensive steps to advertise the Wild Life Sanctuary such as erecting suitable guide marks, etc.
>
> To this end we believe it the part of wisdom to surround about two acres of the camp site by a woven wire fence. A fence exists on one side now. Fencing will be necessary for the other three sides. Two out-door toilets are necessary. The frame cottage should be remodeled by the construction of a porch along the front. One of the rooms of the cottage should be open on the side next to the porch.
>
> To establish a summer fellowship for a suitable student who will prepare a report on the flora of the farm, who will keep a general oversight of the camp, especially at week ends, and who will cooperate with Mr. Hall[7] in whatever represents the best interests of the Sanctuary and of Indiana University.
>
> The stipend should pay the expenses of the recipient of the scholarship. The minimum amount will not be less than $250, as the time of service will extend from Commencement day to the opening of the first semester in September.

On January 30, 1925, ex-Senator Charles W. Lanz, of Bedford, appeared before the Board[8] and presented a plea that the Donaldson

[7] A. B. Hall, custodian of Donaldson Farm.
[8] The Board of Trustees of Indiana University.

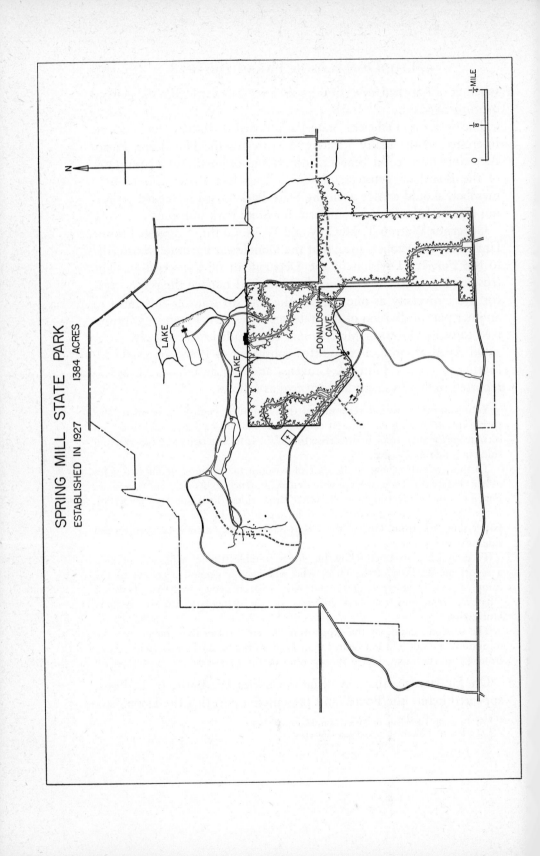

SPRING MILL STATE PARK

ESTABLISHED IN 1927

1384 ACRES

N

LAKE

LAKE

DONALDSON CAVE

0   1/8   1/4 MILE

Farm should be made a state park. President Bryan made a statement giving the idea of the board concerning the use of the farm. After a discussion of matters relating to the Donaldson Farm, President Fesler appointed a committee of three, consisting of Judge Batman, Dr. Samuel Smith, and Mr. Ball, to further consider the use of the Donaldson Farm, this committee to have a consultation or consultations with any committee or persons who may express a desire to have such meetings.

The minutes of the trustees for March 13, 1925, include a letter from the Donaldson Farm committee stating that certain citizens of Mitchell had requested that the Donaldson Farm be made a public park. After careful consideration, the trustees concluded that they had a duty in connection with this property to preserve it as a tract of primeval forest, probably not duplicated in the state. As such it was believed that the farm had more value to the people of the state of Indiana than it could have if utilized for any other purpose.

A committee including members of the legislature appeared before the board on January 24, 1927, and presented arguments in favor of turning over the Donaldson Farm to the Indiana State Conservation Commission. Spokesmen for the committee were Albert Fields and Representative E. Y. Guernsey.

After full consideration, the board decided that if the University were reimbursed for money expended on the Donaldson Farm, the board would consent that the title be taken over by legislative act. Authorization for this transfer was given by the General Assembly, March 11, 1927,[9] and compensation fixed at $9,747.41. It was ordered that the President be authorized to sign the deed.

This farm is now the east central and southeast portion of Spring Mill Park, one of the most interesting and attractive of our numerous state parks.

In making this transfer the preservation of this tract of virgin forest was assured. In the negotiations for the transfer thc University made reservation of the privilege of further study of the blind fauna of the cave and underground stream.

The relation of the Donaldson Farm to the Spring Mill Park area may be understood from a map reproducing the Park site with the irregular Donaldson Farm area in heavy outline.[10]

[9] *Indiana Laws*, 1927, Chap. 252.
[10] Map prepared by Department of Conservation.

The Donaldson Cave is near the central portion of the park, so labeled, in the southernmost part of the northwest portion of the Donaldson Farm. It should not be confused with the cave, and stream issuing therefrom, at the site of the Spring Mill Village. The old mill at the village site has been restored with its overshot water wheel, and still grinds as it did nearly a century ago when my wife's father, James D. Showers, then a boy, carried grain on horseback to this mill from Owensberg, about forty miles distant.

CHAPTER XXXII

STUDENT HEALTH, 1902 - 37

CONTAGIOUS DISEASES

C ARE FOR student health at Indiana University began as emergency care of students suffering from some contagious disease. The chief motive seems to have been the protection of the student body from infection.
President Bryan says:

So far as I now remember, the University did not do anything officially relating to student health until the smallpox epidemic which appeared after the Spanish-American War. It so happened that President Swain was very ill when an incident occurred which made it necessary to take some action. A young woman student who had been exposed to smallpox went home by night train. She was sent back on the next night train to Bloomington. This action was doubtless due to the fear that she would bring the infection to her home town. She came to her physician's office near the public square at four o'clock in the morning. The mayor and council were informed by the physician early the following morning of her presence. They had a great fear that she would spread the disease in the center of the city. Except for this fear, they were not willing to do anything at all in the case. I spent hours that day with the council while they were struggling with the question of what to do. A man who had had the smallpox agreed to take her in his house for $200 a week. The council agreed to pay $100 and the University agreed to pay $100 of this amount. As I remember, she did not come down with the disease and after two weeks was released.

At the meeting of the trustees in November, 1900, the question was raised, "Shall a building suitable for receiving smallpox patients be erected on Jordan Field?" Jordan Field, located northeast of the power plant, was the athletic field, still used for baseball. A more undesirable location for such a purpose it would have been difficult to find. Eight hundred dollars was actually appropriated for the erection of a building for smallpox. Fortunately, there were no cases of smallpox in 1900–1 so the $800 appropriated for that anticipated emergency was not expended. Again in 1901–2 there were no smallpox cases among the students. But the reports from over the state were alarming. The President was justifiably apprehensive. Increasing numbers of students were coming each year from areas in which vaccination regulations were very poorly enforced. Quarantine was often broken with resulting exposure of additional persons. There was always the chance that with the opening of a session of the University or the return of the student body after a vacation, some few of the students might have been exposed, and, after an incubation period, develop smallpox. The few weeks following a vacation or the beginning of a session was a period of watchful anxiety on the part of the administration. Very unfairly, the University was regarded by many as at fault if smallpox or typhoid appeared within the student body. The administration was anxious to leave nothing undone which would minimize this threat to the health of the student body and the good name of the institution.

The President[1] informed the board at their first meeting, a special session, September, 1902, that official reports showed an increase in the number and virulence of cases of smallpox in the state. He believed it unlikely that we could escape having cases develop within the student body during the coming year. In order that the University should not be unprepared he recommended that a fund be placed at the disposal of the Executive Committee. Accordingly, $1,500 was made available for purchase or erection of a house to be used for care of students suffering from smallpox or other contagious diseases.

The Executive Committee met with difficulty in securing a site for a smallpox hospital. An option had been obtained by November 6, but no action had been taken since the site was not free of objections and it was hoped a better site might be discovered. Architect John Nichols had prepared plans for a six-room cottage which could be used for this purpose and cost about $900.

On December 15, 1902, a two-story suburban house on South Henderson Street occupying a five-acre site, far removed from the University and an eighth of a mile from any other residence, was purchased for $2,700. Harvey Pryor, who had had smallpox in his family, was placed in charge to care for the house and provide

---

[1] President Bryan's alarm was well grounded. Official reports show that, in Indiana, deaths from smallpox increased from 1 in 1899 to 75 in 1902, and 195 in 1903. For an excellent account of smallpox during this period see the biography of Dr. John N. Hurty by Thurman B. Rice, A.M., M.D., Chap. XXX.

needed nursing care for patients with smallpox or other contagious diseases.

Mr. and Mrs. Pryor were to occupy the house free of rent and to have an allowance of $50 for fuel. They were to receive $30 a week for the board and nursing of the first patient and $10 a week for each additional patient.

That these precautionary measures were wisely taken was indicated in the President's report in March, 1903. There had been five cases of smallpox and one of scarlet fever. The period of hospitalization of each case had been from seven to fourteen days. The expense had been heavy and the University could ill afford it; but the young men praised highly the care they had received, the scourge had not spread on the campus, and the results were gratifying.

By June, 1905, there was further evidence that the Hospital was functioning satisfactorily. There had been a number of cases of scarlet fever during the year. The cost of care ranged from $30 to $154.25. The total bill for the care of the seven patients was $360.01, including $19.50 for disinfecting.

Sewage Disposal

At the beginning of this century sewage from University buildings and from private houses in Bloomington drained into dry cisterns, the walls of which were laid without cement. But in Bloomington, as in many cities of Indiana of that day and much later days, there were also outside toilets, which were a menace to health.

In June, 1905, a conference was held with the City Council urging establishment of a city sewage system for Bloomington. In November, 1908, the President informed the board:

I am glad to report that a sewer system for the city of Bloomington is in progress of construction and will be completed in the course of the year.

The *Daily Telephone* of June 28, 1909, announced that the work on the sewage plant was finished. But it was not until July 6, as indicated in the local papers, that the sewage system was formally accepted by the City Council and the work of connecting sewage lines from residences with the new system was begun. The sewage assessment roll was adopted by the City Council, August 17, 1909.

SANITARY CONDITIONS

In October, 1910, the President reported on sanitary conditions:

I deeply regret the necessity of reporting an invasion of typhoid fever during the summer of 1910. About twenty students were reported as having this disease. There were three deaths. The Hygiene Committee of the Faculty cooperated actively with the city and state health authorities in determining the cause of the epidemic and seeking for a remedy. The State Health Officer reported his finding that the cases came from a few eating places in one neighborhood, the source of contamination being one or more unprotected vaults. The authorities made a careful examination of the city water and of the water on the University grounds and reported both good. The Hygiene Committee, after careful consideration, recommends that the State Board of Health be requested to send an officer to Bloomington to inspect and report upon sanitary conditions in all boarding places which receive students. The Executive Committee approved of this report and I have asked Dr. Lyons to cooperate with the State Board of Health in this matter. It is a fact that typhoid was very general throughout the State last summer, in many places very much worse than in Bloomington. It is also true that the epidemic here was greatly exaggerated and advertised throughout the State. The enrollment has undoubtedly been affected to a considerable extent by this means. The most important consideration is not, however, the bad name which the town has obtained, not the loss in numbers, but the untimely death of three splendid young men. It is manifestly our duty to leave nothing undone which lies in our power to make the sanitary conditions here as good as possible.

In March, 1911, the committee on hygiene was directed to report to the trustees, in June, plans for improvement of sanitary conditions, especially including student boarding houses.

HYGIENE

In March, 1906, the committee on hygiene had recommended to the faculty that three hours in hygiene should be required of all candidates for graduation, the course in hygiene to be given in the spring of each year, beginning with 1907.

The announcement of three hours of hygiene as a requirement for graduation appeared in the 1906–7 Catalog of Indiana University. For some years this course was in charge of Dr. Rebecca George and Dr. Charles P. Hutchins, chiefly the latter, who was in residence. On Dr. Hutchins' resignation, charge of the course was assigned to Dr. B. D. Myers.

University Physician

Dr. Hutchins resigned as professor of physical training for men in June, 1914, and on December 1 Dr. J. E. P. Holland was appointed University physician. Dr. Holland's duties included the medical examination of entering students, the medical examination of all other students taking gymnasium or athletic work, the prescription of corrective gymnastics. The doctor was also to give medical advice free to students consulting him, but he was not to take charge of cases of serious illness. It was believed that this appointment would promote better health and greater efficiency of University students. The offices were in Maxwell Hall basement, entered from the east.

The work of the University physician grew with the increase in enrollment. As a member of the committee on student health he was in touch with all health activities of the campus. At the beginning of the second semester of the year 1916–17, Dr. Fernande Ida Julia Hachat, M.D. 1912, began her work as assistant University physician. In 1929 the offices of the University physicians were moved to a house[2] on Forest Place known as the Infirmary, where facilities for work were expanded and a few hospital beds were provided for brief occupancy. Here the offices remained until 1939, when they were moved farther south on Forest Place.

During all these years the hospital at the southern limit of the city was retained for contagious diseases.

The Influenza

In the fall of 1918 Indiana University had a larger enrollment than ever before in her history. On October 1 it had reached 1,935, and it was expected to reach 2,000.[3] Of this number, about 60 per cent were enrolled in the Student Army Training Corps, organized that fall. On conclusion of induction ceremonies, October 1, available blankets were issued and the men were instructed to wear warm clothing, keep warm, and report at once to a physician if ill. These instructions were given because alarming reports were coming in from various camps of a virulent outbreak of influenza, and every

[2] The former Kappa house.
[3] See Chap. IX.

precaution was being taken to safeguard the health of the student body. Dr. J. E. P. Holland was already in the Army, and Dr. Fred Batman had taken his place as acting University physician. Suggestions were published in *The Indiana Daily Student* of October 3 for preservation of student health, for it was realized that a bad epidemic of colds was prevalent among the students. Students were admonished to "keep down the flu," to go to Maxwell Hall and get a "cold" shot from the University physician "if you feel badly, your head aches, and you are miserable." "Spanish influenza," as it was often called, was a great menace and student cooperation was sought in avoiding it.

A box notice in *The Indiana Daily Student* of October 4 admonished every S.A.T.C. student to send home for two extra blankets or purchase two at once, as the government blankets might not be available for a few weeks. The following day, though cases of influenza were developing, all classes were directed to continue. Precautions were being taken to prevent the spread of "Spanish influenza" in the University. Certain students had been quarantined.

Then on October 10 the University was closed. The official order read as follows:

> By order of the State Board of Health, the University is closed until October 20th. This order begins at noon today. S.A.T.C. men will remain in barracks under the orders of Captain Dalton. The girls' dormitories will be closed. All students who are not in the S.A.T.C. living in the State are advised to go home, preferably by automobile. All girls living outside the state please see Miss Wells, Dean of Women, before leaving town.
>
> Spanish influenza is a crowd disease. Avoid congregating for any purpose either indoors or outdoors.
>
> William L. Bryan

While the University proper was closed, the S.A.T.C. men, according to Army regulations, were held in barracks. When the first few cases of influenza developed they were placed in quarantine in the University Hospital at the southern suburb of the city. But cases multiplied fulminatingly. It became necessary almost at once to fill the main floor and balcony of Assembly Hall with hospital beds, and a few days later the floor of the auditorium of the Student Building was likewise utilized, and thus the Indiana University S.A.T.C. Hospital was organized.

Matters were in a chaotic state when President Bryan asked me to take charge and organize for the threatened epidemic. The government made this appointment official by appointing me unit surgeon in charge of the hospital.

A staff of local physicians was appointed and a call was sent out for nurses. There was the greatest difficulty in securing competent nurses, for the emergency was general and the death rate in some localities was appalling. Some of the nurses we were able to secure were nurses in "uniform" only. I recall that one nurse who had been sent to us from Cleveland couldn't even take temperatures. In this emergency, faculty women were called on for help. The response was fine and their work most efficient. Here was an epidemic so virulent that, in certain large camps, hundreds were dying. On October 15, 1918, it was reported that there were 250,000 cases of influenza in training camps of the United States, and of these 36,465 had developed pneumonia and 10,741 had died to date. That was a death rate of more than 4 per cent. These faculty women were asked to volunteer their services in this dangerous emergency and they merit unbounded appreciation of their effective response.

The Indiana Daily Student of November 5 carried a box statement by President Bryan in recognition of this service:

An Appreciation

I wish to express the heartiest thanks of the University to those who have helped our soldier boys make the fight against influenza. The almost unequaled record of our University hospital in saving the boys is due to the physicians, nurses, soldier orderlies, and voluntary helpers from the town and the faculty. The work was hard and dangerous. Not a few of the workers broke down with the disease or with exhaustion. Those who are at the battle have not shown more devotion than many who have helped to make the victorious fight here.

While the official notice had stated that the University would be closed for ten days, or until October 20, it was not until November 4 (twenty-five days later) that classes in all departments were again resumed.

Though the situation was improved, it was still very serious. On November 6 there were still thirty-one patients in the University Hospital. Two new cases had been reported on November 4, and only one on November 5. Although the quarantine was lifted, students were urged to stay out of crowds. On November 7 only three cases remained in the hospital.

The peak of the epidemic was reached on October 16 when there were 174 cases. Between October 12 and October 20 there were continuously more than 100 patients and between October 15 and October 20 the number varied from 160 to 174.

Mrs. Fred Batman did heroic service in charge of all the nurses during this period. Those S.A.T.C. men who were to go to officers' training camps about the middle of November were vaccinated for smallpox, typhoid, etc.

All told, there were 350 patients hospitalized. There were only three deaths, i.e., mortality of less than 1 per cent. This was less than one-fourth the average death rate. The University had every reason to be proud of this low mortality in this outbreak of a virulent type of influenza which cost so many lives. The warm quarters had a very unusually large cubic footage of air space in old Assembly Hall and the auditorium of the Student Building. Both had high vaulted ceilings. Another factor conducive to this good result was that students were hospitalized at the first symptom of illness.

A Second Flu Threat

The flu appeared a second time within the student body in January, 1919. The student health committee made a report, approved by the Board of Trustees, read before classes, and published in *The Indiana Daily Student*. Briefly stated, the report stipulated that: vaccination against pneumonia was required and free; gatherings of students on and off the campus were prohibited; trips into town were limited to necessary business; week ends out of town required sanction of deans; and students with increased temperatures, cough, and sore throat were to be regarded as influenza suspects, and required to report to the University physician for examination.

The University physician was authorized to receive acceptable certificates of vaccination issued by outside physicians. Students who refused to be vaccinated were not to remain in the University.

DIPHTHERIA

In 1922 there was at Indiana University an excellent demonstration of the control of an epidemic with the aid of modern science.

Diphtheria was prevalent in many parts of the state that fall. The semester had barely opened when on September 29 three girls in two sorority houses were found to be suffering from this malady. Both houses were quarantined, and students with sore throats were warned to get medical attention. In response to this advice some 150 students visited the office of the University physician over the week end.

Five new cases were reported on Monday, October 2. Dr. Holland, the University physician, announced that there was no foundation for the rumor that the University would have to be closed.

On Friday, October 6, the University physician reported that ten students were in quarantine in the University Hospital. Of these ten students, five were held in quarantine over the week end.

On Monday, October 9, five new cases were ordered into quarantine and announcements were made in classes that we were threatened with an epidemic. Students were advised to present themselves at the office of the University physician to take the Schick test to determine their susceptibility or immunity to diphtheria. In response to this advice, some three hundred students were given this test. Dr. Holland had appealed to the Eli Lilly Company for Schick test material, and that excellent organization had not merely responded immediately, but had sent Dr. E. G. Kyte from their research laboratory to assist Dr. Holland in meeting this emergency.

On Tuesday, October 10, a conspicuous box notice in *The Indiana Daily Student* requested all students to present themselves at once at the University physicians' office for the Schick test. It was reported that seventeen students were in quarantine.

On Thursday, October 12, a total of seventy-five cases had been reported and twenty-one cases were in quarantine. Eight hundred had taken the Schick test, and most of those found to be susceptible had voluntarily taken the immunizing injections. Dr. Holland urged cooperation of students in order to avoid compulsory vaccination.

By Saturday, October 14, this appeal had brought such response from the student body that it was possible to report that 1,500 students had taken the Schick test, of whom about 400 susceptibles had been given the immunizing vaccination. The incidence of new cases was declining. Eight students were in the University Hospital.

On Thursday, October 19, Dr. Holland reported that there had been no new cases for three days. But he warned that approximately one-third of the student body still had a percentage of susceptibles who might be responsible for a recurrence.

On Tuesday, October 24, Dr. Holland reported that the epidemic had been stamped out. Eighty-five cases had developed in nineteen days, only one of which was still in the University Hospital. There were no deaths. The wisdom of establishment of the University Hospital for contagious diseases was again demonstrated.

Great credit was due Dr. J. E. P. Holland for his efficient handling of this epidemic. Thanks were rendered the Eli Lilly Company for their prompt assistance. Credit was also due the student body for the degree of their cooperation at a time when the importance of vaccination was less understood than today.

Procedure in an epidemic, such as described above, would be mere routine today, twenty years later (1943). But in 1923 it was very advanced procedure.

We Do Make Progress

In 1906 the University hospital in Indianapolis was opened a day early in order, as an emergency, to receive thirteen cases of typhoid from Fort Benjamin Harrison. In the hospitals of Indianapolis there were not enough cases of typhoid in 1937 for adequate instruction of medical students. Remarkable decreases have been made in the number of deaths from diphtheria and scarlet fever, and pneumonia may soon be added to this list.

Great credit is due the doctors of Indiana, and the medical profession in general, who have helped to reduce so greatly the mortality from infectious disease. At the beginning of this century a doctor's typhoid practice sometimes amounted to $1,500 per year. Yet no doctor hesitated to lend his full effort to bring about the almost complete eradication of this and other infectious diseases.

Chapter XXXIII

INDIANA UNIVERSITY, 1928 - 30

Ability of Indiana to Support Higher Education

To show the lag of the state of Indiana in support of her institutions of higher education, comparisons were sometimes made between appropriations voted for Indiana University and Purdue University and appropriations for institutions of higher education in other midwest states, Ohio, Illinois, Iowa, Michigan, Wisconsin, and Minnesota.

When statements of the needs of Indiana University were made, it was sometimes remarked that Indiana did not have the population of some of these neighboring states and, therefore, should not be expected to contribute as liberally as other states to a state university. To ascertain the validity of this argument a study was made in the spring of 1928 which revealed its utter fallacy.

Reference to figures found in the United States Bureau of Census showed that whereas the population of Illinois, Ohio, and Michigan exceeded that of Indiana as of July 1, 1928, the population of Indiana exceeded that of Wisconsin, Minnesota, and Iowa. But the combined income of Purdue and Indiana University from the state of Indiana was much below that furnished the state university of either Wisconsin, Minnesota, or Iowa. So it was evident that population did not determine the amount of the appropriation for higher education.

Again it was contended that Indiana was not as rich as some of these neighboring states and, therefore, could not contribute so generously to higher education. But figures from the National Industrial Board showed that the total wealth of Indiana exceeded that of Minnesota and Wisconsin, which states provided $1,500,000 to $2,500,000 more to their universities than the state of Indiana provided for Indiana University and Purdue University combined.

The National Industrial Board presented statistics showing that in per capita wealth Indiana occupied a mid-position in the group of North Central states. The per capita wealth of Iowa, Minnesota, and

371

Illinois exceeded that of Indiana, but the per capita wealth of Indiana exceeded that of Ohio, Wisconsin, and Michigan.

The Bureau of Business Research of Indiana University showed from authoritative statistical reports that the savings accounts in all banks in Indiana in 1927 exceeded the savings accounts of 1920 by $90,000,000; that the growth in building and loan assets of 1927 compared with 1920 amounted to $160,000,000; that the increase in life insurance in force in 1927 compared with 1920 amounted to $1,090,000,000; the increase of life insurance premiums paid in 1927 over 1920 amounted to $25,400,000; and the value of new homes built in 1927 amounted to $25,300,000.

A comparison of figures for 1927 and 1920 showed that there was an increase of expenditures for automobiles of $154,400,000, and the amount spent for state highways in 1925 exceeded the amount of this expenditure in 1920 by $12,300,000.

The Bureau of Business Research showed that in the year 1927 in Indiana $134,400,000 was spent for luxuries, tobacco, ice cream and soft drinks, candy and chewing gum, moving pictures, clubs, etc.

With claims of inability of Indiana to support higher education liberally, based on population, total wealth, and per capita wealth, shown to be untenable, and with evidences of prosperity, as revealed in enormous increases in savings and life insurance in force, expenditures for homes, automobiles, and luxuries, etc., there was still some element in the psychology of Hoosiers that enabled them to tolerate lagging in the position of a poor seventh in this group of North Central states, in amounts spent for higher education.

The explanation of this lag, we believe, is found in the chapter on "Indiana University and the Non-State Schools." The non-state schools were changing rapidly in their attitude toward the state schools. But their graduates of earlier years, in and out of the General Assembly, still retained points of view of their school days, and believed that liberal support of the state schools was prejudicial to the interest and welfare of the non-state schools.

REPORT TO GOVERNOR JACKSON AND THE VISITING COMMITTEE

It was the sense of the board, October 25, 1928, that the University had imperative need of an increase of 100 per cent in its income for operating expenses and that an earnest and determined effort should be made to secure such increase from the next legislature. The following tentative budget, after some consideration, was adopted November 13, 1928:

	Increases Asked for	Total Budget Request
BLOOMINGTON:		
Operating expenses ....$	479,758	$1,426,930
Equipment of all Departments including Library books....................	266,844	316,844
Repairs of buildings and grounds.............	50,872	100,872
INDIANAPOLIS:		
INDIANA UNIVERSITY SCHOOL OF MEDICINE:		
Instructional units:		
Operating expenses ....$	48,200	$ 177,917
Equipment all Departments..........$26,820 Library books 20,000	26,820	46,820
Repairs of buildings, grounds, and tunnel......	42,500	42,500
Nurses Training School......................	20,440	52,974
Service units:		
James Whitcomb Riley Hospital..............		50,000
Robert W. Long Hospital....................		50,000
Coleman Hospital		75,000
Power plant equipment (heat and light)......	80,000	80,000
INDIANA UNIVERSITY SCHOOL OF DENTISTRY:		
Operating expenses	62,754	77,754
STATE EXTENSION SERVICE:		
Extension, social service, and field nursing service	41,984	132,561
TOTAL...........$	1,120,172	$2,630,172

RECOMMENDATION OF BUDGET COMMITTEE TO LEGISLATURE

University authorities were doing an excellent job of calling attention of state officials, legislators, and Indiana people to the lag in support of higher education, and the report of University needs presented to Governor Jackson and his legislative committee, late in 1928, was particularly forceful. This committee recommended an annual appropriation for Indiana University as follows:

General expense $1,400,000
Extension service   35,000
Riley Hospital   75,000
Coleman Hospital   75,000
Long Hospital   50,000
Medical School   110,000
Nurses Training School.............................   20,000
Dental School   50,000
Power plant at Indianapolis.........................   40,000*
   *(The Budget Committee recommends that the total sum
   of $80,000 be paid in the first year of the biennium.) ——————
                              Annually.........$1,895,000

And this was the appropriation finally passed by the General Assembly of 1929 for each year of the coming biennium for Indiana University. While it was an improvement, it fell far short of 100 per cent increase in income for operating expenses which it was the conviction of the Board of Trustees that the University imperatively needed.

EXTENSION OF THE POWER PLANT AT MEDICAL CENTER

In May, after adjournment of the General Assembly, the trustees met to discuss what best could be done with the appropriations granted. Among other things, the board had asked $160,000 for an extension of the heat, light, and power plant at the Medical Center at Indianapolis. The General Assembly appropriated only $80,000. The board cut out every item they could cut and still make even temporary provision for immediate demands. But the bids totaled $103,000, $23,000 in excess of the legislative appropriation. After full consideration, the board felt that no further reductions were possible. In this extremity the vice-president of the board, George A. Ball, said that he would make a gift of $25,000 in order that these absolutely necessary items might be provided. This was the second time within a period of two months that Mr. Ball had come to the aid of the financially hard-pressed Board of Trustees of Indiana University.

Contracts were let to various bidders and the work of expanding the power plant at the Medical Center to render its capacity adequate for the additional load demanded by new construction was pressed to satisfactory, gratifying completion.

THE FIRE IN THE POWER PLANT IN BLOOMINGTON

With the completion of the expansion of the power plant at the Medical Center, the trustees felt that they had solved the problem of power, heat, and light for that biennium. But they were mistaken. On September 25, 1929, the recently remodeled power plant at Bloomington was seriously damaged by a fire. The blaze was discovered shortly after 7:30 p.m. and soon turned the interior of the building into a seething furnace.

The power plant building proper representing an investment of about $50,000 was not badly damaged except for the roof, all of which had to be removed and replaced by a fireproof roof; but much of the equipment costing about $150,000 was damaged by both fire and water. The extent of the damage was believed at the time to be approximately $100,000. Temporary connection was established with the city electric system for lighting buildings and campus. The loss was fully covered by insurance.

The last fire of any consequence on the campus had occurred in 1900 when a part of Wylie Hall was burned.

The first University power plant was constructed in the rear of Wylie Hall in 1885, only to be razed in 1897 when it became inadequate. The second power plant, now occupied by *The Indiana Daily Student* and the University printing plant, was then constructed. In 1905 a power house on the present site was built, originally 98 feet by 82 feet. In 1907 an addition was made at the north end of the building for the storage of coal.

The equipment of the plant had been improved and its capacity increased from time to time. But the margin of surplus capacity was so small that the University was continuously striving to bring capacity of the plant up to the load imposed upon it.

On October 14, 1929, Architect Robert F. Daggett submitted plans for rebuilding and enlargement, and Engineer Charles R. Ammerman made a statement as to the condition of the machinery and gave advice in regard to the equipment. F. H. Sinex, representing the Indiana Inspection Bureau, stated that after a careful examination it was his opinion that the cause of the fire was an electrical short circuit and that better electrical wiring should be installed in a number of buildings. Mr. Ammerman shared this opinion.

Now that the repair of damage caused by the fire had to be under-taken, it was deemed wise by the administration to make provision for considerable expansion in anticipation of the increased load which would follow new construction under the ten-year building program.

On October 31, 1929, it was decided that the south wall of the power plant building should be moved approximately fifteen feet to the south. This provided a material enlargement of the plant. When the reconstruction of the power plant was completed a review of expenditures showed that the damage to the building amounted to $16,000 and the loss to equipment $11,000.

In addition to the insurance, the trustees had allowed $50,000 for enlargement and fireproofing. The final cost of repairs and expansion totaled $173,047.43.

Mr. Ammerman was asked to prepare plans and specifications for an incinerator to be installed in the new power plant at an approximate cost of $3,000. This incinerator was connected with the tall smokestack and provided complete combustion of large laboratory animals without odor on the campus.

THE UNIVERSITY COUNCIL

In the spring of 1928 the first steps were taken by the faculty in the formation of a University senate. In October of 1928 a revised report on a plan of organization of a council,[1] as it was now called, failed of passage. A new committee was appointed, and on January 10, 1929, the report of this committee was adopted by the University faculty. The first report of the University Council made to the faculty on April 29, 1930, covered a meeting held on March 25, 1930, and related to procedure in Freshman week.

At the time this Council was authorized by the faculty, the President stated that its field of activity was distinct from and should in no way conflict with the activity of the committee on promotion of University interests. As time passed, however, the deliberations of the Council did invade the broad field of this committee. This probably was as inevitable as it was unintentional. The committee

---

[1] A University Council without legislative functions had been substituted for a University senate.

on University interests had been authorized to study and offer suggestions on any matter it believed of importance to the University. If the Council were to be anything other than a debating society it should consider matters of vital interest to the institution.

As the Council became more active the meetings of the committee on promotion of University interests seemed more and more a duplication of the work of the Council, and finally committee meetings were abandoned altogether. As chairman of this once constructively active and highly efficient committee, I was chiefly responsible for its unplanned final inactivity and abandonment. In its day it raised the interests of Indiana University to a high place in the thinking of most faculty members and many alumni.

It may be noted that there was a fundamental difference in the composition of the two bodies. Men were chosen for service on the University interests committee because it was felt they had something to contribute. On the Council, representation was by schools, a younger man and an older man from each school, neither of whom might have anything to contribute to promotion of the general interests of Indiana University. It was a time when opinions of the inexperienced were coming to be regarded as important as judgments based on knowledge and experience.

Redefinition of "Alumni"

Mr. Heighway, reporting for the Alumni Association in 1930, urged the preparation of a bill to be presented at the next meeting of the General Assembly (1931), providing that all graduates of the University be allowed to vote for alumni trustee. He asked that such a bill also provide the date of election of alumni trustee, now that Commencement was no longer held on Wednesday. The first change should have been made twenty years earlier, and no doubt would have been if the unenfranchised had been deeply interested in this election.

A part of section 4 of the Act of March 3, 1891, under certain limitations of which the University had operated for forty years, explains this recommendation of Mr. Heighway:

The alumni of the University shall be those persons who have been awarded and on whom have been conferred any of the following degrees:

Bachelor of Arts (A.B.), Bachelor of Letters (B.L.), Bachelor of Science (B.S.), Bachelor of Philosophy (B.Ph.), Bachelor of Laws (LL.B.), Master of Arts (A.M.), Master of Science (M.S.), Doctor of Philosophy (Ph.D.).

Some graduates of schools established after 1891, including M.D.'s who held no baccalaureate degrees, had no right to vote.

Section 4 of the bill passed March 3, 1931, provided a clarification of the election date and this redefinition of alumni:

The Alumni of the University shall consist of those persons who have been awarded and on whom have been conferred the Bachelor's, Master's, or Doctor's degree.

Thus an inequity of long standing was corrected.

STUDENT LOAN FUNDS

By October, 1929, the total student loan funds amounted to $32,629.13, given by fifty-four contributors. An accounting was made of each contribution, showing the name of the donor, the date and the amount of the gift, the number of students accommodated, and the current cash balance of each contribution. Some of the contributions were small, but the identity of each contribution was maintained.

OUT-OF-STATE PREMEDICAL STUDENTS

When in the late twenties the number of applicants for matriculation in the medical schools of the United States became twice as great as the capacity of the schools, some state medical schools limited enrollment to state students. Indiana University continued to accept a few out-of-state students, but charged twice the fee paid by state students and accepted only those out-of-state students with a B grade average both in general and in the sciences. To escape this high scholastic requirement and double fee, some out-of-state students came to Indiana University for their premedical work, expecting then to be admitted to the School of Medicine on the same basis as Indiana boys. To conserve facilities and advantages for Indiana students the trustees in October, 1930, adopted the following rule:

All students from another state who come to Indiana University for the purpose of completing their premedical work shall be required to meet the same qualitative standards as other out-of-state students.

DEATH OF JAMES B. LATHROP

The Reverend James B. Lathrop, of Greensburg, whose death was announced at Commencement, 1929, had held the distinction of being the oldest living graduate of Indiana University. More than that, he had been believed to be the oldest living college graduate in the United States. Born on November 24, 1825, a year and a half after the doors of the institution had been opened for instruction, graduated at the eighteenth Commencement of the University, he was, at the time of his death, June 6, 1929, 103½ years of age. An expression of profound respect for Mr. Lathrop was sent to his family by the President and Board of Trustees.

COMMENCEMENT, 1930

I once entered the office of President Bryan in Maxwell Hall, just as he straightened up at his large, almost square work table, pushing from him two stacks of 8½-inch by 11-inch sheets of paper on which he had been writing. One stack contained about a hundred sheets, the other, half a dozen. Laughingly, he pointed to the big stack, saying, "It has taken all this, to get this"—pointing to the half-dozen pages.

The very interesting address, "Stars and Men," was written in that characteristic way. It was so condensed that it would be impossible to abstract it. It may be found in the *Alumni Quarterly*, Volume XVII, page 294.

The address was particularly apropros, for, following it, Vesto Melvin Slipher and Carl Otto Lampland, both astronomers and graduates of Indiana University, were presented for the honorary LL.D. at the 1930 Commencement, in recognition of their epochal work in locating a ninth planet, Pluto.

OF INTEREST TO THE FACULTY

Three deans were honored in 1928 by election as heads of national organizations. Dean Paul V. McNutt was elected commander of the American Legion, Dean Burton D. Myers president of the Association of American Medical Colleges, and Dean H. Lester Smith president of the National Association of Directors of Summer Schools.

With the consent of Professor Book, Head of the Department of Psychology and Philosophy, this Department in April, 1929, was divided into a Department of Psychology of which Professor Book remained head, and a Department of Philosophy, of which Professor Daniel S. Robinson was made head.

At the meeting of the University faculty on April 26, 1929, the President read portions of a report of the Graduate Council for improvement of the Graduate School. A significant part of this report dealt with qualifications of faculty members prerequisite for appointment or promotion.

A committee consisting of Professors Fred V. Chew, Harold T. Davis, and Walter E. Treanor made a report May 17, 1929, on plans for group insurance for members of the faculty, administrative officers, and employees. It was ordered that the University enter into a contract for this insurance with the Equitable Life Assurance Society of the United States, if satisfactory terms could be agreed upon. A satisfactory agreement was reached. On June 2, 1937, it was ordered that group insurance for those retired or on leave of absence be continued until further orders of the board.

We have quoted the President as saying that increased income to provide faculty salaries which would enable the University to secure and hold superior men was the most important problem confronting the trustees. We have stated that the legislature of 1927 appropriated only about a fourth of the additional million and a half needed. Nevertheless, the administration took advantage of this slight increase in appropriation to make some increase in faculty salaries. The campaign for increased funds as presented to the 1929 legislature was made on the same basis as in 1927. Again in May, 1929, the little addition to income voted by the General Assembly was utilized in part by the administration to make a further slight increase in faculty salaries.

The honorary degree LL.D. was conferred on Frank Clayton Ball, Evans Woollen, John F. Barnhill, Charles Harris, Lafayette Page, Lewis Madison Terman, Clark Wissler, and James A. Woodburn at Commencement, 1929.

Colonel Oliver P. Robinson became commandant of the R.O.T.C. in 1928 when Major Crea was ordered to Fort Thomas.

The chairmanship plan of departmental organization had been of interest to the American Association of University Professors for some time. On recommendation of the local chapter, a faculty committee had been appointed to study the merits of this and of the headship plan of organization. In March, 1929, this committee made its report to the faculty, which adopted a resolution in which the chairmanship plan was endorsed and referred to the President and the trustees with the request that the chairmanship plan be adopted at such time and in such way as would promote the interests of the University without injustice to present members thereof. The Board of Trustees took the recommendation under consideration and investigation.

MISCELLANEOUS

President Bryan recommended (July, 1928) that the Executive Committee, assisted by Professor D. M. Mottier and Charles Hays, the superintendent of building and grounds, be authorized to improve that part of the campus lying between Residence and Memorial Halls. This bit of campus had been an old stone quarry. The committee developed it as a rock garden, making very attractive what had been an unsightly bit of campus.

Professor Wilbur A. Cogshall, Head of the Department of Astronomy, was a member of the U.S. Naval Observatory expedition which sailed from San Francisco on January 23, 1929, for the Philippines to obtain a large-scale photograph of the corona of the sun at the total eclipse, May 9.

A master plan for the University campus was presented by Olmsted Brothers, of Brookline, Mass., in June, 1929. Future building sites, walks, drives, etc. were indicated.

On October 30, 1929, an appropriation of $700 was made for the purchase of two semiportable motion picture machines to be installed in Assembly Hall.

The Senior class of 1930 passed a resolution approving the recommendation of President Bryan that $2.50 of the graduation fees of the Seniors in the University be turned over to the Alumni Association of the University as a membership fee for one year.

Chapter XXXIV

ATHLETICS AT INDIANA UNIVERSITY

A THLETICS[1] is defined as the system of rules or principles employed for physical training, as in running, rowing, boxing, gymnastics, etc. In the development of athletics at Indiana University the field of intercollegiate athletics has had to make its way against the opposition of those whose conception of athletics was limited to the physical development of the individual and who deplored the emphasis laid on competition of groups of individuals functioning as a team, the members of which had different, specialized functions, the success of performance depending largely on the degree in which the group of specialists coordinated and integrated their efforts.

Athletics, 1867–1902
Baseball, 1867–1902

The year 1867 is noteworthy[2] as the year of establishment of *The Indiana Student* and the organization of the first baseball team. It was a fortunate coincidence, for this paper recorded certain interesting items relating to the early days of this major sport, baseball.

The first number of Volume I of *The Indiana Student* was published on February 22, 1867. It was a monthly publication, not *The Indiana Daily Student.* Since the editorial board changed frequently, it had no established editorial or news policy. While *The Indiana Student* cannot be regarded as a very reliable source of historic material, what its staff wrote and failed to write on matters athletic may be accepted as reflecting student thought and interest, as well as lack of interest in athletics.

[1] Woodburn had assigned "Athletics" as a separate chapter for the second volume of the *History of Indiana University.* Happily the manuscript was completed while it was possible to submit it to Professors Moenkhaus, Sembower, Davisson, Clevenger, and President Bryan for suggestions.
[2] It is also noteworthy as the year of the admission of women and of the first legislative appropriation.

Though there are articles on "College Life," on "Student Interests," etc. in Volume I, there are very few references to athletics, or games, or sports. An article on baseball in the issue of May 17, by one who claims that as a leap-frog-ist he has few equals, is quoted as revealing the lack of student interest in and appreciation of this sport, and of those who were making remarkable progress in its development.

Strolling through the suburbs of the city, a few afternoons since, our attention was attracted by a number of persons who were taking vigorous exercise by what appeared, to us, to be chasing butterflies; but, upon approaching them, we found it to be the university baseball club, taking field exercise to the tune of double quick.

This club has been in existence but a short time—yet some of them seem to think themselves perfect in the art, for inquiring of one of the players, to what degree of proficiency they had attained, assuming a tragedical air, he replied that they had just received the thirty-third degree, and, on their own ground, could "beat anything in the State." From what we witnessed, we feel free to say that their excellencies are second to no other club in Bloomington.

We are informed that a challenge has been sent to the Yale, Harvard, Greencastle, and Hindustan (Monroe County) clubs, and we hope will be accepted, as we desire to see the valor of our university club tested. Clubs of this kind are very conducive to the health of the students, and we would be glad to see more of them. As a baseball-ist we do not excel, but as a leap-frog-ist we have few equals. If somebody would organize a club of the latter kind, they would receive our petition "to oncet."

This reporter did not realize that afternoon that he was looking at a remarkable group of men. Happily the personnel and prowess of this first baseball team has been made a matter of record in *I Men's Notes* (Vol. II, No. 2, p. 2), by the captain of that first team, Malcolm A. McDonald, regarded as the "father of baseball" at Indiana University. He says:

The regular team was McIntire, catcher; Allison Maxwell, first base; Richard Maxwell, second base; Fred Howe, third base; McDonald and [Aquilla] Jones, pitchers; Rice, shortstop; Frank Hall, William Bynum, Homer Bothwell, Arthur Twineham, and Shannon Nave, fielders. We had a number of other members of the club, but these I have mentioned were the most prominent players and showed more talent in the game.

McDonald gives an interesting account of the conditions under which the men played and brief biographical sketches of the players and their later successful careers. Articles by Arthur P. Twineham and other players of that early time are found in this same volume of *I Men's Notes*.

One does find in *The Indiana Student* (Vol. I, p. 42) a creditable article on health, in which the importance of physical as well as mental development is emphasized. It is argued that every college should have a gymnasium under the special charge of a professor and that physical training should be required of all. It was recommended that "individuals should supply the deficiency [lack of gymnasium] by taking walks and indulging in such manly sports as will give strength and the powers of endurance to the system."

In *The Indiana Student* (Vol. V, 1871), the only reference to things athletic is found on page 40, the last item in two columns of mere fillers, and reading as follows:

> Baseball season has again arrived. University Clubs are reorganizing, so we will soon be able to witness games of the "manly sport."

On encountering an article in this volume headed "Contest," one is misled momentarily into believing that an athletic contest is the subject of the half-column. On reading the account one discovers that it was a contest between the members of the two literary societies (Athenian and Philomathean). The contestants, three from each society, orated, each on a subject of his own choice. It was not in any sense a debate. This might be regarded as the great indoor sport of the day. Since gestures, watched and criticized, were used freely, with much brow mopping, the "contest" had certain aspects of a physical exercise.

Volumes VI, VII, and VIII of *The Indiana Student* are missing from the University file. Volume IX was published in the school year 1882–83. It follows, therefore, that during the ten years, 1872 to 1882, only three volumes of the paper were published, VI, VII, and VIII. Publication was suspended during seven of those ten years. (Wilkins, Chap. XLVIII, says it was suspended in 1874.)

An article entitled "Match Game of Baseball between the Asbury and Indiana Universities' Nines" appeared in Volume IX of *The*

Indiana Student, May, 1883. It is quoted because for a moment it lifts the curtain dropped by Time over long-ago 1883, and gives a glimpse of nine ununiformed, unpracticed men, a bare-handed catcher, and a pitcher called center, taking a beating.

The *Student's* unsophisticated reporter now realizes the immeasurable distance that lies between his own unpracticed pen and the keen classical pencil of the regular newspaper man. . . .

We venture to say in our own poor way, that nine gentlemanly men from Asbury clad in neat white uniforms, met a hastily collected club of our boys on the campus, and beat them twenty-three to six. For five innings the game was about even—finely played on both sides and intensely interesting. At that point T. W. Wilson's hands were so bruised, that he was compelled to change from the catcher's place to the right field, and the strong point of the home club was broken, as no one else was quite equal to the task of stopping the balls that came from center. It might be further explained that the Bloomingtons were entirely without practice, but we only care to say that it was a gentlemanly game, well and fairly played.

The defeat by Asbury in May of 1883 was avenged in May, 1884, when Indiana beat DePauw[3] both at Greencastle and at Bloomington. The reporting of these games in *The Indiana Student* (p. 148) is the best found in the seventeen years the game had been played on the campus. The reporter tells of bases on balls, of errors, etc., indicating a growth in understanding and appreciation of the game. "However, the club from first to last was treated more shabbily [at Greencastle] than any set of men will ever be permitted to be treated in the rustic village of Bloomington."

By 1884 baseball had become of sufficient interest that the names of the players were printed in *The Indiana Student* (Vol. X, p. 130). This was probably due to the fact that W. J. Bryan (later changed to W. L. Bryan), was editor-in-chief. Bryan had played college baseball and now, in his Senior year, was sympathetic with athletic development. The general faculty attitude at that time, however, was to look upon athletics and games as a very questionable diversion from the real purposes of an educational institution.

I quote this article of 1884, *The Indiana Student* (p. 130):

The following are the members of the Indiana University baseball club: A. Rabb, c.f.; H. G. Stewart, 2b.; D. C. Stewart, 1b.; E. B. Stewart, l.f.; W. J.

[3] The name had been changed from Asbury to DePauw.

Bryan, r.f.; S. M. Ewing, 3b.; W. Holmes, s.s.; T. W. Wilson, c.; G. S. Pritchett, p.; J. A. Payne, 2p.

Briefly, the statistics of the club are as follows: Average weight, 152; average height, nearly 5′10″; average age, 22. Six have light hair, four black. Four have blue eyes, four gray, and two black. The fact that sportsmen of note usually have either blue or gray eyes, strengthens our faith in the club. In politics there are five Democrats and five Republicans. All are righthanded except Payne. Wilson, Rabb, and Pritchett are regarded as especially strong players, though every man fills his place well. D. C. Stewart as a first baseman can hardly be excelled. All the members are good looking, even handsome, but none of them are married or engaged. It is the best club the college ever produced. Those stockings!

That athletics were not universally popular at Indiana University in the fall of '84 is clearly evident from the following editorial:

Athletics have a place in most American colleges and when properly directed are a source of much good. The tendency now, however, is to overdo the matter and the frequent allusions to boat races, baseball matches, etc., by some colleges is disgusting. According to Dr. Sargent, of Harvard gymnasium, modern athletics are on the decline and are degenerating into professionalism. If such is the case their beneficial effects among college students are equally on the decrease.

In *The Indiana Student,* Volume XIII, for the school year 1886–87 the only reference to the University baseball team (p. 226) informs us that:

The College nine for 1887 is as follows: McMullen '90—C. and Captain; Cornell '90—P.; Long '88—1B.; Rabb '87—2B.; Wilsey '89—3B.; Stewart '87—L.F.; Springer '89—C.F.; Starbuck '90—R.F.; Davis—Substitute.

And on page 225 under "Local Notes" we read: "The faculty donated liberally to the baseball club." "The ball grounds were never in better condition."

The pitching of Fred Cornell in a baseball game between Prep students and college Freshmen was featured in an account of the game in *The Indiana Student,* April 15, 1887. "A Prep declared Cornell's balls came like they had wings on their sides."

Cornell was an outstanding athlete. In the *I Men's Notes* (Vol. II, No. 1, p. 3), he writes of "A Great Baseball Game" in which he met a humiliating defeat. The game was between Indiana and Purdue, Decoration Day, 1888. The Indiana team had breezed through undefeated to date. The preceding year a Luther Hord had occasionally come out and practiced with the Indiana boys. He was considered impossible, no speed, no curves, and a joke as a fielder and batsman. When, in this game, the Indiana boys realized that Hord was to pitch for Purdue, it seemed all over but the shouting. But the game at 1 to 1 reached the eleventh inning, when Hord came to bat, and, on a little infield hit, through a series of errors by Indiana men, made a home run, winning the game for Purdue, to the great humiliation of the Indiana boys.

In the spring of 1892 the baseball team won all its games. This championship was not decided until the final game played with DePauw in Bloomington. Both teams had defeated all the other college teams in the Association. DePauw had come to Bloomington on a special train with a brass band. The score was tied four times and in the last inning was made 13 to 11 in favor of Indiana University.

In April, 1893, the *Indiana Student*[4] informs us that the baseball manager had procured Mr. Ikes of Jeffersonville as coach, and the candidates for positions on the team were practicing daily from one to four. The baseball schedule determined by the State Athletic Association was announced.

The baseball season of 1893 was very successful as was also that of 1894. In both seasons Indiana University had championship teams.

The 1894 schedule as determined by the State Athletic Association was announced in the *Indiana Student* of March 13, 1894. An editorial in the issue of April 17, calling attention to the fact that Purdue and DePauw had recently purchased extensive parks for athletic purposes, concludes: "Let us make it our ambition to secure, within the next five years, the Dunn Field north of the University as a playground." This site *was* purchased and developed during the following thirty years.

In the *Arbutus* of 1894, the first ever published, is a brief 3½-page history of athletics at Indiana University in which the names of a few of the celebrities are given: John Rice, A. P. Twineham, George and Malcolm McDonald, Allison and Dick Maxwell, Dr. Sutton, Warren Sherman, Fred Cornell, and Harry McMullen. Lists of

---

[4] The name was changed frequently. See Chap. XLVIII, note 3.

players on baseball teams (1881 to 1894) and on football teams (1886 to 1893) are also given. Further, in this 1894 *Arbutus,* we find a list of the members of the State Athletic Association, a list of members of the University Athletic Association, and the names of the faculty committee on athletics: Martin W. Sampson, Robert J. Aley, and Charles J. Sembower.

The Student of April 23, 1895 (p. 300), states that the faculty had dealt the prospects for a successful baseball season a severe blow by plucking from the team a number of men with poor scholastic records. Nevertheless, in the spring of 1895 the Indiana University baseball team won the state championship. A list of games and scores appeared in *The Student,* May, 1895, pages 328, 352–53.

On January 25, 1896, Fred I. King was elected manager of the baseball team.

The baseball season was terminated in June by victories over Purdue, Wabash, and DePauw. The team had more than held its own though it had played some strong teams.

On the afternoon of January 19, 1899, there was a meeting of the candidates for the baseball team. James H. Horne had recently been appointed trainer[5] and manager by the faculty committee on athletics. This was about three months earlier than baseball men had begun to line up only a few years past. The *Daily Student* of February 13, 1899, announced that a series of matched games of tenpins would be played with a DePauw University team in the near future. The DePauw-Indiana baseball schedule was interesting. DePauw and Indiana University had each won one of the two games played together. So a third game on neutral grounds was played at Crawfordsville and won by DePauw. The Indiana team had beaten Wabash, Purdue, and Nebraska.

In the spring of 1900 Roy O. Pike was captain of the baseball team. He states that the season was only fairly successful, which we may assume is not an understatement.

Baseball in the spring of 1902 was disastrous. One of two games with Ohio State was the only game won against a major team.

---

[5] Though Mr. Horne was appointed trainer, Roy O. Pike, a member of the team, states that he did not act as coach.

Football, 1886–1902[6]

The first mention of football found in *The Indiana Student* appeared in the issue of November, 1884, among local notes (p. 16), in which it was stated that "the football question again was being agitated," and it was hoped that a permanent organization would be formed.

It happened that in the fall of 1885 President Jordan brought to Indiana University as associate professor of economics and sociology, Arthur B. Woodford, a graduate of Yale, who knew something of football. The year 1885–86, the first on the present campus, was a year of organization in a new environment. For Woodford it was a year of orientation during which he ascertained the interest in football and learned something of available material. In the fall of the following school year 1886–87, he introduced football to the Indiana University campus, though it appears that no intercollegiate games were played that year. For three years he did all the coaching.

We find a list of the men forming that first football team on page 14, Volume XIV, of *The Indiana Student* for 1887: Captain Kiplinger, halfback; R. E. Wilsey, halfback; Fred D. Cornell, quarterback; W. M. Butterworth, fullback; Thomas M. Honan, center rusher; Charles Springer, end rusher; William E. Jenkins, rusher; John F. Benham, rusher; Walter W. French, rusher; Joseph H. Shea, rusher.

The team was not successful, however. It was beaten by Franklin 10 to 8. The review at the close of the season complained that the team had had no team to play against in practice and concluded that if the boys of Indiana University have any pride in college athletics, let them go to the grounds, divest themselves of coats and vests, and give the players practice.

The football season of '89 was not successful. The team was defeated by Wabash 40 to 2 and *The Indiana Student* lamented: "Not enough interest was manifest in football to bring a second eleven

---

[6] In the little book *Indiana Football* by Andrew J. Stott, Wabash, '94, published January 1, 1896, is a brief article on "The Beginning [of Football] in Indiana," by Henry T. Mann, Butler captain, 1889–90, in which he states (p. 29) that intercollegiate football was first played in the spring of 1884 between Butler and DePauw.

into the field for practice and at no time had the Indiana eleven played together."

Mr. Evans Woollen, of Indianapolis, the first coach from off the campus, had rendered valuable coaching service for two days.

The football season of 1892 was disastrous. Among the defeats suffered by the team, Wabash beat Indiana by a lopsided score.

The Indiana Student for February, 1893, records an innovation. Though the football team in previous years had occasionally had coaching for a couple of days, in February, 1893, the football manager "was instructed to obtain a good 'coacher' for another year." Difficulties related later were encountered which nullified this plan. The following officers were elected by the Athletic Association to take charge of the work for the remainder of the year: manager of the football team, Jesse W. Mahley; manager of the baseball team, Charles Greathouse; manager of Field Day, Mark Helm. It will be noted that basketball had not as yet become one of the recognized, organized sports.

Manager Mahley reported in the spring of 1893 that he "had received word from an eastern 'coacher' that he would serve in that capacity at Indiana University next year for the modest compensation of $175 per week. The answer to such an offer is a foregone conclusion."

The *Indiana Student* in the fall of 1893 had become a weekly. In the issue of October 17, 1893 (p. 3), is an account of the football game with Purdue, score 64 to 0 in favor of Purdue. The team had left for Purdue at 3 p.m. on Friday and returned to Bloomington at 6 a.m. Sunday. On October 24, 1893, Wabash beat Indiana 24 to 12. On November 4, on the Indiana home grounds, DePauw beat Indiana 34 to 0. And that ended the season for the Indiana team which had had no coaching other than that which the director of the gymnasium, E. C. Syrett, might give. The account of the DePauw game is in excellent spirit. It was a fine game, fairly played.

It appears that an invitation was accepted for a postseason game with the University of Kentucky at Lexington, which resulted in a tie score, 24 to 24. The account praises the treatment of the team and the good spirit of teams and spectators.

The football season of 1894 began auspiciously. The services of Ferbert of Michigan and Hudelson of Purdue had been secured as coaches. On September 25 *The Student* announced editorially the pleasure with which the enthusiasm for football was noted, in marked contrast to passive interest of former years. Under excellent training the team was reported as making unprecedented progress.

The opening game of the season was with Louisville and ended in a score of 0 to 0. The Indiana boys, however, believed that they won the game 2 to 0. But a safety made by the Indiana team was not allowed. A list of the players is found in *The Student,* October 9.

The team lost to DePauw, 20 to 10, but it was considered to have made a splendid showing. The *Greencastle Banner* was very critical of the rooters who had accompanied the team.

The team was beaten by Wabash 46 to 0, in a game described as fairly played, with a fair referee. The Wabash boys played ball. It was, of course, a humiliating defeat, taken without complaint. But it was becoming apparent that editorial boosting, however desirable, did not make a football team.

The boys had met a disaster at Wabash, but on the following Saturday they were defeated by Butler on the home grounds by "a shameful score." The score is not given. But when we recall that Wabash scored against us 46 to 0, and the Butler score against Wabash was high, we may guess the Butler-Indiana score in astronomical figures. From *The Student* account we quote a few sentences:

McGregor is the most promising center Indiana University ever had but he could not practice because he had a recitation from 4 to 5.

Endicott (Carl) played the game for Indiana University.

At present Indiana University is the laughing stock of the Intercollegiate Football Association.

The Student stated that after this game there appeared to be "a complete dissolution of the football team. The players have not been on the grounds since then." The manager of the football team informed the campus that the Athletic Association was $150 in debt to the coach. Eight members of the faculty had subscribed $10 each. The money was finally raised.

The season for which *The Student* had been so enthusiastic ended without a single game being won by the team. This seems to have been the lowest period in early football history. The general student attitude up to this time was that "it was less humiliating to be last in football than to be second in baseball."

In the fall of 1895 *The Student* stated that the prospects for a winning football team had never been better. All that was lacking was the hearty support of the students of Indiana University. The boys lost to and tied DePauw; they lost to Butler; they won their game against Rose Polytechnic. The next week they played Wabash. The score was 12 to 10 in favor of Indiana University. The game ended with the ball on the Indiana University 25-yard line. According to the last paragraph of the write-up of the game

The time agreed upon for closing the game was 4:45 and as that time was now past, Indiana refused to play longer and left the field. Wabash wished to play until dark, and unopposed, went on for a touchdown, and kicked goal; and now, on strength of this last playing claims the game.[7]

Henry T. Stephenson, of the Department of English, was given the management of the football team in 1896.

In 1896–98 an interesting innovation was tried. *The Student* was published as a monthly magazine and as a semiweekly newspaper. The monthly magazine carried no campus news if we except the issue of May, 1898, which contained an article on "Condition of Athletics at Indiana University." The author found the condition not good. "To be sure we hold the football championship, and are going to hold the baseball championship." But Wisconsin had a magnificent three-story gymnasium, a running track, and a swimming pool. It was twenty years later that these facilities were provided at Indiana University, but the teams of the late nineties deserve very great credit in spite of the lack of a three-story gymnasium.

Unhappily, not a single copy of the semiweekly has been preserved. In the fall of 1898 both the magazine and the semiweekly were discontinued and *The Student* appeared first as the *Daily Student*. The first issue, September 26, carried a front page write-up of prospects for the football season, which were regarded as the most promising in the history of the institution. Ex-Captain Emmett ("Fat") King had taken the team through light practice. A list of players included the names of Charles Niezer, Dudley McGovney, Paul Haworth, A. W. Hanson, Roy Pike, and other well-known athletes of that period. Jimmy Horne, the new director, coached.

[7] One may assume that someone was having some fun with the reporter. The official score for that game stands at 12 to 10 in favor of Indiana.

The team was given splendid support in the *Daily Student*. Not only were games well reported but there were daily accounts of football practice. The support of the student body, however, was not good. On October 29, 1898, a tie game, 0 to 0, was played with the University of Cincinnati team, one of the strongest in Ohio. There were 1,050 students registered in Indiana University, but the attendance at this exciting game was only 325.

The season closed with another tie game with the University of Cincinnati on Thanksgiving Day. The team, unfortunately, had lost to Purdue. They had played and beaten Notre Dame on Saturday. They had beaten DePauw the following Monday. Then they played Purdue the following Saturday without having recovered from the preceding games, with a score 12 to 0 against them. But it was a successful football season, and in the *Daily Student* December 14, 1898 (p. 1), is an article "Our Football Team," giving biographical sketches of the players.

On April 14, 1899, we find the *first* notice of spring football practice recorded in the file of the *Daily Student,* with a list of games scheduled for the next fall. Commenting on spring football practice, on April 20 the *Daily Student* states: "Two years ago witnessed our first spring football practice." Spring football practice therefore seems to have been initiated in the spring of 1897, during the literary period of *The Student*.

Tuesday, May 23, 1899, the *Daily Student* announced the formation of the Tri-Collegiate Athletic Association by Notre Dame, Purdue, and Indiana.

The athletic year 1898–99, the first under Director Horne, was very satisfactory. Indiana won a majority of her games, and it appeared that nearly all members of the football team would be back in the fall.

The football season in the fall of 1899 under Captain Hubbard was again very satisfactory. The team lost to Notre Dame and Northwestern but won six games including those with Illinois, Vanderbilt, Cincinnati, and Purdue.

The season of 1900 was, on the whole, successful. In football, Indiana lost to Northwestern and Michigan. The team won from Notre Dame and Purdue, and tied Illinois, 0 to 0.

In the fall of 1901 the football team lost to Michigan, Illinois, and Notre Dame, but won all other games, including those with Purdue and Ohio State University.

The First Field Day, 1888

The first field day was held at Commencement time in June, 1888, under the management of Fred Cornell. The morning was devoted to "lawn tennis." The features of the afternoon program included:

sack race, standing long jump, throwing a baseball, 100-yard dash, throwing a 50-pound weight, running long jump, three-legged race, running hop-step-and-jump, standing jump with 10-pound weight in each hand, running bases, tug-of-war between Freshmen and Sophomores.

At 4 p.m. there was a baseball game.

This field day was so exciting and stimulating that in the October number of *The Indiana Student* (1888) there was a call for a gymnasium at Indiana University. The article ended with a call for men for the teams:

Men of agility and quick perception are wanted for the nine; and men of weight and speed are wanted for the eleven. Our motto is: Indiana University expects every man to do his duty.

It will interest coaches and athletic directors of today that men of quick perception were not regarded as so important for the football team in 1888.

On May 31, 1890, field day exercises were held in Indianapolis. A full baseball schedule was arranged.

A Sophomore-Freshman field meet was held at the University on May 2, 1899. The Sophomores won.

Development of Track, 1898

Track dates its development from the coming of James Horne in 1898 to Indiana University, to succeed as director of the Men's Gymnasium, Madison G. Gonterman, who in 1896 had succeeded Syrett.

Track men (George Teter and Ora Rawlins) in May of that year "first demonstrated that Indiana University athletes, properly trained, could win their share of victories." From that time, thanks to the efficiency of Coach Horne, victories had been crowning the efforts of Indiana contestants (*Arbutus* 1900, p. 111). On January 24, 1899, there was a call for track men by Coach Horne and Manager Charles M. Niezer.[8] On February 20 there was an article in the *Daily Student* by Mr. Niezer on the track meet to be held the following Wednesday.

Under Coach Horne indoor class meets were promoted. On February 23, 1899, an indoor class meet (Juniors vs. Sophomores), held in the New Gymnasium (later called Assembly Hall), was won by the Junior class. This first interclass meet was witnessed by about five hundred students.

A *Daily Student* editorial on April 25 congratulated the Athletic Association on the election of Mr. Niezer as manager of track and field.

On May 18, 1899, the Indiana track team defeated the University of Nebraska, the western champions, and four days later won the track meet from Purdue, 80 to 73.

In the spring of 1900 the development of track and field athletics was exciting much favorable comment and the indoor interclass meet was the great athletic event of the winter term.

Basketball, 1898

The *Daily Student* of May 5, 1899, commented editorially on the fact that a girls' basketball game would be open to the public this year. The previous year it was not open, and tickets were at a premium, exorbitant prices being paid. A picture of the girls' championship basketball team is found in the *Arbutus* of 1902.

Perhaps the most important athletic event of the early months of 1901 was the organization of basketball for men at Indiana University with an intercollegiate schedule. The team was, of course, inexperienced and lost all but one of its intercollegiate games by scores that were not too bad, largely because intercollegiate basketball was new to most of the colleges. The sport won much interest, however, and at the beginning of the season 1901–2 fifty men came out for practice. While the team won four of its eight games it

---

[8] Charles M. Niezer, later a trustee of Indiana University, was an outstanding athlete of his day and of great assistance to Coach Horne in development of track at Indiana University. On leaving Indiana University, he went to Columbia University, where he was a member of the crew.

suffered a staggering defeat at the hands of Purdue, 71 to 25. During these two years coaching was done by men who had had some experience in the game.

The Dunn Meadow Golf Club, 1899

In 1899–1900 Indiana University had the distinction of organizing the first college golf club in the state, the Dunn Meadow Golf Club.

State, Local, and Intercollegiate Athletic Associations

The Indiana Student for April, 1888 (p. 117), gives an account of the formation of a State Athletic Association at Indianapolis by representatives from the different state colleges.

A schedule of baseball games was arranged as follows:

Hanover vs.

State University, at Bloomington, May 2
Butler, at Columbus, April 21
Purdue, at Lafayette, May 26
DePauw, at Greencastle, May 3
Wabash, at Crawfordsville, May 25

Wabash vs.

Butler, at Indianapolis, May 30
Purdue, at Lafayette, April 21
DePauw, at Crawfordsville, May 19
State, at Greencastle, May 3

Butler vs.

Purdue, at Indianapolis, June 8
DePauw, at Greencastle, May 12
State, at Bloomington, May 30

State vs.

Purdue, at Bloomington, May 30
DePauw, at Greencastle, April 21

Purdue vs.

DePauw, at Lafayette, June 2

This schedule is obviously incomplete. But the date, April 14, 1888, is memorable for the formation of this Indiana State Athletic Association.

In February, 1890, appeared the first mention of a local athletic association in *The Indiana Student*:

The Athletic Association met and delegated Hal Reed and Will Bloss to represent the institution at the State meeting.

It seems certain that for a few years the local athletic committee functioned as the local athletic association. The local association gradually became more formal and acquired articles of association called a constitution. We are informed editorially in the *Daily Student* of April 25, 1899, that this constitution was being rewritten by Charles M. Niezer to meet the requirements of the Western Intercollegiate Conference (later the Big Ten) in which Indiana University desired membership.

On January 11, 1895,[9] largely at the insistence of President Smart of Purdue, the presidents of seven universities had met in Chicago, adopted rules, and formed an organization for the control of intercollegiate athletics. The following year, 1896, faculty representatives of this Western Intercollegiate Conference met in Chicago at the Palmer House. These seven institutions were the universities of Minnesota, Wisconsin, Illinois, Northwestern, Purdue, Michigan, and Chicago. In December, 1899, these institutions became the Big Nine by admission of Indiana and Iowa.[10]

The University of Michigan, disapproving of some Conference rule, withdrew from the Conference in 1908. Ohio State was included in 1912, and Michigan returned in 1917,[11] since which time this Western Intercollegiate Conference has been popularly known as "The Big Ten."

ATHLETICS DURING THE BRYAN ADMINISTRATION, 1902–37

When William Lowe Bryan assumed his duties as president on August 1, 1902, the major sports, baseball (1867), football (1886), field day (1888), track and girls' basketball (1898), and intercollegiate basketball for men (1901) all had been established during a period of thirty-five years (1867–1902) but they were not as yet highly organized. Intercollegiate tennis was played and a Dunn Meadow Golf Club had existed. Track and field meets were both interclass and intercollegiate. The second gymnasium had been erected six years earlier, on a site east of Owen Hall, now a parking

[9] *History of the Western Intercollegiate Conference,* by Carl D. Voltmer, 1935, p. 43.
[10] Voltmer, *op. cit.,* p. 5.
[11] *Ibid.,* p. 29.

lot. A competent director of the Men's Gymnasium, James H. Horne,[12] had been appointed, and functioned also as coach (1898–1905).

There was a local athletic association (1890) and a State Athletic Association (1888), which arranged state intercollegiate schedules of games.

The Western Intercollegiate Conference, to which Indiana had been admitted in December, 1899, came to occupy a position of leadership in America in freeing athletics of professionalism and in the establishment of eligibility rules. We learn in Voltmer's *History of the Western Intercollegiate Conference* that so eminent an authority as Caspar Whitney, in the late nineties, commended the western Conference system to eastern leaders.

Tug Wilson, Commissioner of the Western Intercollegiate Conference, states that his records show that from 1900 to 1937 the following men were Indiana University faculty representatives at Conference meetings: 1900–1, Martin W. Sampson; 1901–(November of 1901), Ulysses G. Weatherly; November of 1901, Harold W. Johnston; 1902–6, Sampson; 1906–7, Weatherly; 1907–8, Ernest O. Holland; 1908–12, Johnston; 1912–13, Charles J. Sembower; December of 1913, Schuyler C. Davisson; 1914–19, Sembower; 1919–20, William J. Moenkhaus; 1920–21, Davisson; 1921–24, Moenkhaus; June of 1924, Davisson; 1924–25, Moenkhaus; June of 1925, Davisson; 1925–28, Moenkhaus; December of 1928, Davisson; 1929–38, Moenkhaus.

The chairmen of the standing committee on athletics during the Bryan administration, 1902–37, were: 1902–6, Martin W. Sampson; 1906–7, Ulysses G. Weatherly; 1907–8, Ernest O. Holland; 1908–12, Harold W. Johnston; 1912–19, Charles J. Sembower; 1919–41, William J. Moenkhaus.

Voltmer also tells us (pp. 53, 54) that the first track conference was held in Chicago in 1901. With ten schools represented, there was great difficulty with professionalism, and the Conference re-

---

[12] James Horne writes (May 14, 1948): "I am somewhat surprised that the records show I was director of Gymnasium. I supposed I was director of athletics. I recall that I handled all the business of that line, making all schedules, looking up and hiring coaches, as well as all the business affairs connected with athletics. Stagg at Chicago and Huff at Illinois did the same work under the title director of athletics."

sorted to an interesting procedure for its control. A so-called graduate committee was appointed, composed of a graduate of each of
the schools represented, all resident in Chicago. This committee met
at intervals and considered protests of eligibility of competitors.
Warren D. Howe in 1910 became the Indiana University representative on this committee.

As athletics came into greater and greater prominence, full-time
athletic directors were appointed in the member universities. These
men came into closer and closer touch with eligibility problems and
with one another. In 1925 these directors requested control of the
meets and in 1926 the graduate committee retired from service.[13]

In 1904 the Conference ruled that a full semester's work in residence should be a prerequisite for eligibility to competition in athletic sports and in 1912 prohibited representation in the Conference
by any member of a physical education department.[14]

In 1914 the Conference set aside $2,000 to provide revenue for the
cost of a Conference medal to be given to the Senior of each university in the Conference who had "attained greatest proficiency in
athletic and scholastic work." A list of Indiana University winners
(1915–37) follows:

1915, Matthew Winters; 1916, George Jenks Shively; 1917, DeWitt Mullett;
1918, Wilbur J. Dalzell; 1919, William M. Zeller; 1920, Willard G. Rauschen-
bach; 1921, Everett S. Dean; 1922, William G. McCaw; 1923, Omar C. Held;
1924, John M. Nay; 1925, Harlan D. Logan; 1926, Daniel G. Bernoske; 1927,
Charles F. Benzel; 1928, Arthur J. Beckner; 1929, Wilmer T. Rinehart; 1930,
William E. Clapham; 1931, James E. Hatfield; 1932, Henry A. Brocksmith;
1933, Noble L. Biddinger; 1934, Raymond F. Dauer; 1935, Don A. Veller;
1936, Reed H. Kelso; 1937, Vernon R. Huffman.

For a history of the Western Intercollegiate Conference, one
should read Voltmer's interesting little book. The few references
to it, given above, indicate something of the important influence
of the Conference on athletics, not only in the member universities,
but throughout the United States.

With the completion of the first gymnasium (1892), a director of
the Gymnasium for Men had been appointed and the head of ath-

[13] Voltmer, op. cit., p. 58.
[14] Ibid., p. 5.

letics continued to bear this title until 1910. The title was indicative of the general conception that athletic development was chiefly a matter of dumbbells, Indian clubs, chest weights, horizontal bars, etc. By 1910 it was realized that, while the gymnasium continued to be the center for athletic training, the field was becoming much broader. Dr. Hutchins' title, which he may have suggested, was director of physical training for men and the field of work was that of physical training and hygiene. In 1911 he was given the title, professor of physical training for men. In 1914 the field of work became physical education and hygiene, and Dr. Hutchins' title was made professor of physical education. This title continues.

The following table lists all the men who served as head of athletics at Indiana University, with title and period of service, 1892–1947:

Directors of Athletics

James Zink, Director of Gymnasium for Men............1892–93
E. C. Syrett, Director of Gymnasium for Men.............1893–96
Madison G. Gonterman, Director of Gymnasium for Men...1896–98
James H. Horne, Director of Gymnasium for Men.......1898–1905
Z. G. Clevenger, Acting Director of Gymnasium for Men....1905–6
James Sheldon, Director of Gymnasium for Men..........1906–10
Charles P. Hutchins
   Director of Physical Training for Men.................1910–11
   Professor of Physical Training for Men.................1911–13
   Professor of Physical Education.......................1913–14
James Kase, Instructor in Physical Education,
   and Acting Director of Men's Gymnasium.............1914–15
Ewald O. Stiehm, Acting Professor of Physical
   Education for Men 1916–21
   Professor of Physical Education.......................1921–23
   (died August 18, 1923)
Z. G. Clevenger,[15] Professor of Physical Education
   for Men and Director of Athletics....................1923–47

Coaching and Coaches

In 1888 *The Indiana Student* had stated that "men of agility and quick perception" were needed for baseball and "men of weight and speed" were needed for football. But five years later it was under-

[15] Clevenger was elected June 5, 1923, and given rank of professor on November 23, 1923.

Dancing group of 1923.

Studio of Theodore C. Steele, honorary professor of painting in 1922–26.

The three men who brought music to Indiana University— Edward Ebert-Buchheim, Charles Diven Campbell, Barzille Winfred Merrill.

A group from the 1935 orchestra, which in eighteenth-century costumes gave a performance of Haydn's "Farewell Symphony."

Mitchell Hall and Mitchell Annex were used for music classes until the completion of the new building in 1936.

The first—and present—home of the Printing Plant and *The Indiana Daily Student,* with future journalists at work in the make-up room, 1915.

In 1903 Commencement was held in Assembly Hall. By 1934 it was an outdoor affair with a long procession from Dunn Meadow to the Stadium.

A vocational group of the Student Army Training Corps, learning radio work at I.U. in the fall of 1918.

On January 6, 1922, the voice of Galli-Curci came over the radio, with Professor Rolla R. Ramsey, Professor John L. Geiger, and Frank M. Treat in charge.

stood that something in addition to these qualifications was necessary, that agility and quick perception, weight and speed were of little value apart from training, and the *Indiana Student* (1893) voiced the demand for a "coacher." Finances, however, were low, income small. For many years the director of the Men's Gymnasium was the only full-time man available. He coached in one or more of the major sports if his training or experience made that possible. Otherwise, such coaching as was provided was given by part-time men.

Fortunately, Linnaeus N. Hines, Indiana University, '94, compiled a list of coaches in football at Indiana University, published in the *Alumni Quarterly*, 1934, Volume XXI, page 464. Mr. Hines gives credit for information to old grads and one of the first coaches as follows: Z. G. Clevenger, William A. Alexander, '01, Ulysses H. Smith, '93, William E. Jenkins, '91, Frank C. Dailey, '94, Mark P. Helm, '94, and Joseph R. Hudelson, coach of the football team, 1894.[16]

Football Coaches, 1886–1948 ·

In the fall of 1889 Evans Woollen, of Indianapolis, the first coach from off the campus, coached the team for a few days. Mr. Hines tells us that there was no football in 1890. The complete list of football coaches or head coaches, with their period of service, follows:

Professor Arthur B. Woodford	1886–1889
Evans Woollen	fall of 1889
No football	1890
Joseph Herod (Indianapolis)	1891
John A. Couch (Cornell and Penn)	1892
Edgar C. Syrett (Springfield, Mass., Y.M.C.A.)	1893
Joseph R. Hudelson (Purdue) and G. H. Ferbert (Michigan)	1894
Robert Wren (Harvard) and Winchester D. Osgood (Cornell and Penn)	1895
Madison G. Gonterman (Harvard)	1896, 1897
James Horne (Bowdoin and Harvard) and "Fat" King	1898 through 1904
James (Jimmie) Sheldon[17] (University of Chicago)	1905 through 1913

[16] The information compiled by Mr. Hines has been checked with a file of University Catalogs, a file of the *Indiana Student,* and file of the *Arbutus.*

[17] Sheldon was part-time coach 1910–13. His appointment as it appears in the minutes of the Board of Trustees was in April, 1906 (p. 306). But his picture is shown in the *Arbutus* of 1906 with the team of 1905, and Mr. Clevenger, who was here 1905–6, assures me that this is correct.

Clarence C. Childs (Yale)..1914–15
James Thorpe (Carlisle), Assistant................................1915
Ewald O. (Jumbo) Stiehm[18] (Wisconsin)...............1916 through 1921
James P. (Pat) Herron (University of Pittsburgh)....................1922
William A. (Navy Bill) Ingram.....................1923, 1924, and 1925
Harlan O. (Pat) Page (University of Chicago)............1926 through 1930
Earl C. Hayes (Albion College).........................1931 through 1933
Alvin N. (Bo) McMillin (Centre College of Kentucky).........1934 to 1948

Coaches in Baseball, Track, Basketball, and Wrestling

In order to give as complete a list as possible of baseball coaches, 1867–1937, some fragmentary information relating to baseball coaches in the period prior to 1902, the beginning of the Bryan administration, is repeated here.

It appears that, from 1867 to the spring of 1893, whatever coaching the team received came from some student of recognized ability, like Fred Cornell. In 1893 a Jeffersonville man whom we know only as Ikes was coach of the baseball team. Whether he coached a few days, weeks, or months, we do not know. In 1894 Robert Berryhill and Charles McIntyre coached the team. In 1895 Walter Hottel was manager of the team, and he states that the Captain and second baseman, Harry Scholler, gave the team the only coaching it received. In 1896 and again in 1897 Robert Carothers was baseball coach.

In the spring of 1898 Charles J. Sembower was manager and George Pitcher, captain of the baseball team. Captain Pitcher joins Professor Sembower in stating that there was no coaching in 1898 other than that which they gave.

In January, 1899, James Horne, Director of Men's Gymnasium, was appointed trainer and manager of the baseball team by the faculty committee on athletics. Though Horne acted as manager of the baseball team, Roy O. Pike states that Horne did not act as coach. This statement is verified by Captain Pitcher and by Mr. Horne. Captain Pitcher and Pike state that in that year, 1899, Bart Howard, a minor league professional, was baseball coach.

In 1900 Pike was captain of the baseball team and states that there

[18] Stiehm came to Indiana University from Nebraska where he had been athletic director and coach.

was no professional coach. Horne is pictured in the *Arbutus* as coach of football and track. In the spring of 1901 R. K. Wicker and G. W. Moore coached in baseball. In the spring of 1902, though James Horne was still the coach of baseball by appointment of the athletic committee, there is no evidence that he served in that capacity.

The coaches from 1902 on are listed in the following table:

	Baseball	*Track*	*Basketball*	*Wrestling*
1902	. . . .[19]	James Horne	. . . .	. . . .
1903	Phil O'Neil	James Horne	. . . .	. . . .
1904	. . . .	James Horne	. . . .	. . . .
1905	Z. G. Clevenger	James Horne	. . . .	. . . .
1906	Z. G. Clevenger	No coach[20]	No coach	. . . .
1907	Jake Stahl	Sheldon[21]	Samse–Sheldon[22]	. . . .
1908	R. G. Wicker[23]	Joe Barclay	Ed Cook	. . . .
1909	James Sheldon	Joe Barclay	Robert Harris	. . . .
1910	Ralph C. Roach	At low ebb[24]	John Georgen	Elmer E. Jones
1911	Ralph C. Roach	Dr. Hutchins	. . . .	Elmer E. Jones
1912	John Corbett	Dr. Hutchins	Oscar Rackle	Elmer E. Jones
1913	John Corbett	Dr. Hutchins	Arthur Powell	Elmer E. Jones
1914	Arthur Berndt	Dr. Hutchins	Arthur Berndt	Elmer E. Jones
1915	Arthur Berndt	Clarence Childs	Arthur Berndt	Ed Davis
1916	Frederick L. Beebe	Clarence Childs	E. A. Williford	Ed Davis
1917	Ray M. Whisman	Harvey Cohn	Guy S. Lowman	James A. Kase
1918	Guy L. Rathbun	Dana M. Evans	Dana Evans	Guy Rathbun
1919	Guy L. Rathbun	Dana M. Evans	Dana Evans	Guy Rathbun
1920	Harry M. Scholler	G. L. Rathbun	E. O. Stiehm	Guy Rathbun
1921	George W. Levis	John M. Miller	G. W. Levis	James A. Kase
1922	George W. Levis	John M. Miller	G. W. Levis	Jack Reynolds
1923	Roscoe Minton	Jesse Ferguson	Leslie Mann	Jack Reynolds
1924	Leslie Mann	Jesse Ferguson	Leslie Mann	Jack Reynolds
1925	Everett Dean	E. C. Hayes	Everett Dean	Jack Reynolds
1926	Everett Dean	E. C. Hayes	Everett Dean	Jack Reynolds
1927	Everett Dean	E. C. Hayes	Everett Dean	Jack Reynolds
1928	Everett Dean	E. C. Hayes	Everett Dean	W. H. Thom
1929	Everett Dean	E. C. Hayes	Everett Dean	W. H. Thom
1930	Everett Dean	E. C. Hayes	Everett Dean	W. H. Thom

[19] The *Arbutus* for 1903 credits Phil O'Neil with the coaching.
[20] Trainer Jack O'Brien did what he could.
[21] Sheldon, Samse, and Barclay.
[22] Sheldon took charge after the football season.
[23] Last of March Wicker had to join his team and Sheldon and Boyle took over.
[24] Hutchins came in 1910 but too late to save track.

1931	Everett Dean	E. C. Hayes	Everett Dean	W. H. Thom
1932	Everett Dean	E. C. Hayes	Everett Dean	W. H. Thom
1933	Everett Dean	E. C. Hayes	Everett Dean	W. H. Thom
1934	Everett Dean	E. C. Hayes	Everett Dean	W. H. Thom
1935	Everett Dean	E. C. Hayes	Everett Dean	W. H. Thom
1936	Everett Dean	E. C. Hayes	Everett Dean	W. H. Thom
1937	Everett Dean	E. C. Hayes	Everett Dean	W. H. Thom

Fully to appreciate what this table reveals, one should check it with the list of directors of athletics and the list of football coaches. This check reveals that during the Bryan administration there were different periods in the development of athletics at the University. There is the period prior to 1923 in which there were frequent changes in athletic directors and coaches, and the period since 1923 when a remarkable stabilization of the work in athletics was initiated. In the earlier period, prior to 1923, there were many superior men among directors and coaches. Better days began with the building of a new gymnasium in 1917.

The year 1923 marks the return of Z. G. Clevenger, a former all-round Indiana University athlete, as professor of physical education. Under his direction, baseball and basketball, track, and wrestling were given leadership which with little change has continued for nearly a quarter-century.

Football presented a more difficult problem. Alumni were demanding winning teams. A coach's tenure was just as long as alumni believed him the man to produce winning teams. In Bo McMillin a coach was finally found under whom teams were developed that played good football. They did not always win, for no team does, but they always played good football.

A Great Staff

These coaches, Hayes, Dean,[25] McMillin, and Thom, were not generally thought of by the University faculty as outstanding teachers. Yet they were. Let me speak of Hayes, deceased, as typical of the group. Never boisterous, or ranting, but speaking in a conversational tone, with a little smile showing the deep inner enjoyment he found in his work, he had the faculty of inspiring unbounded con-

---

[25] If it were our function to carry this story beyond the Bryan administration we would, of course, add the name of McCracken, a worthy successor to Dean.

fidence in his men. I knew well some of his men and have in mind
one who stated with conviction that Hayes could tell within fifteen
minutes what time he (the student) had gone to bed the night before, by the way he did track work the following afternoon. Experienced teachers know the importance of motivation. Hayes motivated his protégés. They found his judgment trustworthy, dependable. He told a man what improvement he could make, and
how to do it, and the man did it. He took the mine-run of Hoosier
boys and the best he developed into national figures.

Indiana University had reason to be proud of the personnel of the
Department of Physical Education during this period.

"I" Men Organize

Prior to the Illinois game, 1913, a number of former University
athletes met at the Claypool Hotel, Indianapolis, and formed a permanent organization of "I" men. Every athlete who ever received
a monogram was made a member.

The first officers of the "I" men were: Carl Endicott, president;
Charles J. Sembower, vice-president; George M. Cook, secretary.

State High School Basketball Tournament

The first high school basketball tournament was held in the
Men's Gymnasium on March 10, 1911. Twelve high schools competed. The final was played between Crawfordsville and Lebanon,
and Crawfordsville won, 24 to 17.

In 1912 four teams instead of twelve were invited to the campus.
Lebanon was the winner.

In 1913 thirty-seven high schools entered the contest, which was
won by Wingate. Wingate had defeated Lafayette in the semifinals
and met South Bend in the finals.

In 1914 Wingate won a second consecutive time, defeating Anderson 36 to 8. The general feeling in 1913 was one of pleasure that a
little school had a lucky break. But when Wingate repeated in 1914
by an impressive score, it was recognized as an outstanding team.

This state basketball tournament was held at Indiana University
to and including 1918. In 1919 it was held at Purdue, in 1920 at Indiana University again, and in 1921 it was taken to Indianapolis,
where it has remained.

Establishment of a Department of Athletics

For thirty-one years (1902–33) athletics at Indiana University had been in charge of an athletic board of control, an organization composed of alumni of Indiana University, faculty members, and, for a time, a representative of the student body.

This board of control did not, however, supplant the faculty committee on athletics. It was really the standing committee of the faculty on athletics which existed prior and subsequent to 1902, to which a few alumni and a representative of the student body had been added. The faculty committee never lost control of athletics since they always constituted a majority of this board. A member of this committee always represented the University at Conferences of the Big Ten. In all matters relating to eligibility of players and other matters governed by the Big Ten Conference, the faculty committee on athletics, having a majority on the board of control, was able to report from time to time to the faculty the faithful maintenance of Conference standards. The board of control was merely a device whereby alumni and the student body were assured a hearing through their representatives on matters which seemed, to many, the most important interests of the University.

Athletic affairs were at a low ebb in the spring of 1915, and the manner of choosing alumni representatives on the faculty committee on athletics had become unsatisfactory to the alumni. After preliminary meetings to determine what should be done, there was a call for a general alumni meeting at Indianapolis on May 15, at which a nominating committee was appointed to recommend three alumni for membership on the faculty committee on athletics. The nominees were: George M. Cook, organizer of the "I" men; Frank Jones, of the Equitable Life Assurance Society; Harry M. Scholler, a great athlete of the nineties. These men were welcome members of the faculty committee on athletics.

Further conferences on the campus led to the appointment of class presidents, the presidents of the Indiana Union and the Boosters Club, and the captains of teams to act in an advisory capacity to the faculty committee on athletics. These actions were taken with the belief that it would promote and strengthen athletics to bring alumni representation and student counsel to the assistance of the athletics committee.

The board of control, however, had a degree of autonomy in certain local matters. In maintenance of playing field, equipment, etc., the board of control assumed certain financial obligations, counting on receipts from games for liquidation of these obligations. For illustration, the board urged the erection of the Fieldhouse and paid approximately $71,000 toward the retirement of bonds issued by the University for construction of that building.

In the early 1930's the depression had hit attendance at athletic contests so that receipts from games were materially reduced. This reduction was general among colleges and universities, but at Indiana it occasioned a crisis in the financial affairs of this board of control, in that it had incurred indebtedness of some $60,000 which would be due at an early date and the board was without funds to meet this obligation. It had no recourse but to ask the University for reimbursement of money furnished for bond retirement and other athletic expenditures.

The Fieldhouse bonds were, of course, an obligation of the Board of Trustees of Indiana University. The return to the athletic board of control of funds advanced to pay maturing bonds, though coming at an inopportune time, nevertheless was regarded by the trustees as a reasonable request. Therefore, the secretary of the board, John W. Cravens, was authorized and directed to execute four promissory notes of $15,000 each in the name of the Board of Trustees and on its behalf. These facts are set forth in a resolution, No. 1, on page 196 of the minutes of the Board of Trustees for April, 1933.

But this was only a part of the problem now confronting the trustees. The Fieldhouse had been built after a careful check of the finances of the athletic board of control and on repeated assurances by that body that their income would make it possible to contribute substantially to the retirement of Fieldhouse bonds as they matured. Now it was discovered that the athletic board of control was badly in the red.

A second resolution, therefore, was passed. It recited the fact that this board had made contracts and incurred liabilities for none of which the trustees were responsible or in any way liable. It now appeared that the athletic board of control desired to dispose of its assets with a view to making provision for the payment of its acknowledged liabilities and permanently suspending the further conduct of athletics. Accordingly, it was deemed advisable for the trustees to establish a department of athletics, to acquire the equipment and property of the athletic board of control, and succeed to its rights to conduct intercollegiate contests and games of all kinds, including those now scheduled.

As remuneration for the equipment and all property of whatsoever kind of the board of control, and as partial reimbursement for the sum of $24,800 expended by this athletics board in making permanent improvements to the athletic grounds on the University campus, the trustees assumed liabilities of the board amounting to approximately $40,000.

The trustees in a third resolution (April 12, 1933) then proceeded to establish a department of athletics to be conducted by a committee of twelve[26] members under the control of the President and Board of Trustees. The committee was to be appointed annually by the trustees to serve for one year. They had the right to remove any one or more members at will and to designate one member as chairman. The members of the committee were to serve without compensation, but with reimbursement for traveling expenses if consent of the committee had been previously obtained. The following committee was appointed to serve until the board meeting in June, 1934:

William J. Moenkhaus, chairman

Fred E. Bryan	Roy O. Pike
Severin Buschmann	Charles J. Sembower
Z. G. Clevenger	Ulysses H. Smith
Willis Coval	Henry T. Stephenson
Schuyler C. Davisson	Walter E. Treanor

Willard W. Patty

Thus the activity of the board of control was terminated, but the inclusion of alumni as members of the athletics committee continued to and beyond the close of the Bryan administration.

[26] The number was later increased.

On June 10, 1933, in order to encourage student attendance at scheduled games and supplement the needed income for the retirement of Fieldhouse bonds, it was suggested to the trustees by Director of Athletics Z. G. Clevenger that a yearbook be issued to students at a price of $6 which would be good for admission to all contests held in Bloomington for the year 1933–34. Purchase was to be voluntary, but the price, $6, made the cost of individual games so low that it was felt that these books would have a wide sale among the students. This, indeed, proved to be the case. The income from this source, however, was not immediately as large as anticipated.[27] It had been estimated that the sale of student yearbooks would amount to about $18,000, but the comptroller's office reports that in 1933–34 receipts from this source were only $12,261.85.

It may be recalled, however, that on July 8, 1927, the Board of Trustees had approved the levying of a contingent fee of $2 a student, the proceeds to be set aside for payment on the Fieldhouse. This fee later came to be known as the Fieldhouse fee. The income from sale of student yearbooks supplemented this Fieldhouse fee and other income of the Athletic Association to such an extent that on April 1, 1942, the last of the Fieldhouse bonds was retired.

When the board met in January, 1934, counsels were divided, and various alumni pressure groups were recommending widely differing procedures in connection with athletics. Action was taken by the trustees definitely recognizing the director of athletics as head of that field and responsible for recommendation as to coaches, employees, and other related matters, in accordance with the practice in other departments or schools of the University. The board was informed that this action was the procedure generally followed by other universities and was approved by the Big Ten Conference.

The first major appointment made by Mr. Clevenger was that of A. N. McMillin on May 11, 1934, as football coach for five years. On receipt of assurance from Mr. Clevenger that there would be a balance of $13,000 at the end of the year, the trustees on June 15, 1935, ordered that $10,000 of this balance be applied to the next payment on the Fieldhouse.

In May, 1937, Director Clevenger requested the improvement of

[27] 1933 was a depression year, and the compulsory activities fee had just been abolished.

the football practice field immediately east of the Fieldhouse. The field had been used so many years that the sod was gone and the ground was hard. It was proposed to cover the field with good rich soil and then sod it. Charles Hays, the superintendent of buildings and grounds, estimated the cost from $2,500 to $3,000. This request was granted and the project carried out and paid for out of the athletics fund.

In the period which followed, the athletics committee, of which Dr. Moenkhaus was chairman, did an excellent service in the conduct of athletics at the University. The work done by the chairman of this committee was particularly meritorious. He stood in a position between ambitious, loyal alumni, and the rules committee of the Big Ten. He exercised great wisdom in restraining well-meaning alumni from procedures which would have met the disapproval of the Big Ten, and he succeeded in doing this without losing alumni interest and good will.

Sigma Delta Psi

The following account of the organization of Sigma Delta Psi was prepared by President Emeritus Bryan, a few years before his retirement:

The real founder of the Sigma Delta Psi in America was George Fitch, journalist. It must have been in 1912 that this genial columnist spoke at Indiana University as the guest of the Press Club. He was then at the height of his fame as humorist, and the boys delighted to hear him and to do him honor. In the course of his address he turned aside from whatever else he was saying to tell of a national system of physical education which he had seen in Sweden. He expressed the hope that a similar system would be developed in America. I was an immediate convert to his suggestion. I wrote through our United States Department of State to the government of Sweden, asking for full information concerning their system. I soon received the information desired, had the rules translated into English, and asked Dr. Charles P. Hutchins, who was then director of Physical Education for Men in Indiana University, to use the Swedish rules as a basis for rules suitable to American conditions. Dr. Hutchins proceeded vigorously with this undertaking in consultation with the heads of the departments of physical education at Yale and Minnesota, both of whom warmly approved the new enterprise.

It was decided to organize a society to be named Sigma Delta Psi. Membership in the society was to be open only to those who should meet the rigorous conditions fixed by the rules.

The colleges and universities of the United States were invited to establish chapters in the new society. In the beginning, fewer than a dozen institutions joined; among them Yale, Minnesota, and Indiana. At the present time, forty-two colleges and universities including nineteen state universities have chapters. I think it likely that in a few years the society will be established in all the institutions of learning in the United States.

The Alpha Chapter of the society is at Indiana University, and Indiana has probably more alumni members than any other chapter. Last December, Professor Schlafer received a letter from the National Secretary-Treasurer, Mr. L. W. Olds, in which he says: "At the present time you far excel any of the Western Conference universities in the activities of Sigma Delta Psi." Professor Schlafer adds: "Last year, thirteen different students completed all Sigma Delta Psi requirements, and in due time received their keys and certificates."

What is it all about? Is it just one more way of boosting athletics? No. Is it just one more of the thickening swarm of Greek letter societies? No. There is just one way to gain membership. One must, in the presence of a responsible committee, meet about twenty widely diverse athletic tests. The standards set in these tests are not world records. The standards in each of the twenty tests are within reasonable reach of a strong, well trained youth. But because the tests vary so widely, there is probably not a man in the world who can meet all of them without several years' training, and when by several years' training he has met the twenty diverse tests, he must be a man of splendid all-round physical development.

Men prize the Phi Beta Kappa key. It means that one was once a college man and intellectually one of the best. In like manner the badge of Sigma Delta Psi means that the wearer has been a college man and a man of splendid physical development. A man who wears either badge may be justly proud. A man who wears both is a king.

CHAPTER XXXV

INDIANA UNIVERSITY, 1930 - 32

ALARMING ECONOMIC SITUATION

I N THE fall of 1930 the economic situation in the state of Indiana and in the United States was very difficult, and to many it was alarming. The statement of University needs prepared for Governor Harry G. Leslie and the General Assembly, meeting in January, 1931, was prepared with the conviction that to ask for large increase in appropriation would be unfair and inconsiderate. Therefore the following very conservative statement of needs was presented.

Increases Requested for Biennium
1931–33

Personal Service for additional staff:

Bloomington Division—	Each year	
All Administrative Offices	$ 3,800	
Service Departments and General	3,900	
Arts and Sciences	96,731	
Professional Schools	29,100	
Extension	7,150	
Summer School	20,000	
		$160,681
Indianapolis Division—		
School of Medicine and Hospitals	$18,980	
School of Dentistry	14,100	
		33,080
Total		$193,761

While the General Assembly did not vote even this comparatively small increase, it made no severe reduction in appropriation. For each year of the biennium 1931–33 a total of $1,800,000 was appropriated, an amount only $15,000 less than for each year of the preceding biennium, which, however, was enough to check normal expansion.

412

The legislature of 1931 voted a mill tax for improvement of state fair grounds. Generously supported by Governor Harry G. Leslie, the State Board of Agriculture allocated from this fund an amount sufficient for the erection of a building on the fair grounds to furnish accommodations for Indiana University exhibits.

THE UNION BUILDING, 1929–32

It will be recalled that in the spring of 1924 the building of the Stadium was becoming a major problem. Consequently it is not surprising that, on letting the contract for the women's dormitory (Memorial Hall), the trustees felt that for these two major objectives they had drawn on the slowly accumulating paid-in subscriptions to the Memorial Fund as fully as they dared, and that the Union Building, the third great objective of the Memorial campaign, would have to wait for the financial reservoir to fill again. The construction of the Union Building, therefore, dropped out of the picture temporarily, but was never out of mind.

Five years later, June, 1929, the board approved a recommendation of President Bryan expressing the "earnest wish" that all persons whose pledges to the Memorial Fund were due would pay them at that time. The alumni and other donors were assured that as soon as the trustees were justified by such payments to the Memorial Fund, they would proceed with the erection of the Union Building.

At this time the trustees were considering the construction of an auditorium separate from the Union Building. They were also entertaining, very skeptically, the idea of combining the Administration Building and the Union Building. The board decided (December 27, 1929) to visit and inspect the union buildings of certain neighboring universities: Purdue, Wisconsin, and Michigan.

The early morning of May 16, 1930, was spent in looking over proposed sites for the Union Building, after which the board met in President Bryan's office and further considered matters relating to this project. Officers of the Aeons and of the Indiana Union and also representatives of the Alumni Association and the Alumni Council were invited to confer with the trustees upon the very important and difficult matter of location of this building.

At the same time a full report of the financial resources available for the Union Building was received and considered by the board. Estimates were submitted of the amount that would be raised by an annual fee of $10 or $15 charged each student. Trustees Batman and Niezer were appointed to consider the financial situation and to determine what plan would be best to assure adequate funds for construction.

On June 7, 1930, Alfred Granger, of the firm of Granger and Bollenbacher, of Chicago, went with the board to investigate the proposed sites for the Union Building. After considering these sites, Mr. Granger suggested that the most desirable was the one north of the carpenter shop and Owen Hall, south of the River Jordan, and west of the driveway leading from Seventh Street through the campus.[1] This suggestion was received with favor by the board, but no definite action was taken at this meeting as board members desired to consult further with representatives of the Indiana Union, the Aeons, and the Alumni Council. A sign which would give all visitors an understanding of the location under favorable consideration for this building in which so many were interested was ordered placed on this proposed site.

Two days later a committee consisting of Theodore Dann, president of the Aeons for 1929–30, Max Sappenfield, president-elect of the Aeons for 1930–31, Franklin K. Mullin, president of the Indiana Union for 1929–30, and John Leslie Stuteville, president-elect of the Indiana Union for 1930–31, appeared before the board and expressed satisfaction with the site suggested by Architect Alfred Granger. Alumni Secretary George F. Heighway stated that the site of the Union Building suggested by Architect Granger had been considered by the Alumni Council and that approximately this site met the approval of the members. With evidence of student and alumni approval of this site, the trustees adopted the following very important resolution:

Be it resolved by the Trustees of Indiana University that each student of the University in attendance at Bloomington, Indiana, beginning with the first

[1] The drive from Seventh Street to the power house, at that time, 1930, passed on south between *The Indiana Daily Student* Building and the old Assembly Hall, then to the east to Forest Place drive, and to the west to the Fifth Street entrance. To the west it lay south of Owen and Maxwell Halls.

semester of the academic year of 1930–31, be charged a fee of six dollars per semester as a Union Building fee; to be collected as other student fees are collected; that said fee so charged and collected be segregated from other student fees and held as a separate fund to be known as the "Union Building Fund"; that the same be applied to the payment of the principal and interest of certain bonds to be issued and sold by the Trustees of Indiana University, to procure funds for the completion of a Union Building on land now a part of the University campus at Bloomington, Indiana, and to no other purpose, unless a surplus remains after the payment of the current interest on said bonds, and the payment of the principal thereof as they mature, in which event such surplus may be otherwise applied.

This resolution was in anticipation of the start of construction of the Union Building at an early date. Since alumni, who could not personally enjoy the advantages of this Union Building, had contributed so generously to its erection, it was believed that undergraduates, who would benefit by its facilities, naturally should and cheerfully would wish opportunity to supplement alumni contributions. In a few years, undergraduates would in turn be alumni and feel a deep gratification at having assisted in erection of this very valuable addition to the University campus.

The following day the board authorized the architect to proceed immediately with completion of plans and specifications for the Union Building to be erected on the approximate location indicated, north of the Bookstore, which at that time was housed in a temporary structure between Owen and Maxwell.

On July 9 President Bryan was authorized to write to the architects that it was the opinion of the board that the cost of the Union Building, exclusive of furnishings, should not exceed $600,000. On September 15 Architect Granger submitted revised plans, which were considered at great length. Mrs. Alice Nelson, Director of the Commons, and Ward G. Biddle, speaking for the Bookstore, stated that, from the standpoint of the Commons and the Bookstore (which would be housed in the new building), the plans met their complete approval. The board suggested that dimensions should remain the same but that the architects should consider changes that would reduce the estimated cost of the building. Three months later plans and specifications were approved and ordered advertised for bids, to be opened on or before January 23, 1931.

On December 29 the board accepted the proposition of the Fletcher American Bank to furnish the balance of the funds necessary to erect the Union Building. This proposition provided for a bond issue not to exceed $500,000 at 4½ per cent interest.

When bids were opened on January 23 it was found that the low bid, that of E. A. Carson, was $31,345 in excess of the proposed bond issue. Mr. Carson and Architect Bollenbacher were requested to make a study of the estimates on which Mr. Carson based his bid, and report to the board changes in plans resulting in savings. This report, made on February 14, 1931, covered twenty-eight items and made possible the saving of $53,703.50. Of these possible savings the board made selection to a total of $51,833, which reduced Mr. Carson's bid to $479,512, at which figure a contract was awarded.

This base building bid did not include heating, ventilating, electric wiring, plumbing, kitchen equipment, and elevator, bids for which were opened on February 27 and contracts let totaling nearly $50,000. On November 19 bids for lighting fixtures, furniture, draperies and floor coverings, tables, chairs, etc. for the Union Building were opened and contracts let, totaling about $33,000. When payment was made for the elevator and necessary grading was completed, the cost of the Union Building as of May, 1932, totaled $696,080.69.

The formal dedication of the Memorial Union Building was held at Commencement time, June 13, 1932. The alumni dinner was served in Alumni Hall. A description of the building is found in the *Alumni Quarterly* for July, 1932, page 359.

There are many special features of the Union Building worthy of mention. Outstanding among these is the bronze tablet in the floor of the lobby symbolizing the different branches of military service of the Indiana University men and women memorialized in the erection of the Union Building. Then there is the Golden Book in which are inscribed the names of those who had served in the wars of the Republic and also those who made pledges to the Union Building project. Above the Golden Book is the inscription prepared by President Bryan, cut in the stone wall.

In the construction of any building, and in particular in construction of a union building, the success of the enterprise is its utility plus the general impression derived. This makes it very difficult to compare union buildings since the purpose served varies in certain fundamental particulars from institution to institution. The Purdue union building, for instance, is remarkably adapted for entertainment of the numerous conferences held at Purdue.

The Union Building at Indiana University ranks high from the standpoint of utility, but from the standpoint of impressive beauty it ranks near the top among union buildings in America. The major lounge induces reflection, contemplation, meditation, human faculties little stimulated, little developed in this rushing age.

DIRECTOR OF THE UNION BUILDING

As the Union Building neared completion the administration became increasingly impressed with the necessity of selecting a competent manager who should have responsibility for its operation. Here was a splendid building in which provision had been made for diverse groups and numerous unrelated interests. In order that this structure might fulfil the purpose for which it was erected and become a definite part of the "pride of Indiana," the building must be made to function smoothly and efficiently.

The applications of a number of excellent men were on file for this position. It did not appear that income from the building would be large. With a depression at hand, it was highly desirable that income should meet operating expenses. Was there anyone who could take on the management as an extra load at little or no additional expense?

Attention naturally fixed upon Ward G. Biddle, who, as manager of the Bookstore, would be located in a wing of the Union Building. His Bookstore work was well organized. Could he take on the extra load? President Bryan was requested to have a conference with him on the matter.

The result of this conference was that in February, 1932, Mr. Biddle was selected as director of the Union Building for the year ending July 31, 1933. He accepted this appointment under protest. At the end of the period of appointment he was asked to continue, and did so. In order that he might have more time for his duties as manager of the Bookstore and director of the Union Building, he was relieved of his duties as inspector of men's rooms. At this same meeting, February, 1932, on motion of Judge Wildermuth, seconded by Mrs. Teter, it was ordered that the official name of the Union Building should be Indiana University Memorial Union.

Mr. Biddle did not merely mark time until July 31, 1932, but characteristically began his new job at once. He made an extensive report in May on assignment of rooms, the financial policy of the Union, equipment needed, estimates of expenditures and income, etc. The report met the approval of the board.

Since the official name of the Union Building was Indiana University Memorial Union, it would have been logical to have called the hall in the Union Building, Memorial Hall. But that was the name already in use and accepted as applicable to the girls' dormitory. Mr. Biddle, therefore, recommended that the auditorium of the Union Building be known as Alumni Hall. This suggestion had met the approval of W. A. Alexander, who had directed the Memorial Fund campaign, of Alumni Secretary Heighway, and of other interested persons, and now was approved by the trustees.

New Chemistry Building

The University Catalog of 1841–42 carries the announcement that:

A laboratory and lecture room have recently been erected on the campus, entirely separate from the principal building, for the express accommodation of the department of natural philosophy and chemistry. It offers to young gentlemen who intend ultimately to devote themselves to the medical profession, great advantages.

Professor Robert E. Lyons in a brief "History of Chemistry in Indiana University," published in the *Indiana University News-Letter,* Volume XIX, Number 3, March, 1931, tells us that this two-story building, 32 feet by 48 feet, was erected in 1840 at a cost of $2,000, and that Theophilus A. Wylie was the professor of natural philosophy and chemistry.

A second building for chemistry was erected in 1873, and the following year, Thomas C. Van Nuys, M.D., was appointed as the first full-time professor of chemistry. When, at the opening of the fall session, 1885, the University moved to the new campus in Dunn's Woods, Professor Van Nuys was assigned quarters in Wylie

Hall, which was the third home for the Department of Chemistry. Here he served until 1895, when he retired as professor emeritus and was succeeded by Robert E. Lyons, who served until 1938, when he in turn retired as professor emeritus. It is remarkable that these two men, Van Nuys and Lyons, headed the Department of Chemistry for sixty-four years, 1874–1938.

As the years passed and the enrollment of 202 students, with which the University began the school year 1885–86 on the new campus, became ten and then twenty times that of 1885, although more and more space in Wylie Hall was assigned to the Department of Chemistry, the building became less and less adequate for the accommodation of that growing department.

In a ten-year building program for the University prepared in 1924 by the large faculty committee on promotion of University interests the need for an addition to Wylie Hall was placed second only to the need of the University for expansion of the power plant. On May 20, 1927, Professor Lyons presented to the trustees reasons for the erection of a new building for the Department of Chemistry or, in lieu of a new building, an addition (or additions) to the east side of Wylie Hall.

As months passed the idea of a new building rather than additions to Wylie gained favor with the board. Plans were ordered prepared and a contract for a new building was let in February, 1930. The beautiful new building was completed early in 1931 and formally dedicated on April 2. As part of the dedication ceremonies, the honorary LL.D. degree was conferred upon Leo Frederick Rettger, Oscar Butler Perry, Earl Blough, Oliver Curtis Martin, Fusanobu Isobe, and James Nimrod Currie.

Professor Lyons had the satisfaction of conducting the work of the Department of Chemistry in these new quarters until he retired in 1938. The east wing was assigned to the Department of English.

When in 1931 the Department of Chemistry moved into its new building, changes were made in Wylie Hall amounting to $15,000 for accommodation of departments that would be housed there. Seven departments had requested room in Wylie, but the Department of Home Economics and the Extension Division were the fortunate applicants.

Obligations Outstanding

The President reported, in May, 1932, on properties covered by bond issues. The report showed that, after deduction of payments already made, there were bond issues outstanding as of October 1, 1931, as follows:

At Bloomington:

South Hall	$138,000	
Women's Memorial Hall	112,500	
Fieldhouse	248,000	
Union Building	500,000	
		$998,500

At Indianapolis:

Robert W. Long Hospital	$200,000	
Nurses Home No. 3, Unit 1	3,000	
Nurses Home No. 3, Unit 2	22,000	
Coleman Hospital	175,000	
		400,000

Total $1,398,500

These bond issues, however, were not expected to be a charge on the educational appropriation of the University. South Hall, Women's Memorial Hall, the Fieldhouse all had an earning capacity which was supposed to take care of bonds as they matured; and, in fact, it did so. The Union Building, in addition to Memorial Fund pledges, had an income from certain fees.

The Robert W. Long Hospital bond issue had a backing of real estate the sale of which would more than have canceled the issue. The Nurses' Home obligations were inconsiderable sums. Back of the Coleman bonds again were securities adequate to meet fully the issue. So these particular bond issues could give the University administration little concern.

In addition to these bond issues, however, there were certain property purchases in connection with which there were outstanding obligations. The trustees were wisely gaining possession of the property in Forest Place, houses and lots that once had been entirely outside of the campus, merely bounding the campus on the east, but that now were in the very heart of the campus. There had also been the purchase of the Extension Building in Indianapolis.

Counting outstanding bonds and property purchases, the University had obligations totaling $1,507,500. To meet these obligations it had the conception that $109,000, representing property purchases, would be cared for from the 2-cent tax; $950,500 it was expected would be cared for by income from buildings over a period of years. That left $448,000 an obligation of the board, an obligation the retirement of which was assured by gifts of real estate, subscriptions, and fees.

The courage of the board in assuming new obligations in connection with construction of greatly needed buildings has been mentioned earlier. Emphasis should also be laid on the soundness of judgment exercised by the board in assuming obligations only when there seemed definite sources of income to meet those obligations, sources of income quite apart from the educational funds of the institution, and recognized by bonding agencies and bond purchasers as adequate security.

REWIRING OF UNIVERSITY BUILDINGS AT BLOOMINGTON

On December 27, 1929, Engineer Charles R. Ammerman had submitted a report of a survey of the electric wiring of all University buildings at Bloomington, together with an estimate of cost of repair or replacement. It was decided on January 7, 1930, not to reach a final decision concerning this work until after the bids for the proposed new Chemistry Building had been opened, about the middle of February. It was not until July 9, 1930, that Mr. Ammerman was instructed to prepare plans and specifications with reference to electric wiring. At the October meeting of the board bids on the rewiring of buildings were received and a contract was let to the Sanborn Electric Company of Indianapolis for $143,099.55. This was a very considerable expenditure which the administration undertook on the report of experts that the fire in the power-house probably had been due to a short circuit and that wiring in other University buildings was faulty. The total expenditure was $162,231.44.

THE JAMES B. NELSON ENDOWMENT FOR PHILOSOPHY AND SOCIOLOGY

On February 24, 1930, James B. Nelson, of Indianapolis, made a gift of $200,000 for endowment of the teaching of philosophy, since

increased to $293,000. On December 28, 1931, he made a gift of $200,-
000 for endowment of a chair in sociology. These gifts consisted of
real estate, the income from which is payable to certain annuitants
during their lives. Upon the death of the last annuitant the University will establish chairs or professorships as designated by the donor.
The principal sum, nearly half a million dollars, is to remain unim-
paired.

THE JESSIE SPALDING LANDON GIFT

On December 16, 1930, the board passed a resolution in honor of
the late Mrs. Hugh McK. Landon:

> There are those who give money. There are those who give themselves.
> Mrs. Landon gave both. She has through years given money most generously
> to many good causes, including the development of hospitalization where
> suffering may be alleviated and where many may be restored to lives of health
> and happiness. It was never enough for Mrs. Landon to give money and then
> go her way, leaving the conditions which affect patients to others. Like the
> wise husbandman who keeps his eyes upon his acres, she kept her eye upon
> major hospital policies and also upon the exacting details without which no
> policy is effective. Because of her gifts[2] and her devotion, Mrs. Landon had a
> place in the founding and in the development of the James Whitcomb Riley
> Hospital for Children which is large and which must be permanent. It is
> therefore ordered by the James Whitcomb Riley Memorial Hospital Commit-
> tee and the Board of Trustees of Indiana University that an appropriate
> memorial in honor of Mrs. Landon be placed in a suitable position within
> this hospital.

In compliance with this joint order, a stone tablet was inserted in
the floor of the lobby of the Riley Hospital.

MISCELLANEOUS

In 1930 an appropriation of $3,000 was made for a general labora-
tory building at Winona Lake. This building, available in the summer of 1931, provided a general laboratory and eight research rooms
equipped with electricity, running water, etc., adequate for most
types of limnological work.

---

[2] The financial report of the James Whitcomb Riley Memorial Association included (1)
the bequest of Jessie Spalding Landon of $10,000 to be known as the Linen Fund, and (2)
the creation of a trust of $398,652.55, under the will of Mrs. Landon, the income from
which was payable to the trustees of the James Whitcomb Riley Memorial Association.

In June, 1931, the honorary LL.D. degree was conferred on the Honorable Newell Sanders, who received the degree of Bachelor of Science from Indiana University in 1873, and on Hugh McK. Landon in recognition of his great service to the sick and crippled children of Indiana.

J. B. Howe Martin, Assistant Bursar, was transferred to Indianapolis in charge of the business office of the School of Medicine and Hospitals.

The trustees in November, 1931, concurred in the recommendation of Professor David M. Mottier that the University purchase the herbarium of Indiana plants from Charles C. Deam.

Charles Hays, the superintendent of buildings and grounds, in February, 1932, requested that the Bookstore building be transferred for use as a carpenter shop. This transfer was made, with due credit to the Bookstore for the value of this building.

The trustees approved, May, 1932, the purchase of a replica of the Richard Owen[3] statue now in the state Capitol building at Indianapolis, the statue to be placed in the Union Building and paid for from class funds.

On June 11, 1932, the question of whether the interest on the bonds issued for construction of the Union Building was taxable again came before the trustees and was referred directly to the Commissioner of Internal Revenue at Washington for decision. David Burnett, the commissioner, replied that, in the light of a cited Supreme Court decision, interest on these bonds was not subject to federal income tax.

The Licensing Division of the State Department of Public Instruction added library science to the subject group of high school teachers' licenses in June, 1929. The School of Education of Indiana University made provision for instruction in library science, to make it possible for students to qualify for this license. From 1930 to the close of the Bryan administration, with the exception of the summers of 1933, 1934, and 1935, these courses in library science were given in the summer session only. Later they were given in the regular school year.

[3] Richard Owen was professor of natural philosophy and chemistry, 1863–67; professor of natural science and chemistry, 1867–79. His brother, Robert Dale Owen, was trustee of Indiana University, 1838–46, 1850–52.

Chapter XXXVI

THE UNIVERSITY BOOKSTORE

The Cooperative Bookstore

P RIOR TO 1890, sale of books and supplies had been in the hands of competing book companies. Like the chicken business, it appeared that the enterprise should be profitable. In reality it was unsatisfactory to everyone concerned, students, faculty, and store managers.

The business involved at least three guesses or estimates. There was the guess or estimate of the professor as to the number of books needed. There was the guess of the manager of the bookstore as to how many of the total thought necessary he could safely order. There was also the guess of the manager of the store as to the time he might expect delivery.

In spite of all that he could do, dead stock accumulated on shelves. To protect himself, the manager ordered ultra-conservatively and charged somewhat above list price. Dead stock worried the storekeeper. High prices irritated the students. Delay in providing books for the full class caused delays in getting the course under way and impaired effectiveness of the course, to the annoyance of the instructional staff.

To escape these annoyances, the Indiana University Cooperative Bookstore was organized and incorporated in 1890. It was first located on the second floor of Wylie Hall. By 1897 (possibly earlier) it had been transferred to the east basement of Maxwell Hall, and that was its location when in 1902 the Bryan administration began.

Its purpose as declared in its first constitution was "to supply the students of the University, textbooks, stationery, and other supplies at the lowest practicable cost." During its early years the prices of books and supplies, while usually much below the list prices, were so fixed as to leave a slight margin over operating expenses, in order to accumulate a surplus which should enable the management to buy for cash and secure the most advantageous discounts.

The store was managed for some years by a joint stock company composed of students and members of the faculty who purchased shares of its stock. These shares were sold at $2 each and were redeemable at the end of any term at $1.75 in cash or $2 in books and supplies. The inducement to become a stockholder lay in the fact that books were sold to members at a lower price than to non-members.

Difficulties, however, arose under this management. In November, 1903, President Bryan reported to the trustees:

There are in connection with the University a number of organizations, open to all students, which have in view various useful objects and which are supported by the University. The most important ones are the following:

(1) The Cooperative Association, an incorporated stock company; (2) The Publishing Association, an incorporated stock company; (3) The Lecture Association; (4) The Christian Associations; (5) The Athletic Association; (6) The Arbutus Board.

With the growth of the University, the affairs of all these organizations become more important and complicated, and the amount of money handled by them becomes greater, running into thousands of dollars a year. It is in my opinion an important part of the education of the students to manage such affairs. I believe that the students should be left free to manage them within wide limits. However, as the financial interests have come to be so great, and as the good name of the University may be involved by the mismanagement of any of these organizations, I believe that we should provide for supervision of all of them whenever the authorities of the University find this advisable.

I suggest as a step in this direction that all such organizations be requested to keep a satisfactory system of accounts and to submit these annually, or oftener, to the University to be audited.

The case of the Cooperative Association requires special consideration.

The business of the Association has grown with the growth of the University until it amounts to about fourteen thousand dollars a year. The Association has assets (mostly in the form of books) over and above liabilities, amounting to about thirty-five hundred dollars.

The salesmen in charge of the store are nominated by the President of the University but must be confirmed by a board elected by the stockholders and may be dismissed at will by that board. For the most part college politics has been eliminated from the management of the Association. Not wholly so, however. And within the past year considerable effort has been made to inject politics into the management of the Association, though without success.

In view of the whole situation the question arises whether it is wisest to continue the life of an organization which does a large and constantly enlarging business, which accumulates a large and enlarging property, and which is for the most part under the control of a body of inexperienced men who may at any time attempt to manage the affairs of the Association in the interest of a group rather than in the interest of the whole student body and of the University. For my own part I should be glad if the Cooperative Association were out of existence for the reasons suggested. It is not so clear that we should put it out of existence.

After the most careful consideration with a view to safeguarding the interests of approximately four hundred stockholders, the student body, and the University, a plan was evolved for closing the affairs of the Cooperative Association which was fair to all concerned. This was adopted by the trustees, November 18, 1903, and the Executive Committee was authorized to proceed with the plan for reorganization. From this November meeting, 1903, until the final sale of the Cooperative Association April 2, 1910, this matter was considered in nearly every report of the President to the board. It, therefore, seems desirable to give a summary of the President's reports on a matter which occupied the attention of the administration for so long a time.

The President reported in March, 1904:

In pursuance of the plan for reorganizing the Cooperative Association agreed to by the Board, stockholders were invited to assign their shares to Judge Hogate and to indicate to what student enterprises they wished "the surplus" to go.

Of the total number of shares, 262 had been assigned.

The President then recommended a further plan of procedure which was approved by the trustees:

1. Professor Hogate to assign the shares of stock held by him to the Trustees of Indiana University at the par value, two dollars per share.

2. The Trustees to assume control of the Association through a Board of Directors approved by them. The Board of Directors may be the members of the Board of Trustees, or part of them.

3. All the rights and privileges of remaining stockholders to be fully preserved as under the past and existing management.

4. Meanwhile and pending a final settlement of the affairs of the Association, appropriations to be made to the several student enterprises indicated by those who made assignments of their stock, said appropriation to be in amounts corresponding approximately to what would accrue to those organizations if the affairs of the Association were settled at once.

In accordance with this action the Executive Committee was authorized to work out the details and the sum of $2,500, or so much thereof as might be necessary, was appropriated for that purpose.

On June 16, 1904, the President reported:

In accordance with plans approved at the March meeting of the Board the following steps have been taken in connection with the Cooperative Association:

1. At a regular meeting of the stockholders of the Cooperative Association, the Constitution of the Association was changed in several particulars:

(1) Each share of stock is hereafter entitled to a vote.

(2) The directors of the Association are the Trustees of the University, the President of the University, and two other persons to be elected by the shareholders.[1]

Messrs. E. G. Hogate and S. B. Harding were elected directors.

2. An itemized appraisement of the property of the Association was made by Messrs. Laz Noble of the Bobbs-Merrill Company, S. C. Dodds of the Monroe County Bank, and S. B. Harding. The appraisement which was made under oath showed the net value of the property of the Association to be $3,761.04. The papers in detail are submitted.

3. Members of the Association were promised that an amount of money equivalent to the surplus left after paying for the stock would be appropriated by the Board and distributed as follows:

(1) $1,400 to the payment of debt of the Athletic Association.

(2) The balance pro rata according to the vote of the members. . . .

In accordance with the direction of the Board, there has been paid out $1,449.72 on debts incurred by the Athletic Association. The bills paid were itemized and approved by J. H. Horne and M. W. Sampson.[2] The Athletic Association still has debts amounting to upwards of $500. . . .

Before leaving this question I wish to say that the action of the student stockholders in turning over their property for the use of student enterprises is one of the finest acts in the history of the University. It stands along with their action last year in giving approximately $4,000 to the Student Building.

The following resolution was adopted:

The Board of Trustees of Indiana University desires to place upon record a vote of thanks to the former shareholders in the Cooperative Association for

---

[1] Since the trustees were the owners of three-fourths of the stock of the Cooperative Association, they were the majority of the Association and by these changes in the constitution the University gained control of the Association, the charter of which was still operative, expiring in 1910.

[2] James H. Horne was director of the Men's Gymnasium; Martin Wright Sampson, Professor of English, was chairman of the faculty committee on athletics from 1902 to 1906.

their generous action in transferring their shares to the University for the benefit of public student enterprises.

Reporting to the trustees on the Cooperative Association, November 14, 1904, the President stated that 300 shares had been transferred (some of these were donated) in trust to Professor Hogate, leaving 114 still outstanding. Of the shares outstanding, 109 belonged to nonresidents.

Appropriations had been made in accordance with pledges made to stockholders, who transferred their stock.

Athletics	$1,536.06
Y.M.C.A.	68.87
Y.W.C.A.	30.14
Oratorical Association	32.38
Band	68.06
Student Building	10.98
Undistributed	273.61
On account of 230 shares of $2	460.00
	$2,480.10

The President added:

Two points with reference to the University Bookstore seem to me clear.

1. We ought to stand solidly by the store and the Association as it is until the reorganization of the Association is completed. Moreover, I see no reason for hurrying the reorganization. A hurried reorganization means a heavy sacrifice in the value of the stock. In return for this unnecessary sacrifice, the students would gain no advantage of any sort and no citizen of the State would gain any advantage except the two or three who want to sell books to the students.

2. Under one form or another the University should provide permanently for the sale of University books.

The University has a great many classes. Many of these are elective classes where the enrollment is highly variable and uncertain. These advanced classes have in general the more expensive books. Moreover, frequent changes are necessary to keep abreast with the most recent advances of science. These conditions make the problem of supplying textbooks for the University a very difficult one under any circumstances. On the one hand, there ought to be in stock at the opening of the term enough books in each subject for every student. In proportion as this is not the case, the work of the University is for a time demoralized. On the other hand, an over-supply means money loss which has to be borne by some one. The problem is so difficult that a store which has a complete monopoly can solve it only in a measure. There will always be some mistakes in both directions. Every year we have some complaints that too few books are ordered, and, every year, we sell off dead stock at a heavy discount.

But if this problem is difficult for a store which has a monopoly, it becomes absolutely impossible where several stores are competing for the business. What happens is very simple. The competing firms buy what they consider safe quantities of such books as are used by large classes and make what they can directly and indirectly out of the trade which this brings. But no competing dealer can afford to order an adequate supply of books used in the small elective classes. Accordingly, such books are very generally sent for on individual orders after the term begins. In certain instances which occurred this Fall, the delay caused in this way amounted to two weeks. Such a state of affairs is quite intolerable.

Fourteen years ago our students found it intolerable and organized the Cooperative Association for their own protection. It has seemed best to them as well as to us to reorganize that association. Just what form the business should finally take is a problem for the solution of which there is plenty of time. But under one form or another, I believe that we should protect the students from the undoubted evils of the old system at least as well as they have protected themselves.

If we could secure this protection by an arrangement with a private firm, I should be glad of it. I am now convinced, however, that such an arrangement is not workable and I believe that the wisest course open to us is to maintain, upon our own ground, a store where books shall be supplied.

On January 4, 1906, the President reported:

There has been no change in the management of the Bookstore since the last report. The business is conducted by the joint stock company of which more than two-thirds of the stock is held in trust by Professor Hogate. The service is very satisfactory. The opposition to the new arrangement has disappeared.

On June 18, 1909:

Within the past year a new incident has come up in connection with the Cooperative Bookstore. A book dealer of the city has established a bookstore near the campus and has secured a considerable trade from the students. The sales of the Cooperative Store have been greatly reduced. When the attention of the local board governing the Cooperative Store was called to these facts they took measures to protect the interests of the store and they have no doubt that they can fully protect those interests. Meanwhile Mr. [Claude] Steele has submitted a proposal to take over the book business of the University. I submit his proposal for the consideration of the Board. I suggest that members of the Board meet as a Board of Control of the Cooperative Book Association and that the entire matter be presented for consideration at that time.

After this meeting of the board of control of the Cooperative Association a large student committee was appointed to consider with two faculty members, Professors Ernest H. Lindley and William A. Rawles, the textbook situation at Indiana University.

The report of this committee is found in *Indiana University Bulletin,* Volume VII, Number 9 (November, 1909). The report takes up the criticisms of the Cooperative Association, which included charges of improper disposition of profits, secrecy in management, inefficient management, disregard of the convenience of students, and unnecessarily high prices.

The report states that the committee had been given access to the books of the Cooperative Association and had had repeated conferences with Nicholas O. Pittenger, who had recently been appointed manager. They also had conferences with Claude Steele, proprietor of the Book Nook.

The findings of the committee were that prices had been very low, that since 1904 the management had made annual reports to the University office, which reports were open to inspection. Employment of a regular expert assistant to the manager was recommended. It was shown that the Coop had saved the student body about $2,000 a year for the past six years.

Perhaps the most important part of this report dealt with "The Present Situation":

The great value, therefore, of the past service of the Cooperative Association to the students cannot be doubted. *The question now is, "What shall be the present attitude of the students toward this institution?"* For the past two years, the books show that it has lost money. To secure to the students the benefits of discounting bills, a note for $2,000 was recently given by the directors of the association. . . .

This loss has grown out of the sense of responsibility imposed upon the Cooperative Association to supply the students promptly with textbooks. In order to do this it has had two alternatives: either to order the full number requested by the instructor, or to "order safe," and meet the deficiency by special orders.

In case the first alternative were chosen, the Cooperative Association might find it impossible to dispose of the full stock because of the sales made by competitors, who, having no sense of responsibility to supply the needed number of books, could order whatever number they felt they could dispose of. This dead stock has added to the increased expense.

If an effort were made to evade loss in this way, the Cooperative Association had to resort to the use of special orders. This, also, entailed a loss in added cost of transportation, while at the same time it caused an annoying delay to both instructors and students.

It would seem to be to the pecuniary interests and convenience of the students that the handling of textbooks should be in charge of one reliable dealer, who would assume the responsibility of supplying the desired number at the proper time, and *whose prices would be fixed without any consideration of private profit.* The present Cooperative Association could most easily render these important services.

While it is true that the Cooperative Association is not owned by the students, but by the University, they directly enjoy all the advantages of ownership in the lower prices at which books are sold. It is, therefore, the duty of the students not to permit this institution to fail because of lack of loyal support.

Experience at the University of Illinois has shown that where the handling of books was transferred from a cooperative association to a private institution the prices were materially advanced, in many cases to the full list price.

We have the assurance of the directors that the same service will be maintained by the Cooperative Association even in the event that it gains the exclusive control of the textbook business.

The committee has kept constantly in mind this question: What is the best interest of the students?

In conclusion and in answer to this question, we submit the following *facts:*

(1) That the Cooperative Association is not operated for individual gain. All profits go to the student body in the form of lower prices.

(2) That at no time has the average selling price of textbooks exceeded the net discount price by more than 8 per cent and in many cases it has been less.

(3) Special orders are in most cases supplied at a loss.

(4) The present management, facilities, and hours are satisfactory.

(5) Since its organization the Cooperative Association has saved to the student body approximately $40,000.

We recommend, therefore, that the students of Indiana University support loyally the Cooperative Association, which is in fact their own institution.

It is further the unanimous opinion of this committee that the exclusive control of the textbook business by the Cooperative Association would result in a great saving to the student body.

Nicholas O. Pittenger had taken office as manager of the Bookstore July 1, 1909. His first task was to supervise the moving of the Bookstore to new quarters in the basement of the Library building.

In March, 1910, the President again reported on the Bookstore:

The charter of the Cooperative Bookstore Company, established in 1890, expires in March, 1910. For this and other reasons the whole question of the

University Bookstore should be considered and decided by the Trustees at this time. Within the past year a book dealer—Mr. Claude Steele—has maintained a very vigorous opposition to the store. He has sold a limited number of books and has thus caused the University store to have left upon its hands a corresponding number. The University store has thus been placed in the position where it must lose money or must protect itself by refraining from ordering a full supply. The experience of the year has shown once more that this business cannot be conducted satisfactorily by competing stores.

Meanwhile Mr. Steele has carried on his opposition in a variety of other ways. He has filed a protest with Governor Marshall, accompanied by a legal opinion from Mr. Will R. Wood, of Lafayette, and has stated to me his intention, if necessary, to bring legal proceedings against the continuance of the store.

We learn of the final closing of the affairs of the Cooperative Bookstore from the President's report of June, 1910:

In accordance with the instructions of the Trustees at their March meeting, the Cooperative Bookstore was advertised for sale on April 2, 1910, and was duly sold to Enoch G. Hogate acting for the University, at the price of $3,300. The itemized statement of the property on hand was made public in advance of the sale and bidders were invited to inspect the stock so that the interests of all stockholders should be fully protected morally as well as legally. I submit a financial report of the situation on the day of the sale, April second.

The Cooperative Bookstore Company had a life of twenty years. It began with nothing. It ended with property amounting in round numbers to $3,745.21. It has never cost the University anything except the donation of basement space, heat, and light. It has saved the students approximately $40,000, according to the report of the student-faculty committee of 1909. It turns over to the University the whole of its existing assets. It has been conducted in the past for the most part by student help and, therefore, has been open to various minor criticisms. At present the service is much more satisfactory than ever before in the history of the store. The store can without doubt be carried on without expense to the University treasury and at the same time effect important savings to the students of the University.

Indiana University Bookstore

With the expiration of the charter and the sale of assets of the Cooperative Association, April 2, 1910, that organization passed out of existence and the University Bookstore took its place. The old name clung to the new organization for a time, however, even in official University reports. To patrons of the Bookstore there was no noticeable change, which is understandable when we recall that the

University had had control of the Cooperative since the change of the constitution in 1904. The location of the Bookstore was unchanged and N. O. Pittenger was continued as manager.

At the meeting of the trustees, June 18, 1910, they approved this recommendation of President Bryan:

> I suggest that the Bursar be directed to keep the accounts of the Cooperative Bookstore entirely separate from all other University accounts, to keep a complete and accurate account of all receipts and expenditures of the store, and to make a report of the same to the Trustees at the same time when the regular Financial reports are made to them.

In April, 1923, N. O. Pittenger resigned as manager of the Bookstore and Miss Eleanor Shields was placed in temporary charge. When Mr. Pittenger became manager of the Bookstore on July 1, 1909, the store was insolvent. The stock could not have been sold for enough to pay the store debts. When he retired fourteen years later, April, 1923, in addition to sizable contributions made from Bookstore profits to the purchase of equipment for the cafeteria and for furnishings for Alpha Hall, there was a $10,000 balance on hand, the beginning of the fund which under the management of Ward G. Biddle grew to the $67,500 contributed to the erection of the Bookstore as a part of the Union Building.

On April 26, 1923, it was ordered that the manager of the Bookstore give a bond of $10,000, the fee for which was to be paid from University Bookstore receipts. On July 10 Ward G. Biddle was elected manager.

Since the summer of 1909 the Bookstore had been in the basement of the Library, and that was its location when Mr. Biddle became manager. With the construction of the new wing to the Library (1925–26), it became necessary to find other quarters. At the June meeting of the trustees, 1925, bids ranging from $1,700 to $2,237 for a temporary wooden building, for use of the Bookstore, were submitted. The temporary structure was erected between Owen Hall and Maxwell Hall in the summer of 1925. On May 17, 1928, the board concurred in the recommendation of Mr. Biddle that the north end of the Bookstore building be extended fifteen feet at an estimated cost of $785. This building was occupied until the new quarters were opened in the east wing of the Union Building.

On May 12, 1932, a committee composed of deans and heads of departments was appointed to make a special study of the Bookstore and report its findings. It was believed that the more the faculty and student body knew of the management of the Bookstore the better the Bookstore could serve the faculty and student body. The committee was impressed with the accounting which made it possible to follow details of purchases and sales.

High points of the report, found in the minutes of the faculty, are the following: The Bookstore aimed to make a profit of 5 per cent, and allowed the student a 10 per cent discount. The margin of profit was so small that an overestimate by a faculty member of the number of books needed and thus left in stock could wipe out profit of a period. It was estimated that the Bookstore had saved the students $126,000 in the preceding eight years, an average of about $16,000 per year.

It had been the hope of the management that some day the Bookstore might own its own building. To this end the management had accumulated profits, over a period of twenty-two years, until they amounted to $67,682.25. Of this total, $15,394.42 represented interest. The accumulation represented a profit of approximately 1½ per cent on the business of the Bookstore.

From this sum, since 1923, contributions were made as follows:[3]

For Hospital expenses of students......................$ 699.50
For miscellaneous items................................ 1,476.05
Toward the Union Building.............................. 67,500.00

The New University Bookstore Building

The new Bookstore, opened April 25, 1932, has been called by President Bryan "the most beautiful college bookstore in America." It is a three-story structure constituting the east wing of the Memorial Union Building. The Bookstore proper is entered on the street level. There is no conspicuous supply of books. The store is so arranged that the thousands of books required at the opening of each semester are easily accessible and students are served quickly.

[3] If one adds these contributions he discovers they total about $2,000 more than savings. The difference was a contribution from cash on hand, working capital which enabled the store to discount its bills. This contribution reduced cash to a total a little less than the accumulation prior to 1923.

A broad stairway ascends to the second story where is found a lounge with a fireplace. The main feature of this story is a balcony or mezzanine from which one looks down on the main store display below. This balcony is beautifully adapted and frequently used for art exhibits.

The lounge of this story is now occupied by a bookshop, where current publications of all sorts are on sale and where orders may be placed for anything in print. To the west is the authors' room, containing autographed photographs of authors with autographed copies of books, and the Woodburn room, set aside in honor of Professor James A. Woodburn.

The Bookstore is reached from an outside entrance and from the main lounge of the Memorial Union Building.

Though Mr. Biddle was elected director of the Memorial Union Building in 1932, he continued as manager of the Bookstore until 1936, when he was elected comptroller of Indiana University. His contention that a building could be utilitarian and also beautiful is vindicated in this University Bookstore.

Chapter XXXVII

INDIANA UNIVERSITY, 1932 - 34

The Special Session of 1932

IN THE spring of 1932 the depression was causing the administration of Indiana University increasing apprehension. The small decrease in appropriation for the University voted by the General Assembly in 1931 had been believed to be only temporary. But as the depression continued the question of its possible further effect upon the income and work of the University came before the board when it met in February, together with a consideration of what, if anything, could be done about it.

In May it was agreed that President Bryan and a committee of trustees should meet President E. C. Elliott and a committee of the Purdue board, together with representatives of the other state educational institutions, at the University Club, Indianapolis, on Wednesday, May 25, for a dinner conference on problems created by the depression. The committee named to accompany President Bryan consisted of Trustees Fesler, Ball, and Batman, with Mr. Niezer as alternate.

Governor Leslie was present at this dinner. Perhaps the greatest satisfaction of those present was derived from the assurances of the Governor that he was determined not to call a special session of the legislature. No one knew better than he the possibility of radical action as a result of the mounting concern over the distressing economic situation. Yet within twenty-four hours a special session had been called under insistent pressure of party leaders. The date set for legislators to convene was July 7, 1932.

On July 4, 1932, an alumnus edition of *The Indiana Daily Student* was devoted entirely to a statement of services rendered by Indiana University and the great number of people served by the University. There were charts showing the low cost of this service, and the explanation of the importance of its continuance was forcefully presented. The President's Column was particularly strong. There was

436

a brief quotation from the inaugural address of President Harry W. Chase, of the University of Illinois, in which he said: "Our mission is to our own civilization with its own needs and demands, not to the civilization served by the medieval university or even by those of Europe today."

From time to time during the Bryan administration there had been special sessions of the legislature. This special session of July 7 to August 17, 1932, differed from the four others of the Bryan administration up to that time in that the acts of this session affected seriously the University appropriation.

This is shown in the following table:

	Bloomington	Indianapolis	Total
Appropriation of 1931 for each year of biennium 1931–33	$1,325,000	$475,000	$1,800,000
Appropriation of Special Session 1932, for year 1932–33	1,126,250	403,750	1,530,000
Decrease	15 per cent	15 per cent	15 per cent

The legislative leaders, powerful men of both parties, were united in the effort to prevent the cut for educational institutions from exceeding 10 per cent. But in the middle of the forty-day session it looked as if the appropriation for higher education would be cut 20 per cent; many said it would be 25 per cent; and a few advocated 50 per cent. A leading representative said on the floor of the House that salaries at Indiana University should be reduced 50 per cent and that no one would resign as a result of such reduction.

The attitude of members of the legislature was greatly influenced by the current reports of the results of the depression. There were instances of loss of farms by owners and the serious losses suffered by manufacturers. In their alarm and determination to reduce cost of state government, the legislators introduced many ill-considered measures in the Assembly. A bill was introduced in the Senate to prevent state institutions from belonging to associations having membership outside the state, such as associations of medical schools, law schools, and the North Central Association. One bill proposed to do away with the State Board of Education, upon which so determined an attack had been made in 1897, but which for so many years had functioned most efficiently. The situation seemed grave when a bill was introduced limiting the total tax levy to $1.50 on the hundred dollars. Fortunately none of these radical measures were passed.

Representative Biddle, who, as the President stated, served as the point[1] of a flying wedge (an expression which dates him), made the best fight possible, but his influence was discounted by the fact that he so intimately represented the University.

In August of 1932 the faculty was meeting weekly and Law Professor "Jimmy" Robinson, secretary of the faculty, reached an all-time high in recording the reports of legislative matters presented at those meetings. The meetings had unusual value in giving the faculty an understanding of the attitude of legislators and in preparing them for budget adjustments necessitated by reduced income.

At the faculty meeting of August 17 the President stated his impression that no other form of expansion had been so great as the multiplication of elective courses. He believed the College of Arts and Sciences would be strengthened by a reduction in the range of courses taught.

Mr. Cravens, whose legislative experience was extensive, reported:

We have never before seen conditions like those at this session. Many unkind things were said about the University, but there was not the ill feeling of the session of 1897 when sectarian schools fought the University. At this session the attitude of the sectarian schools was friendly.

Happily, the kindly attitude of the administration toward the denominational schools during the past thirty years had made them allies of great power on this critical occasion.

It was only by a small majority that the bill providing for a 15 per cent cut, instead of 20 per cent or more, passed the House. This decrease meant a reduction of $270,000 in state appropriation for the University for the year 1932-33, and made it necessary for the administration to institute drastic curtailment of expenditures.

The President sat in his office making budget after budget. It was inevitable that faculty salaries should bear part of this cut.[2] Salary

---

[1] In view of Ward's avoirdupois, the President's simile might bear revision.

[2] When President Bryan appeared before the State Budget Committee, he was asked, "Will you cut salaries?" President Bryan replied that he "could see no way to avoid it." The response was "Well, if you do not cut salaries we'll get to them in January." January, 1933, was the time for meeting of the next regular legislative session. (See minutes of President's report to the faculty, August 3, 1932.)

adjustments, long overdue, had been made but recently (1929). The President was in search of a budget adjustment that would affect these still low salaries as little as possible.

Finally on September 1, 1932, the trustees approved the President's recommendations for salary cuts as follows:

> Salaries less than $3,000 were reduced 8 per cent.
> Salaries from $3,000 to $5,000 were reduced 10 per cent.
> Salaries from $5,000 up were reduced 12½ per cent.

This 12½ per cent cut for salaries of $5,000 and above was applicable to the President's salary. But he insisted on a still higher per cent cut of his own salary.

The faculty accepted this adjustment of their salaries in remarkably good spirit. That the state appropriation had been cut 15 per cent, they all knew, and probably all had done a bit of calculating as to what a 15 per cent cut would leave them. It was realized that a straight 15 per cent cut might not be possible in all budget items; therefore, it was conceivable that salaries might have to bear more than 15 per cent of the adjustment.

There was, therefore, a general sense of gratification when the scale of reductions was announced, particularly in view of the President's assurance that the former salary scale would be re-established just as soon as possible. Speaking of this matter recently (1943), the President laughingly remarked that he had never received so many expressions of appreciation when increases in salaries were made as he had received on announcing this cut.

But cutting the appropriation by 15 per cent was not all that this special session of 1932 did to the University.

It will be recalled that the General Assembly of 1927 passed a 2-cent tax for buildings for the state institutions of higher education which was expected to yield about $350,000 annually for the building program of Indiana University. The special session of 1932 suspended this levy for buildings for the years 1932, 1933, and 1934. There was, however, a note of optimism. No one believed the depression other than a temporary phenomenon from which, in time, recovery would follow. Later events proved the correctness of this view.

ADJUSTMENT TO SHRUNKEN BUDGET

Two weeks after adjournment of the special session the trustees met (September 1, 1932) and made a financial survey to determine just what adjustments to this cut of 15 per cent in income would be least disturbing to the work of the University. In this the report of the President was very helpful. The University had been engaged in an extensive building program in connection with which there were outstanding obligations (listed in Chapter XXXV). The President reviewed briefly these obligations and showed the amount due on each bond issue each year. He urged that everything relating to the eight bond issues for which the University was responsible should be scrutinized with the utmost care, so that the University at some later date should not be confronted by an obligation for which no adequate provision had been made.

The administration was concerned not only about the known reduction in income made at the special session of the legislature, but also with the possible reduction in fees which would follow any marked decrease in attendance as a result of the depression. This latter was a matter of particular concern, inasmuch as retirement of certain bonds was dependent in part on a special student fee. Happily, in this instance it was shown that a surplus had already been accumulated, greater than any probable loss due to decreased enrollment.

The President then proceeded to consider every item of expenditure—the *Alumnus,* which had been sent fortnightly to about 25,000 alumni and former students, travel, publications, reduction in personnel, etc.—and made recommendations looking to reduction of expenditures.

It is a significant report, revealing the President's grasp of the minutest details of the budget, involving hundreds of items. A feature of the report is the President's acknowledgment of assistance of deans, department heads, and particularly of Registrar Cravens, Bursar Smith and his staff, and Miss Ruth McNutt, the President's secretary. The acknowledgment is indicative of the extent to which the leadership of the entire institution was drawn into the difficult task of making this revised budget.

During the fall of 1932[3] the Board of Trustees met every month, thus maintaining close touch with the progress being made by the University in this difficult adjustment.

LEGISLATIVE REQUESTS, 1933

But in addition to adjustments to the cut in income made by the special legislative session, the administration in the fall of 1932 was confronted also with the problem of requests to be made of the regular session of the General Assembly, meeting in January, 1933. In the statement of budget needs, stress was laid on restoration of the appropriation of 1931, namely, $1,800,000. The following was the itemized statement of additional income needed, totaling $270,000, which would merely bring University income from the state up to what had been provided for each year of the biennium 1931–32 and 1932–33.

Sustaining Schedule

	Biennium 1933–34	Biennium 1934–35
BLOOMINGTON DIVISION		
1. Restoration of 15 per cent cut in departmental budgets for equipment and supplies	$ 75,000.00	$ 75,000.00
2. Needed repairs and improvements	57,122.52	57,122.53
3. Books and equipment not listed in No. 1	31,127.48	30,127.47
4. Annual building retirement as authorized by Budget Committee	35,500.00	36,500.00
	$198,750.00	$198,750.00
INDIANAPOLIS DIVISION		
Medical School and Hospitals		
1. Covering roof garden of Long Hospital to care for increased service demand	$ 40,000.00	
2. Equipment for above additions	5,000.00	
3. Maintenance of additional space	18,750.00	36,500.00
4. Replacement and repairs to laundry and kitchen equipment		13,746.00
5. Walks, drives, and grading		13,504.00
	$ 63,750.00	$ 63,750.00

---

[3] During the whole year 1832 there was no meeting of the Board of Trustees of Indiana College because of prevalence of cholera in the state.

School of Dentistry
1. Equipment ....$ 7,500.00 $ 7,500.00

Total to restore budget amount in accord with
1931 legislative appropriation. (No restoration
of personal service cut.).......................$270,000.00 $270,000.00

Report of Committee on Promotion of University Interests

The committee on promotion of University interests had prepared a statement supporting this legislative request, a copy of which is found in the files (Budget Requests 1933–35).

This, the last report made by this committee, not only shows the type of matter this committee prepared, but also preserves certain comparative facts of University maintenance of that day, which are quoted below. The introductory paragraphs maintained that, in a time of crisis such as 1932, great leaders alone were not enough; the leader must have intelligent followers.

Our present civilization then depends upon the production of as many well educated people as possible with minds trained and quickened, in the hope that within this group great leaders may be found, and in the hope that we may have produced a citizenship sufficiently enlightened to follow trained leaders.

This means education.

To develop trained leaders, and a citizenship sufficiently intelligent to follow trained leaders, requires the maintenance of the efficiency of our educational institutions. . . .

We have always been economical in higher education in Indiana.

The State of Indiana has invested in Indiana University and Purdue University combined, half as much as Wisconsin, Illinois, Minnesota, Iowa, or Ohio have invested and one-third as much as Michigan has invested in higher education.

.   .   .   .

Valuation of Physical Plant and Equipment, State Schools, 1926
(Latest figures [then] available, and excluding endowments)

State	Total Value	Per cent of Totals
Michigan (Two schools)	$ 31,515,028	22.6
Ohio State (Three schools)	20,102,789	14.5

Iowa

(Two schools) ....$ 19,670,790   14.1

Minnesota

(One school) 19,353,747   13.9

Illinois

(One school) 19,121,444   13.7

Wisconsin

(One school) 18,810,805   13.5

INDIANA

(Two schools) 10,768,304   7.7

Total $139,342,907   100

If the seven million dollars which the ten-year building program was expected to yield Indiana University and Purdue University (3½ million each) had been available and expended as planned, the state of Indiana would still have ranked at the bottom of this list of North Central states in the table given above. Instead of this, the special session of 1932 suspended the levy for buildings.

The following table[4] shows enrollments and appropriations of seven North Central state universities. The appropriation of each exceeds that of Indiana University much more than the enrollment of each exceeds that of Indiana University. Figures from the committee report follow:

University	Students	State Appropriations
University of Minnesota	11,447 (254%)	$4,404,325 (323%)
University of Illinois	11,212 (249%)	5,265,000 (386%)
University of Michigan	10,432 (232%)	4,600,000 (337%)
Ohio State University	9,963 (221%)	4,386,586 (321%)
University of Wisconsin	8,331 (185%)	3,943,650 (289%)
University of Iowa	5,454 (121%)	2,553,405 (187%)
University of Indiana	4,503 (100%)	1,365,000 (100%)

Budget requests for Indiana University and Purdue were compared with those of neighboring state universities in this report:

1927-28 and 1928–29

State	Requested Appropriation for Two Years
Illinois (one school)	$10,500,000
Michigan (two of three schools) (building requests unknown)	10,325,000

[4] Attendance and income at Indiana University are taken as 100 per cent.

		Requested Appropriation
State		for Two Years
Minnesota (one school)	....	$ 9,511,446
Ohio (two of three schools) Ohio University requests unknown	....	10,686,500
Iowa (two schools)	....	14,041,579
Wisconsin (requests unknown)		

Incomplete total for five states for two years............$55,064,525
Average for two years................................ 11,012,905
Indiana University and Purdue together requested
for two years (received far less)..................... 9,226,400

Note: Information for institutions outside state obtained on personal visits to institutions.

Prior to the salary cut of this past summer [July, 1932], the salary scale at Indiana University compared with the average for these six neighboring state universities is shown in the following table:

Salary Scale

	Deans		Professors		Associate Professors		Assistant Professors		Instructors
Iowa.....	20..	$129,750	97..	$516,964	43..	$162,884	73..	$235,352	90.. $187,650
Illinois...	13..	102,401	132..	756,624	72..	295,776	103..	342,372	136.. 296,616
Wisconsin	7..	50,498	173..	925,600	76..	302,850	122..	380,699	194.. 403,900
Ohio.....	11..	84,500	200..	1,052,400	45..	192,195	154..	534,996	193.. 442,163
Michigan.	14..	138,799	176..	1,014,824	97..	409,949	191..	606,249	308.. 569,214
Minnesota	14..	112,000	161..	844,123	86..	326,370	168..	491,904	199.. 417,502
Total..	79..	$617,948	939..	$5,110,535	419..	$1,690,024	811..	$2,591,572	1,120.. $2,317,045
Average......	7,822		5,442		4,033		3,195		2,068
Indiana......	5,680		4,558		3,482		2,954		2,002
Indiana below Average.....	2,142		884		551		241		66
Per cent below Average......	27.3		16.2		13.6		7.5		3.2

This committee report was given wide publicity. While the chairman was entrusted with the writing of the report, he merely put into form ideas expressed by the able and deeply interested members of this large committee.

Governor Leslie, who had been greatly interested in promoting the welfare of the state educational institutions, was succeeded in office in January, 1933, by Paul V. McNutt, Dean of the Indiana University School of Law, equally sympathetic with the aims and needs of the institutions of higher education. Yet with this powerful leadership, in a well disposed legislature, the best the defenders and supporters of higher education were able to do was to limit the further reduction of Indiana University income to $40,000. This meant that the income for each year of the biennium 1933–34 and 1934–35 was $1,490,000, which was $310,000 less than the appropriation of $1,800,000 voted in 1931.

THE EMERGENCY LOAN FUND

An interesting item of bookkeeping appears in the records of the trustees for June, 1933. The University had in its custody certain funds consisting of all or portions of memorial funds contributed by certain classes and by certain organizations. These funds had accumulated over the years beginning with 1908. They varied in amounts from a minimum of $3, the net proceeds of the Sophomore Cotillion of 1929, to $1,206.78 contributed by the class of 1918. There were about forty of these funds, totaling $8,556.97. One of these, $12.40, had been held for twenty-four years. The trustees decided that donors should be requested to designate the use to which it was desired the fund should be devoted. Funds for which no use was designated within sixty days were to become part of an Emergency Loan Fund, to be administered by the board as other loan funds of the University were administered. It was further decided that, in the future, amounts received for which no use was designated by the donors within three years should become part of this Emergency Loan Fund. These facts show the care with which financial trusts, no matter how small, were held of record.

DEFERMENT OF FEES

During the school year 1933–34 state field examiners were making a survey of the financial management of state institutions. At Indiana University one of the recommendations of these field examiners had to do with deferment of fees.

It seems that deferment of fees was in danger of being abused. Deferment was too easily secured, and some students had come to look upon deferment as equivalent to release from any responsibility for fees.

At the meeting of the trustees in May, 1934, a plan concerning deferment of fees, recommended by state field examiners, was adopted.

Under this plan a written application was to be required in which reason for deferment, the time required to complete payment, etc. were to be set forth. A special assistant was to be appointed who would consider each application. This special assistant on examination of the application might issue a temporary permit, to be presented to the Bursar, who was then authorized to permit the student to complete registration.

The student was to receive written notice of action on his application. Emphasis was laid on the temporary nature of the arrangement. The Bursar was required to make monthly reports, and students who failed to meet the deferred obligation were to be barred from classes.

Some questions arose as to certain recommendations of the examiners, and an appeal was taken to their chief. We quote from board minutes of May 11, 1934:

Mr. William P. Cosgrove, head of the State Board of Accounting, O. L. Hayes, and Otto K. Jensen, field examiners, were present. Mr. Cosgrove made a statement that it was the desire of their board to be helpful in every way, and that it was the duty of the field accountants to make examinations and recommendations, but not to determine policies of the University as that was the duty of the Trustees.

Other Effects of the Depression

The Aeons knew that many students were feeling the effect of the depression. Accordingly, in the spring of 1933, after conferring with the chairman of the athletics committee, William J. Moenkhaus, and securing approval of this committee, they recommended that the activities fee, which for some years had been collected from all students, be discontinued at the close of the school year, and that purchase of season books be made optional. The report having been approved by the President, the board on March 8, 1933, concurred in this recommendation.

At this same meeting and for a like reason, the *Arbutus* fee, collected from Juniors and Seniors during the last several years, was discontinued by the board, and subscriptions were made voluntary.

In the early months of 1934 the University was taking steps to help needy students and to cooperate with federal agencies which provided funds for relief of unemployment. See Chapter XLIII.

On May 10, 1934, the board authorized the President to make application for a loan of $400,000 from the Federal Government for construction of an Administration Building. This was a further development of the Federal Government's effort to relieve unemployment resulting from the depression.

MISCELLANEOUS

Trustee Ira C. Batman died on April 10, 1934. The State Board of Education on April 23 elected Paul L. Feltus, of Bloomington, to fill the unexpired term of Mr. Batman. Mr. Feltus was seated at the May meeting of the board, and succeeded Judge Batman as a member of the Executive Committee.

Colonel William R. Standiford was assigned to the University in 1933 when Colonel Robinson was transferred to Fort Benjamin Harrison.

The President submitted with his approval the recommendation of the faculty of the University that there be established a two-year course for students not candidates for graduation. This was approved by the Board of Trustees.

On June 10, 1933, Professor Bernard C. Gavit was elected dean of the School of Law succeeding Paul V. McNutt, who had been elected governor in November. Dean Gavit's duties were to begin June 10, 1933.

In June, 1933, the honorary LL.D. degree was conferred upon: Governor Paul V. McNutt; Elmer B. Bryan, President of Ohio University; Professor Chancey Juday, Professor of Limnology, University of Wisconsin; Dr. Oscar Riddle, Carnegie Station for Experimental Evolution.

Ernest O. Holland, president of the State College of Washington, received the LL.D. at a special convocation on November 20, 1933.

The honorary degree A.M. had been conferred upon Mrs. H. B. Burnet, Fine Arts Department of the Indiana Federation of Clubs, and Jacob Gimbel, humanitarian, at the Foundation Day exercises on May 3.

Ellwood P. Cubberley, formerly Dean of the School of Education, Stanford University, received the honorary LL.D. degree at the Foundation Day exercises on May 2, 1934, and Frank A. Fetter, Professor of Political Economy at Princeton University, was similarly honored at the Commencement of that year.

A bronze tablet was dedicated to Dean Carl H. Eigenmann on Commencement Day, 1933. It hangs in Biology Hall.

The fourteen bedrooms in the Union Building tower were completed in the spring of 1934 as a CWA project in time for use at Commencement.

CHAPTER XXXVIII

THE SCHOOL OF COMMERCE
AND FINANCE, 1920 - 37

WHILE A School of Business, or of Commerce and Finance as it was first called, is something much more than a mere expansion of the courses of a Department of Economics, it is nevertheless true that economics was and remains a basic requirement for all curricula in the School of Business. It is, therefore, a matter of interest to note the development of the course in political economy, or economics, in Indiana University and the expansions and additions by which over a period of eighty years a School of Business was ultimately developed and established.

In the first Catalog of the University, that of 1830–31, we find political economy included in the curriculum as a subject of the Senior year. President Andrew Wylie was professor of mental and moral philosophy, political economy, and polite literature.

The file of Catalogs in the Archives of the University is not complete up to 1853–54 because some of them were destroyed by fire; but every available Catalog (beginning with that of 1830–31) lists political economy as one of the courses for one term of the Senior year (Junior year in a few Catalogs).

The teaching title of President William Daily was professor of mental and moral philosophy and belles-lettres. But the teaching title of his successor, President John Lathrop, was professor of mental, moral, and political philosophy. And this was likewise the teaching title of President Nutt, 1860–75, and of President Moss, 1875–84. And these presidents gave the courses in political economy. President Bryan states that he and William A. Rawles, his classmate, took this course in 1883–84, given by President Moss.

When a "Scientific Course" was offered, political economy was scheduled in either the Junior or the Senior year for students in this course as well as for students of the classics. Students in the "Modern

449

Classics Course," established in 1877–78, also took political economy. But in the Catalog of 1884–85 political economy was announced as an elective for all regular students. This probably reflected the influence of David Starr Jordan, who became president on January 1, 1885.

President Jordan broke the tradition of a president teaching mental, moral, and political philosophy, and became plain "professor of biology." In the University Catalog of 1884–85, in the faculty list we find the title "Mental, Moral, and Political Philosophy" without any appointee to this chair. A year later, 1885–86, mental, moral, and political philosophy had disappeared and instead we find a Department of Philosophy with William Bryan as acting[1] professor scheduling courses in psychology, logic, and ethics in addition to philosophy; and we find Arthur B. Woodford as an "assistant and associate professor in economics and sociology" attached to the Department of History as an instructor in history. This is the first time the term "economics" is used instead of the older term, "political economy," and is the first time the field is recognized by appointment of a member of the faculty, though he gave only part of his time to this subject.

In the Catalog for 1886–87 we find that social science and economics had risen to the status of a Department, with Woodford as a full professor. In the year 1889–90 Woodford was succeeded by Jeremiah W. Jenks, who ten years later was pointed out to me on the Cornell campus as an especially able member of the faculty of that university. Under Professor Jenks the title of the Department appeared as Department of Economics and Social Science.

In 1891–92 Edward A. Ross succeeded Jenks for that one year. He in turn was succeeded by John R. Commons. Three years later the title of the Department appeared as "Department of Political Economy" with John R. Commons as professor of public finance and Frank Fetter as professor of political economy. The title had again become "Department of Economics and Social Science" by 1895–96 with Frank Fetter alone as professor. Assistant Professor Ernest L. Bogart was added to the Department in 1898–99.

---

[1] "Associate professor in philosophy; acting instructor in English" in the full faculty list in the front of this Catalog.

In 1899–1900 Frank Fetter was succeeded by Ulysses G. Weatherly, aided by Ernest L. Bogart and William A. Rawles as assistant professors. Both Weatherly and Rawles had been members of the University faculty for some years, serving in the Department of History.

The work of the Department of Economics and Social Science had expanded during the fifteen years (1887–1902) under the succession of very able men, and in 1902 a number of business courses were introduced. These "Commercial Courses" were announced in the University Catalog published in May, 1902. The announcement stated that the student was expected to devote his first two years at the University to the regular course of studies, during which time he should complete all required subjects. In addition, he was to complete certain courses preparatory for the courses in commerce. A provisional curriculum of the two years' work in commerce followed. From time to time other courses were added. In March, 1904, a "Commercial Course Number" of twenty-four pages was published. It should be noted that these commerce courses constituted the last two years of work of a four-year course of study leading to a baccalaureate degree. The first two years were a pre-commerce requirement and included all the required courses of the Liberal Arts curriculum of that period.

In March, 1916, William A. Rawles, who had been designated as director of the commercial courses, urged that a School of Commerce be established. No action was taken at that time. Additional business courses were introduced in 1919 and at the meeting of the board in March, 1920, it was decided to increase the number of courses, coordinate and organize them as a School of Commerce and Finance, with William A. Rawles as dean. This proved so successful that by June, 1921, a building for the adequate housing of this school had become a necessity. But how should it be financed?

The legislature of 1921 had increased the mill tax for the state educational institutions from 2.8 cents per \$100 to 5 cents on each \$100 of taxable property in the state. Indiana University's share in this tax, two-fifths of the total, was thus increased from 1.12 cents to 2 cents on each \$100 of taxable property. The increase in University income assured by this raise in tax rate promised still further increase in succeeding years from rising property values and rising total of assessments.

Apart from an appropriation to assist in construction of the Riley Hospital, the legislature of 1921 had made no appropriation for buildings at Indiana University. It was believed, however, that the increase in tax rate would produce a surplus beyond maintenance requirements, which surplus might accumulate to meet building needs.

Section 3 of the act increasing the tax rate provided that:

> In case there shall be any unexpended balance at the end of any fiscal year, of the funds provided for by this act, apportioned to any one of said educational institutions, the same shall not revert to the state treasury but shall remain and belong to said institution to which it was apportioned, to be expended in the future for maintenance of said institutions or for improvement of the property of such institutions or for the construction of new buildings, as the board of trustees of said institutions may order.

The need for additional classroom space at the University was so great, however, that the administration believed that building should not be delayed until a building reserve might accumulate but that, if possible, construction should be begun at once.

Accordingly, in June, 1921, formal action was taken by the trustees for erection of a building to be known as Commerce Hall, costing approximately $250,000. In November a site for the building was chosen southeast of Science Hall. In February of 1922 completed plans were approved and a call for bids was ordered.

A deferred payment plan was evolved for financing the construction of this building. This was an innovation and a committee consisting of Trustees S. E. Smith and J. W. Fesler, and Bursar U. H. Smith was appointed to confer with Governor McCray and the Finance Board regarding the bids and the proposed deferred payment contract. On assurance of the Attorney General that the deferred payment plan was legal, the Governor expressed his approval. Under this plan warrants at 6 per cent interest were to be issued to the contractor. Payments of $50,000 each were to be made at six-month intervals, completed in full by January 10, 1925. Fifty thousand dollars each six months was set up as a budget item for building and paid out of increased income derived from increase in tax rate and increase in total assessments.

The title of this school was later changed to School of Business Administration, and since 1938 the School of Business. We now quote from a historical sketch prepared by its first dean, William A. Rawles:

In the organization of the School of Commerce and Finance the Board recognized that it was the function of a State University to discover and train for effective participation in social life the business administrator and the business technician as well as the teacher, the lawyer, the doctor, the scientist, the engineer, the writer, the artist, the political and religious leaders. There was a conviction that there existed an urgent need for the same kind of systematic training in business that was demanded in the older professions.

The School was admitted to membership in the American Association of Collegiate Schools of Business in 1921.

The building for this School, known as Commerce Hall, was dedicated on April 25 and 26, 1923, with appropriate ceremonies. Many eminent business men of the state and nation contributed to the occasion by giving helpful addresses. In commenting upon the event the *Indianapolis Star* in the issue of April 28 in its editorial column carried these words:

"The dedication of Commerce Hall at Indiana University means much more than the ordinary addition of another building to a college campus, devoted to liberal arts, law, or medicine. It typifies the new era of education in its relation to the business world, a physical reminder of the link which binds the modern university to the economic life of the state and nation. From a Hoosier point of view it places Indiana on a plane with other progressive states which have made provision for separate schools of commerce to fit their graduates for specific tasks and to bridge the gap which formerly existed between a degree and practical business equipment.

In 1923 the School was recognized by the establishment here of a chapter of Beta Gamma Sigma, the national honor society in schools of business.

Even prior to the organization of the School of Commerce and Finance the writer had instituted in the office of the Assistant Dean of the College of Arts and Sciences a service for the assistance of graduates—especially those in Economics—in finding positions. This service was continued under the direction of the Placement Bureau in the School of Commerce and Finance and has been instrumental in helping many of its students adjust themselves to the practical business world.

In 1925 the Bureau of Business Research was organized with Professor Lionel D. Edie as Director. In cooperation with the Fletcher American National Bank of Indianapolis, the Bureau began the publication of the *Indiana Business Review,* providing a comprehensive survey of the business conditions in Indiana. This review at once took high rank among the many business reviews published throughout the country. In order to facilitate the publication of the *Review* and to take care of the demands on the part of business for statistical and trade information, the Indianapolis Division of the Bureau was opened in June, 1927.

Upon the resignation in 1927 of Professor Edie to accept a position in the University of Chicago, Professor George W. Starr of Ohio State University was appointed Director of the Bureau of Business Research.

In 1932 the Indianapolis Division of the Bureau was transferred to Bloomington and the manager was made Assistant Director of the Bureau. At the same time the Bureau assumed complete control of the publication of the monthly *Indiana Business Review*.

The specific objectives in mind at the time of creating the Bureau may be summarized as follows: (1) to make general studies of the business conditions in Indiana; (2) to earn the good will and cooperation of the business men of the state by helping them in the solution of their specific problems; (3) to assist chambers of commerce by collecting facts bearing upon commercial conditions in the state; (4) to gather information for the use of the state legislature; (5) to gather material which might be used by teachers and students for the study of the actual conduct of business; (6) to train students in scientific methods of research to create the proper attitude of mind, to arouse an eagerness to analyze the elements of a problem, and to teach them the way to attack a specific problem.

Financial limitations have restricted the activities of the Bureau, but good progress has been made. A continuous study of the monthly conditions of business in Indiana is being conducted. The results of this study are published regularly in the *Indiana Business Review*. This review has wide circulation among the bankers and leading manufacturers and merchants of Indiana. Under the direction of the Bureau or with its assistance many important studies were completed.

In June, 1929, the Bureau was designated by the Secretary of Labor as the official representative of the Bureau of Labor of the United States for the collection of labor turnover and employment data in Indiana.

The Bureau, also, has stood ready to render aid or give information to individuals and private business corporations desiring data on business problems. Officers of the Bureau have been constantly called upon for personal consultation and for presentation of facts before conferences of leading associations of business men in the state.

In formulating the curriculum of the School of Commerce and Finance the main purpose of the course was not the acquisition of a mass of unrelated facts in regard to business procedure, but the attainment of such a mastery of fundamental principles that the graduate, after some practical experience, might know how to meet new contingencies and might take the initiative in devising and applying new methods. This implied that discipline was the paramount thing. But the discipline was to have been acquired in the study of those things bearing immediately upon his future work, and this was where the saving of time would be made.

In order to permit specialization the subjects offered were arranged in eight groups: the General Business Course; and courses in Accountancy, Banking and Finance, Foreign Trade, Insurance, Secretarial Training, Commercial Teacher Training, and Employment Management and Welfare work. After the experience of a few years it was found that 90% of the men pursued the General Business Course and that practically all of the women were enrolled in the Secretarial Training Course or the Course for the Training of Commercial Teachers. It was decided, therefore, to discontinue the specialized courses for men and to arrange the subjects in four groups: the General Business Group, the Secretarial Training Group, the Commercial Teacher Training Group, and the Business-Law Group. The subjects prescribed in the General Business Group were regarded as fundamental in the preparation for any business vocation. Opportunity for some specialization was offered, however, in the senior year by permitting students to select such courses as would prepare them for specific vocations.

From time to time minor modifications in the courses of study were made by omitting certain subjects, by adding some and by expanding others.

The degree granted for the completion of the entire four years of study was Bachelor of Science in Commerce and Finance. The degree Master of Science was also conferred under the direction of the Graduate School upon students who had completed satisfactorily one year of graduate study.

In 1932–33 an important step in the development of the School was taken. The Faculty of the School of Commerce and Finance submitted to the President and Board of Trustees the following recommendations: (1) that the School be made a four-year course so that freshmen would enroll directly in this School instead of the College of Arts and Sciences; (2) that certain changes be made in the curriculum as explained below; (3) that the name of the School be changed to School of Business Administration.

The reasons advanced for favoring the four-year course were these: the School would thus have the unqualified right, subject to the approval of the Board of Trustees, to prescribe entrance requirements, the curriculum and the requirements for graduation; a four-year course would have greater unity in content and would appeal more strongly to the interests of students because they could see more clearly that their studies were directly related to their life purposes; the proposed change was in line with the experiences of most of the schools which were members of the American Association of Collegiate Schools of Business.

The most important changes in the curriculum which were recommended were these: the omission of foreign languages; the transferring of science to the freshman year; and the introduction of more work in the social sciences.

The President and Board of Trustees in March, 1933, approved the recommendations and the changes became effective in September, 1933.

In 1934–35 the Board of Trustees conferred upon the School authority to grant the Master of Science degree and approved the requirements for that degree as recommended by the Faculty.

The School under the two-year plan began with an enrollment of 70 (Juniors, Seniors, and Specials) in the first semester of 1920–21. The attendance for the year 1932–33 (the last under the old plan) was 287. The enrollment for the year 1934–35 under the four-year plan was 733 and in the *first semester* of 1935–36 there were enrolled 822 students. Of this number 125 were women and 697 were men.

There were 14 graduates in the first class (1921) and 94 in 1935. The total number of B.S. degrees granted by the School of Business Administration from its beginning in 1920–21 to October, 1935, was 1,068; the M.S. degrees were 14.

On December 4, 1933, Dean Rawles[2] was seventy years of age and wished to retire at the close of the school year. He was persuaded, however, to continue his administrative duties and was relieved (July 24, 1934) of his teaching duties. In March, 1935, however, his resignation was placed before the Board of Trustees. He died on May 17, 1936.

On May 18, 1935, Herman B Wells was appointed dean of the School of Business Administration. On June 12, 1936, the board authorized Dean Wells to investigate the feasibility of a plan to provide a memorial library in memory of former Dean Rawles. This memorial library was incorporated in the new Business and Economics Building completed in 1940.

Dean Wells had been an instructor in economics in Indiana University, 1930–33. In June, 1933, he was advanced to an assistant professorship in economics, a title which he held 1933–35, on leave of absence. He had expected to spend the summer of 1933 in Europe, but this plan was given up when he was drafted to serve as supervisor of the Division of Banks and Trust Companies of Indiana. To these duties were added those of supervisor of the Division of Research and Statistics of the Department of Financial Institutions of the State of Indiana. Also during this same period (1933–35) he was secretary of the Commission for Financial Institutions for the

---

[2] Dr. Bryan tells this interesting story of William A. Rawles. Mr. Rawles had been called from Mitchell, where he had been teaching, to a position in the Bloomington High School. The president of the school board told him, "You will have to teach a course in accounting." Mr. Rawles replied, "I do not know anything about it; I took Greek in college." The president of the school board replied, "Well, then, you'll have to learn it. Go down at night to Mr. Bollenbacher and he will teach you." Rawles did as directed and later became dean of the School of Commerce and Finance.

State of Indiana. Thus he came to the deanship with this wide acquaintance with people and affairs of importance and with the prestige of these connections. Under his leadership the school of Business Administration continued the remarkable growth which followed the reorganization of 1932, put into effect in the school year 1933–34. The following table shows the increase in attendance which followed reorganization:

Enrollment for the Year

1932–33	287	1935–36	865
1933–34	573	1936–37	1,259
1934–35	733	1937–38	1,546

The School of Business Administration developed so remarkably that the building dedicated in 1923 became wholly inadequate and a new home for this School on a new site became necessary. But that is a story for a later history of Indiana University.

Chapter XXXIX

THE SCHOOL OF LAW

The First Thirty-five Years, 1842–77

ON FEBRUARY 15, 1838, an act of the General Assembly of Indiana was approved, the purpose of which was to convert Indiana College into Indiana University "for the education of youth in the American, learned and foreign languages, the useful arts, sciences (including law and medicine) and literature."

In conformity with the provisions of this act, the Board of Trustees at their organization meeting in September, 1838, having elected a president and faculty, took up the matter of selecting a professor of law. Their unanimous choice (September 25) was Judge Miles C. Eggleston,[1] and a committee of the board consisting of Messrs. Thompson, Law, and Wallace was appointed to communicate this action to Judge Eggleston.

On September 23, 1839, the committee reported that immediately on adjournment of the last session of the board they had, through their chairman, informed Judge Eggleston of his selection and he had respectfully refused. Thereupon they had approached several "gentlemen of distinction and eminent qualifications," but were unable to procure the services of a satisfactory person during the past year. Anxious, however, to be able to fill the chair permanently and in time for the current school year, they had made arrangements with David McDonald, "who has consented to serve on condition that the terms be reduced from four to three months."

The committee recommended adoption of this resolution:

Resolved that there shall be two terms in the Law Department of Indiana University, of three months each, in each and every year. The Winter term shall consist of the months of December, January, and February; the Summer term shall consist of the months of June, July, and August.

[1] Trustee of Indiana University, 1841–48.

458

The price of law tickets was fixed at $20. This resolution was laid on the table. Later that day, on motion of Mr. Howard, the motion was taken up and discussed at length but no action was taken.

After the reorganization of the board by the Act of February 15, 1841, the matter of appointment of a professor of law was again considered, and on July 23, 1841, Tilghman A. Howard[2] was unanimously elected to fill the chair. On September 28, 1841, the letter in which Mr. Howard declined was spread of record. The board, however, did not give up their hope of having him as professor of law, but next day appointed one of their number, Joseph S. Jenckes, to confer with Mr. Howard, and authorized Mr. Jenckes to engage him on terms and salary set forth in the minutes. On June 7, 1842, another letter from Mr. Howard was spread of record. An excerpt from this letter will reveal, in part, why the trustees were anxious to have him fill this chair of law.

> I am profoundly impressed by the action of the Board of Trustees, and their manner of approaching me on the subject of the Law Professorship. My hope is that in yielding to the necessity which compels me to decline a station so honorable I may not be regarded by the Board as having been governed by selfish considerations. My own individual feelings and tastes would be gratified by a different course. To the feelings which you have manifested on this subject, I pray you to accept my sincere acknowledgments.

The board then resolved that the salary of the professor of law should be $1,000, and proceeded to elect a man. Four men, David McDonald, Judge Kinney, Judge Morrison, and Stephen C. Stevens, were placed in nomination. David McDonald was elected, June 7, 1842, on the second ballot, accepted, and under his direction a "School of Law" was established at Indiana University, later called "Department of Law."

The financial situation of the University, however, was becoming increasingly difficult. On October 2, 1846, it was resolved that the salary of the law professor be discontinued, but that Judge McDonald be requested to continue his services on the condition that he receive the fees from the law students ($20 per session of three months) as his compensation, the University to furnish room and firewood. This Judge McDonald agreed to do temporarily.

[2] Trustee of Indiana University, 1838–41.

On August 4, 1853, he resigned to give some attention to the interests of the University in the Vincennes suit. The University had conferred upon him the LL.D. degree in 1852. Judge James Hughes was appointed to succeed him.

The following table is a list of the professors of law from the beginning of the Department in 1842 to its suspension in 1877:

David McDonald .... from 1842 to	1853
William T. Otto................................ 1847	1852
James Hughes 1853	1857
James R. M. Bryant[3]........................... 1857	1861
George A. Bicknell............................. 1861	1870
John U. Pettit................................. 1869	1870
Samuel E. Perkins............................. 1870	1872
Baskin E. Rhoads.............................. 1870	1877
Delana R. Eckles.............................. 1872	1873
David W. LaFollette........................... 1873	1874
Cyrus F. McNutt............................... 1874	1877

During the first thirty-five years, 1842–77, of the history of the Department of Law, there was a remarkably close relationship between the law faculty and the Board of Trustees. Two professors, McDonald (1856–57) and Hughes (1857–60), served as members of the board, and two, Bryant (1855–59) and Rhoads (1866–74), served concurrently as professors of law and members of the board.

During the period 1842–77 there were no published requirements for admission to the study of law. On the contrary, the Catalog of 1842 carried the following notice: "Persons applying for admission as students will not be examined as to their literary ability."

When in 1875 Lemuel Moss succeeded Cyrus Nutt[4] as president of the University he was greatly disturbed by these low entrance requirements to professional study. One of the first acts of this administration was to drop the affiliation with the potentially powerful Indiana Medical College. At the close of the school year 1876–77, the trustees suspended instruction in law until further notice. In the

---

[3] Ambrose B. Carlton, LL.B. '50, is listed on page 575 among alumni appointments to the faculty as professor pro tem of law, probably upon the authority of Theophilus Wylie, *Indiana University, Its History from 1820, When Founded, to 1890*, p. 318. Catalogs of the period, however, do not list Carlton.—I.L.C.

[4] The professor of law was Cyrus McNutt.

Catalog of that year, 1876–77, President Moss made this statement:

I wish further to say that it seems entirely proper and desirable for the State to establish professional schools, as of law and medicine, or to aid in their establishment. There is no reason why the State should not, under proper regulations, teach the elements of these sciences as well as of other liberal and practical sciences. Only they should be so taught as to promote the highest intellectual and moral culture. Our law and medical schools ought to be strictly postgraduate schools—that is, they should require the collegiate course, by way of preparation, and be based upon it. That men should be passed through these professional schools with little or no preliminary training, and little or no preliminary examination—ignorant of language, of literature, of history, of mathematics, of science, of philosophy, and almost wholly destitute of intellectual discipline—is to the disadvantage alike of good morals, good learning, and good professional ability. You will agree with me that there is no present necessity for swelling the ranks of untrained and incompetent lawyers, and physicians, and clergymen. It is with me a grave question whether the State has a right to incorporate a private institution for doing such imperfect and superfluous work; there can scarcely be a doubt that it is unwise and inexpedient for the State to do such work directly and with its own funds. Not, as I have said, that the State should abstain from supporting professional and special schools, but that it should insist upon their being so organized and conducted as to be a constant incentive and aid to general and liberal education. The number of men sent forth from such schools is a very minor matter; their quality and character, whether as specialists and experts or as citizens and leaders in the purification and elevation of public sentiment, is a matter of the very highest importance. It may not be practicable for you at once to require the degree of preparation I have indicated as the condition of admission to a professional school, but surely some requirement may be made, so that persons who would fail in an examination for entrance into an ordinary grammar school may not readily pass, under the patronage of the State, to the study of medicine or law. I would recommend, as the minimum requisition, to be increased as soon as practicable, that any person who wishes to enter any professional school which is or may hereafter be under the control of your board, should pass a preliminary examination equivalent to that required for entrance into the Junior Class in college. This would be a considerable and very much needed step in advance, and would, in the circumstances, be the most difficult step to take. It is always the first step that costs; but the first step must be taken first, and it often counts most as well as costs most. Were this once done it would soon be found feasible to make the professional courses strictly post-graduate courses, and to require the whole college course as their antecedent.

This letter of President Moss is very revealing. He, of course, was right in his attitude regarding the desirability of collegiate requirements for admission to law and medicine, but no school in America was ready for this requirement as yet; indeed, it was a quarter of a century before graduation from a four-year high school was generally required for admission to professional schools. United action was necessary. Unfortunately, President Moss could not see that he had something potentially very desirable in the Indiana University Department of Law and the University affiliation with the Indiana Medical College.

RE-ESTABLISHMENT AND DEVELOPMENT OF LAW COURSES, 1889–1902

On March 20, 1889, Trustee Youche, chairman of the committee on legal affairs, reported that his committee recommended "that a Law School be established as a department of the University."

Instruction in this Department was to be given by two professors of law, one of whom was to be dean. The course in law was to extend over two years and consisted of two three-month terms each year. Applicants for admission were required to be at least eighteen years of age and to pass an examination which would test the applicants' ability to write and speak good English and show a reasonable proficiency in the common school branches. Students who had finished the work of the Junior year in a reputable university were to be granted the diploma of the Law Department on completing the law courses and also the degree of A.B. The fee in the Law Department was fixed at $25 a year.

It will be noted that in the re-establishment of the courses in law no marked increase in entrance requirements was proposed. No high school work was required, so admission to the study of law was far below the requirements for admission to the University, which included completion of a four-year high school course.

On June 11, 1889, the board took up the election of a dean of the Law Department, postponed from the March meeting. The following day, on the third ballot, David D. Banta received seven of the eight votes[5] and was declared elected. Judge Banta was completing his fourth term as a trustee of the University, 1877–89, and was per-

---

[5] It appears that Banta cast his ballot for R. S. Robertson. That Dean Banta was an unusually able man is clearly revealed in the first six chapters of the Woodburn *History of Indiana University, 1820–1902*, which the Dean wrote, and delivered as Foundation Day addresses, 1889–94, inclusive.

suaded by President Jordan to resign as president of the board and assume the deanship of the School of Law. He organized the School, planned the two-year course of study, and directed the development until his death, April 9, 1896.

Having elected a dean, the trustees did not get around to appointment of a second professor until March 6, 1890, when they chose Ernest W. Huffcut.

He was succeeded in 1892 by William P. Rogers. On the death of Dean Banta, Professor Rogers was promoted to the deanship (June 16, 1896), and Judge George L. Reinhard was elected professor of law.

During the period 1889–1902 requirements for entrance on the study of law and the length of the law course were increased.

The title "School of Law" was first used in the Catalog for 1890–91 when the Law School year was increased to three terms and graduates of high schools were excused from entrance examinations.

In the Catalog of 1896–97 it was announced that every applicant would be required to take the entrance examination in English composition. If he failed in this he was required to take English 1 and continue in the course until he passed its examinations.

THE SCHOOL OF LAW DURING THE BRYAN ADMINISTRATION, 1902–37

At the beginning of the Bryan administration the time required for completion of the work of the School of Law had been increased from two years of six months each to three years of nine months each. Applicants for admission had to meet the same entrance requirements as students of the College of Liberal Arts, effective since 1899. The faculty consisted of Dean Rogers, Judge Reinhard, Associate Professor William E. Clapham, and Assistant Professor Herdis F. Clements. The School still occupied quarters in Wylie Hall.

The first serious problem which confronted the Bryan administration arose in the School of Law. The resignation of Dean Rogers[6] was accepted and Judge Reinhard was promoted to the deanship.

On March 27, 1903, Enoch George Hogate was elected professor of law, and on July 19, 1906, he became dean after the death of

[6] For fuller statement see Chap. III.

Judge Reinhard. At this time the law faculty consisted of three professors, two instructors, and four nonresident instructors. On November 10, 1903, Charles M. Hepburn had been elected professor.

The Law School Removed to Maxwell Hall

It may be recalled that the legislature of 1905 made an appropriation of $100,000 to Indiana University for a new library building. Though this appropriation was not available until November, 1905, and though much time would then be required for construction of the new building (two years in fact), the legislature had barely adjourned when the faculty and students of the School of Law held a celebration in anticipation of the great day when the University Library would be moved from Maxwell to its new home and the School of Law might move into the vacated space in Maxwell.[7] Dean Reinhard, the law faculty, and students were taking no chances on some other department or school registering a prior claim to the space to be vacated in this fortress, Maxwell Hall.

Addressing the trustees in April, 1905, the President cited the bright prospects for the School of Law and the definite gain in attendance experienced during the current year. He also called attention to the official jubilee held by the law faculty and students who had rather taken it for granted that the trustees would assign Maxwell Hall to the School of Law on completion of the new Library building. The President added: "I trust you will not be disposed to disappoint them."

Though Maxwell Hall met most of the requirements of the School of Law, it did not have sufficient classroom space. Therefore, in anticipation of the early occupancy of Maxwell Hall by the School of Law, an addition to Maxwell was erected in 1907.

Like Moses, Dean Reinhard did not enter the promised land. He died on July 13, 1906, but his successor, Enoch G. Hogate, in his reports in 1906 and 1907 kept the promise fresh in the minds of the trustees by reiterating how desirable the new home for the School of Law in Maxwell would be. The moving of the Library to its new home was accomplished during the holidays of 1907-8. As the Library was moved out the west door the Law School moved in the

---

[7] In the nineties the School had had some space in Maxwell Hall.

east door of Maxwell Hall. Instruction was begun in these new quarters in January, 1908. When in December, 1936, the Administration Building was occupied, the School of Law took over the whole of Maxwell Hall.

In the new quarters in Maxwell, old needs received new emphasis. In November, 1908, the President recommended the services of a stenographer for two hours a day for the Law School, and called the attention of the board to the pressing need of a larger fund for the library. It was urged that the Law Library fees be devoted to the purchase of books. This continued for some years to be presented as the greatest need of the School of Law. In 1912 Dean Hogate asked for $20,000 for this purpose.

Increase in Entrance Requirements

The School of Law was barely settled in Maxwell when the problem of a marked increase in entrance requirements came before the faculty for discussion. After long consideration a tentative decision had been reached to require for admission one year of collegiate work in 1910 and two years in 1911. But before any publicity had been given this decision a new ruling was made by the Association of American Universities to the effect that member universities must require for admission to professional schools two years of collegiate work for membership in that Association. Desiring not to jeopardize the membership of the University in this Association, the trustees on December 31, 1908, advanced the effective date of these higher entrance requirements to one year of collegiate work in the fall of 1909 and two years of collegiate work in the fall of 1910.

The University administration and the faculty of the School of Law looked forward to a great decrease in attendance as a result of this radical increase in entrance requirements with no advanced notice which might enable students to prepare for the innovation. But in his report to the board in June, 1912, the President showed that the falling off in attendance had been very slight.

Support of Higher Requirements for Study and Practice of Law

Though the falling-off in attendance when two years of collegiate work were required for admission to the School of Law was not as great as anticipated, the subsequent increase in attendance was not as rapid or as great as merited, because of the low state requirements for admission to the Indiana bar. For every school of law in the United States that maintained the high entrance requirements established by the Indiana University School of Law, there were four schools that admitted students directly from high school and to these schools the majority of students continued to go.

For forty-six years, 1889–1935, the School of Law was handicapped in its gradual increase of requirements for entrance on the study of law to two years of collegiate work by a provision of the Indiana Constitution of 1851 that every person of good moral character was entitled to admission to the practice of law. Unsuccessful attempts had been made to correct this situation. In April, 1905, the President directed attention of the trustees to an act of the last legislature authorizing an amendment to the Constitution providing for the establishment of conditions for admission to the bar. But when submitted to vote of the people in 1906 the amendment failed of passage.

In June, 1906, Dean Hogate, reporting on behalf of the School of Law, stated:

> The situation in Indiana is peculiar. In most states of the Union recent legislation has safeguarded the public against incompetency in the practice of the law by requiring of all who seek admission to the bar both a definite prelegal education and a definite professional education. In many states this statutory requirement now calls for four years in the high school and three years in the law school as a minimum. But in Indiana there is not only no requirement either for prelegal education or professional education as preliminary to admission to the bar, but, under the express terms of the Constitution of 1851, every person of good moral character being a voter shall be entitled to admission to practice law in all courts of justice in Indiana.
>
> As an aid in getting the Law School before the people of Indiana, we recommend that the University publish, under the supervision of a special committee appointed by the Law faculty, a pamphlet which, after showing something of the extent and vigor of the present movement in the United States for better preparation for the practice of the law, shall show fully what Indiana University is doing and proposes to do to meet this need.

Furthermore, this School and some thirty other leading schools throughout the United States which had been bearing aloft the banner of higher entrance requirements had been handicapped for many years by lack of support by the Council on Legal Education of the American Bar Association. The legal profession had been satisfied with four years of high school work and three years of law study as preparation for legal practice.

But in September, 1921, the School of Law was jubilant over the fact that the American Bar Association had adopted higher standards by an overwhelming majority vote and had directed the Council on Legal Education and Admission to the Bar to publish from time to time the names of the law schools which complied with the adopted standards and the list of law schools that did not comply. It was directed that, so far as possible, these lists should be made available to students intending to study law. The higher standards adopted applied not merely to entrance requirements, but to important features of the School itself, such as library and the number of full-time teachers. The Association stipulated that the school must not be operated as a commercial enterprise. Compensation of staff must not be dependent on the number of students or on fees received. In time these standards were extended to include financial support, physical plant, University connection, administration, curriculum, teaching methods, quality and character of students accepted for law study, etc.

At the April, 1922, board meeting, members who had visited a number of law schools reported: Frank H. Hatfield on his visit to the University of Iowa Law School; Charles M. Niezer concerning his trip to Columbia Law School; Benjamin F. Long concerning the trip that he and Trustee Fesler made to the law schools of Northwestern University and the University of Chicago.

The lawyers of the board were studying problems of legal education and gaining personal knowledge of physical facilities, library, staff, methods of instruction, and other important features of legal education as developed in leading university schools of law, all of which was of great value and importance to the Indiana University School of Law.

In April of 1935 the high requirements for entrance on the study of law maintained by Indiana University since 1910 received too-long delayed support through a Supreme Court decision. Dean Bernard C. Gavit has written a brief account of this long struggle to raise state requirements for admission to the study of law and to the bar.

The Indiana Constitution of 1851, Art. 7, Sec. 21, contained the following provision: "Every person of good moral character, being a voter, shall be entitled to admission to practice law in all courts of justice." It was assumed by many persons that this provision prohibited educational qualifications for admission to the bar although this proposition was disputed. Beginning in the 1890's, the bar association undertook to resolve the question by an amendment to the Constitution striking out this particular section. The matter was submitted to a popular vote on different occasions—1900, 1906, 1910, 1921, and 1932. At each of those five elections, except 1921, the proposed amendment received a substantial majority of affirmative votes cast on the problem. In no election, however, did it receive a majority of the votes cast in the general election involved at the same time.

In 1931 the General Assembly passed an act giving to the Supreme Court of the state the power to regulate admissions to the bar. Immediately the Supreme Court promulgated rules providing for a state bar examination and conditioning admission to the bar in Indiana on the successful passing of the state bar examination. In January, 1935, one Lemuel S. Todd challenged the validity of this action and insisted upon admission without examination on the theory that under Sec. 21 of Art. 7 of the Indiana Constitution the legislative and court action were unconstitutional. The Supreme Court decided in April, 1935, in an opinion written by Judge Walter E. Treanor (208 Indiana 168) that the section of the Constitution in question had been stricken out by amendment at the 1932 election. The Court overruled a previous case decided in 1880 which had held that the Constitution could not be amended by a majority of voters voting on the amendment but could only be amended by a majority of voters voting in the general election. The Supreme Court held in the Todd case that a majority of the voters voting on a Constitutional amendment could amend the Constitution.

Within a short time after this decision the Supreme Court amended its rules and adopted as a condition for admission to the state bar examinations graduation from a law school approved by the American Bar Association. In general this requires two years of college and three years of law school work although in a limited number of cases the two years of college may be waived in favor of applicants twenty-five years of age or older.

In this manner and at this time, after thirty years of delay, "the final passage" of the amendment to the Constitution referred to by the President in 1905 became effective and higher entrance requirements maintained for so many years by the Indiana University

School of Law received the support of the state of Indiana and became a prerequisite for the state bar examination.

Establishment of a Law Journal

The establishment of a law journal by the School of Law first came under official consideration in June, 1916, and Professor Hepburn was requested to investigate the cost. This investigation revealed so many difficulties that the project did not seem feasible at that time. Two years later (June, 1918) the request of the law faculty for authorization to investigate the demand for a Law School magazine was again approved. It was estimated that the magazine should have a subsidy of $1,500 for the first year. Though again nothing came of this matter, the project was not abandoned.

On March 13, 1925, George H. Batchelor, of Indianapolis, representing the State Bar Association, appeared before the trustees with a proposition for the publication of a law journal under the sponsorship of the School of Law and the Indiana State Bar Association. The following day, March 14, it was ordered that the board enter into a contract with the Indiana State Bar Association for the publication of this law magazine. On May 4 Mr. Batchelor reported that the Indiana State Bar Association proposed to the board that the Association should take over the financial responsibility for the publication, and the members of the faculty of the School of Law should take charge of the editorial work. The matter was referred to a committee consisting of Trustees Batman and Long and President Bryan, who gave it their approval. Arrangements for this joint publication were completed late in 1925.

Of this journal Professor Frank Horack writes:

In 1925 the Indiana State Bar Association decided to edit a publication entitled *The Indiana Law Journal*. This *Journal* was devoted to news of state, district, and local bar meetings, and personal items concerning the members. Before the end of that year it became apparent to the Association that they did not have the manpower to produce the type of publication they desired.

As a result they entered into a contract with Indiana University School of Law for the publication of the *Indiana Law Journal*. This *Journal* first appeared in January, 1926. It was of the law-review type without personals and devoted primarily to scholarly discussions of difficult legal points. The publication was placed in charge of a faculty editor and a student editorial board composed of juniors and seniors of outstanding scholastic attainment.

Further Development of the School of Law

In October, 1912, Dean Hogate stated that the law faculty was looking forward to a time, in the not distant future, when postgraduate work leading to an LL.M. or J.D. might be offered. But it was five years later that this hope was realized. The requirements for the J.D. degree were first announced in the Law Bulletin published in April, 1917, and for the LL.M. in 1918.

In his report to the trustees, March, 1914, Dean Hogate, speaking for the Law School, said:

In my judgment nothing is more necessary at this time than that all three of the Moot Courts should be under the control of one Professor and thoroughly systematized, that the student may get the greatest possible good out of them in applying the principles he learns in lectures to the actual work in the courts. To accomplish this, the School of Law needs another Professor.

On March 23, 1917, because of the serious illness of Dean Hogate, Professor Hepburn was asked to serve as acting dean. When it became evident that Dean Hogate[8] could not resume his duties, Professor Hepburn was elected dean, June, 1918, effective as of August 1, 1918. At this time the law faculty consisted of six professors and one acting professor.

Paul V. McNutt became an instructor in law in the second semester of 1916–17, and was an assistant professor 1917–19. He became professor of law in 1919, and on the retirement of Professor Hepburn as dean,[9] 1925, Professor McNutt was elected to succeed him, May 5, 1925. At that time the other members of the law faculty were: Professors Jesse J. M. LaFollette, Merrill I. Schnebly, Hugh E. Willis, Walter E. Treanor, James J. Robinson, and two nonresident lecturers.

In the fall of 1932 Dean McNutt was elected governor of Indiana. His resignation was submitted November 10, 1932, effective on or before January 9, 1933, when he assumed office. He was given a leave of absence and the board decided not to elect his successor until the following June.

Dean McNutt had suggested on February 17, 1930, that an eighth

[8] Dean Hogate died September 7, 1924, after an illness of seven and one-half years.
[9] Dean Hepburn died July 10, 1929.

member be added to the Law School faculty. At that time there were nine professors and one acting professor listed, three of whom were on leave of absence.

Bernard Campbell Gavit had been appointed acting professor of law for the year 1929–30. He was professor of law, 1930–33, and was elected dean on June 10, 1933, effective as of July, 1933, succeeding Dean McNutt. The active faculty then consisted of seven men, Dean Gavit and Professors Willis, Alfred Evens, Robinson, Robert C. Brown, Fowler V. Harper, and Milo Bowman. The names of Paul V. McNutt and Walter E. Treanor were listed, both on leave of absence. It was a strong faculty of very able men. Dean Gavit has served from 1933 to date (1950).

Like other schools of the University, the Law School from time to time lost, to other schools, members of its faculty, some of whom had distinguished careers elsewhere.

Archibald H. Throckmorton, Professor of Law, 1911–13, resigned to become professor and dean of the Western Reserve University School of Law.

Morton C. Campbell was professor of law, 1916–20. He left to accept a position in the Harvard Law School, where he retired in 1942 as professor emeritus.

Warren A. Seavey, professor of law from 1916 to 1920, left the University to become dean of the University of Nebraska College of Law, 1920–26; professor of law, University of Pennsylvania, 1926–27; and professor of law, Harvard Law School, 1927 to date (1950). He served as president of Association of American Law Schools.

James L. Parks, who became professor of law in 1917, became professor and dean of the University of Missouri School of Law two years later.

Merrill I. Schnebly was professor of law, 1920–26. He subsequently became professor of law at the University of Missouri and later at the University of Illinois, where he still teaches (1950).

William E. Britton, Professor of Law, 1921–24, left Indiana to become professor of law at the University of Illinois, 1924–42.

Each of these men had a distinguished career as a teacher of law. Nearly all have published articles or books well known to the profession.

CHAPTER XL

INDIANA UNIVERSITY, 1934 - 36

THE APPEAL TO THE 1935 LEGISLATURE

F OR MORE than three years Indiana and the nation had been in the grip of a depression. Against his will, Governor Leslie had called a special session of the General Assembly for July 7, 1932, which had cut the appropriation of $1,800,000 made for Indiana University by the regular session of 1931, 15 per cent ($270,000). The next regular session of the General Assembly meeting in January, 1933, made a further cut of $40,000, bringing the total appropriation from the state down to $1,490,000.

In the summer of 1934, though economic conditions were improving, the deep winter of the depression was still near and felt. What would be the attitude of the next General Assembly of 1935, for which a report and budgetary requests were being prepared?

In August, 1934, the needs of the University were presented to Governor McNutt and the State Budget Committee. The University asked for operating expenses at Bloomington $1,100,000 and for operating expenses at Indianapolis $390,000, a total of $1,490,000.

A supplemental statement of University needs which had accumulated during the lean years was also presented:

Raising University dam (present water supply insufficient)
                                                    $61,829.76
Walks, drives, and curbs on campus (entrance to buildings, etc., for which funds have never been available) . 39,370.82
Painting (buildings that should be painted at once). . . . 14,249.80
Steam line to Observatory (repairs to present line) 810.00
Science Hall elevator (replacing worn-out equipment) . . 5,790.00
Wylie Hall elevator (replacing worn-out equipment) . . . 5,330.00
Property notes outstanding (approved by the Finance Committee to be paid from the Educational Improvement Fund suspended by 1932 Special Session during 1932, '33, and '34):
    Elder Property—122 Michigan Street, Indianapolis. . . 10,000.00
    Hepburn Property—Forest Place, Bloomington campus 5,000.00

472

Dental School—Construction $22,927.45
Dental School—Equipment 10,102.75
Additional needs in case Federal Government allows loan
   requested for Administration Building:
Salvaging Assembly Hall......................... 5,000.00
Remodeling and equipping Maxwell Hall for Law
   School 25,000.00
Equipment and furnishings for new Administration
   Building 100,000.00
                    Total.....................————$305,410.58
School of Medicine and Hospitals:
Replacing worn-out equipment for biennium.......$20,000.00
Additional maintenance on quarters being prepared in
   Coleman Hospital for biennium................. 10,000.00
                    Total.....................———— 30,000.00
In order adequately and efficiently to operate, the follow-
   ing additions are needed:
Isolation quarters for Long, Coleman, and Riley
   Hospitals
Housing facilities for residents, interns, nurses, dieti-
   tians, occupational therapists, and X-ray technicians
Central laboratories building with facilities for out-
   patient clinics
Completion of walks, drives, and campus sprinkler
   system
General maintenance and storage building
                    Total............................$335,410.58

When the legislative session of 1935 had adjourned it was found that although $1,490,000 for operating expenses of the University at Bloomington and Indianapolis had been appropriated as requested, no appropriation whatever had been made for supplementary requests. This left the income of the University for the biennium 1935–37 the same as that voted by the session of 1933 for the biennium 1933–35. At least there had been no further reduction.

There was additional legislation the purport of which was not generally understood at once, but which came to be of great importance to Indiana University. This act, passed in the early days of 1935, anticipated the establishment of the Works Progress Administration on May 6, 1935, and gave the University the legal status which enabled it to take full advantage of federal grants made in succeeding years by the PWA. This is discussed in Chapter XLIII.

INSURANCE OF UNIVERSITY BUILDINGS

After the fire in the power plant, September 25, 1929, which was believed due to defective wiring, a survey and report of wiring of the buildings of the campus was made and changes and improvements in wiring were installed as recommended. Later (November, 1934) an insurance committee consisting of Trustees Niezer, Long, and Hatfield was appointed to make a report on insurance carried on University property. On May 17, 1935, this committee made its report, and the following resolutions were unanimously adopted:

BE IT RESOLVED, That the report of appraisals of values submitted by the Insurance Committee of the University properties at Bloomington, Indianapolis, and other locations consisting of valuations of buildings, equipment, furniture, and fixtures in detail, dated May 16, 1935, be and is hereby adopted as the value of the property listed for the purpose of fixing the insurance value thereof.

BE IT FURTHER RESOLVED, That all property of the University be insured against loss by fire or windstorm on the basis of 80% of the insurable value thereof as determined by the Insurance Committee, and that said Insurance Committee be and is hereby authorized to appoint a proper agent to act as an insurance managing agent or representative selected from within or without the personnel of the employees and officers of the University and without any additional cost to the University for such service, that the Insurance Committee be continued for further and final report.

On June 14, 1935, Mr. Niezer, chairman of the insurance committee, read a detailed report of their findings, which was accepted.

On December 7, 1935, Trustees Ball and Nolan were announced as members of the insurance committee of the board in place of Mr. Hatfield, who had resigned, and of Mr. Niezer, whose term had expired.

Mr. Long, acting chairman of the insurance committee, then presented for approval the Group Fidelity bond and the treasurer's bond as recommended by W. P. Ray, acting on behalf of the insurance committee. The matter was referred back to Mr. Long to make investigation in conference with the two newly appointed members of the insurance committee and to report with recommendation after the investigation.

These records of the Board of Trustees are given in rather greater detail than might seem warrantable, because an unfortunate incident in connection with this insurance matter led, on February 26, 1936, to the regrettable resignation of the president of the board, James W. Fesler.

ESTABLISHMENT OF THE OFFICE OF COMPTROLLER

In the spring of 1936 the board informally agreed to establish the office of comptroller, whose function should be to direct the business affairs of the University. Ulysses H. Smith, who had been appointed treasurer, was to continue to act in that capacity. Ward G. Biddle was chosen for the position of comptroller on June 12, 1936. In collaboration with President Bryan, Mr. Biddle presented copies of the statement of the duties to be assigned to the comptroller and the treasurer, which were approved by the board.

CRIMINOLOGY

The President on May 16, 1935, presented to the trustees the contribution which various departments of the University were prepared to make in the field of criminology. The President said:

The University is fortunate in having a considerable number of professors who are from various points of view experts in one of the most important of all social problems, namely—the problem of crime. Criminology is the special field of Professor Edwin H. Sutherland, who succeeds Professor Weatherly as head of the Department of Sociology. Mr. James J. Robinson is Professor of Criminal Law and has wide contacts in the state and nation with persons who are experts in the field of criminal law and the prevention of crime. Dean Gatch reports that several professors in the School of Medicine are experts in the fields which have to do with the detection of crime. It is my view that we should mobilize these forces in the interest of prevention and detection of crime.

At the request of the board, the President presented a plan for organization of an institute of criminology with Professor Sutherland as president and Professor Robinson as director, which was approved June 14, 1935.

A report of the work of the Institute was submitted by Professors Sutherland and Robinson in February, 1936, with the recommendation that professional police training be established, which was approved.

The University Catalog of July, 1937, carried the announcement of this Institute and stated that the work consisted of five divisions:

1. Investigation of causes of crime directed to the prevention of crime. Activities in this field are in charge of Professor E. H. Sutherland, Head of the Department of Sociology.

2. Training for official duties in criminal law administration. Police training is in charge of Professor James J. Robinson, of the School of Law.

3. Cooperation with officials in criminal law administration. Scientific laboratory services are now performed by faculty members of the School of Medicine and of other Schools and Departments of the University.

4. Statutory and administrative improvements in the system of criminal law administration. Drafting of statutes, etc. in charge of Professor Robinson.

5. Increase of public information about criminal law administration through conferences and clinics, etc.

A state-wide conference on criminal law administration was held at Indiana University on March 31, 1936. A feature of the conference was an exhibit of scientific police equipment and operations conducted by the Indiana State police. An exhibit of criminal tools was also shown. Finger printing service was offered to students and citizens. One of the projects of the Institute aims to procure information to be used in formulating a program for reduction of juvenile delinquency.

Four Changes in the Board of Trustees

The number of changes in the Board of Trustees during the biennium 1934–36 was unequaled in any like period of time since organization of the eight-member board in 1855.

The first of the men of this group to be replaced was Frank H. Hatfield, of Evansville, who resigned on May 20, 1935. On June 13, 1935, Val Nolan, elected trustee by the State Board of Education, took the oath of office succeeding Mr. Hatfield.

On June 15 a committee of the Alumni Association called on the Board of Trustees to report that the Alumni Council announced the re-election of James W. Fesler as alumni trustee.

The appointment of Trustee Charles M. Niezer expired on July 1, 1935. He performed his last service as a member of the board at the final Commencement session on June 17. On May 17, 1935, the State Board of Education elected William A. Kunkel, Jr., to succeed Mr. Niezer. Mr. Kunkel took his place on the board on October 9, 1935.

On March 18, 1936, the members of the board were informed by letter that on February 26 James W. Fesler had sent to President Bryan his letter of resignation.

On April 7, all seven members present, the board recorded a long resolution closing with the expression that "Along with all who are interested in Indiana University, the Trustees deeply regret Mr. Fesler's resignation from the Board."

Mr. Fesler, elected alumni trustee in June, 1902, at the same Commencement time that William Lowe Bryan was elected president, became president of the board in 1919 and served in that capacity until his resignation. On the retirement of Edwin Corr in 1924, Mr. Fesler became the senior member of the board. Living in Indianapolis, he had rendered particularly important and valuable service in connection with the establishment in Indianapolis of the School of Medicine, the Robert W. Long Hospital, the School of Dentistry, and as a member of the Joint Executive Committee of the James Whitcomb Riley Hospital for Children. Unreserved tribute is here paid to the fine personal qualities and long service of this loyal alumnus. No one could have given of himself in fuller measure to his Alma Mater.

Vice-President George Ball was elected president of the board on April 7, and, on June 15, John Hastings was elected alumni trustee to fill the unexpired term of Mr. Fesler.

Benjamin F. Long had completed his extended period of service as a trustee on July 1, 1936. On June 19, 1936, Albert Rabb was elected by the State Board of Education to succeed Mr. Long.

RESIGNATIONS WITHIN THE OFFICIAL FAMILY

Losses in the Old Guard were not limited to the Board of Trustees. Within the official family there were two resignations within this biennium.

Dean William A. Rawles, as stated in Chapter XXXVIII, had presented his resignation in the spring of 1935, effective as of June 30. Professor U. G. Weatherly, for many years a colleague of Dean Rawles, retired on the same day.

John W. Cravens had become registrar of Indiana University in 1895 and secretary to the Board of Trustees in 1898. As a member of the Indiana state legislature from 1899 to 1903 he became acquainted with many men of political influence. His position and experience made him very helpful to the new president, William Lowe Bryan.

Mr. Cravens was a man of excellent judgment of men and events. There was nothing devious about him. He was not given to double talk. He could be counted on to express a conservative but frank judgment. If he disagreed or disapproved, he did so courageously, and definitely, yet kindly. He had one great twenty-four-hour interest, and that was Indiana University.

For some time he had been ailing. In the fall of 1935 he would have been unable to carry on his duties but for the efficient organization he had built up. On November 12, 1935, he was granted a leave of absence for the remainder of the semester. When at the June, 1936, meeting of the board he felt it necessary to submit his resignation, it was unanimously voted that Mr. Cravens be given the title of secretary and registrar emeritus.[1]

On June 12, 1936, Thomas A. Cookson, the assistant registrar, was appointed registrar and elected secretary to the board.

WILLIAM LOWE BRYAN

On November 11, 1935, William Lowe Bryan was seventy-five years of age.

Perhaps I can give no better measure of the vigor of the man than to relate the major features of a celebration of the President's seventy-fifth birthday by a foursome of golf. Dean Stout, Hugh Willis (law) President Bryan, and I had driven up to the Indianapolis Country Club. We liked the course because of its natural hazards.

We played the first nine holes before early lunch, rested a short time, and finished the last nine holes about 3 p.m. No one was tired. Someone suggested that we play the first nine holes again. All agreed. That made a total of twenty-seven holes for the day, and President Bryan played those last nine of the twenty-seven in 44, and he was not fatigued, nor were there any other than pleasurable after-effects the next day.

FOUNDATIONS

John S. Hastings and Uz McMurtrie, representing the Alumni Council, submitted to the trustees on June 17, 1935, a proposal for the

---

[1] He died August 10, 1937.

establishment of an Indiana University Foundation. The board approving the plan, Mr. Fesler appointed President Bryan and Judge Wildermuth as a committee to confer with the committee of the Alumni Council regarding articles of incorporation, which were filed in 1936.

On April 3, 1931, William T. Patten, A.B., Indiana University, 1893, had given to the University securities valued at $115,000, the income of which, it was agreed, he should receive during his life. He died on May 3, 1936. This fund is kept intact as the William T. Patten Foundation. As directed in the terms of the agreement, the earnings of this fund are used to bring to Indiana University superior men in various fields. The University will use its own judgment in extending invitations. It may bring a man for a course of lectures, or it may establish another in residence. Mr. Patten believed public education responsible for the growth of our nation.

MISCELLANEOUS

Herman E. Oliphant, A.B., 1909, general counsel of the United States Treasury Department, received the LL.D. in 1936 at Commencement.

On recommendation of O. A. Cora, general commercial engineer of the Indiana Bell Telephone Company, the trustees on April 7, 1936, ordered the installation of a private branch exchange at Indiana University at rates approved by the Public Service Commission of Indiana.

On April 7, 1936, it was decided that when the Departments of Anatomy and Physiology moved into the new Medical Building, Owen Hall should be assigned to the Department of Geology and Geography.

The recommendation of Dean Gatch and Administrator Howe Martin that the official name of the Indianapolis campus be "Indiana University Medical Center," was approved April 7, 1936.

Edmund S. Conklin was appointed head of the Department of Psychology in 1934 on the retirement of Professor William F. Book.

A register of alumni had been prepared for the years 1830–1935 under the supervision and direction of Mrs. John W. Cravens, who was in charge of the Register of Graduates office. This work was continued from June, 1936, under the direction of the Registrar's office. On the recommendation of the President, June, 1936, these important records were transferred to the Archives.

Professor John M. Hill, who joined the faculty in 1916, became head of the Department of Spanish when the Department of Romance Languages was divided in 1934.

In 1936 the construction of a new observatory was begun about two and one-half miles southeast of Bloomington off the Knight Ridge road. It houses a two-foot telescope for photographic purposes, free from interference of night lights of Bloomington.

In the fall of 1935 the Department of Economics and Sociology was divided, with Professor James E. Moffat, who joined the faculty in 1916, heading Economics, and Professor Edwin H. Sutherland chosen for Sociology.

On June 19, 1936, Dean Herman Wells informed the board that the Commission for Financial Institutions of the State of Indiana had asked him to present to them a program of investment counseling that might be offered by the University for the purpose of helping solve this supervisory problem of the Commission. After hearing his proposal the Commission made an informal offer of $5,750 for the nine months, September, 1936, to June, 1937, and $6,500 for the following year as a retainer for service. This proposal was accepted by the board and an Investment Division of the Bureau of Business Research was organized, manned by the faculty of the School of Business.

CHAPTER XLI

THE COURSE OF STUDY, 1824 - 1937

T HE STORY of the course of study of Indiana University consists of two major natural divisions: that prior to 1902, the beginning of the Bryan administration, when, except for a small School of Law, 1842–1877, 1889–1902, the University consisted solely of a College of Liberal Arts, with, in later years, strong emphasis on teacher training; and, the period since 1902, when expansion has consisted in the addition of new departments in the College of Liberal Arts, but chiefly in the development of new schools.

The very detailed factual story of the course of study prior to the Bryan administration, prepared by Professor Lewis C. Carson for *Indiana University, 1820–1904*, is, therefore, almost entirely a story of the development of the curriculum of the College of Liberal Arts. Since this 145-page discussion of the curriculum up to 1904 is available for those interested, this account of the curriculum of that period will be brief and general. Some material derived from sources not previously utilized will be presented and dependence of curricular development upon the economic status of the institution will be emphasized. From this point of view there are three definite periods in the development of the course of study during 1824–1902: 1824–67, 1867–85, and 1885–1902.

THE COLLEGE OF LIBERAL ARTS, 1824–67

During this period the maintenance of the institution was derived from interest on the University Fund (Chap. LIII), supplemented by small fees from students. How very small was the yearly total of student fees in the early years is learned from the report made to the legislature[1] by the treasurer, James Borland, December 10, 1829, which states that between November 26, 1828, and November 28, 1829, student fees amounted to $311.75. The treasurer's report in

---

[1] *Senate Journal*, 1829, p. 56.

1830[2] showed that the receipts for Indiana College in the year 1829–30 were less than $1,000.[3] As Seminary lands were sold and the University Fund increased, interest returns increased. But prior to 1867 interest and fees rarely equaled $7,500.

A report to the legislature[4] by Trustee David H. Maxwell, states that "during the first three years [1824–27 incl.] one teacher only was employed by the trustees, and the Greek and Latin languages alone were taught during that time."

In the spring of 1827 the trustees felt that the time had arrived when a second teacher should be employed. Accordingly, on March 20,1827, the following notice appeared in the *Indiana Journal,* Indianapolis, which reveals the qualifications of a professor of English of that day. This appears to be the first change in the course of study.

STATE SEMINARY NOTICE

A GENTLEMAN of good moral character, and one who is well qualified to teach English Grammar, Geography with the use of Maps and Globes, Natural Philosophy, Trigonometry with its application to Surveying and Navigation; and who can also instruct students in Bookkeeping, is wanted to take charge of the English department in the State Seminary at Bloomington by the 15th day of May next.

The compensation to a teacher at the present time, cannot be very great; but the Trustees of the Institution, hope to have it in their power in a few years to make the superintendence of this department in the Seminary, an object worthy the attention of scientific gentlemen.

By order of the Board of Trustees,
D. H. MAXWELL,
Secretary of Board[5]

P.S. Persons who may wish to correspond with the Board of Trustees, will please to direct their letters to D. H. Maxwell, Bloomington, Indiana.

David D. Banta states that there were a number of applications for this position. John Harney had not only qualifications, but also ideas about education which interested the trustees, so he was employed. It is interesting that instead of getting a professor of English who

[2] *Senate Journal,* 1830, p. 58.
[3] Some salaries, including that of the new president, must have been overdue.
[4] *House Journal,* 1827 (January 2, 1828), p. 284.
[5] He was president of the board, but also served as secretary.

would teach trigonometry, the man chosen was a mathematician who no doubt taught English.[6]

In January, 1828, Dr. Maxwell reported to the chairman of the Committee on Education of the House of Representatives[7] that there were during the "first session of present year [1827–28] twenty-six students, nine of whom studied Mathematical Science only."

Andrew Wylie, elected president of the newly created Indiana College in May, 1928, visited the College sometime in the fall of that year and no doubt made suggestions regarding its organization. But it was not until March 20, 1829, that he finally accepted and it was six months later, October 9, 1829, that he actually arrived in Bloomington to assume his duties. Meantime, Dean Banta tells us, that in the fall of 1828 the trustees required the professors to provide a course of study for the four regular College classes.

A report of the Board of Visitors to Governor Ray, January 1, 1829[8], informs the Governor:

The studies of the Freshman class are, Cicero's Orations, Virgil, Graeca Majora, 1st vol., Adam's Roman Antiquities, Murray's English Grammar, Colburn's Algebra, American Geography, Compositions in English and Latin, Hutton's Geometry.

Those of the Sophomore class are, Walker's Rhetorical Grammar, Horace, Eastern Geography, Hedge's Logic, Blair's Lectures, Graeca Majora, continued, Tytler's Elements of History, Cicero de Oratore, Potter's Grecian Antiquities. The course of studies for the Junior and Senior classes have not yet been established.

It seems, however, that the order of the trustees to provide a four-year course of study was later complied with, for, when President Andrew Wylie arrived in Bloomington, he found a Senior class awaiting him.

President Wylie had been at Indiana College nearly two years when in August, 1831, the first Catalog was published showing a

---

[6] Fifty-eight years later when President Jordan nominated W. L. Bryan as associate professor of English and philosophy, he mentioned Bryan's qualifications as a teacher of logic, rhetoric, composition, philosophy, and history of philosophy, saying, "Mr. Bryan displays a wonderful power in dealing with this class of subjects." Jordan also said that the work of Dr. Bryan was "the best I have ever seen done anywhere" and that he was "one of the most gifted teachers in the state."

[7] *House Journal*, 1827, p. 285.

[8] *Senate Journal*, 1828, p. 229.

considerably changed course of study. The four-year course of study as outlined in that first Catalog was as follows:

Freshman Class

Greek Testament, Minora, Majora 1st vol. Majora 2d vol. commenced. Compositions in English and Latin. Greek Theses.

Sophomore Class

Majora finished, the Iliad. Colburn's Algebra, Cambridge Mathematics. Compositions and Themes, as in the Freshman Class.

Junior Class

Mathematics finished. Mechanics, Astronomy, Physics, Mathematical and Physical Geography. Dissertations, and Themes and Compositions, as before.

Senior Class

Moral and Mental Philosophy, Evidences of Christianity in connexion with Natural Religion, Rhetoric, with a review of select portions of the Greek, Latin and English Classics, Logic, Political Economy, Constitution of the United States. Dissertations, and Composition, in English and Latin.[9]

Each of the four classes attended three recitations or lectures per day. The faculty as announced in that first Catalog of 1831 consisted of the Reverend Andrew Wylie, President and Professor of Moral and Mental Philosophy, Political Economy, and Polite Literature; the Reverend Baynard R. Hall, Professor of Ancient Languages; and Mr. John H. Harney, Professor of Mathematics, Natural and Mechanical Philosophy, and Chemistry. In addition to this faculty of three men, there was a superintendent of the Preparatory Department.

The course in mental and moral philosophy was given by successive presidents until 1885, when President Jordan appointed William Lowe Bryan to teach philosophy and other courses.

In the year 1830–31 the trustees desired to offer courses in chemistry and physics but were handicapped by lack of equipment. In October, 1830,[10] they reported to the legislature that it "is painful to

[9] Hebrew and French were offered by this faculty of three professors, to "such as may wish it and who have completed the Latin course."

[10] *House Journal*, 1830, p. 43.

the Board to be compelled to state that the college has no Philosophical apparaus," and the board had no fund for purchase of such
equipment. It was hoped that the General Assembly would aid with
an appropriation. So far as is known, this was the first vain plea for
supplementary maintenance.

In the Catalog for 1830–31 a course in physics was announced for
the Junior year. The course must have been very elementary. No
course in chemistry was announced, but it was stated that "A chemical and philosophical apparatus has been procured."

In this pitifully inadequate way the work in science was begun.
Much time was to pass before a science course of study coordinate
with the ancient classics course was established. The Catalog of 1840
announced: "The Chemistry lectures as well as those on Natural
Philosophy are illustrated by a course of experiments. A laboratory
and lecture room has recently been erected for the express accommodation of these courses."

In the Catalog of 1854 is printed for the first time the list of courses
necessary to be completed for the degree Bachelor of Science. The
subjects are not arranged by years. German was offered as a special
study. French had been so offered at an earlier date. The Catalog for
1860 states that the scientific courses are the same as those of the
regular course except for the classics. The Catalog for 1860–61 announces that instruction will also be given those who desire it in
French, Hebrew, and German. Later Spanish took the place of
Hebrew.

During the period 1820–67 the legislature had suggested establishment of instruction in law, medicine, and agriculture, but made no
appropriation for this additional work. The legislature of 1852 had
mandated teacher training, described in Chapter XLV. Though a
Department of Law had been established, the sole remuneration of
the professor was, for a time, the fees from students.

THE COLLEGE OF LIBERAL ARTS, 1867–85

In the Catalog published in 1867 there appears the significant
notice:

The above course of study may be modified by the Board of Trustees, at
their coming session, since the Legislature, at their last session, have, by an

appropriation of $8,000 per annum, greatly increased the resources of the University. Some new chairs will likely be established, and the corps of instruction enlarged, and the facilities for education multiplied.

In that year, 1866–67, the faculty consisted of eight professors. The immediate effect of the improved economic status on the course of study will be noted. The legislature of 1869 increased the annual appropriation of the University to $15,000, and the Catalog for 1869–70 calls special attention to the provision for recitations in German every day for two years. Instruction was also given in French. The legislature of 1873 made an *additional annual appropriation* of $15,-000,[11] and in the Catalog of 1873–74 it is specially announced that the Department of Modern Languages had been given equal rank with the Department of Ancient Languages.

By the year 1874–75 three professors had been added to the faculty since 1867 when the first appropriation was made by the state for maintenance of the University. This would not mean much of an addition to a faculty of three hundred or more, but it was a notable increase to a faculty of eight professors.

In 1876–77 the intention to bring the Department of Modern Languages into greater prominence was announced. This was done the following year by offering the Course in Modern Languages leading to the B.L. degree and coordinate with the Classical and Science Courses leading to the degrees A.B. and B.S., respectively.

The short-lived affiliation with the Indiana Medical College was terminated in 1876–77[12] and at the close of the year 1876–77 the Law Course was discontinued by order of the trustees.

Departmental organization begun under the Nutt administration was advanced under the Moss administration, 1875–84, and came into full development with President Jordan.

The College of Liberal Arts, 1885–1902

In the seventeen years between 1885 when Jordan became president and 1902 when the Bryan administration began, the number of departments increased by division and by addition, and within most

---

[11] This was evidently a substitution for the $7,000, for the total received by the University was $23,000 annually.
[12] The Catalog published in the summer of 1876 announced the opening of the Medical Department for October 4, 1876, but whether the affiliation was broken in 1876 or 1877 is unknown.

departments many courses were added. The departmental organization, at first rather indefinite, became thoroughly established by the close of the period.

As illustration of multiplication of departments by division, the Department of Biology was divided into a Department of Zoology and a Department of Botany; the Department of Modern Languages became the Department of Romance Languages and the Department of German; the Department of History became the Department of English History and the Department of American History.

The full story of union and division of history departments follows:

In 1885–86 there was a Department of History and Political Science which the following year became two departments, a Department of History and a Department of Political and Social Science. Political Science held this departmental status for the year 1886–87 only. For five years (1887–92) courses in political science were scheduled along with courses in social science and economics, but in 1892 courses in political science were again given in the Department of American History and continued with the Department of History until 1913 when the Department of Political Science was organized.

In 1886, when History became a department separate from Political Science, it included European history only. In 1888 American history was added with James A. Woodburn as associate professor of American history. In the Catalog of 1890–91 the Department of History became a Department of European History and a Department of American History.

The Catalog of 1892–93 shows a Department of European History and a Department of American History and Politics. The Catalog published in 1895 shows a Department of European History and Institutions and a Department of American History and Politics. One year later courses in European and American history and in political science were offered in the Department of History and Political Science, which continued until 1913 when, as stated above, Political Science was set off as an independent department.

The long-established course in political economy became the Department of Sociology and Economics, and this Department later (1935) became a Department of Economics and a Department of

Sociology. The Departments of Pedagogy, Mechanics and Astronomy, Geology and Geography, Rhetoric and Elocution, and Fine Arts were added. The Department of Rhetoric and Oratory became the Department of English. Although physical training courses were added, they did not have departmental status. In 1889 the School of Law, closed in 1877, was re-established.

The period began with an appropriation of $23,000 from the state, gradually increased to a total of $90,200 in 1901–2. The multiplication of departments reflects this improved economic status.

It is of interest that at the close of the administration of President Moss three Bachelor's degrees were conferred, the A.B., the B.L., and the B.S. But under Jordan the three degrees conferred in 1885–86 were the A.B., Ph.B., and the B.S. The Ph.B. was conferred during the three years, 1886, 1887, and 1888 in spite of the announcement in the Catalog of 1886–87 that the degree A.B. was "the only bachelor's degree now conferred by Indiana University." In actual practice the A.B. degree was the only baccalaureate degree conferred by Indiana University from 1889 to 1913 inclusive.

Curricular Changes During the Bryan Administration

With the inauguration of the Bryan administration (1902–37), expansion of curriculum came through addition of departments to the College of Liberal Arts, through multiplication of courses within departments, but chiefly through the organization of new schools. In organization of new schools nearly every new school owed a great debt to the College of Liberal Arts. In almost every instance the curricula of these new schools consisted, in part, of a group of long-established courses of the College of Liberal Arts, each course being basic to the field of learning of the school. This was a logical elaboration of the group major introduced by Jordan. Superimposed upon these basic courses was the work of a few new departments which revealed and emphasized the professional aspect of the whole group. In some instances these new departments of professional schools also became departments of the College of Liberal Arts.

To the first board meeting of the Bryan administration, September, 1902, the President brought the course of study for consideration. The Student Building, a bothersome project in 1902, would be constructed and put in service and thereafter would be a problem only with respect to routine maintenance. A solution would be found for the alarming smallpox problem. But the consideration of the course of study was to present ever-new aspects, ever-new problems, and from the nature of things would and must continue to be one of the great interests of University administration. At that meeting Dr. Bryan said:

> I have made a study of the occupations of our alumni. At a later time I shall discuss the results in detail. At present I wish to call attention to one principal fact.
>
> From 1830 to 1870, less than ten per cent of our men graduates became teachers. From '71 to '80, fourteen per cent became teachers. From '81 to '90, thirty-nine per cent. From '91 to '95, fifty per cent. From '96 to 1900, sixty-one per cent. To take a single other occupation for comparison: From 1830 to 1870 about forty per cent became lawyers. From '71 to '80, forty per cent. From '81 to '90, twenty-two per cent. From '91 to '95, seventeen per cent. From '96 to 1900, eleven per cent.
>
> This does not include the women graduates, who are practically all teachers or housekeepers. It does not include the graduates in law, unless they were also graduates in the faculty of arts.
>
> I shall not now go further into details. It is obvious, however, that these facts put before us a very important and difficult problem. We are not educating too many teachers. But we are not preparing men for other learned professions in anything like the same proportion. We run the risk of becoming a University Normal School instead of a University. We have met one great modern need of society, that for high school and University teachers, and this is the chief cause of our remarkable growth in the past twenty years. If we are to have the full measure of growth that is possible for us, we must meet equally well, all the needs of society for which the University exists.

Two months later, on November 6, Dr. Bryan continued:

> In my last report I called attention to the fact that within the past ten years more of our alumni have entered the profession of teaching than all other occupations combined and that the disproportion in this regard has been rapidly increasing. I take it for granted no one will be satisfied to have such a state of affairs continue if it can be helped. I believe that it should be our policy to provide as far as we can for the training of men for all the chief occupations which presuppose a University education. As matters stand we have (1) excellent facilities for training teachers, not simply in the department of pedagogy but in all departments. These facilities should by all means be maintained and improved. (2) We have an excellent law school. . . . I

would favor the policy of strengthening the law school to the point of maximum efficiency. (3) We have many courses in zoology, chemistry, bacteriology, physiology, neurology, etc., which are now officially recognized by the best medical schools of the West as first year work in medicine. I hope that the time may not be far distant when by the addition of courses we may have a two year medical school, so that our students could graduate from the best medical schools in the country by two years' professional study. (4) We offer at present some facilities for training for a number of other important established or rising occupations. One who means to be a librarian, a journalist, a business man, a worker in institutions for the pauper or criminal classes, a Y.M.C.A. worker, or a minister, can obtain besides the general college course a considerable amount of work which will tend to prepare him specially for his chosen occupation. It would be possible to increase the facilities in all these fields and it may be advisable to do so at some time within the near future. However, it is evident that we should first do the most necessary things, and that we are not called upon to make doubtful experiments in new fields. In the case of all these professional courses I believe it is a legitimate and wise procedure to allow students to take some such courses as part of their college work.

As indicated in this quotation, President Bryan's earlier study of occupations was now finding a practical application.

At the meeting of the board in March, 1903, the President said:

As a general proposition, it is not essential that we should, as the phrase goes, "cover all the ground." It is not essential that we should have all the different departments which may be included in a university, nor that within any department we should cover all the territory which belongs there.

Let me cite two extreme examples—examples which I should not think of following to the extreme—of what may be done by concentration. Clark University has but five departments, but each of these, when at its best, was conceded to be equal to any in the world.

Dr. Jordan was professor of all the natural sciences here. He deliberately ignored most of his field, gave work to advanced students in nothing but fishes, but sent out more men who became scholars than anyone else has done from this institution.

If it were an original question, I should think that the University would be stronger with a smaller number of departments. We should certainly be slow to add new ones. Within the existing departments we may effect a gradual reorganization by which this may be accomplished by the selection of a smaller number of advanced courses and by the device of giving some advanced courses in alternate years. The resources saved in these ways can be used to raise the level of the collegiate (freshman and sophomore work) and also to permit still more advanced work than we have usually been able to do.

I would not suggest a sudden and general dropping of departments, courses, or men, but that in the readjustments which come each year, we should follow a policy of concentration rather than a policy of expansion. At the present time, for example, there are several changes in this direction.

The President was confronted by an educational situation which disturbed him greatly. Friends of the University had been pleased with its rapid growth during the past seventeen years, but the President's analysis of that growth showed a perilous drift. Various possibilities presented themselves. Which offered the greatest advantage to the University? He called to his assistance certain faculty groups to make special studies of things needed with cost of development of various fields: engineering, journalism, medicine, commerce, etc.

Establishment of the School of Medicine, 1903

The School of Medicine was selected as the first of a series of schools to be organized chiefly because much of the work of the first two years of a medical course had long been given in the College of Liberal Arts. Courses in chemistry, physiology, histology, and embryology, of the College of Liberal Arts, took on a dual status as integral parts of the School of Medicine. Likewise, the new Departments of Anatomy, Physiology, and others, organized to complete the work of the first two years of the School of Medicine, were given a dual status as departments of the College of Liberal Arts.

Since two years of collegiate work were required for entrance on the study of medicine, the precedent of other universities was followed, and on the completion of the two years of premedical work and the first two years' work of the School of Medicine the degree B.S. was granted. This was known as the combined Arts-Medical course. Thus was launched the first of a series of changes in the course of study of Indiana University the combined effect of which was to transform the institution from a College of Liberal Arts to a University in fact.

At the time of the establishment of the School of Medicine (1903) there was very general agreement as to the departments of study of medical schools, but there was considerable variation in the amount of time devoted by various schools to the work of the several departments. With the appointment, in 1902, of the Council on Medical

Education of the American Medical Association a study of curriculum was begun. A Committee of One Hundred, consisting of ten anatomists, ten pathologists, ten surgeons, ten internists, etc., in the year 1908–9, made a report on a standard course of study for schools of medicine. The report was based on the assumption that the four-year course should consist of 4,000 hours' work. The report allocated the number of hours which the committee regarded as proper for each department and suggested the number of hours which should be devoted to lecture, laboratory, and clinics. This report was the guide used in establishment of the work of each department of the School of Medicine.

The adoption of this standard curriculum followed by most schools in organization of medical work greatly increased uniformity of medical work outlined in various schools, and greatly facilitated transfer of students from one school to another of the same grade without loss of time.

Organization of the Graduate School, 1904

The announcement of requirements for graduate degrees which appeared first in the Catalog of 1881–82 was very general. The Master's degree was conferred on completion of the first two years of work in some professional school, or work directed by the faculty or approved by them, in residence or in private. There were no departmental announcements of graduate work. As departments became better organized and course announcements began to be made under the Jordan administration, it is not surprising to find the first course announcement of "Original Research" in 1887–88 in the Department of Zoology of which Jordan was head. But the course was limited to Seniors. Courses in research soon appeared in other departments. Though general announcements of graduate work continued, departmental announcements were limited to "advanced courses" or "research work" without reference to graduate work. Nevertheless, whatever graduate work was done in the pre-Bryan period was done in departments of the College of Liberal Arts.

With the organization, 1904, of the Graduate School, announcements of advanced or research work soon appeared in nearly all departments. In the Catalog for 1906 some departments began to announce certain courses as "courses primarily for graduates." This form of announcement in a few years became very general. In 1908 graduate courses appearing in the departmental announcements of the College of Liberal Arts appeared also in departmental announcements of the Graduate School with identical course numbers, a practice which continued through many years.

The next step in the development was taken when these purely graduate courses in many departments appeared (1917) in the Graduate School only. The evolution of the Graduate School would seem to have been complete. But the Graduate School was manned by staff members of the College of Liberal Arts and was, therefore, largely an extension of the work of that College, known after 1921 as the College of Arts and Sciences.

Curricular changes due to organization of the Graduate School were primarily changes of curriculum of the College of Liberal Arts. From an administrative point of view undergraduate students in the departments of the College of Liberal Arts were under control of the dean of that school who signed their diplomas, whereas graduate students in those same departments were under direction of the dean of the Graduate School, who signed their diplomas.

Meantime, graduate work was becoming a function of all schools in some of which, particularly in the School of Education, considerable numbers were enrolling for graduate work.

Revision of the Course of Study of the College of Liberal Arts, 1906

On April 3, 1905, the President stated to the trustees certain major difficulties confronting the University and reached conclusions of the most vital importance for the future of the institution.

These difficulties were that, like most American universities, Indiana University had expanded too much in the departments of arts and sciences, and that, in contrast with many American universities, Indiana University had expanded too little in professional fields. In support of this conviction, the President submitted three documents.

1. The first was *Indiana University, 1820–1904*,[13] in which he referred to charts prepared by Professors Miller and Bergstrom showing actual expansion in the departments of arts and sciences.

[13] Pp. 48–50.

2. He submitted a table showing which professional schools twelve western state universities had. Indiana University was at the bottom of this list.

3. He resubmitted a manuscript presented first to the board in September, 1902, showing a statistical study of occupations of the graduates of Indiana University. This study showed that in 1900 more of our graduates were entering the teaching field than were entering all other fields combined.

The President concluded:

In my opinion the University's future depends mainly upon a successful change of this situation. The people will make a great University here only upon the condition that the University does many kinds of important things that the people want done. It is useless to discuss this self-evident proposition.

The remedy proposed by the President was a radical change in the course of study, a procedure presenting great difficulties. No serious change in the course of study had been made since Jordan's administration. No one doubted the value of the changes he had introduced. Yet the conviction of the President was so great that he proposed to the faculty a change of course of study whereby the amount of undergraduate work offered by a department should be limited to three years. Each graduate, instead of four years in one department, would have three years in one department and one or more years in some allied department. The President believed that this plan would be better educationally both for those who later became specialists and for those who did not.

Knowing how strongly many faculty members favored the existing organization and expecting spirited opposition, the President was pleased to find acquiescence and in some cases enthusiasm for the plan. A committee of the faculty was appointed to work out in a deliberate and considerate way the revision suggested. A year later, April, 1906, the faculty report was completed and adopted. The 180 hours required for graduation must include the following:

A. Six hours of English Composition.
B. Three hours of Hygiene.
C. Thirty hours of Language.
D. Fifteen hours of Mathematics or Physics.
E. Fifteen hours in some one of the other Sciences.

F. Twenty-four hours from the following subjects: History, Economics, English, Greek, Philosophy, Education, Fine Arts.
G. A major subject and collateral work as follows: (*a*) Forty-five hours within the department elected by the student. (*b*) Thirty hours in closely related departments prescribed by the head of the department. Some exceptions are made to this general rule.
H. Elective work. The student may choose freely enough additional work to make up 180 hours.

The Training School for Nurses, 1914

Instead of using courses of the College of Liberal Arts in the organization of this training school, the University established a combined Arts-Training School course whereby a student who had upon the records of Indiana University ninety hours of credit in the College of Liberal Arts, at least one continuous year of which had been earned in residence at Indiana University, might, under specified conditions, qualify for the A.B. degree and complete the nurses' training course in two years and four months. If the student had not met specific requirements for the A.B. degree but had the subjects prescribed for the B.S. degree, the candidate might receive that degree. The work of the training school was shortened a few months for these young women with collegiate training. The purpose of this arrangement was to encourage University young women to take this nurses' training course.

Organization of the School of Commerce and Finance, 1920

Though a two-years' course in commercial subjects was established in 1902, it was not until March, 1920, that the School of Commerce and Finance was organized. An inspection of the faculty of this school, 1920, shows how fully existing courses of the College of Liberal Arts contributed to its establishment. In a faculty of twenty-nine, twenty-seven were members, some of long standing, in the College of Liberal Arts, one was a member of the faculty of the School of Law, and one, an instructor in stenography and typewriting, was newly added. Other professional appointees were added later.

The degree B.S. in Commerce and Finance, with diploma signed by Dean Rawles, was conferred on those who completed one of the prescribed courses (1921—). This School grew remarkably and in 1936–37 reached an enrollment slightly under that of the whole University at the time Bryan became president, 1902.

Organization of the School of Music, 1921

University credit in certain courses in music was first granted in the year 1910–11 following the establishment of Music as a Department of the College of Liberal Arts in 1910. With the establishment of a School of Music in 1921, the degrees Bachelor of Music, Master of Music, and the degree Bachelor of Arts with Music as major subject began to be conferred. The impress of the College of Arts and Sciences on this School of Music was marked, not for what the former contributed to the organization of the latter but for postponement of the granting of credit in the College for applied music courses.

Establishment of the School of Education, 1923

Instruction in the theory and practice of teaching, given in the Normal Department of Indiana University, established by order of the General Assembly of 1852,[14] was provided entirely by the faculty of the College of Liberal Arts until the work was suspended in 1857. In the late sixties another short-lived effort was made to organize teacher training.

This work was permanently established in 1886 in the College of Liberal Arts as a Department of Pedagogy, which, after several changes, became in 1904 the Department of Education. As the professor in charge of this work, the President was in part responsible for creation of the situation in which so high a percentage of graduates of Indiana University became teachers, a matter which in the early days of his presidency was giving him grave concern.

When the legislature of 1907 made a more formal organization of this educational training necessary, the work was expanded and organized as a School of Education in June, 1908. But the title was misleading, for the status of this work remained departmental. Students completed the work of the School of Education as a major subject and received the A.B. degree from the College of Liberal

[14] Note board action on October 4, 1851 (Chap. XLV, p. 543).

Arts with education as major, just as they had done under departmental organization of this work, 1886 to 1908. And this situation continued until May, 1923, when the School of Education was formally recognized by the trustees as a separate school with the same status as other schools of the University. After reorganization under this new status the School of Education began giving its own degrees in 1925.

After teachers' training instruction was re-established in 1886, this training until 1923, a period of thirty-seven years, was a function of the College of Liberal Arts (College of Arts and Sciences after 1921).

The Dental School Curriculum, 1925

The curriculum of the School of Dentistry, taken over as a part of Indiana University in 1925, received no contribution from the College of Liberal Arts such as the School of Medicine had received on its organization. In 1925 students were admitted from accredited high schools. In 1926 one year of collegiate work and in 1937 two years of collegiate work were added to the high school requirement.

Revisions and Changes in College of Arts and Sciences, 1929–31

The faculty of the College of Arts and Sciences in the spring of 1929 established a system of Reading for Honors, based on the Swarthmore plan. Though regarded as educationally sound and desirable, the plan came into disuse, chiefly because of the work imposed on a teaching staff already heavily loaded. In the same spring a committee was appointed by the President to study the curricula of a considerable number of colleges and universities, with a view to improving the curriculum of Indiana University, which had been adopted in 1906. Revised entrance requirements, comprehensive examinations at graduation, and sharper discrimination between the work of the first two years (Freshman and Sophomore) and that of the last two years (Junior and Senior) of the college course were among the subjects under special investigation.

The report was discussed by the faculty of the College of Arts and Sciences at ten meetings, from November 4, 1930, to March 3, 1931.

The report as finally adopted revised entrance requirements. For many years the sixteen units of high school work required for admission had been divided as follows:

A. Prescribed subjects, 11 units.
  1. English, 3 units.
  2. Mathematics, 2 units (algebra, 1 unit; plane geometry, 1 unit).
  3. Foreign language, 2 units in one language.
  4. History, 1 unit.
  5. Science, 1 unit in one science (general science not accepted).
  6. Two additional units, selected from the above subjects.
B. Elective subjects, 5 units.

In the revised requirements A 1-5 was unchanged. But in B, three units were required from Group A 1-5 leaving four units as free elective. Another social science could be offered instead of history.

The College aptitude rating was required of all entering students.

In addition to revised entrance requirements, certain new principles and procedures were adopted which are still (1940) in use.

The new requirement in English composition made it possible for a student to be freed from all required class work in English, or from some part of it, provided he passed an exemption examination. Failing to pass the exemption examination, he would be required to continue in class work in English composition until his work satisfied the Department of English. There was also this provision:

All students in the College of Arts and Sciences will be given, in addition, at the beginning of the Junior year, an examination to test their ability to use good English. Those unable to demonstrate such ability will be required to do further course work without credit. No student will be granted the A.B. degree until he has passed this Junior examination in English composition.

The new foreign language requirement would be satisfied if the student passed a proficiency examination demonstrating his ability to read moderately difficult prose in the language offered.

The new science requirement provided that the student distribute his fifteen hours of science in such a way that he gain some knowledge of both physical and biological science. Under the old requirement, though the science work had to be in two departments, those two departments might both be in the biological sciences or in the physical science group.

There were also adopted a considerably expanded social science requirement and a new requirement in literature, philosophy, and the arts. Under the old rules each student was required to take fourteen hours in social science or in literature, or the hours might be distributed between the two groups of studies. Under the 1931 rules the total requirement was eighteen hours, of which at least six were to be completed in each group.

It will be noted that in English composition and foreign language, achievement was substituted for the mere accumulation of hours of credit. In the other requirements the aim was to provide rather more broadly the fundamentals of a liberal education.

Departments Added to the College of Arts and Sciences, 1902–37

During the Bryan administration there were added to the College of Arts and Sciences, the Departments of Anatomy, Comparative Philology, Home Economics, Hygiene, Journalism, Physical Education, Physiology, Psychology, and Spanish. The Department of Mechanics and Astronomy was divided. Astronomy became a separate department. Mechanics was in part discontinued and in part was taken over by the Department of Mathematics and in part by the Department of Physics. The Department of History and Political Science became the Department of History and the Department of Political Science, later called Government.

Relation of the School of Law to the College of Liberal Arts

Though the School of Law had been established (1842–77; 1889—) sixty years prior to the Bryan administration and had maintained its curriculum quite independently of the College of Liberal Arts, it was during the Bryan administration that a combined Arts-Law Course was authorized whereby a student might receive the A.B. degree with law as major subject. This combined course consisted of two years of work in the College of Liberal Arts and two years of work in the School of Law. On the completion of this course the student was eligible for admission to the third year of the

School of Law. The arrangement made it possible to secure the A.B. and LL.B. degrees in five years.

In 1909 one year and in 1910 two years of collegiate work were required for admission to the School of Law. In 1910 a course was announced whereby the student might obtain the A.B. and the LL.B. degrees in six years instead of five. The minimum requirement for admission to the School of Law continued to be two years of collegiate work until May, 1934. Students who began collegiate preparation for admission to the School of Law subsequent to May, 1934, were required to present three years of that work for admission.

Journalism

The establishment of a School of Journalism has been proposed and considered from time to time since the first decade of this century. The status of this field of instruction as a department of the College of Liberal Arts was first announced in the Catalog for 1915.

The gradual development of this work to departmental status is typical. The first announcement of this work (1907) was as "Special Courses" following Departmental announcements. Here was outlined a four-year course of study which included all requirements for the A.B. degree and also the special courses in journalism. The work was to be taken with English, history, or economics as major subject. In the 1910 Catalog, these courses were indexed with departments and announced with departmental announcements, but without departmental status; then, as stated above, the work, in 1915, was given departmental status. These developments since 1907 were the result of a growing demand for this work. The demand, however, never was sufficiently great to warrant the next step in this development, which would have been the organization of the work as a school of journalism.

Extension Division and Summer Session

The organization of the Extension Division and establishment of the summer session under a director did not add new courses, departments, or schools, but utilized regularly established courses of the College of Liberal Arts and other schools, which were given at some center off the campus or in the summer period on the campus.

Comment

In describing the organization of new schools by grouping certain long-established courses, the procedure has been oversimplified. In many instances, courses were modified in varying degrees. Let me cite a few illustrations from a field I know best.

In the year 1902–3 Dr. Moenkhaus had given a course in physiology as a member of the Department of Zoology. In 1903–4 the course was modified by giving emphasis to human physiology and was organized as a separate department of the School of Medicine with Dr. Moenkhaus as head.

Prior to 1903 embryology also was given in the Department of Zoology. This course generally throughout America was given by the Department of Anatomy of the School of Medicine as a course of the Freshman medical year. Dr. Eigenmann had accepted the loss of physiology and Dr. Moenkhaus from his Department in good spirit; but at the prospect of losing embryology also he was unhappy. His course was like other courses in this subject in that day, as given in Departments of Biology or Zoology. It began with fertilization. Cell division was illustrated by use of amphibian eggs, and the course ended with the embryology of the chick. Dr. Eigenmann now consented to the addition of mammalian embryology as illustrated by serial sections of a graded series of pig embryos. With this modification, the course met the needs of medical students and was continued in the Department of Zoology as a required premedical course. This procedure was an innovation and necessitated explanation for a few years, but in a decade or two it was adopted by a considerable number of medical schools.

Professor Foley, knowing that the largest group of his students were premedics, volunteered to change the laboratory work for this group by selecting experiments in optics, acoustics, mechanics, electricity, X-ray, etc., of particular interest and value for students expecting to study medicine. He insisted that the laboratory work in physics had been determined in most schools by the needs of engineering students.

Comparable changes and additions were made in the organization of other schools. Meanwhile in the College of Arts and Sciences more and more students were taking only two years' work as premedical, predental, prelaw students. There have been those who, like C. A. Prosser, of the Dunwoody Institute, Minneapolis, have envisioned this as the future of the arts and sciences college in state universities, but that day does not appear imminent.

During the thirty-five years of the Bryan administration, courses, departments, and schools were established in response to a social need, in so far as University income made that possible. Earlier in this chapter President Bryan has been quoted as saying:

I believe it should be our policy to provide, as far as we can, for the training of men for all the chief occupations which presuppose a University education.

The people will make a great University here only upon the condition that the University does many kinds of important things that the people want done.

This policy and conviction are clearly traceable throughout the thirty-five years of the Bryan administration. Bryan believed that opening pathways leading to opportunity for young people to train for useful careers was the mission of democracy. This point of view is repeated in the leading editorial in the *Indianapolis Star* of September 11, 1945:

America is where it is today because this is a land of opportunity and initiative, not one of regimentation. The declaration on which we established our republic is that men "are endowed by their Creator with certain inalienable rights, that among these are life, liberty, and the pursuit of happiness."

It is the right and privilege of every American to make most of his ability and opportunities. The government, under our theory, does not promise to make him happy. The inalienable right to "the pursuit of happiness" is guaranteed to him. Then it is up to him.

The organization of schools and changes of curriculum under the authority of and by the action of the Board of Trustees were not always accomplished with unanimous faculty approval. There were those of the faculty in 1902 who believed that the organization of any new school would be financed by funds which should be expended for expansion and strengthening the College of Arts and Sciences. The opposition, however, was never organized and never represented more than a small percentage of the faculty. The opposition to the School of Education was, I think, most intense.

A beneficent circle of events followed the establishment of opportunity for training as follows:

1. Students came to avail themselves of the opportunity, and numbers increased until

2. Greater facilities for training became desirable, then necessary, which called for

3. An increased legislative appropriation to finance expansion of facilities.

4. The increased appropriation finally was made and the expansion of facilities provided.

With expansion of facilities there were increased enrollments and the circle of events, 1, 2, 3, 4, was repeated, and so on until facilities were adequate for instruction of those seeking this opportunity.

The lag in the circle of events shown above came at 4 (legislative appropriation). It was only by the most vigorous and continuous presentation of University needs to Governor, Budget Committee, members of the General Assembly, and the people of the state, by President and trustees, assisted by informed friends, faculty, students, and alumni, that appropriations were kept semi-adequate.

There was always the hope that the time would come when state support of higher education in Indiana (i.e., the state appropriations for Indiana and Purdue University combined) would equal the appropriations made by neighboring North Central states.

In establishment of the School of Business, the circle of events, 1, 2, 3, and 4, referred to above was repeated under pressure of the demand of the young people of Indiana for business training.

In the School of Medicine, growth for a time was slow, then it became more rapid, until in the early twenties the number of applicants for matriculation began to exceed capacity.

Education, fortunately, is not static, but is constantly growing, expanding. As new fields of knowledge are developed, old fields are abridged, or crowded out, and their values largely lost. Words, however, continue to be the medium for communication of ideas to others, and we continue to turn to the ancient classics in coining new words for new ideas or things, and for understanding of the words derived from the ancient languages in centuries past. We speak of them as dead languages, but they live in the vocabulary of every science, and have utility value justifying far greater consideration than they receive in these midyears of the twentieth century.

CHAPTER XLII

THE YEAR 1936 - 37

NINETEEN THIRTY-SIX being an even year, the President, for the eighteenth time during his administration, was faced by the necessity of interpreting the needs of the University to the Governor and legislature in such manner as to win the means by which the University in fuller measure might provide the more adequate opportunities and facilities for the education of Hoosier young men and women.

The President and trustees were intermediaries between the student body and the University on one hand, and the legislature on the other hand, and were charged with the responsibility of presenting the needs of the former to the latter of these bodies which held the purse strings. The legislators in turn had long been intermediaries between the agencies and institutions of the state on the one hand and the people back home in Indiana. They heard the requests of state institutions for more liberal support, but they also heard the demands of the people back home for economy of administration and keeping down taxes. In such a situation the request for increased support had to carry conviction.

Theoretically, in a democracy, the people get what the majority wants. Chapter XXXVII shows how inadequately the people of Indiana supported their institutions of higher education as compared with neighboring states. Did this mean that Indiana citizens wanted underfinanced institutions of higher education? Not at all. They didn't know they had them. They were the same Indiana citizens who, a score of years earlier, met every quota of soldiers and sailors, doctors and nurses, and oversubscribed every Liberty Loan and Red Cross drive when they were fully informed and convinced of the need.

University officials knew this and for a decade had been putting on a campaign of education, confident that if the people fully understood the needs of modern higher education they would respond as generously as neighboring states which, like Indiana, had been carved out of the same great Northwest Territory. It was with this conviction that the President had prepared his biennial report and on October 19, 1936, addressed it to Edward P. Brennan, Director of the Budget[1], with a letter which we quote:

I beg to submit herewith our budget requests for Indiana University, both the Bloomington and Indianapolis divisions, for the biennium 1937–39.

This represents an honest appraisal of our needs. Each department head was asked to submit what, in his best judgment, was needed to operate his department. In light of the knowledge that we have of these various department needs, we edited the requests, bringing them in line with the needs of the University as a whole and making reductions wherever possible.

We are asking an increase in operating expenses for the following reasons:

1. Our people have not had their salaries restored after the cut in 1932. We understand all other state salaries have been restored. This is all the more important now because of the increased cost of living with which you are familiar. An increase of approximately twenty per cent is requested.

2. Our enrollment has increased from 1931, when we were operating on a budget of $1,875,000, from 4,479 students to the present enrollment of 5,548 students. This, of course, necessitates more teachers, more equipment, and more classroom space. We are asking for an increase over this amount of only twenty per cent, while our enrollment has increased approximately twenty-four per cent,

3. We have extra expense for the upkeep of our five new buildings, four on the Bloomington campus and one in Indianapolis.

4. We have an item of $90,000 per year for needed repairs. During the depression we were unable to keep these up as they should have been.

5. We have an increased expense because of the bond retirement of our new buildings and interest charges.

We have included in this request $185,000 per year for necessary capital outlay. We have also set up as an additional item $500,500 for capital outlay, which is desperately needed, but which will not have to go into the budget if the Educational Improvement Fund[2] is allowed to remain on the statutes.

Indiana University ranks with the best universities in America. The people of Indiana are not willing that by undue restriction of resources their University should ever fall below that rank, to the grave detriment of their children.

Respectfully submitted,
William Lowe Bryan.

[1] A position created by the 1935 legislature.
[2] This refers to the 2-cent tax for new buildings for the educational institutions of the state, passed in 1927. The special legislative session of 1932 suspended this tax for the years 1932, 1933, and 1934, and the moratorium had been continued for two more years.

	1937–38		1938–39	
	Detail	Net	Detail	Net
Bloomington and Extension—				
operating	$1,870,030		$1,870,030	
Stores building—a/c Fire Marshal's recommendation to remove Assembly Hall	50,000		50,000	
Raising University dam to provide adequate water supply	30,000		30,000	
Needed building repairs outlined...	90,000		90,000	
Walks, drives, landscaping—a/c new buildings.....................	15,000		15,000	
Total...............	$2,055,030		$2,055,030	
Less estimated income from fees and Permanent Endowment interest..	338,800		338,800	
		$1,716,230		$1,716,230
Indianapolis — operating School of Medicine, Robert W. Long Hospital, and Training School for Nurses	345,795		345,795	
Less estimated income from student and patient fees...............	95,795		95,795	
		250,000		250,000
James Whitcomb Riley Hospital....	374,865		374,865	
Less estimated per diem income....	299,865		299,865	
		75,000		75,000
William H. Coleman Hospital.....	129,700		129,700	
Less estimated income from patient fees	29,700		29,700	
		100,000		100,000
Clinical Building	40,755		40,755	
Equipment for portion of building being completed under present plans	27,500		27,500	
		68,255		68,255
Total School of Medicine and Hospitals..................		($493,255)		($493,255)
School of Dentistry..............	103,675		103,675	
Less estimated income from student and clinic fees..................	53,675		53,675	
		50,000		50,000
Net operating request........		$2,259,485		$2,259,485

	1937–38 Detail	Net	1938–39 Detail	Net
Capital outlay requests: If the Education Improvement Fund is not allowed to remain on the statutes, the following should be provided in the annual budget for capital outlay:				
Completion of Clinical Building (see detailed outline under Medical Center request).....	$50,000		$50,000	
Equipment of Clinical Building (see detailed outline under Medical Center request).....	12,500		12,500	
Necessary changes ordered by the State Fire Marshal at Medical Center (see Schedule B under Medical Center request)	63,000		63,000	
Classroom building to relieve congested conditions at Bloomington	375,000	500,500	375,000	500,500
Grand total requests.........		$2,759,985		$2,759,985

The legislature for 1937 appropriated for each year of the biennium 1937–38, 1938–39, for maintenance $1,890,000, about 15 per cent less than requested ($2,259,485). For capital outlay, instead of the $500,500 requested, a mere token appropriation, $20,000, or 4 per cent of the asking, was made for 1937–38, and $30,000, 6 per cent for 1938–39. There was, however, an increase over the 1931 appropriation ($1,800,000).

In addition to these appropriations, there was in the General Appropriation Bill of 1937 an item of $50,000 for each year of the biennium 1937–39 for pensions and annuities at Indiana University. This made possible the establishment at Indiana University of a contributory pension and retirement system by a resolution of the trustees on May 18, 1937, effective as of July 1, 1937. This important action, which had been proposed first in 1906, had been considered from time to time since that date and now was brought to a satisfactory conclusion. See Chapter XLIV.

BUILDING PROJECTS INITIATED IN 1936–37

The building activity on the campus in the year 1936–37 was very great. Construction of the seven major buildings described in the next chapter had progressed to the extent that during the year five were accepted as completed as follows:

The power plant extension......................October 2, 1936
Forest Hall ....November 6, 1936
Music Building ....January 5, 1937
Administration Building ....February 9, 1937
Medical Building (Bloomington)................June 14, 1937

The School of Education Building and the Clinical Building (at Indianapolis) were not completed until 1938.

In the closing months and even days of the Bryan administration additional building projects minor in character as compared with those above were initiated and authorized, but actual construction was not begun until after retirement of President Bryan. Most important of these were the new lounge of the Union Building, the women's swimming pool, and the Stores Building.

THE NEW LOUNGE OF THE UNION BUILDING

The first of these projects was the new lounge of the Union Building, which covered part of the north terrace. Preliminary plans were received from Granger and Bollenbacher on October 2, 1936. The architects were requested to prepare a pencil sketch of the north elevation of the Union Building as it would appear with this lounge added.

On November 6 the President was authorized to file an application to the United States of America through the Federal Emergency Administration of Public Works, the PWA, for a grant to aid in financing the construction of an addition to the Union Building, and was designated to furnish such information as the government might request.

Action on this application was slow, and it was not until July 1, 1938, that a grant to aid in this construction was made for 45 per cent of cost, but not exceeding $21,234. This offer was accepted, plans and specifications completed, and an attractive lounge for men was constructed, including provision for display of trophies previously housed in the Men's Gymnasium. The University's share of the cost was paid from a surplus in the Union Building sinking fund.

WOMEN'S SWIMMING POOL

For some years a more adequate swimming pool for women had been needed. On June 11, 1937, one of the last few days of the last session of the Board of Trustees under the Bryan administration, Architects McGuire and Shook were engaged to prepare plans and specifications for a new pool to be located in an addition to the Student Building. It is interesting to note that one of the first major problems of William Lowe Bryan as president of Indiana University was that of erection of this Student Building and that authorization of an addition to this building was one of the last official acts of his administration.

This project was completed with use of WPA labor in demolition of the north wall of the Gymnasium wing of the Student Building and by aid of a grant of $30,000 made by the State Budget Committee from the State Capital Outlay Fund.

THE STORES BUILDING

Another building of this closing year of the Bryan administration was the Stores Building, which had become a "must" project when the old Men's Gymnasium, or Assembly Hall, was judged a fire hazard and its removal recommended. Trustee Wildermuth and Comptroller Biddle were appointed as a committee to make recommendation on location, size, and general construction of a Stores and Service Building.

It was recognized that this building should be close to the power plant. Since it could not be located east of that plant without impairing the use of Jordan Field, it was recommended that the site north of the power plant, occupied by the carpenter shop, the plumbing shop, garages, etc. should be utilized.

Plans were prepared by Architect A. M. Strauss providing for housing the carpenter, plumbing, and electrical shops, office and stores of the superintendent of buildings and grounds, and stores of the comptroller's office. On June 14, 1937, it was decided to proceed with the erection of this Stores and Service Building at a total cost not to exceed $85,000 for the completed project. This building was erected without aid of a PWA grant but was paid for by an allotment of $85,000 made by the State Budget Committee out of the State Capital Outlay Fund.

As Bryan inherited the project of the Student Building from his predecessor, he now left these three minor projects as an inheritance to his successor.

THE PASSING OF ASSEMBLY HALL

An inspection had been made of Assembly Hall by the fire inspector and the chief of the Bloomington Fire Department, and its early removal had been recommended.

This wooden structure had served as an Assembly Hall and a gymnasium for men from 1896 to 1917. Its architecture was much better adapted for use as an assembly hall than as a gymnasium. The pitch of the seats in the balcony was good enough for audience use, but the pitch was so slight that no one back of the first row of balcony seats could see the playing floor. When the New Gymnasium for Men was completed, the use of this old building as an Assembly Hall was continued, the basement was used as a storesroom, 1917–1938, and the building was commonly called the old Men's Gym. With the completion of the new Stores and Service Building, this important stores function would be lost, and Alumni Hall in the Union Building was minimizing the use of the old building as an Assembly Hall.

When erected in 1896 it had stood somewhat apart from University buildings proper. But in recent years new buildings had been erected on every side, in the midst of which stood this wooden relic of earlier years, now considered a fire hazard. It was, therefore, not surprising that on June 14, 1937, the trustees decided that as soon as the Stores and Service Building was completed, Assembly Hall should be razed. Its demolition was begun in the late summer of 1938, and the site of this old landmark which had known the voices of top-flight singers, orators, and actors, as well as of athletes, became a parking lot. *Sic gloria mundi transit.*

The President's Resignation

It had been the purpose of President Bryan to present his resignation in the spring of 1936, shortly after his seventy-fifth birthday (November 11), but a wholly unexpected complication arose in connection with insurance matters pending the adjustment of which the President postponed his resignation.

We have told of a foursome of golf which included President Bryan on his seventy-fifth birthday in which he played twenty-seven holes at the Indianapolis Country Club without fatigue. He was in excellent physical condition and there was no slow-down in his perceptions or judgments.

In the spring of 1937 there were no matters pending making further delay desirable. Accordingly, on March 15, 1937, he addressed the following communication to the Board:

To the Honorable, the Board of Trustees of Indiana University
Mr. President, Mrs. Teter, Gentlemen:

I present herewith my resignation as president of Indiana University with the request that my service may close at the early convenience of the Board of Trustees.

I take this occasion to express my grateful appreciation for the unfailing friendliness and support which the Board of Trustees has given me. I have deeper cause for satisfaction as I retire from this office because of my assurance that the control of the University is in the best of hands. I have served as president under twenty-six trustees. Throughout these changes nothing has changed the disinterested devotion of the Board of Trustees to the highest interest of Indiana University.
Respectfully submitted,
William Lowe Bryan.

Judge Wildermuth moved, with great regret, that the resignation of President Bryan be accepted to take effect at a date to be determined later, but upon condition that the President and Mrs. Bryan continue to occupy the President's House which their generous contribution helped to build, and that Dr. Bryan be given the title of president emeritus of Indiana University, and that his present salary be continued during his life. The motion was seconded by all the other trustees present, and was unanimously carried. The honorary degree LL.D. was conferred upon President Bryan at the June Commencement, 1937.

The President on May 18, 1937, refused the generous provision made for his retirement, but on the urgence of Mr. Ball and other members of the Board of Trustees on June 10, 1937, he accepted less than half of the annual salary, and asked that $6,750 of the amount voted him be retained each year in the treasury of the University at the disposition of the trustees.

On May 25 a dinner was given for President Bryan in the Congress Hotel, Chicago, at which President Bryan, Judge Wildermuth, Vice-President of the Board of Trustees, President Edward C. Elliott, of Purdue University, and others spoke.

On May 27 in Alumni Hall a farewell dinner to the Bryans was given under the sponsorship of the A.A.U.P. Dean Fernandus Payne, of the Graduate School, presided. Professor Robert E. Lyons, who had become an instructor in Indiana University in 1889, spoke for the faculty, and Dean Gatch spoke on the character and career of W. L. Bryan. President and Mrs. Bryan responded. Presentations, addresses, and responses, all of which were of unusual interest, were published in the *Alumni Quarterly* for 1937, pages 353-62, inclusive.

The retirement of William Lowe Bryan marked the end of a period of the history of Indiana University. Men on the Board of Trustees and the administrative staff after long and devoted service were being succeeded by younger and equally devoted men. On the faculty, men who had been young when Bryan was inaugurated had reached, or were approaching, retirement age.

Along with President Bryan, Treasurer Smith and Professors Vos, Osthaus, and Roddy, and, at Indianapolis, Dr. Frank F. Hutchins, had resigned, effective as of June 30, 1937. Under the new retirement plan, Professors Davisson, Rothrock, Hanna, Morris, Jotilda Conklin, Mottier, Foley, Piercy, Merrill, and Geiger, and, at Indianapolis, Alan Hendricks, Librarian of the School of Medicine, were eligible for retirement on June 30, 1937.[3] Dr. William Niles Wishard had retired in the fall of 1936.

Since a dozen other department heads or major professors would reach retirement age in the next five years it was evident not only that the period was one of great change, but that the responsibility of the successor to President Bryan would be very great.

[3] A few of these persons were held beyond the normal date of their retirement.

Election of an Acting President

On May 27, 1937, Herman B Wells, Dean of the School of Business Administration, was elected acting president, beginning July 1, 1937, on the retirement of President Bryan, June 30, 1937. An advisory committee consisting of Ward G. Biddle, Fernandus Payne, William A. Alexander, and Henry L. Smith was appointed to confer with the Acting President at his request and to serve at the pleasure of the trustees.

Miscellaneous

On October 12, 1936, Dean Myers presented to the trustees a letter from Major General W. E. Cole, Commander of the 5th Corps Area, Columbus, Ohio, inviting Indiana University to apply for establishment of a Medical R.O.T.C. unit. Ninety hours of work a year were required. A minimum of fifty students was necessary for establishment of the unit, which was authorized by the trustees. It was expected to establish more advanced work for this unit during the following year at Indianapolis.

A Bureau of Government Research was established in the fall of 1936 under direction of Professor Pressly S. Sikes. The Bureau offers its facilities for various units of government, federal, state, and municipal.

On January 5, 1937, the University purchased land between the University property and Jordan Avenue. These lots, 150 feet deep, became the "front yard" of the Education Building.

The Workmen's Compensation Act of 1915 to which reference was previously made (Chap. XV) was repealed by the Workmen's Compensation Act of 1929. Workmen's compensation insurance was carried from 1930 to 1935 on employees at the Long, Riley, and Coleman Hospitals. On August 5, 1936, the trustees authorized the discontinuance of that insurance. On February 8, 1937, they authorized the purchase of workmen's compensation insurance, covering all employees of the University, in the United States Fidelity and Guaranty Company. This insurance has been in force continuously in the company since that date.

Permission was given the congregation of First Methodist Church to use Alumni Hall on Sundays from April 12, 1937, through June, their beautiful church building having been destroyed by fire.

On June 11, 1937, action was taken providing for the purchase of the Luther Institute building in Fort Wayne as a home for the Extension Division of the University in that city.

In 1937 Comptroller Biddle was elected secretary to the trustees, effective as of July 1, and Registrar Thomas Cookson was elected treasurer.

On November 6, 1936, Olmsted Brothers were requested to make a planting plan for the Union Building and vicinity, Memorial Hall, Music Building, Medical Building, Administration Building, Library, and vicinity, and a plan for widening the entrance to the campus at Kirkwood Avenue; further, the services of Olmsted Brothers, including George Lewis, who was in direct charge of their work on the campus, were to be dispensed with on December 15.

In 1936 Professor Ford P. Hall was made head of the Department of Government after serving as acting head for two years.

Malcolm MacLaren, Jr., took over the work in Greek in 1936 on the retirement of Professor Frank W. Tilden.

On May 18, 1937, word was received that preparations had been completed by which three foreign student exchanges could be established at Indiana University for 1937–38. Beta Theta Pi would give board and room to a Swiss student; Phi Delta Theta to an English student; and Phi Kappa Psi to a German student. The University granted scholarships for these three students for 1937–38.

At Commencement, 1937, the LL.D. was conferred upon Frank Aydelotte and Josiah K. Lilly, Sr., in addition to William Lowe Bryan, mentioned earlier.

A campaign for a fund for fellowships and scholarships in honor of President Bryan was inaugurated in the spring of 1937 by the Indiana University Foundation.

CHAPTER XLIII

THE BUILDING PROGRAM, 1934 - 37

THE CLOSING years of the Bryan administration were remarkable for an extensive program of construction of long overdue, substantial administrative and classroom buildings.

THE ALPHABETICAL EMERGENCY RELIEF AGENCIES AT INDIANA UNIVERSITY

It will be recalled that the Roosevelt administration, 1933–45, was only a few months old when, either by act of Congress or by executive order, a number of emergency relief agencies were created which had a very important influence on the building program and on student employment at Indiana University during the terminal years of the Bryan administration and several years afterwards.

Essential facts concerning five of these emergency relief agencies show the relation of Indiana University to these agencies and may do away with some of the confusion which most people find in them.

FERA

The first of these agencies to be established was the Federal Emergency Relief Administration (the FERA), created by an act of Congress, approved May 12, 1933. The purpose of the act was to cooperate with states, territories, and the District of Columbia in relieving hardships caused by unemployment and drought. It expired June 30, 1938, having been liquidated by the WPA in accordance with provisions of the Emergency Relief Appropriation Act of 1937. (*U.S. Government Manual*, Fall, 1942, p. 611.)

PWA

The Federal Emergency Administration of Public Works was established pursuant to title II of the National Industrial Recovery Act, approved June 16, 1933. Subsequent legislation continued its

515

operation and the Public Works Appropriation Act of 1938, approved June 21, 1938, authorized the continuance of those operations until June 30, 1942. The Independent Office Appropriation Bill for the fiscal year 1943 extended the life of the Public Works Administration to June 30, 1943.

By Part 3 of the President's Reorganization Plan 1, effective July 1, 1939, the Federal Emergency Administration of Public Works and its functions were consolidated into the Federal Works Agency, and it was provided that the Administration and its functions should be administered as the Public Works Administration with a commissioner of public works at the head thereof who should act under the direction and supervision of the Federal Works Administration.

The purpose of the PWA program was to promote and stabilize employment and purchasing power by encouraging the construction of useful public work projects through the making of loans or grants to non-federal public bodies, also to promote interest in long-range planning in the field of public works. (*U.S. Government Manual,* Fall, 1942, p. 407.)

CWA

The Civil Works Administration was established November 9, 1933, by Executive Order, to provide regular jobs on public works for four million unemployed men and women. The function of employment expired July 1, 1934. Function of settling claims continued under WPA. (*U.S. Government Manual,* Fall, 1942, p. 611.)

WPA

The Works Progress Administration was established by Executive Order, May 6, 1935, under the authority of the Emergency Relief Appropriation Act of 1935 and was continued by subsequent yearly acts. The name was changed to Work Projects Administration on July 1, 1939. Subsequent acts extended the Work Projects Administration to June 30, 1943.

The WPA was established to operate in cooperation with local, state, and federal sponsors, a program of useful public works projects and to aid employable needy persons by providing work on such projects. (*U.S. Government Manual,* Fall, 1942, p. 408.)

Offices of the Work Projects Administration were established in each state. A statement of funds available and the types of public projects approved can be found in the *U.S. Government Manual,* Fall, 1942, p. 409.

NYA

The National Youth Administration was established within the Works Progress Administration by Executive Order, June 26, 1935, under authority of the Emergency Relief Appropriation Act of 1935. It was transferred from the WPA to the Federal Security Agency, effective July 1, 1939. Authority and funds for the fiscal year 1943 are provided in the NYA Appropriation Act, 1943.

The NYA operated two programs for youth of ages sixteen to twenty-four:

1. The War Production Training Program.

2. The Student Work Program, which provided part-time employment for needy students in schools, colleges, and universities to enable them to continue properly their education. (For Student Work Program, see *U.S. Government Manual,* Fall, 1942, p. 380.)

Student Employment at Indiana University Under FERA and NYA

On January 3, 1934, the trustees authorized an appropriation of $4,000 to provide employment for needy students.

During the second semester of 1933–34, i.e., from approximately February 1 to early June, FERA funds amounting to $21,414.40 were made available and used for student employment.

Just when and through whose influence the idea of making work relief funds available for students who needed to defray part of the expenses of their education by work it is difficult to say. The need was very general and no doubt the idea presented itself at essentially the same time in a number of places.

One version attributes to Chancellor Ernest H. Lindley, of the University of Kansas, formerly professor of psychology at Indiana University, a major role in making federal funds available for student employment.

The Indiana Daily Student of March 1, 1934, carried an editorial entitled "We Thank You, Professor Lindley." The editorial relates how the Chancellor conceived the idea of providing employment for students under CWA. He presented the idea to his board of trustees, to Governor Alf Landon, and to Harry Hopkins, all of whom approved it. Through his son, Ernest Kidder Lindley, an appointment was made for the Chancellor with the Chief Executive, President Roosevelt, to whom the plan was presented (Harry Hopkins being present).

Recently Paul V. McNutt, then federal security administrator, has written in reply to an inquiry as follows:

I have had a careful check made of the origin of the College Student Aid Program. . . . Proposals for a student aid program were discussed as early as August, 1933. The Program was introduced experimentally in Minnesota by the FERA in December of 1933. On February 3, 1934, Mr. Hopkins authorized the Emergency Relief Administration of all states to draw upon the funds granted them by the FERA for part-time employment of college students in need of aid, advising them that special allotments of funds would thereafter be made available, monthly, for this purpose.

It was Chancellor Lindley's thought that CWA would provide the funds. But CWA was already slated for deletion. Mr. Hopkins, in addition to heading CWA, was also head of FERA and it was from the latter that allocations were made to Indiana University.

During the Bryan administration, ending with the school year 1936–37, federal funds were received by the University for student employment, as follows:

1933–34	FERA (second semester only)	$ 21,414.40
1934–35	FERA	63,720.00
1935–36	NYA	76,725.00
1936–37	NYA	80,334.92
	Total	$242,194.32

These funds were supplemented by certain sums voted by the trustees, totaling about $12,000 during this period.

As a result of this opportunity for employment, many students were able to continue their studies with money earned in doing worth-while work.

CHANGE IN CONCEPTION OF WORK RELIEF PROGRAM

There was, of course, a change in the conception of what could and should be accomplished by the emergency relief agencies as the months passed. For illustration, note the stated purpose of CWA (1933) "to provide regular jobs on public works for four million *unemployed* men and women." Then note the statement of purpose of WPA (1935) "to aid *employable* needy persons by providing work on such [useful public works] projects." Here is a clear advance in thinking from "public works" to "useful public works" and from "unemployed men and women" to "employable needy persons."

In this change in conception of what could be accomplished by emergency relief agencies, I believe Indiana University had a part.

On a trip to Washington, on President Bryan's recommendation, I had had a conference with an individual[1] close in thought to the Chief Executive on this work relief program. I urged that many of the unemployed were unemployable, and that if money were to be spent for public works, the public works should be of an enduring character to which we could later point with the pride and satisfaction of a worth-while accomplishment. I urged that, whereas leaf-raking put money in the pockets of some employable persons, to erect a needed university building gave employment not merely for the men engaged in construction, but for men in stone quarries, glass and furniture factories, and a great number of industries manufacturing materials or equipment used in such construction. Moreover, the resulting structure would fill a real university need of long standing as indicated in our ten-year building program.

This man replied: "Well, we think we know what we are doing. If we do not, it will be too bad."

But before it became too bad the growth in conception of opportunity not merely of giving employment but of constructing "useful public works" had produced the WPA (1935).

THE WORK RELIEF PROGRAM COMES TO THE CAMPUS

The work relief program began in a very simple way on the campus of Indiana University.

[1] Mr. Wayne Coy.

On March 20, 1934, an appropriation of $2,500 was made by the trustees for purchase of materials so that certain work on the Union Building might be completed while the University had the use of CWA funds to pay the workmen.

BUILDING NEEDS AT INDIANA UNIVERSITY IN 1935

There were certain building needs of long standing. As far back as 1927, after a careful survey by the committee on the promotion of University interests, a ten-year building program was outlined for the University at Bloomington and for the Medical Center at Indianapolis. The building program as published at that earlier date was evidence of the validity of the 1935 statement of building needs, evidence that this statement was not something thrown hastily together. For this ten-year building program, see page 342.

THE ADMINISTRATION BUILDING

The building program was revised from time to time and the sequence of buildings shifted as the situation in one school or another became more pressing with the passing of the years and with the increase in enrollments.

An Administration Building had been placed rather far down in the ten-year building program on the theory, long held, that instructional needs took precedence over administrative needs. Administration quarters, however, were cramped. The President's office was on the second floor of Maxwell, outside his door was the Registrar's office, and off the Registrar's office to the south opened the office of the Dean of the College of Liberal Arts. The Bursar's office occupied cramped quarters on the first floor. The crowding in administrative quarters had become so great that an Administration Building came to top the list in the ten-year building program, after the rebuilding of the power plant and provision of adequate accommodations for chemistry by the construction of an entirely new Chemistry Building.

To understand the false starts and changes in plans of the trustees in the first eighteen months of their effort to secure federal assistance in financing the projected Administration Building, it is necessary to realize that during those months the government was in search of a workable plan that would have the greatest appeal to sponsors of public works, the construction of which would relieve unemployment. Unemployment relief was at all times the major objective. Public works were merely a means to that end. Activated in part by sympathy with the government's efforts to get the wheels of industry turning and in part by the desire to take advantage of any opportunity to secure long-needed buildings, the University was all set and ready for action.

After a conference held by the trustees on May 10, 1934, with Architect J. C. Bollenbacher, of Chicago, and Forest Long, of Indianapolis, the acting state engineer for the Federal Relief Administration of Public Works, it was thought that the time for action had arrived, and the trustees made an application for a loan of $400,000 from the Federal Government for the purpose of constructing an Administration Building.

Six months later, since nothing had happened, Judge Wildermuth went to Washington in behalf of this application, and on November 21 the trustees changed the application for a loan to one for a grant and a loan, which conformed with government thought at that time.

A conference with Governor McNutt revealed the wisdom of having legislative authorization to do what might be necessary to meet anticipated government requirements for participation in a public works program. Accordingly, a bill was passed by the 1935 legislature and approved February 19, empowering the University (1) to borrow money, (2) to issue bonds and contracts for repayment, and (3) to accept any grant of money and use the money borrowed or granted in the construction, equipment, and furnishing of any building to be used for University purposes.

On March 4, 1935, the trustees, influenced by information of further changes in plans in Washington, changed once again the form of their application for a grant and a loan to one for a grant only.

With authority of the wise legislation in 1935, the trustees felt they were prepared for any contingency. But the first request of the Federal Emergency Relief Administration of Public Works was for a copy of the bylaws of the Board of Trustees. Neither President

Bryan, nor Secretary Cravens, nor any member of the board had ever seen or heard of bylaws. Indeed it was believed there had never been any bylaws and Washington was so notified. What would be the effect of this disability?

When three months had passed without action on the application of March 4, Judge Wildermuth in June, 1935, had a talk with Wayne Coy, who promised on his return to Washington to look up the status of the application and see what could be done about it.

Again months of uncertainty passed, but on October 9, 1935, the trustees received an offer of the United States of a grant of $180,000 to aid in construction of an Administration Building. They accepted this offer of 45 per cent of the estimated cost.

The federal plan for aid in construction of public works, which at first had been for the government to lend the entire cost of construction, and which some months later was changed to a grant and a loan, and still later to a grant for part of the cost of construction, had finally crystallized in a grant of 45 per cent of the cost of construction, leaving to the sponsor the demonstration of ability to provide the remaining 55 per cent.

The remaining 55 per cent of the cost of the Administration Building was met by a grant of $75,000 from the Governor's Emergency Fund and an issue of $145,000 of bonds, which under authorization of the 1935 legislature the University was empowered to make.

During the seven months that had passed between the filing of the application in its third form, March 4, for a grant, and October 9, when the offer of a grant from the United States was received, the trustees had been proceeding optimistically. On April 4 they had selected a site for the building south of the Library and the entrance to the campus, and tentative plans were discussed. A month later Governor McNutt was quoted by the board (May 16) as saying it was probable large appropriations would be made by the Federal Government for public buildings, in which event the trustees thought it would be necessary to consider:

1. An Administration Building.
2. A building for the School of Medicine at Bloomington.
3. A building for the School of Medicine at Indianapolis.
4. A building at Bloomington for the School of Education.

5. Walks and drives, acoustical treatment for the billiard room and lower hallways of the Union Building, also dining rooms on the second floor and hallways on the third floor.

Deans Smith and Myers made statements of the building needs of their respective schools, and other faculty members wished to be heard regarding building needs other than those of administration. Preliminary floor plans for the Administration Building were examined on May 17, as submitted by Granger and Bollenbacher, who had been retained as architects. Plans and specifications were approved October 10, 1935. This was the day following the offer of the $180,000 grant and indicates the preparation which had been made by the board, knowing that a date was to be fixed by the government for completion of construction. Bids on this building and a proposed women's dormitory were opened and tabulated November 12, 1935, in conjunction with representatives from the PWA office, Indianapolis, and in the presence of bidders. The general contract for the construction of the Administration Building was awarded to Jacobson Brothers, Chicago, on their base bid of $250,000.

On receipt of a letter June 12, 1936, from Governor Paul V. McNutt urging that the new Administration Building be named for President Bryan, the board passed the following resolution:

As a mark of profound devotion, respect, and affection for and gratitude to President William Lowe Bryan, the new Administration Building of Indiana University shall be named for him and called William Lowe Bryan Building; and appropriate inscription thereof shall be made in or upon the building.

PWA rules prevent use of this name during Dr. Bryan's lifetime.

UTILITY TUNNEL

After investigation of the utility tunnels of the campus by Charles R. Ammerman, a consulting engineer, it was recommended, June 14, 1935, that an entirely new tunnel be built for service mains to the Administration Building. A conference with Mr. Hardin, of the Public Works Administration, established cost of this project at $95,500, and an application for a grant-in-aid was filed with PWA.

An offer of $42,975, 45 per cent of the estimated cost, was presented to the board by the United States of America. On October

9, 1935, contracts were let for construction and for the steam heat distributing system, and the following day the board made a contract with Mr. Ammerman for his professional services.

On February 11, 1936, a change order was filed with PWA requesting permission to use an unexpended balance of $25,693.26 of the tunnel grant for construction of a tunnel to the new Medical Building, for which a contract for excavation had been let that day.

Bond Resolution B was spread of record April 27, 1936, authorizing the issuance and sale of $52,000 of general security bonds for the University's share of this installation.

Power Plant Extension

As plans for the Administration Building and other buildings were advanced, the old problem of supplying heat and light to these new buildings again became insistent. After the disastrous power plant fire of 1929, a conservative enlargement had been made with the idea of providing what seemed a reasonable surplus capacity when the plant had been rebuilt under the able guidance of Mr. Ammerman. But with the prospective building program now before the trustees, the need of further expansion was obvious, and in August, 1936, an application for a PWA grant was filed for power plant extension.

The offer of a PWA grant of $37,000 to aid in power plant extension was received on October 16. This whole project had been estimated to cost $123,000. Thirty-seven thousand dollars was approximately 30 per cent of this total instead of the customary 45 per cent. The project, however, was not a pure building project, but involved installation of a turbine generator and a mechanical stoker, the two largest of seven contracts involved, and apparently not considered in making the grant of $37,000. Whatever the reason for a grant of 30 per cent instead of 45 per cent of cost, it was acceptable.

On November 12, 1935, Bond Resolution B authorized issuance of $231,000 of bonds: $145,000 for the University's share of the cost of the Administration Building, and $86,000 for the University's share of the cost of the power plant extension.

Bids for construction of power plant extension were opened on December 3, 1935, and contracts were let. On August 27, 1936, an extension of time for completion of contract was asked for completion of the mechanical stoker and miscellaneous auxiliaries, and granted to September 1, 1936.

Women's Dormitory, Forest Hall

A dormitory for women was the second building project to be advanced during this remarkable period.

In order to show the development of each project we are treating successive projects with an independence that was quickly lost in the rush and overlapping of events.

In this development the Federal Emergency Administration of Public Works was a partner whose final approval was necessary. Two projects launched by the University administration at the same time might be approved by PWA at widely different times. This was true of the Medical Building and the School of Education Building. Two projects approved by the administration at widely different times might come back with PWA approval at essentially the same time, as in the case of the Administration Building and the women's dormitory.

Two houses on Forest Place, in addition to Residence Hall at the corner of Third Street and Forest Place, had been used as dormitories for women. The Indiana Inspection Bureau had recommended that the third floors of these two houses, the Howe and the Hepburn Houses, should not be used for dormitory purposes, and also that Residence Hall should not be used further as a dormitory.

To compensate for this loss, the President thought the use of South Hall as a dormitory for women should be considered. He stated that Dean Agnes Wells and Mrs. Alice Nelson, Director of Halls of Residence, recommended the building of a dormitory for women but "I do not now see the possibility or at any rate the practicability of this proposal."

As the trustees discussed the need of a dormitory for women they became more and more impressed with the desirability of this project; and on May 18, 1935, the board decided to proceed with arrangements for erecting such a dormitory on a site northwest of Memorial Hall, the cost of the building, equipment, and architect's fees not to exceed $125,000. A committee appointed to employ an architect, confer with contractors, receive bids, and arrange for a financing plan was to report at the June meeting. The president of the board appointed on this committee Mr. Niezer, Mrs. Teter, and Mr. Feltus. At this June meeting Mr. Niezer stated that the women's new dormitory could not be built for less than $135,000. After an extended discussion of the matter it was decided to increase the amount for this building to $135,000. All bids on the dormitory submitted on the $125,000 basis were returned to the bidders.

But on further consideration the committee and the board were convinced that $192,000 was necessary to build the dormitory which the University needed, and on that basis an application to the government through PWA was authorized on July 24, 1935.

The official offer of $86,400, 45 per cent of $192,000, was received from the United States of America through PWA on October 16 and formally accepted. Plans and specifications were prepared by Burns and James, architects.

Though application for federal aid in construction of the Administration Building had been made sixteen months earlier than the application for aid in construction of the dormitory for women, bids for erection of these two buildings were opened on the same day, November 12, 1935. On that day a contract was let to E. A. Carson for construction of this dormitory for women.

The grant of $86,400 had been made by the government on an estimated cost of $192,000, which left $105,600 to be provided by the University. But to assure an adequate fund the board on November 12, 1935, authorized a bond issue of $115,000. The bonds sold for a premium of $787, making $202,187 available for the building.

The dormitory, named Forest Hall, was completed on November 23, 1937, at a cost of $1,389 for each girl. This was two-thirds of the cost for each girl in dormitories some institutions were building at that time. Part of this saving was due to our proximity to nearby stone quarries and mills which delivered stone by truck.

Music Building

Dean Merrill made a personal appeal to the board on June 14, 1935, in support of his request for a new building for the School of

Music. The members of the board visited the School of Music in Mitchell Hall.

An application for a grant to aid in construction of a School of Music building was authorized by the board on August 3, 1935. The response was prompt. On October 9 a resolution accepting a grant of $134,212, 45 per cent of the estimated cost of the project, was recorded in the minutes of the board. The acceptance resolutions, copies of which were required by the government, were very formal. This one began as follows:

> Be it Resolved by the Trustees of Indiana University, Section 1: That the offer of the United States of America to the Trustees of Indiana University to aid by way of a grant in financing the construction of a School of Music Building, P.W.A. Project No. Indiana 1087, be and the same is hereby in all respects accepted.

The following day a location for the Music Building was chosen east of Memorial Hall. Plans and specifications were submitted by Architect Daggett on November 12 and approved. Bids were opened on December 3 and found to be very high. Four days later Architect Daggett and Engineer Ammerman made recommendations of cuts to lessen cost, on approval of which the contract for construction was awarded Leslie Colvin on his bid, after deductions of $277,970.

It had been determined that the Music Building would cost $383,-200. The trustees accordingly approved Bond Resolution C for $250,000. Though the grant of $134,212 was made on the belief it was 45 per cent of the cost of the projected building, when construction was completed the grant proved to be less than 35 per cent of the cost. The Music Building was accepted on January 5, 1937.

THE MEDICAL SCHOOL BUILDING AT BLOOMINGTON

As early as 1927 the need of the School of Medicine at Bloomington for more adequate quarters was placed high in the ten-year building program, and by 1935 this need had become acute.

Tentative plans for a new medical building had been drawn by the faculties of the Departments of Anatomy and Physiology based on the Harvard medical buildings, consisting of two wings joined by a unit housing a large lecture room, a library, and other features used by the two departments.

On May 17, 1935, Drs. Myers and Moenkhaus presented to the trustees the need of the School of Medicine at Bloomington for a new building and the following day the board applied to the Federal Government for a grant-in-aid for this project. On December 28, 1935, the offer of a grant-in-aid was received, to cover 45 per cent of the cost of the building upon completion as determined by the Federal Administrator of Public Works, but the grant was not to exceed $211,342.

An acceptance resolution was adopted in approved form. Architect A. M. Strauss, of Fort Wayne, was directed to complete plans, and a site for the building was selected at Forest Place and Third Street as designated in the plat of the campus prepared by Olmsted Brothers, landscape architects.

Ground was broken for the Medical Building on February 28, 1936. On April 6 bids were opened and a contract let to Leslie Colvin on his base bid of $259,000. Alternate contracts were approved, bringing the total up to $267,225. The following day a bond issue of $265,000 was approved for the remainder of the construction cost.

On October 2, 1936, a change order was approved for use of ceramic tile instead of salt-glazed tile in the gross anatomy and mammalian physiology laboratories. This change gave a far better, more hygienic interior finish to these two major laboratories.

On February 20, 1937, an extension of time for completion of this project was requested, which was approved to June 1. The building was given its final inspection on June 14, and the Departments of Anatomy and Physiology moved into the new building, where summer session courses were given.

Dedication exercises at which Governor Clifford M. Townsend presided were held on November 29, 1937. Fred C. Zapffe, secretary of the Association of American Medical Colleges, and Senator Sherman Minton were among the speakers. President Wells spoke in appreciation of the cooperation of state and federal officials in helping to finance this building.

CLINICAL BUILDING, INDIANAPOLIS

On August 3, 1935, the board applied for a grant-in-aid for construction of a Clinical Building at Indianapolis.

On February 11, 1936, an offer from PWA of a grant of $249,750 to aid in construction of this building was received. This offer was accepted and Robert Frost Daggett was employed as architect.

Two months later, April 7, 1936, Mr. Daggett presented sketches of the Clinical Building and made a verbal report upon progress. He was urged to have plans completed by the June meeting. On June 11 Mr. Daggett presented finished plans and specifications, not including plumbing, heating, ventilating, and electric wiring. The plans as completed were approved. He estimated that plumbing, heating, ventilating, and wiring plans could be completed in two weeks. Bids were opened and were found running much above estimates. But it was reported on August 5, 1936, that an agreement had been reached on certain alternate bids which would make it possible to keep within estimated cost. The general construction of the building was awarded to Charles R. Wermuth and Son, Inc., of Fort Wayne, on their base bid of $381,750. Alternate bids were accepted providing for deductions, making the net amount of the contract $322,630.

On August 5, 1936, Bond Resolution C 1936 was approved, providing for the issuance of $315,000 of bonds, to make available the University's share of the cost of construction of the Clinical Building. These 3¼-per cent bonds brought a premium of $3,233.

The new Clinical Building at Indianapolis was completed and occupied in February, 1938, for the work of the spring semester. For a fuller account of the equipment and facilities of this building see Myers, "Medical Education in Indiana" (MS).

SCHOOL OF EDUCATION BUILDING

It will be recalled that on May 16, 1935, the President included a School of Education Building[2] as one of four to be considered if the Federal Government made large appropriations for buildings. Two days later the trustees made application to the Federal Government through PWA for grants-in-aid for construction of a School of Medicine and also a School of Education building.

[2] For a third of a century the administration had been asking for an appropriation for the School of Education Building. In his report to the Governor and Visiting Committee in the fall of 1912, the President said: "We place first the request for an Education Building to house the School of Education, which last year had 17 teachers and 506 students."

When eleven months had passed without action on the application for a School of Education building, Henry L. Smith, Dean of the School, was authorized on April 7, 1936, to make application to the Federal Emergency Relief Administration of Public Works "for such a building for the School of Education as he desired." Application for a grant from the Federal Government again was made by the trustees on June 12, 1936, to aid in construction of a building for the School of Education, and McGuire and Shook, architects, were engaged to prepare preliminary plans.

After some delay a grant of funds was received and accepted on November 6, 1936, and a site for this building was selected north and east of the School of Music. McGuire and Shook were directed to complete plans and specifications, which were presented on January 5, 1937, accepted, and advertised for bids, which were opened on February 8. The day was spent in conference with PWA, the architect, and the engineer.

The following day a contract was let to the Patrick Warren Construction Company for erection of the School of Education and Laboratory School on their base bid of $436,657. Alternates were accepted which brought the total up to $442,369. Bond Resolution 1937A for $425,000 for the University's share of cost was approved. The bonds brought a premium of $2,388. Plans for services were prepared by Bevington-Williams, Inc., Engineers, and heating, ventilating, plumbing, and electric contracts were awarded.

On March 16, 1937, the trustees approved an agreement with the School City of Bloomington covering operation and maintenance of the Laboratory School, patterned after that of Indiana State Teachers College and Ball State Teachers College. Contracts were let on June 11, 1937, for underground steam and electric service mains.

On July 12, 1937, the School of Education and Laboratory building was officially named the University School. The building was completed in 1938.

SUMMARY

To put in tabular form these expenditures at Bloomington and Indianapolis:

At Bloomington

Building	PWA	I.U. Bonds plus premium	Governor's Emergency Fund	Transfer	Total
Administration	$ 180,000	$ 147,400	$ 75,000		$ 402,400
Tunnel	42,975	52,000	I.U. 525	$3,500	99,000
Power plant	37,000	86,000			123,000
Women's dormitory	86,400	115,787			202,187
Medicine	211,342	265,408			476,750
Music	134,212	250,357			384,569
Education	321,925	427,388			749,313
Miscellaneous[3]	185,366		I.U. 33,191		218,557
Total at Bloomington	$1,199,220	$1,344,340	$108,716	$3,500	$2,655,776

Expenditures at Indianapolis

Clinical building	249,750	318,233			567,983
Total for Indiana University	$1,448,970	$1,662,573	$108,716	$3,500	$3,223,759

In addition to the above, the Hydrotherapeutic Pool at the Riley Hospital, costing $72,500, was completed during this period, to the expense of which PWA, the James Whitcomb Riley Association, and the University contributed. All told, the known capital investment of the University, Bloomington and Indianapolis, was increased in excess of three and one-third million dollars during this period.

During this period (1934–37) there were also very extensive improvements of about thirty-five acres of the campus of the School of Medicine, at Indianapolis, even the approximate cost of which we have no knowledge. The work, done during the depression, consisted of filling and grading a major portion of the Indianapolis campus in accordance with the plans prepared by Olmsted Brothers, landscape architects. Between five and ten thousand trees and shrubs were planted. The University and the Riley Memorial Association provided engineering supervision and over-all administration. They also provided the necessary machinery (steam shovels, trucks, etc.). PWA provided the man power. For more than two years, from fifty to one hundred men were employed on this project.

The campus is now the most beautifully landscaped area in the west part of Indianapolis.

[3] President's report of November 4, 1936, p. 8.

CHAPTER XLIV

RETIREMENT AND PENSION SYSTEM AT
INDIANA UNIVERSITY, 1906 - 37

THE ESTABLISHMENT of a faculty retirement and pension system at Indiana University was one of the last major accomplishments of the Bryan administration. This was not a belated thought of President Bryan. On the contrary, it was a problem with which he had been deeply concerned throughout the greater part of his administration.

The story begins on June 16, 1906, when Mr. Rose moved that President Bryan be authorized "to consider and formulate plans for the retirement and pensioning of superannuated professors."

The matter of a retirement and pension system at Indiana University had been brought to the attention of the trustees when in 1905 the Carnegie Foundation for the Advancement of Teaching was established. The Foundation aimed to accomplish the purpose for which it was established, by providing retirement allowances for professors. This was a frontal attack on the problem of superannuation referred to in the motion of Mr. Rose.

It was a time when salaries were small and whatever provision for old age was made was in a medium of exchange the purchasing power of which was gradually diminishing. Tenure, in a sense, increased with advancing years, for in most instances the college officials just as soon would have considered burning one of the college buildings as they would have considered dropping an old professor so long as he could meet his classes. Superannuation, therefore, had become a problem in most colleges and universities.[1]

In 1906 it appeared that state universities would not be included in the list of institutions eligible for the benefit of the Carnegie retirement and pension. This created a situation of much concern to the Indiana University trustees. It was obvious that an institution

[1] For a picture of superannuation at Indiana University see picture facing p. 374, Woodburn, *History of Indiana University.*

532

able to offer social security through the Carnegie retirement plan would have a great attraction for professors quite apart from any immediate increase in salary, or, conversely, a professor in an institution in which he was eligible to a retirement allowance when "the evil days" came would probably refuse to change positions on offer of a higher salary by an institution making no provision for a retirement allowance.

Indiana University had been losing men nearly every year to institutions able to offer higher salaries. The administration was rightly alarmed at this new situation and concluded that the only way of meeting this threat was to establish a retirement system of its own. Hence the action by the board assigning to the President the difficult task of formulating plans for retirement and pensioning of superannuated professors, an action to be interpreted, not so much as a suddenly-awakened interest in the superannuated professor, as an anxiety to protect the University from new raids on its faculty.

On June 15, 1907, on motion of Mr. Shea, President Bryan was again requested to outline a pension system for the faculty and investigate the legal status of the same and to represent the University at any meeting called to discuss the subject if it was advisable to have a representative present.

President Bryan stated to the board on November 5, 1907, that he had recently attended the fourth conference of state universities. Thirty institutions had been represented at the meeting. The relation of the state universities to the Carnegie pension fund had been discussed at length, and it had been decided to make a final attempt to secure the benefits of this Carnegie pension fund for state universities. Meanwhile the President said, "The Cornell plan of retiring old professors as professor emeritus with reduced duties and with the Carnegie allowance has been discussed at Wisconsin."

In the spring of 1908 Professor Eigenmann made a report to the President and trustees in which he discussed the Prussian pension system for teachers. In March, 1910, the President reported:

Since the last meeting of the Board of Trustees, Mr. Abraham Flexner, representing the Carnegie Foundation for the Advancement of Teaching, inspected the Medical School at Bloomington and at Indianapolis. He made no criticism of any kind upon the department at Bloomington, except to recommend an extension of the work in the department. He highly praised the University for what it had accomplished in the unification of medical schools and in laying foundation for the future. If I understand President Pritchett's position, he wishes the Board to state formally its intentions with reference to the development of the Indianapolis School.

In compliance with this request of President Pritchett, Mr. Batman presented a memorandum stating formally the intention of the board in relation to the School of Medicine. This memorandum was adopted by the board.

As matters developed, certain state universities were placed on the list of the Carnegie Foundation for the Advancement of Teaching, and on June 15, 1910, the President announced to the faculty that Indiana University had been placed upon the list accepted by the Carnegie Foundation. On November 28, 1910, President Bryan reported at a special session of the board that he had been greatly surprised to learn of his election as a trustee of the Carnegie Foundation.

It appeared, therefore, that a solution of the problem of pensions for members of the faculty at Indiana University had been found and there was a general feeling of gratification.

This feeling of satisfaction at being made eligible to the benefits of the Carnegie retirement and pension plan was, however, shortlived for on November 17, 1915, the Carnegie Foundation discontinued the acceptance of additional faculty members to participation in the benefits of its retirement and pension system. A few months later, March, 1916, President Pritchett, of the Carnegie Foundation for the Advancement of Teaching, submitted to the teachers and presidents of the educational institutions associated with the Foundation a report entitled "Comprehensive Plan of Insurance and Annuities for College Teachers." On March 15 President Bryan spoke to the faculty on this report of the Carnegie Foundation in which faculties of associated institutions were asked to consider a scheme of insurance in the expense of which the Foundation, the institution, and the teachers should share jointly.

There followed a prolonged discussion in which many participated. Various questions were raised: Would the annuity deposited be a taxable investment? Would a medical examination be waived or be rigid? Would the Foundation be able to care for its share? What would be the cost of conducting the business? etc.

On April 18 a faculty committee reported that they did not feel that the faculty had at hand sufficient details of the plan proposed or the technical knowledge in insurance matters to enable them to pass intelligent judgment on the specific project presented for consideration. The committee submitted:

1. They believed that the first duty of the Trustees of Carnegie Foundation was to keep faith with those persons who had ordered their personal affairs in view of the existing pension plan.

2. The committee favored the establishment for the future of some plan financially sound which should embody the following ideas:
    a. The plan should be contributory.
    b. It should be voluntary.
    c. It should include provision for protection against disability.

President Bryan reported on retirement plans of different institutions and added: "Dean Wigmore, president of the American Association of University Professors, has succeeded in having final action by the trustees of the Foundation postponed until next November."

Since the report proposed radical changes in the relationship existing between the Foundation and the associated institutions, vitally affecting teachers of associated institutions, and less directly affecting all university teachers of the United States, it was very natural that the American Association of University Professors should become deeply interested in the matter.

The Pritchett report had invited teachers and presidents in associated institutions to determine the question "whether the fundamental principles set forth in his report are those upon which sound pension administration and legislation must rest." The American Association of University Professors accordingly appointed a large committee, one from each of twenty-four institutions, with Harlan F. Stone, of Columbia University, as chairman. This committee made a study of the Pritchett report, published in the *Bulletin* of the Association of University Professors, Volume II, Number 5, November, 1916.

This twenty-four-page report included a letter from Chairman Stone to Mr. Pritchett seeking definite information. The letter stated that certain paragraphs of the Pritchett report had been generally construed as meaning that the administration of the Foundation was seriously considering a plan whereby:

(*a*) Teachers under a certain age—the age of 45 being tentatively suggested —who are by existing rules entitled to receive eventual retiring allowances will fail to receive such allowances as the present rules specify; and whereby also,

(*b*) Such teachers, unless they and their institutions qualify under the proposed new plan of contributory pensions will be deprived of any benefit whatever from the pension system of the Foundation.

Mr. Stone stated further that it was of course important for his committee to be sure whether this interpretation was correct before making its report. He added:

I shall therefore be greatly obliged if you will inform me whether any plan which would thus nullify certain of the expectations naturally created by the present rules is under consideration.

From the reply of Mr. Pritchett to this letter of Chairman Stone I quote one sentence, a sentence which did not promote confidence:

It is interesting to remember that, ten years ago when the Foundation announced its pension plan, and reserved in specific terms the power to change these rules in the future in such manner as experience might show to be in the interest of the great body of teachers, some of the teachers sharply criticised the Foundation on the ground that it committed itself to nothing.

Mr. Stone quoted the letter of Mr. Carnegie of April 16, 1905, in which he announced to the Carnegie Foundation trustees the purpose of his gift. He quoted the first report of Mr. Pritchett and the second annual report of the Foundation in all of which the purpose of the founder is clearly expressed. He then quoted Mr. Pritchett's report of 1916 showing in how many respects the conception of the founder is lost sight of.

The report of the American Association of University Professors stated that the unconvincing reasons which were urged for the change in policy of the Foundation had resulted in loss of confidence in the Foundation on the part of American university teachers. To repair this loss of confidence it was the judgment of this large committee representing twenty-four universities that certain things were necessary.

The first is the publication by the Foundation of a definite assurance that it will completely fulfil any expectations held out to teachers in the associated institutions by present rules.

The second is a strict adherence to the fundamental principles and purposes indicated by Mr. Carnegie in his letter of gift and repeatedly enunciated in the early public declarations of the Foundation on the basis of which the existing system was established.

. . . .

Fourth: Finally it seems to us essential, if the Foundation is to enjoy the confidence of the academic profession and attain its highest usefulness, that it should be recognized that for it, even more than for other institutions, definiteness and steadiness of purpose and stability of policy are indispensable.

In the *Bulletin* of the American Association of University Professors, Volume II, Number 6, December, 1916, was published correspondence of Dean John H. Wigmore, of Northwestern University, president of the American Association of University Professors, with Mr. Pritchett, resulting in postponement of action by the trustees of the Carnegie Foundation in order to provide opportunity for "further study of the project in order to avoid another leap in the dark." It will be noted, however, that action was only postponed; it was not changed.

On October 26, 1916, Dean Rawles read before the Indiana University faculty reports from the eastern and western committees of the American Association of University Professors in regard to the pensions system and the proposed modification of the pension system of the Carnegie Foundation for the Advancement of Teaching.

It will be evident that this action of the Carnegie Foundation for the Advancement of Teaching was not accepted with equanimity by the faculties of institutions on the Carnegie list. A meeting was called in New York City and faculty delegates from the member schools were present. I had been elected by our Indiana University faculty to represent them at this meeting. Henry Pritchett, the director, presided, and I think I have never seen a man given a harder one hundred minutes. The delegate from Wisconsin could have retired a few weeks earlier at sixty-five prior to the announcement of the cut in allowances, at a pension considerably higher than became possible at seventy under the new system. Many were present who had refused invitations to other institutions at substantial increase in salary because they felt their later years secure under the Carnegie pension agreement. Resentment was heightened by the fact that back of the Carnegie Foundation for the Advancement of Teaching was another and later-created Carnegie Corporation with funds sufficient to have made a more liberal adjustment possible. It was the belief that the Carnegie board was not correctly interpreting the clearly expressed and repeated wishes of the founder. But nothing was accomplished.

The attitude of the trustees of the Carnegie Foundation was essentially identical with that of the American Association of University Professors in that they urged fulfilment of expectations created under existing rules. In spite of these recommendations, after some delay the new Carnegie pension plan was put in effect in 1918. At a later date new rules published in a confidential report, released May 1, 1929, were as follows:

For professors in associated universities, becoming 65

in	1923–1928	the retirement maximum was	$3,600.00
in	1929	the retirement maximum was	3,000.00
in	1930	the retirement maximum was	2,300.00
in	1931	the retirement maximum was	1,600.00
in	1932	and thereafter maximum was	1,000.00

For this last group, the $1,000 was increased to $1,500 by aid of another Carnegie fund.

How could it happen that ten years after its establishment the Carnegie Foundation found itself committed beyond its ability for fulfilment? The main reason seems to have been an incredible failure to recognize and properly assess the very great increase in attendance at the colleges and universities of America and the accompanying increase in teaching staff entailed.

But this movement was twenty years old when the Carnegie Foundation was established. At Indiana University during the seventeen years, 1885 to 1902, attendance had doubled three times, with corresponding increase in faculty. In the eight years, 1902–1910, attendance doubled again. The go-to-college movement was general and well known to every educator.

On May 14, 1918, President Bryan discussed before the faculty in general terms the new pension and insurance scheme adopted by the Carnegie Foundation for the Advancement of Teaching.

In April, 1919, the President made a report to the trustees on the new Carnegie pension retirement plan, from which we quote:

The new rules provide for participation of full-time professors, associate professors, assistant professors, and officers of similar rank; and for the voluntary participation of any teacher below the rank of assistant professor, who has had not less than three years of service in a degree-giving institution.

In brief, the plan is that the teacher and the university or college that employs him may pay into a retiring allowance fund, monthly payments amounting to one-tenth of the teacher's salary. One-half of each payment is deducted from the teacher's salary and one-half is contributed by the institution in which he teaches. These payments, with compound interest at 4 per cent, provide a retiring allowance fund. If the teacher dies before the retiring age of 65, the amount paid in under the plan, augmented by 4 per cent compound interest, will be returned to his dependents. The plan provides for a policy contract, which allows choice as to date at which the retiring annuity will commence, and choice as to the disposition of that portion of the fund not returned to him prior to his death.

The extent to which the plan affects the institution financially is this: That the institution obligates itself to contribute in monthly installments an amount annually equal to 5 per cent of the combined annual salaries of all its teachers who avail themselves of it.

The main argument in favor of the plan is that it provides a pension retirement for teachers who are not entitled to the old Carnegie pension retirement plan, which closed its doors to newcomers on November 17, 1915.

The plan differs from the ordinary disability policy of the old-line insurance companies in two points favorable to the teachers: (a) no medical examination is required, (b) the institution pays one-half of his premium. On the other hand, it may be pointed out that the teacher does not, under the plan proposed, participate in any surplus earnings over and above the 4 per cent compound interest.

It is but fair to name certain objections offered by a committee of the American Association of University Professors to the adoption of the plan at this time by the universities and colleges: (a) that experience has shown that in great part the intentions announced by the Carnegie Foundation remain unfulfilled; (b) that the resources employed to give the proposed benefits to a new set of teachers may be taken away from the old set; (c) that the new plan has the effect of continuing the supervisory relation of the Foundation, which they consider as possibly undesirable; (d) that if an institution wished to increase salaries to the extent of 5 per cent, the teacher should be granted the increase to use as he pleases and not be forced to invest it in a specified way; (e) that it is more desirable that each institution establish its own retiring pension fund.

Of the state institutions immediately about us, Michigan has announced acceptance of the plan.

On the basis of the combined salaries of our present faculty not eligible to retirement under the old plan, and on the theory that all apparently eligible under the new plan would elect to avail themselves of it, the amount of money necessary to meet the 5 per cent requirement next year would be under $3,500.

It is requested by the Foundation that eligible institutions announce their acceptance to become effective not later than January 1, 1920.

It is my understanding from President Pritchett and from Secretary Fürst that an institution may accept the plan without obligating members of the faculty to participate. It is my understanding also that while an institution accepting the plan obligates itself to pay an amount equal to 5 per cent of the salary of any eligible member of the faculty who wishes to avail himself of it, the institution reserves the right to refuse to recommend for participation members of the faculty not recommended for reappointment in the institution.

It is regrettable that the plan here proposed was not put into effect in 1918 or 1919. In response to President Bryan's urgent recommendation with reference to faculty salaries, substantial salary increases were made in 1920 at the June meeting of the board. It would have been easy to have made salaries 5 per cent less and to have inaugurated the retirement and pension plan without extra drain on University funds. The faculty, however, was not solidly back of the proposition, for reasons stated by the Association of University Professors.

Of the five objections offered by the American Association of University Professors, the first, stating that "in great part the intentions announced by the Carnegie Foundation remained unfulfilled," was far the most important, so far as the faculty of Indiana University was concerned.

Confidence in the management of the Carnegie Foundation had been profoundly shaken. The younger members of the faculty were hesitant to press adoption of a plan which was being introduced at the disadvantage of the older men. The oldest men, those becoming sixty-five before 1923, remained under the Carnegie commitments.

The contributory plan appealed strongly to the great majority. It was indeed essentially the plan adopted eighteen years later, too late to be of any importance to those who would have profited by its adoption in 1919. Undoubtedly some few would have availed themselves of this voluntary plan in 1918, but for their loss of confidence in anything proposed by the Carnegie Foundation.

There followed a period of sixteen years of drifting. In November, 1923, Professor Bert E. Young sent a communication to the trustees, in an effort to revive this dormant project. But nothing came of the effort. And so the matter rested until revived by Governor McNutt in a letter to which the President called the attention of the board in November, 1934. No action was taken at that time, but soon thereafter the President appointed a faculty committee consisting of Raleigh W. Holmstedt, chairman; Burton D. Myers, Bernard C. Gavit, William A. Rawles, and William C. Cleveland. This committee was requested to make a study and report on a retirement system for Indiana University, which it did on December 24, 1934.

The report was presented to the faculty, where it was discussed and suggestions made. There were occasional meetings during 1935. Dean H. L. Smith and Walton S. Bittner were appointed on the committee in place of Professors Rawles and Cleveland. The report in its final form was presented in the late spring of 1936, and was referred to Attorney Edwin Corr for an opinion on the legality of the recommendations, on which he reported September 8, 1936. Finally, on May 18, 1937, a resolution was adopted by the Board of Trustees, providing for a retirement system to go into effect on July 1 of that year.

With new management, confidence in the Carnegie Foundation had gradually been restored, the contributory Annuity Retirement Plan, sponsored by the Foundation, was proving sound, and faculty members accepted it readily. Though, as previously stated, it came too late to be of any importance to the older men, it was very desirable for the younger men and for future generations of the faculty of Indiana University.

The inauguration of this retirement system was one of the finest achievements of the final period of the Bryan administration.

CHAPTER XLV

THE SCHOOL OF EDUCATION[1]

By Velorus Martz

THE NORMAL SCHOOL PERIOD, 1824–64

THE STATE Seminary that opened its doors in 1824 had developed, by 1838, into the Indiana University. During this period, the records disclose no interest in teacher training, though agitation for the professional training of teachers was becoming active throughout the country. At the moment the infant University was making its bow to the public, the Western Literary Institute and College of Professional Teachers was preparing for its eighth annual meeting at Cincinnati, in October, 1838. At this meeting Calvin E. Stowe proposed a resolution on normal schools, which was adopted. The resolution urged the establishment "at the seat of government in each State, and under the patronage of the Legislature, of a Teachers' Seminary and Model School for the instruction and practice of Teachers in the science of Education and the art of Teaching." [2]

President Andrew Wylie, of Indiana University, attended this meeting and may have been impressed by Professor Stowe's presentation of the need for professional training of teachers. At any rate, the Board of Trustees of the young institution, a year later, adopted a resolution requesting from the state legislature "the income from the Saline Fund," in return for which they undertook to establish "forthwith" a normal school in charge of "a Professor specially appointed to that duty." [3] Nothing apparently came of the request, and, when school next opened in the fall of 1840, they urged the matter

---

[1] Professor Martz, of the School of Education, wrote this condensed history from his more detailed account of the development of the School of Education, now in the University Archives.

[2] *Transactions of the Eighth Annual Meeting of the Western Literary Institute and College of Professional Teachers,* Cincinnati, October, 1838, p. 20.

[3] Minutes of the Board of Trustees, Indiana University, September 24–25, 1839, Vol. 1, pp. 37–38, 43.

again upon a committee of the General Assembly,[4] but without success. A decade elapsed before further efforts were made to establish teacher training at the University.

On October 4, 1851, the trustees once more tackled the problem of professional education, this time resolving that "the President and Professors of the University proper be requested to organize a class in Didactics, including the theory and practice of teaching, with a view to the permanent establishment of a Normal Department in connection with the University."[5] A few weeks later, the unexpected and untimely death of President Wylie, November 11, 1851, threw the administrative affairs of the institution into confusion. However, the project was not forgotten, and in their next report (December, 1851) to the legislature the trustees expressed their belief that a normal department "should be made a permanent and essential branch of the State University."

During this eventful year, 1852, the new Constitution of Indiana went into effect and, in the general reorganization of educational affairs, the University acquired a new Board of Trustees. At the first meeting of the new board, April, 1852, a committee report was submitted based more than likely upon suggestions offered at the same meeting by the faculty. This report recommended the addition of courses in agricultural chemistry and in theoretical and practical engineering, as well as the recognition of the existing science offerings as a distinct course leading to graduation and a diploma. Along with these proposals, there was recommended also "a normal Seminary consisting of separate departments for males and females." In support of this proposal the committee asserted "there is no measure more urgently required by public opinion than this. Through this department, the common school system of the State will be brought into connexion and sympathy with the University."[6]

The report of the committee was adopted and $200 was appropriated to fit up a room in the "preparatory building" as a model school for the use of the "male department" of the new seminary. The "female department" offered a somewhat more difficult problem as "females" were not yet eligible to admission as students in full stand-

[4] *Ibid.,* October 1, 1840, p. 86.
[5] *Ibid.,* p. 228.
[6] *Ibid.,* April 14, 1852, p. 246.

ing at the University. So, instead of fitting up a room, it was decided
to appropriate a sum of money for the purpose of erecting a "suitable building or buildings and furnishing same" for the use of the
female department, provided an equal sum should be subscribed for
the same purpose by the citizens of Bloomington.[7]

On the following day (April 15, 1852), in arranging the further
details of the new enterprise, the board authorized the resident trustees (i.e., those residing in Bloomington) and the faculty "to make
all necessary rules and regulations for the organization and good
government of the male department of the Normal Seminary." At
the same time, they were empowered to employ a teacher for the
model school, provided "that such teacher depend solely, for compensation, upon funds derived from tuition fees."[8]

Similar authority over the female department was conferred upon
this same group. But, with an income of $5,200 to meet the entire
budget of the University, the erection of a new building was no light
undertaking. It must have been, therefore, a very happy suggestion
that led the trustees to authorize their committee "to adopt the
Female Seminary of Monroe County, if thought advisable, as the
Female Department of the Normal Seminary, established in connexion with this University."[9] The proviso about payment of compensation from fees was extended likewise to the teachers in this
department.

Later this same month, the new board made a supplemental report
to the General Assembly.

In carrying out their design, the report states, it was their plan to
assign one of the members of the faculty to the work of the Seminary
as "Professor of Didactics." A regular course of studies was to be prescribed, leading to a certificate or diploma. The other departments
of the University were to be open to students enrolled in the Seminary. The model school was intended "to present to the eye of the
learner, a common school, as nearly perfect as possible in its order,
arrangement, furniture, classification, and methods of teaching."
This school was to serve also as a "school of practice, in which to

[7] *Ibid.*, p. 249.
[8] *Ibid.*, p. 252.
[9] *Ibid.*

exercise and test the young teacher's ability and tact." The teacher of this school, they had determined, was to be one who had, himself, been trained in a normal school.[10]

In regard to the contemplated training of young women for the teaching profession, the report has this rather interesting comment:

Inasmuch as it is known that a large proportion of all the teachers in those States, where the common school system is brought to the highest perfection, are females, amounting in some States, it is believed, to five-sixths of the total number; and as it is exceedingly desirable, on every consideration, to increase the proportion of female teachers in Indiana, the Board of Trustees have felt, that without provision for a normal department for females, they would have accomplished less than half their work.[11]

The adoption of the Monroe County Seminary, instead of the establishment of a new department for women within the University, was felt to be the wisest course. The seminary was located on what is now Seventh Street, on the site of the present Masonic Temple. The trustees call attention to the fact that it is "distant over half a mile from the University," presumably to reassure those parents who might feel some concern at the prospect of a too intimate association of boys and girls on the same campus. It was a "fine school" with "an accomplished Principal," an "accomplished corps of teachers." The report assures the members of the legislature that "it is the wish of the Board to place this department upon the most elevated grounds; and to make it subservient both to general education and to the elevation of the female sex." The trustees express the hope that the Assembly will see fit to extend increased financial aid in support of the new project which, it was felt, "will be more efficient, more likely to secure public confidence, will possess more ample means of instruction, than were the entire University fund converted to the sole purpose of the Normal Seminary." [12]

The legislature, which was in session at the time, seemingly was converted to the idea of teacher training at the State University. In

[10] *Report of the Board of Trustees,* April, 1852, pp. 343–44. (The reports of this period are available as reprints from the *House* and *Senate Journals.* This accounts for the numbering of the pages.)

[11] *Ibid.*

[12] *Ibid.,* p. 345.

an act approved June 17, 1852, it not only gave its approval to the project, but made the thing mandatory by enacting that the trustees "shall establish a normal department for instruction in the theory and practice of teaching, free of charge, of such young persons (male and female), residents of the State, as may desire to qualify themselves as teachers of the common schools within the State." [13] The interest of the legislature apparently did not extend to a subsidization of the enterprise, for, in the next annual report of the trustees, the latter express the hope that the Assembly may find a way to give "some additional pecuniary aid to meet the increased expenditure" of their expanded program. [14]

The Catalog of the University for the year 1851–52 [15] announced the institution of the normal department and expressed the hope that it would "soon be organized and go into operation." It was further stated that all college classes would be opened to those who enrolled in this department and that candidates for the teacher's diploma would be afforded opportunity to act as assistants in the model school. "Thus," said the Catalog, "they will go forth to their profession not only themselves *taught* how to teach others, but also with some *experience* as a test of their powers and of their aptness to teach." [16]

The committee, appointed in April to effect the organization of the normal department, reported to the trustees at their meeting held in August in connection with the annual Commencement. The committee had selected Professor Daniel Read as professor of didactics and John Calvin Smith, a graduate of Indiana University in the class of 1851, as teacher of the model school. They asked further time for the consideration of plans and the selection of "fixtures." Their report was accepted and approved. [17]

The new department apparently got off to a good start the next

[13] *Revised Statutes of the State of Indiana*, 1852, Vol. I, p. 508.
[14] *Report of the Board of Trustees*, 1853, p. 316.
[15] In the early years, the Catalogs of the University were issued under varying names in different years, as "catalogues," "circulars," or "reports." In this treatise they will be referred to uniformly as "Catalogs." The Catalog for 1851–52 was issued at the close of that year and contained announcements for the year 1852–53.
[16] Catalog, 1851–52, p. 12. Italics in the original.
[17] Minutes of the Board of Trustees, August 5, 1852, Vol. I, p. 264.

school year (1852–53), with 34 students enrolled in the course in didactics, "22 males, 12 females." The affinity between teachers and summer work must have been noticeable even at that early date, for the trustees report that "the course hereafter will be given in the summer term." [18] The summer term in those days, it might be noted, was the last of three regular terms of the school year, extending from about the first of May to early in August.

A somewhat detailed course was "prescribed for the Normal School." This course seems to have been compounded from courses already offered in the Preparatory Department and the University and certain special courses which were developed for those in preparation for teaching. How extensive these courses were is not definitely known, as they are nowhere reported in terms of credit hours. Neither do we have any information as to who offered the instruction in them. They must have added perceptibly to the teaching load, but apparently no additions to the teaching staff were made to care for them. Whether the whole course was intended to cover two, three, or four years is also not revealed, but we do find the statement that "those who complete the foregoing course, and pass a creditable examination thereon, will be entitled to a certificate or diploma, signed by the Faculty." [19]

The model school for boys was organized and put into operation this same year. It was in immediate charge of John Calvin Smith, though under the "general supervision of the Faculty." [20] A fee of $3.50 a term was charged for tuition. [21]

---

[18] *Report of the Board of Trustees,* January, 1853, p. 315. The Catalog for this year gives the membership in the didactics class as 37, 22 males and 15 females (p. 14).

The presence of "females" in classes at the University as early as 1852 has apparently passed unnoticed by the historians. They may have been a delegation from the Monroe County Female Seminary, recently adopted as the "female department" of the new normal school. As far back as May 3, 1839, the Female Seminary had announced in the *Bloomington Post* that "to facilitate the studies of the Senior Class permission has been obtained for their attending the Philosophical Lectures at the University, and enjoying the benefits of the most extensive apparatus in the State." If this arrangement was ever carried out, the extant records of the University do not disclose it. It is likely that the young women in the didactics class were regarded not as students in full standing, but rather as members of another institution to whom the privilege of attending classes on the campus had been granted. At all events, it seems that there were "co-eds" at I.U. in 1852 in the didactics class, although not in a curriculum leading to a degree.

[19] *Ibid.*

[20] *Ibid.,* p. 316.

[21] *Ibid.,* p. 319.

The arrangements for the "female department" of the normal seminary apparently never got much beyond the paper stage. The trustees report that they "have effected an arrangement with the accomplished principal (Mrs. E. J. McPherson) of the Monroe County Female Seminary, by which this Seminary is placed under the direction of the Resident Trustees and the Faculty of the University, as the female department of the normal school." [22] Unfortunately for this arrangement between the University and the seminary, the new Constitution of 1851 had already stipulated for the sale of the property of the public seminaries, the proceeds to be transferred to the common school fund. Pursuant to this provision, the property of the Monroe County Female Seminary was offered for sale in the summer of 1853. On August 4, of this year, the board rescinded the resolution previously passed authorizing the resident trustees to purchase property to establish a female seminary. [23] From this time on we find nothing in the records about the "female department."

However, the "male department" operated more or less successfully for a number of years. The course of lectures on the theory and practice of teaching given each summer term must have been a very comprehensive affair. In the Catalog for 1854–55 we read:

Lectures are given embracing the following subjects: education, its nature and design; physical education; intellectual education; moral education; aesthetical education; the history of education; an examination of the powers of the mind, especially with reference to receiving and communicating knowledge; schoolhouse architecture, including school furniture, grounds, etc.; organization and classification of schools; graded schools; the proper incentives for the school; rewards and punishments; modes of teaching different subjects; the office of teacher: his duties to himself, his school and the public; duty of the State in reference to educating its citizens; the educational policy of Indiana. [24]

To compress all this within the bounds of one course extending through one term of three months would surely be beyond the powers of any present-day educator. Certainly we can hardly accuse the Catalog of exaggeration when it comments that "it is intended, in this course of lectures, to present, as nearly as may be, the whole duty of the teacher."

[22] *Ibid.*, p. 316.
[23] Minutes of the Board of Trustees, Vol. I, p. 281.
[24] Catalog, 1854–55, p. 22.

On December 4, 1855, Professor Read resigned in order to take a position on the faculty of the University of Wisconsin.[25] With his departure, the class in theory and practice of teaching disappeared after an existence of three years and the activities of the normal department of the University became limited apparently to the model school for boys.

This school continued its somewhat checkered career for two years longer. Its enrollment would appear to have been at all times adequate. In the second year of its existence eighty boys are reported in attendance. This would make it the largest department in the University, as the entire student body of collegiate rank for that year totaled only seventy-five.[26] In spite of a favorable enrollment, the school seems always to have experienced difficulty in retaining its teachers. During the five years of its existence it had five teachers, four of them in the last three years. The chief difficulty here seems to have been financial, as the salary of the teacher was to be paid entirely from the tuition fees.

The University was in severe financial straits, due to the new building that had been made necessary by the fire of 1854. On August 3, 1857, the Board of Trustees resolved "that the 'Model School' as at present constituted is neither a legal nor necessary appendage to the University and that the same be and is hereby suspended."[27] No reason is offered in the minutes of the trustees for this somewhat drastic step, but the Catalog for the following year carries this explanatory note: "The Board of Trustees, at their last annual meeting, abolished the '*Model School*,' having no means at their command for properly carrying on the *Normal Department* at present."[28] With the passing of the model school, the first chapter in the history of professional education at Indiana University comes definitely to a close.

Effort to Reorganize Normal School, 1864–84

The second chapter of our story is a fairly brief one for two reasons: in the first place, there is not a great deal to relate; in the

[25] Minutes of the Board of Trustees, Vol. I, pp. 337–38.
[26] Catalog, 1853–54, p. 13.
[27] Minutes of the Board of Trustees, Vol. I, p. 425.
[28] Catalog, 1857–58, p. 18.

second place, the minutes of the trustees which have been our main reliance hitherto were among the records of this period destroyed in the fire of 1883. For our account of these years we depend primarily upon the annual Catalogs and the reports of the trustees to the legislature or, from 1875 on, to the governor. Unfortunately, these sources usually speak of a department as "recently established," without giving specific dates.

The Catalog for 1864-65 announces that "the Normal Department of Indiana University has been recently reorganized, under the charge of Mr. E. D. [sic] Hunter, Superintendent of the Graded Schools of Bloomington, aided by members of the Faculty." But we find no further account of its activity beyond the additional statement that "There will also be held in connection with this department, a Normal Institute, beginning on the first Monday of August, and continuing three weeks." [29]

Four years later, the annual Catalog lists "Hon. George W. Hoss, A.M., Professor of English Literature and of the Theory and Practice of Teaching," and carries the names of forty students as enrolled in the normal department. Of these, eight or nine seem to be women, "co-eds" having been admitted to the University in 1867.

At the beginning of 1870 the State Normal School at Terre Haute opened its doors and the State Board of Education found itself faced with the problem of determining the respective functions of the two state institutions. Its decision is announced in a resolution adopted June 29, 1870, to the effect that

> The propriety of recommending a discontinuance of the Normal Department of the State University having been urged by a number of members, on motion of Governor Baker, it was, *Resolved,* that the Normal Department of the University should be discontinued, because the money expended in keeping it up can be more profitably employed in imparting instruction in other branches. [30]

Nevertheless, normal work continued at the University during the next school year. But, at the close of that year, Professor Hoss resigned to become president of the Kansas State Normal School. With

[29] Catalog, 1864-65, p. 23.
[30] Minutes of the State Board of Education, Vol. I, p. 90.

his leaving, teacher training work disappeared for the second time from the campus of Indiana University.

Under the administration of President Moss, 1875–84, the University became strictly a liberal arts college. The only activity during this period, bearing upon professional education, was a series of lectures by William T. Harris, of St. Louis, in February, 1881, on the "Philosophy and History of Education." [31] At the opening of the following year, Dr. Harris gave a five-weeks' course in pedagogics to the Junior and Senior classes of the University. At the same time, he apparently repeated the lectures of the year before. [32]

TEACHER TRAINING UNDER BRYAN AND BERGSTROM, 1885–1908

Shortly after David Starr Jordan assumed the office of president, teacher training reappears, this time permanently. In 1885, three courses bearing directly upon the work of the teacher were announced in the Department of Philosophy. They were to be taught by William J. Bryan (later changed to William L. Bryan), a recent graduate of the University, who was acting professor of philosophy, and the only instructor listed in that Department. Apparently he assumed these teachers' courses in addition to his other courses in philosophy. [33]

The following year, the Department of Pedagogy appears with Richard Gauss Boone as professor of pedagogics. The work of the new department was inaugurated with a full complement of ten courses which gave rather complete coverage of the field of education. [34] The same year "specialties" appear and each student was required to select a specialty, which was defined as "a subject in which a four-year course is given." [35] Pedagogy qualified as a specialty.

During the nineties the work in pedagogy steadily expanded. In 1891, "the work known as University extension" was undertaken in a small way. [36] Four years later, pedagogy first appeared in the summer session in a combination course announced as "Psychology and

[31] Catalog, 1880–81, p. 40.
[32] Catalog, 1881–82, pp. 8, 43–44.
[33] Catalog, 1885–86, pp. 32, 50.
[34] Catalog, 1886–87, pp. 10, 48.
[35] Catalog, 1887–88, p. 36.
[36] Catalog, 1891–92, p. 98.

Pedagogy." [37] From that time to the present, education has multiplied its offerings with such regularity that it can now claim with some justification to play the leading role in the summer's activities.

In the midst of all this, Professor Boone resigned to become superintendent of the schools of Cincinnati, Ohio, and the work in pedagogy was suspended for the year 1893–94 pending the selection of his successor. The following year, the Department of Pedagogy reappears with William Lowe Bryan as professor in charge and John A. Bergstrom as assistant professor of psychology and pedagogy. Under the new regime, the offerings in pedagogics were consolidated into four major courses, each extending throughout a year. [38]

Two innovations mark this year in the history of the Department. The first of these was the institution of a pedagogical museum, which was designed to establish and maintain collections of texts, materials, and apparatus used in schools of this country and abroad. This museum was a pet project of Professor Bergstrom's and is mentioned repeatedly with apparent pride. It continued as a feature of the Department during the Bryan-Bergstrom administration. In the history of the University, 1820–1904, written while the museum was still a functioning institution, it is described as containing "a large collection of American textbooks" as well as exhibits from abroad. [39] After the time of Professor Bergstrom, interest in the museum must have waned or difficulties in the way of maintaining it may have arisen. At any rate, it has disappeared, just how or when is not clear either in the records of the University or in the memory of those who were acquainted with the campus in those days.

The second innovation, signalizing the period under consideration, is first mentioned in the departmental report of 1897. Here Bergstrom set forth the need of "an opportunity for the direct study of school work and the problems of different towns." He proposed a scheme "which contemplates using the entire state and probably cities of neighboring states as a laboratory for this purpose." The plan was to arrange for visits to certain cities by students and their instructors, who were there to make "as complete an inventory as

[37] Catalog, 1894–95, p. 90.
[38] Ibid., pp. 58–59.
[39] Lewis C. Carson, in Indiana University, 1820–1904, p. 98.

possible of their educational conditions and problems." It was believed that arrangements could be made for practice teaching by students under "exceptionally fine teachers," in the various systems inspected. Such a course would be of special value in the training of superintendents and at the same time would extend "the influence of the institution and the principles we represent." [40]

The following school year (1897-98), a third member was added to the Department in the person of Elmer B. Bryan, who appears as assistant professor of pedagogy. With his coming, a pedagogical conference is announced comprising "studies in the public schools of Bloomington." [41] In the Catalog of 1898–99, the pedagogical conference has developed into two distinct courses, listed as "Observation and Apprentice Course in Superintendency" and "Observation and Apprentice Course for those who intend to become High School Teachers." The first of these required "visits to about six towns and cities and an equal number of reports on their educational condition," while the second involved "not less than two weeks as an apprentice at some high school to be agreed upon, and a written report upon the work in at least four other schools." [42]

With the elevation of W. L. Bryan to the presidency of the University in 1902, the department over which he had presided was reorganized. Pedagogy was separated from Philosophy and erected into a separate department with Professor Bergstrom at its head, as professor of pedagogy.

In 1904 the Department of Pedagogy became the Department of Education.

It was during the brief period of the Department of Education (1904–8) that we find the beginnings of the work that developed later into systematic supervised teaching. No critic teachers are indicated and most of the time spent in the classroom was devoted apparently to observation, though it was stated that "later the student can be given, for some time, complete charge of the discipline and recitation work of a school." [43] This work must have developed rather

[40] MS report, Department of Pedagogy, June 3, 1897.
[41] Catalog, 1897–98, pp. 73–74.
[42] Catalog, 1898–99, pp. 90–91.
[43] Catalog, 1906, p. 145.

rapidly, for we find that in the year 1907-8 three critic teachers in high school subjects were actually employed and five such were indicated for the following year.[44] The work in the high school was soon expanded but, for some reason, observation in the elementary school was ere long relegated to the summer session.[45]

The development of these courses and the addition of critic teachers to the departmental staff naturally involved the city schools of Bloomington rather intimately in the teacher training program of the University. By logical arrangement, therefore, the superintendent of the local schools, William H. Sanders, became attached to the Department of Education, as "Director of Practice in School Supervision and School Administration," and was so listed for the first time in the Catalog of 1908.

THE SCHOOL OF EDUCATION, 1908-37

Legislation passed at the 1907 session of the Indiana General Assembly marked a decided forward step in the state toward professional training of teachers. A bill, approved March 2, provided for a classification of teachers and established a minimum wage for each class.[46] A second law was enacted, within a few days, constituting the State Board of Education "a state teachers' training board" for the purpose of carrying out the provisions of the preceding act. The training board was empowered "to arrange for a regular system of normal school instruction" and to that end it could adopt courses of study and designate schools and departments to be accredited for the training of teachers. While only twelve weeks of professional training were required for beginning teachers, the law stipulated that the board might provide a two-year training course for elementary teachers, graduates of which might teach without further license.[47] The requirements concerning the training of teachers were to become effective August 1, 1908.

Under the law and the regulations adopted in accordance therewith, Indiana University was approved as an accredited school for

[44] Catalog, 1908, p. 144.
[45] Ibid., pp. 146, 148-49.
[46] Laws of the State of Indiana, 1907, p. 147.
[47] Ibid., p. 451.

the training of all classes of teachers, October 3, 1907.[48] Application had been made to the State Board of Education for accreditment the preceding June and in connection therewith President Bryan had been authorized by the trustees to prepare a course of study and training to conform with the new requirements.[49] In formulating this program, Professor Bergstrom effected arrangements with the Bloomington schools for observation and practice teaching. These arrangements were approved by the trustees in their meeting after the opening of the fall term.[50] As the new law was not to go into force until August 1, 1908, quite likely its full effect would be first felt in the summer session of that year. An urgent demand for the initial twelve weeks of training was anticipated as the deadline approached and preparations were made for an increased enrollment. Though the summer session had been extended to a full term in 1905, it was found insufficient for the requirements of beginning elementary teachers. For this group, accordingly, special courses were provided which were to begin June 15,[51] ten days in advance of the regular session. Specialized courses were planned, likewise, for beginning high school teachers and still others for teachers of experience or previous training.

With a situation such as this developing, the Department of Education, which had administered the teacher training program at the University since 1902, was felt to be inadequate. It was, therefore, erected into a School of Education, just as the summer session was getting under way, at the June meeting of the Board of Trustees, in 1908. In the meantime, Professor Bergstrom had resigned to accept a position at Stanford University and President Bryan was made acting dean of the new school,[52] assuming, for the third time, leadership of Indiana University's activities in the field of teacher training.

The new School of Education got off to its first full academic year in the fall of 1908. It was quartered in Science Hall where the De-

---

[48] Minutes of the State Board of Education, Vol. IV, p. 139.
[49] Minutes of the Board of Trustees, June 17, 1907, p. 365.
[50] Ibid., November 6, 1907, p. 387.
[51] Catalog, 1908, pp. 283–86.
[52] Minutes of the Board of Trustees, June 23, 1908, p. 431.

partment had been accommodated since the completion of that building in 1902.[53] It made its bow to the public with this official announcement:

The enactment of the School Laws of 1907, requiring pedagogical training for all classes of public school teachers of the State, was followed by the segregation and organization of the pedagogic courses and faculty of the University. The result is the present enlarged School of Education.[54]

The requirements for admission to the new School were the same as those for the College of Arts. Students were not admitted to professional courses before the Sophomore year, except those who were in the twelve- and twenty-four-weeks' training courses. Graduates, with a major in education, were granted the A.B. degree, for which forty-five term hours in education were required. The A.M. and Ph.D. degrees also could be earned in this field by advanced work.[55] The Catalog of 1909 reports 189[56] students enrolled in 1908–9.

In this same Catalog we find methods courses appearing for the first time as education courses.[57] Ere long, another new course appears. This is announced as "Research in Education." At the same time, 1909, Henry Lester Smith, the new superintendent of the Bloomington schools, was added to the faculty in the capacity of director of school supervision and administrative practice.[58]

The next few years witnessed a steady expansion in the personnel and work of the new School. By 1911, arrangements had been made again to use the elementary grades of the local schools as a "school of observation," with an instructor from the campus in immediate charge of the work. Something of an innovation was the work in orthogenics which was a project of Professor Elmer E. Jones. It was announced in the Catalog of 1911,[59] as designed "to make a scientific study of all varieties of defectives." Under the plan of its sponsor,

---

[53] Previous to 1902, the Department of Pedagogy had been located in Kirkwood Hall.
[54] Catalog, 1909, p. 252.
[55] Ibid., p. 254.
[56] President Bryan, who was also acting as dean of the new School of Education, in his report to the trustees for this year, gives "a total of 605 students as the enrollment in the School of Education." (See Chap. IX.) This includes all candidates for a teaching license, a majority of whom were registered in the College of Arts and Sciences.
[57] Catalog, 1909, p. 257.
[58] Catalog, 1910, p. 263.
[59] Catalog, 1911, p. 191.

there was an attempt to provide treatment for "a limited number of such defectives," and afford opportunity for observation and "actual laboratory study." To supplement this enterprise, a course in orthogenics was added to the list of educational offerings. In the same year, the title of H. L. Smith was changed to that of "lecturer" in the School of Education and Walter A. Jessup was added to the staff as professor of school administration.

In the spring of 1912 Jessup succeeded President Bryan as dean of the School of Education. On his resignation in the summer of 1912 to go to the University of Iowa, William W. Black was appointed to the deanship and the work of the School was organized with elementary education under Black, the history and philosophy of education under Elmer E. Jones. Courses in school administration and secondary education were assigned to H. L. Smith and William F. Book, respectively. Steps were being taken to raise standards of work, as four-year students were not admitted to professional courses until the Junior year and thirty term hours of undergraduate work in education were required for graduate standing.[60]

With the developing activities and enrollment of the University, an expanded physical plant became an urgent necessity. In their biennial report to the Governor in 1912, the trustees outlined a building program for the immediate future. At the head of a list of five buildings stood the Education building, with this comment, "We place first the request for an education building to house the School of Education, which last year had 17 teachers and 506 students."[61] A site for the new building had already been selected at the corner of Forest Place and Third Street, where the Medical Building now stands. Yet twenty-five years were to pass, and all the buildings but one, on the list of 1912, were to come into being, before an Education building rose on the campus at Indiana University.

Nevertheless, the activities of the School of Education continued unabated. In June of 1913, the Department of Home Economics was established, with Mabel T. Wellman in charge. At the same time a Department of Industrial Education was instituted under the direction of Robert J. Leonard.[62] These departments were the result of

[60] Catalog, 1912, *passim.*
[61] Biennial Report of the Board of Trustees, 1912, p. 6.
[62] Catalog, 1914, pp. 198–99.

a law passed the preceding February by which school corporations were authorized to establish vocational schools or departments and the state undertook to subsidize such work to the extent of two-thirds of the cost involved.[63]

These two new departments occupied a somewhat anomalous position in the organization of the University. They ranked as independent departments, yet in certain administrative details were under the jurisdiction of the School of Education. In the industrial field, courses were soon developed in the "Theory of Vocational Education," "Vocational Guidance," etc. These, in the beginning, were taught by Professor Leonard, but were classified as education courses and were listed among the offerings of the School of Education. At the same time, the shop work involved in this field was announced as belonging in the Department of Industrial Education.[64]

In the same year, 1913, in which these two departments were established, the School of Education apparently began to pay increased attention to extension work. At least, it announced in the current Catalog that "a limited number of extension centers will be organized each year on application."[65]

The next year saw continued changes and development. By "special arrangement" with the local school system, provision was made for the maintenance of a school for backward children.[66] This was an outgrowth of the work in orthogenics inaugurated by Professor Jones some years before.[67] Pupils were assigned to graduate students who had at least a minor in psychology. We have found no record of the enrollment in this interesting course, but at times as many as twenty students were engaged in carrying on the instruction.[68]

Dr. Jones left Indiana in 1914 to go to Northwestern University and with his departure the work with atypical children that he had developed, with such apparent success, seems to have declined. The

[63] "An Act to provide for the encouragement, maintenance and supervision of vocational education in industries, agriculture and domestic science." Approved February 22, 1913. *Laws of the State of Indiana*, 1913, p. 37.

[64] Catalog, 1916, pp. 217–18.

[65] Catalog, 1913, p. 185.

[66] Catalog, 1914, p. 196.

[67] Professor Jones recalls that he organized this work in the fall of 1908, though no mention of it is found in the Catalog until 1911.

[68] Letter from E. E. Jones to F. L. Templeton, department of special education, Bloomington public schools, February 24, 1933.

course in orthogenics was continued for some years, but practice teaching in special education disappeared immediately from the Catalogs and no further mention of it is found. Bloomington did not develop a special school until several years later.

In 1915 Professor H. L. Smith left Bloomington and the University to become assistant superintendent of the schools of Minneapolis. W. W. Black, who had been made dean upon the resignation of W. A. Jessup, was still serving in that capacity, reluctantly. By 1916, he was becoming anxious to lay down the duties of his office and was urging the selection of his successor. This somewhat unusual situation was happily met by recalling H. L. Smith from Minneapolis after one year's absence, and he became dean of the School of Education August 1, 1916, a position which he held continuously for thirty years. Professor Black reassumed his duties as professor of elementary education, in which capacity he served until his retirement in 1925.

At the beginning of 1918 a distinct departure in the field of vocational education was made by the establishment of an Extension Center in Indianapolis which offered "a course for tradesmen who desire to become teachers of their trades." [69] Eventually, similar centers were established in seven industrial cities over the state and two instructors were engaged to devote full time to this work. Professor Leonard resigned in the spring of 1918, just as this work was getting under way. With his leaving, the Department of Vocational Education disappeared as a separate department at Bloomington and the shop work courses were transferred to the Department of Physics. Thus matters stood until 1923,[70] when an agreement was entered into with Purdue University whereby Indiana surrendered all work in industrial and vocational education. In accordance with this arrangement, the equipment and personnel in the new Extension Centers were transferred to Purdue and shop courses were discontinued in the Department of Physics. Only the courses in principles of vocational education, on the advanced level, were retained and these still constitute an important unit in the offerings of the School of Education.

[69] Catalog, 1918, p. 156.
[70] Catalogs, 1918 to 1924.

An enactment of 1913[71] made it possible to count a year of standard college work as professional training. In consequence, the special training courses declined somewhat in importance. This was the situation when Dean Smith assumed control of affairs and it continued without substantial modification until the law of 1919 gave a new aspect to the teacher training problem. This act provided that graduates of an approved two-year elementary training course should be entitled without examination to a four-year provisional certificate good in any elementary school. Likewise, graduates of approved four-year training courses might receive a provisional high school certificate in any subject in which two years of credit had been earned. At the end of the four years, in each case, a life license would be granted if the candidate could show two years of successful experience.[72] The law of 1919 marked the first real step in Indiana, it seems, toward the substitution of professional training for an examination in securing teaching licenses.

While the School of Education was, during this period, assuming a somewhat independent status, the relation between it and the summer session was becoming more closely knit. Ever since the summer of 1908, when the law requiring twelve weeks of training for beginning teachers had gone into effect, education courses had occupied a dominating position in the summer term. Recognition was given this intimate connection with summer work in 1919, in the appointment of Dean Smith as director of the summer session,[73] an office which he administered, in addition to his duties as dean of the School of Education, until World War II brought about the three-semester system.

It was under the law of 1919 that the School of Education began, apparently, to develop some degree of administrative independence and autonomy. Hitherto, it seems, the routine of registration had been cared for in the College of Arts and Sciences, even for those students majoring in education. The two-year elementary students now came to be regarded as a distinct group. They were placed

---

[71] Act approved February 28, 1913. *Laws of the State of Indiana*, 1913, p. 104.
[72] *Laws of the State of Indiana*, 1919, p. 753. This act became a law without the signature of the governor.
[73] Minutes of the Board of Trustees, October 28, 1919.

wholly under the direction of the School of Education and were required to have "a special enrollment card." Only those were admitted to this course who would "make written affirmation" that they wished to qualify to teach in the public schools and intended to teach in grades below the high school after completing their training.[74]

After the Bachman state-wide educational survey of Indiana, the law of 1923 changed fundamentally the basis of teacher licensing and inaugurated our present-day program of teacher training.[75] By this act, the issuing of all licenses after December 1, 1923, was vested in the State Board of Education. Local examining boards and examinations were abolished and licenses were to be granted only on the basis of training. Many different classes of licenses were established.

This statute brought about a decided increase in the work of the School of Education. To equip it better to meet its growing duties, it was erected, shortly after the passage of this act, into an autonomous school with the same status as other schools of the University.[76] This gave it authority to determine its own entrance requirements, establish and grant its own degrees, and in general to administer its own affairs. At the same time, in keeping with the enhanced dignity of a self-governing school, its critic teachers were given the rank of instructor in education in the University faculty.[77]

Perhaps the story of the School of Education since 1923 can best be told by tracing developments along three lines of growth: (1) increasing independence of the school in administrative affairs; (2) raising of standards in the training of teachers; (3) expanding the program of work offered.

When the law of 1923 was enacted, the School of Education was granting no degrees of its own. Undergraduate students taking its courses were registered mainly in the College of Arts and Sciences, where the education required for teaching licenses could be counted as elective work. These students upon graduation received the A.B.

[74] Catalog, 1920, p. 154.
[75] Laws of the State of Indiana, 1923, pp. 36 ff.
[76] Minutes of the Board of Trustees, April 25, 1923.
[77] Ibid.

degree, conferred by the College of Arts and Sciences. Graduate degrees earned in education were similarly granted by the Graduate School under rules and regulations prescribed by that School.

The first step toward administrative independence was taken after the passage of the law of 1919. It will be remembered that the two-year elementary group, created by this law, was placed wholly under the control of the School of Education and was provided with "a special enrollment card." In 1923, when the School was made an autonomous unit in the University, it naturally acquired the right to grant degrees of its own. The first B.S. in Education was granted in October, 1925, to one candidate. For some years thereafter, graduate degrees in education were still granted through the Graduate School. But in 1929 the School of Education was authorized to grant, on conditions to be determined by itself, advanced degrees in education. Two such degrees have been established, the Master of Science in Education and the Doctor of Education.[78] The first M.S. in Education was conferred by the School of Education in October, 1929, upon three candidates. At the June Commencement, the following year, there were eight candidates for this degree.[79] Since then, the number has grown rapidly until, not infrequently, this group constitutes the largest group of graduate students at any degree-granting session. The A.M. degree with a major in education may still be obtained from the Graduate School. The Ed.D. degree was conferred by the School of Education for the first time at the June Commencement, in 1932, upon two candidates.[80]

The other two developments to be noticed in the growth of the School of Education, since the passage of the law of 1923, have been listed as the raising of standards in the training of teachers and a steadily expanding program in the offerings of the School itself. These two movements are closely related since every change in the requirements for teaching licenses necessitates a corresponding change in the work of teacher training institutions.

The raising of standards in licensing requirements is, of course, primarily the work of the State Board of Education. The changes inaugurated have led in two directions: first, to an increase in the

[78] Minutes of the Board of Trustees, May 16, 1929.
[79] Commencement program, 1930.
[80] Commencement program, 1932.

requirements for existing licenses; and, second, to the establishing of licenses for activities that could previously be carried on without them. These licenses, however, were of different grades. Empowered by law to discontinue any licenses below the first grade, the State Board has rather steadily exercised its authority in this direction during the recent years.

The first modification was made by decree of the State Board stipulating that after November 1, 1927, all beginning teachers of academic subjects in high schools must be graduates of a four-year college course, i.e., must qualify for a first grade license. After November 1, 1929, the granting of all second grade licenses for teaching in elementary or high schools was discontinued. Two years later, the final step was taken when all second and third grade administrative and supervisory licenses were likewise discontinued. Thus, after November 1, 1931, all beginning teachers and administrators must be equipped with first grade licenses; no other kind would henceforth be issued.

With second and third grade licenses out of the way, the next steps were to establish licenses for schoolroom services that hitherto had been rendered without special license and to increase the requirements for those licenses already in existence. Thus, beginning with the school year of 1934–35 all coaches in commissioned high schools were required to hold a license in physical education.[81] By action of the State Board of Education, June 7, 1935, a license for public health nurses was to be required after September 1, 1936. On May 8, 1936, similar action was taken looking toward a license for school librarians, to become effective September 1, 1938. The State Board was already giving attention to the problem of additional requirements for teaching and administrative licenses. As early as May 6, 1932, it entertained a recommendation that a Master's degree as well as thirty hours of graduate work be required for administrative licenses. Final action was not taken, however, until September 14, 1934, when it was decreed that such a requirement would become effective January 1, 1935.[82]

An advisory committee on teacher training appointed by the

[81] Minutes of the State Board of Education, June 2, 1933.
[82] *Ibid.*, under dates indicated.

State Board of Education had recently submitted its report, which was adopted by that Board. By this action, the class which began its training September, 1937, was the last class to be accepted under the two-year course. After July 1, 1940, elementary licenses were to be issued only on the basis of four years of preparation. The general outline of a four-year course for this purpose was approved March 12, 1937.

The expansion in the program of the School of Education has been in large degree influenced by the changes just noted. So far as additions to the number of courses offered are concerned, much had been done even before the passage of the law of 1923. The multiplying offerings ere long made it desirable to effect a more systematic numbering of them. Under the new system adopted in December, 1926, the number of a course suggests both its level and its classification. Thus, Education 101 is recognized immediately as a Freshman course in general theory. Education 322 is a methods course on the Junior level, while Education 571 is a graduate course in the field of school finance.

At the beginning of 1926–27, a rural training school was opened through arrangement with Bloomington Township. Here, supervised teaching was carried on in the same general manner as in the city schools. This school was granted a first-class commission, the only one-teacher school in Indiana to hold that classification.

The expanding service which the School of Education was developing during this period was further indicated by the announcement for 1928–29 of a curriculum for school counselors.[83] This is intended to prepare candidates for positions as counselors in junior or senior high schools or as deans of boys or girls in such institutions. It extends through four years of college work and leads to the B.S. degree. Graduate work in this field is now available.

The authorization of graduate degrees in the School of Education naturally has given impetus to the development of graduate work, which has grown so rapidly that, at the present time (1937), the School enrolls 40 per cent of all the graduate students in the entire University.

[83] Announcements, School of Education, 1928, *Indiana University Bulletin*, Vol. XXVI, No. 12, pp. 37–42.

Although a license for school librarians was not required until September, 1938, the State Board, several years previously, recognized library science as one of the subjects in which a high school teacher might earn a license. In consequence, courses in that field were offered under the School of Education in the summer of 1930. They have been continued more or less regularly ever since but, so far (1937), are available in the summer session only.

Physical education has long been available at Indiana University. But with the increased emphasis that it has lately received in the public schools, there arose a feeling that instruction in this field on the campus should be greatly expanded and better organized. With this in view, at the close of the school year 1930-31 a Physical Welfare Training Department was created in the School of Education, with Willard W. Patty as director.[84] This is the only officially recognized department in the School of Education and to it has been allotted, not only the training of physical education teachers and coaches, but also that of teachers of health, hygiene, and safety, as well as the educational phases of the training of public health nurses. Its work extends, likewise, to the field of recreation. Courses have been developed for the training of supervisors of playgrounds, handicraft instruction, and Boy Scout activities. Arrangements were made in 1932 with the Normal College of the American Gymnastic Union, at Indianapolis, whereby that school became affiliated with Indiana University. Under the terms of this agreement, graduates of N.C.A.G.U. are admitted to the University with Senior standing, and by one year of work on the campus at Bloomington may earn the B.S. in Physical Education.

At the same time were announced tentative outlines of courses leading to the Bachelor of Science degree in Education with a major in nursing education. Three curricula are offered and are open only to graduate nurses. They cover two years' work and prepare respectively for a high school teacher's license in health and nursing, for teaching in schools of nursing, and for supervisory and administrative work in hospitals and schools of nursing. Last year (1936), graduate work was offered in this connection leading to an M.S. in Education with a major in nursing education.

[84] Minutes of the Board of Trustees, June 12, 1931. In 1946 it became a School.—Ed.

The Physical Welfare Training Department is one of the rapidly developing departments in the University. It offers work on the graduate level, as well as the undergraduate, and represents a pioneer effort in this direction in the Middle West. It attracts students from other states, many of whom are teachers of physical education in institutions of higher learning and find here an opportunity to secure advanced degrees in the line of their special interest.

Anticipating that four years of training would soon be required for all elementary licenses, those in charge of this work at Indiana University began, some time ago, the study of the problem of an integrated four-year course for the preparation of elementary teachers. By recent action of the State Board, four years of training have been made standard requirement for the elementary license for all candidates beginning training after September, 1937.

For many years a teacher placement service had been maintained on the campus in connection with the Registrar's office. In the summer of 1936 this service was transferred to the School of Education as the Bureau of Teacher Recommendations. Harold E. Moore, the county superintendent of Vigo County, was made full-time director of the work. Its services are offered free of charge to students of the University.

There remains one more development to record, and that is in the field of physical equipment. Until recently, education classes were held here and there in various buildings over the campus, wherever vacant rooms might be available. The School controlled no classrooms and had to accommodate itself in rooms belonging to other schools and departments when such rooms were not otherwise in use. In the summer of 1933, the offices of the School were moved to the old Theta house on Forest Place, where in 1937 they still remained. Some of the rooms in Science Hall which had been used as offices were retained as classrooms. Thus, for the first time, the School of Education has three classrooms that it may claim as its own. As these are quite inadequate for the needs of the School, its classes still meet here and there about the campus.

On October 27, 1936, a federal grant was secured to aid in the construction of an Education building. For several years, plans for such a building had been drafted in some detail and were kept revised from time to time as conditions and needs changed. Because of this, the architects could be put to work immediately. Before winter was over actual construction had begun and is in progress as this is written.

The original project called for a building that would house a laboratory school consisting of a nursery school, a kindergarten, a six-room elementary school, and a junior-senior high school, together with shops, auditorium, gymnasium, and all the customary accessories of a modern school. In addition, offices and classrooms for the School of Education were to be located in a wing which was to be an integral part of the building. However, construction bids exceeded preliminary estimates and a revision of plans became necessary. In consequence, the wing intended for the college classes was eliminated and retrenchments were made in the rest of the building. As a result, the new structure accommodates only the laboratory school. The new building was ready for occupancy in the summer of 1938 and went into operation for its first full year the following September.

The establishment of a laboratory school on the campus of the University entailed some modification of the administrative setup of the School of Education and a rearrangement of its relations with the local public schools in which student teaching had hitherto been carried on. On March 16, 1937, a new contract was entered into by the trustees of the University and the authorities of the school city of Bloomington. This defined the rights and privileges of each party in the new school. For each pupil the city pays to the University three-fourths of the annual per capita cost of educating pupils in similar grades of the public schools. The University determines the course of study and the textbooks for the school, subject only to the condition that all standards for a first-class school be fully met. Pupils assigned to this school attend free of cost, as in any public school. The kindergarten is operated, however, on a tuition basis.

COOPERATIVE RESEARCH AND EDUCATIONAL CONFERENCES

Among the special services rendered by the School of Education are two that extend over a period of years and have been reserved for special treatment. These concern the Bureau of Cooperative Research and the educational conferences that are held regularly on the campus. Both these services were inaugurated in the year 1914 and were in large degree pioneering efforts.[85]

Melvin E. Haggerty, who had been associate professor of psychology and director of the psychological laboratory, became the first director of the new bureau and in that capacity sustained relations with the School of Education while still remaining a member of the Department of Philosophy. In the December, 1914, issue of the *Indiana University News-Letter,* Director Haggerty described the Bureau of Cooperative Research and stated its purpose as follows: "(1) To render assistance to school corporations and officers in increasing the efficiency of school work in Indiana. (2) To further the growth of educational science. (3) To stimulate individuals to the further pursuit of educational research." At the beginning, the bureau operated on a membership basis, members paying a $2 fee annually and obligating themselves to carry on research. Paid memberships were later abolished and the bureau is now supported by the University.

It concerned itself very largely with tests and testing in the early period. More recently, it has developed several standardized tests of its own. The most ambitious effort in this direction was doubtless the development and standardization of the Indiana Composite Achievement Test by Wendell W. Wright. The School of Education, through the bureau, cooperates with the other state institutions of higher learning in developing uniform examinations in high school subjects. The examinations are duplicated and distributed to such high schools as wish to avail themselves of this service.

Another outstanding contribution of the bureau has been its well-known bibliography of educational measurements. A comparable service has been the development of a bibliography of school surveys and references on school surveys, the work largely of Edgar A. O'Dell, and bibliographies of school buildings, grounds, and equipment and of college and university buildings, grounds, and equipment, by Forest R. Noffsinger. Among other services, the bureau maintains a file of educational tests of all kinds. Regular additions have been made to this file until it has become one of the most com-

[85] H. L. Smith, "A Brief Summary of the Essential Facts concerning the Purpose, History, and Work of the Bureau of Cooperative Research at Indiana University." *Bulletin of the School of Education,* Vol. III, No. 6, p. 31.

plete in the country. In the earlier years, the studies of the bureau were published in the *Indiana University Studies*. In 1924, the *Bulletin of the School of Education* was established. Since that date, this has been the avenue of publication for the work of the bureau.

After serving two years as director of the Bureau of Cooperative Research, Dr. Haggerty resigned in the spring of 1916[86] and there seems to have been some difficulty in finding a suitable successor. In 1921 the duties of the position were assigned to Dean Smith,[87] pending continued efforts to find someone for the place. These efforts apparently failing, the dean continued as director down to the time of his retirement.

In the year in which the Bureau of Cooperative Research was established, there was held also, on the campus of the University, the first annual conference on educational measurements. This, like the bureau, was an activity of the School of Education and, like the bureau also, now claims to be the oldest of its kind in the United States. As tests became a commonly accepted device with which teachers were more and more familiar, this conference developed gradually into the general educational conference which it has been for some years past. It meets for a two-day session each April. The proceedings of this conference are published by the Bureau of Cooperative Research in the *Bulletin of the School of Education*.

Two other annual educational conferences have been instituted and maintained by the School of Education. The older of these is the high school principals' conference, which devotes itself to the administrative problems of the high school. Dating from 1922, it holds its meetings in the fall of the year and, to date, has met in fifteen annual sessions. Two years after the inauguration of this conference, a third annual conference was launched, known as the conference on elementary supervision.[88] It met for the first time April 17, 1924, on the day preceding the educational measurements conference of that year. This arrangement has continued ever since and the two conferences have come to constitute, for all practical purposes, one three-day educational conference.

[86] Minutes of the Board of Trustees, March 15, 1916. The Catalog of 1916 gives the date of the resignation as February 15, 1916.
[87] Minutes of the Board of Trustees, June 4, 1921.
[88] *Indiana University News-Letter*, Vol. XII, No. 3, March, 1924.

INDIANA UNIVERSITY THE MOTHER OF TEACHERS

Indiana has long been known as the prolific mother of teachers. Throughout the land, wherever schoolmen foregather, the Hoosier schoolmaster will inevitably be found. It is not surprising, therefore, that the training of teachers has long been a major interest at Indiana University. The School of Education, during the thirties, was the largest professional school in the University, enrolling more than 20 per cent of the entire student body in residence at Bloomington. On the graduate level, the ratio is even higher. More than one-third of all graduate degrees granted throughout the entire history of the University has been conferred upon education majors. During recent years this ratio has risen to more than one-half. The School of Education is especially active in extension work and in the summer session. During the past year (1936–37) the number of graduate students enrolled in extension classes for advanced work in education has aggregated 641. In the summer session, the School of Education has (1937) one-fifth of the entire summer faculty and carries one-third of the entire teaching load, as measured by the number of credit hours earned.

Naturally this constantly increasing volume of work has necessitated an increased personnel. The current Bulletin of the School of Education (1937) lists a staff of fifteen instructors in active service upon the campus and twenty-eight critic and assistant critic teachers attached to the training school. This staff, somewhat augmented in the summer session, and with the assistance of members of various subject matter departments, stands sponsor to some 150 courses carried under the classification of education. Fortunately, not all these courses are offered in any one semester.

A final summary of the nature of the work undertaken by the School of Education will enable us to bring this account to a close. Obviously the major concern of this division of the University is with the preparation of teachers and special workers in education at the various levels. This phase of the work is perhaps more extensive than the ordinary layman might suspect. It deals with the training of those who expect to teach in rural, primary, intermediate, grammar grade, and secondary schools, and with those who plan to become special teachers in commercial subjects, home economics, music, art, physical education, health, or library science, or to work in ungraded schools for backward children. An integral part of this training is the supervised student teaching carried on chiefly in the Bloomington schools under arrangement with the local school authorities. This is in immediate charge of the twenty-eight critic teachers just mentioned and is supervised by three members of the campus staff. During the past year, 335 students were enrolled in this work. In addition to training regular and special teachers, the School of Education extends its efforts to the preparation of graduate students for positions as elementary and high school principals, superintendents, supervisors, school business managers, attendance officers, personnel workers, school and public health nurses, and educational advisers to architects. At the higher levels, courses are offered, also, for training teachers and administrators for normal schools, colleges, and universities, as well as for research workers and directors of public school or college bureaus of educational research.

Beyond the field of teacher training, the School of Education, through its Bureau of Cooperative Research, carries on research and experimental work in elementary, secondary, and higher education. In this connection the bureau maintains a library and museum of educational materials for the use of any interested educators. Among these materials are several thousand educational reports, magazines, and books from all the civilized nations of the globe. The collections of school surveys and educational tests are especially extensive and complete, and probably are exceeded by those of very few other institutions. A somewhat similar collection of public school textbooks has been developed and is housed in a special "Textbook Seminar Room" in the Library. This collection is currently useful and with the passage of time may become a historical exhibit of some value. It may be regarded as a successor to the former "Pedagogical Museum" in which Professor Bergstrom was so deeply interested.

Through the bureau, the members of the staff have conducted studies in school finance, teacher supply and demand, the techniques of handling large classes, and many other problems of school administration. Reports on these studies are published at regular intervals in the bulletin issued by the bureau. The School of Education is ready at any time to aid, to the limit of its facilities, local school districts in conducting surveys, developing building programs, or studying budgetary problems. Without abating its efforts in the field of teacher training, it is coming more and more to recognize its obligation to provide service and leadership for all the educational interests of the state.

CHAPTER XLVI

FACULTY APPOINTMENTS AT INDIANA UNIVERSITY, 1824 - 1937

THE PURPOSE of this study is to determine the facts relative to the number of alumni and non-alumni appointed to the faculty of Indiana University from the beginning of instruction in May, 1824, to the close of the Bryan administration, June, 1937.

The major source of information on which this study is based is a "Who's Who" of the faculty of Indiana University completed in 1936 and kept up to date thereafter. The following form was submitted to and filled in by the members of the current faculty:

John Doe—
1. Now .... Present location and title. (Succeeded ultimately by date and place of death and burial.)
2. Born .... Date and place of birth, with names of parents.
3. Education .... Studied where, when, degrees earned and honorary.
4. Married .... To whom, date, children.
5. Record at Indiana University .. Various titles and period of service under each title.
6. Record elsewhere........... Places, titles, years.
7. Miscellaneous ....

Securing the essential parts of this biographical data for members of the faculty of earlier years presented no difficulty back to July 24, 1883, from which date the minutes of the Board of Trustees are complete. The disastrous fire of July 12, 1883, destroyed all University records except one book of minutes of the trustees, from February 15, 1838, to July 15, 1859.

The History of Indiana University, from 1820, When Founded, to 1890, by Theophilus Adam Wylie, the seventh man appointed to the faculty of Indiana University, was sometimes the only source of

573

information regarding very early appointees. Wylie became a member of the faculty in May, 1837. He retired in 1886 at the age of seventy-six. His history was printed five years before his death. He had known personally and intimately all but three members of the faculty of that early day. Baynard R. Hall, John H. Harney, and Ebenezer N. Elliott had left prior to 1837. This work is a most valuable contribution to the history of the University during those early years. With his feet on the "Western slope," and writing from memory, with most of the records destroyed by fire, it is remarkable that he omitted only three members of the University faculty, included in the University's "Who's Who."

Although the sources mentioned above have been checked, the biographical material for the faculty "Who's Who" was found so carefully prepared that it was relied on chiefly.

Section 7 of an act approved June 17, 1852, reads as follows: "The President, Professors, and Instructors shall be styled 'The Faculty' of the said [Indiana] university." Tutors, teaching fellows, assistants, and faculty of the Preparatory School are therefore not included in this study. The years a man may have served in any minor capacity are disregarded and his faculty connection is considered as dating from the time of his assumption of duties as an instructor or professor.

The members of the clinical faculty of the School of Medicine and of the Departments of Physical Education and Military Training are likewise not included in this study, with a few exceptions. The deans and hospital administrators of the School of Medicine are included. James Sheldon (football) had a teaching appointment in the School of Law. A few military appointees a hundred years ago taught mathematics or surveying and are included.

An alumnus of Indiana University is defined as a person having received a baccalaureate or other degree from Indiana University. An appointee not holding a degree from the University at the time he assumed his duties as an instructor or professor is regarded as a non-alumnus. A number of such non-alumni appointees later received an earned or honorary degree from Indiana University, thus becoming alumni. This did not change the fact that their educational status at the time of appointment was that of non-alumni.

1824–85

Indiana University was the fiftieth college or university to be established in the United States. Although in the following sixty years, 1820–1880, 330 colleges or universities were established, most were small and struggling institutions; and it was not until the close of that period that in the Midwest the career of the scholar acquired a living basis and became sufficiently attractive to compete with law, medicine, and the ministry for some of the ablest young men of the period. For example, the noted mathematician and astronomer, Daniel Kirkwood, had only one pupil, Francis P. Leavenworth (Indiana University, 1880), who became an astronomer, occupying that chair in the University of Minnesota, 1892–1927.

Moreover, prior to 1885 an enrollment of 200 had not been reached and maintained. In the year 1884–85 there were 157 students and a faculty of 18 members. The total number of appointees to this faculty from 1824 to 1885 was only 60, of whom only 7 were alumni of Indiana University. The following table shows the most important data concerning these 7 men:

TABLE 1—*Alumni Appointments, 1824 to January 1, 1885*

Name	Degree	Served	Title
James F. Dodds	A.B., 1834, A.M.	1837–39	Professor of Mathematics
Henry Tanner	A.B., 1842, LL.B., 1846, A.M.	1843–44	Professor of Mathematics and Civil Engineering
James Woodburn	A.B., 1842, A.M.	1853–54	Professor of Mathematics and Civil Engineering
Ambrose B. Carlton	LL.B., 1850	1856–57	Professor pro tem of Law
Amzi Atwater	A.B., 1866, A.M.	1870–93	Professor of Latin
Henry W. Ballantine	A.B., 1856, A.M.	1873–74	Professor of English Literature
		1877–78	Assistant Professor of Greek
Sarah P. Morrison	A.B., 1869, A.M.	1873–75	Assistant Professor of English Literature

Not one of these appointees had made special preparation as was demanded by President David Starr Jordan at a later period. It is true that six of the seven persons had Master's degrees. While these degrees were occasionally earned, it was a common procedure to confer them as a sort of bonus upon holders of the baccalaureate degree who continued for a time in the academic atmosphere, a sort of decoration for a valorous attempt to follow an academic career under very difficult conditions.

Of these seven appointments, six were temporary—for one or two years only. The one person who remained a long time had the equivalent academic training of the others but in addition had a likable personality. The first three appointments indicate a purpose to establish mathematics or mathematics and civil engineering as part of the curriculum.

1885-1937

January 1, 1885, is a date in the history of Indiana University ranking in importance second only to January 20, 1820 (the date of its founding). It marks the end of an early period of foundation, frustration, and near extinction, and the beginning of the present period of gradual progress in the development of the University. A very critical situation in the history of the University was climaxed by the resignation of President Lemuel Moss in November, 1884. A month later, December 19, David Starr Jordan was elected president, effective as of January 1, 1885.

Writing of the beginning of this period in the "Hoosier and City Life" section of the *Indianapolis Star* of February 20, 1916, under the title, "When I Was in Indiana," Jordan said:

> The best things I did there were these two: the introduction of the elective system of study in the "major professor" form, and the selection of the best fitted alumni as professors. . . .
> Hitherto new professors had been mainly sought from the East, and as a rule only the second rate of the young men would accept. After some not very successful attempts to do better I promised chairs to certain alumni on condition that they should adequately prepare in Europe or the East. Among these at the beginning were Swain, Bryan, Hoffman, Woodburn, and Philputt.
> Of these, Joseph Swain and William Lowe Bryan have successfully filled the President's chair. They brought what the University most needed in the teaching staff, character, enthusiasm, and loyalty. And to these and to other alumni professors who followed them a large part of the educational progress of Indiana for these thirty years has been due.

For Jordan's innovation, "the selection of the best fitted alumni as professors," it would have been impossible to have chosen a more

For twenty-five years or more prior to 1937 these fifty-two men and women were teachers and friends to thousands of students.

FRANK MARION ANDREWS
Botany

FRANK GREENE BATES
Government

LILLIAN GAY BERRY
Latin

ERNEST HENRY BIERMANN
German

ALFRED MANSFIELD BROOKS
Fine Arts

OLIVER W. BROWN
Chemistry

ROBERT ELISHA BURKE
Fine Arts

WILBUR ADELMAN COGSHALL
Astronomy

ANNA BROCKMAN COLLINS
English

JOTILDA CONKLIN
French

JOHN WILLIAM CRAVENS
Registrar

EDGAR ROSCOE CUMINGS
Geology

LOUIS SHERMAN DAVIS
Chemistry

SCHUYLER COLFAX DAVISSON
Mathematics

JOHN BENJAMIN DUTCHER
Physics

CARL H. EIGENMANN
Zoology

ARTHUR LEE FOLEY
Physics

JOHN L. GEIGER
Music

ULYSSES SHERMAN HANNA
Mathematics

CORA BARBARA HENNEL
Mathematics

AMOS SHARTLE HERSHEY
Government

HORACE ADDISON HOFFMAN
Greek

WILLIAMS EVANS JENKINS
Librarian; English

ALBERT LUDWIG KOHLMEIER
History

ROBERT EDWARD LYONS
Chemistry

FRANK CURRY MATHERS
Chemistry

CLARENCE EARL MAY
Chemistry

JULIETTE MAXWELL
Physical Education

WILLIAM J. MOENKHAUS
Physiology

GEORGE DAVIS MORRIS
French

CHARLES ALFRED MOSEMILLER
French

BURTON DORR MYERS
Anatomy

CARL W. F. OSTHAUS
German

DAVID MYERS MOTTIER
Botany

FERNANDUS PAYNE
Zoology

JOSEPH WILLIAM PIERCY
Journalism

ROLLA ROY RAMSEY
Physics

WILLIAM A. RAWLES
Economics

MARY ETHELDA RODDY
Physical Education

DAVID ANDREW ROTHROCK
Mathematics

WILLIAM H. SCHEIFLEY
French

WILL SCOTT
Zoology

CHARLES JACOB SEMBOWER
English

ULYSSES HOWE SMITH
Bursar

GUIDO HERMANN STEMPEL
Comparative Philology

HENRY THEW STEPHENSON
English

FRANK WILLIAM TILDEN
Greek

BERT JOHN VOS
German

JAMES M. VAN HOOK
Botany

ULYSSES GRANT WEATHERLY
Sociology

KENNETH POWERS WILLIAMS
Mathematics

JAMES ALBERT WOODBURN
History

CARL H. EIGENMANN   FERNANDUS PAYNE

DEANS OF THE GRADUATE SCHOOL

HORACE ADDISON HOFFMAN   SELATIE EDGAR STOUT

DEANS OF THE COLLEGE
OF ARTS AND SCIENCES

DAVID ANDREW ROTHROCK

MEMORIAL HALL

SOUTH HALL

FOREST HALL

ALPHA HALL

MEMORIAL UNION BUILDING—Bookstore at right

INTERIOR OF BOOKSTORE

BIOLOGY HALL

SCIENCE HALL

LIBRARY

CHEMISTRY BUILDING

ROSE WELLHOUSE

STORES AND SERVICE BUILDING

auspicious moment, for Joseph Swain, William L. Bryan, Horace A. Hoffman, James A. Woodburn, and Allan B. Philputt, recent graduates, were teaching in the Preparatory Department, or the local high school, or, in the case of Hoffman, had already gone east to do postgraduate work.

This plan, introduced by Jordan, was continued during the administrations of John M. Coulter, Swain, and Bryan, and influenced appointments to the faculty during the fifty-two years of these four administrations. Because of the growth of the University, the number of appointments was many times greater during the period 1885 to 1937 than in the years before 1885. In contrast with the 60 appointments to the faculty in the first sixty-one years of the life of the University, there were 897 appointments made in the fifty-two years from 1885 to 1937.

If we consider these 897 appointees from the standpoint of their original appointment we find they are distributed as in the following chart:

TABLE 2—*Alumni and Non-Alumni Appointments, 1885–1937*

	Alumni	Non-alumni
Professors, Heads of Departments, and Deans	22	84
Associate and Assistant Professors	37	142
Instructors	302	274
Directors and Major and Minor Executives	22	14
Total	383	514

Too much significance must not be placed on the figures in the above classification for different people might reach slightly different conclusions and the same person at different times reaches conclusions differing slightly, a variation of .4 of 1 per cent, in the classification of these 897 faculty members. The reason for this slight variation is that dual titles are sometimes given. For example, a man may be a professor or associate professor of ——— and a director of ———, something else. Shall he be classified as director or professor? In which capacity does he function chiefly? Judgments vary.

The significant figures are the totals. Of these 897 appointees 383 (42.7 per cent) were alumni and 514 (57.3 per cent) were non-alumni.

This high percentage of alumni among these 897 appointees is due to the appointment of so many alumni as instructors. Of deans and heads of departments only 20 per cent (22 out of 106) were alumni. Of associate and assistant professors, 21 per cent (37 out of 179) were alumni. But among the instructors 52 per cent (302 out of 576) were alumni. This matter will be considered further a little later.

The 127 Major Appointees, 1885–1937

Among these 897 appointees there were 100 (36 alumni and 64 non-alumni) who, during the period 1885–1937, were appointed as or promoted to be heads of departments or deans, and 27 (14 alumni and 13 non-alumni) who became directors or major executives. Because of the important part played by these 127 leaders during the years 1885 to 1937 it is believed that it will add interest in and understanding of faculty appointments to study these groups in greater detail.

Table 3—*Persons who were appointed or became heads or chief executives*

| | Alumni | | | | Non-Alumni | | | |
	Deans and Heads	No.	Non-Teaching Executives	No.	Deans and Heads	No.	Non-Teaching Executives	No.
Jordan 1885–91	Aley Banta Branner Bryan Eigenmann Foley Gilbert Green Hoffman Lyons Naylor Woodburn	12	Sheeks	1	Barnes Boone Campbell, D. H. Dabney Jenks Karsten Kingsley McCabe Matzke vonJagemann Woodford	11		
Coulter 1891–93	Davisson Mottier Rogers Rothrock Sembower	5			Baillot Commons Fellows Marsters Ross Snow	6		
Swain 1893–1902	Fetter Lindley Miller Moenkhaus Morris Rawles		Cravens		Bergstrom Brooks Cogshall Cumings Hershey Johnston Kuersteiner Merrill, W.A. Reinhard		Babine Bates Breed Danforth	

	Alumni		Non-Alumni	
	Deans and Heads	Non-Teaching Executives	Deans and Heads	Non-Teaching Executives
	No.	No.	No.	No.
			Sampson Stempel Stephenson Tilden Weatherly	
	6	1	14	4
Bryan 1902–37	Book Burke Campbell, C.D. Edmondson Forry Gatch Kohlmeier Maxwell, A. McNutt Payne Rice Smith, H.L. Wells, H.	Alexander Biddle Cavanaugh Chamness Elliott Goodbody Heighway Jenkins Neff, R.E. Smith, S.E. Smith, U.H. White, C.	Alburger Bates, F. Black Carter Conklin Emerson Gavit Hall Harger Henshaw Hepburn Hill Hills Hogate Howe Jessup Leonard MacLaren Manwaring Merrill, B.W. Moffat Moon Myers Nollen Piercy Rea Robinson Stout Sutherland Turner Vos Wellman Young	Cookson DeNise Holland, J.E.P. Mason Martin Monroe Pettijohn Thompson Wells, A.
	13	12	33	9
Totals	36	14	64	13

It will be noted that within this group of deans and heads, alumni constituted 52 per cent of Jordan's appointees (12 of 23), 45 per cent of Coulter's appointees (5 of 11), 30 per cent of Swain's appointees (6 of 20), and 30 per cent of Bryan's appointees (13 of 46).

It is of further interest to break down the alumni and non-alumni groups of each administration into smaller groups in which each man is placed in the faculty rank of his initial faculty appointment. The result is shown in Tables 4 and 5.

TABLE 4—*Initial Ranks of Appointees*

Jordan, 1885–91

	Alumni	No.	Non-Alumni	No.
Heads and Deans	Banta Branner Gilbert Hoffman Woodburn	5	Barnes Boone Campbell, D.H. Dabney Jenks Karsten Kingsley McCabe Matzke von Jagemann Woodford	11
Assistant Professors	Naylor	1		
Instructors	Aley Bryan Eigenmann Foley Green Lyons	6		
Directors or Executives	Sheeks	1		

Coulter, 1891–93

	Alumni	No.	Non-Alumni	No.
Heads and Deans	Rogers	1	Baillot Commons Fellows Ross Snow	5
Associate Professors			Marsters	1
Instructors	Davisson Mottier Rothrock Sembower	4		

Swain, 1893–1902

	Alumni	No.	Non-Alumni	No.
Heads and Deans	Fetter Miller	2	Johnston Kuersteiner Merrill, W.A. Reinhard Sampson	5
Assistant Professors			Bergstrom Hershey Tilden Weatherly	4
Instructors	Lindley Moenkhaus Morris Rawles	4	Brooks Cogshall Cumings Stempel Stephenson	5

	Alumni	No.	Non-Alumni	No.
Directors or Executives	Cravens		Babine	
			Bates, H.S.	
			Breed	
		1	Danforth	4

Bryan, 1902–37

	Alumni	No.	Non-Alumni	No.
Heads and Deans	Book		Alburger	
	Maxwell, A.		Black	
	Smith, H.L.		Carter	
			Conklin	
			Emerson	
			Gavit	
			Henshaw	
			Hepburn	
			Hills	
			Hogate	
			Howe	
			Jessup	
			Leonard	
			Merrill, B.W.	
			Nollen	
			Piercy	
			Robinson	
			Stout	
			Sutherland	
			Vos	
		3	Young	21
Associate Professors	Gatch		Bates, F.	
			Hall	
			Hill	
			Manwaring	
			Moon	
			Myers	
			Rea	
			Turner	
		1	Wellman	9
Assistant Professors	Payne		Harger	
		1	MacLaren	2
Instructors	Burke		Moffat	
	Campbell, C.D.			
	Edmondson			
	Forry			
	Kohlmeier			
	McNutt			
	Rice			
	Wells, H.	8		1
Directors or Executives	Alexander		Cookson	
	Biddle		DeNise	
	Cavanaugh		Holland	
	Chamness		Martin	
	Elliott		Mason	
	Goodbody		Monroe	
	Heighway		Pettijohn	
	Jenkins		Thompson	
	Neff, R.E.		Wells, A.	
	Smith, S.E.			
	Smith, U.H.			
	White	12		9

It should be borne in mind that the 100 men considered in the preceding tables are the men who were appointed or promoted to be heads of departments or deans during the years 1885-1937.

If during the fifty-two years of these four administrations, alumni were recipients of special consideration, it should appear in connection with these 100 most important appointments to the faculty of Indiana University. To summarize:

Table 5—*Initial Status of Appointees becoming Heads of Departments, 1885 to 1937*

	Alumni		Non-Alumni		
	No.	Per Cent	No.	Per Cent	Total
Heads of Departments and Deans	11	20	42	80	53
Associate Professors	1	9	10	91	11
Assistant Professors	2	25	6	75	8
Instructors	22	79	6	21	28
Total	36		64		100

The table shows that only 20 per cent, 11 out of 53, who were appointed as heads of departments were alumni. Nine per cent of associate professors and 25 per cent of assistant professors who were later promoted to headships of departments were alumni. Seventy-nine per cent of instructors who ultimately became department heads were alumni. This means alumni instructors were appointed with a better evaluation of ability than were non-alumni.

According to President Bryan:

The initial suggestion and recommendation of those appointed as instructors came, in nearly all cases, not from the president but from heads of departments to the president, and through him to the trustees.

Whatever motives influenced heads in their recommendations, a chief motive must have been the securing of satisfactory assistance.

Recommendations of department heads in many instances were made under the emergency of unexpectedly large enrollments in certain departments, as will be shown later. Distribution of this group as to numbers and percentage of alumni and non-alumni is shown in Table 2. The later history of these appointees shown elsewhere in this report indicates that these appointments, whether alumni or non-alumni, were generally justified or of short duration.

President Bryan also stated:

The initial suggestion and recommendation of those appointed as assistant or associate professors came usually from heads of departments. These appointments were well considered in each case by the head concerned and the president, and then by the trustees.

TABLE 6—*Training of Alumni Heads and Deans*

	A.B.			Masters					Doctors														
	Butler	DePauw	Indiana U.	Columbia	Cornell	Harvard	Indiana U.	Stanford	Bonn	Chicago	Clark	Columbia	Cornell	Halle	Harvard	Heidelberg	Indiana U.	Johns Hopkins	Leipzig	Miami Med.	Penn. U.	Strassburg	Tubingen	U. of Paris
Aley			X				X															X		
Banta			X																					
Book			X				X				X													
Branner																		X						
Bryan			X				X				X													
Burke			X				X																	
Campbell, C.D.			X																				X	
Davisson			X				X																	X
Edmondson			X				X										X							
Eigenmann			X				X										X							
Fetter			X	X											X									
Foley			X				X						X											
Forry		X															X							
Gatch			X															X						
Gilbert	X						X										X							
Green			X				X																	
Hoffman			X	X																				
Kohlmeier			X	X												X								
Lindley			X				X			X														
Lyons			X				X									X								
Maxwell, A.			X				X													X				
McNutt			X																					
Miller			X					X		X														
Moenkhaus			X				X			X														
Morris			X				X																	X
Mottier			X				X		X															
Naylor							X																	
Payne			X				X					X												
Rawles			X	X								X												
Rice			X				X											X						
Rogers			X																					
Rothrock			X				X												X					
Sembower			X																		X			
Smith, H.L.			X				X					X												
Wells, H.			X				X																	
Woodburn			X				X											X						

The large majority of these 36 alumni heads and deans enjoyed the broadening influence of some years' contact with other universities as was shown in Table 6.

It will be noted that seven European universities, six Eastern universities, and three midwestern universities provided the graduate training of this group. Only six had the Doctor's degree from Indiana University. Two of these, Frank Forry and Thurman B. Rice, received the degree Doctor of Medicine and in time became heads of departments in the School of Medicine. John C. Branner, Clarence E. Edmondson, Carl H. Eigenmann, and Charles H. Gilbert received the Ph.D. degree at Indiana University and had long careers as educators.

Branner had never been a student at Indiana University. His Ph.D. was his only degree and that was honorary, though well merited. He had been state geologist to Brazil and was regarded as the most eminent American on the geology of South America. He followed Jordan to Stanford, where, in Jordan's absence, he was acting president.

Edmondson and Eigenmann had all their formal academic training at Indiana University, where Edmondson became dean of men, and Eigenmann, organizer and dean of the Graduate School. Eigenmann's work is so well known that no comment is needed. Edmondson's work is less well understood (Chap. LIV, p. 761).

Gilbert followed Jordan to Stanford where he was professor of zoology from 1891 to 1928, the time of his death. Joseph P. Naylor had never been a student at Indiana University. His only degree was the honorary Master's degree from Indiana University. He left the institution in 1891 for DePauw where for thirty-two years he was professor of physics.

The non-alumni appointees of this group of deans and department heads enjoyed great diversity of training. Two universities, Cornell and Harvard, each furnished the graduate training of four of these appointees. Eight earned a Doctor's degree at Johns Hopkins, four each at the University of Chicago and Cornell University, and three each at Princeton and Yale. The scholastic training of these 64 non-alumni faculty members who became deans or department heads is shown in the following table.

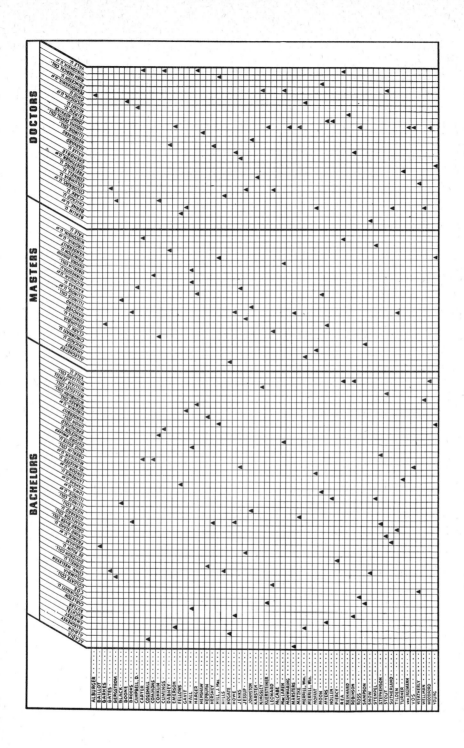

Of the total number of directors or executives the 27 named in Tables 3 and 4 had major responsibilities. Of this number 14 were alumni and 13 non-alumni. These 27 directors, as a rule, were not members of the faculty under the act approved June 7, 1852. There were, however, a few exceptions in which, in addition to the title as director or executive, the individual also had a professorial title carrying faculty membership. Known efficiency of the appointee was the sole consideration involved in making these appointments.

Instructors, 1885–1937

The number of instructors was so large that this class of appointees deserves further study to determine what became of them. The following table presents the important facts about their relations with the University.

TABLE 8—*Instructors, 1885 to 1937*

	Alumni	Non-Alumni	Total
Remained at I.U. 1 to 4 years	168	176	344
Remained at I.U. 5 to 25 years	36	34	70
Earned some professorial rank	76	58	134
Became head or dean	22	6	28
Total	302	274	576

Of the 28 instructors who became heads or deans, 79 per cent were alumni. Of the 134 instructors who won some professorial rank, 76, or 56.7 per cent, were alumni. The 36 alumni instructors and 34 non-alumni instructors, a total of 70, who remained at Indiana University five to twenty-five years have all but disappeared. No large group of them were in the faculty at any one time. Though they rendered service commensurate with their rank and remuneration, rules relating to employment of personnel in force since 1940 will in the future limit the number in this group.

A further check was made on what became of the 344 instructors who remained in Indiana University one to four years only. Of these, 209 (60.8 per cent) had nonacademic careers, and 135 (39.2 per cent) had successful careers as professors or deans in other colleges or universities. Of the latter, 74 were alumni and 61 were non-alumni. These facts are summarized in the following table:

TABLE 9

	Alumni	Non-Alumni
Assistant professors	12	16
Associate professors	15	12
Professors	38	27
Deans	8	6
President	1	
Total	74 (54.8%)	61 (45.2%)

The fact that 74 of these 168 alumni instructors, as contrasted with 61 of the 176 non-alumni instructors who left Indiana University in four years or less, had successful academic careers in other universities and colleges would seem to indicate that the alumni group of appointees during these fifty-two years was somewhat the stronger.

The largest group of short-term instructors of Indiana University had nonacademic careers. There were 209 of these, of whom 94 were alumni and 115 non-alumni. The careers of some were cut short by early death. The remainder are found as businessmen, chaplains, directors of various departments and enterprises, editors, judges, lawyers, physicians, surgeons, superintendents of city schools, heads of departments in city schools, research specialists in various fields, employees in various departments of the United States government, and in a considerable range of other activities. The major difference in the nonacademic careers of these 209 persons was that there were many more lawyers and doctors in the alumni than in the non-alumni group.

These facts indicate that the instructorship at Indiana University was a proving ground and that advancement to higher faculty rank has been commendably difficult. The University has had no length-of-service policy of promotions. Demonstration of superior ability as a teacher or as an investigator in some independent field, not a mere rehash of the doctorate thesis, or performance of some service important to the University and the commonwealth have been fairly consistently required as a basis of promotion.

Presidents

Previous to 1885 there were six presidents, of whom William Daily was an alumnus of Indiana University. Presidents, as such, have not been included in any count of the faculty. Alfred Ryors and David Starr Jordan are included in the count of faculty prior to 1885 since both were professors prior to becoming president. Bryan is included since his appointment as instructor was effective as of January 1, 1885. He served seventeen years as a faculty member, to June, 1902.

When Jordan was elected president there were forty-seven applicants for the position. In 1884 it was not considered a breach of good form to apply for this position.

Coulter, of course, was never a student or member of the faculty at Indiana University. The minutes of the trustees show that John M. Coulter was elected professor of botany and geology on April 14, 1885. He evidently refused the appointment, for on June 6, 1885, Branner was elected professor of geology and instructor in botany. The Ph.D., which was granted Coulter in June, 1884, the minutes of the trustees indicate to have been "pro merito." During his brief stay of two years at the University, Coulter had to make a comparatively large number of appointments because Jordan had taken with him to Stanford six men from the faculty he had built up, five of them department heads.

Coulter was never a member of the so-called "Specialists' Club," nor was Swain. James A. Woodburn gave the membership of this club as "Jordan, its organizer, representing biology; Charles H. Gilbert, zoology; Horace A. Hoffman, Greek; William Lowe Bryan, philosophy; Rufus Green, mathematics; and James A. Woodburn, history." Bryan and Hoffman, members still living (1940), have been consulted without adding to this list. The purpose of the club was not the meeting of specialists but the stimulation of young men to become specialists. It fitted in with Jordan's idea of selecting superior alumni and sending them away to qualify for their specialty. An instance of this was the appointment of Swain as associate professor of mathematics, with a leave of absence of one year in which "to qualify for mathematics work." As the mission of this very informal club was fulfilled, Jordan's catholic interest was transferred to other matters and the club faded out.

Jordan deliberately started at Indiana University what commonly has been called inbreeding, a term adopted from the biologists. But it must be noted that Jordan, in his autobiographical sketch in the

Indianapolis Star, was not talking of promiscuous inbreeding which has given rise to the deduction that all inbreeding led inevitably to degeneration, but of selective inbreeding by which the best qualities of a strain are emphasized and perpetuated.

Jordan, Coulter, Swain, and Bryan were searching for men of superior ability and had the keenness to recognize and the courage to develop them, even if found on their own campus. Adaptability was a factor of great importance in the selection of new faculty members, but adaptability was not a quality confined to alumni. Some of the most adaptable men were found among the non-alumni appointees, while the greatest opposition to the initiation of a program for making Indiana University a university in fact was encountered in some ultraconservative alumni faculty members. It was not expected, of course, that the appointee would be complacent on encountering inadequate facilities. It was hoped that he would grasp the vision and share the conviction, bordering on certainty, that in time conditions at Indiana would be made adequate and that it was going to be worth while to help bring about that better day.

Seventy-four alumni[1] of Indiana University have been called to some normal school, college, or university as president (1937). Boards of trustees of these widely distributed institutions have recognized these individuals as men of superior ability and attainment by selecting them for the high office of president. Since Indiana men have received this recognition from seventy-four groups of trustees throughout the United States, would not the trustees of Indiana University have been unpardonably short-sighted if some of the best of these had not been retained as long as possible as faculty members?

After an absence of many years, Jordan pointed with pride to the establishment of this procedure as one of the best things he did while in Indiana and expressed the conviction that to it was due "a large part of the educational progress of Indiana University."

Peculiar Difficulties, 1885–1937

In addition to these facts with reference to appointments during the 113 years of the institution's existence (1824–1937) with special emphasis on the fifty-two years of the administrations of Jordan,

---

[1] In addition to the 74 alumni there were 7 non-alumni members who were called to the presidency of some educational institution.

Coulter, Swain, and Bryan, there are other factors necessary to an evaluation of the innovation introduced by Jordan. There was a rapid increase in enrollment, calling for additions to the teaching staff. Appropriations did not keep pace with the need for additional teachers and the instructional staff became increasingly inadequate.

The gain in enrollment is shown by the following tables:

TABLE 10—*Doubling of Enrollment, 1885–1937*

For the Year	Enrollment
1884–85	157
1888–89	300—doubled
1894–95	633—doubled again
1901–2	1,285—doubled still again
1909–10	2,564—doubled a 4th time
1924–25	5,067—doubled 5 times
1936–37	7,005

TABLE 11—*Acceleration of Enrollment During the Periods Noted Above*

Period	Gain	Average Gain Per Year
1885–89	143	36
1889–95	333	55
1895–1902	652	93
1902–10	1,279	160
1910–25	2,503	167
1925–37	1,938	161

It will be noted that there was an acceleration in the average annual gain in enrollment up to 1925. Because of the great increase in the number of matriculants, an unexpectedly large enrollment in a number of departments at the opening of nearly every year constituted an emergency calling for relief. This emergency was met in 52 per cent of the cases by appointment of some recent graduate, available on short notice, as instructor. A special study of 576 instructors shows that 60 per cent of these appointments were temporary and that advancement to professorial rank was difficult.

During those fifty-two years of most rapid increase in enrollment, the increase in budget was not commensurate with the increase in teaching load. The report of the committee on finance, made under date of January 3, 1885, estimated the income for 1884–85 at $56,676. With a budget of this size, Bryan was offered an instructorship in the fall of 1884 for the year at $250, which he declined. In June, 1885, he was made associate professor at a salary of $1,000. Jordan's salary for 1884–85 had been $1,800.

The inadequacy of state support of the University is further indicated by the fact that when the fire of 1883 destroyed the main University building, the legislature voted a paltry $15,000 for its rebuilding. It was not until 1895 that a tax of one-sixth of a mill (on the dollar) was imposed by the legislature for support of Indiana University, Purdue University, and Indiana State Normal. By the close of the school year 1900–1901, the enrollment had doubled three times since January 1, 1885, while the University income had a little more than doubled. In the year 1884–85 the budget of $56,676, though small, was in excess of $400 per student. The budget of 1901–2, $129,-000, was slightly in excess of $100 per student. When confronted by the necessity of appointing an emergency instructor, a better alumnus than non-alumnus could usually be secured for the small salary available. With the waning of non-state school opposition, the mill tax was increased and, though Indiana has never been as generous as some neighboring states in support of higher education, state appropriations did improve. The dissipation of non-state school misapprehension and opposition was one of the finest fruits of the tactful and friendly attitude of the Bryan administration. We believe that, in any effort to evaluate the policy introduced by Jordan, the peculiar difficulties of the period as sketched briefly above should be considered.

NEPOTISM

This study was undertaken to determine the degree to which alumni had been appointed to faculty or administrative positions in Indiana University. Nepotism has not been considered. Instances could be cited in most universities in which brothers, or parent and child, or husband and wife were concurrently members of the same faculty. This is not nepotism. The appointive body is the Board of Trustees, unrelated to appointees. To review the relationship, if any, of members of the teaching or administrative staff to the Board of Trustees throughout the 113 years of the history of Indiana University, 1820–1937, is impossible, for relationships are not known in early cases.

During the past seventy years certain appointments have been regarded as instances of nepotism, which, according to Webster, is bestowal of patronage on the basis of relationship rather than of merit.

One of the earliest cases is that of Allan B. Philputt, son-in-law of James D. Maxwell. Mr. Maxwell was a trustee, 1861–92. Allan B. Philputt, A.B., Indiana University, 1880, served as instructor in Greek, 1884–87, and associate professor, 1887–89. Between 1880 and 1884 he had been a graduate student at Indiana University, Harvard University, and elsewhere. Considering the excellent preparation of Mr. Philputt for this appointment and taking into account the fine career of this superior man, one must conclude the appointment was made on merit.

Louise Maxwell, daughter of Trustee James D. Maxwell, served as card cataloguer in the Library of Indiana University, 1889–93. Her father died in 1892. In 1893 she became acting librarian. With the exception of one year spent at Leland Stanford University on leave of absence, she spent the remainder of her life as acting librarian or assistant librarian of Indiana University, where she rendered superior service.

In 1899, fifty years ago, the administration was in search of a competent person as keeper of grounds. Since the heart of the campus was twenty acres of primitive forest, there was needed a man who, among his other accomplishments, was part forester. A person with the knowledge, experience, and judgment desirable had not been found. In this emergency, Robert A. Ogg, a trustee, said: "I do not like to suggest my brother, but he knows all about doing what we are needing here." An investigation was made and William R. Ogg was appointed and served most acceptably for many years.

All three of these cases—and others might be cited—had one feature of nepotism, viz., the appointee was related to a person in the group having appointive power. But there is no evidence that any one of these appointments was on a basis of relationship instead of merit. On the contrary, the trustees refused to permit themselves to be handicapped by the fact of relationship when a person of superior merit was available.

The appointment of Sarah Parke Morrison, daughter of Trustee John I. Morrison, has been looked upon erroneously as an example of nepotism. John I. Morrison served as trustee, 1846–55, 1874–78. Miss Morrison's appointment was made in 1873 when her father was not a member of the board. She served only two years.

Closely Related Faculty and Staff Members

Within the faculty there have been instances of closely related persons. John P. Foley, brother of Professor Arthur L. Foley, had been appointed and was serving as electrician for the campus. His work often overlapped that of the man in charge of building maintenance and there were occasional clashes between them. Both were good men. The President solved the problem of clashing personalities by assigning John Foley as technician in the rapidly expanding Department of Physics, of which his brother was head.

For some years Mrs. Myrtle E. Stempel taught in the Department of Comparative Philology, which was headed by her husband, whose hearing was failing and who might have to be replaced at any time. There was never any question regarding the high quality of her work.

There were other instances in which husband and wife, or parent and child, or other closely related persons were concurrently on the faculty or staff of Indiana University. Among these were Mr. and Mrs. John Cravens (Mrs. Cravens, Miss Mellie Greene, had been the efficient secretary of the President before her marriage). There were Mr. and Mrs. Clarence Edmondson, Mr. and Mrs. Walton S. Bittner, Mr. and Mrs. Robert E. Burke, and other like instances in all of which superior service was secured by the University through appointment of someone closely related by blood or marriage to some faculty or staff members. Among these cases I know of not a single instance of nepotism. No appointee was related to the appointive body, the trustees, and in every case superior service was rendered. Yet employment of closely related persons did give rise to criticism.

Rules Relating to Employment of Personnel

To avoid even the appearance of procedure open to criticism, the trustees, on May 31, 1940, adopted a resolution governing employment of personnel under which employment of closely related persons was discontinued entirely. Since 1940 is a date beyond the period covered by this Volume II of the *History of Indiana University* the resolution[2] is not discussed here. It is, however, a matter of interest to

---

[2] This resolution does not apply to cousins or to persons more distantly related.

ascertain to what degree appointments would have been affected by this resolution had it been in effect throughout the period of this study.

To make this determination the following procedure was adopted. Starting with a complete list of faculty members, 1824 to 1937, the list was carefully checked by several persons whose long association with the University and whose wide acquaintance rendered their judgment valuable. Every person in the list who was known to be or thought to be in any way related to any other faculty member, administrative officer, or trustee was marked for careful study. The list was then checked by President Bryan and by Dean H. L. Smith, both of whom have lived in Bloomington all their lives, and by Professor William J. Moenkhaus, appointed under the Swain administration in 1894.

Instances of supposed relationship were carefully checked by contacting the individuals or their relatives. Likeness of name does not mean family relationship. For instance, Professor Rolla R. Ramsey and Earl E. Ramsey, at one time principal of Bloomington High School, are not related in any known degree. The Barbours, Elizabeth and Humphrey, were not related despite the identical spelling of the family name.

Carelessness in checking facts of relationship can lead to great error. As an illustration, Lillian Gay Berry (1902–43) was the sister of Burton Bowers Berry (1893–94). Her appointment followed that of her brother after an interval of eight years. Merely stating the fact of relationship, though truthful, may still lead to a very false impression. The period of employment of all related persons was, therefore, painstakingly ascertained in order to determine whether appointments were concurrent. Dr. William J. Moenkhaus, for example, was not related to Ernest W. Rettger at the time their appointments were concurrent. At a later date they became brothers-in-law.

The study reveals the fact that during the years 1824–1937 there were 54 persons on the faculty who were related but whose periods of service were not concurrent. Therefore these 54 persons are given no further consideration. There are 122 persons whose appointments were concurrent and who were related as follows:

By blood:
Parent-child 32
Brother-sister 21
Uncle or aunt, nephew or niece........................ 4
                                                            — 57
Cousins 3
Second cousins 7
                                                            — 10
                                        Total........67
By marriage:
Husband-wife 38
Brother- or sister-in-law............................... 7
Father-, mother-, son-, or daughter-in-law............... 2
Child and step-parent.................................. 0
                                                            — 47
Cousins 7
Second cousins 1
                                                            — 8
                                        Total........55

Omitting 18 cousins and second cousins, not included in the board rules, there were 104 persons (122 less 18) related in the degree covered by the resolution of the Board of Trustees. If the resolution of the board had been limited to parent-child, brother-sister, husband-wife, brother- or sister-in-law, it would have applied to 94 per cent of cases they included. If the resolution had included all degrees of relationship up to and including second cousins by marriage, it would have applied to only 18 additional persons in 113 years.

One should not leave this subject without stating that in the most frequent faculty relationship, husband and wife, the wife in most instances proved eminently fitted for and adapted to the work for which she was appointed. For the greater part, the child-parent and brother-sister appointments were of brief duration. In a few instances in which the appointments extended over a considerable period of years, contemporary faculty members knew a very worth-while service was being demanded and rendered.

Conclusion

The story here related conforms to type for the development of an old culture, such as art, literature, or education, in a new territory.

The culture was first imported, but bringing it to America did not make it American. It was still European culture, only transplanted, and it remained so for half a century or more until a new generation began to write stories and paint pictures. Some of these new Americans went across the water to learn what Europe had to teach of art and literature, and came back to write and draw. People liked what they wrote and painted and finally even Europe said it was good, and so we knew it was good. We bought the stories and books and paid the artist for his painting, and the author and artist paid the grocer, and a culture was established in new territory on a living basis.

Essentially this process was repeated when education was carried across the mountains to a new frontier in the great Northwest Territory, a territory larger than Germany or France, a territory in which education was subsidized in township and state by federal land grants. During the first sixty years only a few graduates of the state school succeeded in establishing themselves in the field of university education. But with the election of Jordan came the dawn of that new period when the transplanting process was completed and education had taken root in the new soil.

CHAPTER XLVII

THE INDIANA UNIVERSITY LIBRARY

By William A. Alexander

THE HISTORY of the Library of Indiana University may be divided into three parts: 1824, the date of the opening of the Seminary, to the fire of 1854; 1855 to the fire of 1883; and 1884 to the present.

1824 TO 1854

There is no record of the origin of the Library, but we can be reasonably certain that on May 1, 1824, the ten boys who entered the Seminary as its first student body had access to the private library of the Reverend Baynard R. Hall, the first professor of the new school. Professor Hall doubtless brought with him into the new state a number of valuable books dealing with courses of higher learning. Judge David D. Banta states that Professor Hall himself said that he was "the very first man since the creation of the world that read Greek in the New Purchase."[1] It is safe to assume that there are no records extant of the library of the Seminary, during its short existence of four years.

On January 24, 1828, the Indiana state legislature gave the State Seminary the status of a college, Indiana College. On May 5, 1828, Andrew Wylie, D.D., was selected as its president.[2]

The first mention of a library in any of the publications of Indiana University is found in *Indiana University, Its History from 1820, When Founded, to 1890*, by Professor Theophilus Adam Wylie:

In 1838, the last year under the college charter, a member of the Board brought charges against the President for maladministration; the principal charge seems to have been with reference to the purchase of books for the

---

[1] Woodburn, *History of Indiana University, 1820–1902*, p. 332, n. 5.

[2] Banta, in Woodburn, *op. cit.*, p. 64, tells us that President-elect Andrew Wylie spent the summer of 1829 in the seaboard states begging books and money for books, for a library in Indiana College. There can be no doubt that there was a library in Indiana College with the coming of President Wylie.—Ed.

Library. It was asserted that more money than had been appropriated by the Board had been spent, and improper books had been bought. The President, however, was fully acquitted, and was thanked by the Board for what he had done, instead of being censured.

The first annual Catalog of the University to contain any reference to the Library is that for the year 1839–40,[3] in which it is stated that "a library, not large indeed, but rich in a choice collection of the most invaluable books is provided." The Catalog of the following year announced the establishment of a library fee, a circulation system, and the acquisition of new volumes as follows:

The collegiate library is open to all the students on paying a subscription of fifty cents per session. Each subscriber is permitted to take out a volume every Saturday.

This library has recently been augmented by a purchase of about two thousand dollars' worth of books, some of them rare and valuable. It embraces a choice collection of Greek, Latin, French, and English Classics; the best standard works on History, Biography, and the Sciences; together with a selected variety of miscellaneous literature.

The earliest known catalog of the Library is the fifty-page publication printed by order of the trustees in Bloomington in 1842. It is a classified catalog (in contrast to the dictionary catalog now used) arranged under highly technical terms, many of which are now rarely used or are obsolete. The entries under each class are by the

---

[3] Earlier references to the Library are found in the minutes of the first meeting of the University Board of Trustees, September 27, 1838, p. 15, as follows:

"Mr. Owen from the Library Committee offered the following report:

Report

" 'The Committee on the Library report that they have examined the Library of the University and find the same in good order and preservation. While your Committee were pleased to find in the Library many interesting and useful, and some rare and curious works, they regretted to perceive that many others of a standard character, and some especially useful to us as American citizens, were still deficient. In looking over the works on the shelves, they noticed one (the Thesaurus) which, however valuable in itself, and however essential as a work of reference, in a very extensive and complete Library did not seem to your committee as useful, in the present stage of the institution as its price ($300) expended in other, less costly works would be. They recommend therefore, that if the said work can be sold (as your Committee have been informed it can be) for the same it cost, the president of the University be empowered and instructed so to sell it, and to invest the proceeds chiefly in works connected with the early history of our country—in voyages and travels, and in other standard English Works. They would especially recommend the following: . . .' [For an interesting list of these books see original manuscript of B. D. M.]

"At this same meeting of the Board of Trustees, on motion of Trustee Owen it was resolved that Professor Dodds be appointed Librarian of the University to serve one year from this date (September 27, 1838)."—Ed.

title instead of author, and they are not arranged alphabetically, nor even chronologically by date of publication. The preface of this catalog is quoted in full:

In the preparation of the following catalogue, the exemplar catalogue given by Professor Park of the University of Pennsylvania in his Pantology has been taken as a guide. As many of the terms used in his classification are new, it will be necessary to explain, as concisely as possible, their meaning.

Under the head Pantology and General Bibliography are comprised all those works of a general nature such as Encyclopedias, Libraries, etc., which treat to a greater or less extent of branches of knowledge in every department.

Under the head Psychonomy, all those works which treat of the laws of mind, or of the intellectual sciences. This province is divided into four departments; viz. 1. Glossology: under which head we arrange all works which relate to the study of language. 2. Psychology: those which treat of mental science. 3. Nomology: those which treat of law or government. 4. Theology: those which treat of religion, using the term in its widest sense.

Under the head Ethnology are arranged those books which treat of nations, geographically or historically. This province is also divided into four departments. 1. Geography: under which head are placed all voyages, travels, and statistical works, as well as geographical, commonly so called. 2. Chronography: works treating of civil history and antiquities. 3. Biography: the lives of eminent men. 4. Callography: poetical works, romances, and miscellaneous literature.

Under the head Physiconomy we place those works which relate more immediately to the material world. In this province are three departments: 1. Mathematics. 2. Acrophysics, or Natural Philosophy: under this head all works relating to natural phenomena. 3. Idiophysics, or Natural History: works treating chiefly of natural productions. 4. Androphysics, or Medical science: works which have reference to the structure, functions, etc., of the human frame.

The fourth and last province is Technology: Under this head we place those works which relate to the physical arts, either useful or ornamental. This province in like manner is divided into four departments. 1. Architecnics: under which head we would arrange, if we had them, works treating of the art of Construction and Communication. 2. Chreotechnics: works on Agriculture, Manufactures, and Commerce. 3. Machetecnics: works on the arts of war. 4. Callotechnics: works on the Fine Arts such as Music, Painting, etc., exclusive of Poetry and Romance. There are still further divisions of these various heads, which the size of the library renders unnecessary to regard.

According to this first library catalog, the number of volumes in the Library in 1842 and the entries in each class are shown by the following table:

	No. of Vols. by subjects	No. of Vols. by groups
I. Pantology and General Bibliography	108	108
II. Psychonomy—		
General works	47	
I. Glossology	37	
II. Psychology	72	
III. Nomology	217	
IV. Theology	201	574
III. Ethnology—		
I. Geography	35	
II. Chronography	106	
III. Biography	97	
IV. Callography	196	434
IV. Physiconomy—		
General works	12	
I. Mathematics	5	
II. Acrophysics	28	
III. Idiophysics	21	
IV. Androphysics	8	74
V. Technology—		
II. Chreotechnics	3	
IV. Callotechnics	6	9
Total	1,199	1,199

On April 9, 1854, the largest and newest University building containing the Library was destroyed by fire. Not a book was saved from about 1,200 valuable volumes.[4] The rooms of the Athenian and Philomathean Societies with their small libraries were also destroyed.

1855 TO 1883

By the last day of November, 1856, a new building was ready for occupancy and a room on the second story was assigned to the Library. Soon after the fire,[5] Henry W. Derby, a prominent bookseller and publisher of Cincinnati, Ohio, wrote the following letter to President Daily:

Reverend William M. Daily, D.D., President of Indiana University

Dear Sir—Upon a recent visit to Bloomington, the calamity which had befallen the University in the total destruction of its library was brought to my

[4] See note 8, below.
[5] Wylie says September 25, 1855.—Ed.

attention. In aid of repairing a loss so serious to an institution of learning, I beg you to select from our general catalogue of books to the amount of fifteen hundred dollars, which are hereby placed to your order.

> Respectfully, your obedient servant,
> H. W. Derby.

Needless to say, this generous offer was gratefully accepted.

At about the same time W. H. Jones, of Fort Wayne, Ind., presented to the Library a valuable collection of law books of the seventeenth and eighteenth centuries. There were about 800 volumes in the Derby collection and about 200 volumes donated by Mr. Jones.

In 1864 about 1,000 volumes, brought by Professor Richard Owen, were placed in the Library to be used by students under the same regulations which applied to the books owned by the University.

The annual Catalog of 1870 solicited donations of books for the Library. By 1873 the whole number of volumes in the Library was 7,000, including the 1,000 volumes of Dr. Owen's library and about 600 volumes in each of the two literary societies.

In a Commencement address[6] at Indiana University, June 11, 1924, Dr. James Albert Woodburn, Professor Emeritus of American History, who entered as a Freshman in the fall of 1872, said:

> In that one building also was the library, the whole of it in one small room. There were no departmental libraries. A busy member of the faculty, Professor T. A. Wylie, acted as librarian, the library being open one forenoon a week, on Saturdays. . . .
>
> The little library room of the time was crowded and cluttered. There was no reading room, no chairs to tempt the students to linger and read, and stack permits to enable them to browse among the books were as unnecessary as the practice was unknown. So far as I recall there were no periodicals to induce the interest of students in current affairs. The students went in (or a few of them did) only long enough to return a book and to take out another for a week. In no direction is the progress of the University more striking than in the growth and use of the Library over those days. Now we think of the Library as the heart of the University which must grow with the body, and we are quickly sensitive to the danger of heart pressure or cramped conditions that may prevent further expansion.

In 1876 President Moss presented to the trustees his views of the aims and needs of the University and stated that the greatest need

[6] *Alumni Quarterly,* Vol. XI, p. 298.

was the enlargement of the Library. He asked for a minimum of $6,000 but added that $10,000 could be wisely expended and then leave the necessities of the Library far from satisfied. In the same report he recommended that the contingent fee for students be increased from $3 a term to $5 a term and that of this sum $3 a term be applied to the Library[7] for constant additions of books. By 1882 the size of the Library had increased to more than 12,000 volumes. The book stacks were open to all. The Library was open every day during term time (except Sunday, Saturday p.m., and examination days) from 9 a.m. till noon and from 1:30 p.m. till 5 p.m. In this year the Library became a designated depository of all public documents published by the state and by the United States.

1883 to Date

On the night of July 12, 1883, the main University building erected in 1873 was destroyed by fire. The Library of about 13,000 volumes was destroyed, and also the library of Professor David S. Jordan.

At the beginning of the present accession record, opposite accession Number 52, is found the statement: "The only volume rescued from the fire of 7/12/83."[8] This book is a government document, valuable today because of the difficulty of obtaining documents of so early a date and also because of its rescue. The book is U.S.—Patent Office. Annual Report of the Commissioner, 1848. The volume is in good condition at this date. In starting a new library collection in October, 1883, there were 59 books on hand for a beginning, all belonging to the old Library. These books were probably in circulation at the time of the fire. From among these books, Pedestrian in France and Switzerland, by G. Barrell, Jr., was given accession Number 1 and begins a new record. Today, this book seems to have been given a place of signal honor, but was undoubtedly selected haphazardly enough at the time of recording. The volume is in the Library today, and is in excellent condition.

The first librarian[9] of Indiana University was Theophilus Adam

[7] The board did not approve this recommendation at once but by 1883–84 there was a $5 contingent fee and a $1 library fee.—Ed.

[8] See Woodburn, op. cit., p. 332, n. 5, for the story of another book which survived the fires.—Ed.

[9] See note 3, above.—Ed.

Wylie, who came to Indiana College in 1837 as professor of natural philosophy and chemistry. Professor Wylie supplemented his teaching duties by acting as librarian from 1860 to 1879. While the annual Catalog of the University for 1860 is the first to record his name as librarian, it is generally understood that he served in that capacity for a number of years prior to that date.

The Catalog for 1880–81 lists the name of William Wesley Spangler as librarian, the second to occupy this office in Indiana University. His name is recorded in the same publication as secretary of the Board of Trustees. In 1884 he also served as registrar. Mr. Spangler was born near Auburn, Ind., November 15, 1855. He was graduated from Indiana University in 1880 with both the Bachelor of Arts and the Bachelor of Letters degrees, and in 1886 received the A.M. degree. In his second year as librarian he started the first card catalog, classified according to the decimal system.

After the fire of July 12, 1883, which destroyed nearly the entire collection of books, the Library opened the year 1884–85 with about 1,200 volumes and an annual expenditure from $2,000 to $3,000 for its increase. Several liberal donations of valuable works were made. Among these was a nearly complete set of Professor Louis Agassiz' scientific works, given by his son, Professor Alexander Agassiz.

The trustees had purchased twenty acres in what was known as "Dunn's Woods," on the eastern edge of Bloomington. Two new buildings had been erected on the new campus and in the larger one, Wylie Hall, the Library was placed, when in the fall of 1885 the University moved to this new site. At this time the Library contained nearly 7,000 volumes. On June 7, 1887, the trustees enacted the following rules for the Library:

The Library shall be under the general charge of the Librarian.

The Library rooms shall not be a place for loafing, nor for the transaction of any business not connected with the legitimate purposes of the Library.

The doors shall be open (on all college recitation days) at 8:15 o'clock a.m. and remain open during the day until 4 p.m., except for an hour at the noon recess.

No loud talking, laughing, or other noises shall be allowed in the library rooms. The Librarian is empowered to call upon the janitor to enforce strict observance of this rule.

The Faculty shall designate and set apart such books as belong to a reference library, which books shall not be removed from the library except by permission of the President of the University, for special work, to be returned in such time as he shall designate in such permit.

Books belonging to a particular department solely, and so designated, may be taken by the heads of departments for classwork, to be returned as soon as no longer needed.

Books not belonging exclusively to some one department may be so taken by permission of the President, he designating the time for the return of the same, and to have power to direct the same to be returned sooner, if needed, for use in any other department or for any other purpose.

Books not reserved as reference books strictly may be taken by the Faculty and students of the University, on their receipting to the Librarian therefor, to be returned in two weeks from date of such receipt.

Any person not connected with the University desiring the use of the Library shall be permitted the free use thereof in the library rooms under the same restrictions as apply to others regarding good order, but shall not have the privilege of taking books away unless by permission of the President, who shall be responsible therefor.

Any person losing, defacing, writing in, or otherwise injuring any book belonging to the Library shall be fined the cost of replacing such book, and shall be debarred from all privileges of the Library until the same shall be paid.

A new Library building, Library Hall, renamed Maxwell Hall in 1894, was dedicated on January 20, 1891. The central part, or book room, having a capacity of 60,000 volumes, served the double purpose of stack room and reference reading room. The north half of the room was occupied by students' tables and chairs and the other half by iron cases, on which were shelved all books except those of the Law School. Four rooms on the first floor of the west end of the building were used for the official and mechanical work of the Library, newspaper reading room, and storage of periodicals and pamphlets. The first and second floors of the east wing and the second floor of the west end were used as classrooms by various departments of the University. As the enrollment of students increased the Library gradually acquired all space in the building except the second floor of the west wing, which came to be used for the general administrative offices. In late December, 1907, the Library was moved to its present location.

Mr. Spangler retired as librarian in 1892–93, and in the fall of 1893 Louise Maxwell became acting librarian. Miss Maxwell was an alumna of Indiana University, class of 1878, and was a daughter of

Dr. James D. Maxwell, in whose honor the Library building of 1891 was named.

The first record of Library assistants had appeared in the Catalog in 1888–89 when Miss Maxwell was listed as "Library Card-Cataloguer," Florence Hughes, as "Card-Cataloguer," and John Roscoe Mutz as "Library Accessions Cataloguer." To Miss Maxwell belongs the distinction of the longest period of service in the Library of anyone who has served the institution. She was acting librarian, 1893–96, 1903–4, and 1909–10, and in 1896 was made assistant librarian. She was on leave of absence in 1900–1 to serve as classifier in the library of Leland Stanford University. She was on active duty for thirty years and from 1918 to her death, August 24, 1926, was on leave of absence on account of ill health. Thus Miss Maxwell was officially connected with the Library for thirty-eight years. She was a cultured, broad-minded, sympathetic official who might have had a long and successful career as permanent librarian had she desired to assume the full responsibilities of that position.

At this time there were 19,000 volumes in the library, the Dewey Decimal system of classification was used, and a complete card catalog was in operation. The books were on open shelves accessible to everybody seven hours a day, six days a week. The reading room provided about 150 periodicals.

For the years 1896–98 Alexis Vasilievich Babine was librarian. He was born in Russia, March 22, 1866. In 1888 he came to America and entered Cornell University where he earned the A.B. degree in 1892 and A.M. in 1894. He arrived at Cornell University with the sum of $15 and a slight reading and writing knowledge of English but no acquaintance with the spoken language. However, his knowledge of Latin, Greek, French, German, Italian, Spanish, and Russian with the related Slavic languages was outstanding, and he was assigned to assist in the cataloging of Russian books. He was an assistant in the Cornell library from 1890 to 1896.

Mr. Babine's services at Indiana were of a high scholarly and practical order. He was systematic, thorough, and direct. In his relations to his subordinates as well as to his superiors he was patient and kind. At the same time he was rigorous in maintaining discipline with the former and in executing instructions from the latter.

After two years at Indiana he resigned in order to accept the position of associate librarian at Leland Stanford University, where he remained until 1901. From 1902 to 1910 he served in the cataloging and classification division of the Library of Congress.

His service in the Library of Congress was interrupted in 1910 by his desire to return to Russia to devote himself there to teaching and writing. He published a two-volume history of the United States in the Russian language. While in Russia he secured for the Library of Congress the famous Yudin collection of books in Russian history, literature, and bibliography comprising more than 80,000 volumes. Caught in Russia by the World War and the ensuing revolution, after suffering five years of starvation, cold, risk of imprisonment and of wanton execution without trial, he with difficulty secured his release and returned to the Cornell library in 1922, where he served until 1927 as supervisor of accessions. In 1927 he became chief of the Slavic Division of the Library of Congress, serving until his death on May 10, 1930.

Referring to Mr. Babine's appointment as the head of the Slavic Division, Herbert Putnam, Librarian of the Library of Congress, writes in his annual report for 1930:

Scholarly, methodic, industrious, punctilious, and versed in the necessary technique; familiar also with administration, and liking it, his professional qualifications for the post were in that field very unusual. And they were complemented by personal qualities which won great respect, and among his intimates warm affection. A peculiar uprightness of mind, character, and bearing gave him distinction and inspired confidence and liking. With it a sensitive modesty and a loyalty always to be relied upon.

In his will dated the day before his death, after specifying a bequest of $500 to his stepmother in Russia, Mr. Babine left the entire residue of his estate to the Library of Congress Trust Fund Board "for the use of the division of Slavic literature in the increase of its collections in Russian literature, Russian political and social history, and the history of Russian fine arts."

In the account of the change of the classification of books to the Library of Congress system given below, it is noted that a few schedules have not been finished by the Library of Congress. One of these is Russian literature. The delay is due to the death of Mr. Babine on whom the Library of Congress had counted for a scheme of Russian literature.

George Flavel Danforth succeeded Mr. Babine as librarian of Indiana University in 1898. He was graduated from Cornell University in 1890 with the degree of Bachelor of Philosophy and from the Auburn Theological Seminary in 1893. He did graduate work at Yale and Cornell universities and while at Cornell he was an assistant in the Library.

After the fire of 1883 new records were started in the Library (October 1, 1883). The Dewey Decimal system, in use at the time of the fire, was still in use when Mr. Danforth became librarian, but he was not satisfied with this system. Among some of the University libraries there was a feeling that the Dewey classification system was inadequate for academic purposes, and, consequently, various other classifications were used. Cornell University was using the British Museum notation, which, according to their own statement, "can hardly be called a classification." Voicing the general dissatisfaction among universities with the Dewey schedules, Mr. Danforth undertook the task of compiling a classification of his own, using the one at Cornell as his basis. The main divisions of this classification were thought out very carefully, the arrangement was logical and scientific, not unlike that of the Library of Congress, and overcame many objections to the Dewey. But the Dewey classification was a practical one, had the continuity and elasticity of application in which this newly devised classification was entirely lacking. Miss Maxwell, Assistant Librarian, who had charge of the classification at that time, saw the defects in the application of the new system and objected to the discontinuance of the Dewey. However, the change was made. At the time there were 30,154 books in the Library classified in Dewey which had to be reclassified; besides, the current incoming books at the rate of from 2,000 to 3,000 books a year had to be handled.

Mr. Danforth retired as librarian in June, 1903, and William Evans Jenkins came as librarian in the summer of 1904. Mr. Jenkins received the A.B. from Indiana University in 1891 and the A.M. from Leland Stanford University in 1894. Until his appointment as librarian he was engaged in business in Richmond, Ind., and brought to his new position a rare combination of scholarship and practical business ability which resulted in an unusually successful career as a librarian. Before beginning his duties as librarian he spent five months at the Albany Library School as a special student under Melville Dewey.

The first event of importance in this period was the erection of a new building for the Library, which was finished January 1, 1908, at a cost, including equipment, of $137,000. The site made possible the placing of the first floor in the vertical middle of the stack tower. The building was built in the form of an "L." The main reading room 56 by 94 feet has seats for 204 readers while around the walls is shelving for 6,000 volumes in the open reference collection. In the basement under the reference room are eight small rooms for seminar purposes. The stack tower provided for seven levels, three of which were installed in the new building. The third level is continuous with the floor of the main reading room. The circulation desk was placed at the north end of the main reading room. The offices and staff working rooms were located on the first floor of the wing extending to the east. The second floor of this wing was used by the Department of Fine Arts for studio and classrooms.

The Library was moved to the new building in the holidays of 1907–8. The book collection was moved in three days, thought to be a record for a library of that size, and service was suspended for only one hour during the moving. When the Library was moved there were 64,000 accessions.

The opening of the new building marked the beginning of expert reference service as distinguished from competent delivery and circulation desk service.

The second important work under Mr. Jenkins' librarianship was the change of the classification system to the plan devised and used by the Library of Congress. In 1916–17 Ida Wolf became acting classifier and in 1918 was classifier. Until the fall of 1918 the system of classification devised by Mr. Danforth had been in use long enough for its deficiencies in detail to become apparent. At any rate, the system was breaking down and something had to be done. The Library of Congress classification was receiving universal recognition and was considered best for large libraries. Such libraries as the University of Chicago, Leland Stanford, and the University of Michigan were using it. If the Dewey system had been in use at this time, there would have been no change. But in view of the former change it seemed unwise to reinstall Dewey, especially when there was a recognized better system in process, the Library of Congress system. At this time, too, the United States had entered the World War, and the Library was not ordering so many books. Consequently, if the change ever was to be made, it was a particularly propitious time for it. The Board of Trustees in the spring of 1918 authorized the installation of the Library of Congress classification. Reclassification was begun September, 1918. There were 125,600 books in the old classification when the transition was made. The work was effected by adding approximately 16,000 books a year to the Library of Congress classification, which included the current books immediately added to the new classes. The Library was annually receiving from 6,000 new books in the early days of the change to the recent 13,000, the greater number of new books balancing the smaller number of reclassified books that needed to be added as the years advanced.

For all practical purposes the Library of Congress system is completed at the present time. But the system itself is still in process of formation. The Library of Congress has not as yet completed certain classes and fragments of classes. However, Indiana University has been supplied with manuscript forms of the classification not yet printed, and in this way the work has been very materially speeded.

And so the Library at present is classified under the Library of Congress plan, the most modern, scholarly, and definitive system used by large libraries today. It is difficult to foresee a time or a development in library technique when this classification will become inadequate. The work has been very competently carried on by the regular staff in addition to the routine work of the Library without a special appropriation for that purpose. Ida Wolf has been the head of the classification department throughout the entire process of reclassification and deserves great credit for this work.

In the summer of 1921 Mr. Jenkins retired as librarian and was appointed professor of English literature, preferring to devote his entire time to teaching. He engaged in this work until his death in 1939. Mr. Jenkins was succeeded as librarian by William Albert Alexander,[10] writer of this sketch.

From 1921 to 1937 Indiana University has enjoyed a period of steady and substantial growth. In this period the Library has kept pace with the general growth of the University. The School of Law maintains a separate library under competent supervision. The staff of the main Library has been increased gradually from eleven in 1921 to twenty full-time members and thirty student assistants in 1937. The number of accessions has increased in sixteen years from 144,000 volumes to 300,000 volumes.

The four additional levels in the stack towers provided for in original plans were erected between the years 1922 and 1926.

In January, 1927, an addition to the Library was opened for use. The session of the state legislature of 1925 appropriated $325,000 for the new addition, of which approximately $225,000 was used for the building and $100,000 for equipment.[11] The addition provides new reading room facilities for 180 students, a larger newspaper room, additional seminar rooms, more space for the cataloging and classification departments, new rooms for the bindery and bound newspapers, and increased space for general storage. The new reading room became known as the reserve book room. The circulation desk was moved from the reference room to a new room called the circulation room. The general card catalog is located in this room.

In addition to the central Library where the general literary and historical collections are housed, there are seventeen departmental collections of varying sizes, kept in the different University buildings. These collections are: Anatomy, Astronomy, Botany, Chemistry, Dentistry, Fine Arts, Geology, Hygiene, Law, Mathematics, Medicine, Music, Physical Training for Men, Physical Training for Women, Physiology, Physics, and Zoology.

A recent innovation of the classification department is the acquisition of fireproof safes to house the shelf records and the accession books. For advantage in insurance security, the state fire in-

[10] During his student days, 1895 to 1901, Mr. Alexander had been a library assistant. From 1901 to 1905 he had served as reference librarian. He served as librarian from 1921 until his death July 8, 1943.—Ed.
[11] See Chap. XXV, p. 303.—Ed.

surance department required that one Library record be kept fire-proof. In compliance with this demand, the shelf list and accession records are locked in steel safes while staff members are not on duty. While this in no way safeguards the books in the Library from burning, it does give the Indiana University Library a safe check of the volumes the Library contains.

The 300,000th volume in the Library was accessioned on February 23, 1937. President William L. Bryan was asked to select one of the books which he had written as the 300,000th accession. Accordingly, he chose *Plato the Teacher,* edited jointly by Mrs. Bryan and himself. They autographed the book. This 300,000th book represents a period of growth of 53 years and 7 months. It took 31 years and 6 months to collect the first 100,000 volumes, viz., from July, 1883, to January, 1915; 13 years, 10 months, for the second 100,000 volumes, from January, 1915, to November, 1928; 8 years, 3 months, for the third 100,000 volumes, November, 1928, to February, 1937.

The Library budget for the fiscal year 1936–37, excluding the cost of heat, light, repairs on building, and janitor service, follows:

Salaries	$36,575.50
Student assistants	9,825.00
General books and continuations	3,750.00
Departmental books and continuations	14,815.25
Binding	4,125.00
Equipment and supplies	3,000.00
Total	$72,090.75

Recent grants of special appropriations by the Board of Trustees have enabled the Library to add some invaluable sets to its collection: *The Times* (London) from 1835 to 1933, almost a complete run, was bought for $2,850; the Senate Legislative documents 1-25 were purchased at a cost of $800; the *Cincinnati Daily Gazette* from 1849 to 1882 cost $1,000; the *Cincinnati Daily Commercial* from 1849 to 1927, incomplete, was purchased for $673.75, and the *Monumenta Germaniae* cost $3,088.10. A special appropriation of $2,500 has been made and apportioned among the various departments for the purchase of material needed for graduate study.

Chapter XLVIII

THE INDIANA DAILY STUDENT [1]

*Compiled, May, 1937, for Professor Joseph W. Piercy by
Lloyd Wilkins, A.B. '39*

A N OIL lamp sputters in a stuffy little room in the Fee building.[2] "Leatherwood" Duncan tilts his chair against an already heavily marked wall. Bob Richardson sprawls across a couch. "Sol" Meredith stands at the oil-smoked window. Three other upperclassmen loll in the yellow glow.

Meredith wheels, his eyes flash enthusiasm, "Student!" he cries, "Indiana Student!"

The year was 1867. Out of that meeting, seventy years ago, came the first issue of *The Indiana Daily Student*[3] on February 22, 1867.

Weeks, perhaps months, of planning preceded the meeting. For years students at the then struggling University had recognized the need for a school publication, but financial difficulties had made the establishment of a paper impossible Then, one evening, half a dozen members of the Junior and Senior classes of the University gathered together to work out final details. Unanimously, the members of the two classes had agreed to found what was to become one of the earliest of college papers.

No reference treats the story of the founding more lucidly than that written by "Leatherwood" Duncan himself more than four

---

[1] While the material in the following pages has been checked for accuracy as closely as possible, the facts themselves, in the main, came from the files of *The Indiana Daily Student* itself.

These files often disagreed in various accounts of the history of the paper. No account was complete. Many obviously were in error. In some cases, the files for three or four years were missing entirely, and information had to be taken from whatever sources were available.

Consequently, the chances for error were great, particularly in the early history. Nowhere, so far as can be learned, has there been printed a list of all the editors of the paper.

[2] Now the Breeden building, Bloomington, at the northeast corner of Sixth and College. —Ed.

[3] The publication, which began as *The Indiana Student*, changed name frequently, as follows: 1867, *The Indiana Student*; 1873, *Indiana Student*; 1882, *The Indiana Student*; 1893, *Indiana Student*; 1894, *The Student*; 1898, *Daily Student*; 1903, *The Daily Student*; 1912, *The Indiana Student*; 1914, *The Indiana Daily Student*. In this manuscript it is referred to informally as the *Student*.—Ed.

years after the paper was established. He wrote from Emporia, Kan., in 1871, where he had gone following his graduation from the University, to the current editor of the paper, who published the letter:

I was glad to get the *Student*. It reminded me of auld lang syne. The time when half a dozen met in Fee's building, in the room lately occupied by Chancellor Gillmore, to organize a college organ, we were unanimously of the opinion we should have a paper. That was agreed on. Next came the name. The infant was born and had to be christened. We puzzled our brains, all of us, in names beginning with "A" and running to "Z," but no name appeared suitable until the big senior from Cambridge City—"Sol" Meredith; you remember him, or at least Dr. Nutt and W. F. Browning where he used to "hash," do; he was a jolly, big-hearted popular student, and is now driving the pen for the *Cambridge Tribune*—put his giant intellect to bear on the subject, struck an attitude, and sang out "Student"—"Indiana Student!" And so it was christened.

The first number was issued February 22, 1867, under auspices of the senior and junior classes and was a four-page sheet about 8 by 10.[4] But it was spicy. "Sol" was good on locals. By a little political manipulating, it was agreed to divide the honor between the "Betas" and "Sigs." It doesn't just now occur to me how the dispositions were made, but I remember the Betas got one, R. D. Richardson[5] on the editorial staff, and the Sigs two, "Sol" and myself. It started out under rather unfavorable circumstances, but by hard work we managed to make both ends meet, barring a little deficit the members had to foot. But then the honor!

That year we managed to get up a spicy paper generally. "Sol" was excellent on locals, though sometimes he got off things not very suitable for a first-class paper, as, for instance, the "vegetable poetry" and the "Ode to the Lady Hill." Bob was a good writer, but inclined to be sarcastic. He could beat any of us on criticism. As for my own productions, about all they ever did was to get an invitation to spend an hour with Dr. Nutt. . . !

Amusingly, in the light of the many errors newspapers are charged with today, Duncan wrote the letter in complaint of an item in the *Student* he received mentioning that he recently had visited in Bloomington. The mistake was fortunate, for his information concerning the founding is all that is to be found in the many volumes of the *Student*. Thus, he atoned for the *Student's* failure, in the first issue, to carry a true account of the establishment of the

---

[4] Actual size: 8½ by 12.
[5] Robert Dale Richardson, Trustee of Indiana University, 1879–91.—Ed.

paper. The article the *Student* did carry concerning itself in the first issue treated the establishment and naming facetiously.

Since 1867 the *Student* has seen many changes. It failed financially and was abandoned in 1874, only to be revived eight years later by a student who was to become the University's president—William Lowe Bryan. Previously a monthly and semimonthly publication, it became a weekly in 1893; in 1896 it was transformed into two publications—a semiweekly newspaper and a monthly magazine. Once the official University yearbook—in 1888—ten years later it became the University daily. It has been owned by literary societies, the University Librarian, publishing associations, and student editors. Its life has been eventful, but before tracing it step by step it first is necessary to look into earlier journalism at the University.

There were at least two papers that preceded *The Indiana Daily Student*. For this information, it is necessary to turn once again to the columns of that publication, and, there again, it was an editorial oversight that resulted in valuable material later being included.

In the November, 1882, issue of the *Student,* Professor James K. Beck wrote what was entitled a "History of Journalism at Indiana University." Covering only the early history of this publication, it brought, in the January issue of 1883, a remonstrance from David D. Banta, then a member of the Board of Trustees of the University.

Pointing out that Professor Beck had erred in not including in the article a reference to publications earlier than 1867, Banta explained that journalism at the University really began in the 1840's. Banta said that Andrew Wylie, then president of the University,

published a journal called *The Equator*[6] through the columns of which he presented to the public the claims of the University for its patronage, and also vindicated himself in his change of church relations. The journal was printed in the Old College building, according to the memory of Professor M. M. Campbell.

When Matthew Simpson, D.D., first President of Asbury [DePauw] University, delivered his inaugural on the thirteenth of September, 1840, he cast some reflections upon the Indiana University. At least, his remarks were so interpreted by President Wylie, who, according to the memory of the Honorable G. M. Overstreet, who was, at the time, a student in Bloomington

[6] See Chap. LII for additional information concerning this paper.—Ed.

—wrote, and published in *The Equator,* a caustic review of President Simpson's address.

I have never seen a copy of *The Equator,* and cannot say how long it was published, nor whether it was a weekly, monthly, or quarterly; but, it was, I think, the first of Indiana University college journalism.

In December, 1845, the Athenian Society began the publication of *The Athenian,* which was the second venture entitled to be classed as a college journal coming from the University.

In 1854, and after the second Old College building, with the college and society libraries, had been destroyed by fire, the Athenians, as also the Philos, donated, of their own scant stores and begged of their friends, books with which to begin a new society library. Among the contributors was Professor James Woodburn,[7] of fragrant memory, who presented an unbound volume of *The Athenian,* with the money to pay for its binding. The volume was bound and went into the Athenian library, but afterward, it seems, the library was gobbled up, and the only volume of *The Athenian* I ever saw went the way of the other books.

I have in my possession, however, the first number of that venture, and as it was unquestionably the pioneer in Indiana University college journalism, insofar as being projected and carried on by students, I venture to say something of it.

The first number bears the date of December, 1845. It is a pamphlet of twenty-four single column pages, well printed in long primer. The title page, without display, is as follows:

THE
ATHENIAN;
Edited by a Committee
of the
ATHENIAN SOCIETY
of
INDIANA UNIVERSITY
Vol. I—1845
"Delectando Pariterque Monendo"

BLOOMINGTON
Printed at the Christian
Record Office
1845

The names of the committee editing the publication, Banta said, appeared nowhere in the issue. The paper included articles of the

[7] The father of James Albert Woodburn.—Ed.

literary type, as: "A Synopsis of the Education of the Ancient Greeks and Romans."

"Not a word of college news was in it," Banta complained in his article, "save that which appeared inferentially." "*The Athenian* died at the close of its first year," he concluded, "and the world most likely lost nothing by it. . . ."

Hardly had Banta's lambasting of *The Athenian* appeared in print when the *Student* received a communication from Dr. T[heophilus] Parvin. "As one of the progenitors, still living, of *The Athenian,*" Parvin defended the paper on the grounds that Banta's criticism was based on the first issue. To prove that the paper had carried well-written articles in later numbers, Parvin recalled, he said, that among contributors were Samuel T. Wylie, Daviess Batterton, Barton W. Wilson, James Scott Hester, and Dr. Andrew Wylie.

With its contemporary college publications, however, the facts tend to show that *The Athenian* was not highly esteemed. Parvin reveals that the Princeton paper—the *Nassau Monthly*— greeted the first issue of the Indiana University publication with editorial jeers that eventually were carried to the ears of *The Athenian* editorial staff. It was a day when exchanges were commented upon freely, and when one of the major tasks of editors appeared to be that of criticizing other college publications. Undaunted by the adverse reception, the *Athenian* editor, Parvin recalled, retaliated by terming the Princeton paper the "Nausea Weakly," with appropriate remarks concerning its quality.

Whether any publication existed at the University during the period from 1845 to 1867 is not known; at least there is no record which would tend to show there was a college paper.

Thus things were when the *Student* was founded. Two papers had been attempted; both had failed. There were 128 students enrolled in the University,[8] and Bloomington businessmen did not appear to be any too eager to advertise in a student publication. The *Student* had no financial backing; it was controlled by student politics. Offsetting these facts, however, was the desire of the student body, small as it was, for some paper that would represent the University along with other papers of the college world.

[8] Exclusive of Preparatory students.—Ed.

In answer to that wish of the students came the first issue of *The Indiana Student*. The first issue listed H. C. Meredith, H. C. Duncan, both members of Sigma Chi fraternity, and R. D. Richardson, Beta Theta Pi, as the editing committee. Duncan, in his letter previously included, recalled that the three were on the "editorial staff." Professor J. K. Beck, in a later history, said that, in the winter of 1866–67, presumably with the beginning of the paper, Meredith and Richardson were named editors and Duncan made associate editor for the Junior class.[9]

The next year the constitution was changed so that, in the following seven years, there was only one chief editor and two associates each year. There apparently was one exception even to this in 1867–68, and in 1871–72 there seems to be some doubt as to whether there were one or two editors.

In the first issue, editorials were carried under a page-2 masthead. Included was one appealing to alumni for support of the paper; another briefly reviewed the history of the University.[10] The facetious article on the founding of the paper occupied two columns on page 1 along with a list of the names of the members of the faculty.

Page 3 contained a miscellaneous assortment of articles, with a few of them coming under a general classification as news items. One, "Rain and Sunshine," complained of the incessant rain and of the hardships it brought to the "unfortunate swain who must make a call." Other matter included a poem, "The Spirit of Beauty," and an article, "About Visitors," advocating that literary societies of the University open their meetings to women so as to make the gatherings more interesting. Page 4 listed the various literary societies thriving on the campus. Greek social orders and their members also were named. At this time, only Phi Delta Theta, Beta Theta Pi, Sigma Chi, and Delta Psi Theta were represented. Editorial paragraphs were sprinkled through the columns and, as was the custom, what news matter there was was handled from an editorial viewpoint rather than as news.

Typographically, the paper was very clean. The single-line heads

[9] The latter appears to be the case, as Duncan was a Junior and was advanced to the post of editor in 1867–68. He served as co-editor with Allison Maxwell.
[10] A copy of the first editorial of *The Indiana Student* is found in a manuscript copy of this chapter in the University Archives.—Ed.

were set in boldface, seven-point type and were centered at the tops of the columns. The initial letter was set in on the first word of articles of major importance. Advertising was in paragraph form, usually as "advice" to readers. A typical advertisement was as follows:

LOOK HERE, STUDENT—Throw away that old, rusty, corroded cast-iron pen which you have been blotting with for ten years, and which makes a mark like an iron weed dipped in a tan vat, and get one of Tobe Smith's fine gold pens, which will write your "pumpkin blossom" a letter if you give it the ink and let it go. We've tried it.

Following are the advertising and subscription rates quoted:

Single copy, one college year (40 weeks)	$1.50
Single copy, one college term	.50
Single numbers	.50

One square, one insertion	1.00
Each subsequent insertion	.50
Half square, one insertion	.50
Each subsequent insertion	.25
One square, three months	3.00
Half square, three months	1.75
Legal notice, one insertion	.25
Legal notice, three months	1.00

A note in the first issue revealed that the editors "hoped to do better in the future." Here, too, in the first issue, the editors sounded an ideal that has followed down through most of its years, that of: "Owing allegiance to no faction . . . subservient to no personal motives of exaltation, pure in tone, seeking the common good. . . ."

The second number was released on March 8 and consisted of eight pages, including eighteen advertisements. According to the few comments regarding how subscriptions were selling, the paper immediately had found backers. The *Bloomington Republican* commented editorially: ". . . the first number of a very neat little paper has been laid upon our doorstep. . . ." The editorial offices, too, appeared soon to become a loafing place for students, for the editors complained in an early issue that "boys seem to be inclined to visit the sanctum during office hours, and, hereafter, we ask they relieve us of their company at such times." Peculiarly, the second issue shows, it was the practice to number the pages of the various issues from paper to paper. That is, the first issue was numbered 1 to 4, the second 5 to 12, etc.

With the resignation of Henry Meredith on May 17, 1867, Vinson Carter became co-editor in his place. The paper remained approximately the same throughout the first year. How faintly it dealt with news as news can only be realized through inspection of the papers themselves. Names were seldom used, and all news events were told in a manner that seemed to accept the reader's previous knowledge of the event. The paper consisted chiefly of literary material, with news matter subordinated. The scope of the paper's contents perhaps can best be appreciated by a brief survey of the 1867–68 volume's contents. Subjects discussed included "The Distance of Fixed Stars"; "Kingdom of God"; "Labor and Genius"; "Select Your Reading"; "Letters from Graduates"; "Indian Summer"; "Vandalism"; and "The Ladrones of Mexico."

J. Glass McPheeters, Bloomington postmaster, bookseller, news dealer, and stationer, assumed financial responsibility for the paper with the November, 1867, issue. His name at this time was inserted in the masthead as publisher. The paper was printed by J. P. Luse and Company of New Albany, Ind.

Through an error, the issue of January 24, 1868, was dated with the year 1867, a mistake that for some time caused some to believe that the founding of the paper was a month earlier than it actually was. During this period, there were frequent errors in the numbering of both volumes and issues, a fact that makes a study of the papers more difficult and less certain.

There are only scattered issues of Volumes II, III, and IV, a lack which necessitates securing even the names of the editors during these years from other sources. From the few issues, however, it appears that as early as November, 1867, an attempt was made to make the publication semimonthly. Evidently, some months passed without any issues at all, and, in 1870, according to a later news item, the paper died completely from April until the following September. After the first year, also, the size of the paper was reduced slightly.

In the college year 1869–70 Walter A. Foland was one of the editors.

With the beginning of Volume V, in 1870–71, the *Student* was reduced to 9½ inches by 6¾ inches, was two columns, and was published monthly under the auspices of the Athenian and Philomathean societies. Walter Houghton was chief editor with Robert A. Ogg[11] serving as assistant editor. There is no explanation of the change in the publishers of the paper, but it is assumed that the literary societies took the paper over after the financial failure of the former editors. The groups elected the editor from within their own membership, the individual serving six months. At the same time, two associate editors were chosen. The paper was larger from the standpoint of pages, most of the issues running as large as sixteen. It carried many columns, including "entertainments," "University News," "Law Department," "personals," and "local." Stilted in the front of the paper, the writing was tapered off to humor toward the back.

In 1871 an editorial requested the Board of Trustees to purchase a press for the University, giving the argument that the paper had been forced to reduce its size because of lack of finances. Asking financial aid and moral support from the University, the paper charged that "the compensation of the editors is nothing, minus a few degrading marks in the class standing."

Editors took errors far more seriously than at the present time; even typographical mistakes received correction notices in the following issues. At this time the paper was printed by A. A. Stevens at Salem, Ind.

In November of 1871 the paper was further reduced in size, being cut down to 9¼ inches by 5½ inches, although still retaining the two columns and using smaller type. On November 15, 1871, however, the paper went back to its previous size, 9½ inches by 6¾ inches. Individuals were listed as publishers, although the publication still was issued under auspices of the literary societies. At this time, incidentally, Houghton urged that the Hesperian Society—a women's literary organization—be allowed to take part in the paper's

[11] Robert A. Ogg, Trustee of Indiana University, 1896–1902.—Ed.

operation "since ladies are taking such a prominent place in college." The society was admitted.

Although there are no files available, the paper evidently prospered until 1874, when, in the latter part of James W. Head's administration as editor, it was discontinued because of lack of funds and as a result of the "political farce of leaving it in the hands of societies." While there is little available material concerning this phase of the *Student's* life, later notes tend to show that the method of selecting the editor had degenerated until political machinations eventually brought about its abandonment as a publication.

Then came a long period when there was no school paper, either carried on by the University or, as far as can be ascertained, through independent enterprise. From 1874 until the fall of 1882, as a substitute for a school paper, a column of University news was carried in the Bloomington publications. At this time, however, other sources tend to show that there were frequent "bogus" publications issued at intervals. Libelous, anonymous sheets, the boguses, as they were termed, were given wide campus and city circulation during the night. Even as late as 1894, when the *Student* had resumed publication, there was an occasional reference to this type of paper. The *Dagger* of Commencement week, 1875, was one of the most noted of these. It denounced certain members of the faculty and called for their removal.

In November, 1882, stronger than ever and more ably written and edited, *The Indiana Student* again appeared on the campus under its original name. Published monthly by what was known as the University Publishing Company, it was printed at the Palladium Press, Richmond. It was by far the best publication that the University had seen as its own student product.

Of magazine type, the paper was 6 inches by 9½ inches and was two columns wide. It carried twenty-eight pages, plus a gray front cover with an illustration of the old University grounds. Clarence L. Goodwin and William J. (Lowe) Bryan were editors, with Librarian William W. Spangler as business manager. The trio founded and conducted the paper as a private enterprise. The paper eliminated much of the lofty language and style of earlier issues and even carried many personal notes. Often, in speaking of itself, the paper was termed a magazine rather than a newspaper, and the names frequently were used interchangeably.

While articles and essays were featured, these issues included hundreds of personal items concerning alumni and students. Much of the news itself was presented in almost the present accepted form, although no headlines were used and the items all ran approximately the same length—about seventy-five words. The paper usually carried eighteen to twenty pages of advertising, depending on the local merchants to a great extent.

With the destruction of the new University building by fire on July 12, 1883,[12] all the back numbers of the *Student* were destroyed and for a time, according to the paper, there was some thought of discontinuing publication. The decision to move the school to Dunn's Woods, however, resulted in a vote to continue, with the editorial corps not selected on a basis of church affiliation, county, faction, or fraternity affiliations.

Dr. Bryan took over the full editorship in 1884 and, either because of his interest or because of complaints of the business office, a circulation campaign was opened which included several unique offers to subscribers. Among them, the *Student* offered a free subscription to *Health and Home* to all past purchasers of the paper who would pay their delinquent subscriptions.

Also, the

mammoth pipe of peace, smoked on class day by all members of the class of 1873, was recently found, and will be presented to the first member of that class that subscribes for the *Student,* as soon as the subscription of the last member of the class is turned in.

Circulation, one item revealed, ran between "five hundred and one thousand."

If, during this time, the editors kept one eye on the magazine style of publication, they kept the other on guard for innovations in the collegiate publishing field. "Is it true," the *Student* commented in 1884,

that those college journals which have adapted a newspaper form are to be still further improved by the insertion of "patent insides"? If so, the last step

[12] Since that time a file has been partly built up from private sources.—Ed.

into the field of real journalism will have been taken. They will then easily rank with the country weekly.

Later, the *Student* takes notice that publication was begun at Nashville, Tenn., of an all-college journal, promising to steer clear of the "negative success" of many other college papers—"flat personals and local comicalities."

The time element in news meant little. If the report barely made the issue, it was not given better or greater space because of the late development, but rather placed somewhere inside the paper with an explanation of why a longer account was not carried. Sports news was covered regularly, with the following a good example of the type of lead used:

This is the score by innings of the game played on the DePauw University campus on Saturday, May 10. But it does not tell the whole story of the trip. There are some interesting things about which it does not speak. It does not reveal that the Indiana University pitcher sent fifteen DePauw batters to base on balls—and the consequent fact that not many of their thirteen tallies were made by hitting the puzzling balls he pitched. . . .

The "local notes" column was an effort that apparently relied upon the knowledge of the reader for any effect it might have. A characteristic sample ran like this:

——Mumps
——Baseball
——The hobgoblin
——Two ice creams
——Two high screams
——Ne, mater, et suam
——The students did vote
——Meek brought up the rear . . .

The *Student* also carried in its columns at this time original plays written by students. Included are two by Dr. Bryan.

With the beginnings of the issues of the school year 1885–86, the masthead of the paper said that it was published by the Indiana University Lecture Association. Formed independently by a group of students eager to bring prominent lecturers to the then financially handicapped University, the organization was an active agent in promotion of University affairs.

The size of the paper varied slightly through these years, although it always ranged around 9 to 11 inches in length and from 6 to 8 inches in width. The paper changed but little from the previous two years' issues, and through the country's schools it began to attract considerable attention. The *Indianapolis Journal* made the following comment in 1886:

> *The Indiana Student,* the organ of Indiana State University, Bloomington, for January, is received. We were about to say that it avoided that mild form of juvenile idiocy on local notes, which usually begin with: "Scat," "Who tied the dog loose?" "Where will sweetie spend Sunday nights now?" etc. The *Student* falls from grace only once, and says, "Observe the obtuse angle of that moustache." The offense is not great, but it is a fly in the ointment nevertheless. . . .

In December of 1886 the *Student* was taken over by the University Librarian, although no explanation was given for the change. An editorial explained that the enthusiastic response of the alumni to the paper and the increased enrollment of the University justified expenditure of more money on the publication. In accordance with the policy, the paper was changed into a semimonthly, the first issue appearing January 15, 1887. It and subsequent issues ran from fourteen to eighteen pages.

The Librarian evidently assumed responsibility for the *Student* until as late as October, 1887, when the publication line was dropped entirely from the masthead. Again a monthly, the paper, according to a later note, was "the personal property of the editors-in-chief." At this time the Board of Trustees purchased one hundred copies of each issue for distribution to high schools throughout the state.

Primarily, as it had been in the past few years, the *Student* was a magazine. Occasionally the publication carried a magazine type cover with a picture of some member of the faculty or of an administrative officer. The first cut of this type ever to appear in the paper was a picture of Daniel Kirkwood in the issue of January, 1888. Later in the year, the paper began carrying a few comic illustrations, the first being a one-column cut of a tall, ungainly individual labeled "I.U. Junior."

In June of this year the *Student* became the first Indiana University yearbook ever to appear. Thirty-seven pages, the issue carried a full page each for the listing of the various literary societies and their respective members. There also were numerous illustrations, each social organization being allowed a full page for insertion of a cut of its coat-of-arms and insignia. A first-page article carried an announcement declaring that "such a thing as a college annual never has gone out from the University, but the *Student* hopes to continue this beginning in later years."

Primarily because of the fraternity versus non-fraternity ill feeling, and also because it was felt unfair to sell the paper from editor to editor, soon there arose a demand among the student body that the paper be re-established on a different basis. On October 1, 1889, a meeting was called at the National Hotel in Bloomington at which the various elements among the students were represented. Two representatives were selected from each element, the *Student* says, and this body drew up and submitted a plan for the reorganization of the paper. The plan later was ratified at a mass meeting held in Maxwell Hall [later—1894—called Mitchell Hall] on October 4 of the same year.

Under the new plan, the ownership of the *Student* was to be vested in a board of directors consisting of eleven members. The board was made up of one member each from the eight fraternities and sororities, two from the non-fraternity group, and one from the faculty. The faculty member was Professor Richard G. Boone, of the Department of Pedagogics.

Immediately after adoption of the plan, the board convened and divided itself into two classes. The first class held office for one year and the second class for two years. Officers of the directors included president, always to be a faculty representative, a vice-president, and a secretary.

Bylaws stipulated that the president should be required to call a meeting at the request of three members of the board; that eight directors should constitute a quorum, and that election of officers should be held each year on the second Saturday in April. Voting was to be by ballot and no element was to succeed itself. Seventy-five paid-up subscriptions from each faction were required before that faction was to be considered eligible for an editor.

Following are the main clauses under the new organization:

The Board of Directors, before the close of each year, shall select two students to whom *The Indiana Student* shall be leased for the following year in consideration of one dollar, duly in hand paid; said lease to be made on conditions imposed by the board of directors.

Lessees shall conduct the business of publishing *The Indiana Student,* be liable for all debts contracted and entitled to all moneys accruing under their management.

Students so selected shall not be from the same fraternity or sorority, each of whom shall have one representative in every period of five years. Nor shall they both be from the non-fraternity element, which shall have two representatives in every period of five years. . . .

Under this plan, Walter W. French, of Mount Vernon, and Edward O'Donnell, of Mitchell, became the first editors. The paper did not change in size and retained the two-column style of makeup. There were many personals, alumni notes, and news items, still in paragraph form without headlines. The front pages were given over to book reviews, speeches, and long articles. Athletics were given more emphasis, however.

The primary object, apparently, was to furnish more of a record of the University than to provide a newspaper. Local news, although carried, still was not complete in itself. The editors in 1891 admitted that they felt the literary inclusions were not interesting to alumni, that the locals were too old for the students but sought by graduates, and that other matter was interesting to neither but necessary for the records. A trend to more regular presentation was seen as early as 1892, when the paper began publication of three- and four-paragraph exchange stories, with date lines, from other schools. At this time, the Indiana College Press Association was formed with representatives from Earlham, Rose Poly, DePauw, Butler, Purdue, Wabash, and Indiana.

Notice that the *Student* was to change to a weekly publication of eight to twelve pages was carried in the June, 1893, issue. An editorial said the paper would include the same general features and that

an attempt would be made to make it the official organ of the faculty, that is, the means of announcing the proceedings of the faculty with regard to college work. While avoiding those things that are calculated to create sensations, the right to criticize certain practices in college life that are known to be objectionable will be more fully exercised.

The change was made with the October 3, 1893, issue. The paper at this time went to four columns and was released every Tuesday morning. It resembled a newspaper more than any of the prior issues, although there were still no news headlines and the entire front page usually was given over to a single article. Page size was 14 inches by 10 inches. Advertisements, for the first time, were scattered throughout the pages, while previously they always had been carried solidly in the back. It continued this way until the January, 1894, issue, when announcement was made that it would be cut from twelve to eight pages because "of the finances and work involved."

On June 21, 1894, another reorganization was effected. An editorial signed by Werter Dodd and Claude G. Malott, incoming editor and business manager, respectively, said that the former plan had proved unsuccessful. The students at this time cooperated with the University faculty in forming a stock company with a capital of $1,000. The company was called the Publishing Association of Indiana University and the paper termed *The Student* rather than *Indiana Student*. Under the new plan, the stockholders elected nine directors, who in turn selected an editor, a business manager, and a revising editor. The paper, according to Dodd and Malott, was to be "literary" primarily. It was, however, to contain some news "for the benefit of alumni."

As early as 1896 a movement was opened for the establishment of a daily paper, to be prepared by the class in reporting opened at the University the previous year. An editorial at this time advocated that the instructor of this class be made the permanent editor and general manager. As a result, in October of that year *The Student* began publication of both semiweekly and monthly editions, the latter a literary publication and the former, presumably, following closer along newspaper lines. Unfortunately, no copies of the semiweekly edition are available, all files evidently having been lost. The monthly editions, however, carried the name *The Student* and contained only articles and poetry. The issues ran about thirty-four pages and were 10 inches by 6¾ inches in size. In 1897, under the same organization, Florence Myrick, of Richmond, became the first woman editor, although there is no record of whether she was editor of the semiweekly, monthly, or both.

With the issue of September 26, 1898, the paper appeared as a three-column, four-page daily, on newsprint. At this time the first regular headlines also were used. The size was 11¼ inches by 8¼ inches. The paper was published five afternoons a week, Monday through Friday. While the front-page flag called the paper *Daily Student,* the editorial masthead termed it *Indiana Student.* Headlines were of the type used by the *Cincinnati Enquirer.* The following example is typical:

GENEROUS WELCOME

WAS EXTENDED BY DR. SWAIN
TO THE NEW STUDENTS

After Which Mr. R. B. Gruelle, of Indianapolis, Gave an Interesting Lecture on "The Beautiful, Where and How it is Found."

At this time the *Student* began publication of a summary of state, national, and city news, and a review of college news was carried under a stock headline. The paper was printed at the *World-Courier* office in Bloomington. Issues were released irregularly, according to later notes, until the school year 1899–1900. In respect to the issues at this time, there are no available files from June, 1899, to 1903.

Walter H. Crim, of Salem, editor of the paper in 1899–1900, later said that in 1899, with Claude Malott as business manager and R. H. Brandon as editor, the present *Daily Student*—the second attempt at a daily publication—was launched. The writer (Crim), who was associate editor, took charge after a few weeks, as Brandon suddenly left school. Crim said he thus became the first editor of the first *"Daily" Student.* This material came from a letter Mr. Crim had printed in the paper after he had left school.

Along in the years when the files are missing, the *Student* became a four-column, six-day afternoon paper. It was delivered at 7 p.m. through use of a regular carrier system. Publication offices still were at the *World-Courier* office, while campus editorial rooms were maintained in Kirkwood Hall, Room 16. The Association considered publication of a monthly to supplement the daily, but this evidently never was carried out.

There was frequent mention of the sales of stock of the *Student* among the "barb" and fraternity elements, each attempting to secure enough control to place an editor or business manager. Announcement of caucuses and candidates for the posts were made openly through the columns of the paper, and the elections attracted more attention than perhaps any other campus activity.

Then came what was to be one of the most interesting phases of the *Student's* career, not because of progress, but because of the attitude toward news and news honesty. In the year 1905–6, and in the following few years, a mythical Ambrose Wilkins drifted through the local column, took an active part in campus political affairs, according to the paper, and expounded his views on a variety of topics. The *Student* went so far as to print his picture and list his world-wide achievements on March 5, 1906. Later his death was reported.

Ambrose, the editor said, was greatly appreciated by the student body in that he served to offset "the dullness of the paper otherwise." Unsatisfied with the comment aroused by their development of this character, the paper began making stories, generally of a sensational type. Perhaps the most flagrant example of this manufacturing of news occurred on April 16, 1906, when the *Student* appeared with a long, purportedly factual front-page article describing the annual Panthygatric dance, open only to coeds. A colorful account, the story implied that at least part of the program was a trifle improper, and that, on one occasion, those attending were thrown into terror when a suddenly released window shade revealed that the proceedings had been observed by parties outside.

In the next issue a letter to the editor charged University officials with lack of discipline. This brought another letter, this time from the dean of women, denying that the story in the paper had been true. Investigation revealed that the news story had been manufactured almost entirely. On April 20 an editorial explained that the story had been exaggerated for color. But faculty members demanded further retraction. Robert Thompson, editor, refused to comply, claiming that the one retraction was enough and that he had not known, himself, that the story was to be printed. The story, it was implied, was written by W. C. Mattox. The University ordered suspension of Thompson and George Osborn, business manager, but students circulated a petition demanding their reinstatement. Both Thompson and Mattox resigned from the staff, however, and were permitted to remain in the University. Lewis A. Harding was named editor and Osborn was reappointed business manager.

More of an effort to get late news in the paper was evident about this time, with frequent insertion of bulletins, usually at the bottom of the story with which they were connected or at the bottom of the first page. They usually concerned events which occurred in the late afternoon, since the paper was published in the early evening. Campus election results usually were handled in this manner.

During these years the editor of the paper received fifteen hours of credit for his work. On May 1, 1906, however, the University announced that no further credit would be given, the editors receiving only whatever financial benefits they might earn. The result, according to an editorial at this time, was that there was an immediate decrease in the number of applicants for the position.

There continued, however, intense political maneuvering for the editorship of the paper. So politically active did the students become at the close of the 1906–7 school year that the faculty interceded and supervised the election in an effort to eliminate part of the activity. Julian J. Behr, who, in his year's term of office already had edited an unusually good paper, was renamed and became the only *Student* editor to serve two complete years.

Several changes were instituted in regard to the management of the *Student* in the fall of 1907. As a result of the institution of the journalism course, a reorganization of the staff was effected and various department editors named. The offices of the *Student* again were moved back into Kirkwood after some time spent in the Student Building. On December 12 announcement was made that the paper was to be changed into a six-day morning publication with the opening of the next school year. The morning issues were not actually started, however, until April 10, 1908. There evidently was an effort made at this time to make the paper larger, but facilities were not available.

The paper remained about the same until 1909–10, when a conference between Dr. William Lowe Bryan, Fred Bates Johnson, faculty adviser, and Walter Greenough, editor, resulted in the decision to make the *Student* the product of the journalism course the next year. Students in the practical course in journalism were to make up the staff. With the opening of school in the fall, an editorial said that there had been "a departure in newspaper work at the University" and that the *Student* would be published "under direction of the editor-in-chief and the instructor in journalism." The publication was still owned, however, by the Indiana University Publishing Association. It was issued every morning except Sunday and was printed at the *World-Courier* building.

But there was a continuance of politics, and several additional changes brought the paper closer under University supervision. On May 3, 1910, after a meeting between President Bryan, the faculty committee on publications, and the board of directors of the University Publishing Association, it was announced that the ownership of the *Student* [13] was to be signed over to the Board of Trustees of the University. The time of the transfer was set for May 15 of the same year. Although the University offered payment for outstanding shares of stock, most of the holders donated their shares toward the creation of a fund to establish a University printing plant. Also at this time there was an effort made to have entrance fees raised so as to include a subscription to the paper.

The first issue under the ownership of the University was published September 22, 1910. The paper retained the same general form and release dates. There was a definite effort to get later news, however, and on October 1 a football extra was sold at gates as spectators filed away after a DePauw-Indiana football game. In previous years,[14] when the paper was published in the late afternoon, it had been the policy to suspend publication to enable the staff and printers to attend the games. Wire stories of out-of-town games were used frequently in later extras. On Saturday, October 22, the first page of the *Student* was carried on the front page of the *Indianapolis News* extra as an example of the type of work being done and as a presen-

[13] See Chap. IX, p. 81.—Ed.
[14] Three pink editions were published on football days between 1907 and 1909.—Ed.

tation of the *Student's* account of the Wisconsin-Indiana game played at Wisconsin.

The paper became five columns in 1911. For a time, in 1912, it became as large as twelve columns with no explanation of change, but this size was not maintained. The editors used many three-, four-, and five-column headlines, and the practice was, if the head would not count, to use large and small type in the same line so that the words could be worked in. During the month of January of the latter year, notice was given that the *Student* had acquired United Press telephone bulletin service from Indianapolis. There was no evidence of this service in later issues, however.

Professor Joseph W. Piercy took over the Department of Journalism on August 1, 1911. At the close of the school year he announced that several editors were to be appointed each year, rather than one, to give more students the benefit of the training. Consequently, three editors were named for the school year 1912–13. At this time, there were frequent occasions when boilerplate was used on the front page, along with an occasional advertisement.

New headline type was purchased and make-up improved. The name again was changed to *The Indiana Student* rather than *The Daily Student*. During this time, full play was given important national news stories, with the accounts carrying "Special to *The Indiana Student*." These may have been United Press stories, but credit was not stated. Full city coverage also was given in these years.

The long struggle for a University printing plant which would enable publication of the *Student* on the campus came to a close in 1914. On December 4, 1913, the Board of Trustees discussed the purchase. In March, 1914, the Board announced that the expenditure had been approved, with the *Student* moving into its "new" plant on September 30, 1914. At this time it became, finally, *The Indiana Daily Student,* marking the first time that the titles all had been used together.

The paper was six columns wide and the head type evidently was the same generally used up to 1935 and the purchase of the Ludlow equipment. In general make-up, the paper appeared very similar to the *Student* of recent years. Four pages, it was published every morning except Sunday and weekly during the summer term. It was interesting to note that the office's first phone number, conveniently, was Main 0000.

The paper improved constantly following establishment of publication offices at the University printing plant. It was better edited throughout. Comments from other papers placed it as one of the outstanding college publications of the country. The paper's modest motto, rather than the "W.G.C.D.," [15] was "Best in the Middle West." Make-up was conservative, with even the news of the United States entry into the World War held to what would correspond to the *Student's* present Number 1 (full) headline.

President Bryan agreed to write a column on the editorial page as early as 1916, according to a news item at that time. It was to be called "Notes by the President." The articles did not appear regularly, however, and he evidently discontinued writing this column for the paper.

As the war brought a shortage of supplies, including paper, the *Student* discontinued Monday editions. The masthead continued to state, however, that the paper was published daily except Sundays. Along with other papers throughout the nation, the *Student* carried on a campaign to raise war funds. The Monday editions were not revived with the close of the war.

During all these years the *Student* paid little attention to the day of its founding, and even on its fiftieth anniversary, in 1917, there was no comment. One evident reason for this oversight is that for many years no edition was issued on Washington's birthday, a holiday. Observance of the *Student's* founding, therefore, was overlooked. In 1910, and in some later years, the observance was held February 19, with the error not caught.

The name of W. L. Reeves was carried on the masthead as business manager for the first time on January 3, 1919. Prior to this time, business managers had been students.

The paper became more and more liberal in make-up and gradually became larger. On October 22, 1920, the *Student* received approval for Associated Press telephone service from Indianapolis. The service consisted of a fifteen-minute phone call nightly from Indianapolis, and the first news from this new source was carried No-

---

[15] World's Greatest College Daily.—Ed.

vember 2, 1920. Simultaneously, the paper became an "earlier" morning publication, although exact times are not given.

Several consecutive changes in page size were attempted in 1921. There was an increase to seven columns on November 29 of that year, although the page size remained the same. In December, however, the page size was increased to approximately that used today. Following these alterations, for several months there was no consistent size, the papers varying considerably from issue to issue. The number of pages also varied.

In September, 1922, the first state fair issues of the paper came out, with Ernie Pyle as the editor.

Saturday night editions—in addition to Saturday morning editions—were established in 1925, the first of these being released on February 7. In reality a Sunday paper, the issues consisted of two six-page sections and included complete news, literary and feature sections with excellent student-drawn cartoons. Russell E. Campbell was editor at the time, with the magazine sections of the Saturday issues under separate direction. The regular paper was cut from six to four pages. The Saturday night issues were not profitable from the business standpoint, according to W. L. Reeves, while Campbell recently declared the work involved in getting material ready for publication was too exacting for students in school. These issues were discontinued after May 9, 1925.

President Bryan's first official column appeared September 15, 1926. It was this column that resulted many years later in the Sigma Delta Chi den being dedicated in memory of Don Mellett, of Canton, Ohio, editor and former Indiana University student who was slain by gangsters in the Ohio city.

With the school and state fair issues of the school year 1927–28, the *Student* went to eight columns. The following year, its motto, "He Serves Best Who Serves the Truth," appeared for the first time. Later, in 1929–30, the slogan was changed to " 'Tis the Truth That Makes Men Free," but this later was discarded and the first motto used.

In keeping with a style introduced at that time, and which now is gaining headway, an attempt was made in the *Student* issues to use all capital and lower case headlines. A half-page was given over to art and city news. With these additions, the *Student* was practically the same as it is at present [1937] with the exception of full Associated Press wire service. The complete service was assured, however, when the Board of Trustees voted on December 5, 1930, to have an automatic printer installed in the office. The first news over the new equipment was carried January 6, 1931.

Through all these years, since the establishment of the University printing plant in 1914, there had been few changes in headline style. The paper had become more liberal; there were more streamer headlines and the headline type faces were larger, but the general appearance of the paper remained about the same. The purchase of a Ludlow typograph and an Elrod slug and rule caster in 1935 by the University printing plant, therefore, came as a major development in the *Student's* history. For the first time, it made the *Student* an all-slug newspaper, the hand-set type being abandoned. Used as an experiment in the state fair issues of the paper in 1930, the equipment was not adopted definitely until the state fair issues and school year of 1935–36.[16]

---

[16] In the manuscript of this chapter found in the Archives of Indiana University is a list, believed to be as accurate as possible, of the editors of *The Indiana Daily Student,* from date of founding to 1937. The list does not include the state fair issues or the summer session issues of this publication.—Ed.

Chapter XLIX

THE GRADUATE SCHOOL FROM ITS BEGINNING TO 1937

By Fernandus Payne

General Historical Facts

ESS THAN sixty years after the founding of Indiana University in 1820, evidence of a fundamental interest in work beyond the Bachelor's degree is found. It is true that between 1834 and 1876 the Master of Arts degree *in cursu* had been conferred upon a number of graduates of Indiana University; but as this degree was granted three years after the Bachelor's degree and without further work at the University upon the part of the recipient, the fact is not especially significant in the history of the Graduate School.

In the school year of 1880–81 the University Catalog listed A. B. Philputt, A.B., 1880, as a "Resident Graduate" student, the first to be so listed. The University was then manned by a faculty of fourteen headed by the Reverend Lemuel Moss, President, and included such outstanding educators as Theophilus A. Wylie, Professor of Natural Philosophy; Daniel Kirkwood, Professor of Mathematics; Thomas C. Van Nüys, Professor of Chemistry; David S. Jordan, Professor of the Natural Sciences; John G. Newkirk, Professor of History; and Rufus B. Richardson, Professor of the Greek Language and Literature. For that year the enrollment in the Collegiate Department was 188, and three courses in "Liberal Culture" were offered, namely: "The Course in Ancient Classics," "The Course in Modern Classics," and "The Course in Science," leading to the degrees, Bachelor of Arts, Bachelor of Letters, and Bachelor of Science, respectively. During that same year S. Brown Wylie, A.B., Indiana University, 1876, served as assistant in the Department of Physics and Chemistry, and was awarded the *honorary* degree of Master of Science in 1881. In 1882 the first *earned* Master's degrees (by examination and approved thesis) were awarded to Alembert W. Brayton, W. Webster-Butterfield, and Charles H. Gilbert. Mr. Gilbert was added to the faculty of the University in 1880 as an assistant in the Departments of Natural Sciences and the Modern Languages, and, after receiving his Master of Science degree in 1882, was the recipient of the first Ph.D. degree granted by Indiana University, which honor he received in 1883. Within five years after graduate work began, 12 M.S. degrees, 18 A.M. degrees, and 6 Ph.D. degrees had been granted.

Although graduate work first appeared as an outgrowth of the undergraduate curriculum, definite plans for its continuation by qualified students were formulated in 1882 and have varied only in details of administration over a period of fifty-five years. It is interesting to note that the original objectives were thorough study and development of independent thought through freedom in the pursuance of studies. Scholarly production was early recognized as sufficient evidence of the fulfilment of these objectives, as the only criteria of attainment employed were the presentation of a satisfactory thesis and an examination.

Under the stimulus of David Starr Jordan, who became president of the University January 1, 1885, many fundamental advances in graduate study were inaugurated along with the general expansion of the institution. When the University was moved to its new location in September, 1885, several new professorships were instituted, the faculty was increased in numbers, and other developments were begun in accordance with "the increased numbers of students and the requirements of the times." The most significant features of President Jordan's administration as it affected graduate study are:

The development of special courses whereby each professor has some opportunity to give advanced instruction in the direction of his specialty, and the student has an opportunity to do something more than to secure mere elements of a subject. The arrangement of the work is such that each student has a wide range of choice among elective studies, while at the same time he is required to take up special work of some one department and continue it for three or four years, thus making it the backbone of his education.

At that time there were fourteen departments, fully organized and equipped to offer a four years' course to be pursued as a "specialty," and consequently an equal number of opportunities for advanced study.

Between 1883 and 1893 the degree Doctor of Philosophy was conferred upon fourteen individuals, including such well-known persons as John Merle Coulter, John Casper Branner, Joel Asaph Allen, Oliver Perry Hay, Carl H. Eigenmann, Oliver Peebles Jenkins, and Barton Warren Evermann. While all these degrees were merited, not all were earned by residence within the University. Between 1893 and 1908 the faculty of the University was hesitant, apparently, about conferring a degree of the magnitude of Doctor of Philosophy, and candidates for that degree were sent elsewhere. Between 1908 and 1923, after the formal segregation of the Graduate School, at least one or two, and sometimes as many as six, Ph.D. degrees were granted annually. In 1924 the postwar enrollments in universities and colleges began to show marked increases, and a rapid rise in the number of Ph.D. degrees is to be noted.

Honorary degrees flourished during the early years of the University and by 1886 a total of 45 honorary Doctor of Divinity degrees, 47 honorary Doctor of Laws degrees, and 32 honorary Master of Arts degrees (*in cursu*) had been conferred. After the beginning of graduate study on a formal organized basis and the awarding of earned degrees, a period of marked conservatism in awarding honorary degrees prevailed. Not until in 1905 was such an honor bestowed again, and at that time the degree of Doctor of Laws was conferred upon John Watson Foster, the jurist. Others followed: James Whitcomb Riley, our Hoosier poet, in 1907; David Starr Jordan, zoologist and university president, in 1909; and Theodore Clement Steele, the artist, in 1916. Since 1920 many eminent educators, scientists, statesmen, authors, and others have received this recognition. With the discontinuance of Master of Arts degrees *in cursu* in 1876, the honorary Master of Arts degree has rarely been granted. The few exceptions have been Nebraska Cropsey, 1913, and Mrs. H. B. Burnet and Jacob Gimbel, 1933. In 1911 honorary Master of Arts degrees *privatim* were granted to a group of seventeen faculty members of Indiana University.

In 1937 the Graduate School embraced twenty-eight departments including the School of Education and the School of Music, and was manned by a faculty of ninety-two members chosen on the basis of accomplishment in the fields of research, graduate teaching, and directing of theses of graduate students. Advanced work was offered leading to the Master of Arts, Master of Science, and Doctor of Philosophy degrees. With increased enrollments more detailed requirements in regard to credit, residence, and scholarly production became necessary. Nevertheless, considerable liberty continued and was even encouraged.

DEVELOPMENT OF THE ADMINISTRATION OF THE GRADUATE SCHOOL

Because the entire University in 1882 had not outgrown the conservative figures of 200 students and 15 faculty members and because graduate study was in its initial stages of development, only an occasional student was involved. In consequence the entire faculty was able to serve as an advisory body, to approve theses, and to conduct final examinations of candidates for degrees.

In 1890, however, it was provided that the work for the Master's degree

be done not under the direction of the Faculty, as hitherto, but "under the direction and supervision of the professor in charge of the Department in which studies are carried on" and the work for the Doctor's degree had also to be done "under the direction and supervision of the appropriate member of the Faculty." [1]

This change was in keeping with the increasing tendency toward specialization. The course of study for the doctorate, however, was still subject to final approval by the general faculty.

A standing committee on advanced degrees was first appointed in 1894, and applications were referred to this committee of six members of the faculty, together with the head of the department having charge of the major subject. The committee was appointed by the President of the University, two members from each of the three general groups, as follows: (1) Greek, Latin, Romance Languages, Germanic Languages, English; (2) European History, American History, Economics and Social Science, Pedagogics, Law; (3) Mathematics, Physics, Chemistry, Geology, Zoology, Botany. The original committee was composed of Professors Thomas C. Van Nüys, Gustaf E. Karsten, William L. Bryan, John R. Commons, David M. Mottier, and Horace A. Hoffman.

[1] *Indiana University, 1820–1904*, p. 164.

With a few changes in personnel from year to year the committee continued to approve candidates for advanced degrees and assumed, in 1895, the additional responsibility of planning programs. On May 15, 1902, the committee voted to establish a Graduate School "in order to give dignity and coherence to the graduate work." It was further recommended that in an annual report to the President the governing body of the Graduate School should "suggest plans for organizing, advancing, and conducting the work leading to the Doctorate in Philosophy."

Formal organization of the Graduate School was authorized by the faculty on February 1, 1904, and the organization was completed in March, 1904, the real purpose being to "emphasize the facilities offered by the University for work of an advanced nature." The committee on advanced degrees continued to function as the governing body of the Graduate School until 1908 when the office of dean was created. Dr. C. H. Eigenmann, then Head of the Department of Zoology and Director of the Biological Station, was appointed the first dean of the Graduate School. After this action the committee on advanced degrees emerged as the administrative committee of the Graduate School and in 1909 became the Graduate Council.

Meetings of the Graduate Council were held upon the call of the dean to consider questions pertaining to admission, advanced degrees, and numerous other problems arising from the complexity of an expanding school in which each graduate student, because of the diversity of training and interests, had to be considered for the most part on an individual basis in respect to any general regulations. From a committee of seven the Council expanded eventually into a committee consisting of a representative from each department and school offering graduate work.

In 1925, because of the illness of Dean Eigenmann, a major change in the administration of the Graduate School occurred. Fernandus Payne, Professor of Zoology, was appointed assistant dean, with full responsibility. He was made dean upon the death of Dean Eigenmann in 1927. Perhaps it is not out of place in this brief historical sketch to say a few words about Dean Eigenmann. His dynamic and stimulating personality and his intense interest in research made him the logical choice for dean when the Graduate School was organized. These same characteristics enabled him to influence both faculty and students throughout his entire career. They could not come into his presence without being stimulated to greater efforts. He was a man of vision but was not always able to carry out his plans. He laid well the foundations for future growth and development. Those who followed owe him much.

In 1934 the Graduate Council was discontinued when an official Graduate School faculty was organized to administer the affairs of the School. Although various groups had been listed in previous University Catalogs as constituting the Graduate School faculty, none had been given official recognition and authority. The new faculty members were selected from schools and departments offering graduate work and were appointed by the President upon recommendation of the dean of the Graduate School after consultation with respective deans of professional schools or with heads of departments involved.

Evolution of Requirements for Admission and Advanced Degrees

In the University Catalog for 1882 we find the following announcement of the first definite scheme for graduate degrees:

For Masters' Degrees

1. Any graduate of this University as Bachelor of Arts, Letters, or Science, who subsequently completes a course of study of not less than two years in any reputable professional school of Theology, Law, Medicine, Literature, Music, Advanced Science or the Mechanic Arts, on presenting to the Faculty of this University satisfactory evidence that he has thus completed any of the professional courses named, and that he has maintained a good character, may receive from the University the Master's Degree of the same name as the Bachelor's Degree he has already received.

2. Any graduate of this University, or of any similar and equal Institution, who does not pursue a professional course as above described, may receive from this University a Master's Degree, corresponding to his Bachelor's Degree, at the expiration of three years from the date of graduation; *provided,* he gives evidence of good character and completes a course of study fairly equivalent to any of the professional courses above named under the direction of the Faculty of this University, either in residence at the University or in private, or partly in residence and partly in private. The satisfactoriness of the work to be determined by an examination of each candidate by the Faculty

of this University, and by the presentation on his part of a creditable Thesis on some theme prescribed by this Faculty. *Provided further,* that the three years herein required may be reduced to two, if the entire time is spent by the candidate in residence at this University, or under the immediate direction of its Faculty.

For Degree of Doctor of Philosophy

The degree of Doctor of Philosophy may be received by the graduate of this University, or of any other Institution of like character and equal rank, five years after graduation; *provided,* the candidate, in addition to the requirements for the Master's Degree, as above recited, shall still further pursue studies under the direction of the Faculty of this University, pass satisfactory examinations in the same, present *in print* a satisfactory Thesis upon some prescribed or accepted subject, embodying original work, and maintain a good character. Provided further, that the five years herein required may be reduced to three, if the entire time is spent in residence at this University, or under the immediate direction of its Faculty.

An interesting item concerning the diploma appeared in the Catalog for 1884–85. It states that "the fee for a diploma for an advanced degree or honorary degree is *ten* dollars. If no diploma is desired, no fee is charged. In accordance with State statute, these fees are applied to the Library Fund." These statements did not appear after 1886.

As early as 1885 "a bound copy of each thesis presented for a Master's degree" was required "to be deposited in the University Library." It was also stipulated then that "the degree of Doctor of Philosophy will not be given as an honorary degree, and it will be given to no one who has not obtained prominence as a special student in some department of learning." In 1886 the time requirement for the degree Doctor of Philosophy was omitted altogether, and the last part of the stipulation just mentioned was modified to read: "It will, further, not be given as a result of any examinations or of any course of study alone, but only on evidence of original work actually done, by some person who has achieved prominence as a special student in some department of learning."

Evidence of the lack of preparation by all departments to offer instruction of a graduate character appears in the following statements in the Catalog for 1885:

Students holding a degree from Indiana University, or from any college having similar requirements, may select for themselves a course of advanced work, in any one or more departments of the University which may be able to provide for them. Facilities for such advanced work are offered in most departments of the University, especially in the Departments of Mathematics, Chemistry, and Biology.

In the following year the latter part of this announcement was changed to read:

Special courses, leading to the Master's degree (M.A., M.S.), will be arranged to meet the needs of each individual student. The advantages offered in the University for special advanced or original work are now very great, and it is the aim of those in control of the affairs of the University to make it the center of such work in the State in all departments within its scope.

In 1887 the following explanation also was added:

As a rule, no degree of any sort will be given by the University to any person who has not, at some time, been a matriculated student in residence at the University. It is not desired to create at the University an "examining board" to certify to the value of work done elsewhere.

As thus modified and enlarged, this announcement regarding the character of the graduate instruction appears also in the Catalogs for 1888 and 1889.

In 1887 the requirements for graduate degrees were newly defined as follows:

Master of Arts

Any graduate of this University, or of any similar institution, may receive the degree of Master of Arts (A.M.) upon the completion of a course of advanced study, of not less than one year, in residence at the University, under the direction of the Faculty, the value of the work to be determined by an examination of each candidate, and by the presentation of a satisfactory thesis on some theme prescribed or accepted by the Faculty; but graduates of this University may, in special cases, be excused from residence though not from examination at the University.

Any graduate of this University of three years' standing, who has completed the course of study in a reputable professional school, on presenting to the University Faculty a creditable nonprofessional thesis, with satisfactory evidence that he has maintained a good character, may receive the degree of Master of Arts.

Doctor of Philosophy

The degree of Doctor of Philosophy (Ph.D.) may be received by the graduate of this University, or of any other institution of similar character and rank, upon the completion of an advanced course of study of not less than three years, at least one of which must be spent in residence at this University, the value of the work done to be shown by a final examination and by the presentation of a satisfactory thesis in print upon some prescribed or accepted subject embodying original work.

The requirement regarding evidence of good character was omitted after 1888.

A definite influence of the major subject system upon the plan of graduate instruction began to be felt in 1891. The Master's degree then required

the successful completion of three full courses of study occupying at least one year of three daily recitations, or the equivalent thereof, in residence at the University, such courses to be chosen under the advice of the head of the Department in which the major part of the work is to be done, and to be subject to the approval of the general Faculty.[2]

In 1893 provision was made, moreover, that

if at any time during the year an undergraduate has completed the requirements for graduation, a written statement to this effect is given him by the President of the University, and his work for the remainder of the year may be counted toward his higher degree.[3]

With the organization of the Graduate School in 1904 the requirements for the Master of Arts and Doctor of Philosophy degrees were set forth in the Catalog as follows:

Master of Arts

The degree of Master of Arts may be conferred upon graduates of this University, or of any other institution of the same standing, upon the completion in residence of fifteen hours per term, carried during at least one entire college year. Thirty of the total of forty-five hours must be in one department, or in closely allied departments. Fifteen hours must be distinctly graduate in character.

The Master's degree may be conferred upon graduates of this University upon the completion in absence of fifteen hours per term, or their equivalent, carried during at least two full years under the direction of the Faculty, hours of private work done in absence being estimated at one-half the credit value of work done at the University.

Professional studies are not accepted for this degree, but research work on professional subjects may be accepted at the option of the professor in charge of the major subject.

A thesis may be required at the option of the professor in charge of the major subject.

---

[2] *Indiana University, 1820–1904*, p. 164.
[3] *Ibid.*

Doctor of Philosophy

The degree of Doctor of Philosophy may be conferred upon graduates of this University, or of any institution of similar character and rank, upon the completion of an advanced course of study of not less than three years. In exceptional cases, on the recommendation of the professor in charge of the major subject and with the concurrence of the Committee on Advanced Degrees, part of this time may be spent in study at other universities.

The course of study for the degree of Doctor of Philosophy must be pursued under the direction of a committee consisting of the heads of the Departments in which the work is done, and its value shall be determined by a final examination and by the presentation of a satisfactory thesis embodying original work upon some prescribed or accepted subject. In each case a detailed statement, which must be endorsed by the professor in charge of the major work, must be submitted to the Committee on Advanced Degrees not later than May 10th of the year in which the candidate presents himself for examination.

The thesis of every candidate for the degree of Doctor of Philosophy must be presented to the Committee on Advanced Degrees on or before the first day of June of the year in which he proposes to take the degree. The thesis must be endorsed by the head of the Department as being in its final form and ready for the press. Examinations of each candidate for this degree will be conducted before a committee consisting of all the instructors under whom graduate work has been taken. If the candidate is recommended for the degree, five printed copies of the thesis shall be deposited in the library before the degree is conferred.

Formal application for the degree of Master of Arts must be filed with the Dean at least three months before the time when the degree is to be given. Formal application for the degree of Doctor of Philosophy must be on file at least one year before the candidate is admitted to the examination.

After the establishment of the office of the dean of the Graduate School in 1908 and the Graduate Council had taken over the former duties of the committee on advanced degrees, a few changes in requirements for advanced degrees followed. Concerning admission to the Graduate School, definite statements appeared for the first time in the Catalog for 1909, and were slightly modified to read as follows in 1910:

Students holding a bachelor's degree in Arts or Science from Indiana University, or the same degree or its equivalent from institutions of equal rank, are admitted to the Graduate School on presentation of the proper credentials. Persons holding the bachelor's degree from institutions whose requirements are considered to lack a year or more of being the equivalent of the A.B. from this institution, are not admitted to the Graduate School. They may enter the College of Liberal Arts and are referred to the Dean of the

College for their standing. Holders of the A.B. or its equivalent from institutions whose requirements lack less than a year of being the equivalent of the A.B. from this institution, may be admitted to the Graduate School. In such cases, work in addition to the minimum of forty-five hours for the degree, will be demanded. The amount will be determined in each case by the Council of the Graduate School.

All graduate students will enroll at the beginning of each term, and those entering regularly organized classes will submit to the same regulations as undergraduate students. Work will in many cases be individual and not controlled by a recitation schedule. At the time of entrance to the Graduate School the student must submit a plan of the entire work he wishes to present for the master's or doctor's degree. This plan must be approved by the professor of the major subject and the Dean of the Graduate School.

Candidates for the A.M. degree were allowed to pursue their work during summer terms "with the reservation that the student must be in residence during three out of four successive Summer terms. Single half-terms will not be counted toward the residence requirement."

It was also stated that

In or before June, 1910, the Master's degree may be conferred upon graduates of this University upon the completion in absence of fifteen hours a term, or equivalent work, carried during at least two full years under the direction of the Faculty, hours of private work done in absence being estimated at one-half the credit value of work done at the University. After June, 1910, no degrees will be conferred for work in private nonresidence study.

At the same time candidates for the Ph.D. degree were required to present a unified program of studies involving the selection of a major subject "consisting of the work of some one Department or recognized subdivision of a Department; and not less than two minors at least one of which must be in some related but different Department from that of the major subject." The need of a knowledge of French and German was also recognized as a real aid in the work of graduate students; hence, the following ruling concerning the doctorate went into effect in 1910: "At least one year before the final examination the candidate shall satisfy the professor in charge of the major subject of his ability to use French and German for purposes of investigation."

In 1915 more emphasis was placed on the actual content of course work submitted for advanced degrees as well as the fulfilment of other requirements; thus, we find the following rulings:

Freshman courses shall not be counted on advanced degrees. The first ten hours in beginning French and German do not count on advanced degrees except by permission of the Graduate Council, on the written recommendation of the professor in charge of the major subject. The Council shall in such cases fix the amount of credit to be given. The amount of credit that a student may receive for elementary courses in other subjects is determined by the professor in charge of the major subject.

Graduate students were strongly urged to gain some proficiency in modern foreign language before entering the Graduate School, and credit for ten hours in a modern foreign language was made a prerequisite for admission. Candidates for the A.M. degree were required to make up the deficiency in addition to the thirty semester hours required for the degree. (The University had during the course of the previous year changed from the "term plan" in which forty-five term hours were considered the equivalent of a year of work to the present "semester plan.")

During the next five years requirements for advanced degrees were altered only slightly. For the Master's degree an optional oral examination was introduced, a five-year time limit was placed upon the work, and theses were required in all departments. For the Ph.D. degree it was definitely stated that at least one of the three years required must be spent in residence at Indiana University. Further, the degree could be conferred without the publication of the thesis in advance if *arrangements* were made to deposit five printed copies in the Library.

A postwar educational trend brought many students into the Graduate School with irregularities of training or plans for further work of one sort or another which were to necessitate special action. Some wished to continue their work after receiving a Bachelor's degree, but not necessarily for an advanced degree. Such students were allowed to enter the Graduate School as "Graduate Students, not Candidates for a Degree." Work of the University was being extended to many students over the state through the various centers of the Extension Division. Thus, persons qualified to do graduate work who were employed full-time either as teachers or in business were allowed to pursue not more than five semester hours per semester either on the campus or by extension work.

In 1922 provision was made in the Graduate School for students who lacked not more than five hours on the A.B. degree at Indiana University to begin their advanced studies immediately. This ruling applied particularly to those who were able to complete practically all of the requirements for a Bachelor's degree by the end of the first semester of their Senior year. The work of each candidate for the Ph.D. degree was placed under the direction of a committee composed of the heads of the departments in which the work was to be done. The final examination for the doctorate was also conducted by a committee consisting of all the instructors under whom graduate work had been taken, in the presence of such members of the faculty of the Graduate School as cared to attend. (At this time the Graduate School faculty was considered to be made up of those members of the University faculty of professorial rank who devoted a part of their time to research and a part to graduate instruction.)

With the admission of students who were not interested in advanced degrees came the question whether admission to the Graduate School also meant admission to candidacy for a degree should the individual later decide to pursue a program of studies leading to a higher degree. Consequently, the Graduate Council in 1926 made a definite distinction on these points with the following statements:

Admission to the Graduate School does not imply admission to candidacy for a degree. Admission to candidacy for a degree is determined after the student has been in residence one or more semesters. If the student is a candidate for one of the higher degrees, he must, in all cases, complete to the satisfaction of the department of the major subject the graduate work required in that department for the degree.

At the same time work of the Extension Division which was offered through regularly organized Centers was allowed to be counted toward the A.M. degree "under the same conditions and to the same extent as the same work when offered at the University." Work done by correspondence was ruled not applicable on an advanced degree. A provision was made whereby Indiana University graduates were allowed to transfer a third of their work on the A.M.

degree "from other accepted institutions." Similarly, candidates who were assistants or instructors in the University were given the privilege of transferring a maximum of fifteen hours of credit earned at other accepted institutions toward the A.M. degree.

For the Ph.D. degree a bond filed in the Bursar's office was required to insure publication of the doctoral dissertation "within a reasonable length of time." The following year supervision of the course of study for the Ph.D. degree was delegated to special committees appointed for each applicant by the dean of the Graduate School in consultation with the head of the major department. In each case the committee was composed of at least three members whose duties were "to assist in outlining the applicant's program of studies, supervise his work, admit him to candidacy, and certify the completion of the work for the degree."

Certification for the language examinations was shifted from the departments of the major interest of the candidate to the language departments concerned, and each candidate "unless exempted by the committee in charge of his work for the doctorate, shall, at least one year before he is allowed to take the final examination, have a reading knowledge of French and German" with the provision that "another foreign language may be substituted for one of the required languages by consent of the student's committee." The privilege of exemption was revoked in 1936.

In 1929 the doctoral dissertation assumed an importance suggestive of the degree which it represents. To be acceptable it was designated that it should be "the result of an investigation in an unknown field, must be a real contribution to knowledge," and "of sufficient value to warrant publication." The acceptability was to be passed upon by the candidate's committee and then submitted to the Graduate Council for final approval. Permissible forms of publication are "in some reputable journal or in book form," mimeographing, or through an abstract or digest published at the expense of the candidate. A bond for the amount of $100 was fixed as security.

In 1930 certain qualitative as well as quantitative limitations were placed upon extension work as it affected graduate students. Although all of the work for an A.M. degree might be completed by extension work if the proper courses could be secured, only one year of such work or work completed *in absentia* was approved for application on the Ph.D. degree. An allowance of one and one-half years of such work was made in the case of students doing their major work in the field of education.

As a reading knowledge of either French or German became indispensable in research, even in the first year, a definite requirement on the A.M. degree was established in 1933.

In February, 1936, the Graduate School faculty approved the following regulations concerning admission to candidacy for advanced degrees:

Admission to the Graduate School does not imply admission to candidacy for a degree. Before a student is admitted to candidacy for the A.M. or M.S. degree, certain requirements must be met. (1) At least one semester before the completion of work for these degrees, the major department must certify to the Dean of the Graduate School that the student is qualified for advancement to candidacy (a preliminary qualifying examination may be required) and must indicate what member of the staff is to serve as the student's major professor. (2) In the case of the A.M. degree the language department involved must certify to the Dean of the Graduate School that the student has met his language requirement; in the case of the M.S. degree the language requirement of the major department must be met and certification made to the Dean of the Graduate School by the student's major professor. After these requirements have been met, the Dean of the Graduate School shall notify the student, the major professor, and the head of the major department that the student has been admitted to candidacy.

Before a student is admitted to candidacy for the Ph.D. degree certain requirements must be met. (1) At least one year before completion of work for the doctorate, the Ph.D. advisory committee must certify to the Dean of the Graduate School that the student has passed a preliminary qualifying examination. The examination shall cover the major and may cover the minor subjects also. Students transferring to Indiana University for the last year of work for the doctorate may be permitted to take the preliminary qualifying examination not later than eight months before completion of work for the degree. (2) Before the preliminary qualifying examination may be taken (*a*) the Ph.D. advisory committee must approve the subject of the student's thesis and must file it with the Dean of the Graduate School, and (*b*) the language departments involved must certify to the Dean of the Graduate School that the student has met his language requirements. After these various requirements have been met, the Dean of the Graduate School shall notify the student, the chairman of the Ph.D. advisory committee, and the head of the major department that the student has been admitted to candidacy.

Promotion of Research

Since "the function of the Graduate School is to carry on research and to train students to become teachers and investigators," no small part of the School's energies, financial as well as intellectual, has been devoted to research. In most departments there is no exact line of demarcation between teaching and research. Certain facilities such as laboratories, libraries, and equipment are provided for both pursuits, and cooperatively their interlinking interests are promoted advantageously.

Special incentives, however, have been provided from time to time to encourage research on the part of both graduate students and faculty. As might be expected, the first evidences of promotion of scholarly work were very modest. With the establishment of the Graduate School in 1904 came the following announcement of scholarships:

From among the seniors and graduate students of special promise, Scholars may be appointed who will be given an opportunity to gain a familiarity with the University work and administration, which can not be obtained in any of the regularly announced courses. To this end the Scholar may be given an opportunity to assist in laboratory courses, to supervise departmental libraries, and to assist in museum administration. No other remuneration than the experience gained and the recommendation the appointment carries with it will be received by a Scholar.

For 1904–5 four students were given these scholarship appointments. The scholarships, themselves, were discontinued after 1908.

Assistantships were first instituted to encourage research as well as to care for certain duties in the various departments. The 1904 Catalog also carried this announcement:

Assistantships, in some universities designated "Fellowships," or "University Fellowships," or "Teaching Fellowships," are available in some of the departments. These carry a remuneration of from $150 to $300 annually. Appointment to an assistantship is primarily a recognition of merit and an encouragement to research. At least half the time of an assistant must be given to research. The assistants are members of the Graduate School, not members of the Faculty.

In 1908 teaching fellowships made their appearance with special emphasis on the graduate work of the student over and above the time which the student would be asked to spend in rendering service to the University. "Teaching fellows" were apparently understood to cover the general field of assistants or tutors, according to the following announcement:

The Teaching Fellows are relieved from all term fees and the fellowship carries with it an honorarium of between $200 and $500 annually. The highest amount will ordinarily be paid only if the incumbent is appointed for a third year. A Teaching Fellowship is primarily a recognition of scholarship. Not less than two-thirds of each Fellow's time must be devoted to work leading to the Doctorate in Philosophy. A Fellow may be appointed for three separate years, but not for more. Appointments are for one year, and do not imply a reappointment. Teaching fellows will be required to render service to the University as assistants, tutors, or instructors.

In 1910 two special fellowships were made available, one each for work in zoology and astronomy. The Donaldson fellowship, valued at $500, was

open to students who are in large measure capable of doing independent work in biological subjects. The fellowship implies residence for twelve months at the cave farm of the University, at Mitchell, Indiana. A certain amount of supervising work is required of the incumbent.

This fellowship was not offered after 1913.

The Lawrence fellowship in astronomy was established by Mr. Percival Lowell, of the Lowell Observatory, Flagstaff, Ariz., upon the following terms and conditions:

1. The fellowship shall be known as the Lawrence Fellowship, in remembrance of the donor's mother, and is established in perpetuity, revocable, however, at any time at the will of the founder.

2. It shall be annually available and shall cover the college calendar year, that is, from commencement to commencement of the same.

3. The applicant shall be appointed by the Department, the donor reserving the right of final passing upon the suitability of the candidate so presented.

4. The Fellow shall be given time and opportunity for an original thesis on some astronomical subject looking to the taking of a Master's degree, the nature of which shall be decided by the Director and the Fellow. But the Fellow shall be expected to give general assistance in the observatory's work during the period of his fellowship.

5. The Fellowship will pay $600 and the Fellow's traveling expenses to and from the Observatory at Flagstaff, Ariz.; and a furnished room at the Observatory shall be free to the Fellow's use.

The Lawrence fellowship is still available to qualified applicants.

At the March, 1910, meeting of the Board of Trustees ten graduate fellowships worth $200 each plus exemption from fees were established for graduates of other Indiana colleges. The policy was

to assign them to the most promising students, irrespective of the special field of study in which they wish to work, or the particular institutions from which they come. As between cases of equal merit, however, attention will be given to securing a distribution of the awards among different departments of study and different colleges of the State.

In 1919 these fellowships were withdrawn and a number of University fellowships were made available to applicants who had completed at least a year of graduate study. These fellowships carried with them an honorarium of $300 to $500 annually. At the same time holders of fellowships and scholarships, while they were expected to render some service to the University, were not allowed, without special permission of the Graduate Council, to do other work for remuneration. In 1925 these fellowships were discontinued in favor of six $600 University fellowships for graduate students who had completed at least one year of graduate work. In 1932 these, too, were withdrawn because of current economic conditions and of the necessity for a reduced budget.

Special research fellowships were authorized in 1912. These were to be "awarded to students who have shown marked ability and who desire to investigate definite problems in which they are interested. Each case is decided on its merits." For 1911–12 seven research fellows were appointed with compensations fixed by the Board of Trustees, on the recommendation of the Graduate Council. In 1914 the compensation was limited to $300 to $500, but in 1915 these amounts were changed to $500 to $1,000, with the total number of recipients limited to three a year. It was further stipulated that "these fellowships were created only for men of exceptional ability and merit, who may or may not have received the Ph.D. degree." The value of these fellowships was increased in 1920 to $1,000 to $1,500 and were maintained at this level until 1929 when the financial condition of the institution did not seem to permit their continuation.

At a meeting of the trustees of the University on May 18, 1915, Dr. Luther Dana Waterman, Professor Emeritus of Medicine in the

School of Medicine, presented to the trustees deeds for property amounting in value at that time to $100,000, on the following conditions:

1. That he shall retain the management and income from the property during his lifetime.
2. That the proceeds from the property be devoted to the establishment and permanent maintenance of an Institute for Scientific Research.
3. That the Trustees bind themselves to appropriate annually an amount of money for the Institute equal to the annual proceeds from the property.

The trustees accepted the proposal of Dr. Waterman and pledged the faith of the University to carry out the conditions designated therein. The original gift was later supplemented, under the same conditions, by bonds for $11,000. In October, 1917, it was decided to inaugurate the work of the Institute at once. Dr. Arthur L. Foley, Professor of Physics in Indiana University, was elected Waterman research professor and given full time for the work; he continued until 1925. After 1925 the proceeds from this Institute were used to further investigations by various members of the faculty, although in most cases for only a summer or semester at a time. In 1933, however, the Institute again supported a full-time appointment when Dr. Stanley A. Cain, of the Department of Botany, became Waterman associate and continued until 1935. Dr. William R. Breneman, of the Department of Zoology, was appointed assistant professor in the Waterman Institute beginning with the school year 1936–37. Such appointments are now approved by both the dean of the Graduate School and the President, and every effort is made to carry forward the work of the Institute to the best advantage of both the University and the individual involved with fundamental progress in research as their mutual objective.

Since 1925 a number of special fellowships have been sponsored at different times by various individuals or companies for research in specific fields.

Growth of the Graduate School

During the fifty-seven years, 1880–1937, in which graduate study has developed at Indiana University, the total number of enrollments and earned degrees granted have gradually increased, even though certain factors have caused fluctuations.

From the beginning of graduate work until 1910, students were privileged to pursue individual work "in absence." Enrollment statistics show, however, that only during a five-year period, 1889–1893, was this privilege used to any extent. Since graduate work "in absence" has played so small a part, it has been ignored completely in compiling enrollment data, and the term "enrollments" is understood to mean "enrollments in residence."

Although graduate work has been steadily on the increase, certain factors have caused significant shifts. After the Graduate School was officially organized in 1904, a marked rise in enrollments occurred and continued until 1916 when the influence of World War I is to be noted. The decrease in enrollments at that time was not very great and in 1918 started to rise again—this time to project upward quite rapidly until 1929. The postwar desire for further education coupled with the state license laws inaugurated in 1923 contributed to this sudden expansion.

Two advanced degrees, the Master of Science in Education and the Doctor of Education, were authorized by the trustees in 1929 to be conferred by the School of Education; hence, a large group of students withdrew from the Graduate School to work for these new degrees with their different standards. Previous to 1935 graduate work in the School of Business Administration was included in the Graduate School. In 1935, however, this School withdrew to give its own degree, Master of Science in Business Administration.

With the beginning, in 1929, of a serious financial depression it is of special significance to note that the level of average enrollments during the period 1930–35 represented an increase over the previous five-year period. The main negative factor, the economic status of the country, supplemented by a division of enrollments for advanced work in education between the Graduate School and the School of Education, was more than balanced by enrollments resulting from a special incentive to secure employment as a result of specialization in advanced study. During the decade 1925–35 162 Ph.D. degrees were conferred—almost twice as many as have been granted during the entire previous existence of graduate work.

The following lists of enrollments in the Graduate School and advanced degrees conferred since 1880 were compiled from the annual lists published in the University Catalog and supplemented by information recorded in the office of the Graduate School.

	Enrollments		Degrees Granted			
	In Absence	In Residence	M.S.	A.M.	Ph.D.	Total
1880–81	—	1	—	—	—	0
1881–82	—	1	3	—	—	3
1882–83	—	2	2	4	1	7
1883–84	—	2	1	—	2	3
1884–85	—	1	3	4	1	8
1885–86	—	6	3	10	2	15
1886–87	—	8	—	5	1	6
1887–88	—	5	—	6	—	6
1888–89	19	9	—	7	2	9
1889–90	29	12	—	14	—	14
1890–91	17	19	—	16	2	18
1891–92	24	28	—	17	2	19
1892–93	23	22	—	16	1	17
1893–94	—	47	—	11	—	11
1894–95	—	49	—	15	—	15
1895–96	—	62	—	15	—	15
1896–97	—	65	—	10	—	10
1897–98	—	84	—	14	—	14
1898–99	—	77	—	15	—	15
1899–1900	—	69	—	11	—	11
1900–1	—	69	—	21	—	21
1901–2	—	82	—	18	—	18
1902–3	—	84	—	19	—	19
1903–4	—	77	—	19	—	19
1904–5	—	87	—	30	—	30
1905–6	—	86	—	25	—	25
1906–7	—	112	—	34	—	34
1907–8	—	127	—	30	3	33
1908–9	—	125	—	29	3	32
1909–10	—	141	—	45	—	45
1910–11	—	167	—	35	2	37
1911–12	—	148	—	50	4	54
1912–13	—	175	—	56	3	59
1913–14	—	172	—	49	4	53
1914–15	—	220	—	72	6	78
1915–16	—	200	—	55	4	59
1916–17	—	230	—	53	4	57
1917–18	—	186	1	27	4	32
1918–19	—	153	—	29	1	30
1919–20	—	163	—	32	5	37
1920–21	—	200	1	37	2	40
1921–22	—	278	—	48	5	53
1922–23	—	288	—	53	6	59
1923–24	—	341	—	64	10	74
1924–25	—	400	—	84	10	94
1925–26	—	518	4	93	9	106
1926–27	—	620	3	100	14	117
1927–28	—	788	4	116	15	135
1928–29	—	880	15	104	22	141

	Enrollments		Degrees Granted			
	In Absence	In Residence	M.S.	A.M.	Ph.D.	Total
1929–30	—	837	11	134	16	151
1930–31	—	879	9	114	17	140
1931–32	—	845	3	111	20	134
1932–33	—	781	3	82	22	107
1933–34	—	689	7	85	15	107
1934–35	—	644	5	81	12	98
1935–36	—	694	1	81	18	110
1936–37	—	688	1	70	18	89

CHAPTER L

THE EXTENSION DIVISION[1]

By Cedric C. Cummins

BEING NEITHER completely academic nor secular, the Extension Division was variously interpreted by those who knew it. Appraisal by instructors in more orthodox divisions of the University ranged through a service to the state, source of extra income when a new rug or baby was imperative, department of public relations, recruiting stations for campus enrollment, threat to academic standards, chance to teach students with less passive viewpoints, teaching jobs for their Ph.D. graduates, or performer of tasks which otherwise each department would have to shoulder. Weary cynics regarded it as an unavoidable accompaniment of becoming a Big university to be accorded the same resigned tolerance shown to new deans and administrative units.

Apostles of adult education classified it with libraries and museums as among the solid, continuous, but somewhat inflexible carriers of their work. To its many clients throughout Indiana, it was an available branch of the University. The small, evangelistic group that guided the child from birth to maturity viewed the Extension Division as an agency that provided university methods and materials to a number of Indiana citizens in a practical and democratic manner.

As a matter of record, academic learning had been carried beyond campus bounds as soon as the Indiana Seminary opened its building to ten students in 1824. For, in addition to his duties as president and sole teacher, the Reverend Baynard R. Hall undertook to shepherd the Presbyterians of Bloomington in return for $150 a year in "articles of trade." Considering the prevailing association of education and religion, his labors had at least some of the attributes of extension work. After two and a half years, however, the Seminary trustees advanced his salary to $400 and forbade the preaching.[2]

---

[1] Mr. Cummins completed this chapter after he had severed his connection with the Indianapolis Center, where he taught history, to go to the University of South Dakota.

[2] D. D. Banta, in James A. Woodburn, *History of Indiana University, 1820–1902*, pp. 15–19.

In succeeding years as the Seminary grew into a College and then a University, staff members were called upon with increasing frequency for extramural lectures. Institutes, historical societies, Fourth of July celebrations, and other gatherings took advantage of a professor's supposed ability to talk upon all subjects. The ministerial instructor—and practically all staff members were of that category —taught Sunday School, held midweek services, and preached twice on the Lord's Day as a matter of course. The President became virtually an instructor to the state at large. His major addresses newspapers carried as part of the wisdom and literature of the time.[3]

The immediate background of the organized extension movement, however, was the "Great Awakening" in education of the thirty years following the Civil War. The frontiersman's opinion that the scholar was poorly fitted to repair a chimney or plow "new ground" gradually gave way to a demand that schooling be available to all as a natural fruit of democracy. At the same time, industrialization produced an urban population that had time and need for more formal education. Mere participation could not fit its youngsters into job and society as had been true of their fathers on the farm; teachers and books must take up the slack. Education became, therefore, a crusade of that generation.

Consequently, grade schools lengthened their sessions, and commissioned high schools reached one hundred by 1890. The office of county superintendent of schools was created, teachers' institutes gained state aid, lyceums flourished, and reading circles were organized. Special schools for the handicapped appeared. Higher education (1) accepted coeducation, (2) diversified its curriculum to admit such newcomers as modern languages, history, and chemistry, and (3) deepened the educational stream with the seminar method, research laboratories, and graduate degrees. The state created Purdue and Indiana State Normal (Terre Haute) and began legislative grants to Indiana University for current expenses. There existed a search for more education and a cautiously increasing willingness that it be provided at general expense with public—that is to say, democratic—control.[4]

---

[3] Woodburn, *op. cit.*, pp. 77, 174, 175.

[4] See W. O. Lynch, "The Great Awakening," *Indiana Magazine of History*, XLI, pp. 107–30.

Under the impact of this spirit Indiana University underwent such sweeping curricular revisions and so augmented its enrollment that it could almost be said to have been founded anew. Moreover, staff members were drawn more and more into such general services as helping to establish commissioned high schools and lecturing to various societies, "county normals," and teachers' institutes.[5] Therefore, when Professor Richard Boone undertook to give two non-credit lectures on pedagogy each month to the teachers of Bloomington during 1889–90,[6] he probably regarded his efforts as little different from previous institute work. But his lectures constituted quasi-extension teaching.

The transition was completed the next year, when Chairman May Wright Sewall and Secretary-Treasurer Amelia W. Platter persuaded the Indianapolis Association of Collegiate Alumnae to invite Professor Jeremiah W. Jenks to give a series of lectures on economics. Beginning, therefore, in January, 1891, Professor Jenks took his way to Indianapolis on twelve Friday evenings to explain away the mysteries of the "dismal science" to a large audience, apparently much intrigued by the demonstration. A few took advantage of the University's offer of two term hours of credit for those who did the prescribed reading, met the instructor for a weekly recitation, and passed the written examinations. All expense and administration were shouldered by the Association. The claim has been made—and perhaps rightly—that these lectures constituted the first university extension work west of the Allegheny Mountains.[7]

By this time the native Hoosier stream was being joined by the waters of an extension river that had begun in Cambridge, England, as early as 1867 and run its course through such varied American institutions as Johns Hopkins University, the larger city libraries, and Chautauqua.[8] Therefore, before Professor Jenks completed his course,

---

[5] Woodburn, *op. cit.,* pp. 287 ff.

[6] Departmental Report, Pedagogy, 1890. School of Education. The writer is indebted to Professor Velorus Martz for this information.

[7] Letters of Amelia W. Platter and James A. Woodburn to Almon R. Buis are included in his The History and Work of the Extension Division of Indiana University, unpublished Master's thesis, Indiana University (Bloomington, 1928), Appendix A, pp. 120–37. Mr. Buis' valuable study has been repeatedly consulted in the preparation of this account.

[8] James Creese, *The Extension of University Teaching* (New York, 1941), pp. 21–40.

President David Starr Jordan was explaining to the trustees that there was a general movement afoot known as "University Extension," by which the colleges enlarged "their usefulness as well as their reputation with the public at large." The board approved his recommendation that the faculty be given permission to undertake such teaching as seemed to them "wise and desirable," and so arranged as "not to interfere with classroom work." The only expense to be assumed by the University was for general advertising.[9] To administer the venture, a University extension standing committee of vague responsibility was appointed, consisting of Ernest W. Huffcut, Orrin B. Clark, and Edward A. Ross.[10]

By July, 1891, an Extension Teaching Circular was in press proclaiming an ambitious program of weekly lectures, summer schools, and correspondence. "Education," the circular argued, "has rightfully come to be regarded like politics and religion, as a lifelong matter and, as properly democratic, the concern of all."[11] That fall the annual Catalog, 1891–92, offered the benefits of higher education to those who could "find a little leisure from the exactions of business and domestic cares for the pursuit of some liberalizing study." A teacher would be sent to those unable to seek the teacher on the campus. "This does not mean," it was cautiously added, "that the University is to detach itself from its base and resolve itself into a staff of itinerant lecturers. On the contrary the University will maintain and strengthen all its existing departments and courses. It will simply reach two classes of students instead of one." Presaging what was later to be a characteristic aspect of Indiana University extension was the hope that "when permanent centers are established consecutive courses may be given that will enable more earnest students to do continuous University work."[12]

The newly appointed president, John M. Coulter, proved to be an enthusiastic convert to the extension movement. "The advantages

---

[9] President's Reports and Reports to Legislative Visiting Committees, 1881–91, V, Archives, Administration Building. Reports of the President's office will be cited hereafter as President's Reports.

[10] *Indiana University Extension Teaching Circular*, 1891, No. 1, p. 3. Unless otherwise indicated, publications of the University are assumed to have been published in Bloomington.

[11] *Ibid.*, pp. 2–3.

[12] Indiana University Catalog, 1891–92, pp. 98–101.

to the University," he assured the Board of Trustees, "are known to be very great in the way of advertising its work, attracting students, and arousing a general interest in its welfare."[13] Further evidence of President Coulter's enthusiasm was his early demonstrated willingness to teach his share of off-campus courses. Moreover, in December, 1891, he dispatched young and suave Professor James A. Woodburn to the Philadelphia conference that organized the American Society for the Extension of University Teaching. Here it was discovered that twenty-eight states and territories had almost simultaneously begun extension in some form.[14]

Meanwhile, the University's extension classes were going forward in five cities,[15] despite the fact that the initiative and administration rested on the audience. Classes had been scheduled only upon petition of a local group that could guarantee an audience and all expenses and perform such tasks as securing a meeting place, keeping attendance, selling tickets, and distributing local announcements. The instructor received his traveling expenses and ten dollars for each lecture.

During this year (1891–92) four instructors gave nine courses of six or twelve lectures to an average audience of approximately one hundred students. President John M. Coulter lectured on botany at Louisville, New Albany, and Evansville; Professor Orrin B. Clark on Shakespeare and James Russell Lowell at Louisville; Professor James A. Woodburn on American history at Indianapolis and Chicago (two series); and Professor Edward A. Ross on economics and sociology at Indianapolis. Most subjects were from the more recent curricular additions and designed primarily for auditors who had already been exposed to considerable education. Five of the nine courses were given outside the state and apparently were the first extension classes held in Louisville and Chicago.[16]

Very seriously did the instructor regard his responsibility; most

[13] President's Reports, 1891–95, pp. 4–5.
[14] Louis E. Reber, "University Extension in the United States," *Bureau of Education Bulletin*, 1914, No. 19 (Washington, 1914), pp. 5–6.
[15] Indiana University Catalog, 1891–92, pp. 99–101; *Indiana University Extension Teaching, Announcements*, 1892–93, pp. 3–7.
[16] George F. James, *Handbook of University Extension*, American Society for the Extension of University Teaching (Philadelphia, 1893), p. 164.

assuredly did he earn his stipend. For greatest success he must combine in proper quantities the erudition becoming his training and the platform manner of the lyceum speaker. It was considered essential to distribute a syllabus of each lecture containing an outline, penetrating questions, and a bibliography. An hour's question and review session was held before or after the open lecture, and required of those wishing credit. They must also write at least one lengthy report, take a final examination, and meet all prerequisites.

"The subjects and their treatment," the Catalog had warned, "are the same as at the University itself, and regular university methods and standards are maintained in all extension courses."[17] This formal, course-credit approach to extending the University's services followed the pattern impressed upon the extension movement by its English originators. It was also the type of off-campus activity most readily acceptable by the campus staffs. Actually, a very small minority of those who enrolled for lectures went on to qualify for credit.

Encouraged by the large audiences, an expanded program was arranged for the following year, 1892–93, and a new standing committee appointed: Woodburn, John R. Commons, and William E. Henry. Fourteen of the courses listed in the Catalog found sponsors scattered among ten different cities, and to the teaching staff of the previous year were added Commons (economics), Richard G. Boone (pedagogy), and Edward H. Griggs (literature). Audiences were large, but out of an enrollment of seventy-five the instructor could count on only about six or seven credit students. Attendance at the quiz hour varied disconcertingly from week to week.[18]

Compared with the previous year, there had been an increase in the number of courses, in departments represented, in total enrollment, and in centers to which instructors traveled. The University's extramural program appeared, therefore, to have found permanent footing. Actually, not a single extension class was conducted by Indiana University the following year, nor for many years thereafter. The same debacle struck the whole mushrooming extension movement throughout the country, including the virtual crusade of Presi-

[17] Indiana University Catalog, 1891–92, p. 99.
[18] *Ibid.*, 1892–93, pp. 97–101; *Indiana University Extension Teaching, Announcements,* 1892–93, pp. 2, 8–21; Buis, *op. cit.,* 18–21.

dent William R. Harper at the University of Chicago. Such a general failure implied generally applicable causes. But neither the dusty catalogs nor the memories of participants furnish explanations that are entirely satisfying.

One lecturer explained later that because of the slow train rides, two days' absences from home each week, and campus duties "a man seemed to be confronting the alternatives of devoting himself entirely to extension work or taking none of it." [19] That University policy-makers were also concerned about the implications of this remark was demonstrated by the resolution of the trustees on June 9, 1893, that no extension work be undertaken except on "Friday evenings or Saturday, unless in the judgment of the President it seems advisable." [20] Certainly the spectacular growth of campus responsibilities at the very time extension made its appearance tended to monopolize time, energy, and money. The graduating class of 1894, for example, had seen the faculty grow from 28 to 45, enrollment from 321 to 636, and the library from 13,000 to 20,000 volumes.[21] Furthermore, the innate conservatism of university thought and the fear that extension meant lower standards and "education without tears" caused many to withhold support.

It is possible, also, that the English-born impetus to extension work struck the American educational world before the changes of the "Great Awakening" had matured, thereby pushing the extension movement into a premature trial run. In addition, performance remained in the hands of volunteer enthusiasts who tired of missionary labor in a cause that was everybody's business and nobody's responsibility. The University had not launched a positive program but had merely permitted the state's citizens to call upon staff members for limited help. Finally, less emphasis on formal courses and more on noncredit services might have found a larger audience.[22]

Fragmentary evidence indicates that the extension idea did not pass entirely from memory during the succeeding years of its long depression. The University Catalog invited those who wished to

[19] James A. Woodburn to Almon R. Buis, November 27, 1926.
[20] Minutes of the Board of Trustees, July 24, 1883–June 16, 1897, V, p. 438, Archives.
[21] Woodburn, op. cit., p. 425.
[22] Creese, op. cit., pp. 49–50; Robert E. Cavanaugh to Cedric Cummins, October 14, 1947.

secure extension lecturers to correspond with the relevant department heads.[23] In 1896 the Board of Trustees officially sanctioned "more extension work by professors throughout the state" and authorized the payment of their traveling expenses.[24] It is unlikely that credit courses were held, but single lectures may have been given under this provision. There is more substantial evidence that beginning about 1904 a few students gained correspondence credits.[25] Moreover, with each year the educational trends of the past half-century were providing a broader potential base for extension work.

After almost fifteen years of somnolence the extension movement was gradually bestirring itself throughout the country. There was no sweeping epidemic of activity such as had occurred in 1891, and, significantly, much of the pattern of the revived program stemmed from the grass roots of the Midwest. Inspired by existing educational opportunities and the ideology of the Progressive Era, the University of Wisconsin took the lead, initiating an ambitious program in 1906 that exerted a continuing influence upon its sectional neighbors.[26]

A renewal of the offensive on the extension front by Indiana University was signaled by an official bulletin in 1908 advertising correspondence courses in English literature. During the next four years similar offerings were added in history, political science, German, and philosophy.[27] Having accorded these cautious steps his sympathetic support, President William Lowe Bryan now concluded that the time had come for more comprehensive action. Upon recommendation of a special committee, he appointed Dean William A. Rawles as acting director of extension work for 1912–13.

The nominating committee had recommended Dean Rawles on the ground that it was "vitally important" that the director "be a man who knows the University from the inside, and whom the members of the University know and trust."[28] During his progres-

---

[23] Indiana University Catalog, 1894–95, p. 84. This shifting of responsibility to department heads occurred for the first time in this Catalog; it was carried without change to 1909.
[24] Minutes of the Board of Trustees, July 24, 1883–June 16, 1897, p. 528.
[25] Sarah D. Kirby, "A Brief Review of the Work of the Correspondence Study Bureau, 1912–1920." Correspondence Study Bureau, Buis, op. cit., p. 23.
[26] Creese, op. cit., pp. 51–55.
[27] Indiana University Correspondence Study, July, 1911, pp. 3, 4.
[28] Samuel B. Harding and others to President William L. Bryan, April 12, 1912. Archives.

sion from a modest post in the Preparatory Department to an associate dean of the College of Liberal Arts, he had undoubtedly met those qualifications. His earnest integrity and emphasis on detail insured as responsible performance as would be possible for one who continued to fulfil his duties as dean and teach more than half a load. Thirty years later his secretary still vividly recalled the picture of Dean Rawles patiently and painstakingly recording correspondence grades and registrations in what moments he could find during and after a crowded work day.[29] His desk in Maxwell Hall was Extension headquarters.

Correspondence study received first attention, forming the solid core around which the new extension program was built. By June, 1913, 144 registrations had been added to the 60 inherited from previous years. Outlines and assignments were wheedled from faculty members and intricacies of records attacked with the aid of Rawles' ebullient secretary, Miss Sarah Kirby. Neither received extra remuneration the first year.

Lectures got under way more slowly. But by the second year, 1913–14, two credit courses were being given in Indianapolis and successful arrangements were made to furnish speakers for the Indiana Federation of Clubs.[30]

The remainder of Rawles' program consisted of informal, noncredit undertakings new to extension. A High School Discussion League of 178 schools was formed under the direction of Ross F. Lockridge. All pupils spoke on the same topic in progressive elimination contests that ended with the choice of state champion in the spring at Bloomington. The first contest was held in 1913–14 on the subject, "A New Constitution for Indiana."

Mr. Lockridge also made innumerable appearances before teachers' institutes and other groups urging the formation of Civic Discussion Clubs. Considerable success was achieved, for ninety-five groups wrote to the Extension Division for further aid. An additional venture into adult education was a vigorous attempt to assist

[29] William A. Rawles, "Preliminary Report of the Director of the Extension Division, October 1, 1912, to June 1, 1913," pp. 1–12. Correspondence Study Bureau. Conference with Sarah Kirby, June, 1946.

[30] William A. Rawles, "Report of the Director of the Extension Division for June 1, 1913, to June 1, 1914," pp. 3–15. Correspondence Study Bureau.

women's clubs in devising yearly programs that would be systematized and meaningful. From these efforts grew the first package libraries. In order to get factual data into the hands of club members and high school contestants, magazines, pamphlets, bulletins, newspaper clippings, and a few books were assembled by topic and lent with no charge other than postage. Most of these items were acquired by gift from publishers of leading periodicals, pressure groups, individual faculty members, and the out-of-date magazines of the Faculty Club.[31]

Loans of visual aids to schools and libraries were experimentally begun with a few paintings assembled by Professor Alfred M. Brooks. Through the campus Y.M.C.A. a speakers' bureau was formed for near-by churches. Eight Bloomington boys' clubs and three classes in English for the foreign-born quarry workers were organized. These projects, however, attracted only a small part of the attention accorded the special conferences that began in 1914 on the campus. In February a large group assembled for a study of "Taxation in Indiana"; a conference in April discussed "Educational Measurements" (featuring Professor E. L. Thorndike of Columbia University); and one in June plunged into the controversial question, "Shall a Constitutional Convention be Called in Indiana?"[32]

The Extension Division was assuming such proportions that for some months the director had been urging the selection of a full-time head. After Rawles' declination, John J. Pettijohn was appointed to take office August 1, 1914. "When I assumed it," Dean Rawles wrote in retrospect, "I was totally inexperienced in work of this character and felt the lack of preparation and technical knowledge."[33] Perhaps so, but he had initiated the major lines of activity which the Extension Division would thereafter follow. Furthermore, as a trusted "insider" he had won campus tolerance (relatively speaking) for extension education.

Pettijohn assumed his duties with a budget of more than $18,000[34] and a host of ideas. Four formative years on the extension staff of

[31] *Ibid.,* pp. 5–6.
[32] *Ibid.,* pp. 6–7.
[33] *Ibid.,* p. 6.
[34] Minutes of the Board of Trustees, June 30, 1914, p. 52.

the University of Wisconsin had given direction to his basic liberalism (of the Robert LaFollette, Theodore Roosevelt, Woodrow Wilson school). In his eyes, the currently expanding participation in education was a democratic movement, and one which the universities could materially assist through their extension divisions. He had, therefore, a pulpit as well as a religion. His good humor, seemingly inexhaustible energy, and quick mind soon made his name and tall, rangy figure known to all.

That his ability was also recognized outside the state was indicated the next year when he helped organize the National University Extension Association and became its first secretary. Chiefly interested in policy formation, he generally left the burdens of administrative detail to his chief aids, Walton S. Bittner, Public Welfare Service; Sarah D. Kirby, Correspondence Study; Grace Thompson, Bureau of Public Discussion; Bert C. Riley, Field Organizer; and Irene Langwill, Office Manager.[35] Offices were moved to Kirkwood Hall.

Work of the Division was sorted into two main categories of Extension Teaching Service and Public Welfare Service. The second lay much closer to the heart of the new director, for it contained the adult, informal, and noncredit aspects of extension that could reach wider audiences than the minority with college interests and prerequisites. Like the racers in *Alice in Wonderland,* each Hoosier would be encouraged to start where he was and run as fast as he could. As extension workers knew, just such aid was being successfully furnished to farmers by land-grant colleges through institutes, lectures, pamphlets, and demonstrations.[36]

Central to Pettijohn's plans was the organization of community centers, after exploratory interviews by the field organizer. If possible, an Extension Center Association was formed in each locality with a president, secretary, and an executive council to plan programs of education and entertainment. The Extension Division cooperated with the Association at all stages, encouraging the drafting of a three-part program consisting of academic lectures in series; a

---

[35] Indiana University Catalog, 1915–16, p. 344; conferences with Robert E. Cavanaugh, Mary B. Orvis, and Albert L. Kohlmeier, 1946.

[36] John J. Pettijohn, "Report to the President" in President's Reports, 1914–15, pp. 149–78.

lyceum menu of dramatic readings, music, and travelogues; and a community institute. The first two were to be held at periodic intervals during the school year and the last on three or four successive days. The projects were to be self-supporting except for extension staff work and circulars.[37]

Final results were uneven. Difficulty was experienced in finding community leaders to assume the rather heavy burden of keeping the associations going. Lectures in series were considered dull, and popularity of lyceum programs fluctuated. The institutes, however, combined Chautauqua methods and local pride to achieve success, twenty-three being held before American entry into the First World War turned energies into other channels. Lectures, community sings, stories for children, stereopticon views (e.g., Yellowstone Park), musical recitals, exhibits, and dramatic readings provided diversified fare from mid-morning to bedtime.[38] Much of the program was conducted by local talent.

Other phases of Public Welfare Service appeared in amazing number, financed by staff energy when the budget proved inadequate. State-wide conferences and local child welfare expositions were held in many cities. The various noncredit endeavors begun during the Rawles period were enlarged and pamphlets and booklets distributed by the score. Community surveys were made in cooperation with civic societies, and, upon request, professors visited and counseled with public school teachers.[39]

Extension Teaching Service, the other major part of the Division, consisted of correspondence courses, class study, academic lectures, and club study. Correspondence registrations climbed steadily until checked by the war, then recovered to reach 631 in 1920–21. Classroom study lagged in the early years because of neglect by a staff preoccupied with noncredit projects. Yet each year a few more courses were given to those who took advantage of the standing offer to

[37] E.g., First annual program of the Indiana University Extension Center Association, Washington, Ind., 1915–16. Archives.

[38] Ibid: Community Institute, Colfax, Ind., June 21, 22, 1916. Archives. Conference with Walton S. Bittner, June, 1946.

[39] Various annual reports of John J. Pettijohn, 1915–20, in President's Reports; Indiana University Extension Division, Announcements, 1915–20. Hereafter referred to as Extension Announcements.

send an instructor to any group "of not less than fifteen persons in any Indiana community [who would] organize to study a subject offered as an extension course."[40]

A precedent-making step in class work was taken early in 1916 with the establishment of an extension teaching center in Indianapolis. Free rooms on the tenth floor of the Merchants' Bank Building and $1,000 were donated by the Chamber of Commerce, and civic organizations added their blessing. In charge of the center at first was Ray S. Trent, followed in 1918 by Robert E. Cavanaugh, and in 1921 by Mary B. Orvis. Both course-credit and informal services were undertaken.[41] The differences between this venture and the extension community centers are apparent.

A second extension center was founded in 1917 at Fort Wayne, sponsored by the Commercial Club, city school board, and county commissioners. Free rooms and utilities were provided on the third floor of the Allen County courthouse. Frank W. Shockley, in charge the first year, was transferred to the Bloomington office in 1918 and succeeded by Floyd R. Neff, who was teaching in Fort Wayne Central High School.[42]

The World War, 1917–18, was both a disruptive force and an opportunity for a wider role to the Extension Division. Many of its established services declined or leveled off. On the other hand, most of the methods and devices laboriously created or appropriated by the extension movement during the past decade were used to mobilize opinion and to train skilled workers, soldiers, and sailors in this first "all-out-war."[43] Specifically, valuable aid was given the Indiana State Council of Defense in two respects. Its child welfare committee drew upon the Extension Division for exhibits, lecturers, conferences, and assistance in planning. Still more significantly, a Speakers' Bureau of gargantuan size was staffed and run by the Extension Division, the Defense Council furnishing office and supplies. Pettijohn was bureau director, with Cavanaugh as his assistant and later his successor. A good share of the Extension Division staff was even-

---

[40] Extension Announcements, 1917–18, p. 10.
[41] Ibid., p. 21.
[42] President's Reports, 1916–17, p. 83; Indiana University Catalog, 1917–18, p. 229.
[43] Walton S. Bittner, The University Extension Movement (Washington, 1930), p. 25.

tually drawn into some phase of this work, and funds of $5,500 were appropriated by the University to meet extra expenses.

Mr. Cavanaugh, already in Indianapolis, undertook much of the active direction. More than four hundred volunteer speakers from over the state were channeled to committees and meetings in need of their voices. Some of their addresses were full length, but a majority were much shorter—for these were the Four Minute Men! Speaking throughout the state each week on a common topic selected by the national office, they talked for exactly four minutes before almost every kind of audience on "Where Did You Get Your Facts?" "Food Conservation," "Liberty Loan," and similar subjects. At the movie house, when the hero and heroine had walked hand in hand into the sunset at the end of the first show of the evening, the pianist would shift from "Hearts and Flowers" to "Over There," the lights would come on, and one of Cavanaugh's Four Minute Men take the stage.[44] They helped secure Middletown's [45] cooperation with the weekly drives and long-range goals of national policy.

Extension personnel was drawn into still broader war effort. In 1918 Pettijohn was called to Washington, D.C., as associate director of the National Four Minute Men, and later director of the Speakers' Bureau of the National Committee on Public Information. Thanks to his ability and gregariousness he soon "knew everyone." He remained on after the war, becoming in 1919 director of the Federal Division of Educational Extension in the United States Department of the Interior. For assistance he called two of his Indiana staff to Washington: Bittner was made associate director and Miss Mary B. Orvis did research, editing, and writing.[46] Some of the secretarial and clerical assistants also came from the Extension Division staff: Lelah Whitted, Edith Huntington, and Helen Duncan.

Pettijohn returned to Indiana in 1920 with a national reputation and his biography in the elect of *Who's Who*. He plunged into the

[44] James R. Mock and Cedric Larson, *Words That Won The War* (Princeton, 1939), Chap. 5; *Indiana University Extension Bulletin,* "The Speakers' Bureau of the State Council of Defense," March, 1920, pp. 7, 8; conferences with Mr. Cavanaugh, June, 1946.

[45] The typical American town, as depicted in *Middletown,* by Lynd.—Ed.

[46] President's Reports, 1919–20, pp. 42–43; conversation with Mary B. Orvis, June, 1946. Pettijohn was also director of the National University Extension Association, Inc.

difficult task of resuscitating the noncredit services that had lapsed during the war. He placed the Division among the first to adopt Home Reading Courses and made cooperative arrangements with the Indiana Parent-Teacher Association. His was the spirit behind *Educational Issues*,[47] an unaffiliated magazine begun in 1920 for the discussion of Indiana educational problems in the forthright fashion of "personal journalism." As usual, he was soon straining at the outer walls of his budget. But despite this activity his intimates were aware that he was growing restless and somewhat disheartened. They were not surprised, therefore, when he accepted an offer from the University of Minnesota to become assistant to the president and director of the summer session, resigning December 31, 1920.[48] The University had lost a bellwether.

Robert E. Cavanaugh was immediately appointed acting director, becoming full director on June 6, 1921.[49] Cavanaugh well understood the realities of the Hoosier educational world. Born near Salem, he had taught eight years in Indiana rural schools, received his Bachelor's degree from Indiana University in 1908, gone on to the University of Chicago for his graduate work, and returned to Salem as superintendent of schools in 1909. There Pettijohn met him in 1917. Impressed by his administrative record and by his cooperation with the noncredit extension program in Salem, Pettijohn invited him to become head of the Indianapolis Center the next year. To the regular duties of this post were soon added his previously described labors with the Four Minute Men and the direction of the Indianapolis Extension Center during Pettijohn's absence in Washington.[50] He was to remain in charge of the University's Extension Division until 1946, tripling the combined years of his two predecessors.

"Pettijohn and Cavanaugh both put their trust in education," summarized one observer after Cavanaugh had resigned as director. Yet they differed in many respects. Pettijohn was quick in decision but not very much interested in running something after he had begun it. Cavanaugh moved more slowly, carefully testing his ideas in his mind before applying

[47] *Educational Issues*, 1920–22. Indiana State Library.

[48] John J. Pettijohn, Faculty History. Archives. Pettijohn continued at Minnesota until his early death, March 20, 1923.

[49] Minutes of the Board of Trustees, June 6, 1921, p. 112.

[50] Faculty History, "Robert W. Cavanaugh," Archives. Conferences with Cavanaugh, Bittner, and Orvis, April and June, 1946.

them, and then followed through. He was extremely able, and, above all, thoroughly honest and fair. If he hadn't been, he could not have kept the same staff for twenty-five years.

To this picture a campus administrator added that "Cavanaugh fulfilled more than he promised. Another thing, he made it a point to consult the departments here in all matters." [51]

Though campus staffs may not have fully appreciated the uniqueness of their Extension Division on this last score, the results were fruit enough. By such methods, Cavanaugh took an experimental (though already significant) division and made it an integral part of the University structure. Recognition in the national extension field came in the form of innumerable committee appointments and the presidency of the National University Extension Association in 1931–32.

The new director took up his headquarters in the strategically located offices of the Indianapolis Extension Center, ceaselessly moving over the state and making frequent periodic trips to Bloomington. Most of the administrative offices remained on the campus under the general supervision of Bittner as associate director. Already widely known, Bittner was to be elected secretary-treasurer of the National University Extension Association in 1928 and annually re-elected for over twenty years. Because he leaned toward noncredit extension activities and Cavanaugh toward course-credit work, their efforts supplemented each other's. It was to the credit of both that a team of two nationally recognized figures pulled together so excellently throughout the entire time.

Change of directors had made easier the transition that was taking place in the extension program of Indiana (and other schools). The experimental days, the exuberant days, the days when a fundamental change in the nature of the University service was envisioned that would make the campus literally as big as the state, were past. Noncredit work was giving way to credit, and the noncredit activities that did survive were the institutionalized, tangible services such as visual aids, package libraries, home reading courses, and high school contests. Community institute programs were dying out while the

[51] In 1946 the writer collected characterizations of Cavanaugh by his associates; these are typical of the high praise encountered.

resident Extension Centers founded cautiously at Indianapolis and Fort Wayne were taking hold in substantial fashion. Their work was preponderantly course-credit in nature, which had the advantage of paying much of its way and of acquainting many faculty members with extension education through participation as instructors. "Solid university course work," Cavanaugh observed, "has been the core around which the informal services have been built, financially and administratively." [52]

Public Welfare Service, therefore, tended to lose precedence to the Extension Teaching Service of classroom instruction, correspondence, lectures, and, for a time, Winona and Gary summer courses. Total class enrollments were pushed from 3,353 in 1920–21 to 11,188 in 1936–37 by taking advantage of a number of supporting influences. Automobiles, improved highways, and interurbans extended the area served by classes, and continued expansion of secondary education enlarged the pool of eligibles for college courses. Need for additional high school teachers, plus higher license requirements, created an extraordinary demand for evening or Saturday courses for teachers. Lastly, and fundamentally, postwar prosperity and mechanization was strengthening those economic, technological, and social changes that had called the educational crusade and extension work into being in the first place.

EXTENSION TEACHING SERVICE [53]

Year	Class Study							Correspondence		Lectures
	Total Enrollments	Total Students	Indianapolis Enrollments	Fort Wayne Enrollments	Calumet Enrollments	South Bend Enrollments	Other Enrollments	Enrollments	Students	
1920–21	3,353	2,254	1,110	674			1,569	790	617	90
1926–27	8,008	5,873	2,485	1,457	416		3,650	2,229	1,878	103
1931–32	8,432	5,253	3,355	1,789	1,701	206	1,390	1,854	1,504	93
1936–37	11,188	5,495	3,554	2,271	2,308	669	2,386	1,673	1,370	90

Under the guidance of its new executive, Mary B. Orvis, the Indianapolis Center reached an enrollment of 3,554 by the end of

[52] Robert E. Cavanaugh to Cedric Cummins, April 12, 1946.
[53] Statistics in this table were compiled from the *Extension Announcements* of the relevant years.

Bryan's administration. In addition to instruction of extension students, academic instruction was supplied for the John Herron Art Institute and, in lesser extent, for the Normal School of the North American Gymnastic Union near by. The Center had the city and neighboring towns to draw from, and as early as 1920 began to emphasize commercial courses. Popular lectures, short courses for basketball coaches, and other noncredit activities added variety. As the nearest Center to Bloomington, it was able to draw much of its teaching staff from the University.

Headquarters were moved to the old Medical College Building, 102 North Senate, in 1920. But this location proved to be on the edge of "a less desirable part of the city," so that the offices were transferred the following year to 319 North Pennsylvania Street. In January, 1928, the University purchased the building formerly occupied by the Bobbs-Merrill Company which had been moved from the Plaza to 122 East Michigan Street. The new quarters were occupied before the end of the year, the staff thereby escaping the fish fries of Democratic headquarters adjacent to the building's previous location.[54]

Experiences of other Centers paralleled that of Indianapolis in most respects, but they could not rely on commuters from Bloomington for as many of their instructors. Fort Wayne Center continued its solid growth—2,271 enrollments by 1937—with Neff in charge throughout the entire period. Extension classes were held in Gary and neighboring cities as early as 1917, but the first step toward formal organization did not come until five years later. At that time an office was established in the Gary Memorial Auditorium with the assistance of the city board of education, which printed extension bulletins and provided classrooms and administrative aid. Albert Fertsch, the director of adult education of the Gary schools, supervised the work in his spare time. In 1932 a second step was taken by the creation of the Hammond, Whiting, East Chicago Extension Center with Hugh W. Norman as executive secretary. In 1936 its name was changed to Calumet Center

---

[54] Minutes of the Board of Trustees, December 27, 1927, p. 309; interviews with Cavanaugh, Miss Orvis, and Mrs. Gertrude Heberlein. In the early part of the period there was a decentralization of academic responsibility; Miss Orvis was in charge of Arts and Science courses, Frank H. Streightoff of commerce, and Ralph E. Carter of education.

with offices in Roosevelt High School of East Chicago and an enrollment of 2,308. Significantly, establishment of this Extension Center
was followed shortly by an increase in campus registration from
this populous corner of the state.[55]

The South Bend-Mishawaka Center was not completely institutionalized until after the period covered by this study, but its early
history during the 1920's paralleled that of Gary. Gertrude Kaiser
from the Indianapolis Center, Helen Duncan, and Laura Alexander,
the secretary of the Bureau of Class Instruction, in turn, helped to
organize classes, with Galen B. Sargent, the assistant to the superintendent of the South Bend schools, acting as liaison officer with the
local schools. Classes were held in Central High School.

These special Centers did not contain all the class work and for a
time, in fact, seemed to be becoming the less important part of it.
Directed from Bloomington, by Professor Ernest M. Linton in the
early period, classes were meeting in as many as eighty-five different
towns by the middle twenties. Most of them were held in conjunc-
tion with teachers' institutes. An effort to reorganize and revitalize
the township teachers' institutes in 1921, plus an increase in teacher
requirements in 1923, had resulted in a half-day of the monthly institute being reserved for the study of a professional subject for
credit under the direction of an instructor approved by one of the
colleges in the state. Subjects and books were chosen annually by the
Indiana Teachers' Reading Circle Board and approved by the State
Board of Education. Popularly termed "Saturday Institute Courses,"
they were pursued with vigor by Indiana University, through its
Extension Division, to an extent that 105 institute classes were given
to 2,558 students in 1924–25. Enrollment declined soon thereafter,
as teaching requirements were further modified.[56]

Allied to class study was the stable, less dramatic work of the Cor-

[55] Extension Announcements, 1926–27, p. 5; Classes Offered by Indiana University Cooperating with the Gary Public Schools, Gary, 1923; Buis, op. cit., pp. 53–54.

[56] Extension Announcements, 1928–29, pp. 20–24; Announcements, 1930–31, p. 20; Emmett W. Arnett, Some Educational and Financial Phases of the Indiana University Extension
Classes, unpublished Master's thesis, Indiana University (Bloomington, 1927), pp. 4–7.
Included in Arnett's study was a comparison of the grades made by 64 students in extension classes with those they made after coming to the campus. The result showed them
to be almost identical in average, with campus grades slightly higher. A larger percentage
of these 64 graduated with honors than did those who had had no extension classes.

respondence Study Bureau. Mary Pratt had followed Miss Kirby as its head in 1920, and she in turn was succeeded by Louise Rogers in 1923. Like so many of Cavanaugh's staff, Miss Rogers was to continue in office throughout his directorship and beyond. Correspondence study paid its own expenses to an even greater extent than did extension class work. It possessed the further advantage of being able to reach the student isolated by geography or subject interest. Some students profited much, some little—just as their brethren on the campus. But amidst the myriad private correspondence schools of varying and often undeterminable value, the University was providing authentic courses staffed usually by those who were teaching the same subjects in the classroom.

Correspondence enrollments rose gradually to the high point of 2,229 in 1926–27, then fell off slightly until the depression forced them down to 1,118 in 1933–34. Recovery set in soon, however, and the enrollment climbed back to 1,673 three years later. College courses formed the backbone of the bureau's work, the students demonstrating a preference for English, education, and history in that order. But noncredit, adult education courses were given to a few and high school ones annually to approximately 150 pupils. The high school correspondence courses were accepted by Indiana University as entrance credits and by the State Board of Education in lieu of the state equivalency examination, as well as by individual high schools.[57]

Included also within the Teaching Service were approximately ninety noncredit lectures arranged by the Division each year, many of them given in the resident Centers. A fourth phase of the Teaching Service was the summer school conducted by the Extension Division at Winona Lake for three years, 1928–30, and at Gary for two years, 1931–32, for "vacationing" students and faculty.[58] Professor Linton and Helen Duncan managed this offering in the respective Centers.

Emphasis on course-credit education did not exclude the under-

[57] "Report of the Correspondence Study Bureau, 1934–1937"; "Correspondence Study at Indiana University." Copies of both reports are in the Correspondence Study Bureau.
[58] *Extension Announcements,* 1929–30, pp. 4, 37–38.

taking of many informal tasks by the Public Welfare Service. So varying were they that neither the accompanying table nor the following description pretends to include all of their ramifications. Much of the service was performed in cooperation with state associations or societies. In one year, for example, some member of the Extension Division staff was chairman of the reciprocity committee of the Indiana Federation of Clubs, chairman of the child welfare committee of the Indiana League of Women Voters, corresponding secretary of the Indiana Council of Women, executive secretary of the Indiana Child Welfare Association, president of the Indiana Council of Social Agencies, executive secretary of the Indiana Municipal League, secretary of the adult education committee, vice-president of the Indiana Endorsers of Photoplays, and a member of the State Health Council. In addition, extension workers occupied three key offices in the Indiana Parent-Teacher Association.[59]

PUBLIC WELFARE SERVICE[60]

Year	Films Distributed	Lantern Slide Sets	Exhibits	Package Library Loans	Plays Lent	High School Contests Enrollments—Schools			
						Discussion	Latin	Mathematics	Music
1920–21..	2,135	571	71	1,639	165	204			
1926–27..	11,291	4,031	124	6,270	3,570	175	455		
1931–32..	6,215	6,871	135	7,745	3,331	123	379	393	74
1936–37..	10,675	7,777	150	5,544	3,401	82	289	456	168

The Bureau of Public Discussion, one of the early divisions of noncredit work, sought with limited funds "to stimulate intelligent discussion of current political, economic, and social questions." One of its most important undertakings was the previously mentioned loan service of Package Libraries consisting of magazine clippings, pamphlets, and reports. As a special service, technical reprints and articles were supplied members of the Indiana State Medical Associa-

[59] *Ibid.*, 1926–27, p. 32.
[60] *Extension Announcements* for the relevant years. The figures for high school contests refer to the number of schools participating.

tion, municipal officials, and members of the Indiana Parent-Teacher Association.[61]

Also within the jurisdiction of the Bureau of Public Discussion were its Club Study and Discussion projects which prepared sample club programs, bibliographies, and outlines, and cooperated with the *Indianapolis Star* in judging annual club program contests. The State High School Discussion League, Latin contests, music contests, mathematics contests, and the Thomas A. Edison Scholarship Contests for Indiana were also administered by this bureau. Likewise worthy of note was its Drama Loan Service. As a result of numerous requests for assistance in play selection the bureau had begun collecting plays in the fall of 1920 for loan. Once a play was chosen, copies for use had to be ordered from the publisher. Beginning in 1932 the first annual drama conference was held, and in 1936 appeared the first issue of "Stage Door," a monthly, mimeographed bulletin containing reviews of new plays and notes of interest to directors. Advisory assistance to community dramatics was developed, directors of production were employed, and a traveling theatre was sent on tour.

After being directed in turn by Harriet N. Bircholdt (before 1920), Grace Thompson, Mary Pratt, and Dorothy Huntington, the Bureau of Public Discussion came under the control of Mrs. Adela K. Bittner in 1926.[62]

A second major division of the Public Welfare Service was the Visual Instruction Bureau. Its lantern slide collection numbered 715 subject collections by 1936, containing 30,000 slides that were lent to high schools, libraries, and clubs. Its motion picture film service received a marked impetus from the many war films distributed after the war and continued to grow until it overshadowed slide distribution in the eyes of many patrons. Further aspects of the Visual Instruction Bureau were the exhibits of posters, drawings, original paintings, and copies of masterpieces and the yearly poster contest that put grade and high school pupils at work on such subjects as

[61] E.g., *Extension Announcements*, 1929–30, p. 49.
[62] Interview with Helen Duncan, June, 1946; Buis, *op. cit.*, pp. 86–95. The Drama Loan Service was designated Play Loan Service for a time.

"Safety" and "The Kindergarten." An advisory service of demonstrations, lectures, and special circulars on the use of films was maintained, and films were furnished to University departments. Hugh W. Norman headed the bureau until his transfer to the Calumet Center led to the appointment, first, of Mrs. Pauline Jones Ellis, and, later, of Ford Lee Lemler.[63]

Numerous other noncredit services were performed, many of which were eventually cataloged under the all-inclusive term of General Welfare Service. Particularly important in the years immediately following the First World War was the child welfare work to which Mrs. Edna H. Edmondson made special contributions. Stressed in the same period were the educational programs on behalf of public health nursing and on play and recreation, the latter under the leadership of Professor George E. Schlafer. Art education was pushed after 1930 with the assistance of the Department of Fine Arts and the Indiana Federation of Art Clubs, under the direction of Mrs. Avis Burke. A few public conferences were held, and a valuable information service was maintained that reached the public by way of bulletins on such topics as *Art Guide to Indiana, Aids to Latin Teachers,* and *Indiana Local History.*[64]

Another general service consisted of Home Reading Courses carried out in cooperation with the State Library and the United States Bureau of Education for a nominal fee. Upon completion of the prescribed ten or twelve books on a given topic the reader received a certificate (but not academic credit) from the Extension Division.[65] Management of this work was lodged in the capable and busy hands of Helen Duncan, office manager of the Division since 1921, and later was transferred to Mrs. Burke, who was also active as a liaison officer with the Federation of Women's Clubs and Indiana Federation of Art Clubs.

The depression of the thirties affected the Extension Division, as it did other branches of the University. Enrollments fell off in class study and correspondence, salaries were decreased, and "nonessen-

---

[63] "Bureau of Audio-Visual Aids, Indiana University Extension Division, 1914–1937," special report prepared by Carolyn Guss.

[64] For a record of these services see the *Extension Announcements* and special bulletins for the years concerned.

[65] Interviews with Helen Duncan, June, 1946.

tials" pared away. At the same time, because the Extension Division represented the University in the field, it was called upon to assist state and local authorities in organizing adult education classes in the FERA and WPA projects. National Youth Administration assistance was given to students at the Extension Centers, and Bittner was appointed chairman of the NYA work of the University as a whole.[66]

To summarize, if the major functions of the University are to discover knowledge and to disseminate it, most labors of the Extension Division fell within the latter category. It helped to lessen the gap between the known and what was commonly known. But more than facts were carried from the campus, for the university viewpoint (restraint, objectivity, perspective, etc.) accompanied in some small or larger way almost every activity. In a sense, extension work constituted a progress report of the University to its owners.

This close contact between public and Extension Division, however, carried a danger as well as an opportunity. In a discerning Commencement address on the campus, historian Frederick J. Turner had spoken of the peculiar role of the state-supported university to serve the needs of the time without yielding to them. It must, according to him, "recognize new needs without becoming subordinate to the immediately practical, to the shortsightedly expedient. It must not sacrifice the higher efficiency for the more obvious but lower efficiency." It must find "the wisdom to make expenditures for results which pay manifold in the enrichment of civilization, but which are not immediate and palpable."[67] Because of the nature of its work, the problem here posed was especially applicable to the Extension Division. That it maintained its balance was indicated by the fact that the early press of teacher training did not turn the Centers into normal schools nor the later emphasis on business courses transform them into trade schools.

A backward view of the extension movement reveals that it had appeared in those countries that had undergone the dual changes of industrialization and political democracy. It was natural, therefore,

---

[66] Interview with Bittner, June, 1946; *Extension Announcements,* 1938–39, p. 11.
[67] Frederick Jackson Turner, *The Frontier in American History* (New York, 1920), pp. 283–84.

to the times and to Indiana, and it was a product of the same forces that produced compulsory secondary education, more varied curriculums, and the professional schools. Despite modest funds and the suspicion of the orthodox who regarded it as the Salvation Army of education, the Extension Division was particularly adapted to furthering the goal expressed by President Bryan in his inaugural. "What the people want," he said at that time, "is open paths from every corner of the state, through the schools, to the highest and best things which men can achieve."

CHAPTER LI

THE COLLEGE OF ARTS AND SCIENCES

T HE COLLEGE of Arts and Sciences has played a very important part in the development of Indiana University, and those who have written the history of this institution have been mindful of this fact. Paradoxically, however, there is no chapter on the College of Arts and Sciences in Volume I of the *History of Indiana University, 1820–1902*, or in *Indiana University, 1820–1904*.

To understand this seeming omission it must be explained that the title "College of Arts and Sciences" was first used in 1921; that for twelve years prior to that date, 1909–21, the title "College of Liberal Arts" was in use; and that for seventy-one years, 1838 to 1909, this one school functioned as Indiana University.

In 1828 Indiana College was established by the General Assembly of the state of Indiana. The organization of Indiana College was very simple. There was no use of the term "College of Liberal Arts" and there were no departmental announcements. There were no course announcements, but merely a list of subjects studied each of two sessions[1] of each of four years. When, by legislative act of 1838, Indiana College became Indiana University, there was, for three years, no change in Indiana College except in name, Indiana University, although a struggling School of Law was established in 1842.

As the years passed there were unsuccessful attempts at establishment of other schools. Courses in agricultural chemistry were given for a few years, 1853–59, in the hope of establishing a school of agriculture. There was a Normal Department announced in the Catalog

---

[1] These two sessions at first were of unequal length. As stated in the Catalog of August 17, 1831, the first session extended from the first of November until the last of April, six months. The second extended from the first of June to the last of September, four months. But in the next Catalog extant, that of September, 1835, the sessions were of equal length, five months each.

This division of the year into two equal sessions was superseded in 1849–50 by a division of the year into three terms, a procedure followed until the year 1915–16 when there was a return to the two-semester plan.

of 1851, which was suspended in 1857. An effort was made to revive it in 1865, which, in 1869, seemed successful, but it expired the next year. Instruction in engineering was announced, 1853–58, but apart from long established courses in mathematics and physics, the effort ended in promise. From 1871 to 1874 the course was revived briefly as civil engineering. The pitifully small budget of the institution foredoomed these efforts to failure.

An affiliation with the Indiana Medical College (1871) was ended (1876–77)[2] and the School of Law was closed in 1877, not reopened until 1889. During the twelve years, 1877–89, the institution was in reality a College of Liberal Arts, called Indiana University.

During the years 1872–76 there was the nearest approach to a university organization of any time prior to 1909. Within the University Catalogs of that period there were scheduled three departments, a Collegiate Department, a Law Department, and a Medical Department. Here the word "Department" was used as a division of the University as we use the word "School" today. But this promising organization developed by the President Nutt administration quickly succumbed because of the opposition of President Moss and of inadequate funds.

A division of the University of less importance than schools was the Department of Military Science and Engineering. The term "Department" as applied to a division of instruction of a school, such as the Department of Greek, or Department of Chemistry, was first generally used in the Catalog of 1874–75, the last year of the Nutt administration. Prior to that time the subjects studied each term constituted the sole course announcement. These departmental announcements of 1874–75 were general, not detailed, statements and this division of the Catalog bore no heading until the Catalog of 1884–85, the first under the Jordan regime, which bore the heading "Departments of Instruction." The following year the heading became "Departments of Study" and so remained until 1891 when the heading "Courses of Study" was used. In 1894–95 this heading became "Departments and Courses of Study." In 1903–4 the heading became "Departments of Liberal Arts," and this in 1909, as stated above, became "College of Liberal Arts."

[2] See Chap. XLI, p. 486, n. 12.

When, in 1894–95, Horace A. Hoffman became dean, his title was Dean of the Departments of Liberal Arts. This title in 1908 became Dean of the College of Liberal Arts, though this heading for departmental announcements was not used until the following year.

When Woodburn wrote the *History of Indiana University, 1820–1902,* including Banta's account of the early days, it was really the College of Liberal Arts of which they wrote, since, except for the small School of Law, that is all there was of Indiana University during that period. And when Professor Rawles wrote the brief "Historical Sketch," and Professor Carson wrote the 162-page Part II of *Indiana University, 1820–1904,* entitled "Development of the Course of Study," it was chiefly the sketch and course of study of the College of Liberal Arts of which they wrote.

So it becomes apparent that instead of the College of Liberal Arts being omitted, nearly everything that has been written prior to the Bryan administration has been of the College of Liberal Arts, though it had not as yet acquired that title. Our present task, therefore, is not to repeat a story that has been so well and extensively told, but to bring the story up to date, to tell the essentials of the development of the College of Liberal Arts (now the College of Arts and Sciences), during the Bryan administration. (The development of the course of study of the College of Liberal Arts during this period is described in Chapter XLI.)

In the early days of the Bryan administration the School of Law functioned very much as the Department of Chemistry or of History. Students registered in the University and presented their certificate of registration to the dean of the School of Law where they enrolled for law courses. In faculty meetings, particularly, the College of Liberal Arts was dominant. But as a School of Medicine, a Graduate School, a School of Education took their places along with Law as schools of Indiana University, it began to be apparent that the liberal arts departments were not Indiana University, but a division of Indiana University for which an appropriate title should be found. These facts contributed to the adoption in 1909 of the title "College of Liberal Arts."

In 1902 the University consisted of a large College of Liberal Arts with a small School of Law. President Bryan believed it was of the highest importance to the welfare of the institution to initiate those developments whereby the institution which was a university in name only should become a university in fact. As events proved, the time was opportune for this development.

During the years 1902–37 this transformation took place. In this evolution, emphasis, naturally, was placed on changes that were occurring, but in these changes the College of Liberal Arts was not lost nor was it adversely affected as some felt sure would be the case. On the contrary, it exists today stronger than when this period began.

When we look back over the years, it seems clear that in 1902 the College of Liberal Arts was about to burst its bounds. Within it were the germs of other schools, ready to come into being, germs of a Graduate School, of a School of Medicine, of a School of Commerce and Finance, of a School of Education, and of a much better organized summer school and Extension Division. To all of these the College of Liberal Arts made important contributions. Indeed it seems no exaggeration to say that but for the College of Liberal Arts the organization of these other schools would have been impossible at that time.

The contribution of the College of Liberal Arts to each one of these schools has been noted in connection with its organization and pointed out in the chapter on "The Course of Study." Though the College of Liberal Arts of 1902 made no contribution to the School of Music or the School of Dentistry or to the Training School for Nurses, all three of these schools later made contacts with the College. The School of Music functioned for a time as a Department of the College during its evolution into School status. Predental students spend two years in the College in preparation for the study of dentistry, and the work of the Training School for Nurses may, under certain circumstances, count as the fourth year of the College leading to a baccalaureate degree. So we see the College of Arts and Sciences as the mother college of the professional schools, contributing to their organization and providing preliminary training for their student body.

An examination of the development of Indiana University, 1902–37, shows that emphasis was laid on graduate and professional work. This was the avowed policy of President Bryan. It was also the recommendation of the non-state school presidents at the important conference called by Governor Marshall in 1909. For a list of new departments added to the College of Liberal Arts, 1902–37, see Chapter XLI, "The Course of Study." At the close of the Bryan administration, June, 1937, the College of Arts and Sciences consisted of the following departments:[3] Anatomy, Astronomy, Botany, Chemistry, Comparative Philology, Economics, English, Fine Arts, French and Italian, Geology and Geography, German, Government, Greek, History, Home Economics, Hygiene, Journalism, Latin, Mathematics, Military Science and Tactics, Philosophy, Physical Education, Physics, Physiology, Psychology, Sociology, Spanish, Zoology, and the Institute of Criminal Law and Criminology (later called Institute of Criminal Law Administration, and still later, Department of Police Administration).

These twenty-nine departments represented an increase of eleven over 1902. An examination of the eleven departments added shows that two of them, the Department of Anatomy and the Department of Physiology, were formed in the development of a professional school, that of medicine, and both departments consisted largely of courses formerly given in the Department of Zoology. Other departments arose by division of dual or composite departments without any considerable increase in courses offered. The Departments of Comparative Philology, Psychology, and Spanish arose in this way.

Approximately 50 per cent of the increase in the number of departments of the College of Arts and Sciences was merely a matter of bookkeeping. Other departments such as Home Economics, Hygiene, and Physical Training were organized in response to an obvious need. It seems clear, therefore, that no emphasis was laid on the development of the College of Arts and Sciences, yet it grew, since there was an increase in the number of students desiring a baccalaureate degree, and most professional schools of Indiana University required work in a College of Arts and Sciences as a prerequisite for entrance. But this preprofessional work could be taken in any college

---

[3] "Department" here includes "Military Science and Tactics," which did not carry that designation in the Catalog, but was listed, with its courses, along with Arts and Sciences departments, and later came to be carried under the heading "Unattached Departments." Physical Education was treated this way until its incorporation into the School of Health, Physical Education, and Recreation. Likewise, the Institute of Criminal Law and Criminology, until its later organization as a Department in the College of Arts and Sciences.

of good standing and thus was of importance to all colleges of arts and sciences of the state of Indiana. Thus it transpired that the College of Arts and Sciences of Indiana University as in 1902, so in 1937, was still the largest, the dominant school of Indiana University through which a high percentage of the student body passed to enter some professional school.

CHAPTER LII

INDIANA UNIVERSITY PUBLICATIONS

By Ivy L. Chamness

IN THESE latter days, universities have gone rather extensively into the publishing business. Some of them have their presses and even put out spring book lists. It was not always so. In the earliest days the annual Catalogs and occasional sermons or addresses were probably the only pamphlets produced by or for the colleges.

At least these are all that have come down from the earliest days of Indiana University and there likely was little else. What was destroyed by the two fires (1854 and 1883) which burned University buildings, including the libraries, will never be known. There is, to be sure, a copy of the catalog of the Library published in 1842, but there may have been other materials, as well as the books acquired between 1842 and 1854, of which there is now no record.

THE CATALOG

The oldest Catalog[1] in the University files was printed in 1831, during the Indiana College period, and is believed to be the first one published. The Library file of Catalogs lacks those between 1832 and 1834, inclusive. Officials have made every effort to locate copies of the missing numbers.

Throughout the years the Catalog has had various titles: Annual Catalogue of the Officers and Students of Indiana College; Catalogue of the Officers and Students of Indiana University; Catalogue of the Trustees, Officers, and Students; Annual Circular of the University of Indiana comprising the Catalogue; Annual Report of Indiana University Including (or Comprising) the Catalogue; Annual Catalogue of Indiana University for the Year ———; Catalog Number (of *Indiana University Bulletin,* Official Series).

[1] Spelled Catalogue until the adoption of "simplified spelling" early in 1915.

689

Editing and Publishing

The first Catalog was probably written by the President; at least some later and larger numbers are known to have been prepared by the head of the institution. As the University expanded, other arrangements were made. In the Catalog of 1891–92 there appeared, among the standing committees, a catalog committee; in 1900 this gave way to the publications committee. In April, 1906, an editor of University publications, which by this time included the *Bulletin* series, was appointed. The next year's Catalog showed that the editor would be on leave of absence for a period, and an assistant editor was appointed. Both of these persons were faculty members who of course had teaching duties. It was not until 1914 that a full-time editor—the author of this sketch—was appointed. The University was expanding at this time, and the publishing work was very much increased by the establishing of new series. The spread of extension, the increasing number of conferences held at Indiana University, the addition of more professional schools, the encouragement of research —these were some of the reasons for an enlarged publishing program at that time and through the years since that time.

In 1937 the Publications Office was handling the *Indiana University Bulletin,* the *Indiana University News-Letter,* the *Indiana University Studies* (succeeded in 1939 by three new series for the humanities, social sciences, and folklore, and the Science Series, established in 1935), the *Bulletin of the School of Education,* and the *Bulletin of the Extension Division.* In addition, there were every year numerous small folders, the Commencement program, and the annual telephone directory, from the fall of 1936. Of these, the publications appropriation covered the *I.U. Bulletin,* the *News-Letter,* the *Studies,* and the Science Series.

The dean of the Graduate School and his committee pass upon the manuscripts submitted for publication in the series for research papers and usually ask an outside scholar to give his opinion.

The School of Education and the Extension Division originate their bulletins, but the editing and printing are in charge of the Publications Office.

The responsibility for the *Indiana University Bulletin* series, which includes the Catalog and the separate bulletins announcing courses and requirements in the schools, lies with the Publications Office and the various schools and departments which are asked to furnish copy, which must be edited, correlated, cross-referenced, and "whipped into shape" for a printer.

Many other printing jobs of various size and importance are produced for divisions and departments by the Indiana University printing plant without going through the Publications Office, although there is and has been considerable sentiment in the publications committee for more centralization of budgeting for printing and of editorial work. Obviously any further centralization would not include professional journals nor such student publications as the *Folio,* the *Arbutus,* and the like, but might include the numerous promotional pieces put out independently by schools and departments from time to time.

During the Bryan administration major printing jobs were done under state contract. A printing plant was established in 1914, to print *The Indiana Daily Student,* but it also did small University jobs. Gradually, with additional equipment, more pamphlet work was done, and six years after the close of this administration the plant began to print the Catalog and its component bulletins.

The place and method of distribution of publications vary with their purpose. Divisions and schools having their own series do their own mailing; the Library sends out the research publications in exchange for other valuable material received from other libraries and universities; and the registrar is responsible for distributing the Catalog and various bulletins announcing courses.

THE EQUATOR

Did the University attempt some publishing about 1840? The minutes of the Board of Trustees for April 6, 1839, show a motion made to "procure and establish a literary paper, at this place, under the direction of the board," but the motion was laid on the table until the next regular session, the minutes of which, however, make no mention of the proposal. According to D. D. Banta, Andrew Wylie published the *Equator,* presenting to the public through its columns the claims of the University for its patronage and vindicating himself in his church relations. In the 1904 history of the University, the bibliography of former faculty members has for Andrew Wylie, "numerous sermons and translations from Plato. In *Equator*."

One copy of this very rare publication is in the University Archives. It is so rare that a Library of Congress copy of another issue of the periodical "has been withdrawn from circulation" and was not even available for examination by the Chief of the Periodicals Division (letter of October 4, 1943).

The copy in the Library of Congress is the *Bloomington Weekly Equator* for May 8, 1841, Volume I, Number 21. The editor and publisher was A. E. Drapier, editor and publisher of Volume I, Number 1, which is in the University Archives. This latter number dated November, 1840, was advertised (August, 1840) in the I.U. Catalog for that year:

The Equator, a weekly paper, devoted to the interests of science and literature, which was last year commenced and discontinued by Mr. J. Dale,[2] is now revived, in popular folio size, and conducted by the undersigned [A. E. Drapier]. . . . An Extra (50 to 100 pages 8vo) of choice matter and well put up, will be furnished gratuitously to agents and subscribers, some time toward the close of the volume.

The issue owned by the University is called "The Extra Equator: devoted to the Interests of Science and Literature in the West." I am told that in campaign years extra numbers of periodicals were often issued. This particular one contains 84 pages and is "printed and published by the Editor in the Old College Building." In the Preface the editor speaks of "the present series of the Weekly Equator" and of "the bustle of a new printing house." He called the Extra Volume I, Number 1.

The University copy is bound in a volume with sixteen other miscellaneous pamphlets of the period, 1829–43.

An entry in the manuscript history of the newspapers of Indiana prepared by the late Logan Esarey says: "Equator of the Weekly Press and Gazette of Our Family, School and Church Interests (August, 1840 to ——). Founded by Jesse Brandon and A. E. Drapier,

---

[2] A John Dale from Logansport was graduated in 1837. J. Dale was printer of the 1839 Catalog. See also Chap. XLVIII, p. 614.

publishers. J. Dale was editor at some time in its career. It was primarily a school paper. It was a weekly and sold for $1.50 per year.[3] What became of it does not appear." Where Dr. Esarey gathered this information one cannot now ascertain; it contradicts Drapier's advertisement as to the founder.

It is interesting to speculate about the printing of this paper. David D. Banta says that Jesse Brandon brought to Bloomington the press on which he and his brother, the second Indiana state printers, printed the Acts of the General Assembly and other state documents for many years and that J. Brandon printed a paper in Bloomington as early as 1824 and his press was here as late as 1854. He printed the 1835 Catalog. At least one extant pamphlet (1839) and the Catalog for 1840 were printed by the "Equator Press" ("Office" on the pamphlet). The name of A. E. Drapier appears as the printer of the Catalog on the title page. An 1840 address by Andrew Wylie was printed in the Old College Building, as was the *Extra Equator*.

THE INDIANA UNIVERSITY BULLETIN

Just as the Catalog seems to have been the first publication, so the *Indiana University Bulletin,* the official series carrying the Catalog and pamphlets for the schools of the University, seems to be the oldest continuous series of the several series which the University has published. (The *Student* and *Arbutus* are student publications.)

The present series of the *Indiana University Bulletin* seems to have been first issued in May, 1903, and bimonthly publication was announced in the second-class postal entry made under the Act of Congress of July 16, 1894.

Earlier than this, however, at least two efforts were made to establish a series of bulletins.

On June 7, 1887, trustees appropriated money for the publication of a bulletin, which had been "asked for by the faculty." The faculty minutes for February 19, 1887, show that a committee was appointed to report to the board a plan for the publication of an official organ. A paragraph in *The Indiana Student* for October, 1887, quoted from *The Telephone* informs us:

---

[3] In advance, according to the advertisement mentioned above. *The Indiana Student,* January, 1883.

The *I. U. Bulletin* is the title of a new publication which will soon appear from the University press. It is to be conducted on the plan of the Johns Hopkins *Bulletin,* and will be the only publication of the kind in the State. It will appear six times during the year in the form of a 16-page pamphlet. It will be the organ of the Faculty. It will be edited by a committee of three of the Faculty elected by sealed ballots. The Board of Trustees have appropriated $100[4] toward its support, the remaining expenses to be made from subscriptions at 25 cents per year, and guaranteed by the Faculty. The committee having the matter in charge are Professors von Jagemann, chairman, Clark, Woodburn, Spangler, and Dabney.

This publication appeared in November and December, 1887, in February, March, May, and June, 1888. Volume II, Number 1, appeared in November, 1888, Numbers 1 and 2 (a repetition of Number 1 with added material) in February, 1889 (Number 3 is missing in files), and Numbers 4, 5, 6 in July. These are all the issues on file. The doubling up of numbers may be an indication that for some reason or other there was less enthusiasm for this project, and on November 2, 1889, the trustees ordered that there be no appropriation made for the *University Bulletin* "this year." The Catalogs of 1888 and 1889 described the *Bulletin,* but no mention was made in 1890.

The contents of the second volume included "Practical Education," by John M. Coulter; "Education and the State," by David S. Jordan; "Study of Indiana University Records," by A. D. Moffett; a table of matriculation for 1879–88; notes of the faculty; the faculty for 1889–90; schedule of recitations for the winter term of 1889.

The second effort to establish a series was in 1901. A perusal of these bulletins presents a puzzling study for one who deals in publications which have been admitted to second-class postal privileges or for a librarian who must catalog "continuations."

The Catalog for 1901, issued in May, carried "University Bulletins [note the plural] Number 1, May, 1901," at the top of the front cover and at the bottom stated that application had been made for entry at the post office at Bloomington, Ind., as second-class matter. Page 2 of the cover announced the *University Bulletins* as a bimonthly publication. Number 2 of this series came out in July and was devoted to

---

[4] Although the financial report for the fiscal year ending October 31, 1888, shows that $200 was paid out for this publication, the dates for the vouchers fall in two academic years.

the School of Law; Number 5, in January, 1902, announced courses in the spring term, summer session, and Biological Station.

In May, 1902, the Catalog came out, called Series 2, Number 1, of *I.U. Bulletins,* and the second-class entry seems to have been granted. In July, 1902, a number for the School of Law was called Volume I, Number 2, which seems erroneous. In January, 1903, Series 2, Number 5, served the same purpose as Number 5 for January, 1902.

There must have been some technical difficulty with the postal authorities or some confusion somewhere, for the 1903 Catalog, published as before in May, came out as a *"Supplement"* in the "Appendix" to the *Indiana University Bulletin* [note singular], Volume 1, Number 1, which was a six-page bulletin of recent news concerning the University. The second-class entry was "in accordance with the provisions of the Act of Congress of July 16, 1894." Presumably the earlier numbers were not "in accordance." Volume I, Number 2, *et seq.* of the *Bulletin* gave the date of the postal entry as July 23, 1903.

By 1908 new schools and courses must have created a need for doubling the number: two issues in April, May, and June, and one each in January, February, March, July, September, and November. The date of entry changed from July 23, 1903, to May 16, 1908, in Volume VI, Number 5.

In July, 1910, a subseries was announced in the Prefatory Note as the *I.U. Studies,* which studies are numbered independently; that is, Volume VIII, Number 7, of the *I.U. Bulletin* carried *Studies* 1–8; Volume VIII, Number 8, *Studies* 9, 10, etc. From the beginning the *Studies* carried *Indiana University Studies* on the cover in larger type than was used for *I.U. Bulletin,* of which it was a subseries. Numbers 18 and 19, however, were published simply as *Studies* and carried no second-class entry. Perhaps that accounts for some apparent confusion, for the next study after Number 18, back in the *Bulletin* series, was also published as Number 18 (marked 18a by hand later), but the first page carries the volume number (XI, No. 7) of the *Bulletin* under the *I.U. Studies* line. In January, 1916, the *Studies* became an independent series.

To go back to the *Bulletin* per se. Beginning with March 1, 1914, eighteen issues a year were announced in the entry. The date of entry, however, did not change from May 16, 1908, to March 2, 1914, until Volume XII, Number 8 (July 1, 1914) where the Act of Congress under which the *Bulletin* was admitted to second-class privileges changed from July 16, 1894, to August 24, 1912, evidence perhaps of a new or revised law.

In 1915 (Vol. XIII) the same entry was carried throughout the year, but only thirteen numbers were published and Number 1 was dated March 15, as was Number 1 of Volume XII. It might be noted that at first Number 1 of each volume was issued in May; in 1908 it changed to April; in 1914 to March, and in 1916 to January. There was an announcement in January, 1916, of pending application for change of frequency of issue to twelve numbers[5] a year, beginning with January, 1916, which was granted January 28, 1916, and so announced in the next number.

Since January, 1916, the *Bulletin* has been called the Official Series, to distinguish it from the *Bulletin of the Extension Division, Indiana University,* established in 1915. Later—1924—another *Bulletin*—the *Bulletin of the School of Education, Indiana University*—was established.

The varied and interesting contents of Volume I (1903) included: President Bryan's inaugural; a 36-page compilation of laws governing the University; 1903 legislative acts affecting the University, including provision of money for macadamizing Indiana Avenue and making sidewalks and tree plats; addition of the Theodore Roosevelt bird collection and loan of the Austin Thompson collection of Indiana antiquities to the museum; list of the first fifty-eight contributions from the zoological laboratory; policy on chapter house government; financing of the Student Building; a sixty-two-page illustrated report of work done at the Biological Station in 1902.

There were announcements of Commencement exercises, of a change in requirements for English majors, of summer field work in geology, of additions to the faculty, of a journalism prize, and of new courses in Dante, journalism, architecture, and manual training.

---

[5] In January, 1942, the number of issues was changed to thirteen, after the merger of the Normal College of the American Gymnastic Union with the University. Four years later, when the series absorbed the twelve annual issues of the *Indiana University News-Letter* and added five new numbers, application was made for thirty issues of the *Bulletin* each year, distributed as follows: four times each in January, February, March; three times each in April, May, June; twice each in July, August, December; monthly in September, October, November.

The "systematic enlargement of the facilities in medical education" accounts for announcements describing the policy and for biographical sketches of men in charge of anatomy and physiology.

Notes from the School of Law included news of new and retiring professors, announcement of the new ten-weeks' summer term, Law School Commencement affairs, reduction of fees, and equipment of the courtroom.

Number 6 of the *Bulletin,* the Commercial Course Number, contained the staff of instructors, statement of the purpose, scope of the curriculum, requirements for admission and graduation, sequence of studies, description of courses, fees and expenses, and, of no small interest, a four-page extract from a paper written by William A. Rawles and published in the *Indianapolis Journal* of December 14, 1903, which is called "A Consideration of Some Objections."

An illustrated number for the then new Medical School and a Register of Graduates (the fourth) (1820–1904 classes) edited by W. A. Alexander appeared in Volume II.

The 1904 Catalog is inexplicable. The first eight pages carry an extract from a paper published by Law Dean George L. Reinhard in *The Green Bag* explaining the case method of teaching law. Extension of work in physics, mention of graduate degrees and of the combined A.B.-LL.B. account for another two pages preceding the formal beginning pages.

Another Commercial Course number of thirty-one pages, in Volume III, repeated Dr. Rawles' *Indianapolis Journal* article and carried letters from prominent businessmen giving their opinions on the value of a commercial course in a state university. Number 4 of this volume contained the Commencement address (1905) of Hon. John W. Foster, '55, and the reports of the Christian Associations. Tributes to some of the great men of Indiana University in early days were paid by Mr. Foster, himself a man of eminence.

An "extra number" in Volume IV for the School of Medicine used full-page half-tones to show views of various laboratories in which students in medicine did their work (same pictures as in Vol. II, No. 3). After a picture book showing University campus views came out in September, 1906, the School of Law immediately (November) followed suit with a picture book of the same size and shape, size and shape quite different from that of the other numbers in this volume.

In July, 1907, an issue devoted to the School of Medicine was followed by a 52-page picture book published as a supplement which carried pictures of laboratories and other facilities at both Bloomington and Indianapolis.

Facilities for professional training in education at the University, a follow-up of changes made by the legislature of 1907, are described in the issue of January, 1908.

The Graduate School had a separate bulletin for the first time in June, 1908; other numbers that year were used for "supplementary announcement regarding courses for professional training in education," extension and correspondence study, the new journalism course, the Christian Associations, and the Cooperative Bookstore.

In April, 1909 (Vol. VII) a four-page number for the School of Law was immediately followed by a detailed bulletin for the same school. Can the explanation lie in this paragraph in the earlier one, set in italics?

Beginning with the Fall term, 1909, one year of college work in addition will be required for admission to the School of Law. With the beginning of the Fall term, 1910, the requirements will be raised to two years of college work.

"History Teaching in the High School" (Vol. VII, No. 8), a report on a questionnaire sent out by the Department of History and the School of Education, probably represents one of the earliest efforts of the University to be of professional assistance to high school teachers through publications.

The Report of a Committee Appointed to Consider the Textbook Situation in Indiana University (Vol. VII, No. 9) was of considerable interest at that time because of student agitation on that subject.

The fifth Register of Graduates (Vol. IX, No. 5) included the class of 1910. Another interesting number carried the 1911 Commencement address of President Edward J. James, of the University of Illinois; the addresses for the School of Law Commencement and the alumni, and the address made in connection with the presentation of the sword of General Walter Q. Gresham.

A separate bulletin for the Extension Division, as such (in Vol. X), was devoted chiefly to announcements concerning correspondence study.

The interest manifested about 1913 in a new constitution for Indiana is reflected in one number (Vol. XI, No. 6) concerned with debating and public discussion and indeed a manual for civic discussion clubs, an activity of the expanding Extension Division. This particular bulletin was written by Ross F. Lockridge, in charge of extension debating and public discussion. Civic discussion clubs were invited, through this bulletin, to consider the question of a new constitution for Indiana, a question which the legislature of 1913 was putting before the voters to decide in 1914. A later bulletin (No. 10) devotes sixty-four pages to an abstract of historical and political facts and conditions concerning the making of Indiana constitutions, by Ernest V. Shockley, and sixteen student speeches made in an interclass discussion contest. The School of Education bulletin in this volume (March 1, 1914) carries announcements for the new departments of home economics and industrial education, authorized in June, 1913.

Proceedings of conferences held at the University appear in Volume XII, a reminder of the fact that the 1913 legislature greatly increased the appropriations of the University, and expanding services and activities resulted. Two conferences on taxation, one on educational measurements, and one on constitutional convention are reported. Two bulletins for the Extension Division carry an outline for the study of current problems and announcements concerning public discussion activities.

The ambitious program of eighteen bulletins a year announced in March, 1914, was discontinued with Volume XIII, Number 13, December, 1915. Proceedings on conferences on vocational education, educational measurements, and newspaper work, a manual of pageantry, and two publications on history teaching ("History Teaching in the Secondary Schools" and "History Consultation Service") are included in the thirteen issues of this volume.

After the number of issues each year dropped back to twelve in 1916, almost all of the numbers (up to 1946) were devoted to official announcements of courses and curricula. The omission of proceedings of conferences and similar publications may be explained by the launching of the *Bulletin of the Extension Division* in September, 1915, and the *Bulletin of the School of Education* in 1924. Indeed, some of the proceedings already included in previous issues of the *I.U. Bulletin* had been published under the auspices of the Extension Division.

From 1916 on, among the few publications outside of official announcements carried in this series are an illustrated General Circular and the Sixth Register of Graduates in 1917; Military Life at Indiana University (Ralph L. Rusk) in 1918; A Syllabus in Industrial Relations, 1920; the Centennial Memorial Volume, in 1921; Educational Publicity (John W. Cravens), 1922.

The News-Letter

The *Indiana University News-Letter* was established as a twelve-times-a-year publication in January, 1913, as the *Alumni News-Letter,* and was edited for almost two years by Professor Samuel B. Harding. The first five numbers, all appearing in January and February, appealed to the alumni and former students of the University to use their influence in procuring increased appropriations for the University. The first number is a letter from forty-two faculty members—with facsimiles of their signatures—plus an appended paragraph from President Bryan, setting forth the needs and possible services of the University. Among the former may be noted some needs which have been filled, the oft-repeated one only recently filled—an auditorium. After the legislative session, a *News-Letter* informed alumni about the increased appropriations and discussed questions of policy.

One number of the first volume is devoted to social welfare work of the Christian Associations. The remaining numbers take up the alumni movement, then assuming form, with the adoption of a constitution in June, 1913, and the launching of the *Indiana University Alumni Quarterly* in January, 1914.

The name was changed in Volume II, Number 2, to *Indiana University News-Letter,* and so it remained throughout the Bryan administration. The contents of the *News-Letter* were diversified and often very interesting and valuable.

RESEARCH PUBLICATIONS

The *Indiana University Studies,* which, as noted above, began in 1910 as a subseries of the *Bulletin* (Vol. VIII), became an independent series in January, 1916 (started as Vol. III since twenty-seven studies had been published already and had been bound in two volumes), appearing six times a year until January, 1919, when the number was reduced to four. Papers from many departments of the University have been published as *Studies.* One hundred twenty-four numbers, some quite sizable, were published in this series, the last one appearing in April, 1942.

In order to expedite the publication of the research work of faculty members, a new series was established in 1935 called *Indiana University Publications, Science Series.* (To publish research in other areas, three other series were begun in 1939: Humanities, Social Science, and Folklore.) No second-class mailing privileges were sought for these series.

Mention should be made of scientific research papers published in various journals elsewhere but credited to Indiana University laboratories.

In 1892 Professor Carl H. Eigenmann began the practice of numbering papers from his laboratory, published elsewhere, as "Contribution No. —— from the Zoological Laboratory of Indiana University," and the practice has continued to the present. By the end of the Bryan administration 265 papers had been published.

Likewise the papers growing out of research conducted by the Waterman Institute for Scientific Research, published in outside journals, have been credited as "Contribution No. —— from the Waterman Institute." The first paper so published was by Professor Arthur L. Foley in 1919, and the last paper appearing during the Bryan administration was No. 76.

PUBLICATION OF ENDOWED LECTURES

The first volume of lectures given under the Powell endowment, addresses by William E. Hocking, came from the Yale Press in 1937. The next year saw publication by Harper of the first Patten lectures, given in 1936–37 by Alfred Manes.

PUBLICATIONS BY PRESIDENT BRYAN

William L. Bryan, with Mrs. Bryan, published *Plato the Teacher* in 1897. During his administration as president he published two books. The first, *The Spirit of Indiana,* 1917, contained his Commencement addresses from 1902 to 1917, inclusive, and five other addresses "in the hope that they express in one or another way some part of the spirit of Indiana." The 1934 book, *The President's Column,* reprinted 204 "columns" (one by Mrs. Bryan) written for *The Indiana Daily Student* and the *Indiana Alumnus* "as a means of saying whatever I wished to say to members of the University in residence or elsewhere." In 1938 after his retirement he published *Farewells,* a 167-page book containing his Commencement addresses from 1919 on and a half-hundred or more of his "Columns" from *The Indiana Daily Student.* In 1941 a scientific study made by Dr. Bryan and the late Ernest H. Lindley in 1899–1900 was published as No. 11 of *Indiana University Publications, Science Series.* His *The Measured and the Not-Yet-Measured* was published in 1947 as No. 17 of the *Humanities Series.*

Several of President Bryan's addresses have been published in pamphlet or booklet form. Those found include some which are not printed in any book of his essays: "Capital in Nerves," a chapel sermon; Foundation Day messages to alumni—"Patriotism for Indiana" (1916), "The Era of Gifts" (1917), "A War Message" (1918); "The Life of the Professor," read as the president's address before the National Association of State Universities, in 1912; "Out of the Jungle—Straight On," a temperance lecture. Some of these and many Commencement addresses were also published in the *Indiana University Alumni Quarterly. Paradise* is a beautiful booklet printed in 1927, carrying the Commencement address of 1920.

THE BULLETIN OF THE SCHOOL OF EDUCATION

In 1924 the School of Education established the *Bulletin of the School of Education,* issued six times a year to publish the proceedings of conferences held by the School and the results of investigations of various kinds carried on by the Bureau of Cooperative Research. The frequency of issue was reduced to four late in 1932 after the legislative cut ordered by the special session of that year, but was changed again to six three years after the close of the Bryan administration.

This series has carried proceedings of conferences of high school principals, on educational measurements, and on elementary supervision; bibliographies on educational measurements, school budgets, school surveys and references on school surveys, college and university buildings, literature on the teaching of English, literature on education in countries other than the United States of America, school buildings, grounds, and equipment; studies of the results of tests, of school surveys, analyses of old public school textbooks; and other topics of interest to educators. Through 1946 the complete list of titles was carried in each number.

A "Bibliography of Educational Measurements," compiled by the Bureau of Cooperative Research, was published by the University in 1923, before the School of Education had established its series. Another publication, in 1923, for the School of Education was the "Proceedings of the High School Principals' Conference," held at Indiana University in December, 1922.

PUBLICATIONS OF THE EXTENSION DIVISION

In September, 1915, the expanding Extension Division established its own publication, called the *Bulletin of the Extension Division.* It was issued twelve times a year until the legislative cut of 1932 necessitated retrenchment, and the number was reduced to eight. With the addition of more Extension Centers, and the decrease in frequency of publication, most of the issues are now used for announcements of courses offered over the state, but the earlier numbers were very frequently devoted to papers on subjects of current and perhaps permanent interest in diversified fields.

Under the auspices of the Extension Division there was published, in 1914, *Readings in Indiana History,* an illustrated volume of 463 pages, containing "the best original or first-hand materials for some study of Indiana history." The book was compiled and edited by a committee of the history section of the Indiana State Teachers Association.

A series of pamphlets, at least twenty-nine, called *Circular of In-*

formation was issued by the Extension Division beginning in 1915, and seems to have been discontinued about 1922. These covered a variety of topics, indicative of the different lines of work carried on by the Extension Division: loan exhibits of pictures with notes, club-study, lists of lectures, community institutes, public discussion and package libraries, debating, visual instruction, play and recreation, correspondence study, children's health conferences, business courses, training teachers for service in the vocational schools of the state (1920).

Other pamphlets (1916 and 1917) announce community institutes and children's health conferences in various towns of the state.

PUBLICATIONS OF THE SCHOOL OF BUSINESS

The Indiana Business Review, a monthly, summarizes trade and industry in Indiana and is sent free to business concerns in the state. Launched in March, 1926, it was published in cooperation with the Fletcher American National Bank, Indianapolis, until August, 1932, when it first appeared, as it now does, under the auspices of the University only. From a four-page publication it has trebled its size.

Indiana Business Studies consist of research papers, published from time to time. Some studies have been published at irregular intervals since 1924, but they did not bear the title of any series until about 1939. These earlier studies, however, have now been assigned numbers and are listed in later numbers in chronological order.

The Investment Bulletin, a monthly, was launched in the last year of the Bryan administration (January, 1937).

The *Hoosier Journal of Business,* launched in December, 1925, was designed to further the interest of graduates in the progress of the School, to establish a connecting link between businessmen and students in training at the University, and to spread the knowledge and experiences of leaders in various fields of business. The magazine appeared in December, 1925, January, March, and May of 1926, and was then discontinued.

THE INDIANA MAGAZINE OF HISTORY

The *Indiana Magazine of History,* owned by Indiana University, is published quarterly by the Department of History in cooperation

with the Indiana Historical Society. It was founded in 1905 by
George A. Cottman, and published by him for three years (1905–7).
Beginning with 1908 it was sponsored by the Indiana Historical Society and was turned over to Indiana University between the March
and June issues of 1913. It was called the *Indiana Quarterly Magazine of History* until June, 1913. Professor Logan Esarey was the first
editor under University auspices. He was succeeded by Professor
William O. Lynch.

THE INDIANA LAW JOURNAL

See Chapter XXXIX for an account of this journal.

THE QUARTERLY BULLETIN

Two copies of the *Quarterly Bulletin* of the State College of Physicians and Surgeons, then affiliated with Indiana University, are on
file. These are Numbers 1 and 2 of Volume I and were published in
August and November, 1906.

MISCELLANEOUS PUBLICATIONS

In 1923–24 the Indianapolis Chamber of Commerce and Indiana
University cooperated in preparing the *Indianapolis Vocational Information Series,* seven pamphlets dealing with the opportunities
(for women) in the telephone service, department store service, the
profession of nursing, banking, teaching, the printing trades, and
journalism. Professor Harry D. Kitson served as adviser.

The first Register of Graduates—this one called Names, Addresses,
and Occupations of the Graduates of I.U.—was published in 1897.
The next one appeared in 1899. The third appeared in 1901 as Number 3 of *University Bulletins.* Later Registers have already been mentioned.

Indiana University *News Notes* was another series which ran for
some years. Volume IV, Number 8 (January 24, 1918) says, to editors, that the University news is being sent to them in convenient
form for immediate use and urges them to make known, through
their papers, the facts about Indiana University.

The Regimental Review, official organ of the R.O.T.C. unit of
Indiana University, first appeared in March, 1929. It was published

irregularly during the school year and seems to have been discontinued in May, 1934.

"I" Men's Notes is a series established by the "I" Men in June, 1916. No *Notes* were published in 1918, and the last issue in the Library file bears date of October 15, 1919.

The Commencement programs are interesting and valuable. The University has all except those for the years before 1840 and those for 1852 and 1863.

The earlier volumes dealing with University history are described pictorially in the beginning pages of this work.

Pamphlets, large and small, some very valuable, which have been preserved are too numerous to list, except in a library catalog. And yet many of these seemingly unimportant publications may prove to contain a missing bit of information which some future University historian may be seeking.

A four-page leaflet carries the address of Isaac Jenkinson, then a trustee, made at the dedication of Kirkwood Hall, January 25, 1895.

An undated leaflet contains three pages of opinions of eminent educators concerning the standing of Indiana University among other universities. Those quoted are William R. Harper, Benjamin I. Wheeler, John M. Coulter, Edward A. Ross, J. McK. Cattell, Jacob G. Schurman, Stephen A. Forbes, J. M. Stillman, T. C. Mendenhall, Stanley Hall, W. G. Hale, Charles D. Marx.

The "Reminiscences" of George G. Wright, 1839, are almost a history in brief of Indiana University's first seventy years. It is his address delivered before the Alumni Association on June 11, 1889. Mr. Wright was a brother of Joseph A. Wright, one of the first students in the Indiana Seminary, who later became governor.

An address on "Old Age," delivered in the Chapel on March 30, 1879, by Professor Elisha Ballantine, was published at the request of a number of students.

The inaugural address of President Joseph Swain, delivered at Commencement, June 14, 1893, and another address by him on "Higher Education and the State," delivered before the Fortnightly Club of Bloomington, date not given, have also been preserved.

Two small books of historical interest are *The Pageant of Bloomington and Indiana University, 1916,* and *The Centennial Pageant of Indiana University, 1920,* both written by William Chauncy Langdon. The second edition of the earlier book includes the dramatis personae of the performance and the committees. A four-page folder announces an illustrated address on pageantry, given by Mr. Langdon in Caleb Mills Hall, Indianapolis, February 18, 1916, and in the Student Building four days later. The program contains notes concerning the music from the pageants of Cape Cod, Mass.; Meriden, N.H.; Austin, Tex.; St. Johnsburg, Vt.; and the Foundation Day Ceremonial of Indiana University in 1916, played by Indiana University orchestra, led by Charles D. Campbell. Mr. Campbell composed the Foundation Day Ceremonial music. Mr. Langdon wrote the Ceremonial which was printed by the University in 1916 and reprinted in 1920.

An attractive booklet published by the University in 1916, *In Honor of Shakespeare,* was a dramatic tribute by Mr. Langdon for the Shakespeare Tercentenary celebration of the University, held on April 26, 1916.

The small program of the 1929 ceremonies commemorating the one-hundredth Commencement is of historical interest, carrying the dramatis personae of the bit of pageantry. Descendants and relatives of the members of the first graduating class—1830—took part in the ceremonies.

A grim reminder of the World War is the three-page Indiana University Memorial Masque, produced on the campus June 6, 1922, also written by Mr. Langdon. Another grim reminder is a six-page pamphlet devoted to books of the war—poetry, novels, short stories, speeches, essays, and personal experiences.

The program of a memorial service on April 13, 1919, for Charles D. Campbell is of unusual interest in that the University orchestra and chorus rendered two of his musical compositions.

An eight-page pamphlet announces the opening of the first dormitory for men in 1924, and a similar one does the same for the Memorial Hall a year later.

We read a brief history of the Y.W.C.A. in a four-page folder put out in 1916, the fiftieth anniversary of the founding of the organization.

An elaborate illustrated booklet was published preceding the campaign for the Memorial Fund.

A booklet dated October 1, 1917, recording the organization (October 24, 1913) of the "I" Men's Association, carries their constitution and a list of members with their addresses. It was compiled by George M. Cook.

An attractive booklet of forty pages was issued in 1925, containing the addresses made at the dedication of the James Whitcomb Riley Hospital for Children (October 7, 1924) and an eight-page historical sketch of the movement to honor the poet which culminated in the building of the hospital.

A thirty-two-page pamphlet listed the various departmental exhibits held as the first all-University exposition at Commencement time, 1922.

The Department of Journalism issued, in 1921, a sixteen-page pamphlet called *Instruction in Journalism at Indiana University*. Along with information concerning this work, one finds a list of graduates and former students engaged in newspaper or magazine work, Walter Williams' "The Journalist's Creed," and Warren G. Harding's twelve points for reporters.

A small booklet of seventy-four pages lists the rules and regulations of the faculty as they were on January 23, 1917.

Small pamphlets of the School of Education give rules governing theses for the A.M. degree; rules and suggestions relative to graduate degrees in that School and the preparation of theses (1924); and requirements for the preparation of theses and research reports (1931).

The work of the School of Law was described in pamphlets published in 1893, 1896, 1899, 1900, and 1903; announcements for spring and summer in 1895, 1898, 1899, 1900 (Biological Station work included from here on), and 1901; special announcements for the Biological Station in pocket-size pamphlets from 1920 through 1937.

A copyrighted publication (1916) by George F. Reynolds, then associate professor of English, is an outline for the study of European drama. There is no imprint on this pamphlet showing whether or not this was published by the University, but another Reynolds pamphlet listing suggestive questions for use in the study of a modern play was published by the University Department of English.

Other study helps include two pamphlets by Professor Frank W.

Tilden: *Greek Literature in English* and *Greek Life,* and one by Professor William T. Morgan, *Syllabus on Modern European History.*

A twelve-page pamphlet published in 1908 is devoted to a general statement of facilities and resources. There are paragraphs stating the requirements for admission and graduation and for the academic training of faculty members, describing the equipment and financial resources, and outlining in brief the history of the University.

Miscellaneous pamphlets found include "Leased Lives," the baccalaureate address in 1918 by Lloyd C. Douglas; "R.O.T.C. Rules and Regulations."

Two picture books of the University, other than those published as numbers of regular series, show the University as it was in 1896 and in 1900.

In June, 1914, a small pamphlet was issued to announce the curriculum of the Training School for Nurses in the then newly-opened Robert W. Long Hospital.

The Commencement address of David Starr Jordan, delivered on June 7, 1888, "The Ethics of the Dust," was published, presumably by the University, the printing being done by a Richmond firm.

Students of political science will be interested in a pamphlet published in 1914, "New Constitution for Indiana," which reports the speeches made by the thirteen Indiana district contestants in the first annual High School Discussion Contest.

There has been preserved a pamphlet, "Indiana University and the State: A Review of the Legal History of the University," by M. E. Forkner, of New Castle. There is nothing to indicate where this address was delivered—if it was a delivered address—and nothing to indicate the place of publication, or who published it.

Men of Indiana was a sizable illustrated publication (July, 1930) financed from proceeds of *The Athletic Review,* the official football program and athletic magazine which has been published for home football games since the early twenties.

In the Library collection may be found the following pamphlets of historical interest: an address made before the Philomathean Society, August 5, 1856, by Daniel Read, then of the University of

Wisconsin; a Fourth of July address, 1840, by Andrew Wylie, "printed in the Old College Building"; an address on the "Study of the Law," delivered in the Chapel of Indiana University, December 5, 1842, by David McDonald, assuming at that time the professorship of law; sermon on "The Union of Christians for the Conversion of the World," April 20, 1834, by President Andrew Wylie; other sermons by him, one dated 1830; the Funeral Discourse delivered in the University Chapel, November 13, 1851, "over the remains of the late Rev. Andrew Wylie," by Rev. William M. Daily, published by request; "Justice," a discourse to the students of the Law Department by Andrew Wylie, February 26, 1850, on conferring upon the graduating class their diplomas and published at their request; a memorial booklet containing the addresses delivered at the Gymnasium on May 11, 1908, in memory of Nathaniel Usher Hill; one pamphlet containing the argument of George H. Dunn before the Supreme Court of Indiana, November term, 1849, in the case of the State of Indiana versus the Vincennes University, in chancery; also a bill in chancery by Senator O. H. Smith.

FINANCIAL REPORTS

In the beginning the reports of the Board of Trustees were submitted to the Governor and by him to the legislature and printed in the *House Journal*. The law of June 17, 1852, under which the University operates, requires the Governor to

order the printing annually of five thousand copies of the annual report of the Board of Trustees, twenty-five hundred of which shall be for the use of the members of the General Assembly, and twenty-five hundred for the faculty. Such report shall contain what is now included in the annual catalogue, with such other matters as may be deemed useful to the cause of education, connected with the University.

An attorney general's opinion of 1886 says that this report is embraced in the *Documentary Journal* printed and distributed by the state. None of this expense is to be borne by the University. All copies of reports printed for distribution and not embraced in the *Documentary Journal* must be paid for out of funds appropriated for the State University.

Another opinion of 1900–2 says that

the State Printing Board may eliminate from any report such matters as they may deem unnecessary to be published.

A volume of these reports, beginning in 1875, shows variation in content. For example, the 1875 report consists of four pages, and sets out a financial statement, a table on the number of students, and a résumé of improvements and accomplishment—all over the signature of the secretary to the Board of Trustees, and dated January 11, 1876. The title page of the next report says "including the Catalogue for the Academical Year 1876–77." It is a Catalog and nothing more, except an eight-page letter from the President to the board. For many years these reports varied greatly in contents, but in the early part of this century they became standardized.

These biennial financial reports continued until 1931, since which time reports have been published annually.

ALUMNI PUBLICATIONS

The first *Alumnus,* a quarterly magazine, was published by the Alumni Association for at least one year, the issues appearing in August and November, 1898, and in February and May, 1899. The subscription price was fifty cents a year.

In the fall of 1921 the weekly *Indiana Alumnus* was founded, replacing the *Weekly Student,* which had been published for one year. In the spring of 1927 the *Alumnus* was discontinued, and the "Alumnus Issue" of *The Indiana Daily Student* was resumed. In 1932 this was discontinued, and *The Indiana Alumnus* was resumed. It aimed to keep the alumni in close touch with campus activities of the University and was sent only to those who subscribed.

The Alumni Association published the *Indiana University Alumni Quarterly* from January, 1914, to October, 1938—one hundred issues. Its first editor—and indeed he might be called the father of the magazine—was Professor Samuel B. Harding, who served until the summer of 1916. The printing of this publication was financed by the Alumni Association, but the editorial work was done by persons in the employ of the University.[6]

---

[6] In the fall of 1938, the *Quarterly* and *The Indiana Alumnus* were discontinued to give place to the *Indiana Alumni Magazine,* published nine times a year at present, with an editor paid by the Association.

STUDENT PUBLICATIONS

The official publications are grist in the mill of the historian, but provide no chuckles. For a picture of the lighter side of University life, we go to available student publications.

Probably the first student publication was *The Athenian,* devoted to the interests of the University and founded in 1845 by the Athenian Society, "to be published monthly during term" and to use only articles of a "high literary character: nothing abusive or personal." It lived at least one year. Volume I, Number 1, appeared in December, 1845, and the eleven succeeding numbers have been preserved.[7]

The Indiana Daily Student, founded in 1867 (not as a daily), is the subject of another chapter in this book.

The *Arbutus* of 1894, the first one, is very, very different from that of 1937. Historical sketches, original verse, class histories, "write-ups" of all the "activities" and student organizations, and many jokes and other humor features throw the emphasis of the book on student work, not on mechanical reproduction of pictures by a commercial concern. The 1894 book carries pictures, too, of Greek and "barb" organizations, of faculty members, of athletic teams, of all seniors, of campus buildings, but accompanying these is plenty of interesting reading matter. The binding is crimson and cream, with the arbutus leaf and flower reproduced on the cover on a background of gold. The book was dedicated to the people of Indiana, "who have so generously provided us with the many privileges and opportunities that we enjoy at Indiana University."

An *Arbutus* has been published every year since it was established in 1894. By the late teens and early twenties the book had become very large, but had lost all literary content. Where earlier editors searched their Shakespeare and other classics for quotations suitable for describing their fellow-students, present-day boards burn their midnight oil in fitting names to pictures by the hundreds.

The editorial foreword to the 1894 book distinctly implies that there had been earlier annuals, and such a one has been found. *The Indiana Student* for June, 1888, is a rather large, illustrated number, with a separate cover. It is called a "modest beginning" of a college

[7] See also Chap. XLVIII, p. 615.

annual, and we are told that such a thing as a college annual had never before gone out from the University. The authors of the foreword, D. Driscoll and Frank B. Foster, "hope that those who follow us may improve upon it from year to year until Indiana University may each year send out an annual second to none." They imply that their aims were to advertise the University, to swell her enrollment, and to awaken interest and enthusiasm in the alumni. Cartoons, lists of organization members, personal items, and so on were used.

The *Arbutus* is not the only class publication. The class of 1891, three years before the first *Arbutus* was published, put out a book containing their pictures, class autographs, pictures of faculty and of buildings (new and old).

Junior annuals were published from time to time. In April, 1900, the class of 1901 published the *Megaphone,* a Junior annual, "to our beloved selves who, since childhood, have been a constant source of pleasure and self-satisfaction, this volume is admiringly dedicated." Stella Marshall was editor-in-chief, and Homer McKee was illustrator. Most of the material was written in a facetious vein. An earlier number was that published in 1899 by the class of 1900.

The Junior published in 1905 by the class of 1906 contained pictures, class history, class names, articles on athletics and "Frat Man and 'Barb,'" and jokes. The class of 1907 put out a book, *The Junior,* on the occasion of the Junior Prom in 1906—a souvenir. There were pictures, the class history, articles on the "scrap" and on athletics.

"The Chile Con Carne Number" of the Juniors, published in 1911 by the class of 1912, was also a souvenir of the Junior Prom. It carried cartoons by Don Herold, historical sketch of the class, scrap records, articles on athletics, and a feature called "The University Skeleton."

The late lamented Keith Preston, who once wrote a little stanza about "the graves of little magazines that died to make verse free," might have written companion lines on the student magazines that have been born and, after a few struggling gasps, have died and passed into oblivion. But not oblivion for the historian, for the Library has several copies of such magazines, carefully guarded.

One copy of *The Bumble Bee* of March, 1899, says in "A Foreword": "Students need a paper in which they can say a word for themselves...we all need to be laughed at occasionally and have our faults pricked...to buzz about and maybe light at intervals...point out the shortcomings of the learned gentlemen who sit in the seats of the mighty." It contains poetry, stories, and short articles. Whether it used all its ammunition in the first issue, met a destructive reception, or whether the Library salvaged only one copy we know not, but there is only one number in the Library collection, an interesting situation in view of the fact that it was announced to be "published whenever the publishers happen to feel like it."

The I.U. Illustrator, launched in November, 1897, was intended to be "a general illustrator of the happenings, social, political, and industrial, in and about the University of Indiana" and as such "to add a progressive feature to University life." Jack H. Smith was evidently its editor, manager, illustrator, and staff, all in one. It was a very interesting magazine, carrying pictures, jokes, cartoons, as well as verse and editorials. Three issues of this are in the Library files.

One issue of *As She Is* (October, 1901), "being a report of the Committee of Students on Affairs," is included in the Library collection. "*As She Is* will remain as she is unless she gets better....If a discerning student body sees fit to nip us in the bud, as it were, 'we will fold our tent like the Arab and silently stifle our warble.'" It contains yells, an article on "The Athletic Regeneration," sketches, and comments on I.U. situations.

A dignified publication was *The Hoosier "Lit."* The only issue on file is the first, January, 1901. Walter H. Crim was editor-in-chief. The articles, stories, poems were furnished chiefly by the editors.

Hot Shots, June, 1901, was published by the class of 1903. As in many other cases, there is now no way of ascertaining whether there was more than one issue.

The Bored Walk, a campus humor magazine, was launched in January, 1931, with Bernard O. Nordberg as editor-in-chief the first two years. It continued to the fall of 1942.

Volume I, Number 2 of *The Crimson* (May 5, 1909), a literary magazine, carries many interesting articles and stories in its thirty-six pages. How long this magazine lasted is not known. The Library has a copy dated April 6, 1909 (Vol. I, No. 1), carrying President Bryan's picture, stories, alumni notes, poetry, nonsense, Dr. Bryan's

"Capital in Nerves," and other material including a plan proposed for putting the *Arbutus* on a business-like, representative basis. There were a faculty critic and advisory board for this issue.

The Hoosier, of later date, lasted at least two years, but the issues were not consecutive. It first appeared in November, 1916, published by the Writers' Club, with this staff: J. Harold Schuler was to be its first editor, and worked upon the first issue until the last hours of his life (he died on October 4). Mary H. Mack, vice-president, became editor; and Kenyon Stevenson, business manager. The magazine appeared regularly each month through May, 1917, and then was doubtless interrupted by the World War. In October, 1919, it was resumed with Andrew H. Hepburn as editor-in-chief. Eight issues appeared, through May, 1920. Its aim was "to furnish a medium of expression for the literary life of the University, and its columns are open to undergraduates, alumni, and members of the faculty."

The Crimson Bull, a humor magazine, was launched by Sigma Delta Chi in October, 1920. It seems to have lasted only a year, more or less.

The Vagabond appeared in the fall of 1923, as a bimonthly student publication, carrying poems, essays, short stories, sketches, and humor. Its twofold object was to offer "a medium of expression for the literary life of the campus; and it hopes to hasten a rebirth of interest in science, art, and life at Indiana." Its first editor-in-chief was Mauck Brammer, and Philip B. Rice, later Rhodes scholar, was from the beginning one of the most active associate editors and later became editor-in-chief. The magazine did not always achieve its aim of appearing five times a year, and in the fall of 1926 it was published occasionally. The last issue in the Library file bears date of March, 1931.

The *Crimson Quill* appeared intermittently for a few times about 1927. Some of the contributions had appeared as papers in Professor Henry T. Stephenson's classes in narrative writing.

A publication called *High School Journalist,* issued bimonthly by the local chapter of Sigma Delta Chi in cooperation with the Department of Journalism and the Publicity Office, appeared for four or five years in the late 1920's and early 30's. It was sent to high school papers.

Booklets comparable to what has been known for a score or more of years as the *Red Book* were published as far back as 1893–94. That particular one was called the *Students' Hand Book* and was published, like its successors, by the Y.M.C.A. (the Y.W.C.A. also participated in this one, as in some others). Some were called *The Student Directory*; others *The Directory, Indiana University Student Directory, Directory of Indiana University,* the *Indiana Red Book,* and later *The Red Book.* The earliest publications did *not* carry the list of students enrolled, but did carry the information which the Christian Associations wished to get into the hands of the students.

Three University song books have been published in the last few years—in 1921, 1926, and 1930, by the Association of Women Students and its predecessor, Women's Self-Government Association.

A Freshman handbook to aid new women students is published each year. It has been supervised at different times by the A.W.S., Y.W.C.A., and W.A.A., and dates back at least to 1912, when the Woman's League put out such a book. It has been variously named: *Women Students' Handbook, Indiana Freshman Handbook, W.S.-G.A.*

The *Freshman Guide* for men students was published each summer by the Y.M.C.A. from about 1925 to 1941.

The *Y News* was a little paper issued in the interests of the Y.M.-C.A. in 1930. According to the best information available, it survived only a year, or perhaps less.

The Library collection contains a number of miscellaneous student publications: a catalog of the Athenian Society of Indiana University (founded in 1830), published in 1860; Athenian Society certificate of honorable dismissal from the Society, presented to John R. Cravens, 1840 (Latin original, with typewritten translation); Athenian Society letter dated September 29, 1842, to J. R. Cravens, thanking him for address delivered to graduates of the Society in 1842; Garrick Club constitution and bylaws, compiled by Sherwood Blue in February, 1928; four-page leaflet on El Club Español, 1916; a recipe book compiled and edited by the Home Economics Club; constitution and bylaws of the Women's Athletic Association, adopted in February, 1929; the books of the *Jordan River Revue* for 1929, 1930, and 1931, with orchestrations, clippings, music scores, etc.; a booklet published by Oscar Ewing in honor of the silver anniversary, 1935, of the 1910 class; the Sigma Xi (Indiana chapter) lists of officers and members and programs for 1906, 1907, 1908, and 1909.

What the not-too-distant future will bring—who knows? Will science provide new media which will decrease the importance of the printed page?

CHAPTER LIII

THE ESTABLISHMENT AND MAINTENANCE
OF INDIANA UNIVERSITY

THE STORY of the establishment and maintenance of Indiana University begins with the constitutional convention of 1816 and the offer by the Federal Government of two townships of land for establishment of a State University. This offer was accepted by the convention, and Indiana, just emerging into statehood, was pledged to the founding of such an educational institution and to making the two townships of land productive for its benefit.

Bearing in mind that one township had been reserved for this purpose in Gibson County[1] under an act of Congress, March 26, 1804, the convention promptly appointed a committee, June 19, 1816, which was instructed to select a second township to be recommended for reservation. At that time, 1816, Indiana was approximately one-third its present size. But all Hoosiers were confident that the state would expand northward by successive purchases of land from the Indians. With this idea in mind, the committee made its way northward to within six miles of the Ten O'Clock Line, which was a major boundary between the state of Indiana and the Indian lands to the north. Here, near the little village of Bloomington, in the County of Monroe, the committee selected a township, Perry, and made its report to the convention. This report was submitted, properly endorsed, to President Madison, who, on July 10, 1816, under authority of a Congressional Act of April 19, 1816, reserved this township, Perry, in addition to the township previously reserved.[2]

---

[1] Part of this township in Gibson County had been sold and the proceeds used to erect a building for Vincennes University, established by the Territorial General Assembly in 1806.

[2] Section 6 of this act contains a proposition for free acceptance or rejection by the constitutional convention. The fourth article of this proposition reads as follows:

"That one entire township, which shall be designated by the President of the United States, in addition to the one heretofore reserved for that purpose, shall be reserved for the use of a seminary of learning, and vested in the legislature of said state, to be appropriated solely to the use of such seminary by the said legislature."

718

Thus Congress, President Madison, and the constitutional convention all understood that Indiana was receiving two townships, one in Gibson County and one in Monroe County, to be made productive by the new state, for the benefit of a State University, and for thirty-five years successive sessions of the Indiana General Assembly legislated on that theory and understanding.

The subject matter of the establishment and maintenance of Indiana University falls in three markedly different periods: (1) The period from January 20, 1820, when the bill was approved founding Indiana University, to May, 1824, when instruction began. (2) The period 1824 to 1867, when the first appropriation was made by an Indiana General Assembly for maintenance of the University. During this period the institution was maintained solely by rental of lands or interest on the proceeds of sale of land, supplemented by small student fees. (3) The period 1867 to date, 1945, during which period various plans were tried for supplementing the income derived from interest on proceeds of sale of Seminary lands.

ESTABLISHMENT OF INDIANA UNIVERSITY, 1820–24

The act approved January 20, 1820, under which Indiana Seminary was established authorized the successive steps necessary to the organization of the Board of Trustees and the erection of necessary buildings.

1. The act named six men who were to qualify, organize, and function as a Board of Trustees. This board, properly qualified and organized, was directed:

2. "To repair to the reserved township of land in said county [Monroe], and proceed to select an eligible and convenient site for a state seminary."

3. To appoint an agent, who, having given bond, should lay off and sell, under sanction of the Board of Trustees, not to exceed one section of the reserved township most contiguous to the seminary site, taking payment and security therefor.

4. With the proceeds of this sale the trustees were directed, as soon as they deemed it expedient, to erect "a suitable building for a state seminary, as also a suitable and commodious house for a Professor."

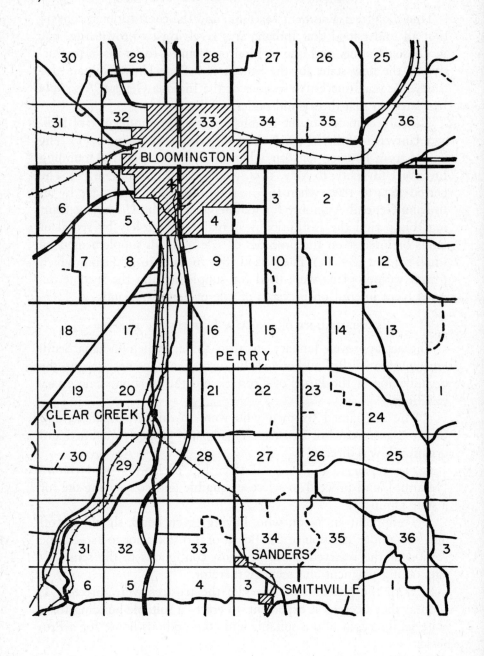

James Borland was the agent appointed under this act of January 20, 1820, and in the *Corydon Gazette*[3] of September 17, 1820 (p. 3), is a notice of sale of lots on the second Monday in November, 1820, of not less than one-half an acre nor more than twenty acres each.

The position of the Seminary township (Perry Township) and the Seminary site are shown on the accompanying map of Perry Township.

The city of Bloomington lies partly in Perry Township and partly in the township north of Perry (Bloomington Township). The heavy line passing east and west through Bloomington is the northern boundary of Perry Township. It is about seventy-five feet south of Third Street where that street intersects Walnut and College. Seventy-five feet is a distance too small to be shown on a map of this scale, so this heavy line is approximately Third Street. The heavy broken line passing southward from Bloomington is Highway 37, known in Bloomington as Walnut Street.

The numbering of the sections of the township, 1 to 36, gives the key to the scale of the map, since each section is, of course, one mile square. "The eligible and convenient" ten-acre site selected by the trustees is in section 4 indicated in the shaded Bloomington area of the map by †. It is a quarter of a mile south of Third Street and just west of Walnut. At a later date sections 3, 9, and 5 were reserved. These sections lay east, south, and west of section 4.

With the organization of Indiana Seminary as Indiana College (1828), James Borland was chosen by the new Board of Trustees as the first treasurer of the College. As treasurer he made a brief and informative report to the Board of Visitors of his service as agent which gives the sales price of the first reserved section, Number 4.

The agent for the late Trustees of the State Seminary of Indiana, respectfully reports:
That the seminary section (sold in the year 1820,)
    for the sum of $4 822 00
Received one year's rent for the seminary 16 00
Received of J. Robinson for clay and cablin[4] 15 00

---

[3] Corydon at that time was the state capital.

[4] Evidently meant for cablish—windfall timber. Report is quoted from *Senate Journal*, 1828, p. 230, exactly as it appeared there. There evidently was an error in addition when $243.50 was obtained.

do. D. Rawlings for rails...................... $ 7 00
Interest received............................   316 80

When added makes....................................$5 176 80
Of which there has been expended.............. 4 409 53
Agent's per cent on the same....................   220 47   4 630 00

Leave due of said fund.....................................$ 546 80
Tuition fees received prior to May, 1828.........   143 50
Tuition fees received since......................   99 62   243 50

                                                            $ 790 30
Of which there has been paid to orders........................   152 50

Leaves due the institution......................................$ 637 80

JAMES BORLAND, *Treasurer*

Honorable Board of Visitors, Indiana College.
October 31, 1828

The $4,409 expended included the cost of the College building and
the "commodious house for a Professor" as stipulated in the Act of
January 20, 1820. The erection of these buildings completed the first
episode in making the Seminary lands productive for the benefit of
the Seminary. It should be noted that the trustees of Indiana Seminary appointed the agent, directed the sale, received and expended
the proceeds, as dictated by the Act of January 20, 1820. Three other
contiguous sections, one east, one south, and one west of this first
section, were handled in this manner, and these four sections were
the only sections handled in this manner.

An act approved January 9, 1821, authorized the trustees or agent
of the Seminary to lend at interest on good land security the money
in their possession. The sale of the reserved section 4 had taken place
on the second Monday in November, 1920. On January 9, 1821, they
must have had on hand most of the cash received. The above act
was probably passed at the request of the trustees. The Borland report quoted above shows receipt of $316.80 interest received, a thrifty
procedure. With the exception of this one section 4, no land in Perry
Township was sold until 1827.

In this act establishing a state Seminary in Bloomington, the
Seminary township in Gibson County is not mentioned; but two

days later on January 22, 1820, a joint resolution was adopted appointing Jesse Emmerson as superintendent to rent the improved lands in the reserved township in Gibson County, and he was directed to account to the state for the proceeds. Thus it was provided that the reserved township in Gibson County was first made to yield an income by rentals.

The sale of Seminary lands in Gibson County was first authorized on January 2, 1822. The General Assembly appointed three commissioners to superintend this sale. The commissioners were directed to make a complete report of their proceedings to the General Assembly, on or before the first Monday of December, annually, and to pay over to the State Treasury all money by them received that it might be made a productive fund for the benefit of the State Seminary. It was provided that no land should be sold at less than $5 an acre. This was the beginning of the University Fund.

In order to relieve a situation which developed in connection with sale of Seminary lands in Gibson County, as the board of trustees of Vincennes University ceased to function, section 7 was written into this Act of January 2, 1822:

> Whereas it is stated to this General Assembly that the former Board of Trustees of the Vincennes University sold certain quarter sections of the seminary township without making and executing deeds therefor, and that the said Board have expired by the negligence of its members; for remedy whereof: the said commissioners . . . are hereby authorized . . . to make and execute deeds, . . .

In anticipation of the early completion of the college buildings and readiness for instruction the trustees, late in 1823, selected the first professor. His annual salary was only $250, but with his appointment the problem of maintenance of the Seminary was at hand. Accordingly, early in 1824, the General Assembly made the first provision for maintenance of Indiana Seminary out of proceeds of Monroe County Seminary lands.

Renting of Seminary Lands, 1824

On January 31, 1824, a bill was approved authorizing the agent for the reserved township in Monroe County to rent the land and deliver the rental (payable in corn or other grain) to the trustees of

Indiana Seminary, who were authorized to receive the profits arising in any way from the Seminary lands and apply them to the support of the State Seminary. Sections 3 and 4 of this act empowered the agent of the Gibson County Seminary lands, "now under control of the State," to rent same and report to the Speaker of the House. All rents and profits arising from the reserved township in Gibson County were to be paid over to the state treasurer.

Obviously it was the conviction of the legislators that the rental from the Monroe County township should provide adequately for maintenance of the Seminary. When it is considered that during the first three years there was one professor, who for the greater part of that time received only $250 a year for teaching service, and that there were some 23,040 acres of land in a township six miles square, it is evident how legislators might estimate that even a small rental on the fraction of the township free of forest and available for cultivation would provide the small maintenance budget of that day.

On February 10, 1825, the "act [of 1824] concerning the Seminary lands in Gibson and Monroe counties," referred to above, was amended. The amendment stipulated that rentals of lands in the reserved township in Monroe County were to be paid in money, and none of the land was to be rented for less than 62½ cents an acre.

Section 2 of this amendment authorized the trustees to receive all the profits arising in any way from the land "and in addition thereto they shall be entitled to receive the legal interest, that may be due from this state on seminary moneys now in its treasury... the Treasurer to pay the same, on the twentieth day of December of each year." This act made the state responsible for interest.

THE PERIOD 1824–67

This period began in May, 1824, with the opening of Indiana Seminary for instruction. During the whole of this period the maintenance of Indiana Seminary, College, University was derived from the two Seminary townships as rentals or as interest on the proceeds of sale of land, supplemented by small fees from students.

There are two major sources of information relating to the manner in which the Seminary lands in Gibson and Monroe counties were made to yield an income for establishment and support of the Seminary: (1) the acts of successive sessions of the General Assembly supplemented by reports in *House, Senate,* and *Documentary Journals* together with contemporary publications; (2) the extensive reports in the minutes of the trustees, when available, particularly the report of the finance committee, May, 1840, and that of George Dunn as treasurer of state, recorded September 22, 1842, on pages 136 to 147. These two sources supplement each other, giving together an understanding of the handling of the lands of these Seminary townships, not furnished by either alone.

Sale of Seminary Lands, 1827

With the exception of section 4 in Perry Township sold in 1820 for money with which to erect Seminary buildings, no Seminary land was sold in Monroe County prior to 1827. The sale of Gibson County lands had been ordered by the General Assembly in 1822.

Then an act of January 25, 1827, provided for appointment of commissioners to make sale of Seminary lands in both Gibson and Monroe counties. These commissioners were to pay to the treasurer of state the proceeds of sales directed by the treasurer, who was required to pay to the Indiana Seminary trustees the interest on money in his hands derived from these sales.

Legislators apparently were becoming impatient to complete the sale of these Seminary lands. On January 26, 1836, the legislature again required the commissioners of the reserved township of Seminary lands in Monroe County to sell the unsold lands.

Three Reserved Sections in Monroe County

The Act of January 25, 1827, carried a further important provision. Section 10 reserved from the sale of Seminary lands in Monroe County, three sections, one east, Number 3, one south, 9, one west, 5, all three adjacent to section Number 4 sold in 1820 and in which the Seminary site and buildings were located. The relation of these three reserved sections to section 4 is seen in the map of Perry Township, page 720.

The Act of January 29, 1830, made provision for sale of reserved section 9, in the reserved township in Monroe County, lying "adjoining to, and immediately south, of the one heretofore sold, for the purpose of erecting the Seminary buildings in said county."

The commissioners were authorized to lay out said section, to give public notice, and to furnish the secretary of Indiana College and the treasurer of state with a full statement of the amount arising from the sales of the section aforesaid (No. 9, see map).

Section 6 provided that all money arising from the sales hereby authorized should be paid

to the Treasurer of the Indiana College, and shall be paid out to the order of the Board of Trustees of said College, and be by them applied to the finishing of the college chapel, at this time erecting, and for purchasing a philosophic apparatus and library for said college, and for other purposes.

An act approved January 26, 1836, authorized the sale of the residue of the reserved section 9 in Perry Township, put on sale in 1830. Evidently the sale ordered in 1830 had been dragging.

Sale of East and West Reserved Sections

An act approved February 4, 1837, required the commissioners to lay off and sell the *east* reserved section of Seminary lands. All money received from the sale was to be paid over to the treasurer of the Indiana College "to be applied by them in the way and manner which shall most conduce to the advancement of the interests of the said institution."

Section 7 of this act authorized the trustees of Indiana College

(if in their discretion they may deem it to be for the interest of said college) at their next regular annual meeting to order the commissioner to sell the section of reserved land in said township commonly called the *west* section. [No. 5, see map.]

The sale of the west reserved section was ordered at the next annual meeting of the Board of Trustees, for in the minutes for September 25, 1838 (p. 9), there is found the report of the committee on ways and means, containing reference to the survey of the west section and the estimate of the commissioner that in the following November there would be due about $1,050 from the sale of the west section.

Sales Price of Four Reserved Sections in Monroe County

Fortunately we have a very definite statement of the sales price of these four reserved sections in the Seminary township in Monroe County, found in the Dunn report.

George Dunn had been a trustee of Indiana University, 1828–36. In 1842 he was treasurer of state and when the trustees of the State University called upon him for a report on the University Fund he knew exactly what they wished and made a report copied in the minutes of the board under date September 22, 1842 (pp. 136–47 inclusive), consisting of eight statements.

Statement 4 of this report is a statement of principal derived from sale of four College sections in Monroe County, the amount paid upon first-, second-, third-, fourth-, and fifth-year notes, and the balance outstanding on August 1, 1842, as exhibited by new books prepared for the commissioner of the Seminary township.

Amount of sales.................................. $33,568.71¼
Amount paid in hand............................... 8,454.45¾
Balance due at sale in 5 annual installments.......... 25,114.25½
  Deduct from above for payments as follows:
    On 1st notes, 1 year...................... $3,540.74
    On 2d notes, 2 years...................... 3,110.22½
    On 3d notes, 3 years...................... 1,924.55¾
    On 4th notes, 4 years..................... 755.44½
    On 5th notes, 5 years..................... 182.64½   9,513.61¼

Leaving balance due on principal........................ $15,600.64¼
                                                                     (*sic*)

This statement reveals that, though the sales price of these four reserved sections was $33,568.71, only $8,454.45 had been paid. Notes were taken for $9,513.61, which left $15,600.64 due on principal, which, under legislative instructions, must have been secured by mortgages on land. We know from reports that ten years later interest was still being paid on some of these notes, but what losses ultimately were sustained we do not know.

The University Fund, 1822 to Date

The University Fund is defined in the Revised Statutes of 1852[5] as consisting "of the lands in Monroe and Gibson Counties, and proceeds of sales thereof." When the Indiana Seminary was established it was believed that the sale of this grant of federal lands would yield $200,000, and that the interest on that sum would provide

[5] Chap. CXIV, p. 508.

amply for necessary buildings and for maintenance. In reality this fund never amounted to half the estimate, though it might have done so had not the needs of the institution led to sale of lands too soon. The fund accumulated very slowly and the interest on this fund in the Seminary period was very small. State Treasurer Samuel Merrill reports[6] that up to December, 1827, interest on the University Fund amounting to $387.81 had been paid on order of the president of the Board of Trustees. Up to that time, 1827, the state treasurer had received $729 from the Gibson County township as rents. Rental of Monroe County Seminary lands was paid directly to the trustees and constituted the greater part of maintenance budget.

For five years, 1822–27, the University Fund was derived solely from sale of Gibson County Seminary lands. Except for section 4 of the Seminary township in Monroe County, no Seminary lands in Monroe County were sold until 1827.

From May, 1824, when the Seminary was opened, until 1867, income from these two Seminary townships, as rentals or interest, supplemented by small fees, was the sole source of maintenance of the institution. A very determined effort was made to learn the total of the University Fund. This will be discussed later.

Loan Office Established for University Fund, 1828–97

Another act approved on January 24, 1828, authorized establishment of a loan office "for the state of Indiana, in the town of Indianapolis, to be connected with, and kept at the office of the state Treasurer." Section 3 provided:

That the funds for the loan office hereby established, shall consist of the principal of all monies the proceeds of the sales of the seminary lands in Gibson and Monroe counties, which now are, or shall hereafter, agreeably to the laws of this state, be paid into the state treasury; together with all grants, etc.

Section 4 provided that "The treasurer of state, as superintendent of the loan office aforesaid, shall have power" to make loans to citizens of Indiana on real estate security.

[6] *House Journal*, 1827, p. 48.

Section 15 made it

the duty of the superintendent aforesaid [*i.e.,* the treasurer of state], at all times, to pay over to the order of the board of trustees of the Indiana College . . . any interest of monies accruing from loans herein contemplated. . . .

This is a change from earlier procedure in which the state itself paid interest on this fund in the State Treasury.

Section 17 authorized payment to the treasurer of $75 a year for his services as superintendent of the loan office.

On January 23, 1829, an act, supplemental to the above act of January 24, 1828, set up for the treasurer the legal procedure and safeguards to be observed in conducting the affairs of the loan office. Later, 1843, the loan office was transferred to the office of the auditor of state. The Revised Statutes for 1843[7] made it the duty of the auditor of state to make all loans from the University Fund. The state treasurer as custodian of the fund merely paid over the money as directed by the auditor. The home of the University Fund was the State Treasury. In 1897 the auditor was directed to allocate the University Fund to the counties.

Relationship of State and University to University Fund

In the Act of January 24, 1828, in which Indiana Seminary was given college status, the legislators deemed it important to define the relations of the state of Indiana and Indiana College to the University Fund. In section 12 of this act they indicated very clearly and definitely

that all monies, arising from the sale of the Seminary townships, in the counties of Monroe and Gibson, shall be, and forever remain a permanent fund, for the support of said College, and the interest arising from the amount of said sales, together with the three reserved sections in the Seminary townships situated in the county of Monroe . . . shall be, and hereby are forever vested in the aforesaid trustees and their successors. . . .

This act established the University Fund, which was in the custody of the treasurer of state as a permanent fund, the interest on which was to be turned over to the College trustees for College maintenance. The act repeated that the reserved sections of the Seminary

[7] Chap. XIII, p. 244, sec. 28.

township in Monroe County were in the custody of the trustees of Indiana College and their successors.

Further Safeguards to the University Fund

To provide a double check on this University Fund an act of January 23, 1829, provided that the auditor of public accounts, i.e., the state auditor, be brought into the picture. Section 2 reads:

It shall be the duty of the commissioners aforesaid, within three months after the taking effect of this act, severally to transmit to the auditor of public accounts, a correct statement of all monies by them heretofore paid, on account of the sales of said lands, into the state treasury; and forever thereafter, the said commissioners, shall when they make payment of any seminary monies, into the state treasury, also furnish the auditor of public accounts, with a correct statement of the amount thereof; and the said auditor shall enter all the reports so made, or which shall hereafter be made, on his books, in the same manner as he is now required by law to do, in regard to the state revenue.

Amount of University Fund

Let us recall that the University Fund as defined in the Revised Statutes of 1852 consists "of the lands in Monroe and Gibson Counties, and proceeds of sales thereof."

In Statement 1 of the George Dunn report of 1842 we find an analysis of the sale of Seminary lands with a record of the total sales price of these lands. This total sales price brings us close to the total of what the University Fund should be. Statement 1 follows:

STATEMENT No. 1

Township	Number Acres Sold	Average per Acre	Total Sales Price	Number Acres Unsold	Value of Unsold Lands
Gibson	16,529.64 A	$1.37	$22,639.83½	2,480 A	$1,860
Monroe.........	21,214.51 A	1.40	39,713.06¼	40 A	30
	37,744.15 A		$62,352.89¾	2,520 A	$1,890
Reserved College Sections	2,406.38 A	13.95	33,568.71¾	1 A	40
Total	40,150.53 A		$95,921.61½	2,521 A	$1,930
Adding Unsold..	2,521 A		1,930.00		
Total Sold and Unsold	42,671.53 A		$97,851.61½		

The table above shows that on the date of this report, early in 1842, only one acre of the four reserved sections remained unsold. The total number of acres of Seminary lands in the two townships was 42,671.53. Two full townships should be 46,080 acres. The shortage was in Gibson County. Add Gibson County lands sold (table above) to Gibson County lands unsold and we get a total of 19,009.64 acres. This shortage is explained in Statement 3 by Mr. Dunn in which he tells us that under earlier enactments of the Territorial period 4,640 acres of the Gibson Township were sold, "the proceeds of which went to the erection of a college edifice at Vincennes," except that part of the proceeds ($2,371.96) was deposited in the State Treasury. Adding the 4,640 acres to the 19,009.64 we get a total of 23,649.64, which is 609.64 acres in excess of a full township.

The acres sold, unsold, and reserved in the Monroe Township total 23,661.89 acres, which was 621.89 acres in excess of a full township. This is an error of nearly one section, one square mile, and though it could be the error of the surveyor whose instruments sometimes were far from perfect, there were other opportunities for error in reporting and copying records of the many transactions involved.

This Statement 1 of Mr. Dunn would seem to indicate that the possible University Fund was the total sales price, $97,851.61½. But this total included $33,568.71¾ derived from the sale of the four reserved sections in Monroe County, the proceeds of the sale of which were not to be added to the University Fund, but were turned over directly to the trustees of the University for erection of the first buildings, and later for completion of a chapel, the purchase of philosophical apparatus, etc. Subtracting the $33,568.71¾ derived from sale of four reserved sections from the total sales price, we get $64,282.89¾ as the total University Fund. Two other statements follow which it is believed give a more accurate evaluation of this fund.

There are two statements of the productive fund of the University at this period, 1840–42, one by Mr. Dunn, Statement 8 of his report, and one prepared by the finance committee of the Board of Trustees, both of which are based on a careful examination of records. The Dunn Statement 8 is headed, "an estimate of the whole fund of the University." The statement follows:

Cash on hand in Loan Office................................$ 6,418.48
Outstanding Loans Statement No. 6.......................... 55,376.39
Balance due from purchasers in Gibson Township and on interest
    per Statement No. 3....................................: 7,819.44½
Balance due from purchasers in Monroe Township and on interest
    per Statement No. 2.................................... 13,161.57
Balance due from purchasers of College Sections and on interest
    per Statement No. 4.................................... 15,600.64½
Balance due from Mr. Alexander to State Treasury as per his
    account current in that office (sued on)..................... 776.97

                          Total.....................$99,153.50

It should be noted that the fifth item, $15,600.64, is an amount due on College Sections, i.e., the four reserved sections in Perry Township, and the sixth item, $776.97, is due from Mr. Alexander, former commissioner of the four reserved sections. Subtracting these two amounts totaling $16,377.61 from $99,153.50 we have the University Fund, $82,775.89.

On page 66 of the minutes of the trustees (May 5, 1840) is found Document F, a report of their finance committee, giving an estimate of the productive fund of the University.

Amount in hands of treasurer of state and commissioners..........$80,946.00
Amount of notes due from purchasers of the reserved sections..... 10,094.23
Interest on above notes (about 3 years on each note).
    Hands of J. Berry.. 1,816.92
Other notes for collection like those above...................... 294.39
Amount of notes at 10% interest in hands of Treasurer of the
    University.. 1,336.00
Balance due from William Alexander, former commissioner...... 1,151.11
Balance in hands of treasurer of University...................... 333.19
60 Lots unsold valued at.. 2,500.00

                                             $98,471.84

                  Signed:

                      Robert Dale Owen
                      James Blair
                      D. H. Maxwell

Items 2 to 7 inclusive in this report have to do with proceeds of the four reserved sections of Perry Township, Monroe County. Subtracting the total of these six items, $15,025.84 from the total in the report, $98,471.84, we have $83,446.00.

This total of the University Fund deduced from this report of the finance committee of the trustees differs from the total deduced from the report of Treasurer Dunn (Statement 8) by only $670.11. If one considers that the time difference of the two reports is about eighteen months, and if one considers that in a review of old accounts some may be regarded worthless one year that a year later may be believed in part collectible, and vice versa, the two reports of the University Fund are remarkably alike.

Other statements of the Dunn report are also very interesting. Statement 5 is a "Statement of interest derived from loans of college funds, the amount disbursed as expenses of College, either as salaries of Professors or expenses incident to management of fund, from the time of receiving the first interest in 1822 to close of the fiscal year 1841."

From the twenty annual reports in Statement 5 two are selected, those of 1828 and 1841, which follow:

Year 1828

Amount of interest received		$1,685.51
Amount of expenses of College	$1,160.81	
Amount of specific appropriations	295.14	
Amount of superintendent's salary	48.80	1,504.75
Amount undrawn at close of 1828		$ 180.76

This statement shows the income from the University Fund, $1,685.51 in 1828. Add to this sum the small fees from students, approximately $150, and we have the budget for this year, about $1,835.

The term "Specific Appropriations" seen in this report does not mean an appropriation from the state but some special expenditure charged to the University interest or income. In the year 1828 there were two professors. President Wylie arrived in 1829.

The 1841 statement shows a considerable increase in the amount of interest received.

Year 1841

Balance on hand	$ 603.00	
Interest received	4,665.59	$5,268.59
Expenses	$5,146.00	
Interest on hand	152.59[8]	$5,268.59

By 1841 the institution had become a University. The budget for the year was $5,268.59 plus student fees.

Further evidence of the pitiful inadequacy of the maintenance budget of the University is secured from the report of David H. Maxwell, president of the board, to the General Assembly, handed down in the House, January 14, 1852. The report, in part, follows:

State of Finances

On this subject the General Assembly is respectfully referred to the annual report of the Auditor of State. The Trustees are wholly dependent upon that report for information in regard to the condition of the funds in the Loan Office. The average amount derived from that fund, say since the year 1843, has been somewhat less than $4,000 a year; which, with the tuition fees of about $1,200 per year, constitutes the fund for the payment of Professors, etc. (*House Journal,* 36th session, p. 491.)

Statement 6 of the Dunn report accounts for loans of Seminary funds (the University Fund) made each year beginning with 1828.

Number 7 is a "Statement of the Receipts of the Seminary Funds [University Funds] derived from rents, sales, and interest on sales of Seminary Townships, in Gibson and Monroe Counties, and the disbursement thereof from 1st Receipts in 1822 to close of financial year 1841—as exhibited by the Books of the Loan Office and State Treasury."

A report of great interest, made by Trustee Robert Dale Owen, chairman of the committee on ways and means, shows the probable receipts and expenditures of the University for the year 1840–41.

This estimate of Mr. Owen shows that the University was still receiving in 1841 interest on outstanding notes taken on sale of reserved sections of Seminary lands in Monroe County together with some principal.

---

[8] Obviously there is an error of $30 somewhere in this statement. Probably the amount undrawn at the close of 1841 was $122.59.

REPORT OF COMMITTEE ON WAYS AND MEANS

Probable Expenditures	
Still due the faculty..........$	440.00
Due ensuing year	
for salaries	5,950.00
Janitor's wages	100.00
Legislative expenses	400.00
Treasurer . . say.............	125.00
Repairs and Incidental........	150.00
	$7,165.00
$2,000 drawn from N. B. Palmer would leave in the University Treasury	154.37
	$7,319.37

Probable Income	
From Notes in Mr. Berry's hands[9] in next 6 months....$	1,400.00
And in following 6 months....	1,000.00
McCalla's Notes and Int.......	440.00
Due by William Alexander[10] on Mr. Palmer's[11] draft......	440.00
Three notes in Treasurer's hands	1,151.00
Five months interest on same	38.37
Tuition fees; say 50 @ $17	850.00
	$5,319.37
It will then be necessary to draw from funds in the hands of N. B. Palmer during the ensuing year.........	2,000.00
	$7,319.37

Further Legislation Bearing on the University Fund

An act was approved January 9, 1842, making it the duty of agents to report annually the amount of land sold and unsold, the amount of money both principal and interest received for lands sold, the amount of land leased, etc. It was made the duty of the state treasurer to report on the same to the legislature, annually, sending a duplicate report to the trustees of the State University.

On January 17, 1846, an act was approved to authorize the trustees of the Vincennes University to bring suit against the state of Indiana and for other purposes. This act opened the way to litigation, which was carried to the Supreme Court of the United States.[12]

An act approved June 17, 1852,[13] presents an interesting variation in procedure in disposal of Seminary lands. Under this act the care and disposition of *unsold Seminary lands* was vested in the commissioners of the reserved townships of the respective counties (sec. 55) who were directed to rent or sell same on such terms as the trustees

---

[9] Mr. Berry was a commissioner.
[10] Mr. Alexander was a commissioner.
[11] Mr. Palmer was treasurer of state.
[12] See page 737.
[13] *Revised Statutes,* Chap. CXIV, p. 504.

of the University should prescribe, turn proceeds, principal, and interest direct to the treasurer of the trustees, taking duplicate receipts, one of which was sent to the state auditor to be used by him in his settlement with such treasurer. Up to this time money derived from sale of unreserved sections of Seminary land had been paid directly to the State Treasury.

This unusual procedure with reference to unsold lands was modified on March 2, 1859, by an act providing that the trustees should have lands appraised and record same and file a copy with the county auditor, who should, when so required, by the Board of Trustees, offer the lands for sale. The county treasurer was directed to pay the principal to the treasurer of state and interest to the treasurer of the Board of Trustees on the first Monday of each month.

The auditor of state was directed to lend such principal in the same manner as required by law for other portions of the University Fund.

The procedure authorized in these Acts of 1852 and 1859 applied to only a small remnant of Seminary land. We know from Statement 1 of the report of Treasurer Dunn that in 1842 only 2,521 acres out of nearly 43,000 remained unsold. Nearly all of these 2,521 acres were in Gibson County and they must have been very undesirable for they were valued in 1842 at $1,930, less than 77 cents an acre. At the time these acts were approved it is probable that only a few hundred acres and a few hundred dollars were involved.

The University Fund Imperiled

The University Fund was in almost constant danger of loss arising from loans made on inadequate security. This will be discussed in some detail in connection with appointment by the University, in 1899, of a financial agent.

Peril of the University Fund and of the University reached an all-time high in the early fifties of the nineteenth century. To the constitutional convention, 1851, certain delegates came with the avowed purpose of destroying Indiana University. A determined effort was made to dissipate the University Fund. It was with difficulty that this purpose was foiled by powerful friends in the convention who succeeded in writing into Section 7, Article VIII, the declaration that "All trust funds held by the State shall remain inviolate and be faithfully and exclusively applied to the purpose for which the trust was created."

Barely had the institution escaped that peril, when in the December (1852) term of the United States Supreme Court (decision made January 25, 1853) the claim of Vincennes University was sustained. Later it was decreed that $66,000 be paid Vincennes University[14] from the University Fund. In this emergency the legislature accepted the argument and recommendation of Governor Wright and authorized an issue of state bonds in satisfaction of this claim, thus preserving the University Fund for the purpose for which it was intended.

A report of the finance committee in 1852 gave the amount of the University Fund as $72,400. If $66,000 had been taken from this fund, the remainder, $6,400 would have been so entirely inadequate as a productive fund for University maintenance that the doors would unavoidably have been closed.

The trustees had scarcely recovered from this threat of disaster when on April 9, 1854, the main University building with the valuable library was destroyed by fire. The situation was so grave that, to complete a fund of $18,000 for rebuilding, a mortgage for $6,000 was put on the University campus.

Summary of Difficulties of 1824–67

The difficulties of the period 1824–67, which were many and great, stemmed chiefly from the pitifully inadequate maintenance budget of the University. The Law School, established in 1842, except for a room and firewood furnished by the University, was maintained for a time by fees from students. Other schools which were almost mandated by the General Assembly, such as Agriculture and Medicine, could not be started because of inadequate maintenance. There were many changes in the Board of Trustees. Superior men appointed to the board must have found it impossible to do things which challenged their interest. They became irregular in attendance and dropped out. New boards were appointed in 1828, 1838, 1841, 1852, 1855.

[14] R. S. Robertson, trustee of Indiana University, 1882–94, states (Wylie's *History of Indiana University*, p. 30) that this suit was brought under a contract with Samuel Judah, attorney for Vincennes University, under which he retained one-fourth of the amount recovered, $16,625, as his fee.

THE PERIOD 1867-1937

During this period, the Indiana General Assembly first recognized its obligation to supplement the income derived from the University Fund for maintenance of the University.

Income from the University Fund was supplemented:

By annual appropriations...............................1867–95
By creation of a Permanent Endowment Fund.............1883–95
By a varying mill tax.................................1895–1925
By a budget system...................................1925–

Beginning with an annual appropriation of $8,000 in 1867, the supplemental part of the University income grew until the income derived from the University Fund in 1867 represented about one-half of one per cent of the maintenance derived from the state in 1937.

Annual Appropriations, 1867–95

There is much evidence that the members of the constitutional convention of 1816, who accepted the federal grant of two townships of land and pledged that the state would establish a University, believed the proceeds of the sale of 46,080[15] acres of land would be an endowment so great that the interest on that endowment, some of which was lent at 10 per cent, would constitute an income sufficient for the permanent support of the institution. In fact, the interest on this University Fund, plus small fees, *was* the sole support of Indiana University until 1867.

How limited was the vision of legislators of that day with regard to an educational institution is revealed in a legislative act of 1833 establishing the Christian College of New Albany. One of the provisions of that act was that the institution should never hold property in excess of $10,000. It never did.

Measured by present standards, the 1867 appropriation of $8,000 seems a pitifully small appropriation. But it approximately doubled the income during the early sixties, which is a major accomplishment of any administration. In fact it was an epochal event in the history of Indiana University, of great credit to President Nutt and

[15] It was really only 41,440 acres. The Gibson County township was 4,640 acres short.

his Board of Trustees. In 1869 this appropriation was increased to $15,000 and in 1873 to $23,000 annually. And at that figure it stood throughout the nine and one-half years of the Moss administration and until the fifth year of the Jordan administration, when in 1889 it was increased to $30,000 annually.

Accumulation of Permanent Endowment Fund, 1883–95

Still laboring under the impression that maintenance of the State University would be provided most satisfactorily by income from endowment, the legislature of 1883 passed an act providing that "there shall be assessed and collected . . . in the year of 1883, and in each of the next succeeding twelve years" a tax of one-half of one cent on each $100, proceeds of which were to accumulate for twelve years, and provide a greatly increased permanent endowment fund for Indiana University. It was believed that this tax would yield $540,000 and that this fund at prevailing rates of interest would yield as much or more than the annual appropriation of that day. The fund thus collected was known as the Permanent Endowment Fund. Interest on Permanent Endowment Fund appears first in the financial report of the Board of Trustees, as of October 1, 1887. The fund exceeded the $540,000 estimated.[16] There is no record of its exact amount. The University Fund was later merged with the Permanent Endowment Fund under the title of the latter. The total of these two funds, now known as the Permanent Endowment Fund, is carried today (1945) at $768,575.69.

University Bonds

The term "University bonds" is a misnomer. These bonds are state bonds, issued to the University for a part of the Permanent Endowment Fund, accumulated under the Endowment Act of 1883.

As the Permanent Endowment Fund accumulated in the early eighties, the trustees, alarmed by losses in the University Fund and concerned for the safety of the Permanent Endowment Fund, at their meeting on June 9, 1885, "resolved that Messrs. Mitchell and Banta be appointed a committee to secure execution of bonds of the

---

[16] A tax of one-half cent on each $100 of the total taxable property of the state (real and personal), 1883–95, would have yielded $578,864.49.

state for the funds of the University collected under the endowment act of 1883."

On November 7, 1887, a report was made by a committee of the board that up to that time fifty-year, 5 per cent state bonds had been issued as follows:

Bonds of October 11, 1885 ....$ 60,000
Bonds of February 15, 1887 60,000
Bonds of September 1, 1887 24,000
                                                       _____
                        Total...................$144,000

A copy of one of these bonds is found in the minutes (p. 255). We find no explanation as to why state bonds were not issued for the balance of the Permanent Endowment Fund.

For many years the interest on the University bonds and the interest on the Permanent Endowment Fund were reported separately, though both were derived from the Endowment Act of 1883. For instance, in the report of President Swain to the trustees on November 5, 1895, he includes a letter from A. C. Daily, the auditor of state, estimating the income of the University for the year ending October 31, 1896, quoted in part:

College Fund[17] interest ....$ 8,000
Interest on University bonds.............................. 7,200
Permanent Endowment Fund interest.................... 26,000

The University Fund, or College Fund as it is here called, was derived from a gift of federal lands in 1816, and is just as much a permanent Endowment Fund as the funds accumulated under the Endowment Act of 1883. All three items in the report quoted above are carried today (1945) very properly as Permanent Endowment Fund.

Mill Tax Period, 1895–1925

Obviously the plans of 1883 were no longer adequate for 1895, and, accordingly, a new plan of supplementing University income from endowment was devised. For the first time (1895) a tax of

[17] The terms "College Fund," "College Endowment Fund," and "University Endowment Fund" were used interchangeably for the "University Fund."

6⅔ mills on $100 (sometimes expressed as 1/15 mill on $1) was voted by the legislature for Indiana University in substitution for the annual appropriations. In the year 1901–2, the last year of the Swain administration, this tax yielded $90,200. It was the tax in force when the presidency of William Lowe Bryan was begun.

In 1903 the General Assembly amended the 1895 tax act, increasing the levy to 2¾ cents on every $100 of taxable property of the state, and giving Indiana University 4/11 of the total, or 1 cent on every $100.

Then in 1913 the General Assembly, under leadership of Governor Ralston, voted the 7-cent tax for support of the institutions of higher education, giving 2/5 to Indiana University. This was, for Indiana University, 2.8 cents on each $100. In the first year this tax was in full effect, 1914–15, it yielded for the University the sum of $537,340.90.

In 1919 the General Assembly cut this 7-cent rate to 2.8 cents for each $100. Two-fifths of this tax, the amount allocated to Indiana University, was 1.12 cents for each $100. This, of course, was a radical cut in the educational tax rate. It was not expected, however, to yield a decreased income. The explanation of this paradox is found in the lengthy (200 pp.) completely revised tax bill of 1919, one provision of which was that all lands and the improvements and buildings were assessed at their full, true cash value, "at the price they would bring at a fair, voluntary private sale." It was expected that this would give a total value of taxable property two and one-half times as great as under the former assessment plan. If this estimate were correct, then a tax rate of 2.8 cents on the $100 on the greater total would yield exactly the same income as the 7-cent rate on the lesser valuation.

In 1919 the total of taxable property in Indiana was $2,233,761,065. In 1920, with property assessed at its full value, the total was $5,749,258,800. It appears, therefore, that the estimate of the legislators was remarkably accurate.

At the legislative session of 1921 the University sought to have the 7-cent tax restored. The General Assembly, however, fixed the rate at 5 cents, which gave Indiana University 2 cents on each $100 of assessed values in the state.

Expressed in tabular form:

Educational Tax

YEAR	Tax on Each $100	When Passed	Indiana University Share on Each $100	Yielded	Total Income from State	Remarks
1901–2	1⅔c	1895	6⅔ mills	$90,200.00	$ 90,200.00	I.U. received ²/₅ of total
1911–12	2¾c	1903	1c	183,937.98	258,937.98	I.U. received 4/₁₁ of total
1912–13	7c	3/'13	2.8c	189,214.29	291,414.29	I.U. was to receive ²/₅ of 7-cent tax
1913–14	7c	3/'13	2.8c	294,997.08	457,674.62	End of 2¾-cent and beginning 7-cent tax
1914–15	7c	3/'13	2.8c	537,340.90	543,303.05	7-cent tax in full effect
1915–16	7c	3/'13	2.8c	560,884.65	642,526.99	
1916–17	7c	3/'13	2.8c	574,199.71	537,623.98	
1917–18	7c	3/'13	2.8c	587,163.37	586,671.48	
1918–19	2.8c	3/'19	1.12c	615,850.13	845,655.65	
1919–20	2.8c	3/'19	1.12c	638,504.12	703,127.29	End 7-cent and beginning 2.8-cent tax
1920–21	5c	3/'21	2c	637,308.96	823,658.80	2.8-cent tax in full effect
1921–22	5c	3/'21	2c	892,942.99	1,062,995.03	End 2.8-cent and beginning 5-cent tax

In addition to the educational tax tabulated above, the state occasionally made supplementary maintenance appropriations, and also special appropriations for buildings, land, repairs, the Graduate School, the School of Medicine, the Robert W. Long Hospital, etc. It follows, therefore, that the total receipts from the state were usually somewhat in excess of the yield of the educational tax; sometimes much in excess of the educational tax.

In the years 1916–17 and 1917–18 the total received from the state was less than the yield of the educational tax. Unexpended balances on hand September 30 were held in the State Treasury to be used for building or other purposes, subject to approval of the State Finance Board, according to a provision of the educational tax act.

During the first ten years of the Bryan administration income from the educational tax doubled, increased 100 per cent. But during the second decade it increased almost 500 per cent.

Biennial Appropriations, 1925 to Date (1945)

In 1925 the mill tax for maintenance of the state institutions of higher education gave way to the biennial budget system which is in force today (1945). Under this system *annual* budgets are voted biennially.

University Fund Apportioned Among the Counties

The experiments of seventy years (1867 to 1937) in supplementing income from the University Fund have been presented in succession in order that a better grasp of these procedures might be secured. But while these different plans were being tried the loan office in the auditor's office was continuing in its effort to make the University Fund productive for the benefit of the University. Though legislation was enacted from time to time the purpose of which was to safeguard the University Fund, loans were made on insufficient security and losses were incurred which affected the University income.

The interest received by the University on the University Fund for the year 1877–78 was $6,500; for 1882–83, $5,000; for 1883–84, $3,500. This, of course, was alarming to the University administration. President Coulter and his Board of Trustees (1891–93) were much distressed by fund losses, but were unable to propose any remedy. President Swain met the situation in 1893. Not only the University Fund but the Permanent Endowment Fund was imperiled. By 1897 a plan had been evolved for maintaining the integrity of the University endowment. On March 2, 1897, an act of the General Assembly was approved making a new provision for the lending of this University endowment. The act was introduced by a "Whereas" explaining the reason for its passage, which, in part, follows:

Whereas, A large amount of the permanent endowment fund of the State University located at Bloomington has been loaned by Auditors of State upon securities which have, in many instances, proved insufficient, by reason of which there has been great difficulty in collecting the interest and principal; a great many of said loans being now long past due and uncollected, already entailing considerable loss and great danger of further impairment of the principal of said fund, ...

The treasurer of state was ordered to collect all outstanding loans belonging to the Permanent Endowment Fund of the State University which might be due, and all other loans as fast as they became due, and the auditor of state was directed to apportion the fund among the several counties of the state according to population. The counties were required to pay interest on this fund to the treasurer of the state in the same manner that interest was paid on the School Fund, and the treasurer of state was directed to pay this interest to the treasurer of Indiana University.

Appointment of Financial Agent

It was soon realized, however, that the collection of many outstanding loans presented major difficulties, including numerous "hot potatoes." President Swain had been warned that pressing collection of overdue loans of the University Fund would be to the disinterest of the University and interfere with appropriations. But President Swain was a man not easily frightened. Still it must have taken courage for the Board of Trustees on November 17, 1899, to appoint William T. Hicks, of Bloomington, as financial agent to assist the Executive Committee "in getting the loans of the University Fund in better shape." Mr. Hicks was a retired banker who made the boast that he had never lost a loan, and though not a lawyer he had a lawyer's keen understanding of the legal aspects of loans.

On November 1, 1901, Mr. Hicks made a report showing:

Delinquent interest on the College and Endowment Fund which, by
    proper effort, ought to be collected...............................$15,500
College and Endowment Fund Loans outstanding.................. 34,000

In June, 1902, Judge Hadley, of the Indiana Supreme Court, handed down a decision in the case of Fisher vs. Brower in which the University Fund was declared entitled to the same protection by the state as the School Fund. This decision is quoted on page 747.

It was expected that the fund collected under the Endowment Act of 1883 would be made productive for the benefit of the University, but this was not always done, for in November, 1904, President Bryan was much concerned over the fact that some $74,000 of University endowment lay in the State Treasury, unlent, unproductive. With the trustees he discussed the preparation of a bill to make this fund available for a dormitory for women. Mr. Hicks, the financial agent of the University, was requested to prepare a statement of all outstanding loans from the College[18] Fund.

On November 16, 1904, Mr. Hicks was directed by the Board of

[18] See note 17.

Trustees to prepare a statement of all College Funds, to be preserved in a book to be kept in the administrative office. He also was directed to confer with the auditor of state with a view to pushing collection of College Endowment Fund loans.

In June, 1908, Mr. Hicks made a final and complete report of the Permanent Endowment Fund under which title the University Fund was of record in the office of the auditor of state.

This eight-page report gave a list of twenty-eight loans[19] of the University Fund still outstanding and ranging from $100 to $600, for a total of $10,182. There was a list of fifty-two pieces of real estate[20] appraised at $8,492, held in trust by the state for the University. The report closes with a summary as follows:

Distributed to the counties	$602,532.74
In Auditor's office for distribution	251.87
Borrowed by state (state bonds)	144,000.00
Loans outstanding	10,182.00
Appraised real estate	8,492.00
Total	$765,458.61

This report when compared with that of November 1, 1901, shows an improvement of nearly $40,000 in loans and interest outstanding.

Though no one could question the voluntary effort of the trustees in collecting long overdue loans, their position was entirely extra-legal, as was also that of Mr. Hicks, who never brought suit for recovery. But we note that, after five years of persuasion, he was directed by the Board of Trustees to confer with the auditor of state with a view to pressing collections of outstanding loans. It must have been obvious at all times that this was a logical next step, if persuasion failed.

The plan of lending the University Permanent Endowment Fund to the counties, and making the counties responsible for the loan, insured the integrity of the fund. Though many county auditors handled the part of the Permanent Endowment Fund prorated to

[19] By June, 1913, the number of loans had been reduced to four and a total of $1,057.55. By June, 1916 (p. 13, President's Report), $735.55 was still outstanding on these four loans.
[20] By June, 1916 (p. 182, President's report), certain lots had been sold for a little more than the appraised value, leaving 40 lots with an appraised value of $5,314.12. By 1929-30 only 26 lots remained, appraised at $4,023. These same 26 lots are listed in the 1944 financial report, p. 134, and carried at $4,023.

them under the act of 1897[21] in a highly efficient and commendable manner, some made bad loans and incurred losses which the counties had to make good. As the years passed this became a source of increasing irritation to the counties, and in 1943 a change in procedure again became desirable.

Return of University Fund to State Treasury Permissive

On March 8, 1943, an act was approved making the treasurer of state the exclusive custodian of the Common School Fund and the Indiana University Permanent Endowment Fund not held in trust by the counties. The act provided that the counties might elect to surrender, to the treasurer of state, custody of the Permanent Endowment Fund. A State Board of Finance was authorized with directions for investment of this fund.

Special Appropriations

In the early days it took a great disaster such as a fire to win from the legislature a grudging, tiny appropriation for building. Appropriations were usually 40 to 60 per cent of the amount really needed.

Happily, a more generous attitude toward support of higher education developed during the Bryan administration, a more generous attitude toward provision for educational opportunities for Indiana boys and girls.

One of the most important provisions for building was made in the Educational Improvement Act of March 7, 1927. This act provided a levy of 2 cents on each $100 of taxable property, 7/20 of which was allocated to Indiana University, and yielded for Indiana University about $350,000 per year. The act was to be in effect ten years and provide for a ten-year building fund. It made a long-range program of construction possible. Unfortunately, depressed economic conditions led the legislature to suspend the act in 1932, and again in 1935, and finally to repeal it. It was a program of great merit.

---

[21] The act approved March 7, 1927, had nothing whatever to do with the Permanent Endowment Fund, and is mentioned only to guard against possible confusion. The fund provided in this act, known as the Educational Improvement Fund, had as its purpose the improvement of the physical property of the state institutions of higher education. The funds at intervals were to be paid to the trustees of the respective institutions and used as directed. On the Indiana University campus it was known as the Building Fund. Section 3 provided that: "Nothing in this act shall affect in any way any endowment or permanent fund."

Supreme Court Decision, 1902

On June 24, 1902, i.e., a week following the election of William L. Bryan as president of Indiana University, but before he had taken office (August 1, 1902), the Indiana Supreme Court handed down a decision[22] defining the relation of Indiana University and its endowment fund to the state. Though this decision presented nothing new to those acquainted with the history of the University, a question had been raised, and this clearly expressed official reply was believed to have had much influence in the more adequate support of the University in the following session of the General Assembly (1903) and in succeeding legislative sessions.

Since the historic background for this decision is given with references revealing a constancy of purpose on the part of the General Assembly and the people of Indiana throughout the long history of the University, it is believed that the decision should be made available in this book.

In July, 1893, the lands described in the complaint were mortgaged to the state for a loan from the Permanent Endowment Fund. In 1898 the auditor of state sold to Abraham G. Brower the mortgaged lands to recover loan and interest. But in 1897 the county treasurer had sold the lands for taxes. In 1900 Brower brought suit against Samuel S. Fisher, purchaser at tax sale, to quiet title and won, whereupon Fisher appealed.

In writing his decision Judge John V. Hadley felt it desirable to review the status of this Permanent Endowment Fund, which in turn called for a consideration of the relation of the State University to the state of Indiana.

Judge Hadley said:

As ancillary to main question, appellants urge that the permanent endowment fund is a private fund, and not entitled to the constitutional and statutory protection accorded to public school funds, and that with respect to this particular fund the State acts merely as a trustee in making and collecting loans. An inquiry into the origin of the State University, for the maintenance of which institution the permanent endowment fund is exclusively designed, reveals the unmistakable purpose of the people to make the university a part of our public school system. Article 9, Section 2, of the Constitution of 1816 provided: "It shall be the duty of the General Assembly, as soon as circum-

[22] 159 Indiana 139 ff.

stances will permit, to provide by law for a general system of education, ascending in regular gradation from township schools to a state university, wherein tuition shall be gratis, and equally open to all."

In compliance with this mandate of the Constitution the legislature in 1820 established the State Seminary at Bloomington. Acts 1820, p. 82. In 1828 this institution was advanced to the dignity of Indiana College, an endowment fund established, its trustees required to report receipts, expenditures, etc., to the Governor, for submission to the General Assembly, and the constitution of the college declared to be unalterable by any law or ordinance of the trustees, "nor in any other manner, than by the legislature of this State." Acts 1828, p. 115. By an act of 1838 (Local Laws 1838, p. 294), the General Assembly conferred upon the institution the name of Indiana University, and the same body in 1842 adopted a joint resolution—reciting in terms section 2 of article 9 of the Constitution of 1816 above quoted,—requiring the trustees of the Indiana University to report to the next legislative session, whether, in their opinion the resources of said university are sufficient to enable the legislature to pass a law making tuition gratis, in compliance with the constitutional mandate. Acts 1842, p. 174. In order that the special relation of the university to the state might be continued unquestioned, under the new Constitution of 1851, the General Assembly of 1852 enacted that "The institution established by an act entitled 'An act to establish a college in the State of Indiana,' approved January 28, 1828, is hereby recognized as the university of the State." 1 R.S. 1852, p. 504, 1 G. & H., p. 660. And again in 1867 the legislature asserted that it should be the pride of every citizen of the State to place the State University in the highest condition of usefulness and make it the crowning glory of our present great common school system. Acts 1867, p. 20.

The maintenance fund is in no smaller sense a state fund. It has its origin from the sale of certain lands of the State acquired by gift from the government for educational purposes. Acts 1828, p. 117. It has been augmented from time to time, as the needs of the university increased, by specific appropriations from the state treasury,—first in 1867 (Section 6159 Burns 1901); again in 1873 (Section 6160 Burns 1901); and by general taxation for twelve years beginning in 1883 (Section 6161 Burns 1901), and again in 1895 (Acts 1895, p. 171).

The University as well as its endowment has always been under the supervision of the State. Five out of its eight trustees are chosen by the state board of education. Section 6060 Burns 1901. Its trustees are required to report to the State. Section 6081 Burns 1901. The Governor shall annually cause 5,000 copies of the report to be printed, at the expense of the State, for distribution. Section 6084 Burns 1901. The trustees are required to provide for special instruction in certain branches. Sections 6088, 6089 Burns 1901. The State Librarian shall supply books to its library. Section 6092 Burns 1901. The State Geologist shall collect specimens of mineralogy and geology for its cabinet. Section 6093 Burns 1901. The home of the fund is the state treasury, and prior to April, 1897, it was loaned and collected by the state officers (Acts 1852, Sections 6095–6107 Burns 1901), and the annual interest thereon applied to the expenses of the university, upon warrants drawn on the Treasurer of State by the Auditor of State upon requisitions of the trustees. Section 6094 Burns 1901.

And as further evidence of character of the fund, as construed and held by the people themselves, the legislature of 1897, with a prefatory declaration that "the people of the State are equally entitled to the use of said fund, and to its permanent protection," passed a law for the distribution of the fund to the several counties of the State, to be loaned and collected by the several county auditors, and the accruing interest annually reported and paid into the State treasury, at the time and in like manner as interest on the common school fund is paid; the second section of which act reads as follows: "The said moneys so distributed and paid to said counties, as provided by Section 1 of this act, shall be loaned by the auditors of the respective counties in the same manner, and on the same terms and conditions, and under the same restrictions, subject to the same limitations, and said loans shall be again collected from the borrower, as the common school funds are now loaned and collected. And the said several counties shall be liable in the same manner and to the same extent, for the principal and interest of said fund, and for the payment of the same, as they are now liable for payment of the interest and principal of the common school funds." Acts 1897, p. 117, Section 6116b *et seq.* Burns 1901.

We therefore conclude from the foregoing review of the subject that the Indiana University is an integral part of our free school system; that it was the special creation of the Constitution; that the protection and preservation of the funds belonging to it have been the special care of the General Assembly; and that its permanent endowment is in every material sense such a public educational fund as the Constitution declares "shall remain inviolate," and is perforce entitled to the same constitutional and statutory favoritism that is shown to other public educational funds. We are strengthened in this view by the manifest and uniform legislative purpose to treat the common school fund and the university fund as distinct, but as belonging to the same class.

While some hold that this decision was *obiter dictum,* merely an incidental opinion given by Judge Hadley, yet the opinion reviews the facts so fully and the conclusions are so obvious that they have been accepted without question from that day. This decision, therefore, has been looked upon by the University as one of the important events of 1902.

SUMMARY

For forty-seven years, 1820–67, Indiana University was built and maintained by the proceeds of its first endowment, two townships of land granted by the Federal Government and accepted by the constitutional convention of 1816, supplemented by small fees from students. This land was given to the state, to be made productive for a State University, and everything that was done in making this land and the University Fund, derived from sale of this land, productive for the benefit of the State Seminary, College, University, was done as directed by successive acts of the Indiana General Assembly.

Ten acres in section 4 (see map of Perry township, p. 720) of the reserved township in Monroe County were selected as a site for the State Seminary, and the remainder of this section was sold by an agent appointed by the trustees, the proceeds being delivered to the treasurer of the Seminary and expended by the trustees for erection of a Seminary building and a "suitable and commodious house for a Professor."

With the exception of this one section, none of the Perry Township land was sold prior to 1827, when the sale of all the Perry Township land was authorized, except for three sections, one south (9), one east (3), and one west (5) of the section previously sold (4). These three reserved sections were later sold like section 4, by a commissioner appointed by the Board of Trustees; the proceeds were delivered directly to the treasurer of the State College, and used by the trustees for further building and equipment. These four sections 3, 4, 5, and 9, were the only lands handled in this manner. All other lands of Perry Township and all the lands of the reserved township in Gibson County were sold by commissioners appointed by the state. Proceeds were delivered to the treasurer of state and made productive as a University Fund, for the benefit of the University.

The lands of the reserved township in Gibson County were put on sale in 1822. When the Seminary became Indiana College in 1828, the University Fund amounted to less than $16,000. But in September, 1842, George Dunn, a former trustee of Indiana University, reported that in Gibson County only 2,480 acres remained unsold; in Monroe County only 40 acres remained unsold. These unsold lands, 2,520 acres, were valued at $1,890. By 1846 the value of unsold lands was only $1,000.

During the Seminary period, 1824–28, these Perry Township lands and the unsold lands of the reserved township in Gibson County were made productive by rental at not less than 62½ cents per acre.

On January 24, 1828, a loan office was established in the office of the state treasurer, for the purpose of lending the University Fund. In 1843 the auditor of state was assigned the duty of making the loans, while the treasurer of state remained custodian of the fund. The time came when this plan was not working well. Bad loans gave rise to losses in fund and income. Interest on this fund had dropped from $6,500 in 1877-78 to $3,500 in 1883-84, which was for the University a serious loss in income, and a matter of much concern to Presidents Coulter and Swain. Therefore, on March 2, 1897, an act was passed calling into the State Treasury all loans of the University Fund, about $75,000, made to individuals, and providing for the distribution of the University Fund and the Permanent Endowment Fund (1883-) pro rata to the counties of the state, which were made responsible for principal and interest.

In 1943 the counties were authorized to surrender, to the treasurer of state, custody of the Permanent Endowment Fund, if they so chose.

The two funds, the University Fund, about $75,000, and the Permanent Endowment Fund, raised by a small tax, 1883-95, about $690,000, remain today as a minor source of University income. They are carried (1945) on the books of the University under the single title Permanent Endowment Fund, at $768,575.69. State bonds were issued for part, $144,000, of this Permanent Endowment Fund. Though the income from these two endowments is small, historically they are important in that they date back to days when interest on the University Fund plus small fees was the sole maintenance of Indiana University, and to 1883 when it was believed that the creation of an endowment of something over half a million dollars would provide adequate income for Indiana University.

The income from the University Fund was supplemented, 1867-95, by annual appropriations. The income from the combined University and Permanent Endowment Fund has been supplemented, 1895-1925, by a varying mill tax, and 1925 to date (1945), by annual appropriations voted biennially at legislative sessions.

CHAPTER LIV

CHANGES AND ACCOMPLISHMENTS, 1902–37

THE BOARD OF TRUSTEES DURING THE BRYAN ADMINISTRATION

IT IS remarkable that during the thirty-five years of the Bryan administration, 1902–37, there were only eighteen changes in the Board of Trustees. Of these eighteen trustees thirteen were elected by the State Board of Education, and five were elected by the alumni. Including the eight men of the board that elected William L. Bryan as president of Indiana University, some of whom served many years, twenty-six trustees were associated with the Bryan administration.

The thirteen men elected by the State Board of Education were: Theodore F. Rose, James E. Watson, Ira C. Batman, Samuel R. Lyons, Benjamin F. Long, Frank H. Hatfield, Howard Sandison, Charles M. Niezer, George A. Ball, Paul L. Feltus, William A. Kunkel, Val F. Nolan, Albert L. Rabb.

The five trustees elected by the alumni were: James W. Fesler, Samuel E. Smith, Nellie Showers Teter, Ora L. Wildermuth, John S. Hastings.

These eighteen changes in the board were in marked contrast to the first thirty-five years of the history of Indiana University, 1820–55, during which eighty-five men were appointed. This was a period characterized by small resources, difficulties of travel, and experimentation by the General Assembly as to the size of the board. By 1902 great changes had occurred and no man chosen for trustee declined the appointment.

LAND—THE GROWTH OF THE CAMPUS AT BLOOMINGTON

In 1902 the campus consisted of 50.82 acres, the total of five land purchases made since the University was moved from South College Avenue. Although these purchases antedated the Bryan administration, an account of the circumstances and conditions which led the board to buy or not to buy land in those days is deemed worthy of record.

On November 5, 1883, the trustees authorized the special committee on location of the New College campus to purchase the tract of land in Dunn's Woods

commencing at a point where the south line of 6th street intersects with the line designated by Mr. Dunn, 375 feet east of the street, now laid out (Indiana Avenue), then running east on a line with the south line of the continuation of 6th street to the cemetery [Dunn], then south to the turnpike [3d St.], then west to the said west line, thence to the place of beginning—so as to enclose a parallelogram.

The deed for this twenty-acre tract in Dunn's Woods bears the date November 11, 1885. But the final clause of the recorded deed recites:

In witness whereof said grantors have hereunto set their hands and seals this 11th day of November, 1885, to relate back to and take effect from the 4th day of February, 1884.

February 4, 1884, the effective date of the recorded deed, is therefore the date of acquisition of this site. Wylie Hall and Owen Hall were built, furnished, and occupied at the beginning of the fall session of 1885. The trustees were much too good businessmen to build structures like Owen and Wylie on ground they did not own.

But we do not have to depend on inference. In the minutes of the trustees for March 25, 1884, the president of the board was authorized to sign, on behalf of the board, the contract for erection of buildings we know as Owen Hall and Wylie Hall. Attention of the board on June 7, 1884, was "called to the fact that Mr. Moses Dunn has not yet received any pay for the land which he has deeded to the University and that he desires to know when he may be paid." Accordingly, on June 10, 1884, a recommendation was approved by the board that $3,000 be paid Mr. Dunn on account and the balance in the following November (1884).

We can be certain that before this payment was made the trustees had a deed or a contract for a deed which, whenever given, was effective on February 4, 1884. The deed originally may have been defective in some respect. It may have been given by Moses Dunn alone and later it may have been learned that his brother George and wife had an interest in the property. Delay may have been occasioned by the refusal of George Dunn to sign a warranty deed, which Moses had given, for the recorded deed is signed:

Moses F. Dunn, unmarried,
George G. Dunn and
Euphemia Dunn his wife convey,
and said Moses Dunn conveys
and warrants.

The campus as it was in 1902 is shown in the map inside the front cover. In that map is shown also the relation of the new campus to Dunn Meadow and to the original campus of 1820.

In 1884 when the first purchase of land was made in Dunn's Woods, the only house between Third and Tenth streets and between Indiana Avenue and Jordan was the old brick home of Moses Dunn,[1] which stood about where the west part of the Gymnasium for Men is now located.

The campus site selected in 1820 was a tract of ten acres. In November, 1883, the new campus site selected by the Board of Trustees was a tract just twice as large. At that time, 1883–84, there were 143 college students. There was as yet no indication of the rapid growth which was imminent. If there were trustees who thought more land should be purchased, it is evident that a majority of the board was of the opinion that $6,000 was as much of the small fund available as could be justifiably expended for land.

But with a new campus, a new president, and new buildings, attendance doubled twice in the first ten years, 1884–94. In 1896 there were 944 college students, 800 more than in 1883–84. In the year 1897 the trustees purchased 30 additional acres of land, plots 2, 3, and 4 (shown on the map inside the back cover), and the campus then contained a little more than 50 acres. By that time it was obvious that much additional land should be purchased, but the trustees were not able to convince the legislature of that fact.

When the second plot of ground was purchased in 1897, President Swain had built his house on Third Street near Indiana Avenue[2]

---

[1] The Dunn farm consisted originally of 160 acres, lying between Third and Tenth streets, and between Dunn Street and Fee Lane projected southward.
[2] Later purchased by the Phi Gamma Delta fraternity.

and other houses had been built in that neighborhood. This left a number of lots at the corner of Third and Indiana which for fifty years the University has tried to purchase and only a part of which she has succeeded in getting.

The following is a list of the thirty-two successive purchases of land which made up the campus on June 30, 1937, when William Lowe Bryan retired. Beginning with purchase No. 1, the growth of the campus from a plot of 20 acres to a campus of 136.89 acres may be followed without difficulty. Numbers on the map at the end of the book show the location of each purchase.

1.	February 4, 1884	20 acres	Total acres, 20
2.	March 29, 1897	8⅓ acres	28⅓
3.	June 22, 1897	9.56 acres	37.89
	June 22, 1897	10.43 acres	48.32
4.	November 23, 1897	2½ acres	50.82
5.	September 27, 1905	19½ acres	70.32
6.	October 4, 1905	1 lot	70.50
7.	May 5, 1913	21 acres	91.50
8.	October 5, 1914	26.03 acres	117.53
9.	June 28, 1919	10 lots	
10.	July 26, 1921	27 lots	
11.	February 24, 1922	1 lot	
12.	February 28, 1922	6 lots	
13.	May 15, 1922	1 lot	
14.	June 22, 1923	21 lots	
15.	June 23, 1923	1 lot	
16.	June 23, 1923	1 lot	
17.	June 23, 1923	1 lot	
18.	June 23, 1923	1 lot	
19.	June 23, 1923	1 lot	
20.	June 23, 1925	8 lots	
21.	July 21, 1925	1 lot	
22.	April 26, 1926	1 lot	
23.	April 11, 1927	1 lot	
24.	February 7, 1928	1 lot	
25.	May 12, 1928	1 lot	
26.	September 14, 1928	1 lot	
27.	November 26, 1929	1 lot	
28.	February 16, 1931	2 lots	
29.	September 15, 1936	4 lots	
30.	January 1, 1937	1½ lots	

31. January 11, 1937......... 9 lots ....
32. June 11, 1937 ....½ lot ....

Total acres 136.89

The list of purchases show that during the Bryan administration 86.07 acres were added.[3] The campus at Indianapolis on June 30, 1937, consisted of 48.43 acres and there were 250.13 acres in the University Waterworks drainage area.

EMPHASIS ON PROFESSIONAL AND GRADUATE WORK

At the first regular meeting of the trustees under the presidency of William Lowe Bryan, in November, 1902, the President began his long campaign for the expansion of the University along lines of professional and graduate work. Good progress had been made along these lines when, in 1909, Governor Marshall called a conference of state and non-state school presidents (Chap. X) at which a resolution was adopted recommending that in the future the development of Indiana University should be along lines of professional and graduate work.

This resolution was very welcome to President Bryan for it conformed perfectly with the plan he had been advocating for the development of Indiana University. An examination of the following table shows the distribution of the faculty and student body in 1902 and 1937:

School	Faculty 1902	Faculty 1937	Students 1902	Students 1937
Graduate	93		82	688
Arts and Sciences	57	201	1134	2505
Law	4	12	69	201
Education		39		754
Medicine		103		430
Nursing		13		210
Business Administration		20		1274
Music		11		107
Dentistry		40		190
Extension Division		7		5495

[3] President Bryan relates: "Captain John Alexander, an alumnus of the University and a relative of Moses Dunn, told me he had drawn two wills for Mr. Dunn. In the first Mr. Dunn bequeathed to the University all of the Dunn farm not already purchased by the University. Later Mr. Dunn was angered by a ruling of the town council of Bloomington that the Dunn farm was city lot property, to be assessed for taxes, streets, sewage, etc., on that basis. So Mr. Dunn changed his will disposing of his property otherwise."

It should be noted that in 1902 the faculty was found in only two schools, those of Arts and Sciences and of Law, but some of the students in that year were found also in the Graduate School. In 1937 faculty and student body were widely distributed with the majority in the combined Graduate School, professional schools, and Extension Division organized during the Bryan period. The School of Medicine (1903), the School of Education (1908), and the Graduate School (1904) had already been established with a combined enrollment of 611 students, when the Marshall conference was called in 1909.

A further examination of the table shows that in 1937 the enrollment in the College of Arts and Sciences was a little more than twice as great as in 1902, whereas the enrollment in the Graduate School (688) was more than eight times that of 1902. But the 688 students in the Graduate School were not all the graduate students in Indiana University in 1937. There were also graduate students, candidates for advanced degrees, in the professional schools as follows:

School of Business 27
School of Music 6
School of Education 407
                                                                                  ———
                                        Total 440

The total number of graduate students in Indiana University in 1937 was therefore 688 plus 440, or 1,128. In fact, the total was in excess of 1,128 since the graduate students in the School of Medicine are not included in that number.

In January, 1885, when Jordan became president, the Law School had not been re-established and the College of Arts and Sciences with an enrollment of 157 was 100 per cent Indiana University. In 1902 the enrollment in the College of Arts and Sciences was 88 per cent of the total University enrollment. In 1910 it was 70.5 per cent, and in 1937 it was only 37 per cent of the total University enrollment.

These figures show, in a negative way, how fully the development of Indiana University during the Bryan administration had been in fields of graduate and professional education. Though the enrollment in the College of Arts and Sciences had more than doubled from 1902 to 1937, that enrollment was an ever smaller and smaller fraction of the total University enrollment because of the rapid development of graduate and professional schools.

Furthermore, during this period, 1902–37, two years of collegiate work for matriculation in the School of Law and three years of collegiate work for entrance on the study of medicine had become the minimum requirement. Many students were coming to professional schools with four years of collegiate work. In 1937 there were nearly 300 students holding a baccalaureate degree, but not candidates for a graduate degree, enrolled in the professional schools of the University. All told, there were in the whole University in the last year of the Bryan administration, 1936–37, 1,417 students holding a baccalaureate degree, a number greater than the enrollment of the entire University in 1902, when Bryan became president.

Survey of Accomplishments, 1902–37

A survey of the period 1902–37 reveals a remarkable series of accomplishments. Schools were added as follows:

1903. The Indiana University School of Medicine.
1904. The Graduate School.
1908. The School of Education.
1912. The Extension Division.
1914. The Training School for Nurses.
1920. The School of Commerce and Finance (Business).
1921. The School of Music.
1925. The School of Dentistry.

In addition to the organization of these eight schools, the status of the summer session was strengthened and improved by the appointment of a director. Buildings were erected as follows:

1903. Science Hall (begun in 1901) dedicated January 21, 1903.
1905. New Power-house erected.
1906. Student Building completed. (Contributions.)
1907. New Library building erected.
    Annex to Maxwell Hall constructed.
1908. Rose Wellhouse erected.
1910. Biology Hall erected.
    University Waterworks constructed (250 acres bought).
1911. Owen Hall remodeled.

1914. Robert W. Long Hospital completed.
Old power plant remodeled as Journalism Building.
1917. Men's Gymnasium completed.
1919. New building for School of Medicine (Indianapolis) completed.
1923. Commerce Building completed (now Social Science).
1924. South Hall dormitory completed.
First unit of James Whitcomb Riley Memorial Hospital completed.
President's House completed.
1925. Women's Memorial Hall completed.
Memorial Stadium completed.
1926. Addition to Library completed.
1927. Home Economics Practice House purchased.
Coleman Hospital completed.
1928. Ball Residence for Nurses completed.
Addition to Medical School Building (Indianapolis) completed.
Extension Division Building purchased (former Bobbs-Merrill Building).
Fieldhouse completed.
1929. Power-house remodeled.
Kappa Kappa Gamma House (Forest Place) purchased.
The Howe House (Forest Place) purchased; became (1939) Student
Health Service.
1930. Kiwanis Wing of Riley Memorial Hospital dedicated.
1931. Chemistry Building completed.
Kappa Alpha Theta House (in Forest Place) purchased and became
School of Education offices.
Rotary Convalescent Unit of Riley Hospital completed.
1932. Union Building (Memorial) completed.
Bookstore completed.
Hepburn House (Forest Place) purchased.
1934. New School of Dentistry Building completed.
Fourteen bedrooms in Union Building Tower completed.
1935. Hydrotherapeutic pool at Riley completed.
1936. Administration Building completed.
School of Music Building completed.
Forest Hall dormitory completed.
Addition to Power-house equipment installed.
New tunnels (for heat) constructed.
Alpha Hall (Forest Place) purchased by University.
Louden House (Forest Place) purchased.
1937. New Medical School Building (Bloomington) completed.
New Clinical Building (Indianapolis) under construction.
Contract let for construction of University School building (February 8,
1937).
Stores and Service Building, plans accepted June 14, 1937.

GIFTS

As a part of his message to Foundation Day alumni gatherings in January, 1917, President Bryan sent a "provisional" list of gifts made to the University, the earliest of which was made in 1841. This "Era of Gifts" message was published in the *Alumni Quarterly* for April of that year.[4]

The Bryan administration was indeed an era of gifts. The largest ones, such as foundations and named buildings, have been considered in detail in this work, but the thousands of other gifts, both large and small, must needs be omitted in detail. Many small ones may represent greater sacrifices than larger ones. Some sizable gifts have been anonymous.

More than $100,000 has been given for loan funds, of which there were none at the beginning of the Bryan administration. Likewise, large sums of money for scholarships, fellowships, research projects, and scientific expeditions have been given by individuals, organizations, and business firms who were interested in a special field of work or in the work of a particular individual.

Collections of books and periodicals, many very rare, have come to the University; portraits and art objects, furnishings, Senior class gifts, scientific collections, loving cups, oxygen rooms, baby clinics, money for prizes, have been donated by alumni and groups or individuals who never had any connection with the University.

The names of the donors to the Riley Hospital building fund are filed in a special memorial room near the entrance. During the years since the erection of the building many other gifts—large and small— have been made. Some are real estate or other property to be available on the death of the donor.

The Memorial Fund campaign brought thousands of pledges, ranging from one dollar to several thousand, some of which, as is always the case in such campaigns, were not paid. On the basis of pledges, however, work on the Memorial structures was begun. The names of all who pledged are inscribed in the Golden Book, in the lobby of the Union Building.

[4] The University Catalog, from 1911 through 1932, carried a list of gifts and bequests. It was discontinued, along with some other sections of the Catalog, after the legislative appropriation was cut by the special session of 1932.

The Indiana University Foundation, incorporated one year before Dr. Bryan retired, was created to obtain, hold, and administer gifts of all sorts for the benefit of Indiana University.

THE FACULTY A DISCIPLINARY BODY

For one hundred years the faculty, in addition to its function as an instructional body, was also a disciplinary body. Recently a minute book of the faculty for the years 1835 to 1844 has come into possession of the University. In that early day, and indeed for many years later, the faculty as a whole considered breaches of good conduct. The faculty heard and considered evidence and imposed punishment.

From time to time in the eighties, committees were appointed to study and report back to the faculty on some disciplinary matter, but it was not until the meeting of the faculty on September 25, 1891, that President Coulter announced the appointment of a committee on discipline.

On September 23, 1893, newly-elected President Joseph Swain also announced the appointment of a committee on student affairs in place of the committee on discipline. This committee was composed of three members, William L. Bryan (chairman), Horace A. Hoffman, and Robert J. Aley. The personnel of this committee is indicative of the high importance attached to it. Bryan remained chairman of this committee until he became president, when the dean of the School of Law was assigned to this honor and responsibility.

The committee on student affairs considered cases and made recommendations to the faculty, which retained the power of review and final decision. The saving of time and energy of the faculty, however, was not as great as might be supposed. Faculty meetings were held frequently and the major business on many occasions was the discussion of the report of the committee on student affairs. There were always faculty members who would impose harsh penalties. Others advocated penalties so light that they had no disciplinary value. Much time was consumed finding a mid-course between these extremes.

In 1918 Agnes E. Wells, a woman of superior ability, wisdom, and judgment, was appointed dean of women, and a year later Professor Clarence E. Edmondson was appointed dean of men, and in 1920 became chairman of the committee on student affairs, a position which he filled to the close of the year 1942–43. In the summer of 1921 Charles J. Sembower also was appointed dean of men with duties beginning on August 1. This appointment made it possible for two fair-minded men, tolerant, sympathetic, yet firm and courageous, to consult in cases of marked difficulty. Dean Sembower became the counselor of men, while Dean Edmondson's time was devoted chiefly to disciplinary matters. With appointment of these three deans, only contested decisions were brought before the faculty.[5]

Growing Complexity of Administration

In the early years of the Bryan presidency, administrative matters were still relatively simple, though not so simple as at the beginning of the Jordan administration in 1885, seventeen years earlier, when grade cards were made out by Jordan. Changes in administration from 1885 to 1902 were occasioned by increase in size of the College of Arts and Sciences and of the School of Law, re-established in 1889.

Up to the time of the election of David Starr Jordan as president, there had been but one officer, a librarian, in addition to the faculty. In 1885 the librarian, William W. Spangler, was also the registrar. In 1890 the office of registrar was separated from that of librarian and Sophia M. Sheeks was appointed registrar. She was succeeded by Henry Bates. In 1895 John W. Cravens became registrar. In the fall of 1899 U. H. Smith became assistant to the registrar and in 1906 his title was assistant to the registrar and accountant. Then in June, 1908, U. H. Smith was made bursar.

Mr. Smith writes:

One of the duties assigned me when I became Assistant to the Registrar in the fall of 1899 was the collection of fees, which were deposited at the First National Bank to the credit of Indiana University. All regular University funds were disbursed by checks signed by John W. Cravens, secretary to the

---

[5] The Act of February 15, 1838, defining the faculty and its powers, was revised, *Indiana Revised Statutes,* Chap. 114, p. 505, approved June 17, 1852, as follows:

"SEC. 7. The president, professors and instructors shall be styled 'The Faculty' of said university, and shall have power:

"*First.* To enforce the regulations adopted by the trustees for the government of the students.

"*Second.* To which end they may reward and censure, and may suspend those who continue refractory, until a determination of the board of trustees can be had thereon."

Board of Trustees, or by the President[6] of the University. After my appointment as Bursar, several Bursar's Funds were established, such as Student Loan Funds and Temporary Deposits. These funds were disbursed by Bursar's checks signed by me. After the addition of the Indianapolis center—Medical, Hospital, and Dental—checks from those units, by order of the Board of Trustees—see record—were signed by me as Bursar.

The increasing complexity of administration during the Bryan presidency was due not so much to increase in size of schools existing in 1902 as to the organization of new schools. With the organization of each new school, new problems of staff and maintenance presented themselves. There was always the question whether requests of new schools for staff and maintenance were made on the same conservative, economic, non-lavish basis which the oldest school of the University, the College of Arts and Sciences, had long known to be necessary. From the beginning of the Bryan presidency there were members of the Arts faculty who were sure that the organization of new schools was to the disinterest of the College of Arts and Sciences and to its faculty. The small faculty of the School of Law had constituted a minority group in the administration of the University by the faculty of the College of Liberal Arts, which was somewhat jealous of its prerogatives resting on its early organization. For so many years it had functioned as a University faculty that it was not easy to accept another school as having equal voice in University matters. As the University grew, allocation of duties became necessary.

When I came to Indiana University in the second year of the presidency of William Lowe Bryan, September, 1903, I consulted him regarding my departmental budget. The President said: "Let us not set up any definite budget. When you need something, come and see me and we will talk it over." From an administrative point of view this was an ideal way of keeping check on expenditures which the General University Budget would not permit. From my point of view if I could not make a convincing statement of needs, then a reconsideration was warrantable. The plan was for me an

[6] President Bryan states that this authority conferred by the Board of Trustees was never exercised except in some emergency during illness or absence of Secretary Cravens.

education in the economy of Indiana University. But with the multiplication of schools the above procedure became quite impossible.

Stenographic assistance came slowly to administrative offices and schools. In July, 1911, it was ordered "that Judge Hogate be authorized to use such funds as are necessary from the appropriation made for the law library last October to procure a typewriting machine." Much later the day came when each school had a typewriter and the part-time assistance of some student, and still later the school had a full-time stenographer.

This development was typical of many other administrative matters. Take the telephone as another example. When in 1900 a fire in Wylie Hall severely damaged that building, there was only one telephone on the campus. That was in the office of the President. It was necessary to reach this phone in order to notify the downtown fire department. President Bryan tells the story. His class was in the north end of Kirkwood. He noted the blaze in adjacent Wylie and with Professor Morton rushed to the President's office. But someone had notified the President of the fire, and he had locked his office and had gone to investigate. So when Professors Bryan and Morton reached the President's office, they found it locked. But the transom was open. So Professor Morton stood on Professor Bryan's shoulders and was boosted through the high transom and gave the alarm.

In 1909 a contract was let for a local telephone installation which made it possible to reach other departments in a four-story building or on the campus, and finally another installation made it possible to reach downtown.

Struggle to Make Facilities Equal to Demands

There was an interminable struggle to make educational facilities of the University keep pace with the ever-increasing numbers of students seeking the educational advantages of the University. The Registrar had from department heads reports on the use of every lecture room and office for every hour of the day and every day of the week. Schedules of courses were studied and restudied with the purpose of using buildings and equipment with maximum efficiency. It seemed that during the Bryan administration the power plant was being remodeled almost continuously. It was following the fire in the power plant in 1929 that it was made adequate.

William Lowe Bryan as an Administrator

Any brief statement of the factors chiefly responsible for the success of William Lowe Bryan as an administrator must take into account the background under which the Bryan administration began.

We have discussed the antagonism of denominational groups which began in the first decade of the history of Indiana University, hampered every administration, and flared into a united attack only a few years before Bryan's election to the presidency. To this eighty-two-year-old hostility had been added further antagonism by Jordan's support of evolution. Jordan was so constituted that he had to voice his advocacy of any matter concerning which he had a deep conviction. In evidence, witness his Peace Address in Baltimore during World War I.

These old antagonisms, recently augmented, Bryan inherited. They did not disappear overnight. Indeed, it appeared for a time during the governorship of Thomas Marshall that they might again flare into open and united attack. On the contrary, however, the conference of state and non-state school presidents (October 14, 1909) came to be regarded as definitely marking the beginning of better relations between state and non-state schools.

Perhaps nothing contributed more to the success of the Bryan administration than the laying of these old antagonisms. In his attitude toward the non-state schools Bryan was motivated by a sincere sympathy with their difficulties and by the conviction that education, both state and non-state, had not been supported as generously in Indiana as in neighboring states. He believed also that the growing educational demands of young people of Indiana would tax the combined resources and facilities of both state and non-state schools. His kindly good will gave opportunity for the convictions of the straightest thinkers among non-state school leaders to be understood and finally accepted. These straightest thinkers were saying that instead of growth of the state schools being a menace to the very existence of the non-state schools, as had been believed for so many years, growth of state schools could be helpful to the non-state schools in emphasizing their needs and in opening hearts and purses in their support.

Chapter III, "The First Year of the Bryan Administration," reveals how Bryan's conception of the educational needs of the state led naturally to his conviction that the establishment of new schools at the University was necessary to meet those educational needs. Nothing is more characteristic of Bryan's technique in establishment of new schools than his willingness and wisdom in starting something potentially great in a very simple, inexpensive way.

Where many would have said that we cannot think of starting a School of Commerce and Finance (later called Business) with less than a quarter or half a million dollars, he dared make the start at an expenditure of a few hundred dollars. But the school grew, demonstrated that it met a demand for such instruction, and financial support came.

The same was true of the organization of the School of Medicine. The entire additional budget required for the organization of the School of Medicine in 1903 did not exceed $2,500. The last two years of the School of Medicine were organized in Indianapolis in 1906 with a hospital of 65 beds and run for two years at a cost of $2,500 in excess of receipts. The time came about 1930 when the capital investment of the Indiana University School of Medicine in Indianapolis was equal to that of the campus at Bloomington.

Some faculty members did not share Bryan's convictions regarding establishment of new schools. Only a few were opposed to the organization of all new schools. Opposition of others was limited to organization of some particular school only. There was never any organized opposition. A few of the most controversial developments came before the faculty for consideration and were approved by decisive majorities. In this faculty as in most faculties there were sharp differences of opinion on many matters. Yet Bryan succeeded in welding this faculty into a cooperative and harmonious unit whose spirit on University matters was that of a big family, each member of which, with very few exceptions, gave unreservedly of time, energy, and thought to furthering the interests of Indiana University.

SUMMARY

The history of Indiana University during this period, 1902–37, is the history of a rapidly growing institution in which there is the never-ending plea for more generous legislative appropriations to enable the University to meet the ever-growing demands of the young people of Indiana for broader educational opportunities. It is the story of the organization of eight new schools, the organization of the summer session under a director, and establishment of new departments some of which threaten to expand into schools. It is the story of the erection of forty new buildings, a third of which were gifts of individuals or groups of individuals varying in number from a few to 40,000.

Each of these major accomplishments began as a hope for fulfilment of a University need, then became a major project which, for a time, occupied the center of the stage. Some projects were long-drawn-out, were for a long time shoved into the background by competing needs considered more pressing. For illustration, the need of better accommodations for the administrative offices was first voiced when plans were being considered for the new Library in 1905. The need was obvious. Administration quarters were cramped, inadequate. But again and again for thirty-one years the needs of administration were weighed and subordinated to educational expansion, providing educational opportunities for Hoosier boys and girls. So it was not until 1936 that the Administration Building was erected.

Other illustrations could be cited. Some of the most important objectives of the administration were intangible, such as the development of better public relations, particularly the development of confidence, good will, and cooperation between the University and the non-state schools.

With the resignation of President Bryan and the appointment of President Wells, a great administration of Indiana University came to an end and a new administration was inaugurated, giving promise of still greater service. The new officers were well acquainted with the problems of Indiana University—and were widely and favorably known throughout the state.

The resignation of William Lowe Bryan meant more than the retirement of one man to inactive status. It marked the end of a period of the history of Indiana University. John W. Cravens, the confidant and adviser of the President from his inauguration, had retired in June, 1936, because of an affliction which a little later proved fatal. On the Board of Trustees, James W. Fesler, who was elected trustee on the same day that W. L. Bryan was elected President, Frank Hatfield, Charles M. Niezer, and Benjamin F. Long, all men of long and distinguished service, had been succeeded recently by younger men equally devoted to Indiana University. On the faculty the men who had been young in 1902 now in 1937 had reached or were approaching retirement age, and had been or were about to be replaced by young successors.

When Bryan assumed the presidency of Indiana University in 1902, he found the income of the institution approximately $150,000, derived from the following sources:

Educational tax levy	$ 92,000
Interest on endowment, etc.	49,000
Student and sundry fees	8,500
	$149,500

On his retirement President Bryan left Indiana University with an income for 1937–38 in excess of 2¾ million, derived as follows:

For maintenance from state	$1,890,000
Interest on endowment, etc.	38,200
Student fees	511,766
	$2,439,966

In addition to the above, the state also contributed for Indiana University for the year 1937–38:

For land and buildings	$240,300
For repair of old buildings	30,000
For a retirement fund	50,000
	$320,300
Grand total	$2,759,866

This was an increase in state support of more than two million dollars, about twenty-four times what the state had contributed to the support of Indiana University at the beginning of the Bryan administration.

It will be noted there was a very great increase in student fees due in part to increase in enrollment, but in greater part to an actual increase in the annual fees paid by the student. The increase was from an average of $7 a year for each student in 1902 to an average of $75 a year in 1936–37.

This statement of income takes no account of further receipts of considerable sums having no direct connection with the educational activities of the campus, such as receipts from dormitories fixed on a maintenance cost basis, any small profits from which are reinvested in repairs, improvements, or conveniences for the students concerned. For further illustration, thousands of dollars are received by our hospitals for services already rendered on a nonprofit basis; Extension Division fees which in part reimburse that Division for expenses incurred; Fieldhouse fees, Union Building fees, etc.

The increase in University maintenance noted above, while gratifying, is not impressive when compared with maintenance of neighboring state universities, the support of which for many years has been more generous than that of the state of Indiana for Indiana University and Purdue University combined.

In *The Spirit of Indiana,* Bryan had written:

What the people need and demand is that their children shall have a chance —as good a chance as any other children in the world—to make the most of themselves, to rise in any and every occupation, including those occupations which require the most thorough training. What the people want is *open* paths from every corner of the State through the schools to the highest and best things which men can achieve. To make such paths, to make them open to the poorest and make them lead to the highest, is the mission of democracy.

In this great ambition to open to Indiana boys and girls, pathways to opportunity for development, the administration of William Lowe Bryan achieved a remarkable degree of success. Happily as those paths increased in number, they led not only to Indiana University, but to sister educational institutions of our great state.

INDEX

Permanent Endowment Fund—*Continued* 739; what included in 1945, 740; Hicks 1908 report on loans, 745; act of 1943 concerning, 746, 751; Judge Hadley reviews status of, 747

Perring, Roy Henderson, instructor in 1902-3, 9

Perry, Oscar Butler, receives LL.D., 419

Perry Township: second Seminary township, 101n., 718; one section sold in 1820, 719, 721, 722; shown on map, 720; manner of handling four sections, 722, 750; rental of Seminary lands in, 723, 724; 1827 legislation ordering sale, 725; 1830 legislation, 725; 1836 legislation, 725, 726; sale of south section, 725; sale of east and west sections, 726; sales price of four reserved sections, 726; loan office to handle funds, 728; reserved sections in custody of trustees, 730; report of Robert Dale Owen for 1840-41, 734; Seminary site in, 750; funds from unreserved sections in University Fund, 750; see George H. Dunn.

Pettijohn, John J.: appointed director of the Extension Division, 178, 667; first summer session director, 182; Indianapolis office, 183; war service, 213; leaves, 251, 672; appointed by Bryan, 579, 667; training, 667; director of war speakers' bureau, 670; goes to Washington, 671; postwar activities, 672; contrasted with Cavanaugh, 672

Pettit, John Upfold, professor of law, 460

Pfaff, Orange Garrett: enters war service, 200; chair endowed for, 336

Phelps, William Lyon, convocation address at I.U., 184

Phi Beta Kappa, chapter organized at I.U., 147

Phi Gamma Delta, negotiations with, to purchase property, 88, 141-45

Philosophy, Department of: Book heads, 207; separated from Department of Psychology, 380; Nelson endowment of chair in philosophy, 421; mental and moral philosophy taught by presidents, 484

Philputt, Allan Bearden: appointment, 592; first "resident graduate student," 636

Physical Education: training courses added, 488; departmental status, 488, 499; requirement that coaches be licensed, 563; training of physical education teachers, 565, 566

Physics: course announced in 1831, 485; courses for premedics, 501; Department offers shop courses, 559

Physiology, Department of: added, 499; came from Department of Zoology, 501

Piercy, Joseph William: director of Department of Journalism, 145, 632; 1913 report on need of printing plant, 167; war service, 213; eligible for retirement in 1937, 512; appointed by Bryan, 579

Pike, Roy Oakley: leads campaign for Bloomington water supply, 290; captain of the baseball team, 388, 402; statement about coaching, 402; member of committee to manage Department of Athletics, 408

Pitkin, Edward Meyer, in Methodist student work, 130

Pittenger, Nicholas Otto: "Y" officer, 126; manager of Bookstore, 430, 431, 433; resigns, 433; successful management of Bookstore, 433

Placement Bureau, established, 453

Pohlman, Augustus Grote, reports on student health procedure, 180

Political Science, Department of, relation with Department of History, 487, 499

Porter, James Pertice, instructor in 1902-3, 9

Porter, Miles F., on committee to choose first I.U. Medical School faculty, 68

Post office, board requests substation for I.U., 251

Powell, Arthur, basketball coach, 403

Powell, Mahlon: establishes a professorship in philosophy, 308; publication of first Powell lectures, 701

Power-house: value of building in 1902, 5; built in 1897, 19; facilities inadequate in 1902, 19; enlargement and improvement asked for, 20; $20,000 granted for improvement, 21; decision to begin a new plant, 29, 32, 759; 1904 need for special appropriation, 32; 1907 legislative grant for completing, 45; 1909 legislative grant, 77; old plant used for Journalism Department, 168, 759; plans for enlargement ordered, 183; new one needed in 1916, 202; needed in 1918, 213; needed in 1920, 247; plans for rebuilding, 248; cost of 1921 improvements, 251; needed in 1924, 301; money for improvement in 1925, 303; 1928 survey and remodeling, 347; fire in 1929, 375, 421; other power plants, 375; rebuilding, 375-76, 759; extension in 1936, 508, 759; PWA aid in building, 524, 531; see School of Medicine.

Practice teaching: arrangements for, in 1907, 85; see School of Education.

Pratt, Mary, in charge of correspondence study, 677, 679

Preparatory Department: superintendent in 1831, 484; courses used in 1853 Normal School, 547

Salaries, Faculty—*Continued*
  I.U. scale compared with that of other midwest colleges, 444; salary of first law professor, 459; restoration of 1932 cut asked in 1936 report, 505; in 1884-85, 590; salary of first professor, 658, 723, 724

Sampson, Martin Wright: professor in 1902-3, 8; submits plan for courses in journalism in 1903, 27, 52; faculty representative in Big Ten, 398; chairman of standing committee on athletics, 398, 427n.; appointed by Swain, 579

Samse, Leroy: basketball coach, 403; track coaching, 403n.

Sanders, Newell, receives LL.D., 423

Sanders, William Henry, University connection, 554

Sandison, Howard: succeeds Robert I. Hamilton as trustee, 206; death, 224; Bryan's tribute to, 259; elected by State Board of Education, 752

Sargent, Galen B., helps to organize South Bend classes, 676

S.A.T.C.: organized, 208-10; influenza strikes, 365-68

Schellschmidt, Adolph, becomes instructor in cello, 238

Schlafer, George Ezra, leads extension programs in play and recreation, 680

Schmuck, Adolph, director of work in journalism, 81

Schnebly, Merrill Isaac: on law faculty in 1925, 470; resigns, 471

Scholarships: county scholarship provisions amended, 221; for Latin-American students, 225; funds pledged for, in 1920, 250; for Mexican, Spanish, and Spanish-American students, 252; for Swiss, English, and German, 514; campaign for funds to honor Bryan, 514; "Scholars" appointed in 1904-5, 651

Scholler, Harry M.: baseball coaching, 402; coach in 1920, 403; elected to athletic board of control, 406

Schortemeier, Frederick E.: first secretary of Riley Memorial Association, 309; story of beginning of Riley Hospital, 309; secretary-treasurer of Joint Executive Committee of Riley Hospital, 313; retires, 313

Schuler, John Harold, work on *The Hoosier*, 715

Science, requirement changed in 1931, 498

Science Hall: value in 1902, 5; dedicated, 5n., 758; money needed to complete in 1902, 20; special appropriation for completion, 21; appropriation for another science building, 76, 149; another science building needed, 300-1

Scott, Will, in charge of Donaldson Farm, 354

Scribner, (Mrs.) Josephine Pittman, suggests naming dormitory for first coed, 181

Seavey, Warren Abner: helpful in promoting military training, 197; enters war service, 201; resigns, 471

Sectarianism: an issue in early days of I.U., 89; House investigation of, 90; Senate investigation, 90; in the University of Michigan, 92; church and state in the American colonies, 96, 97; colonial colleges, 98; church and state in Virginia, 113; denominational criticism, 123

Segar, Louis Harold, enters war service, 201

Sembower, Charles Jacob: assistant professor in 1902-3, 8; appointed by Coulter, 9, 578; on faculty in 1937, 10; interested in Fieldhouse, 191; dean of men, 252, 762; faculty representative in Big Ten, 398; chairman of standing committee on athletics, 398; member of committee to manage Department of Athletics, 408

Sembower, Mrs. Charles Jacob, helps to write Senior induction ceremonial, 264

Semester system, adoption, 182, 647

Seminary lands: see Federal Government, Legislature, Gibson County, Perry Township, George Hedford Dunn, Income.

Shake, Curtis Grover, "Y" officer, 126

Shakespeare, William, celebration of tercentenary of death, 184, 707

Shea, Joseph Hooker, becomes ambassador to Chile, 179

Sheeks, Sophia May: appointed by Jordan, 578; registrar, 762

Sheldon, James: director of gymnasium, 400; football coach, 401; baseball, basketball, and track coach, 403; teaches law, 574

Shields, Eleanor, in temporary charge of Bookstore, 433

Shively, Benjamin Franklin: makes motion for establishment of medical department, 24, 25; death, 179; Bryan's tribute to, 258

Shively, George Jenks, winner of Conference medal, 399

Shockley, Ernest Vivian: Bryan's letter to, 142; writes bulletin on constitution making, 699

Shockley, Frank William, extension work, 670

Showers, James D., calls meeting to aid Medical School, 64

Sigma Delta Chi, publications by, 715

Sigma Delta Psi, history of, 410

Sigma Xi: chapter established at I.U., 36; get appropriation for purchase of journals, 88; programs, etc. for 1906-8, 717

Sikes, Pressly Spinks, directs Bureau of Government Research, 513

Skjerne, Axel, joins music faculty, 239

Slipher, Vesto Melvin, receives LL.D., 379

Sluss, John William, war service, 200

Smith, Henry Lester: becomes dean of School of Education, 178; helpful in promoting military training, 197; war service, 213; director of summer session, 223, 560; president of the National Association of Directors of Summer Schools, 379; on President's advisory committee, 513; on committee to work on retirement plan, 541; joins School of Education faculty, 556; title changed, 557; leaves and returns as dean, 559; director of Bureau of Cooperative Research, 569; appointed by Bryan, 579; checks faculty list (1824-1937) for relationships, 594

Smith, Jack H., responsible for *The I.U. Illustrator*, 714

Smith, John Calvin, first teacher of model school, 546, 547

Smith, Luella (Mrs. Sam Hepburn), work at clearing for new gymnasium, 188

Smith, Samuel Edwin: becomes trustee, 179; vice-president of the board, 224; appointed provost, 263; part in Stadium rebuilding, 295; on Joint Executive Committee of Riley Hospital, 313; appointed by Bryan, 579; elected trustee by alumni, 752

Smith, Ulysses Howe: on staff in 1902-3, 9; interested in Fieldhouse, 191; member of committee to manage Department of Athletics, 408; treasurer, 475; resignation, 512; appointed by Bryan, 579; posts at I.U., 762; duties, 762

Snow, Benjamin Warner, appointed by Coulter, 578

Snow, Charles Wilbert, enters war service, 201

Social Service: work begun, 148; development, 159; expansion asked for, in 1916, 203; progress in 1916, 205

Sociology: Nelson endowment for chair, 422; Weatherly succeeded by Sutherland as head of Department of, 475, 480; development of Department, 487

Sollitt, Ralph Victor: first alumni secretary, 167; Indianapolis office, 183

Sororities: regulations for houses in 1909, 78; request for building chapter house on campus, 181; publication on policy of chapter house government, 696

South Hall: erected, 261, 759; how financed, 261, 262; naming, 262; students ask for additions to, 351; debt in 1931, 420; use for women suggested, 525

Spangler, William Wesley: librarian, secretary to trustees, and registrar, 603, 762; retires, 604

Spanish: replaces Hebrew in curriculum, 485; Department added, 499

Specialties: defined, 551; Specialist Club membership, 588; developed under Jordan, 637

Springer, Francis M., begins service under Bryan, 7, 8

Stadium: dedication, 190, 298, 759; story of building and rebuilding, 291-99; members of repair committee, 292; lawsuits, 296-99; cornerstone laying, 296

Stahl, Jake, baseball coach, 403

Standiford, William Russell, assigned to I.U., 447

Starr, George W., director of Bureau of Business Research, 454

State Athletic Association: determines 1894 baseball schedule, 387; members in 1894, 388; 1888 schedule for baseball, 396; organization, 396, 398; arranged intercollegiate contests, 398

State Board of Education: non-state schools feared power of, 105; function in Geeting Bill, 107; meets with non-state school presidents, 109; bill passed modifying composition of, 110; meeting with new members, 110; composition prior to 1899, 110; orders I.U. to discontinue normal department in 1870, 550; action on license requirements, 562; requirements for elementary teachers, 564, 566

State College of Physicians and Surgeons: organized, 36, 64; union with I.U., 67

State schools: committee grows out of joint I.U.-Purdue committee of Chicago, 190; meet for joint action on mill tax, 245, 310; efforts of I.U. to join in legislative appeal, 339, 341; representatives meet in 1932, 436

State Tax Board, actions in Bloomington water problems, 276, 277, 279-82, 290

Steele, Claude: proposition on sale of textbooks, 429; proprietor of Book Nook, 430; opposed to I.U. Bookstore, 432

Steele, Theodore Clement: receives LL.D. degree, 184, 638; becomes honorary professor of painting, 252

Stempel, Guido Hermann: assistant professor in 1902-3, 8; on faculty in 1937, 10; Head of Department of Comparative Philology, 37; receives A.M. Privatim, 146; charter member of Phi Beta